CLASSICAL ECONOMICS

To
my mentors,
Ludwig von Mises
and
Joseph Dorfman

Classical Economics

An Austrian Perspective on the
History of Economic Thought
Volume II

Murray N. Rothbard

Professor of Economics
University of Nevada
Las Vegas, US

Edward Elgar

Published by
Edward Elgar Publishing Limited
Gower House
Croft Road
Aldershot
Hants GU11 3HR
England

Edward Elgar Publishing Company
Old Post Road
Brookfield
Vermont 05036
USA

British Library Cataloguing in Publication Data
Rothbard, Murray N.
   Classical Economics: Austrian Perspective
   on the History of Economic Thought
   I. Title
   330.153

Library of Congress Cataloguing in Publication Data
Rothbard, Murray Newton, 1926–
   An Austrian perspective on the history of
economic thought.
   Includes bibliographical references.
   Contents: v. 1. Economic thought before
Adam Smith — v. 2. Classical economics.
   1. Economics–History.   2. Austrian
school of economists.   I. Title.
HB75.R6726   1995   330'.09   94–15922

ISBN 1 85278 962 X

Printed and bound in Great Britain by
Hartnolls Limited, Bodmin, Cornwall

Contents

Introduction

As the subtitle declares, this work is an overall history of economic thought from a frankly 'Austrian' standpoint: that is, from the point of view of an adherent of the 'Austrian School' of economics. This is the only such work by a modern Austrian; indeed, only a few monographs in specialized areas of the history of thought have been published by Austrians in recent decades.[1] Not only that: this perspective is grounded in what is currently the least fashionable though not the least numerous variant of the Austrian School: the 'Misesian' or 'praxeologic'.[2]

But the Austrian nature of this work is scarcely its only singularity. When the present author first began studying economics in the 1940s, there was an overwhelmingly dominant paradigm in the approach to the history of economic thought – one that is still paramount, though not as baldly as in that era. Essentially, this paradigm features a few Great Men as the essence of the history of economic thought, with Adam Smith as the almost superhuman founder. But if Smith was the creator of both economic analysis and of the free trade, free market tradition in political economy, it would be petty and niggling to question seriously any aspect of his alleged achievement. Any sharp criticism of Smith as either economist or free market advocate would seem only anachronistic: looking down upon the pioneering founder from the point of view of the superior knowledge of today, puny descendants unfairly bashing the giants on whose shoulders we stand.

If Adam Smith created economics, much as Athena sprang full-grown and fully armed from the brow of Zeus, then his predecessors must be foils, little men of no account. And so short shrift was given, in these classic portrayals of economic thought, to anyone unlucky enough to precede Smith. Generally they were grouped into two categories and brusquely dismissed. Immediately preceding Smith were the mercantilists, whom he strongly criticized. Mercantilists were apparently boobs who kept urging people to accumulate money but not to spend it, or insisting that the balance of trade must 'balance' with each country. Scholastics were dismissed even more rudely, as moralistic medieval ignoramuses who kept warning that the 'just' price must cover a merchant's cost of production plus a reasonable profit.

The classic works in the history of thought of the 1930s and 1940s then proceeded to expound and largely to celebrate a few peak figures after Smith. Ricardo systematized Smith, and dominated economics until the 1870s; then the 'marginalists', Jevons, Menger and Walras, marginally corrected Smith–

Ricardo 'classical economics' by stressing the importance of the marginal unit as compared to whole classes of goods. Then it was on to Alfred Marshall, who sagely integrated Ricardian cost theory with the supposedly one-sided Austrian–Jevonian emphasis on demand and utility, to create modern neoclassical economics. Karl Marx could scarcely be ignored, and so he was treated in a chapter as an aberrant Ricardian. And so the historian could polish off his story by dealing with four or five Great Figures, each of whom, with the exception of Marx, contributed more building blocks toward the unbroken progress of economic science, essentially a story of ever onward and upward into the light.[3]

In the post-World War II years, Keynes of course was added to the Pantheon, providing a new culminating chapter in the progress and development of the science. Keynes, beloved student of the great Marshall, realized that the old man had left out what would later be called 'macroeconomics' in his exclusive emphasis on the micro. And so Keynes added macro, concentrating on the study and explanation of unemployment, a phenomenon which everyone before Keynes had unaccountably left out of the economic picture, or had conveniently swept under the rug by blithely 'assuming full employment'.

Since then, the dominant paradigm has been largely sustained, although matters have recently become rather cloudy. For one thing, this kind of Great Man ever-upward history requires occasional new final chapters. Keynes's *General Theory*, published in 1936, is now almost sixty years old; surely there must be a Great Man for a final chapter? But who? For a while, Schumpeter, with his modern and seemingly realistic stress on 'innovation', had a run, but this trend came a cropper, perhaps on the realization that Schumpeter's fundamental work (or 'vision', as he himself perceptively put it) was written more than two decades before the *General Theory*. The years since the 1950s have been murky; and it is difficult to force a return to the once-forgotten Walras into the Procrustean bed of continual progress.

My own view of the grave deficiency of the Few Great Men approach has been greatly influenced by the work of two splendid historians of thought. One is my own dissertation mentor Joseph Dorfman, whose unparalleled multi-volume work on the history of American economic thought demonstrated conclusively how important allegedly 'lesser' figures are in any movement of ideas. In the first place, the stuff of history is left out by omitting these figures, and history is therefore falsified by selecting and worrying over a few scattered texts to constitute The History of Thought. Second, a large number of the supposedly secondary figures contributed a great deal to the development of thought, in some ways more than the few peak thinkers. Hence, important features of economic thought get omitted, and the developed theory is made paltry and barren as well as lifeless.

Furthermore, the cut-and-thrust of history itself, the context of the ideas and movements, how people influenced each other, and how they reacted to and against one another, is necessarily left out of the Few Great Men approach. This aspect of the historian's work was particularly brought home to me by Quentin Skinner's notable two-volume *Foundations of Modern Political Thought*, the significance of which could be appreciated without adopting Skinner's own behaviourist methodology.[4]

The continual progress, onward-and-upward approach was demolished for me, and should have been for everyone, by Thomas Kuhn's famed *Structure of Scientific Revolutions*.[5] Kuhn paid no attention to economics, but instead, in the standard manner of philosophers and historians of science, focused on such ineluctably 'hard' sciences as physics, chemistry, and astronomy. Bringing the word 'paradigm' into intellectual discourse, Kuhn demolished what I like to call the 'Whig theory of the history of science'. The Whig theory, subscribed to by almost all historians of science, including economics, is that scientific thought progresses patiently, one year after another developing, sifting, and testing theories, so that science marches onward and upward, each year, decade or generation learning more and possessing ever more correct scientific theories. On analogy with the Whig theory of history, coined in mid-nineteenth century England, which maintained that things are always getting (and therefore must get) better and better, the Whig historian of science, seemingly on firmer grounds than the regular Whig historian, implicitly or explicitly asserts that 'later is always better' in any particular scientific discipline. The Whig historian (whether of science or of history proper) really maintains that, for any point of historical time, 'whatever was, was right', or at least better than 'whatever was earlier'. The inevitable result is a complacent and infuriating Panglossian optimism. In the historiography of economic thought, the consequence is the firm if implicit position that every individual economist, or at least every school of economists, contributed their important mite to the inexorable upward march. There can, then, be no such thing as gross systemic error that deeply flawed, or even invalidated, an entire school of economic thought, much less sent the world of economics permanently astray.

Kuhn, however, shocked the philosophic world by demonstrating that this is simply not the way that science has developed. Once a central paradigm is selected, there is no testing or sifting, and tests of basic assumptions only take place after a series of failures and anomalies in the ruling paradigm has plunged the science into a 'crisis situation'. One need not adopt Kuhn's nihilistic philosophic outlook, his implication that no one paradigm is or can be better than any other, to realize that his less than starry-eyed view of science rings true both as history and as sociology.

But if the standard romantic or Panglossian view does not work even in the hard sciences, *a fortiori* it must be totally off the mark in such a 'soft science' as economics, in a discipline where there can be no laboratory testing, and where numerous even softer disciplines such as politics, religion, and ethics necessarily impinge on one's economic outlook.

There can therefore be no presumption whatever in economics that later thought is better than earlier, or even that all well-known economists have contributed their sturdy mite to the developing discipline. For it becomes very likely that, rather than everyone contributing to an ever-progressing edifice, economics can and has proceeded in contentious, even zig-zag fashion, with later systemic fallacy sometimes elbowing aside earlier but sounder paradigms, thereby redirecting economic thought down a total erroneous or even tragic path. The overall path of economics may be up, or it may be down, over any give time period.

In recent years, economics, under the dominant influence of formalism, positivism and econometrics, and preening itself on being a hard science, has displayed little interest in its own past. It has been intent, as in any 'real' science, on the latest textbook or journal article rather than on exploring its own history. After all, do contemporary physicists spend much time poring over eighteenth century optics?

In the last decade or two, however, the reigning Walrasian–Keynesian neoclassical formalist paradigm has been called ever more into question, and a veritable Kuhnian 'crisis situation' has developed in various areas of economics, including worry over its methodology. Amidst this situation, the study of the history of thought has made a significant comeback, one which we hope and expect will expand in coming years.[6] For if knowledge buried in paradigms lost can disappear and be forgotten over time, then studying older economists and schools of thought need not be done merely for antiquarian purposes or to examine how intellectual life proceeded in the past. Earlier economists can be studied for their important contributions to forgotten and therefore new knowledge today. Valuable truths can be learned about the content of economics, not only from the latest journals, but from the texts of long-deceased economic thinkers.

But these are merely methodological generalizations. The concrete realization that important economic knowledge had been lost over time came to me from absorbing the great revision of the scholastics that developed in the 1950s and 1960s. The pioneering revision came dramatically in Schumpeter's great *History of Economic Analysis*, and was developed in the works of Raymond de Roover, Marjorie Grice-Hutchinson and John T. Noonan. It turns out that the scholastics were not simply 'medieval', but began in the thirteenth century and expanded and flourished through the sixteenth and into the seventeenth century. Far from being cost-of-production moralists, the scholastics believed that the just price was whatever price was established on the 'common estimate' of the free market. Not only that: far from being naive labour or cost-of-production value theorists, the scholastics may be considcred 'proto-Austrians', with a sophisticated subjective utility theory of value and price. Furthermore, some of the scholastics were far superior to current formalist microeconomics in developing a 'proto Austrian' dynamic theory of entrepreneurship. Moreover, in 'macro', the scholastics, beginning with Buridan and culminating in the sixteenth century Spanish scholastics, worked out an 'Austrian' rather than monetarist supply and demand theory of money and prices, including interregional money flows, and even a purchasing-power parity theory of exchange rates.

It seems to be no accident that this dramatic revision of our knowledge of the scholastics was brought to American economists, not generally esteemed for their depth of knowledge of Latin, by European-trained economists steeped in Latin, the language in which the scholastics wrote. This simple point emphasizes another reason for loss of knowledge in the modern world: the insularity in one's own language (particularly severe in the English-speaking countries) that has, since the Reformation, ruptured the once Europe-wide community of scholars. One reason why continental economic thought has often exerted minimal, or at least delayed, influence in England and the United States is simply because these works had not been translated into English.[7]

For me, the impact of scholastic revisionism was complemented and strengthened by the work, during the same decades, of the German-born 'Austrian' historian, Emil Kauder. Kauder revealed that the dominant economic thought in France and Italy during the seventeenth and especially the eighteenth centuries was also 'proto-Austrian', emphasizing subjective utility and relative scarcity as the determinants of value. From this groundwork, Kauder proceeded to a startling insight into the role of Adam Smith that, however, follows directly from his own work and that of the scholastic revisionists: that Smith, far from being the founder of economics, was virtually the reverse. On the contrary, Smith actually took the sound, and almost fully developed, proto-Austrian subjective value tradition, and tragically shunted economics on to a false path, a dead end from which the Austrians had to rescue economics a century later. Instead of subjective value, entrepreneurship, and emphasis on real market pricing and market activity, Smith dropped all this and replaced it with a labour theory of value and a dominant focus on the unchanging long-run 'natural price' equilibrium, a world where entrepreneurship was assumed out of existence. Under Ricardo, this unfortunate shift in focus was intensified and systematized.

If Smith was not the creator of economic theory, neither was he the founder of *laissez-faire* in political economy. Not only were the scholastics analysts of, and believers in, the free market and critics of government intervention; but the French and Italian economists of the eighteenth century were even more *laissez-faire*-oriented than Smith, who introduced numerous waffles and qualifications into what had been, in the hands of Turgot and others, an almost pure championing of *laissez-faire*. It turns out that, rather than someone who should be venerated as creator of modern economics or of *laissez-faire*, Smith was closer to the picture portrayed by Paul Douglas in the 1926 Chicago commemoration of the *Wealth of Nations*: a necessary precursor of Karl Marx.

Emil Kauder's contribution was not limited to his portrayal of Adam Smith as the destroyer of a previously sound tradition of economic theory, as the founder of an enormous 'zag' in a Kuhnian picture of a zig-zag history of economic thought. Also fascinating if more speculative was Kauder's estimate of the essential *cause* of a curious asymmetry in the course of economic thought in different countries. Why is it, for example, that the subjective utility tradition flourished on the Continent, especially in France and Italy, and then revived particularly in Austria, whereas the labour and cost of production theories developed especially in Great Britain? Kauder attributed the difference to the profound influence of religion: the scholastics, and then France, Italy and Austria were Catholic countries, and Catholicism emphasized consumption as the goal of production and consumer utility and enjoyment as, at least in moderation, valuable activities and goals. The British tradition, on the contrary, beginning with Smith himself, was Calvinist, and reflected the Calvinist emphasis on hard work and labour toil as not only good but a great good in itself, whereas consumer enjoyment is at best a necessary evil, a mere requisite to continuing labour and production.

On reading Kauder, I considered this view a challenging insight, but essentially an unproven speculation. However, as I continued studying economic thought and embarked on writing these volumes, I concluded that Kauder was being confirmed many times over. Even though Smith was a 'moderate' Calvinist, he was a staunch one nevertheless, and I came to the conclusion that the Calvinist emphasis could account, for example, for Smith's otherwise puzzling championing of usury laws, as well as his shift in emphasis from the capricious, luxury-loving consumer as the determinant of value, to the virtuous labourer embedding his hours of toil into the value of his material product.

But if Smith could be accounted for by Calvinism, what of the Spanish–Portuguese Jew-turned-Quaker, David Ricardo, surely no Calvinist? Here it seems to me that recent research into the dominant role of James Mill as mentor of Ricardo and major founder of the 'Ricardian system' comes strongly into play. For Mill was a Scotsman ordained as a Presbyterian minister and steeped in Calvinism; the fact that, later in life, Mill moved to London and became an agnostic had no effect on the Calvinist nature of Mill's basic attitudes toward life and the world. Mill's enormous evangelical energy, his crusading for social betterment, and his devotion to labour toil (as well as the cognate Calvinist virtue of thrift) reflected his lifelong Calvinist world-out-look. John Stuart Mill's resurrection of Ricardianism may be interpreted as his fileopietist devotion to the memory of his dominant father, and Alfred Marshall's trivialization of Austrian insights into his own neo-Ricardian schema also came from a highly moralistic and evangelical neo-Calvinist.

Conversely, it is no accident that the Austrian School, the major challenge to the Smith–Ricardo vision, arose in a country that was not only solidly Catholic, but whose values and attitudes were still heavily influenced by Aristotelian and Thomist thought. The German precursors of the Austrian School flourished, not in Protestant and anti-Catholic Prussia, but in those German states that were either Catholic or were politically allied to Austria rather than Prussia.

The result of these researches was my growing conviction that leaving out religious outlook, as well as social and political philosophy, would disas-trously skew any picture of the history of economic thought. This is fairly obvious for the centuries before the nineteenth, but it is true for that century as well, even as the technical apparatus takes on more of a life of its own.

In consequence of these insights, these volumes are very different from the norm, and not just in presenting an Austrian rather than a neoclassical or institutionalist perspective. The entire work is much longer than most since it insists on bringing in all the 'lesser' figures and their interactions as well as emphasizing the importance of their religious and social philosophies as well as their narrower strictly 'economic' views. But I would hope that the length and inclusion of other elements does not make this work less readable. On the contrary, history necessarily means narrative, discussion of real persons as well as their abstract theories, and includes triumphs, tragedies, and con-flicts, conflicts which are often moral as well as purely theoretical. Hence, I hope that, for the reader, the unwonted length will be offset by the inclusion of far more human drama than is usually offered in histories of economic thought.

Murray N. Rothbard
Las Vegas, Nevada

Notes

1. Joseph Schumpeter's valuable and monumental *History of Economic Analysis* (New York: Oxford University Press, 1954), has sometimes been referred to as 'Austrian'. But while Schumpeter was raised in Austria and studied under the great Austrian Böhm-Bawerk, he himself was a dedicated Walrasian, and his *History* was, in addition, eclectic and idiosyn-cratic.
2. For an explanation of the three leading Austrian paradigms at the present time, see Murray N. Rothbard, *The Present State of Austrian Economics* (Auburn, Ala.: Ludwig von Mises Institute, 1992).
3. When the present author was preparing for his doctoral orals at Columbia University, he

had the venerable John Maurice Clark as examiner in the history of economic thought. When he asked Clark whether he should read Jevons, Clark replied, in some surprise: 'What's the point? The good in Jevons is all in Marshall'.

4. Joseph Dorfman, *The Economic Mind in American Civilization* (5 vols, New York: Viking Press, 1946–59); Quentin Skinner, *The Foundations of Modern Political Thought* (2 vols, Cambridge: Cambridge University Press, 1978).

5. Thomas S. Kuhn, *The Structure of Scientific Revolutions* (1962, 2nd ed., Chicago: University of Chicago Press, 1970).

6. The attention devoted in recent years to a brilliant critique of neoclassical formalism as totally dependent on obsolete mid-nineteenth century mechanics is a welcome sign of this recent change of attitude. See Philip Mirowski, *More Heat than Light* (Cambridge: Cambridge University Press, 1989).

7. At the present time, when English has become the European *lingua franca*, and most European journals publish articles in English, this barrier has been minimized.

Acknowledgements

These volumes were directly inspired by Mark Skousen, of Rollins College, Florida, who urged me to write a history of economic thought from an Austrian perspective. In addition to providing the spark, Skousen persuaded the Institute for Political Economy to support my research during its first academic year. Mark first envisioned the work as a standard Smith-to-the-present moderately sized book, a sort of contra-Heilbroner. After pondering the problem, however, I told him that I would have to begin with Aristotle, since Smith was a sharp decline from many of his predecessors. Neither of us realized then the scope or length of the ensuing research.

It is impossible to list all the persons from whom I have learned in a lifetime of instruction and discussion in the history of economics and all its cognate disciplines. Here I shall have to slight most of them and single out a few. The dedication acknowledges my immense debt to Ludwig von Mises for providing a mighty edifice of economic theory, as well as for his teaching, his friendship, and for the inspiring example of his life. And to Joseph Dorfman for his path-breaking work in the history of economic thought, his stress on the importance of the stuff of history as well as of the theories themselves, and his painstaking instruction in historical method.

I owe a great debt to Llewellyn H. Rockwell Jr for creating and organizing the Ludwig von Mises Institute, establishing it at Auburn University, and building it, in merely a decade, into a flourishing and productive centre for advancing and instructing people in Austrian economics. Not the least service to me of the Mises Institute was attracting a network of scholars from whom I could learn. Here again I must single out Joseph T. Salerno, of Pace University, who has done remarkably creative work in the history of economic thought; and that extraordinary polymath and scholar's scholar, David Gordon of the Mises Institute, whose substantial output in philosophy, economics and intellectual history embodies only a small fraction of his erudition in these and many other fields. Also thanks to Gary North, head of the Institute for Christian Economics in Tyler, Texas, for leads into the extensive bibliography on Marx and on socialism generally, and for instructing me in the mysteries of varieties of millennialism, a-, pre- and post. None of these people, of course, should be implicated in any of the errors herein.

Most of my research was conducted with the aid of the superb resources of Columbia and Stanford University libraries, as well as the library at the University of Nevada, Las Vegas, supplemented by my own book collection accumulated over the years. Since I am one of the few scholars remaining who stubbornly cleave to low-tech typewriters rather than adopt word processors/computers, I have been dependent on the services of a number of typists/word processors, among whom I would particularly mention Janet Banker and Donna Evans of the University of Nevada, Las Vegas.

1 J.B. Say: the French tradition in Smithian clothing

1.1   The Smithian conquest of France

One of the great puzzles in the history of economic thought, as we have indicated, in Volume 1, is why Adam Smith was able to sweep the field and enjoy the reputation of 'founder of economic science' when Cantillon and Turgot had been far superior, both as technical economic analysts and as champions of *laissez-faire*. The mystery is particularly acute for France, since in Britain the only schools competing with the Smithians were the mercantilists and the political arithmeticians. The mystery deepens when we realize that the great leader of French economics after Smith, Jean-Baptiste Say (1767–1832), was *really* in the Cantillon–Turgot tradition rather than that of Smith even though he greatly neglected the former and proclaimed that economics began with Adam Smith. He, Say, was supposedly only systematizing the wonderful but inchoate truths found in the *Wealth of Nations*. We shall see below the precise nature of Say's thought and his contributions, as well as his decidedly 'French' non-Smithian, and 'pre-Austrian' logical clarity and emphasis on the praxeologic axiomatic–deductive method, on utility as the sole source of economic value, on the entrepreneur, on the productivity of the factors of production, and on individualism.

Specifically, in his brief treatment of the history of thought in his great *Treatise on Political Economy*, Say makes no mention whatever of Cantillon. Despite the considerable influence of Turgot on his doctrine, he brusquely dismisses Turgot as sound on politics but of no account in economics, and asserts that political economy in effect began with Adam Smith's *Wealth of Nations*. This curious and wilful neglect of his own forbears is made obscure by the scandalous fact that there is not a single biography of Say in the English language, and precious little even in French.

Perhaps we can understand this development given the following. In France, economics had long been associated with the physiocrats, *les économistes*. The ouster from the controller-generaliship of the great Turgot in 1776 and the consequent demise of his liberal reforms served to discredit the entire physiocratic movement. For Turgot was unfortunately considered in the public eye as merely a fellow-traveller of physiocracy and its most influential follower in government. After this loss of political influence, the French *philosophes* and the leading intelligentsia felt free to heap mockery and ridicule upon the physiocrats. Some of the fanatical cult aspects of physiocracy left it vulnerable to scorn, and the *encyclopédistes*, though themselves generally pro-*laissez-faire*, led the attack.

The advent of the French Revolution accelerated the demise of physiocracy. In the first place, the Revolution was itself too intensely political to allow much sustained interest in economic theory. Second, the physiocrats' strategic devotion to absolute monarchy tended to discredit them in an era when the monarch had been toppled and destroyed. Moreover, the physiocrats, with their emphasis on the exclusive productivity of land, were associated with devotion to the landed, aristocratic interest. The French Revolution against aristocratic rule and against feudal landholding had no patience for physiocracy. The impatience was aggravated by the emergence of industrialism and the Industrial Revolution, which increasingly rendered obsolete the physiocratic devotion to the land. All these factors served to discredit physiocracy totally, and since Turgot was unfortunately identified as a physiocrat, his reputation was dragged down at the same time. This situation was aggravated by the fact that Turgot's former aide and close friend, editor and biographer was the last of the physiocrats, the statesman Pierre Samuel DuPont de Nemours (1739–1817), who added to the problem by deliberately distorting Turgot's views to make them appear as close to physiocracy as possible.

Originally, Smith's *Wealth of Nations* was poorly received in France. The then dominant physiocrats scorned it as a vague and poor imitation of Turgot. However, the great libertarian Condorcet, who had been a close friend and biographer of Turgot, wrote admiring notes appended to several French translations of the *Wealth of Nations*. And Condorcet's widow, Madame de Grouchy, continued the family interest in Smithian studies by preparing a French translation of the *Theory of Moral Sentiments*. Later, in the 1790s, the physiocratic remnants latched gratefully on to the Smithian coat-tails. Smith, after all, favoured *laissez-faire*, and he was almost outlandishly pro-agriculture, holding that agricultural labour was the chief source of wealth. As a result, most of the later physiocrats became early Smithians in France, led by the Marquis Germain Garnier (1754–1821), the first French translator of the *Wealth of Nations*, who presented Smithian doctrine to France in his *Abrège elementaire des principes de l'économie politique* (1796).

1.2 Say, de Tracy and Jefferson

The leadership of the French Smithians was quickly gained by Jean-Baptiste Say, when the first edition of his great *Traité d'Économie Politique* was published in 1803. Say was born in Lyons to a Huguenot family of textile merchants, and he spent most of his early life in Geneva, and then in London, where he became a commercial apprentice. Finally, he returned to Paris as an employee of a life insurance company, and the young Say quickly became a leader of the *laissez-faire* group of *philosophes* in France. In 1794, Say became the first editor of the major journal of this group, *La Décade Philosophique*. A champion not only of *laissez-faire* but also of the burgeoning *industrielisme* of the Industrial Revolution, Say was hostile to the absurdly pro-agricultural physiocracy.

The *Décade* group called themselves the 'ideologists', later sneeringly dubbed by Napoleon the 'ideologues'. Their concept of 'ideology' simply meant the discipline studying all forms of human action, a study meant to be a respecter of individuals and their interaction rather than a positivistic or scientistic manipulating of people as mere fodder for social engineering. The ideologues were inspired by the views and the analysis of the late Condillac. Their leader in physiological psychology was Dr Pierre Jean George Cabanis (1757–1808), who worked closely with other biologists and psychologists at the *École de Médecine*. Their leader in the social sciences was the wealthy aristocrat Antonie Louis Claude Destutt, Comte de Tracy (1754–1836).[1] Destutt de Tracy originated the concept of 'ideology', which he presented in the first volume (1801) of his five-volume *Éléments d'idéologie* (1801–15).

De Tracy first set forth his economic views in his *Commentary* on Montesquieu, in 1807, which remained in manuscript due to its boldly liberal views. In the *Commentary*, de Tracy attacks hereditary monarchy and one-man rule, and defends reason and the concept of universal natural rights. He begins by refuting Montesquieu's definition of freedom as 'willing what one ought' to the far more libertarian definition of liberty as the ability to will and do what one pleased. In the *Commentary*, de Tracy gives primacy to economics in political life, since the main purpose of society is to satisfy, in the course of exchange, man's material needs and enjoyments. Commerce, de Tracy hails as 'the source of all human good', and he also lauds the advance of the division of labour as a source of increasing production, with none of the complaints about 'alienation' raised by Adam Smith. He also stressed the fact that 'in every act of commerce, every exchange of merchandise, both parties benefit or possess something of greater value than what they sell'. Freedom of domestic trade is, therefore, just as important as free trade among nations.

But, de Tracy lamented, in this idyll of free exchange and commerce, and of increasing productivity, comes a blight: government. Taxes, he pointed out, 'are always attacks on private property, and are used for positively wasteful, unproductive expenditure'. At best, all government expenditures are a necessary evil, and most, 'such as public works, could be better performed by private individuals'. De Tracy bitterly opposed government creation of and tampering with currency. Debasements are, simply, 'robbery', and paper money is the creation of a commodity worth only the paper on which it is printed. De Tracy also attacked public debts, and called for a specie, preferably a silver, standard.

The fourth volume of de Tracy's *Elements*, the *Traité de la volonté (Treatise on the Will)*, was, despite its title, de Tracy's treatise on economics. He had now arrived at economics as part of his grand system. Completed by the end of 1811, the *Traité* was finally published at the overthrow of Napoleon in 1815, and it incorporated and built upon the insights of the *Commentary* on Montesquieu. Following his friend and colleague J.B. Say, de Tracy now heavily emphasized the entrepreneur as the crucial figure in the production of wealth. De Tracy has been sometimes called a labour theory of value theorist, but 'labour' was instead upheld as highly productive as compared to land. Furthermore, 'labour' for de Tracy was largely the work of the entrepreneur in saving and investing the fruits of previous labour. The entrepreneur, he pointed out, saves capital, employs other individuals, and produces a utility beyond the original value of his capital. Only the capitalist saves part of what he earns to reinvest it and produce new wealth. Dramatically, de Tracy concluded: 'Industrial entrepreneurs are really the heart of the body politic, and their capital is its blood.'

Furthermore, all classes have a joint interest in the operations of the free market. There is no such thing, de Tracy keenly pointed out, as 'unpropertied classes', for, as Emmet Kennedy paraphrases him, 'all men have at least their most precious of all properties, their faculties, and the poor have as much interest in preserving their property as do the rich'.[2] At the heart of de Tracy's central emphasis on property rights was thus the fundamental right of every man in his own person and faculties. Abolition of private property, he warned, would only result in an 'equality of misery' by abolishing personal effort. Moreover, while there are no fixed classes in the free market, and every man is both a consumer and a proprietor and can be a capitalist if he saves, there is no reason to expect equality of income, since men differ widely in abilities and talents.

De Tracy's analysis of government intervention was the same as in his *Commentary*. All government expenditures are unproductive, even when necessary, and all embody living off the income of the producers and are therefore parasitic in nature. The best encouragement government can give to industry is to 'let it alone', and the best government is the most parsimonious.

On money, de Tracy took a firm hard-money position. He lamented that the names of coins are no longer simple units of weight of gold or silver. Debasement of coins he saw clearly as theft, and paper money as theft on a grand scale. Paper money, indeed, is simply a gradual and hidden series of successive debasements of the money standard. The destructive effects of inflation were analysed, and privileged monopoly banks were attacked as 'radically vicious' institutions.

While following J.B. Say in his emphasis on the entrepreneur, de Tracy anticipated his friend in rejecting the use of mathematics or statistics in social science. As early as 1791, de Tracy was writing that much of reality and human action is simply not quantifiable, and warned against the 'charlatan' application of statistics to the social sciences. He attached the use of mathematics in his *Mémoire sur la faculté de penser* (*Memoir on the faculty of thought*) (1798), and in 1805 broke with his late friend Condorcet's stress on the importance of 'social mathematics'. Perhaps influenced by Say's *Traité* two years earlier, de Tracy stated that the proper method in the social sciences is not mathematical equations but the drawing forth, or deduction, of the implicit properties contained in basic 'original' or axiomatic truths – in short, the method of praxeology. To de Tracy, the fundamental true axiom is that 'man is a sensitive being', from which truths can be obtained through observation and deduction, not through mathematics. For de Tracy, this 'science of human understanding' is the basic foundation for all the human sciences.

Thomas Jefferson (1743–1826) had been a friend and admirer of the *philosophes* and ideologues since the 1780s when he served as minister to France. When the ideologues achieved some political power in the consular years of Napoleon, Jefferson was made a member of the 'brain trust' Institut National in 1801. The ideologues – Cabanis, DuPont, Volney, Say, and de Tracy – all sent Jefferson their manuscripts and received encouragement in return. After he finished the *Commentary* on Montesquieu, de Tracy sent the manuscript to Jefferson and asked him to have it translated into English. Jefferson enthusiastically translated some of it himself, and then had the translation finished and published by the Philadelphia newspaper publisher William Duane. In this way, the *Commentary* appeared in English (1811), eight years before it could be published in France. When Jefferson sent the published translation to de Tracy, the delighted philosopher was inspired to finish his *Traité de la volonté* and sent it quickly to Jefferson, urging him to translate that volume.

Jefferson was highly enthusiastic about the *Traité*. Even though he himself had done much to prepare the way for war with Great Britain in 1812, Jefferson was disillusioned by the public debt, high taxation, government spending, flood of paper money, and burgeoning of privileged bank monopolies that accompanied the war. He had concluded that his beloved democrat–republican party had actually adopted the economic policies of the despised Hamiltonian federalists, and de Tracy's bitter attack on these policies prodded Jefferson to try to get the *Traité* translated into English. Jefferson gave the new manuscript to Duane again, but the latter went bankrupt, and Jefferson then revised the faulty English translation Duane had commissioned. Finally, the translation was published as the *Treatise on Political Economy*, in 1818.[3]

Former President John Adams, whose ultra-hard money and 100 per cent specie banking views were close to Jefferson's, hailed the de Tracy *Treatise* as the best book on economics yet published. He particularly lauded de Tracy's chapter on money as advocating 'the sentiments that I have entertained all my lifetime'. Adams added that

> banks have done more injury to the religion, morality, tranquility, prosperity, and even wealth of the nation, than they ... ever will do good.

> Our whole banking system, I ever abhorred, I continue to abhor, and shall die
> abhorring ... every bank of discount, every bank by which interest is to be paid or
> profit of any kind made by the deponent, is downright corruption.

As early as 1790, Thomas Jefferson had hailed *The Wealth of Nations* as the best book in political economy, along with the work of Turgot. His friend Bishop James Madison (1749–1812), who was president of William & Mary College for 35 years, was the first professor of political economy in the United States. A libertarian who had emphasized early that 'we were born free', Bishop Madison had used the *Wealth of Nations* as his textbook. Now, in his preface to de Tracy's *Treatise*, Thomas Jefferson expressed the 'hearty prayer' that the book would become the basic American text in political economy. For a while William & Mary College adopted de Tracy's *Treatise* under Jefferson's prodding, but this status did not last long. Soon Say's *Treatise* surpassed de Tracy in the race for popularity in the United States.

The calamitous 'panic' of 1819 confirmed Jefferson in his stern hard-money views on banking. In November of that year, he elaborated a remedial proposal for the depression which he characteristically asked his friend William C. Rives to introduce to the Virginia legislature without disclosing his authorship. The goal of the plan was stated bluntly: 'The eternal suppression of bank paper'. The proposal was to reduce the circulating medium gradually to the pure specie level; the state government was to compel the complete withdrawal of bank notes in five years, one-fifth of the notes to be called and redeemed in specie each year. Furthermore, Virginia would make it a high offence for any bank to pass or accept the bank notes of any other states. Those banks who balked at the plan would have their charters forfeited or else be forced to redeem all their notes in specie immediately. In conclusion, Jefferson declared that no government, state or federal, should have the power of establishing a bank; instead, the circulation of money should consist solely of specie.

1.3   The influence of Say's *Traité*

J.B. Say was made a member of the governing tribunate during the Napoleonic consulate regime in 1799. Four years later, his *Traité* was published, soon establishing him as the outstanding interpreter of Smithian thought on the continent of Europe. The *Traité* went through six editions in Say's lifetime, the last in 1829, then double in size from the original edition. In addition, Say's *Cours complet d'économie politique* (1828–30) was reprinted several times, and the extract from the *Traité* printed as the *Catéchisme d'Économie politique* (1817), was reprinted for the fourth time shortly after Say's death. Every great European nation translated Say's *Traité* into its own language.

In 1802, Napoleon cracked down on the ideologues, a group he had once courted, but had always detested for its liberal economic and political views He recognized the ideologues as the staunchest opponents, in theory and practice, of his intensifying dictatorship.[4] Napoleon forced the senate to purge itself and the tribunate of the ideologues, thus ousting J.B. Say from his tribunal post. The ideologues were philosophers, and the Bonapartists saw philosophy itself as a threat to dictatorial rule. As Joseph Fievée, editor of the Bonapartist *Journal de l'Empire*, put it, 'philosophy is a means of complaining about the government, of threatening it when it departs from the principles and the men of the Revolution'.[5]

Two years later, shortly after becoming emperor, Napoleon again went after Say, refusing to allow a second edition of the *Traité* to be published unless Say changed an offending chapter. When Say refused to do so, the new edition was suppressed. Ousted from the French government, Say became a successful cotton manufacturer for ten years. In fact, Say became one of the leading new-style manufacturers in France As his biographer writes, Say was 'intimately involved in the emergence of large scale industry. He was, in effect, one of the most remarkable types of these manufacturers of the Consulate and of the Empire, of these first great entrepreneurs who sought to place the new technological processes in operation'.[6]

After Napoleon's fall in 1814, the second edition of the *Traité* was finally published, and in 1819 Say embarked on a new professorial career, first at the Conservatoire National and finally at the College de France. The admiring Jefferson, himself steeped in *laissez-faire* economic thought, assured Say that he would find a hospitable climate in the United States. Jefferson was joined in those wishes by President Madison. Indeed, Jefferson wanted to offer Say the professorship of political economy at his newly founded University of Virginia.

Say's *Traité* exerted great influence in Italy. At first, Smith's *Wealth of Nations* had little impact on Italian economics. Italy had already had a flourishing free trade tradition, notably in the systematic *Meditations on Political Economy* (1771) (*Meditazioni sull'economia politica*) of the Milanese Count Pietro Verri (1728–97). There was no mention of Smith in the 1780 work of the Neapolitan Gaetano Filangieri (1752–88), in the writings of Count Giovanni Battista Gherardo D'Arco (1785), or even as late as Francesco Mengotti's free trade work *Il Colbertismo* (1792) – and even though the *Wealth of Nations* had been translated into Italian in 1779.

The spread of the French revolutionary regime into Italy brought Adam Smith's influence along with the soldiers. Smith became the leading economic authority during the early Napoleonic years. After 1810, Say and de Tracy swept Italian economics into their camp. The views of Say were propounded in the lucid treatise, the *Elementi di economie politica* (1813) by

Luca De Samuele Cagnazzi of Altamura (1764–1852), and in the treatise by Carlo Bosellini of Modena, *Nuovo esame delle sorgenti della privata e della pubblica richezza* (1816). The courageous Abbate Paolo Balsamo (1764–1816) spread Smithian and later Say's views throughout Sicily, calling for free trade in agriculture, and for the freeing of Sicilian agriculture from the restrictions of feudalism (particularly in his *Memorie economiche ed agrarie*, Palermo, 1803, and his *Memorie inedite di pubblica economia*, Palermo, 1845).

Say's friend and colleague Destutt de Tracy also wielded enormous influence in Italy. His *Elements* was translated into a ten-volume edition (Milan, 1817–19) by the former priest Giuseppe Compagnoni (1754–1833). Furthermore, high up in the revolutionary government of Naples in the 1820s were the elderly statesman and philosopher Melchiorre Delfico, head of the provisional revolutionary junta and correspondent and admirer of de Tracy, and the follower of de Tracy, Pasquale Borelli, head of the Neapolitan revolutionary parliament.

Spain and the new Latin American countries were also influenced by de Tracy. One of the leaders of the liberal Spanish revolution of 1820 against absolute monarchy was Dom Manuel Maria Gutierrez, the translator of the *Traité* into Spanish (1817), and professor of political economy at Malaga. Furthermore, a member of the revolutionary Spanish Cortes of 1820 was Ramon de Salas, the translator of de Tracy's *Commentary*, who returned from exile in France to take part in the struggle. And still another member of the Cortes, J. Justo Garcia, had translated de Tracy's book on *Logic*., In Latin America, de Tracy's admirer and follower, Berardino Rivadavia, became president of the newly independent Republic of Argentina.[7] Tracy also became highly popular in Brazil as well as Argentina, and in Bolivia his 'ideology' became the official doctrine of the state schools in the 1820s and 1830s.

It is hardly surprising that the second wave of Smithian writers in Germany were strongly influenced by J.B. Say's *Traité*. Ludwig Heinrich von Jakob (1759–1827) was, like Kraus, a Kantian philosopher as well as economist. Studying at the University of Halle, he became professor of philosophy there. Von Jakob published a Smithian treatise on general economic principles, the *Grundsätze der Nationalökonomie* (Principles of Economics) (Halle, 1805). Later editions, up to the third, published in 1825, incorporated Sayite emendations. Furthermore, von Jakob was so impressed with Say's work that he translated the *Traité* into German (1807) and into Russian. Von Jakob, indeed, helped spread enlightened views in Russia in more ways than by publishing a translation of Say. He taught for a while at the University of Kharkov, and was a consultant to several official commissions at St Petersburg.

The most interesting and thoroughing Sayite in Germany was Gottlieb Hufeland (1760–1817). Hufeland was born in Danzig, where he became mayor, and studied at Göttingen and Jena, where he became professor of political economy. In his *Neue Grundlegung der Staatswirtschaftskunst* (Giessen, 1807–13), Hufeland adopted all the important innovations of J.B. Say – or rather his return to the French–continental, pre-Smithian tradition. Thus, Hufeland brought back the entrepreneur, and carefully separated his pure profits from confronting risk, from his interest return and from the rent or wage for his managerial abilities. Furthermore, Hufeland adopted a utility–scarcity theory of value, stressing the cause of value as the valuations of a stock of goods by individual consumers.

The influence of Say and de Tracy in Russia strikes an ironic note. In 1825, one of the leading liberal Decembrists, Pavel Ivanovich Pestel, who considered de Tracy's *Commentary* as his Bible, tried to assassinate the absolute ruler Csar Nicholas I. Nicholas, in turn, proceeded to have Pestel hanged, even though he himself was educated in the Smithian and Sayite *Cours d'Economie Politique* of Heinrich Freiherr von Storch.[8]

The English translation of the fourth edition of Say's *Traité* appeared in London in 1821, as *The Treatise on Political Economy*. The free trade Boston journal, the *North American Review*, reissued the *Treatise* in the United States the same year, with American annotations by the free trade champion Clement C. Biddle. Say's *Treatise* quickly became and remained the most popular textbook on economics in the United States down through the Civil War.[9] Indeed, it was still being reprinted as a college text in 1880. During that period, the *Treatise* had gone through 26 American printings, in contrast to only eight in France.

The untranslated writings of the ideologues had an unexpected influence in Great Britain. Thomas Brown, friend and successor to Dugald Stewart in the chair of moral philosophy at Edinburgh, was fluent in French, and was heavily influenced by the philosophy of de Tracy. Furthermore, James Mill was a philosophic disciple of Dr Brown, and was himself an admirer of Helvetius, Condillac and Cabanis. It is not surprising, therefore, that Mill should have been the first in Great Britain to appreciate the importance of Say's law of markets.

It is no wonder that the Say version of Smithianism became the most popular economics work on the European continent and in the United States. Not being able to call himself a physiocrat, Say called himself a Smith follower, but he was one largely in name only. As we shall see, his views were really post-Cantillon and pre-Austrian rather than Smithian classical.

One crucial difference between Say and Smith was in the limpid clarity and lucidity of Say's *Treatise*. Say quite justly called the *Wealth of Nations* a 'vast chaos', and 'a chaotic collection of just ideas thrown indiscriminately among a number of positive truths'. At another point, he calls Smith's work 'a promiscuous assemblage of the soundest principles ..., an ill-digested mass of enlightened views and accurate information'. And again, with great perceptiveness, Say charges that 'almost every portion of it [the *Wealth of Nations*] is destitute of method'.

Indeed, it was precisely Say's great clarity which, while winning him world wide popularity, lowered his stock among the British writers who unfortunately ruled the roost of economic thought. (The fact that he was not British himself doubtless added to this deprecation.) In contrast to the inchoate Smith, or to the tortured and virtually unreadable Ricardo, Say's clarity and felicity, the very ease of reading him, made him suspect. Schumpeter puts it very well:

> His argument flows along with such easy limpidity that the reader hardly ever stops to think and hardly ever experiences a suspicion that there might be deeper things below this smooth surface. This brought him [Say] sweeping success with the many; it cost him the good will of the few. He sometimes did see important and deep-seated truths; but when he had seen them, he pointed them out in sentences that read like trivialities.

Because he was a splendid writer, because he avoided the rough and tortured prose of a Ricardo, because, in Jefferson's phrase, his book was 'shorter, clearer, and sounder' than the *Wealth of Nations*, economists then and later tended to confuse smoothness of surface with superficiality, just as they so often confound vagueness and obscurity with profundity. Schumpeter adds:

> Thus he never got his due. The huge textbook success of the *Traité* – nowhere greater than in the United States – only confirmed contemporaneous and later critics in their diagnosis that he was just a popularizer of a Smith. In fact, the book got so popular precisely because it seemed to save hasty or ill-prepared readers the trouble of wading through the *Wealth of Nations*. This was substantially the opinion of the Ricardians, who ... put him down as a writer – see McCulloch's comments upon him in the *Literature of Political Economy* – who had been just able to rise to Smithian, but had failed to rise to Ricardian, wisdom. For Marx he is simply the "insipid" Say.[10]

1.4   The method of praxeology

A particularly outstanding feature of J.B. Say's treatise is that he was the first economist to think deeply about the proper methodology of his discipline, and to base his work, as far as he could, upon that methodology. From previous economists and from his own study, he arrived at the unique method of economic theory, what Ludwig von Mises was, over a century later, to call 'praxeology'. Economics, Say realized, was not based on a mass of inchoate particular statistical facts. It was based, instead, on very general facts (*fait généraux*), facts so general and universal and so deeply rooted in the nature of man and his world that everyone, upon learning or reading of them, would give his assent. These facts were based, then, on the nature of things (*la nature des choses*), and on the deductive implications of these facts so broadly rooted in human nature and in natural law. Since these broad facts were true, their logical implications must be true as well.

In his introduction to the *Treatise*, which sets forth the methodological nature and implications of his work, Say begins by being critical of the physiocrats and of Dugald Stewart for confounding the sciences of politics and of political economy. Say saw that if economics, or political economy, was to progress, it must stand on its own feet as a discipline without being intimately mixed from the start with political science – or the science which sets forth the correct principles of the political order. Political economy, wrote Say, is the science of wealth, its production, distribution and consumption.

Say goes on to mention the popularity of the Baconian method of induction from a mass of facts in the formation of a science, but then adds that there are two kinds of facts, 'objects that exist' and 'events that take place'. Clearly, objects that exist are primary, since events that take place are only movements or interactions of existing objects. Both classes of facts, noted Say, constitute the 'nature of things', and 'a careful observation of the nature of things is the sole foundation of all truth'.

Facts may also be grouped into two kinds: *general* or *constant*, and *particular* or *variable*. About the same time as Stewart, but far more comprehensively, Say then launched into a brilliant critique of the statistical method, and of the difference between it and political economy. Political economy deals with general facts or laws:

> Political economy, from facts always carefully observed, makes known to us the nature of wealth; from the knowledge of its nature deduces the means of its creation, unfolds the order of its distribution, and the phenomena attending its destruction. It is, in other words, an exposition of the *general facts* observed in relation to this subject. With respect to wealth, it is a knowledge of effects and of their causes. It shows what facts are constantly conjoined with; so that one is always the sequence of the other.

Say then added an important point, that economics 'does not resort for any further explanation to hypothesis'. In short, unlike the physical sciences, the assumptions of economics are not tentative hypotheses which, or the deductions from which, must be tested by fact; on the contrary, each step of the logical chain rests on definitely true, not 'hypothetical', general facts. (It might be added that it is precisely this crucial difference between the method of economics and of physical sciences that has brought so much contumely on the head of praxeology during the twentieth century.) Instead of framing hypotheses, economic science must perceive connections and regularities 'from the nature of particular events', and 'must conduct us from one line to another, so that every intelligent understanding may clearly comprehend in what manner the chain is united'. 'It is this', Say concludes, 'which constitutes the excellence of the modern method of philosophizing'.

In contrast, statistics exhibit particular facts, 'of a particular country, at a designated period'. They are 'a description in detail'. Statistics, Say added, 'may gratify curiosity', but they can 'never be productive of advantage' if they do not indicate the 'origin and consequences' of the collected facts and this can only be accomplished by the separate discipline of political economy. It is precisely the confounding of these two disciplines that made Smith's *Wealth of Nations*, in Say's perceptive words, an 'immethodical' and 'irregular mass of curious and original speculations, and of known demonstrated truths'.

A crucial difference between statistics and political economy, Say goes on, is that the latter's general principles or 'general facts' may be discovered, and therefore may be known with certainty. The principles of political economy, wherever they rest on 'the rigorous deductions of undeniable general facts', 'rest upon an immovable foundation'. They are what von Mises would later call 'apodictic'. Political economy, indeed, 'is composed of a few fundamental principles, and of a great number of corollaries or conclusions, drawn from these principles'. The particular facts of statistics, on the other hand, are necessarily uncertain, incomplete, inaccurate and imperfect. And even when true, Say correctly notes, they 'are only true for an instant'. Again, on statistics, 'how small a number of particular facts are completely examined, and how few among them are observed under all their aspects? And in supposing them well examined, well observed, and well described, how many of them either prove nothing, or directly the reverse of what is intended to be established by them[?]' And yet the gullible public is often dazzled by 'a display of figures and calculations ... as if numerical calculations alone could prove anything, and as if any rule could be laid down, from which an inference could be drawn without the aid of sound reasoning'.

Say goes on to a blistering critique of the use of statistics without theory:

> Hence, there is not an absurd theory, or an extravagant opinion that has not been supported by an appeal to facts; and it is by facts also that public authorities have been so often misled. But a knowledge of facts, without a knowledge of their mutual relations, without being able to show why the one is a cause and the other a consequence, is really no better than the crude information of an office-clerk ...

Say then denounces the idea that a good theory is not 'practical', and that the 'practical' is somehow superior to the theoretical:

Nothing can be more idle than the opposition of *theory* to *practice*! What is
theory, if it be not a knowledge of the laws which connect effects with their
causes, facts with facts? And who can be better acquainted with facts than the
theorist who surveys them under all their aspects, and comprehends their relation
to each other? And what is practice without theory, but the employment of means
without knowing how or why they act?

Say then brilliantly points out why it is impossible for peoples or nations to
'learn from experience' and to adopt or discard theories correctly on that
basis. Since the early modern era, he notes, wealth and prosperity have
increased in western Europe, while at the same time nation-states have compounded restrictions of trade and multiplied the interference of taxation.
Most people then superficially conclude that the latter *caused* the former, that
trade and production increased as a result of the interference of government.
On the other hand, Say and the political economists argue the reverse, that
'the prosperity of the same countries would have been much greater, had they
been governed by a more liberal and enlightened policy'. How can facts or
experience decide between these two clashing interpretations? The answer is
that they cannot; that only correct theory, theory deducible from a few universal general facts or principles, can do so. And that is why, notes Say,
'nations seldom derive any benefit from the lessons of experience'. To do so,
'the community at large must be enabled to seize the connexion between
causes and their consequences; which at once supposes a very high degree of
intelligence and a rare capacity for reflection'. Thus, to arrive at the truth,
only the complete knowledge of a few essential general facts is important;
'every other knowledge of facts, like the erudition of an almanac, is a mere
compilation, from which nothing results'.

Furthermore, in arguments about public policies, when 'facts' are allegedly set against the 'system' of economic theory, it is actually one theoretical
'system' poised against another, and, again, only theoretical refutation can
prevail. Thus, said Say, if you talk about how free trade between nations is
advantageous to all the participants, this is accused of being a 'system', to
which is opposed worry about deficits in the balance of trade – itself a
system, but a fallacious one. Those who assert (as had the physiocrats) that
luxury fuels trade whereas thrift is ruinous, are setting forth a 'system', and
then, in an exact prefiguring of the Keynesian multiplier, 'some will assert
that circulation enriches a state, and that a sum of money, by passing through
twenty different hands, is equivalent to twenty times its own value' – also a
system.

In a surprising and perceptive prefigurement of modern controversies, Say
goes on to explain why the logical deductions of economic theory should be
verbal rather than mathematical. The intangible values of individuals, with
which political economy is concerned, are subject to continuing and unpredict-

able change: 'subject to the influence of the faculties, the wants and the desires of mankind, they are not susceptible of any rigorous appreciation, and cannot, therefore, furnish any *data* for absolute calculations'. The phenomena of the moral world, noted Say, are not 'subject to strict arithmetical computation'.

Thus we may know absolutely that, in any given year, the price of wine will depend on the interaction of its supply, or stock to be sold, with the demand. But to calculate the two mathematically, these two elements would have to be decomposed precisely into the separate influence of each of their elements, and this would be so complex as to be impossible. Thus:

> it is not only necessary to determine what will be the product of the succeeding vintage, while yet exposed to the vicissitudes of the weather, but the quality it will possess, the quantity remaining on hand of the preceding vintage, the amount of capital that will be at the disposal of the dealers, and require them, more or less expeditiously, to get back their advances. We must also ascertain the opinion that may be entertained as to the possibility of exporting the article, which will altogether depend upon our impressions as to the stability of the laws and govern-ment, that vary from day to day, and respecting which no two individuals exactly agree. All these data, and probably many others besides, must be accurately appreciated, solely to determine the *quantity* to be put in *circulation*; itself but one of the elements of *price*. To determine the *quantity* to be *demanded*, the price at which the commodity can be sold must already be known, as the demand for it will increase in proportion to its cheapness; we must also know the former stock on hand, and the tastes and means of the consumers, as various as their persons. Their ability to purchase will vary according to the more or less prosperous condition of industry in general, and of their own in particular; their wants will vary also in the ratio of the additional means at their command of substituting one liquor for another, such as beer, cider, etc. I suppress an infinite number of less important considerations, more or less affecting the solution of the problem ...

In short, the enormous number of imprecise, changing and quantitatively unknown determinants make the application of the mathematical method in economics impossible. And therefore those who

> have pretended to do it, have not been able to enunciate these questions into analytical language, without divesting them of their natural complication, by means of simplifications, and arbitrary suppressions, of which the consequences, not properly estimated, always essentially change the condition of the problem and pervert all its results; so that no other inference can be deduced from such calculations than from formula arbitrarily assumed.

Mathematics, seemingly so precise, inevitably ends in reducing economics from the complete knowledge of general principles to arbitrary formulas which alter and distort the principles and hence corrupt the conclusions.

But how then is the political economist, knowing the general principles with certainty, to apply these principles to specific problems such as the

condition of the wine market? Here, too, Say anticipated the brilliant conclusions of Ludwig von Mises on the proper relationship between theory and
history, theory and specific application. Such applied theory in economics,
Say indicated, is an art rather than a strict science:

> What course is then to be pursued by a judicious inquirer in the elucidation of a
> subject so much involved? The same which would be pursued by him, under
> circumstances equally difficult, which decide the greater part of the actions of his
> life. He will examine the immediate elements of the proposed problem, and after
> having ascertained them with certainty (which in political economy can be ef-
> fected), will approximately value their mutual influences with the intuitive quick-
> ness of an enlightened understanding, itself only an instrument by means of which
> the mean result of a crowd of probabilities can be estimated, but never calculated
> with exactness.[11]

J.B. Say then relates the fallacies of the mathematical method in economics to the teachings of his great mentor, the physiologist Cabanis. He quotes
Cabanis on how writers on mechanics grievously distort matters when they
deal with the problems of biology and medicine. Citing Cabanis:

> The terms they employed were correct, the process of reasoning strictly logical,
> and, nevertheless, all the results were erroneous ... it is by the application of this
> method of investigation to subjects to which it is altogether inapplicable, that
> systems the most whimsical, fallacious, and contradictory, have been maintained.

Say then adds that whatever has thus been pointed out about the fallacies
of the mechanistic method in biology is *a fortiori* applicable to the moral
sciences, which is why we are 'always being misled in political economy,
whenever we have subjected its phenomena to mathematical calculation. In
such case it becomes the most dangerous of all abstractions'.

Finally, Say perceptively points to another problem that, then as now, leads
learned people to dismiss the principles and conclusions of economics. For
they

> are too apt to suppose that absolute truth is confined to the mathematical and to
> the results of careful observation and experiment in the physical sciences; imagin-
> ing that the moral and political sciences contain no invariable facts or indisputable
> truths, and therefore cannot be considered as genuine sciences, but merely hypo-
> thetical systems, more or less ingenious, but purely arbitrary.

To bolster this view, the critics of economics point to a great many differences of opinion in that discipline. But so what? Say asks. After all, the
physical sciences have always been rent by controversy, sometimes clashing
'with as much violence and asperity as in political economy'.

The mathematical method was not the only system of abstraction to suffer a trenchant demolition by J.B. Say. For Say was also sharply critical of verbal methods of logic that took off into the empyrean without continuing ground-work in, and repeated checking by, reference to general and universal facts. This was Say's main methodological stricture against the physiocrats. 'In-stead of first observing the nature of things, or the manner in which they take place, of classifying these observations, and deducing from them general propositions' – that is, instead of being praxeologists, the physiocrats

> commenced by laying down certain abstract general propositions, which they styled axioms, from supposing them to contain inherent evidence of their own truth. They then endeavoured to accommodate the particular facts to them and to infer from them their laws; thus involving themselves in the defence of maxims evidently at variance with common sense and universal experience...

In short, a system of economic theory must not only be axiomatic–deductive; it must always make sure to ground those axioms in 'common sense and universal experience'.

In his Introduction to the fourth edition, Say levelled similar strictures against David Ricardo and the Ricardian system. Ricardo, too, 'sometimes reasons upon abstract principles to which he gives too great a generalization'. Ricardo, he charged, begins with observations founded on facts, but then 'pushes his reasonings to their remotest consequences, without comparing their results with those of actual experience'. After a certain point in the reasoning, 'the facts differ very far from our calculation' and 'from that instant nothing in the author's work is represented as it really occurs in nature'. 'It is not sufficient', Say concludes, 'to set out from facts; they must be brought together, steadily pursued, the consequences drawn from them constantly compared with the effects observed', so that

> the science of political economy ... must show, in what manner that which in reality does take place, is the consequence of other facts equally certain. It must discover the chain which binds them together, and always, from observation, establish the existence of the two links at their point of connexion.

1.5   Utility, productivity and distribution
In contrast to the Smith–Ricardo mainstream of Smithians who set forth the labour theory (or at very best, the cost-of-production theory) of value, J.B. Say firmly re-established the scholastic–continental–French utility analysis. It is utility and utility alone that gives rise to exchange value, and Say settled the value paradox to his own satisfaction by disposing of 'use-value' altogether as not being relevant to the world of exchange. Not only that: Say adopted a subjective value theory, since he believed that value rests on acts of valuation

by the consumers. In addition to being subjective, these degrees of valuation are relative, since the value of one good or service is always being compared against another. These values, or utilities, depend on all manner of wants, desires and knowledge on the part of individuals: 'upon the moral and physical nature of man, the climate he lives in, and on the manner and legislation of his country. He has wants of the body, wants of the mind, and of the soul; wants for himself, others for his family, others still as a member of society'. Political economy, Say sagely pointed out, must take these values and preferences of people as givens, 'as one of the *data* of its reasonings; leaving to the moralist and the practical man, the several duties of enlightening and of guiding their fellow-creatures, as well in this, as in other particulars of human conduct'.

At some points, Say went up to the edge of discovering the marginal utility concept, without ever quite doing so. Thus he saw that relative valuations of goods depends on 'degrees of estimation in the mind of the valuer'. But since he did not discover the marginal concept, he could not fully solve the value paradox. In fact, he did far less well at solving it than his continental pred ecessors. And so Say simply dismissed use-value and the value paradox altogether, and decided to concentrate on exchange-value. As a result, how- ever, he could no more than Smith and his British successors, devote much energy to analysing consumption or consumer behaviour.

But whereas Say simply discarded use-value, Ricardo made the value paradox and the unfortunate split between use- and exchange-value the key to his value theory. For Ricardo, iron was worth less than gold because the labour cost of digging and producing gold was greater than the labour cost of producing iron. Ricardo admitted that utility 'is certainly the foundation of value', but this was apparently of only remote interest, since the 'degree of utility' can never be the measure by which to estimate its value. All too true, but Ricardo failed to see the absurdity of looking for such a measure in the first place. His second absurdity, as we shall see further below, was in think ing that labour cost provided such a 'true' and invariable measure of value. As Say wrote in his annotations on the French translation of Ricardo's *Prin- ciples*, 'an invariable measure of value is a pure chimera'.

Smith, and still more Ricardo, were pushed into their labour cost theory by concentrating on the long-run 'natural' price of products. Say's analysis was aided greatly by his realistic concentration on the explanation of real market price.

Costs, of course, are intimately related to the pricing of factors of produc- tion. One question that cost-value theorists have difficulty answering is if, indeed, costs are determining, where do *they* come from? Are they mandated by divine revelation?

One of the anomalies of Say's discussion is that, even though a subjective value and utility theorist, he uncomprehendingly rejected the insight of

Genovesi and of his own ideologue forbear Condillac, that people exchange one thing for another because they value the thing they acquire more than what they give up – so that exchange always benefits both parties. And in denying this mutual gain, Say is inconsistent with much of his own position on utility.

In spurning Condillac, Say is being not only ungenerous but almost wilfully obtuse. First he notes that Condillac 'maintains that commodities, which are worth less to the seller than to the buyer, increase in value from the mere act of transfer from one hand to another'. But Condillac insists, for example, that 'equal value is really given for equal value', so that when Spanish wine is bought in Paris, 'the money paid by the buyer and the wine he receives are worth one another' – to which we might ask, to *whom*? He then admits that the selfsame wine is worth more in Paris than it had been when grown in Spain, but he insists that the increase in the value of the wine took place not 'at the moment of handing over the wine to the consumer, but comes from the transport'.

But St Clair trenchantly takes Say to task: 'In reality, the transfer to the consumer is the essence of the transaction; the long transport is subsidiary to this purpose; the change of locality is merely a means to this end, and would not have been necessary if consumers willing to buy the same quantity and pay the same price could have been found on the spot'.

Say continues obstinately to assault Condillac's insight: 'The seller is not a professional cheat, nor the buyer a dupe, and Condillac is not justified in saying that if the values exchanged were always equal neither party would gain anything by exchange'. But in reality, of course, Condillac was perfectly right; why *should* anyone bother exchanging *X* for *Y* of equal value?

St Clair reacts brilliantly in exasperation:

> Lord, how these economists do misunderstand one another! Condillac does not suggest that the wine merchant is a rogue and the customer a fool; he does not suggest that the merchant robs either the consumer or the producer; his doctrine is that products increase in utility and value by being transferred from the producer to the consumer, and that both parties benefit by the intervention of the merchant who brings about the exchange. To the producer the merchant is a consumer-finder; to the consumer he is a commodity-finder; with the merchant as medium of exchange, the producer gets a better price for his produce and the buyer better value for his money.[12]

One of Say's great contributions was to apply utility theory to the theory of distribution, in brief by discovering the productivity theory of the pricing, and hence the income, accruing to factors of production. In the first place, Say pointed out that, in contrast to Smith, *all* labour, not just labour embodied in material objects, is 'productive'. Indeed, Say brilliantly pointed out that *all* the services of factors of production, whether they be land, labour, or capital, are *immaterial*, even though they might result in a material product. Factors, in short, provide immaterial services in the process of production. That process, as Say pointed out clearly for the first time, was not the 'creation' of material products. Man cannot create matter; he can only *transform* it into different shapes and moulds, in order to satisfy his wants more fully. Production is this very transformation process. In the sense of such transformation, all labour is productive 'because it concurs in the creation of a product', or, metaphorically, in the creation of 'utilities'. If, as can happen, labour has been expended to no ultimate benefit, then the result is error: 'folly or waste in the person bestowing' the labour. One example of unproductive labour is crime, not only a non- but an anti-market activity: there 'trouble [effort] is directed to the stripping another person of the goods in his possession by means of fraud or violence...[it] degenerates to absolute criminality and there results no production, but only a forcible transfer of wealth from one individual to another'.

J.B. Say also put clearly for the first time the insight that wants are unlimited. Wrote Say: 'there is no object of pleasure or utility, whereof the mere desire may not be unlimited, since every body is always ready to receive whatever can contribute to his benefit or gratification'. Say denounced the proto-Galbraithian position of the British mercantilist Sir James Steuart, in extolling an ascetic reduction of wants as a solution to desires outpacing production. Say heaps proper scorn on this doctrine: 'Upon this principle, it would be the very acme of perfection to produce nothing and to have no wants, that is to say, to annihilate human existence.'

Unfortunately, Say proceeds to fall prey to this very Galbraithian trap by attacking luxury and ostentation, and by maintaining that 'real wants' are more important to the community than 'artificial wants'. Say hastens to add, however, that government intervention is not the proper road to achieving proper affluence.

On the valuing or pricing of the services of the factors (or as Say would put it, 'agents') of production, Say adopted the proto-Austrian in direct contrast to the Smith–Ricardo tradition. For since subjective human desire for any object creates its value, and reflects its utility, productive factors receive value because of their 'ability to create the utility wherein originates that desire'. Ricardo, writes Say, believes 'that the value of products is founded upon that of productive agency', i.e. that the value of products is determined by the value of their productive factors, or their cost of production. In contrast, Say declares, 'the current value of productive exertion is founded upon the value of an infinity of products compared one with another ... which value is proportionate to the importance of its cooperation in the business of production ...'. In contrast to consumer goods, Say points out, the demand for productive factors does not originate in immediate enjoyment, but rather in the 'value of the product they are capable of raising, which itself originates in the utility of that product, or the satisfaction it may be capable of affording'. In short, the value of factors is determined by the value of their products, which in turn is conferred by consumer valuations and demands. The causal chain, for Say as for the later Austrians, is *from* consumer valuations *to* consumer goods prices *to* the pricing of productive factors (i.e. to costs of production). In contrast, the Smithian, and especially the Ricardian, causal chain is *from* cost of production, and especially labour cost, *to* consumer goods prices. By speaking of the 'proportionate' value of each factor, Say once again comes to the edge of a marginal productivity theory of imputation of consumer to factor valuations, and to the edge of a variable proportions analysis. But he does not reach it.

Say did not rest content with a general, even if pioneering, analysis of the pricing of productive factors. He goes on to virtually create the famous 'triad' of classical economics: land (or 'natural agents'), labour (or 'industry' for Say), and capital. Labour works on, or employs 'natural agents' to create capital, which is then used to multiply productivity in collaboration with land and labour. Although capital is the previous creation of labour, once in existence it is used by labour to increase production. If there are classes of factors of production, what easier trap to fall into than to maintain that each class receives the kind of income attributed to it in common parlance: i.e. labour receives wages; land receives rent; and capital receives interest? Surely a common-sense approach! And so Say adopted it. While useful as a first attempt (excepting the forgotten Turgot) to clarify production theory out of Adam Smith's muddle, this superficial clarity comes at the expense of deep fallacy, that would not be uncovered until the Austrians. In the first place, these three rigidly separated categories already begin to break down in Say's interesting insight that labourers 'lend' their services to owners of capital and land and earn wages thereby; that landowners 'lend' their land to capital and labour and earn rent; and that capitalists 'lend' their capital to earn interest. For how exactly do these payments differ? How does rent as a 'loan' price compare with interest as a loan? And how do wages differ from interest or rent? In fact, the muddle is even worse, for workers and landowners don't 'lend' their services; they are not creditors. On the contrary, in a deep sense, capitalists lend *them* money by giving them money in advance of selling the product to the consumers; and so workers and landowners are 'debtors' to the capitalists, and pay *them* a natural rate of interest. And finally, this classical triad rests on a basic equivocation, as Böhm-Bawerk would eventually point out, between 'capital' and 'capital goods'. Capital as a fund of savings or lending may earn interest; but capital *goods* – which are the real physical factors of production rather than money funds – do *not* earn interest. Like all other factors, capital goods earn a price, a price per unit of time for their services. If you will, capital goods, land, and labourers *all* earn such prices, in the sense of 'rents', defining a rental price as a price of any good per unit of time. This price is determined by the productivity of each factor. But then where does interest on capital funds come from?

Thus, in grappling with the problem of interest, Say criticizes Smith and the Smithians for focusing on labour as the sole factor of production, and neglecting the cooperating role of capital. Tackling the Smith–Ricardian (and what would later be the Marxian) riposte: that capital is simply accumulated labour, Say replies yes, but the services of capital, once built, are there and continue anew and must be paid for. While satisfactory enough on one level, the answer does not solve the problem of where the net return on capital funds comes from, a return which Turgot and then the Austrians explained as the price of time-preference, of the fact, in short, that capital is not only accumulated labour but also 'accumulated time'.

Despite the lack of resolution of the problem of interest, Say set forth an excellent analysis of capital, in the sense of capital goods, and its crucial role in production and in increasing economic wealth. Man, he pointed out, transforms natural agents into capital, to work further with nature to arrive at consumer goods. The more he has built capital goods – the more tools and machinery – the more can man harness nature to make labour increasingly productive. More machinery means an increase in productivity of labour and a fall in the cost of production. Such increase in capital is particularly beneficial to the mass of consumers, for competition lowers the price of product as well as the cost of production. Furthermore, increased machinery permits a superior quality of product, and allows the creation of new products which would not have been available under handicraft production. The enormous increase in production and rise in the standard of living releases human energies from the scramble for subsistence to permit cultivation of the arts, even of frivolity, and most importantly for 'the cultivation of the intellectual faculties'.

Say follows Smith in his discussion of the division of labour, and in pointing out that the degree of that division is limited by the extent of the market. But Say's discussion is far sounder. He shows, first, that expanding the division of labour needs a great deal of capital, so that investment of capital becomes the crucial point rather than its division *per se*. He also points out that, in contrast to Smith, the crucial specialization of labour is not simply *within* a factory (as in Smith's famous pin factory) but ranges over the entire economy, and forms the basis for all exchange between producers.

Say also saw that the essence of investing capital is *advancing* money payments to factors of production, an advance that is repaid later by the consumer. Thus 'the capital employed on a productive operation is always a mere advance made for payment of a productive service, and reimbursed by the value of their resulting product'. Here he captured the essence of the Austrian insight into capital as a process over time and one that involves payment in advance for production. Say also anticipated the Austrian concept of 'stages of production'. He pointed out that, instead of waiting a long time for reimbursement by the consumer, the capitalist at each stage of production purchases the product of the previous stage and thereby reimburses the previous set of capitalists. As Say lucidly puts it:

> The miner extracts the ore from the bowels of the earth; the iron-founder pays him for it. Here ends the miner's production, which is paid for by an advance out of the capital of the iron-founder. This latter next smelts the ore, refines and makes it into steel, which he sells to the cutler; thus is the production of the founder paid, and his advance reimbursed by a second advance on the part of the cutler, made in the price of the steel. This again the cutler works up into razor-blades, the price for which replaces his advance of capital, and at the same time pays for his productive agency.

Generalizing:

> Each successive producer makes the advance to his precursor of the then value of the product, including the labour already expended upon it. His successor in the order of production, reimburses him in turn, with the addition of such value as the product may have received in passing through his hands. Finally, the last producer, who is generally the retail dealer, is compensated by the consumer for the aggregate of all these advances, *plus* the concluding operation performed by himself upon the product.

In the end, the money paid by the consumers for the final product, say razor blades, repays capitalists for their previous advances for the various services of the factors of production.

Turning to wages and the labour market, Say pointed out that wages will be highest relative to the price of capital and land, where labour is scarcest relative to the other two factors. This will be either whenever land is virtually unlimited in supply; and/or when an abundance of capital creates a great demand for labour. Furthermore, wage rates will be proportionate to the danger, trouble, or obnoxiousness of the work, to the irregularity of the employment, to the length of training, and to the degree of skill or talent. As Say puts it: 'Every one of these causes tends to diminish the quantity of labour in circulation in each department, and consequently to vary its' wage rate. In recognizing the differences of natural talent, Say advanced far beyond the egalitarianism of Adam Smith and of neoclassical economics since Smith's day.

In the long run, capital will earn the same return in all firms and industries; but this is only true in the long run, since for one thing there are inevitable immobilities of land, labour and capital. To Say, the 'profits' or interest, on capital stems from its productive services – again, a fundamental confusion between capital as a fund, which earns interest, and capital goods, which are productive factors and earn prices and incomes for their productivity. But despite this basic error, Say had many shrewd things to say about interest. He was possibly the first economist, for example, to show that risk premiums are added to the basic interest rate, so that riskier debtors will pay higher interest. Risk, he pointed out, depends on expected safety of the investment, the personal credit and character of the borrower, the past record of the borrower, and the ability or willingness of the government of the debtor's country to enforce the payment of debt. Furthermore, Say introduced an innovation theory of profit by stating that since new methods of employing capital are more uncertain they are especially risky, and hence they will tend to be more profitable. Thus, innovation profits are subsumed under risk.

Say was also insistent that interest on the loan market is determined by the demand for capital (to which it is directly proportional) and the supply of capital (inversely proportional). A champion of freedom of the loan market – 'usury' is no worse morally than rent or wages – he also demonstrated that it was a fallacy that the quantity of money either lowers or raises the rate of interest. Say perceptively pointed out that it is 'an abuse of words to talk of the interest of money'; it is really interest on savings, not money, and loans can and do occur in kind as well as in money. Wrote Say: the 'abundance or scarcity of money or of its substitutes ... no more affects the rate of interest, than the abundance or scarcity of cinnamon, or wheat, or of silk'.

1.6 The entrepreneur

If Adam Smith purged economic thought of the very existence of the entrepreneur, J.B. Say, to his everlasting credit, brought him back. Not quite as far back to be sure as in the days of Cantillon and Turgot, but enough to continue fitfully and 'underground' in continental economic thought even though absent from the dominant mainstream of British classicism.

Emphasis on the real world rather than on long-run equilibrium almost forced a return to the study of the entrepreneur. For Say, the entrepreneur, the linchpin of the economy, takes on himself the responsibility, the conduct, and the risk of running his firm. He almost always owns some of the firm's capital, Say being familiar with the fact that the dominant entrepreneur and risk-taker in the economy is the one who is also a capitalist, an owner of capital. The owner of capital or land or personal service hires these services out to the 'renter' or entrepreneur. In return for fixed payments to these factors, the entrepreneur takes upon himself the speculative risk of gaining profit or suffering loss. 'It is a sort of speculative bargain, wherein the renter takes the risk of profit and loss, according to the revenue he may realize, or the product obtained by the agency transferred, shall exceed or fall short of the rent or hire he is to pay'.

The entrepreneur, Say adds, acts as a broker between sellers and buyers, applying productive factors proportionate to the demand for the products. The demand for the products, in turn, is proportionate to their utilities and to the quantity of other products exchanging for them. The entrepreneur constantly compares the selling prices of products with their costs of production; if he decides to produce more, his demand for productive factors will rise.

Part of the profits accruing to the capitalist–entrepreneur will be the standard return on capital. But apart from that, Say declared, there will be a return to the 'peculiar character' of the entrepreneur. The entrepreneur is a manager of the business, but his role is also broader in Say's view: the entrepreneur must have judgement, perseverance, and 'a knowledge of the world as well as of business', as he applies knowledge to the process of creating consumer goods. He must employ labourers, purchase raw material, attempt to keep costs low, and find consumers for his product. Above all, he must *estimate* the importance of the product, the probable demand for it, and the availability of the means of production. And, finally, he 'must have a ready knack of calculation to compare the charges of production with the probable value of the product when completed and brought to market'. Those who lack these qualities will be unsuccessful as entrepreneurs and suffer losses and bankruptcies; those who remain will be the skilful and successful ones earning profits.

Say was critical of Smith and the Smithians for failing to distinguish the category of entrepreneurial profit from the profit of capital, both of which are mixed together in the profits of real world enterprises.

Say also appreciated entrepreneurship as the driving force of the allocations and adjustments of the market economy. He summed up those workings of the market by stating that the wants of consumers determine what will be produced: 'The product most wanted is most in demand; and that which is most in demand yields the largest profit to industry, capital, and land, which are therefore employed in raising this particular product in preference; and, *vice versa*, when a product becomes less in demand, there is a less profit to be got by its production; it is, therefore, no longer produced'.

Such astute analysts as Schumpeter and Hébert are critical of Say as having a view of the entrepreneur as a static manager and organizer rather than as a dynamic bearer of risk and uncertainty. We cannot share that view. It seems to us that Say is instead foursquare in the Cantillon–Turgot tradition of the entrepreneur as forecaster and risk-bearer.

From his analysis of capital, entrepreneurship, and the market, J.B. Say concluded for *laissez-faire*: 'The producers themselves are the only competent judges of the transformation, export, and import of these various matters

and commodities; and every government which interferes, every system calculated to influence production, can only do mischief.'

1.7 Say's law of markets

While J.B. Say has been almost totally ignored by mainstream economists
and historians of economic thought, this is not true for one relatively minor
facet of his thought that became known as 'Say's law of markets'. The one
point of his doctrine that the active and aggressive British Ricardians got out
of Say was this law. James Mill, the 'Lenin' of the Ricardian movement (see
below), appropriated the law in his *Commerce Defended* (1808), and Ricardo
adopted it from his discoverer and mentor.[13]

Say's law is simple and almost truistic and self-evident, and it is hard to
escape the conviction that it has stirred up a series of storms only because of
its obvious political implications and consequences. Essentially Say's law is
a stern and proper response to the various economic ignoramuses as well as
self-seekers who, in every economic recession or crisis, begin to complain
loudly about the terrible problem of general 'overproduction' or, in the common language of Say's day, a 'general glut' of goods on the market. 'Overproduction' means production in excess of consumption: that is, production
is too great in general compared to consumption, and hence products cannot
be sold in the market. If production is too large in relation to consumption,
then obviously this is a problem of what is now called 'market failure', a
failure which must be compensated by the intervention of government. Intervention would have to take one or both of the following forms: reduce
production, or artificially stimulate consumption. The American New Deal in
the 1930s did both, with no success in relieving the alleged problem. Production can be reduced, as in the case of the New Deal, by the government's
organizing compulsory cartels of business to force a cut in their output.

Stimulating consumer demand has long been the particularly favoured
programme of interventionists. Generally, this is done by the government and
its central bank inflating the money supply and/or by the government incur-
ring heavy deficits, its spending passing for a surrogate consumption. Indeed,
government deficits would seem to be ideal for the overproduction/
underconsumptionists. For if the problem is too much production and/or too
little consumer spending, then the solution is to stimulate a lot of unproductive consumption, and who is better at that than government, which by its
very nature is unproductive and even counter productive?

Say understandably reacted in horror to this analysis and to the prescription.[14] In the first place, he pointed out, the wants of man are unlimited, and
will continue to be until we achieve genuine general superabundance – a
world marked by the prices of all goods and services falling to zero. But at
that point there would be no problem of finding consumer demand, or, in-

deed, any economic problem at all. There would be no need to produce, to work, or to worry about accumulating capital, and we would all be in the Garden of Eden.

Thus Say postulates a situation where all costs of production are at last reduced to zero: 'in which case, it is evident there can no longer be rent for land, interest upon capital, or wages on labour, and consequently, no longer any revenue to the productive classes'. What will happen then?

> What then, I say, these classes would no longer exist. Every object of human want would stand in the same predicament as the air or the water, which are consumed without the necessity of being either produced or purchased. In like manner as every one is rich enough to provide himself with air, so would he be to provide himself with every other imaginable product. This would be the very acme of wealth. Political economy would no longer be a science; we should have no occasion to learn the mode of acquiring wealth; for we should find it ready made to our hands.

Since, apart from the Garden of Eden, production always falls short of man's wants, this means that there is no need to worry about any lack of consumption. The problem that limits wealth and living standards is a deficiency of production. On the market, Say points out, producers exchange their products for money and they use the money to buy the products of others. That is the essence of the exchange, or market, economy. Therefore the supply of one good constitutes, at bottom, the demand for other goods. Consumption demand is simply the embodiment of the supply of other products, whose owners are seeking to purchase the products in question. Far better to have demand emerging from the supply of other products, as on the free market, than for the government to stimulate consumer demand without any corresponding production.

For the government to stimulate consumption by itself 'is no benefit to commerce; for the difficulty lies in supplying the means, not in stimulating the desire for consumption; and we have seen that production alone, furnishes the means'. Since genuine demand only comes from the supply of products, and since the government is not productive, it follows that government spending cannot truly increase demand:

> a value once created is not augmented ... by being seized and expended by the government, instead of by an individual. The man, that lives upon the productions of other people, originates no demand for those productions; he merely puts himself in the place of the producer, to the great injury of production ...

But if there can be no general overproduction short of the Garden of Eden, then why do businessmen and observers so often complain about a general glut? In one sense, a surplus of one or more commodities simply means that *too little* has been produced of *other* commodities for which they might exchange. Looked at in another way, since we know that an increased supply of any product lowers its price, then if any unsold surplus of one or more goods exists, this price should fall, thereby stimulating demand so that the full amount will be purchased. There can never be any problem of 'overproduction' or 'underconsumption' on the free market because prices can always fall until the markets are cleared. While Say did not always put the matter in these precise terms, he saw it clearly enough, particularly in his *Letters to Malthus*, in his controversy with the Rev. Thomas Robert Malthus over Say's law. Those who complain about overproduction or underconsumption rarely talk in terms of price, yet these concepts are virtually meaningless if the price system is not always held in mind. The question should always be: production or sales *at what price*? Demand or consumption *at what price*? There is never any genuine unsold surplus, or 'glut', whether specific or general over the whole economy, if prices are free to fall to clear the market and eliminate the surplus.

Moreover, Say wrote in his *Letters to Malthus*, 'if the quantity sent in the slightest degree exceeds the want, it is sufficient to alter the price considerably'. It is this notion of what we would now call 'elasticity', and resulting sharp changes in price, that for Say leads many people to mistake a 'slight excess' of supply 'for an excessive abundance'.

The policy implications of attending to the price system are crucial. It means that to cure a glut, whether specific or pervasive, the remedy is not for the government to spend or create money; it is to allow prices to fall so that the market will be cleared.

In his *Letters to Malthus*, Say offers the following example. One hundred sacks of wheat are produced and exchanged for 100 pieces of cloth (or rather, each is exchanged for money and then for the other commodity). Suppose that productivity and output of each is doubled, and now 200 sacks of wheat are exchanged for 200 pieces of cloth. How is superabundance or overproduction going to affect either or both commodities? And if by producing 100 units of each product, the producer made 30 francs' profit, why couldn't the resulting increase of production and fall in the price of each product *still* reap 30 francs' profit for each seller? And how can general glut arise? Yet Malthus would have to maintain that part of the new production of cloth would find no buyers.

Say then notes that Malthus in a sense conceded the point about prices falling due to increased production, and then fell back on a second line of defence: that 'productions will fall to too low a price to pay for the labour necessary to their production'. Here we come to the nub of the overproductionist/underconsumptionist complaints – if we can get past their foggy aggregate concepts and their real or seeming neglect of the fact that a lower price of any product can always clear the market.

In reply, Say noted that Malthus, having unfortunately adopted the labour theory of value, neglected to add the productive services of land and capital to labour in the costs of production. So that the assertion is that selling prices will fall below the costs of production.

But where do 'costs' come from? And why are they somehow fixed, exogenous to the market system itself? How are they determined? Although Ricardo joined with Say on the question of overproduction, it was easy for a British follower of Smith and Ricardo (such as Malthus) on cost theories of value to fall into this trap and to assume that costs are somehow fixed and invariant. Say, believing as we have seen that costs are determined by selling price rather than the other way round, was impelled to a far clearer and more correct picture of the entire matter. Returning to his example, Say points out that if the wheat and cloth producers double the quantity produced with the same productive services, this means not only that the prices of wheat and cloth will fall, but also that factor productivity has risen in both industries. A rise of factor productivity means a lowering of cost. But this means that an increase in output will not only lower selling price; it will *also* lower costs, so there is no reason to assume grievous losses or even a lessening of profit if prices fall.

Apparently, Say continued, Malthus is worried about the prices of productive services remaining high and therefore keeping costs too high as production increases. But here Say brings in a brilliantly perceptive point: prices of productive factors must be high *for a reason*; they are not preordained to be high. But this high wage or rent in itself precisely 'denotes that what we seek for exists, that is to say, that there is a mode of employing them so as to make the produce sufficient to repay what they cost'. In short, factor prices being high means that they have been bid up to that height by alternative uses for them. If the costs of these factors seriously impinge upon or erase the profits of a firm or industry, this is because these factors are more productive elsewhere and have been bid up to reflect that vital fact. Say's reasoning is strikingly similar to the modern free trade reply to the 'cheap labour' argument for protective tariffs. The reason why labour is *more* expensive, say, in the United States or other industrialized country, is that *other* American industries have bid up these labour costs. These industries are therefore more efficient than the industry suffering from competition, and hence the latter should cut back or shut down and allow resources to shift to more efficient and productive fields.

In more peripheral but still relevant areas, J.B. Say engaged in some lovely and powerful examples of *reductio ad absurdum* argument. Thus, on the importance of demand *vis-à-vis* supply, and on the question of gluts, he asked what would have happened if a merchant shipped a current cargo to the site of New York City in the early seventeenth century. Clearly, he wouldn't have been able to sell his cargo. Why not? Why this glut? Because no one in the New York area was producing enough *other goods* to exchange for this cargo. And why would this merchant be sure to sell his cargo nowadays in New York City? Because there are now enough producers in the New York area to make and import products, 'by the means of which they acquire that which is offered to them by others'.

It would have been absurd to state that the problem about the seventeenth century cargo was there was *too many* producers and *not enough* consumers. Say adds that 'the only real consumers are those who produce on their part, because they alone can buy the produce of others, [while] ... barren consumers can buy nothing except by the means of value created by producers'. He concludes eloquently that 'it is the capability of production which makes the difference between a country and a desert'.

The other potent *reductio*, also in his *Letters to Malthus*, is part of his defence of innovation and machinery against charges of overproduction. Malthus, Say notes, concedes that machinery is beneficial when the production of the product is so increased that employment in that field increases also. But, Say adds, new machinery is advantageous even in the seeming worst case, when production of the particular good is not increased and labourers are discharged. For, first, in the latter case as well as the former, productivity increases, selling prices fall, and standards of living rise. Besides, writes Say, bringing in the *reductio*, tools are vital to mankind. To propose, as Malthus does, to limit and restrain the introduction of new machinery is to argue implicitly that 'we ought (retrograding rather than advancing the career of civilization) successively to renounce all the discoveries we have already made, and to render our arts more imperfect in order to multiply our labour by diminishing our enjoyments'.

As to labourers disemployed by the introduction of new machinery, Say writes that they can and will move elsewhere. After all, he adds caustically, the employer who brings in new machinery 'does not compel them [the labourers] to remain unemployed, but only to seek another occupation'. And many employment opportunities will open up for these labourers, since income in society has increased due to the new machinery and product.

Echoing Turgot, Say also counters the Malthus–Sismondi worry about the leaking out of savings from vital spendings, pointing out that savings do not remain unspent; they are simply spent on other productive (or *re*productive) factors rather than consumption. Rather than injuring consumption, saving is invested and thereby increases future consumer spending. Historically, savings and consumption thereby grow together. And just as there is no necessary limit to production, so there is no limit to investment and the accumulation of capital. 'A produce created was a vent opened for another produce, and this is true whether the value of it is spent' on consumption or added to savings.

Conceding that sometimes the savings might be hoarded, Say was for once less than satisfactory. He pointed out correctly that eventually the hoard will be spent, either on consumption or investment, since after all that is what money is for. Yet he admitted that he too deplored hoarding. And yet, as Turgot had hinted, hoarded cash balances that reduce spending will have the same effect as 'overproduction' at too high a price: the lower demand will reduce prices all round, real cash balances will rise, and all markets will again be cleared. Unfortunately, Say did not grasp this point.[15]

Say, however, was again powerful and hard-hitting in his critique of Malthus's belief in the importance of maintaining unproductive consumption by government: income and consumption by government officials, soldiers, and state pensioners. Say argued that these people live off production, whereas productive consumers add to the supply of goods and services. Say continued sardonically: 'I cannot think that those who pay taxes would be at a loss what to do with their money if the collector did not come to their assistance; either their wants would be more amply satisfied, or they would employ the same money in a reproductive manner'.

In contrast to his opponents, who wished the government to stimulate consumer demand, Say believed that problems of glut, as well as poverty in general, could be solved by increasing production. And so he inveighed in many passages against excessive taxation, which raised the costs and prices of goods, and crippled production and economic growth. In essence, J.B. Say countered the statist proposals of the underconsumptionists Malthus and Sismondi by an activist programme of his own: the libertarian one of slashing taxation.

Say combined his anti-tax insights with his critique of Malthus's fondness for government spending via a trenchant attack on Malthus and the public debt. Say noted that Malthus, 'still convinced that there are classes who render service to society simply by consuming without producing, would consider it a misfortune if the whole or a great part of the English national debt were paid off'. On the contrary, rebutted Say, this would be a highly beneficial event for England. For the result would be

> that the stock-holders [government bond-holders], being paid off, would obtain some income from their capital. That those who pay taxes would themselves spend the 40 millions sterling which they now pay to the creditors of the State. That the 40 millions of taxes being taken off, all productions would be cheaper, and the consumption would considerably increase; that it would give work to the labourer, in place of sabre cuts, which are now dealt out to them; and I confess that these consequences do not appear to me of a nature to terrify the friends of public welfare.

1.8 Recession and the storm over Say's law

We come now to a final, critical question about Say's law. Why did the storm over the law appear only in two massive clusters? For the timing of the swirling controversy over the law is no accident. J.B. Say coined the law in 1803, and James Mill brought it to Britain in 1808, converting Ricardo and his disciples. But why was there no particular controversy over the law until much later? Specifically, the storm erupted in 1819, when the French–Swiss economist Jean Charles Leonard Simonde de Sismondi (1773–1842) published his *Nouveaux principes d'économie politique* (*New Principles of Political Economy*). Sismondi's book was followed the next year by the Rev. Thomas Robert Malthus's (1766–1834) *Principles of Political Economy* (1820). The odd point is that both these men had been ardent Smithians for two decades; why publish these heretical underconsumptionist views at virtually the same moment?

Sismondi's aristocratic Florentine family had settled in France, only as Huguenots to be driven by persecution to settle in Geneva, the Calvinist heartland. Sismondi was born in Geneva, the son of a Calvinist clergyman. When the radical influence of the French Revolution reached Geneva, the Sismondis moved to London, where young Sismondi had a chance to study and participate in English business affairs.

Sismondi settled down as a farmer in Tuscany in the late 1790s, publishing a physiocratic tract on Tuscan agriculture in 1801. Soon after, he became an ardent follower of Adam Smith, and published his two-volume Smithian work, *De la richesse commerciale* (*On Commercial Wealth*) in Geneva in the same year – 1803 – that Say published his famous *Traité*. While Say skyrocketed to influence and fame, Sismondi's work was ignored, and remained totally unknown outside France. Perhaps resentment at this fate played a role is Sismondi's radical conversion, embodied in his *Nouveaux Principes*. But the timing, the prompting for this conversion, was critical, namely: the end, in 1815, of a generation of massive war and inflation in Europe led quickly and inevitably to a post war deflation and depression. Recessions, especially on such a grand scale, were new phenomena in Europe; there was therefore no body of theoretical explanation, and hence the typical business cry of 'glut' or 'overproduction' struck a chord among many observers. In the case of Sismondi, it led him straightaway and permanently into a thoroughgoing and lifelong statism, including the advocacy of a comprehensive welfare state, a deep hostility to capitalism and the factory system, and a call for return to a simple agrarian economy. In the second edition of his *Nouveaux Principes* in 1827, Sismondi, in his preface, proclaims the 'new economics' or 'new liberalism' which 'invokes government intervention' instead of *laissez-faire*.

Sismondi was offered a professorship of political economy at the University of Vilna on the strength of his first book; the *Nouveaux Principes* brought him an offer from the Sorbonne. But Sismondi preferred to remain in Geneva, churning out a remarkably prolific series of historical works (including a 16-volume history of the Italian republics in the Middle Ages, and a 31-volume history of the French), and tending to the life of a gentleman farmer. On his farm he fought against overproduction in his own dotty way: making sure that production would be as low as possible by choosing the feeblest workers for employment on the farm, and deliberately having his house repaired by an incompetent worker. One wonders why he did not go all the way in his living the exemplary life of underproduction, and stop working or producing altogether. Thoroughly embittered at the lack of recognition of his socialistic views, Sismondi write shortly before his death in 1842: 'I leave this world without having made the slightest impression, and nothing will be done'. Would that he had been right.

Far more of an impact at the time was made by the simultaneous conversion to underconsumptionism by the Rev. Malthus. Malthus, son of an aristocratic country gentleman, graduated from Cambridge with honours in mathematics, and was ordained in the Anglican clergy. After serving as a fellow of a college in Cambridge, Malthus became a country curate, writing his famous *Essay on Population* in 1798. Malthus was more than the gloomy population theorist that made his name: he was also an ardent Smithian economist. In 1804, Malthus became the first academic economist in England, taking up a chair of history and political economy at the new small East India College of Haileybury, established by the East India Company to train future employees. Not only was he the first, Malthus was to remain the only academic political economist in England for the next two decades.

Malthus was a firm friend of Ricardo, and his break with the Smith–Ricardo tradition on underconsumption did not mar their close friendship. The controversy gave rise to a famous correspondence between them, and when Ricardo died in 1823 he left Malthus a small legacy as a token of their *camaraderie*. More important is the fact that Malthus lost interest in his underconsumptionist heresy after 1824, and quickly reverted to being a leader of Smithian classical economics. Clearly the reason for Malthus's loss of interest was the fact that Britain recovered from the post-Napoleonic depression after 1823, and the first storm over Say's law was over.

Despite the fact that Malthus's interest in his underconsumption theory was generated and maintained solely by the postwar recession, his doctrine was, oddly enough, not a cyclical theory at all but an alleged tendency of free markets to a permanent depression. It should also be noted that Malthus was not worried about savings leaking out into hoarding and remaining unspent. He was an overproductionist as well as an underconsumptionist, so that invested savings only made matters worse by increasing production: 'If ... commodities are already so plentiful that an adequate portion of them is not profitably consumed, to save capital can only be still further to increase the plenty of commodities, and still further to lower already low profits'.

While Say, in reply to critics, did not of course come up with a full-fledged theory to explain the general recession and 'overproduction' in relation to a profitable selling price, he did offer some remarkably prescient insights which have been completely overlooked by historians, perhaps because they were presented in his *Letters to Malthus* rather than in his *Treatise*.

First, Say takes up the postwar depression in the United States, for Malthus had claimed in response to Say, that since the US enjoyed low taxes and free markets, their absence could not be the reason for the glut suffered there. Say very sensibly attributes the basic problems in the US to the great prosperity that country had enjoyed as a neutral during most of the Napoleonic wars, so that, unburdened by blockade, its exports and its commerce enjoyed unusual prosperity. Thus, with the end of the wars in 1815, and the swift return of European maritime trade in both hemispheres, the US was found to have overexpanded its mercantile products and, in contrast, *under*produced agricultural or manufactured goods. So in a deep sense, the problem is not general overproduction, but an overproduction of some goods and underproduction of others. What the United States is suffering from, then, is *under*production of these other goods. The Americans could have used the increased production to exchange for more of the goods offered by the resurgent European maritime trade. Prophetically, Say predicted that 'A few years more and their [American] industry altogether will form a mass of productions, amongst which will be found articles fit to make profitable returns or at least profits, which the Americans will employ in the purchase of European commodities'. And then Americans and Europeans will each produce whatever they are best and most efficient at.

> Those commodities which the Europeans succeed in making at least expense will be carried to America, and those which the American soil and industry succeed in creating at a lower rate than others, will be brought back. The nature of the demand will determine the nature of the productions; each nation will employ itself in preference about those productions in which they have the greatest success; that is, which they produce at least expense, and exchanges mutually and permanently advantageous will be the result.

And how about European business? What is the problem there? Why is it depressed? Here, Say put his finger on the heart of the problem: 'costs of production multiplied to excess'. In short, the problem with the European depression was not that there was a 'general overproduction' but that entrepreneurs had bid up costs of production (factor prices) too high, so that consumers were not willing to purchase the products at prices high enough to cover costs. The problem, in fact, was neither the producing of too many goods nor not buying enough, but a bidding up of costs to too high a level. Say goes on to say that these excessive costs created 'disorders ... in the production, distribution, and consumption of value produced; disorders which frequently bring into the market quantities greater than the want, keeping back those that would sell, and whose owner would employ their price in the purchase of the former'. In short, the bidding up of excess costs in some way distorted the production structure so as to cause a massive overproduction of some goods and an underproduction of others.

After these passages, pregnant with hints of the later Austrian theory of the trade cycle, Say unfortunately goes off on a tangent in ascribing the excess costs to the taxation of industry and the market. But then he returns with a remarkably perceptive passage, attributing seeming 'superabundance' to massive ignorance and error on the part of the entrepreneurs:

> This superabundance ... depends also upon the ignorance of producers or merchants, of the nature and extent of the want in the places to which they sent their commodities. In later years there have been a number of hazardous speculations, on account of the many fresh connexions with different nations. There was everywhere a general failure of that calculation which was requisite to a good result ...

In short, the problem centres on a general failure of entrepreneurial forecasting and 'calculation' leading to what turns out to be an excessive bidding up of costs. Unfortunately, Say does not pursue this crucial point to query why such an unusual entrepreneurial failure should have taken place. But he does go on to anticipate von Hayek's important point about entrepreneurs and producers employing the market as a learning experience, to become better at estimating costs and demands on the market. Say writes:

> but because many things have been ill done does it follow that it is impossible, with better instruction, to do better? I dare predict, that as the new connexions grow old, and as reciprocal wants are better appreciated, the excess of commodities will everywhere cease; and that a mutual and profitable intercourse will be established.

With the recovery of Europe from the postwar depression, Say's law – at least in the rather vulgarized form adopted by the British classical school[16] – became absorbed into the mainstream of economic thought and was challenged only by cranks and crackpots who properly constituted what Keynes later called 'the underworld' of economics. These denizens were resurrected by John Maynard Keynes in his *General Theory*, which, written during the depths of another and even more intense depression (1936), hailed them all – from Malthus to later underconsumptionists and to the egregious German-Argentinian merchant Silvio Gesell (1862–1930), who urged that the government force everyone to spend money in a brief period of time after receiving it. Gesell's objective, as in the case of all the most flagrant money cranks, was to lower the rate of interest to zero, a goal Keynes was later to echo in his call for the 'euthanasia of the rentier [bond-holder]'. It is perhaps fitting that this Gesell, whom Keynes called 'the strange, unduly neglected prophet', capped his dubious career by becoming the finance minister of the short-lived revolutionary Soviet republic of Bavaria in 1919.

Keynes's own doctrine followed in the line of Malthus and the others, except that underspending in general was substituted for underconsumption as the allegedly critical economic problem. Keynes made a denunciation of Say's law the centrepiece of his system. In stating it, Keynes badly vulgarized and distorted the law, leaving out the central role of price adjustments[17], and had the law saying simply that total spending on output will equal total incomes received in production[18].

Since Keynes's day, economists have managed to obfuscate Say's rather simple notion with a welter of turgid discussions of Say's alleged 'principle' or 'identity', made all the more obscure by a plentiful use of mathematics, a form of alleged explication particularly out of place when dealing with such an anti-mathematical theorist as J.B. Say.

1.9 The theory of money

Say's excellent discussion of money, like most of the rest of his doctrine, has been grievously neglected by historians of thought. He begins by setting forth a theory of how money originates that was later to be developed in a famous article by Carl Menger and would form the basis of the first chapter in every money and banking text for generations. Money, he pointed out, originates out of barter. To facilitate exchanges and overcome the difficulties of barter, people on the market begin to use particularly marketable commodities as media of exchange. Specifically, under barter everyone, in order to buy a product, must find someone who desires his own specific product, and this soon becomes very difficult. Thus: 'The hungry cutler must offer the baker his knives for bread; perhaps, the baker has knives enough, but wants a coat; he is willing to purchase one of the tailor's with his bread but the tailor wants not bread, but butcher's meat; and so on to infinity'.

How to overcome this problem of what later came to be called the 'double coincidence of wants?' By finding a more generally marketable commodity which the seller will take in exchange:

> By way of getting over this difficulty, the cutler, finding he cannot persuade the baker to take an article he does not want, will use his best endeavours to have a commodity to offer, which the baker will be able readily to exchange again for whatever he may happen to need. If there exist in the society any specific commodity that is in general request, not merely on account of its inherent utility, but likewise on account of the readiness with which it is received in exchange for the

necessary articles of consumption ... that commodity is precisely what the cutler will try to barter his knives for; because he has learnt from experience, that its possession will procure him without any difficulty, by a second act of exchange, bread or any article he may wish for.

That commodity is precisely the money in that society.

Say then goes into a by now familiar analysis of which commodities are most likely to be chosen on the market as monies. A money commodity must have a high inherent value – this is, value in its pre-monetary use. It must also be physically easily divisible, preserving a proportionate quota of its value when divided; it should have a high value per unit weight, so that it will both be scarce and valuable, and easily portable; and it must be durable, so it can be retained as value for a long time. Of course, once a commodity is chosen as a general medium of exchange, its value becomes much higher than it had been in the pre-monetary state.

Say follows the continental tradition of assimilating money to all other commodities; i.e., the value of money, as of all other commodities, is determined by the interaction of its supply and its demand. Its value, its purchasing power on the market – moves directly with its demand and inversely with its supply. While he lacked the marginal approach, Say pointed the way to the eventual integration of a utility theory of goods with money. Since money, too, is an object of desire, its utility is the basis for its demand on the market. Say also criticized Ricardo and the British classical school for attempting to explain the value of money, not by utility or supply and demand, but, as in the case of all other goods, by its cost of production. In the case of money, only the supply of money and not the demand was considered important and the supply was supposedly governed by the cost of mining gold or silver.

Say was a hard-money man, insistent that all paper must be instantly convertible into specie. Irredeemable paper expands rapidly in quantity and depreciates the value of the currency, and Say pointed to the recent issue by the revolutionary French government of the *assignats*, inconvertible paper that depreciated eventually to zero. Say was thus able to analyse one of the first examples of runaway inflation.

If the national money is deteriorated, it becomes an object to get rid of it in any way, and exchange it for commodities. This was one of the causes of the prodigious circulation that took place during the progressive depreciation of the French *assignats*. Everybody was anxious to find some employment for a paper currency, whose value was hourly depreciating; it was only taken to be re-invested immediately, and one might have supposed it burnt the fingers it passed through.

Say also pointed out that inflation systematically injures creditors for the benefit of debtors.

Say was highly critical of the Smith-Ricardo yen to find an absolute and invariable measure of the value of money. He pointed out that while the relative values of money to other prices can be estimated, they are not susceptible to measurement. The value of gold or silver or coin is not fixed but variable as is that of any commodity.

One of the splendid parts of Say's theory of money was his trenchant critique of bimetallism. He was insistent that the government's fixing the ratio of the weights of the two precious metals was doomed to failure, and only caused perpetual fluctuations and shortages of one or the other metals. Say called for parallel standards, that is, for freely fluctuating exchange rates between gold and silver. As he pointed out: 'gold and silver must be left to find their own mutual level, in the transactions in which mankind may think proper to employ them'. And again, the relative value of gold and silver 'must be left to regulate itself, for any attempt to fix it would be in vain'.

While at one point Say inconsistently looks with favour on Ricardo's plan for a central bank redeeming its notes only in gold bullion and not even coin, the general thrust of his discussion is for ultra-hard money. On the whole, Say comes out for 100 per cent specie money, for a money where paper is only a 'certificate' backed fully by gold or silver, 'A medium composed entirely of either silver or gold, bearing a certificate, pretending to none but its real intrinsic value, and consequently exempt from the caprice of legislation, would hold out such advantages to every department of commerce' that it would be adopted by all nations. So insistent was Say on separating money from government that he called for changing the national names of monies to actual units of weight of gold or silver e.g. *grams* instead of *francs*. In that way, there would be a genuinely worldwide commodity money, and the government could not impose legal tender laws for paper money or debase currency standards. The entire current monetary system, Say writes happily, 'would thenceforth fall to the ground; a system replete with fraud, injustice, and robbery, and moreover so complicated, as rarely to be thoroughly understood, even by those who make it their profession. It would ever after be impossible to effect an adulteration of the coin ...'. In short, Say concludes eagerly, 'the coinage of money would become a matter of perfect simplicity, a mere branch of metallurgy'.

Indeed, the only role that Say would, inconsistently, reserve for government is a monopoly of the coinage, since that coinage was to be this simple 'branch of metallurgy' that government could presumably not cripple or destroy.

There is not a great deal of analysis of banking in Say's *Treatise*. But despite his aberration in being favourable to the Ricardo plan for a central bank bullion standard, the main thrust of his discussion is, once, again, to separate government from bank credit expansion, *either* by a 100 per cent reserve banking system, or by freely competitive banking, which would presumably approximate that condition. Thus Say writes highly favourably of the 100 per cent reserve banks of Hamburg and Amsterdam. Free banks of circulation (issuing bank notes) he holds to be far better than a monopoly central bank, for 'the competition obliges each of them to court the public favour, by a rivalship of accommodation and solidity'. And if these banks are not to be based on 100 per cent specie reserve, which Say indicates would be the best system, competition would keep them investing in sound, very short-term credit which could easily be used to redeem their bank notes.

1.10   The state and taxation

Amidst the morass of bland economic writings on taxation, Jean-Baptiste Say stands out like a beacon light. It is true that he was unusually devoted – even in that generally liberal era – to *laissez-faire* and the rights of private property, and only waffled a very few times in that creed. But for some reason, most *laissez-faire* and libertarian thinkers in history have not really considered taxation to be an invasion of the rights of private property. In J.B. Say, however, an implacable hostility to taxation pervades his work; he tended to make it responsible for all the economic evils of society, even, as we have seen, for recessions and depressions. Say's discussion of taxation was brilliant and unique; and yet, as with almost all his work, it has received no attention whatever from the historians of economic thought.

In contrast to almost all other economists, Say had an astonishingly clearsighted view of the true nature of the state and of its taxation. In Say there was no mystical quest for some truly voluntary state, nor any view of the state as a benign semi-business organization supplying services to a public grateful for its numerous 'benefits'. No; Say saw clearly that the services government indubitably supplies are to *itself* and to its favourites, and that all government spending is therefore consumption spending by the politicians and the bureaucracy. He also saw that the tax funds for that spending are extracted by coercion at the expense of the tax-paying public.

As Say points out: 'The government exacts from a tax-payer the payment of a given tax in the shape of money. To meet this demand, the tax-payer exchanges part of the products at his disposal for coin which he pays to the tax-gatherers.' The money is then spent for the government's 'consumption' needs, so that 'the portion of wealth, which passes from the hands of the tax-payer into those of the tax-gatherer, is destroyed and annihilated'. Were it not for taxes, the tax-payer would have spent his own money on his own consumption. As it is, the state 'enjoys the satisfaction resulting from that consumption'.

Say goes on to attack the 'prevalent notion' that tax monies are no burden on the economy, since they simply 'return' to the community via the expenditures of government. Say is indignant:

This is gross fallacy; but one that has been productive of infinite mischief, inasmuch as it has been the pretext for a great deal of shameless waste and dilapidation. The value paid to government by the tax-payer is given without equivalent or return: it is expended by the government in the purchase of personal service, of objects of consumption ...

Thus, in contrast to the naive Smith's purblind assumption that taxation always confers proportional benefit, we see J.B. Say treating taxation as very close to sheer robbery. Indeed, at this point Say revealingly quotes with approval Robert Hamilton's likening of government to a large-scale robber. Hamilton had been refuting this very point: taxation is harmless because the money is recirculated into the economy by the state. Hamilton had likened such impudence to the 'forcible entry of a robber into a merchant's house, who should take away his money, and tell him he did him no injury, for the money, or part of it, would be employed in purchasing the commodities he dealt in, upon which he would receive a profit'. (Hamilton might have added a Keynesian touch: that the robber's spending would benefit his victim manyfold, by the benign operations of the magical multiplier.) Say then comments on Hamilton's point that 'the encouragement afforded by the public expenditure is precisely analogous'.[19]

Say then bitterly goes on to denounce the 'false and dangerous conclusion' of writers who claim that public consumption (government expenditures) increases general wealth. But the damage is not really in the writing: 'If such principles were to be found only in books, and had never crept into practice, one might suffer them without care or regret to swell the monstrous heap of printed absurdity ...'. But unfortunately, these precepts have been put into 'practice by the agents of public authority, who can enforce error and absurdity at point of the bayonet or mouth of the cannon'. In short, once again, Say sees the uniqueness of government as the exercise of force and coercion, particularly in the way it extracts its revenue.

Taxation, then, is the coercive imposition of a burden upon the members of the public for the benefit of the government, or, more precisely, of the ruling class in command of the government. Thus Say writes:

> Taxation is the transfer of a portion of the national products from the hands of individuals to those of the government, for the purpose of meeting the public consumption or expenditure ... It is virtually a burthen imposed upon individuals, either in a separate or corporate character, by the ruling power ... for the purpose of supplying the consumption it may think proper to make at their expense; in short, an impost, in the literal sense.

He is not impressed with the apologetic notion, properly ridiculed in later years by Schumpeter, that all society somehow voluntarily pays taxes for the general benefit; instead, taxes are a burden coercively imposed on society by the 'ruling power'. Neither is Say impressed if the taxes are voted by the legislature; to him this does not make taxes any more voluntary: for 'what avails it ... that taxation is imposed by consent of the people or their representatives, if there exists in the state a power, that by its acts can leave the people no alternative but consent?'

Moreover, taxation cripples rather than stimulates production, since it robs people of resources that they would rather use differently:

> Taxation deprives the producer of a product, which he would otherwise have the option of deriving a personal gratification from, if consumed ... or of turning to profit, if he preferred to devote it to an useful employment ... [T]herefore, the subtraction of a product must needs diminish, instead of augmenting, productive power.

Say engages in an instructive critique of Ricardo, which reveals the crucial difference over the latter's long-run equilibrium approach and the great difference in their respective attitudes toward taxation. Ricardo had maintained in his *Principles* that, since the rate of return on capital is the same in every branch of industry, taxation cannot really cripple capital. For, as Say puts it, 'the extinction of one branch by taxation must needs be compensated by the product of some other, towards which the industry and capital, thrown out of employ, will naturally be diverted'. Here is Ricardo, blind to the real processes at work in the economy, stubbornly identifying a static comparison of long-run equilibrium states with the real world. Say replies forcefully and trenchantly:

> I answer, that whenever taxation diverts capital from one mode of employment to another, it annihilates the profits of all who are thrown out of employ by the change, and diminishes those of the rest of the community; for industry may be presumed to have chosen the most profitable channel. I will go further, and say, that a forcible diversion of the current or production annihilates many additional sources of profit to industry. Besides, it makes a vast difference to the public prosperity, whether the individual or the state be the consumer. A thriving and lucrative branch of industry promotes the creation and accumulation of new capital; whereas, under the pressure of taxation, it ceases to be lucrative; capital diminishes gradually instead of increasing; wealth and production decline in consequence, and prosperity vanishes, leaving behind the pressure of unremitting taxation.

Say then adds a charming sentence, taking a praxeological slap at Ricardo's fondness for what might be called his method of utterly unrealistic, verbal mathematics, 'Ricardo has endeavoured to introduce the unbinding maxims of geometrical demonstration; in the science of political economy, there is no method less worthy of reliance'.

Say then goes on to heap scorn on the argument that taxes can positively stimulate people to work harder and produce more. Work harder, he replies, to furnish funds to allow the state to tyrannize still further over you! Thus:

> To use the expedient of taxation as a stimulative to increased production, is to redouble the exertions of the community, for the sole purpose of multiplying its privations, rather than its enjoyments. For, if increased taxation be applied to the support of a complex, overgrown, and ostentatious internal administration, or of a superfluous and disproportionate military establishment, that may act as a drain of individual wealth, and of the flower of the national youth, and an aggressor upon the peace and happiness of domestic life, will not this be paying as dearly for a grievous public nuisance, as if it were a benefit of the first magnitude?

What, then, is the bottom line; what is Say's basic prescription for taxation? Indeed, what is his prescription for total public spending? Basically, it is what one might expect from a man who believed the state to be a 'grievous public nuisance' and 'an aggressor upon the peace and happiness of domestic life'. Quite simply, 'the best scheme of [public] finance, is to spend as little as possible; and the best tax is always the lightest'. In the next sentence, he amends the latter clause to say 'the best taxes, or rather those that are least bad ...'.

In short, J.B. Say, unique among economists, offered us a theory of total government spending as well as a theory of overall taxation. And that theory was a lucid and remarkable one, amounting to: that government is best (or 'least bad') that spends and taxes least. But the implications of such a doctrine are stunning, whether or not Say understood them or followed them through. For if, in the Jeffersonian phrase, that government is best that governs least, then it follows that 'least least' is zero, and therefore, as Thoreau and Benjamin R. Tucker were later to point out, that government is best that governs – or in this case, spends and taxes – not at all!

1.11 Notes

1. We should also mention as prominent in the ideologue group the historian Constantin François Chasseboeuf, Comte de Volney (1757–1820).
2. Emmet Kennedy, *Destutt De Tracy and the Origins of 'Ideology'* (Philadelphia: American Philosophical Society, 1978), p. 199.
3. It might be noted that de Tracy's intermediary in the negotiations with Jefferson on the translation was their mutual friend, the last of the physiocrats, DuPont de Nemours, who had emigrated to Wilmington, Delaware in 1815 to found his famous gunpowder manufacturing dynasty.
4. Thus in a famous speech in February 1801, Napoleon denounced the ideologues as the most harmful class of men. They were 'windbags and ideologues. They have always fought the existing authority', he thundered. 'Always distrusting authority, even when it was in their hands, they always refused to give it the independent force needed to resist revolutions'. See Kennedy, op. cit., note 2, pp. 80ff.
5. Or as Emmet Kennedy commented, 'political theory could not be tolerated in a state where politics was not'. Ibid.

6. Ernest Teilhac, *L'Oeuvre économique de Jean-Baptiste Say* (Paris: Librairie Felix Alcan, 1927), pp. 24–6. Quoted and translated in Leonard P. Ligglio, 'Charles Dunoyer and French Classical Liberalism', *Journal of Libertarian Studies*, 1 (Summer 1977), pp. 156–7.
7. For a while, Rivadavia was also working on a translation of Bentham.
8. Storch's *Cours*, published in Russia in 1815, was reprinted in Paris in 1823, with notes appended by Say. Storch accused Say of theft in publishing the French edition without his consent, whereupon Say riposted that Storch lifted the bulk of the work from himself, de Tracy, Bentham, and Sismondi.
9. The sixth and last American edition of 1834, edited by Biddle, incorporated changes made in the final French edition of 1826.
10. J.A. Schumpeter, *History of Economic Analysis* (New York: Oxford University Press, 1954), p. 491.
11. This distinction between certain theory and its application by an 'enlightened understanding' approximates von Mises's later distinction between conceptual theory (*'Begreiffen'*) and understanding (*'Verstehen'*).
12. Oswald St Clair, *A Key to Ricardo* (New York: A.M. Kelley, 1965), pp. 295–6.
13. In the first annotated biography of economics ever written, John R. McCulloch, along with James Mill, the leading British Ricardian, noted of Say that he was a lucid writer but stubbornly refused to accept all the great advances of Ricardo. The only creative insight McCulloch credited to Say was his law. John Ramsay McCulloch, *The Literature of Political Economy* (1845, London: London School of Economics, 1938), pp. 21–2.
14. Discussion of Say's law is made more complicated by the fact that Say, of course, did not set aside some particular passage or sentence and call it 'my law'. The *locus classicus* of Say's law is generally held to be Book I, Chapter XV of the *Treatise*, and it indeed has been anthologized as 'the' statement of the law. *Treatise*, pp. 132–40. Actually, there are important and relevant passages scattered throughout the *Treatise*, especially pp. 109–19, 287–8, and pp. 303–4.

    Moreover, almost all of Say's *Letters to Malthus*, in particular p. 1–68, are taken up with defence of Say's law and his critique of Malthus's (and the Frenchman Simone de Sismondi's) worry about general overproduction and complaint about alleged underconsumption. Historians of economic thought have often found Say's *Letters* superficial and erroneous, but in fact his being forced to give attention to the law carried him to the heart of the differences and led him to express his views in a lucid and pungent manner. See J.B. Say, *Letters to Mr. Malthus* (1821, New York: M. Kelley, 1967).

    For an anthologizing of Book I, Chapter XV as *the* statement of Say's law, see Henry Hazlitt (ed.), *The Critics of Keynesian Economics* (1960, New Rochelle, New York: Arlington House, 1977), pp. 12–22.
15. But Schumpeter and other historians are grossly unfair in ridiculing one of Say's arguments against Malthus: that there cannot be overproduction because 'to create a thing, the want of which does not exist, is to create a thing without value; this would not be production. Now from the moment it has a value, the producer can find means to exchange it for those articles he wants'. While this appears to eliminate the problem by defining it out of existence, there are two comments that may be made on Say's behalf. First, this is indeed a charming but unconvincing argument, but it is tangential, and does not vitiate the value of Say's law or its creator's crushing arguments on its behalf. In the heat of debate, Say, like many another intellectual combatant, sometimes used any argument that came to hand. But second, this point is not wholly valueless. For it focuses attention on a key question which Say raised but did not fully answer: *why* in the world did the producers make goods that, it turned out later, the consumers did not want to buy – at least at profitable prices? Needless to say, Say's opponents provided no satisfactory answer. For Schumpeter's attitude, see Schumpeter, op. cit., note 10, pp. 619–20.
16. The vulgarization took two forms. Most of Say's emphasis on price adjustments was omitted, as was any hint of entrepreneurial failure in bidding up costs, or in the idea that specific classes of overproduction and underproduction might be the hallmark of recessions. Another item was the Mills's formulation that 'commodities pay for commodities'

rather than all supplies of goods and services pay for each other. This was a legacy of Smith's stress that the only productive labour was that embodied in material objects, or commodities.

17. By leaving out three important sentences in his quotation from John Stuart Mill's summary of Say's law, Keynes omits any hint of the price system as equilibrating force. John Maynard Keynes, *The General Theory of Employment, Interest, and Money* (New York: Harcourt, Brace, 1936), p. 18. On this point, see Hazlitt, op. cit., note 14, p. 23.

18. Keynes also summed up Say's law as holding that 'supply creates its own demand' – a formulation followed by virtually all economists since Keynes, including Schumpeter, Mark Blaug, Thomas Sowell and Axel Leijonhufvud. As Professor Hutt writes, in correcting this distortion: 'But the supply of plums does not create the demand for plums. And the word "creates" is injudicious. What the law really asserts is that the supply of plums *constitutes* demand for whatever the supplier is destined to acquire in exchange for the plums under barter, or with the money proceeds in a money economy'. W.H. Hutt, *A Rehabilitation of Say's Law* (Athens, Ohio: Ohio University Press, 1974), p. 3 and 3n.

19. The quotation comes from a critique of the British national debt by the Scottish mathematician Robert Hamilton (1743–1829). This work was *An Inquiry Concerning the Rise and Progress, the Redemption and Present State, and the Management of the National Debt of Great Britain and Ireland* (Edinburgh, 1813, 3rd ed., 1818). Hamilton was born in Edinburgh and, after leaving college, worked as a banker. Shifting to academic pursuits, he became rector of the Academy of Perth in 1769. Ten years later he became professor of mathematics at the University of Aberdeen.

2 Jeremy Bentham: the utilitarian as big brother

2.1 From *laissez-faire* to statism

Jeremy Bentham (1748–1832) began as a devoted Smithian but more consist-ently attached to *laissez-faire*. During his relatively brief span of interest in economics, he became more and more statist. His intensified statism was merely one aspect of his major – and highly unfortunate – contribution to economics: his consistent philosophical utilitarianism. This contribution, which opens a broad sluice-gate for state despotism, still remains as Bentham's legacy to contemporary neoclassical economics.

Bentham was born in London the son of a wealthy lawyer, whiled away his youth at Oxford, and was admitted to the bar in 1772. But it soon became clear that Bentham was not interested in a career as an attorney. Rather, he settled down for life with his inherited wealth to become a cloistered philoso-pher, legal theorist, and 'projector' or crank, eternally grinding out schemes for legal and political reform which he urged upon the great and powerful.

Bentham's first and enduring interest was in utilitarianism (which we shall examine further below), and which he launched with his first published work at the age of 28, the *Fragment on Government* (1776).

Most of his life, Bentham functioned as the Great Man, scribbling chaoti-cally on endless and prolix manuscripts elaborating on his projected reforms and law codes. Most of the manuscripts remained unpublished until long after his death. The affluent Bentham lived in a capacious house surrounded by flunkies and disciples, who copied revision after revision of his illegible prose to get ready for eventual publication. He conversed with his disciples in the same made-up jargon with which he peppered his writings. While a cheery conversationalist, Bentham brooked no argument from his aides and disciples; as his precocious young disciple John Stuart Mill later recalled with kindly understatement Bentham 'failed in deriving light from other minds'. Because of this trait, Bentham was surrounded not by alert and knowledgeable disciples but by largely uncomprehending aides who, in the perceptive words of Professor William Thomas, 'looked on his work with a certain resigned scepticism as if its faults were the result of eccentricities beyond the reach of criticism or remonstrance'. As Thomas continues:

> The idea that he was surrounded by a band of eager disciples who drew from his system a searching critique of every aspect of contemporary society, which they were later to apply to various institutions in need of reform, is the product of later liberal myth-making. So far as I know, Bentham's circle is quite unlike that of any other great political thinker. It consisted not so much of men who found in his work a compelling explanation of the social world around them and gathered about him to learn more of his thoughts, as of men caught in a sort of expectant bafflement at the progress of a work which they would have liked to help on to completion but which remained maddeningly elusive and obscure.[1]

What Bentham needed desperately were sympathetic and candid editors of his work, but his relationship with his followers precluded that from happening. 'For this reason', adds Thomas, 'the steadily accumulating mass of manuscripts remained largely a *terra incognita*, even to the intimate members of our circle'. As a result, for example, such a major work in manuscript, *Of Laws in General*, astonishingly remained unedited, let alone unpublished, until our own day.

If anyone could have played this role, it was Bentham's outstanding follower, James Mill, whom we will deal with more fully below (Chapter 3). In many ways, Mill had the capacity and personality to perform the task, but there were two fatal problems: first, Mill refused to abandon his own intellectual work in order to subordinate himself exclusively to aiding the Master. As Thomas writes, 'Sooner or later all Bentham's disciples faced the choice of absorption or independence'. Though he was a devoted follower of Benthamite utilitarianism, Mill's personality was such that absorption for him was out of the question.

Second, the slipshod and volatile Bentham desperately needed shaping up, and the brisk, systematic, didactic, and hectoring James Mill was just the man to do the shaping. But, unsurprisingly, Bentham, the Great Man, was not about to be shaped up by anyone. The personality clash was too great for their relationship to be anything but arm's length, even at the height of Mill's discipleship, before Mill achieved economic independence from his wealthy patron. Thus, in exasperation, Mill wrote to a close mutual friend about Bentham: 'The pain he seems to feel at the very thought of being called upon to give his mind to the subject, you can have but little conception of'. At the same time Bentham, even long afterwards, confided his lingering resentment of Mill to his last disciple, John Bowring: 'He will never willingly enter into discourse with me. When he differs he is silent ... He expects to subdue everybody by his domineering tone – to convince everybody by his positiveness. His manner of speaking is oppressive and overbearing.' There is no better way to summarize the personality clash between them.[2]

Bentham's first published work, the *Fragment on Government* (1776), gained young Bentham an *entrée* into leading political circles, particularly the friends of Lord Shelburne. These included Whig politicians like Lord Camden and William Pitt the younger, and two men who were quickly to become Bentham's close friends and earliest disciples, the Genevan Etienne Dumont and Sir Samuel Romilly. Dumont was to be the main carrier of Benthamite doctrine to the continent of Europe.

While utilitarian political and legal reform continued to be his main interest throughout his life, Bentham read and absorbed *The Wealth of Nations* in the late 1770s or early 1780s, quickly becoming a devoted disciple. Although Bentham praised practically no other author, he habitually referred to Adam Smith as 'the father of political economy', a 'great master', and a 'writer of consummate genius'. In the early 1780s, Bentham's brother Samuel, a wealthy engineer, was engaged by the Empress Catherine the Great to organize various industrial projects. Samuel invited Jeremy to stay with him in Russia, which he did from the mid-1780s to the end of 1787, with a view to presenting an 'all-comprehensive [legal] code' to enable that despot to govern her realm more efficiently.

Bentham characteristically never completed the code for Catherine, but, while in Russia he learned – falsely, as it turned out – that William Pitt, now prime minister, was preparing to urge a reduction in the legal maximum rate of interest from 5 to 4 per cent. Agitated, Bentham wrote and soon published, in 1787, his first, and only well-known work on economics: the scintillating and hard-hitting *Defence of Usury*. Trying to bring more consistency into Smithian *laissez-faire*, Bentham argued against all usury laws whatever. He grounded his view squarely on the concept of freedom of contract, declaring that 'no man of ripe years and of sound mind, acting freely, and with his eyes open, ought to be hindered … from making such a bargain, in the way of obtaining money, as he thinks fit'. The presumption, in any situation, is for freedom of contract: 'You, who fetter contracts; you, who lay restraints on the liberty of man, it is for you … to assign a reason for your doing so.' Furthermore, how can 'usury' be a crime when it is exchange by mutual consent of lender and borrower? 'Usury', Bentham concludes, 'if it must be an offence, is an offence committed with consent, that is, with the consent of the party supposed to be injured, cannot merit a place in the catalogue of offences, unless the consent were either unfairly obtained or unfreely: in the first case, it coincides with defraudment; in the other, with extortion.'

In his appendix to the *Defence of Usury*, Bentham restates and sharpens the Turgot–Smith defence of savings. Savings results in capital accumulation: 'Whoever saves money, as the phrase is, adds proportionately to the general mass of capital … The world can augment its capital in only one way: viz by parsimony.' This insight leads to the principle that 'capital limits trade', that the extent of trade or production is limited by the amount of capital that has been accumulated. In short: 'the trade of every nation is limited by the quantity of capital.'

The *laissez-faire* implication, as Bentham saw, is that government action or spending *cannot* increase the total amount of capital in society; it can only divert capital from free market to less productive uses. As a result, 'no regulations nor any efforts whatsoever, either on the part of subjects or governors, can raise the quantity of wealth produced during a given period to an amount beyond what the productive powers of the quantity of capital in hand … are capable of producing'.

Defence of Usury had a great impact in Britain and elsewhere. Dr Thomas Reid, the distinguished Scottish 'common-sense' philosopher who succeeded

Adam Smith to the chair of moral philosophy at Glasgow, strongly endorsed the book. The great Comte de Mirabeau, the leading force in the early stages of the French Revolution, had the work translated into French. And in the United States, the tract went into several editions, and it inspired several states to repeal their laws against usury.

In the course of the *Defence*, there are hints of valuable analysis. Lending is defined as 'exchanging present money for future', and other intimations of time-preference or waiting as a key to saving include such phrases as the saver having 'the resolution to sacrifice the present to [the] future'. Bentham also intimates that part of interest charged includes a risk premium, a kind of insurance premium for the risk of loss incurred by the lender.

During the 1780s, Bentham was also writing his 'Essay on Reward', published only a half-century later as the *Rationale of Reward*. In it, Bentham expounded enthusiastically on 'Competition as rewards', and hailed the 'advantages resulting from the most unlimited freedom of competition'. It was on this principle of free competition and opposition to governmental monopolies that 'the father of political economy' had, in Bentham's over-enthusiastic words, 'created a new science'.

In his next economic work, the unpublished 'Manual of Political Economy' (1795), Bentham continued the *laissez-faire* theme of 'No more trade than capital'. The government, he emphasized, can only divert investment funds from the private sector; it cannot raise the total level of investment. 'Whatever is given to any one branch, is so much taken from the rest ... Every statesman who thinks by regulation to increase the sum of trade, is the child whose eye is bigger than his belly.' Towards the end of the same work, however, a cloud no bigger than a man's hand appeared that would eventually take charge of Bentham's economic analysis. For Bentham began his rapid slide down the inflationist chute. In a kind of appendix to the work, he states that government paper money could increase capital if resources were not 'fully employed'. There is no analysis, as of course there never is in the inflationist canon, of *why* these resources were 'unemployed' in the first place, i.e. why their owners withheld them from use. The answer must be: because the resource owner demanded an excessively high price or wage: inflation is therefore a means of fooling resource-owners into lowering their real demands.

It did not take long for Jeremy Bentham to slide down the slippery slope from Adam Smith and what would be Say's law back to mercantilism and inflationism. Shortly afterwards, in an unpublished 'Proposal for the Circulation of a [New] Species of Paper Currency' (1796), Bentham happily wedded his 'projecting' and constructivist spirit to his new-found inflationism. Instead of floating bonds and paying interest on them, the government, he proposed, should simply monopolize all issue of paper notes in the kingdom.

It could then issue the notes, preferably non-interest bearing, *ad libitum* and save itself the interest.

Bentham was scarcely at his best answering the question of what limit there might be to this government paper issue. The limit, he answered, would obviously be 'the amount of paper currency in the country'. Bentham's modern editor is properly scornful of this patent claptrap: 'It is like saying "the sky's the limit" when we do not know how high the sky may be.'[3]

In his later writings on the subject, Bentham searched for some limits to paper issue, if unsuccessfully. But his commitment to a broadly inflationist course deepened further. In his unfinished 'Circulating Annuities' (1800), he developed his government paper scheme further, and hailed the serviceability of inflation in wartime. Indeed, Bentham makes an all-out assault on the Turgot–Smith–Say insights and actually declares that employment of labour is directly proportional to the quantity of money: 'No addition is ever made to the quantity of labour in any place, but by an addition made to the quantity of money in that place ... In this point of view, then, money, it should seem, is the cause, and the cause *sine qua non*, of labour and general wealth.' Quantity of money is all; so much for Smithian doctrine! In fact, Bentham went further in *Circulating Annuities*, heaping scorn on his alleged mentor for denouncing the mercantilist preoccupation with the state's piling up of gold and silver and with a 'favourable' balance of trade. There is no absurdity, averred Bentham,

> in the exultation testified by public men at observing how [great] a degree of what is called the balance of trade is in favour of this country ... Seduced by the pride of discovery, Adam Smith, by taking his words from the kitchen, has attempted to throw an ill-grounded ridicule on the preference given to gold and silver.

After once again calling for the elimination of bank paper for the benefit of a government monopoly of paper issue (in the fragmentary 'Paper Mischief Exposed', 1801), Bentham reached the acme of inflationism in his 'The True Alarm (1801). In this unpublished work, Bentham not only continued the full-employment motif, but also grumbled about the allegedly dire effects of hoarding, of money saved from consumption that went into hoards instead of investment. In that case, disaster: a fall in prices, profits and production. Nowhere does Bentham recognize that hoarding and a general fall in prices also means a fall in costs, and no necessary reduction in investment or production. Indeed, Bentham worked around to the Mandeville fallacy about the beneficial and uniquely energizing effects of luxurious spending. In the mercantilist and proto-Keynesian manner, saving is evil hoarding while luxury consumption animates production. How capital can be maintained, much less increased, without saving is not explained in this bizarre model.

James Mill and David Ricardo have been considered loyal Benthamites, and this they were in utilitarian philosophy and in a belief in political democracy. In economics, however, it was a far different story, and Mill and Ricardo, sound as a rock on Say's law and the Turgot–Smith analysis, were firm in successfully discouraging the publication of the 'The True Alarm'. Ricardo scoffed at almost all of later Benthamite economics and, in the case of money and production, asked the proper questions: 'Why should the mere increase of money have any other effect than to lower its value? How would it cause any increase in the production of commodities ... Money cannot call forth goods ... but goods can call forth money.' Bentham's major theme ... 'that money is the cause of riches' – Ricardo rejected firmly and flatly.

In his penultimate work of importance on economics, Jeremy Bentham came full circle. He had launched the economic part of his career with a hard-hitting attack on usury laws; he ended it by defending maximum price control on bread. Why? Because the mass of the public would favour cheap bread (assuredly so!), and so there would then be a 'rational' and 'determinate standard' for the good and moral price of bread, a standard which apparently free contract and free markets cannot set. What would such a standard be? Showing that for Bentham his *ad hoc* utilitarianism and cost–benefit analysis had totally driven any sound economics out of his purview, he answered that it would have to be empirical and *ad hoc*. Casting economic logic to the winds, Bentham maintained that the authorities should set a 'moderate' maximum price, which would weigh the costs and benefits, the advantages and disadvantages, of each possible price. And Bentham assured his readers of his moderation: he did 'not mean it [his proposal] as a whip or scorpion for the punishment of the growers or vendors of corn'. But that would be the inevitable result.

Ad hoc empiricism was now rampant in Bentham. Admitting that all previous attempts at maximum price control were disasters, like any later institutionalist or historicist Bentham denied any relevance, since the circumstances of each particular time and place are necessarily different. In short, Bentham denied economics altogether – that is, denied the possibility of laws abstracting from particular circumstances and applying to all exchanges or actions everywhere.

In arguing against the opponents of price control, Bentham often used reasoning that was tortuous and even absurd. For example, to the charge that maximum price control would lead to attempted consumption exceeding supply (one of the greatest problems with price control), Bentham insisted that this could not happen in Britain, where the Poor Law ensured welfare payment to the poor with an increase in the price of bread. The opinion that, at some time or other, the demand curve can be vertical and not falling is in every century the hallmark of an economic ignoramus, and Bentham now passed that test. For centuries, writers and theorists knew that demand increased as price fell, and Bentham was now writing as if economics had never existed – and could never exist.

Since consistency was the realm of despised deductive logic, Bentham denied that his opposition to usury laws had any relation to his defence of price control on bread. But while he still maintained that his earlier analysis had been correct, he now offered a crucial revision: he had overlooked that a notable advantage of a usury law is that the government can then borrow more cheaply (at the expense, of course, of squeezing out marginal private borrowers). And he went on to admit that he now found this 'advantage' decisive, so that now he would place usury laws on the governmental agenda: 'I should expect to find the advantages of it in this respect predominate over its disadvantages in all others.' In short, Bentham, the alleged 'individualist' and exponent of *laissez-faire*, finds that advantage to government outweighs all private disadvantage!

Again treating his earlier views on usury, Bentham denied that he had ever believed in any self-adjusting and equilibrating tendencies of the market, or that interest rates properly adjust saving and investment. He went on in a revealing diatribe against *laissez-faire* and natural rights, to demonstrate to one and all the incompatibility between utilitarianism on the one hand and *laissez-faire* or property rights on the other:

> I have not, I never had, nor shall have, any horror, sentimental or anarchical, of the hand of government. I leave it to Adam Smith, and the champions of the rights of man ... to talk of invasions of natural liberty, and to give as a special argument against this or that law, an argument the effect of which would be to put a negative upon all laws. The interference of government, as often as in my jumbled view of the matter the smallest balance on the side of advantage is the result, is an event I witness with altogether as much satisfaction as I should its forbearance, and with much more than I should its negligence.

One wonders by what mystical standard the 'scientific' Bentham managed to weigh the advantages and disadvantages of every particular law.

Three years later, in 1804, Jeremy Bentham lost interest in economics, a fact for which we must be forever grateful. It is only unfortunate that this waning of zeal had not occurred a half-decade before. The case of Jeremy Bentham, however, should be instructive to that host of economists that attempt to weld utilitarian philosophy with free market economics.

One would think that the master of utilitarianism would have contributed to utility analysis in economics, but oddly enough Bentham proved to be interested only in the 'macro' realms of economic thought. The only exception came in the largely unfortunate *True Alarm* (1801), in which Bentham not only declared that 'all value is founded on utility', but also enters into a cogent critique of Adam Smith's alleged 'value paradox'. Water, Bentham noted, can and does have economic value, while diamonds *do* have value in use as a foundation of its economic value. Continuing on, Bentham approaches the marginalist refutation of the value paradox:

> The reason why water is found not to have any value with a view to exchange is that it is equally devoid of value with a view to use. If the whole quantity required is available, the surplus has no kind of value. It would be the same in the case of wine, grain, and everything else. Water, furnished as it is by nature without any human exertion, is more likely to be found in that abundance which renders it superfluous; but there are many circumstances in which it has a value in exchange superior to that of wine.

2.2   Personal utilitarianism

As we have seen, Jeremy Bentham's strictly economic views, especially when he slid back to mercantilism, had no impact on economic thought, even upon his own philosophic disciples such as James Mill and Ricardo. But his philosophic views, introduced into economics by these same disciples, left an unfortunate and permanent impact on economic thought: they provided economics with its underlying and dominant social philosophy. And that dominance would be no less powerful for being generally implicit and unexamined.

Utilitarianism provided economists with the ability to square the circle: to allow them to make pronouncements and take firm positions on public policy, while still pretending to be hard-headed, 'scientific', and therefore 'value-free'. As the nineteenth century proceeded and economics began to become a separate profession, a guild with its own code and practices, it became possessed of an overwhelming desire to ape the success and the prestige of the 'hard' physical sciences. But 'scientists' are supposed to be objective, disinterested, unbiased in their scientific work. It was therefore assumed that for economists to espouse moral principles or political philosophy was somehow introducing the virus of 'bias', 'prejudice', and an unscientific attitude into the discipline of economics.

This attitude of crude imitation of the physical sciences ignored the fact that people and inanimate objects are crucially different: stones or atoms don't have values or make choices, whereas people inherently evaluate and choose. Still, it would be perfectly possible for economists to confine themselves to analysing the consequences of such values and choices, *provided* they took no stand on public policy. But economists burn to take such stands; in fact, interest in policy is generally the main motivation for embarking on a study of economics in the first place. And advocating policy – saying that the government *should* or *should not* do A, B or C, – is *ipso facto* taking a value position and an implicitly ethical one to boot. There is no way of getting around this fact, and the best that can be done is to make such ethics a rational inquiry of what is best for man in accordance with his nature. But the pursuit of 'value-free' science precluded that path, and so economists, by adopting utilitarianism, were able to pretend or to delude themselves that they were being strictly scientific, while smuggling unanalysed and shaky ethical notions into economics. In that way, economics embraced the worst of both worlds, implicitly smuggling in fallacy and bias in the name of hard-nosed value-freedom. The Benthamite infection of economics with the bacillus of utilitarianism has never been cured and remains as rampant and as predominant as ever.

Utilitarianism consists in two fundamental parts: *personal* utilitarianism, and *social* utilitarianism, the latter being built upon the former. Each is fallacious and pernicious, but social utilitarianism, which we are more interested in here, adds many fallacies, and would be unsound *even if* personal utilitarianism were to be upheld.

Personal utilitarianism, as launched by David Hume in the mid-eighteenth century, assumes that each individual is governed only by the desire to satisfy his emotions, his 'passions', and that these emotions of happiness or unhappiness are primary and unanalysable givens. The only function of man's reason is use as a *means*, to show someone how to arrive at his goals. There is no function for reason in setting man's goals themselves. Reason, for Hume and for later utilitarians, is only a hand-maiden, a slave to the passions. There is no room, then, for natural law to establish any ethic for mankind.

But what, then, is to be done about the fact that most people decide about their ends by ethical principles, which cannot be considered reducible to an original personal emotion? Still more embarrassing for utilitarianism is the obvious fact that emotion is often a hand-maiden of such principles, and is patently *not* an ultimate given but rather determined by what happens to such principles. Thus someone who fervently adopts a certain ethical or political philosophy will feel happy whenever such philosophy succeeds in the world, and unhappy when it meets a setback. Emotions are then a hand maiden to principles, instead of the other way round.

In grappling with such anomalies, utilitarianism, priding itself on being anti-mystical and scientific, has to go against the facts and introduce mystification of its own. For it then has to say, *either* that people only *think* they have adopted governing ethical principles, and/or that they *should* abandon such principles and cleave only to unanalysed feelings. In short, utilitarianism has either to fly in the face of facts obvious to everyone (a methodology that is surely blatantly unscientific) and/or to adopt an unanalysed ethical view of its own in denunciation of all (other) ethical views. But this is mystical, value-laden, and self-refuting of its own anti-ethical doctrine (or rather, of any ethical doctrine that is not a slave to unanalysed passions).

In either case, utilitarianism is self-refuting in violating its own axiom of not going beyond given emotions and valuations. Furthermore, it is common human experience, once again, that subjective desires are *not* absolute, given and unchanging. They are not hermetically sealed off from persuasion, whether rational or otherwise. One's own experience and the arguments of others can and do persuade people to change their values. But how could that be if all individual desires and valuations are pure givens and therefore not subject to alteration by the intersubjective persuasion of others? But if these desires are not givens, and *are* changeable by the persuasion of moral argument, it would then follow that, contrary to the assumptions of utilitarianism, supra-subjective ethical principles *do* exist that can be argued and can have an impact on others and on their valuations and goals.

Jeremy Bentham added a further fallacy to the utilitarianism that had grown fashionable in Great Britain since the days of David Hume. More brutally, Bentham sought to reduce all human desires and values from the qualitative to the quantitative; all goals are to be reduced to quantity, and all seemingly different values – e.g. pushpin and poetry – are to be reduced to mere differences of quantity and degree. The drive to reduce quality drastically to quantity again appealed to the scientistic passion among economists. Quantity is uniformly the object of investigation in the hard, physical sciences; so doesn't concern for quality in the study of human action connote mysticism and a sloppy, unscientific attitude? But, once again, economists forgot that quantity is precisely the proper concept for dealing with stones or atoms; for these entities do not possess consciousness, do not value and do not choose; therefore their movements can be and should be charted with quantitative precision. But individual human beings, on the contrary, are conscious, and do adopt values and act on them. People are not unmotivated objects always describing a quantitative path. People are qualitative, that is, they respond to qualitative differences, and they value and choose on that basis. To reduce quality to quantity, therefore, gravely distorts the actual nature of human beings and of human action, and by distorting reality, proves to be the reverse of the truly scientific.

Jeremy Bentham's dubious contribution to personal utilitarian doctrine – in addition to being its best known propagator and popularizer – was to quantify and crudely reduce it still further. Trying to make the doctrine still more 'scientific', Bentham attempted to provide a 'scientific' standard for such emotions as happiness and unhappiness: quantities of pleasure and pain. All vague notions of happiness and desire, for Bentham, could be reduced to quantities of pleasure and pain: pleasure 'good', pain 'bad'. Man, therefore, simply attempts to maximize pleasure and minimize pain. In that case, the individual – and the scientist observing him – can engage in a replicable 'calculus of pleasure and pain', what Bentham termed 'the felicific calculus' that can be churned out to yield the proper result in counselling action or non-action in any given situation. Every man, then, can engage in what neo-

Benthamite economists nowadays call a 'cost–benefit analysis'; in whatever situation, he can gauge the benefits – units of pleasure – weigh it against the costs – units of pain – and see which outweighs the other.

In a discussion which Professor John Plamenatz aptly says 'parodies reason', Bentham tries to give objective 'dimensions' to pleasure and pain, so as to establish the scientific soundness of his felicific calculus. These dimensions, Bentham asserts, are sevenfold: intensity, duration, certainty, propinquity, fecundity, purity and extent. Bentham claims that, at least conceptually, all these qualities can be measured, and then multiplied together to yield the net resultant of pain or pleasure from any action.

Simply to state Bentham's theory of seven dimensions should be enough to demonstrate its sheer folly. These emotions or sensations are qualitative and not quantitative, and none of these 'dimensions' can be multiplied or weighted together. Again, Bentham raised an unfortunate scientistic analogy with physical objects. A three-dimensional object is one where each object is linear, and therefore where all these linear units can be multiplied together to yield units of volume. In human valuation, even with pleasure and pain, there is no *unit* common to each of their 'dimensions' and therefore there is no way to multiply such units. As Professor Plamenatz trenchantly points out:

> the truth is that even an omniscient God could not make such calculations, for the very notion of them is impossible. The intensity of a pleasure cannot be measured against its duration, nor its duration against its certainty or uncertainty, nor this latter property against its propinquity or remoteness.[4]

Plamenatz adds that it is true, as Bentham states, that people often compare courses of action, and choose those they find most desirable. But this simply means that they decide between alternatives, not that they engage in quantitative calculations of units of pleasure and pain.

But one thing can be said for Bentham's grotesque doctrine. At least Bentham attempted, no matter how fallaciously, to ground his cost–benefit analysis on an objective standard of benefit and cost. Later utilitarian theorists, along with the body of economics, eventually abandoned the pleasure–pain calculus. But in doing so, they also abandoned any attempt to provide a standard to ground *ad hoc* costs and benefits on some sort of intelligible basis. Since then, the appeal to cost and benefit, even on a personal level, has necessarily been vague, unsupported and arbitrary.

Moreover, John Wild eloquently contrasts utilitarian personal ethics with the ethics of natural law:

> Utilitarian ethics makes no clear distinction between raw appetite or interest, and that deliberate or voluntary desire which is fused with practical reason. Value, or pleasure, or satisfaction is the object of any interest, no matter how incidental or

distorted it may be. Qualitative distinctions are simply ignored, and the good is conceived in a purely quantitative manner as the maximum of pleasure or satisfaction. Reason has nothing to do with the eliciting of sound appetite. One desire is no more legitimate than another. Reason is the slave of passion. Its whole function is exhausted in working out schemes for the maximizing of such interests as happen to arise through chance or other irrational causes ...

As against this, the theory of natural law maintains that there is a sharp distinction between raw appetites and deliberate desires elicited with the cooperation of practical reason. The good cannot be adequately conceived in a purely quantitative manner. Random interests which obstruct the full realization of essential common tendencies are condemned as antinatural ... When reason becomes the slave of passion, human freedom is lost and human nature thwarted ...

(T)he ethics of natural law sharply separates essential needs and rights from incidental rights. The good is not adequately understood as a mere maximizing of qualitatively indifferent purposes, but a maximizing of those tendencies which qualitatively conform to the nature of man and which arise through rational deliberation and free choice ... There is a stable universal standard, resting on something firmer than the shifting sands of appetite, to which an appeal can be made even from the maximal agreements of a corrupt society. This standard is the law of nature which persists as long as man persists – which is, therefore, incorruptible and inalienable, and which justifies the right to revolution against a corrupt and tyrannical social order.[5]

Finally, in addition to the problems of the pleasure–pain calculus, personal utilitarianism counsels that actions be judged not on their *nature* but on their *consequences*. But, in the non-Bethamite, mere cost–benefit (rather than 'objective' pleasure–pain) analysis, how is anyone to gauge the consequences of any action? And why is it considered easier, let alone more 'scientific', to judge *consequences* than to judge an act itself by its nature? Furthermore, it is often very difficult to figure out *what* the consequences of any contemplated action will be. How we are to find the secondary, tertiary, etc. consequences, let alone the more immediate ones? We suspect that Herbert Spencer, in his critique of utilitarianism, was correct: it is often easier to know what is *right* than what is expedient.[6]

2.3   Social utilitarianism

In extending utilitarianism from the personal to the social, Bentham and his followers incorporated all the fallacies of the former, and added many more besides. If each man tries to maximize pleasure (and minimize pain), then the social ethical rule, for the Benthamites, is to seek always 'the greatest happiness of the greatest number', in a social felicific calculus in which each man counts for one, no more and no less.

The first question is the powerful one of self-refutation: for if each man is necessarily governed by the rule of maximizing pleasure, then why in the world are these utilitarian philosophers doing something very different – that is, calling for an abstract social principle ('the greatest happiness of the greatest number')?[7] And why is *their* abstract moral principle – for that is what it is – legitimate while all others, such as natural rights, are to be brusquely dismissed as nonsense? What justification is there for the greatest happiness formula? The answer is none whatever; it is simply assumed as axiomatic, above and beyond challenge.

In addition to the self-refuting nature of the utilitarians clinging to an over-riding – and unanalysed – abstract moral principle, the principle itself is shaky at best. For what is so good about the 'greatest number'? Suppose that the vast majority of people in a society hate and revile redheads, and greatly desire to murder them. Suppose further, that there are only a few redheads extant at any time, so that their loss would entail no discernible drop in general production or in the real incomes of the non redheads remaining. Must we then say that it is 'good', after making our social felicific calculus, for the vast majority to cheerfully slaughter redheads, and thereby maximize their pleasure or happiness? And if not, why not? As Felix Adler wryly put it, utilitarians 'pronounce the greatest happiness of the greatest number to be the social end, although they fail to make it intelligible why the happiness of the greater number should be cogent as an end upon those who happen to belong to the lesser number'.[8]

Furthermore, the egalitarian presumption of each person counting precisely for one is hardly self-evident. Why not some system of weighting? Again, we have an unexamined and unscientific article of faith at the heart of utilitarianism.

Finally, while utilitarianism falsely assumes that the moral or the ethical is a purely subjective given to each individual, it on the contrary assumes that these subjective desires can be added, subtracted, and weighed across the various individuals in society so as to result in a calculation of maximum social happiness. But how in the world can an objective or calculable 'social utility' or 'social cost' emerge out of purely subjective desires, especially since subjective desires or utilities are strictly ordinal, and cannot be compared or added or subtracted among more than one person? The truth, then, is the opposite of the core assumptions of utilitarianism. *Moral principles*, which utilitarianism claims to reject as mere subjective emotion, are intersubjective and can be used to persuade various persons; whereas utilities and costs are purely subjective to each individual and therefore *cannot* be compared or weighed between persons.

Perhaps the reason why Bentham quietly shifts from 'maximum pleasure' in personal utilitarianism to 'happiness' in the social realm is that talking about the 'greatest pleasure of the greatest number' would be too openly ludicrous, since the emotion or sensation of pleasure is quite clearly not addable or subtractable between persons. Substituting the vaguer and looser 'happiness' enabled Bentham to fuzz over such problems.[9]

Bentham's utilitarianism led him to an increasingly numerous 'agenda' for government intervention in the economy. Some of this agenda we have seen above. Others items include: a welfare state; taxation for at least a partial egalitarian redistribution of wealth; government boards, institutes and universities; public works to cure unemployment as well as to encourage private investment; government insurance; regulation of banks and stockbrokers; guarantee of quantity and quality of goods.

2.4 Big brother: the panopticon

Utilitarian economists have often been – in my view properly – accused of trying to substitute 'efficiency' for ethics in advocating or developing public policy. 'Efficiency', in contrast to 'ethics' sounds unsentimental, hard-nosed and 'scientific'. Yet extolling 'efficiency' only pushes the ethical problem under the rug. For in *whose* interests, and at *whose* expense, shall social efficiency be pursued? In the name of a spurious science, 'efficiency' often becomes a mask for exploitation, for plundering one set of people for the benefit of another. Often, utilitarian economists have been accused of being willing to advise 'society' on how to build the most efficient 'concentration camps'. Those who have held this charge to be an unfair *reductio ad absurdum* should contemplate the life and thought of the prince of utilitarian philosophers, Jeremy Bentham. In a profound sense, Bentham was a living *reductio ad absurdum* of Benthamism, a living object lesson of the results of his own doctrine.

It was in 1768, at the age of 20, when Jeremy Bentham, returning to his *alma mater*, Oxford, for an alumni vote, chanced upon a copy of Joseph Priestley's *Essay on Government*, and came across the magical phrase that changed and dominated his life from then on: 'the greatest happiness of the greatest number'. But, as Gertrude Himmelfarb points out in her scintillating and devastating essays on Bentham, of all his numerous schemes and tinkerings in pursuit of this elusive goal, the one closest to Jeremy's heart was his plan for the panopticon. In visiting his brother Samuel in Russia, in the 1780s, Bentham found that his brother had designed such a panopticon, as a workshop, and Bentham immediately got the idea of the Panopticon as the ideal physical site for a prison, a school, a factory – indeed, for all of social life. 'Panopticon', in Greek, means 'all-seeing', and the name was highly suitable for the object in view. Another Benthamite synonym for the panopticon was 'the Inspection House'. The idea was to maximize the supervision of prisoners/school children/paupers/employees by the all-seeing inspector, who would be seated at a tower in the centre of a circular spider-web able to spy on all the cells in the periphery. By mirrors and other devices, each of the spied-upon could never know where the inspector was looking at any given time. Thus the panopticon would accomplish the goal of a 100 per cent inspected and supervised society without the means; since everyone *could* be under inspection at any time without knowing it.

Bentham's apologists have reduced his scheme to merely one of prison 'reform', but Bentham tried to make it clear that all social institutions were to be encompassed by the panopticon; that it was to serve as a model for 'houses of industry, workhouses, poorhouses, manufactories, mad-houses, lazrettos, hospitals, and schools'. An atheist hardly given to scriptural citation, Bentham nevertheless waxed rhapsodic about the social ideal of the panopticon, quoting from the Psalms: 'Thou art about my path, and about my bed; and spies out all my ways ...'

As Professor Himmelfarb aptly puts it:

> Bentham did not believe in God, but he did believe in the qualities apotheosized in God. The Panopticon was a realization of the divine ideal, spying out the ways of the transgressor by means of an ingenious architectural scheme, turning night into day with artificial light and reflectors, holding men captive by an intricate system of inspection.[10]

Bentham's goal was to approach, or simulate, the 'ideal perfection' of complete and continuous inspection of everyone. Because of the inspector's 'invisible eye', each inmate would conceive himself in a state of total and continuing inspection, thus achieving the 'apparent omnipresence of the inspector'.

Consistent with utilitarianism, the social arrangement was decided upon by the social despot, who acts 'scientifically' in the name of the greatest happiness of all. In that name, his rule maximizes 'efficiency'. Thus, in Bentham's original draft, every inmate would be kept in solitary confinement, since this would maximize his being 'safe and quiet', without chance of unruly crowds or planning of escape.

In arguing for his panopticon, Bentham at one point acknowledges the doubts and reservations of people who appear to want maximum inspection of their children or other charges. He recognizes a possible charge that his inspector would be excessively despotic, or even that the incarceration and solitary confinement of all might be 'productive of an imbecility', so that a formerly free man would no longer in a deep sense be fully human: 'And whether the result of this high-wrought contrivance might not be constructing a set of *machines* under the similitude of *men*?' To this critical question, Jeremy Bentham gave a brusque, brutal and quintessentially utilitarian reply: who cares? he said. The only pertinent question was: 'would *happiness* be most likely to be increased or diminished by this discipline?' To our 'scientist' of happiness, there were no doubts of the answer: 'call them soldiers, call them monks, call them machines; so they were but happy ones, I should not care.'[11] There speaks the prototypical humanitarian with the guillotine, or at least with the slave-pen.

Bentham was only willing to modify the solitary confinement of each inmate in the panopticon because of the great expense of constructing an entire cell for each person. Economy was an overriding concern in running the panopticon – economy and productivity. Bentham was concerned to maximize the coerced labour of the inmates. After all, 'industry is a blessing; why paint it as a curse?' Seven-and-a-half hours a day sufficed for sleep, and an hour-and-a-half total for meals, for after all, he admonished, 'let it not be forgotten, meal times are times of rest: feeding is recreation.' There is no reason why inmates should not be forced to work 14 or even 15 hours a day, six days a week. Indeed, Bentham wrote to a friend that he had been 'afraid' of revealing many of his proposed savings, 'for fear of being beat down'. He had in mind working the inmates no less than 'sixteen and a half profitable hours' a day, dressing them without stockings, shirts or hats, and feeding them exclusively on potatoes, which at that time were regarded even by the poorest citizens as fit only for animal fodder. Bedding was to be as cheap as possible with sacks used instead of sheets, and hammocks instead of beds.

Bentham's overriding concern with economy and productivity is made understandable by a crucial element in his panopticon plan – an element often neglected by later historians. For the Great Inspector was to be none other than Bentham himself. Prisons of the realm, and presumably eventually schools and factories, were to be contracted out to Bentham, who would be contractor, inspector and profit-maker from the scheme. It is no wonder then, that Bentham had such supreme confidence in the ability of the inspector to maximize his own happiness along with the happiness of the 'greatest number' of panopticon inmates at the same time. Bentham's long-term gain, if not the 'greatest happiness' of the prisoners, was also to be ensured by long-run provisions that would keep 'released' prisoners in the almost permanent thrall of the inspector. In Bentham's final plan for his panopticon, no prisoner would be released unless he enlisted in the army; enlisted in the navy; or had a bond of £50 posted for him by a 'responsible householder'. It must be realized that £50 was a handsome sum at a time when the average unskilled labourer received a wage of about 10 shillings a week – or about two year's salary. The bond was to be renewed annually, and any failure to renew would subject the prisoner to be shipped back to the panopticon, 'though it should be for life'. Why would any responsible householder be interested in posting a £50 bond for an ex-prisoner? To Bentham, the answer was clear: only if the prisoner was willing to contract his labour to that householder, with the understanding that the householder would have the same power over the labourer as that 'of a father over his child, or of a master over his apprentice'. Since this mammoth bond had to be renewed every year, the ex-prisoner was envisioned by Bentham as a perpetual slave to the householder. If there was no bond, the prisoner would have to shipped to a 'subsidiary establishment', also run on panopticon principles. And who better to run such establishments than the main prison contractor, i.e. Bentham himself? Indeed, all the conditions of the panopticon were designed to induce the prisoners or other inmates to be enslaved to the contractor (Bentham) virtually for life.

In view of Bentham's overriding concern with the panopticon, and of his explicit identification of himself as the contractor, we must remark on what Himmelfarb points to as:

> the strange, almost willing inattentiveness of biographers and historians to the most striking feature of the plan and the decisive cause of its rejection. To them Bentham was a philanthropist who sacrificed years of his life and most of his fortune to the exemplary cause of penal reform and who was inexplicably, as one biographer put it, 'not to be allowed to benefit his country'. Most books on Bentham and even some of the most respectable histories of penal reform do not so much as mention the contract system in connection with the Panopticon, let alone identify Bentham as the proposed contractor.[12]

Finally, Bentham's panopticon was supposed to be intimately connected with a woodworking machine that his brother Samuel had invented in Russia about the same time as the panopticon workshop. What better use for thousands, if not many thousands of inmates than to be busily and cheaply at work making an enormous amount of wood? Samuel's woodworking machine proved to be too costly to be built and powered by a steam engine; so why not, in Bentham's own terms, 'human labour to be extracted from a class of person, on whose part neither dexterity nor good will were to be reckoned upon, ... now substituted to the steam engine ...?'

That Bentham scarcely aimed to confine the panopticon to the class of prisoners is shown particularly by his panopticon poorhouse scheme. Written originally in 1797 and reissued in 1812, Bentham's *Pauper Management Improved* envisioned a joint-stock company, like the East India Company, contracted by the government to operate 250 'Industry Houses', each to house 2 000 paupers subject to the 'absolute' authority of a contractor–inspector–governor, in a building and suffering under a regimen very similar to the panopticon prison.

Who would constitute the class of paupers living under the slave labour regime of the panopticon poorhouse? To Bentham, the company – of which he, of course, would be the head – would be assigned 'coercive powers' to seize anyone 'having nether visible livelihood or assignable property, nor honest and sufficient means of livelihood'. On that rather elastic definition, the average citizen would be legally encouraged to aid and abet the coercive powers of the poorhouse company by seizing anyone he considered of insufficient livelihood and trundling him off to the panopticon poorhouse.

Bentham's envisioned scale of the network of panopticon poorhouses was nothing if not grandiose. The houses were to confine not only 500 000 poor but also their children, who were to continue bound to the company, even if their parents were discharged, as apprentices until their early 20s, even if married. These apprentices would be confined in an additional 250 panopticon houses, bringing the total number of inmates in the industry houses up to no less than one million. If we consider that the total population of England at that time was only nine million, this means that Bentham envisioned the confining in slave labour, regimented and exploited by himself, of at least 11 per cent of the nation's population. Indeed, sometimes Bentham envisioned his panopticons as incarcerating up to three-fifths of the British population.

Jeremy Bentham conceived of his panopticon in 1786 at the age of 38; five years later, he published the scheme and fought hard for it for two more decades, also urging France and India in vain to adopt the scheme. Parliament finally rejected the plan in 1811. For the rest of his long life, Bentham mourned the defeat. Near the end of his life at the age of 83, Bentham wrote a history of the affair, paranoiacally convinced that King George III had sabotaged the plan out of a personal vendetta arising from Bentham's opposition, during the 1780s, to the king's projected war against Russia. (The book's title is *History of the War Between Jeremy Bentham and George III* (1831), By 'One of the Belligerents'.) Bentham lamented, 'Imagine how he hated me … But for him all the paupers in the country, as well as all the prisoners in the country, would have been in my hands'.[13] A tragedy indeed!

Jeremy Bentham started out in life as a Tory, a typical eighteenth century believer in 'enlightened despotism'. He looked to the enlightened despots, whether Catherine the Great of Russia or George III, to put his reforms and crank schemes for the 'greatest happiness of the greatest number' into effect. But the failure to push through the panopticon soured him on absolute monarchy. As he wrote, 'I … never suspected that the people in power were against reform. I supposed they only wanted to know what was good in order to embrace it'. Disillusioned, Bentham allowed himself to be converted, partially by his great disciple James Mill, to radical democracy, and to the panoply of what came to be known as philosophic radicalism. As Himmelfarb summed up the new radicalism, its innovation 'was to make the greatest happiness of the greatest number dependent upon the greatest power of the greatest number', the greatest power to be lodged in an 'omnicompetent legislature'.[14] And if, as Himmelfarb puts it, the 'greatest happiness of the greatest number' might require 'the greatest misery of the few', then so be it.

It seems scarcely an exaggeration when Douglas Long compares Bentham's social outlook with that of the modern 'scientific' totalitarian, B.F. Skinner. Bentham wrote toward the end of his life that the words 'liberty' and 'liberal' were among 'the most mischievous' in the English language, because they obscured the genuine issues, which are 'happiness' and 'security'. For Bentham, the state is the necessary cradle of the law, and every individual citizen's duty is to obey that law. What the public needs and wants is not liberty but 'security', for which the power of the sovereign state must be unbounded and infinite. (And who is to guard the citizen from his sovereign?) For Bentham, as Long puts it:

> by its very nature the idea of liberty more than any other concept posed a continual threat to the completeness and stability Bentham sought in his 'science of human nature'. The indeterminate, open-ended quality of the libertarian view of man was alien to Bentham. He sought rather the perfection of a neo-Newtonian social physics.[15]

It is certainly apt if grandiloquent that Bentham saw himself as the 'Newton of the moral world'.

The philosophic radicals, despite their proclaimed devotion to *laissez-faire*, adopted not only Bentham's later democratic creed, but also his devotion to the panopticon. John Stuart Mill, even when most anti-Benthamite in the course of his eternally wavering career, never criticized the panopticon. More starkly, Bentham's brilliant 'Lenin', James Mill, despite his eagerness to bury Bentham's statist economic views, admired the panopticon with the extravagance of the Master himself. In an article on 'Prisons and Prison Discipline', written for the *Encyclopedia Britannica* in 1822 or 1823, Mill praised the panopticon to the skies, as 'perfectly expounded and proved' on the great principle of utility. Every aspect of the panopticon received Mill's plaudits: the architecture, the hammocks instead of beds, the all-seeing inspection, the labour system, the contract system, the perpetual slavery of the 'released prisoners'. Mill's lavish praise was private as well as public, for in a letter to the editor of the *Encyclopedia*, Mill insisted that the panopticon 'appear(s) to me to approach perfection'.

2.5 Notes

1. William E.C. Thomas, *The Philosophic Radicals: Nine Studies in Theory and Practice 1817–1841* (Oxford: The Clarendon Press, 1979), p. 25.
2. See, ibid., pp. 35–6.
3. Werner Stark, 'Introduction', in Stark (ed.), *Jeremy Bentham's Economic Writings* (London: George Allen & Unwin, 1951), II, 18–19.
4. John Plamenatz, *The English Utilitarians* (2nd ed., Oxford: Basil Blackwell, 1958), pp. 73–4.
5. John Wild, *Plato's Modern Enemies and the Theory of Natural Law* (Chicago: University of Chicago Press, 1953), pp. 69–70.
6. Herbert Spencer, *Social Statics* (New York: Robert Schalkenbach Foundation, 1970), pp. 3ff.
7. As Plamenatz points out, Bentham and his followers assert 'that no man can desire any pleasure except his own', and yet, paradoxically, 'they both insist that the greatest happiness, no matter whose, is the only criterion of morality'. Plamenatz, op. cit. note 4, p. 18.

And Professor Veatch points out that 'the utilitarians have always had some difficulty in showing why anyone has any obligation to think about others. If one begins by basing one's ethics on straightforward hedonistic principles, asserting that pleasure is the only thing of any value in life and recommending that the moral agent simply do as he pleases, it is patently difficult to make the transition from such a starting point to the further assertion that this same moral agent ought to concern himself not merely with his own pleasure, but equally with the pleasure of others'. Henry B. Veatch, *Rational Man: A Modern Interpretation of Aristotelian Ethics* (Bloomington, Indiana: Indiana University Press, 1962), pp. 182–3.

8. Felix Adler, The Relation of Ethics to Social Science', in H.J. Rogers, (ed.), *Congress of Arts and Science* (Boston: Houghton Mifflin, 1906), VII, p. 673. Peter Geach also makes the point that what if, even in utilitarian terms, more social happiness can be obtained by following the wishes of the *smaller* number? See Peter Geach, *The Virtues* (Cambridge: Cambridge University Press, 1977), pp. 91ff.

9. There are many other deep flaws in utilitarianism. For one, even assuming that happiness can be added or subtracted between persons, why couldn't more total social happiness be obtained by following the wishes of the *smaller* number? And what then? See Geach, op. cit., note 8. And further, the utilitarian assumption of complete moral indifference among subjective utilities or preferences will often prove counter-intuitive. How many people, for example (the majority?) will stubbornly hold with the utilitarians that someone's desire to see an innocent person hurt should count as fully in the social calculus as other, less harmful, preferences? Cf. Murray N. Rothbard, *The Ethics of Liberty* (Atlantic Highlands, NJ: Humanities Press, 1982), p. 213.

10. Gertrude Himmelfarb, *Victorian Minds* (1970, Gloucester, Mass.: Peter Smith, 1975), p. 35.

11. Ibid., p. 38.

12. Ibid., pp. 58–9.

13. Ibid., p. 71.

14. Ibid., p. 76.

15. Douglas C. Long, *Bentham on Liberty* (Toronto: University of Toronto Press, 1977), p. 164. And Long wrote: Bentham 'broadened his view of the functions attributable to a lawmaker until they ... seemed to include every imaginable form of social control over the universe of human actions'. Ibid., p. 214.

3 James Mill, Ricardo, and the Ricardian system

3.1 James Mill, the radicals' Lenin

James Mill (1771–1836) was surely one of the most fascinating figures in the history of economic thought. And yet he is among the most neglected. Mill was perhaps one of the first persons in modern times who might be considered a true 'cadre man', someone who in the Leninist movement of the next century would have been hailed as a 'real Bolshevik'. Indeed, he was the Lenin of the radicals, creating and forging philosophical radical theory and the entire philosophical radical movement. A brilliant and creative but an insistently Number 2 man, Mill began as a Lenin seeking his Marx. In fact, he simultaneously found two 'Marxes', Jeremy Bentham and David Ricardo. He met both at about the same time, at the age of 35, Bentham in 1808 and Ricardo around the same date. Bentham became Mill's philosophic Marx, from whom Mill acquired his utilitarian philosophy and passed it on to Ricardo and to economics generally. But it has been largely overlooked that Mill functioned creatively in his relationship with Bentham, persuading the older man, formerly a Tory, that Benthamite utilitarianism implied a political system of radical democracy. David Ricardo (1772–1823) was an unsophisticated, young, but retired wealthy stockbroker (actually bond dealer) with a keen interest in monetary matters; but Mill perceived and developed Ricardo as his 'Marx' in economics.

Until he acquired his post at the East India Company in 1818, at the age of 45, Mill, an impoverished Scottish emigré and freelance writer in London, lived partially off Bentham, and managed to keep on good enough formal terms with his patron despite their severe personality conflicts. An inveterate organizer of others as well as himself, Mill tried desperately to channel Bentham's prolific but random scribblings into a coherent pattern. Bentham meanwhile wrote privately to friends complaining of the impertinent interference of this young whippersnapper. Mill's publication of his massive *History of India* in 1818 won him immediate employment to an important post at the East India Company, where he rose to the head of the office in 1830 and continued there until his death.

As for David Ricardo, self-taught and diffident, he scarcely acted as a Great Man. To the contrary, his admiration for Mill, his intellectual mentor and partly his mentor in economic theory, allowed him to be moulded and dominated by Mill. And so Mill happily hectored, cajoled, prodded and bullied his good friend into becoming the 'Marx', the great economist, that Mill felt for whatever reason he himself could or should not be. He pestered Ricardo into writing and finishing his masterpiece, *The Principles of Political Economy and Taxation* (1817), and then into entering Parliament to take an active political role as leader of the radicals. Mill was then delighted to become the leading and highly devoted Ricardian in economics.

As a 'Lenin' then, James Mill had a far more active intellectual role than the real Lenin would ever enjoy. Not only did he integrate the work of two

'Marxes'; he contributed substantially to the system itself. Indeed, in endless conversations Mill instructed Ricardo on all manner of topics, and Mill looked over, edited, and undoubtedly added to many drafts of Ricardo's *Principles*. We have already seen, for example, that it was Mill who first absorbed and adopted Say's law and passed it on to his pupil Ricardo. Recent researches indicate that James Mill may have played a far more leading role in developing Ricardo's *magnum opus* than has been believed – for example, in arriving at and adopting the law of comparative advantage.

Mill's stance is surely unique in the history of social thought. Very often theorists and writers are anxious to proclaim their alleged originality to the skies (Adam Smith being an aggravated though not untypical case). But what other instance is there of a man far more original or creative than he liked to claim; how many others have insisted on appearing to be a mere Number 2 man when in many ways they were Number 1? It is possible, it should be noted, that the explanation for this curious fact is simple and materio-economic rather than depth-psychological. Mill, son of a Scottish shoemaker, was an impoverished Scot without steady employment trying to make his way and raise a family in London.. Bentham was a wealthy aristocrat who functioned as Mill's patron; Ricardo was a wealthy retired stockbroker. It is certainly possible that Mill's posture as devoted disciple was a function of a poor man keeping his wealthy mentor–disciples happy as well as maximizing the public's reception for their common doctrines.

As a pre-eminent cadre man, Mill possessed all the strengths and weaknesses of that modern type. Humourless, eternally the didact, but charismatic and filled with prodigious energy and determination, Mill found enough time to carry on an important full-time job at the East India House, while yet functioning as a committed scholar–activist on many levels. As a scholar and writer, Mill was thorough and lucid, committed strongly to a few broad and overriding axioms: utilitarianism, democracy, *laissez-faire*. On a scholarly level, he wrote important tomes on the history of British India, on economics, on political science, and on empiricist psychology. He also wrote numerous scholarly reviews and articles. But strongly committed, as Marx would be, to changing the world as well as understanding it, Mill also wrote countless newspaper articles and strategic and tactical essays, as well as tirelessly organizing the philosophic radicals, and manoeuvring in Parliament and in political life. With all that, he had the energy to preach and instruct everyone around him, including his famous and failed attempt to brainwash his young son John. But it must be noted that Mill's fierce and fervent education of John was not simply the crotchet of a Victorian father and intellectual; the education of John Stuart was designed to prepare him for the presumptively vital and world-historical role of James's successor as leader of the radical cadre, as the new Lenin. There was a method in the madness.

James Mill's evangelical Calvinist spirit was tailor-made for his lifelong cadre role. Mill was trained in Scotland to be a Presbyterian preacher. During his days as a literary man in London he lost his Christian faith and became an atheist, but, as in the case of so many later evangelically trained atheist and agnostic intellectuals, he retained the grim, puritanical and crusading habit of mind of the prototypical Calvinist firebrand. As Professor Thomas perceptively writes:

> This is why Mill, a sceptic in later life, always got on well with (Protestant) dissenters [from the Anglican Church] ... He may have come to reject belief in God, but some form of evangelical zeal remained essential to him. Scepticism in the sense of non-commitment, indecision between one belief and another, horrified him. Perhaps this accounts for his long-standing dislike of Hume. Before he lost his faith, he condemned Hume for his infidelity; but even when he had come to share that infidelity, he continued to undervalue him. A placid scepticism which seemed to uphold the *status quo* was not an attitude of mind Mill understood.[1]

Or perhaps Mill understood Hume all too well, and therefore reviled him.

Mill's Calvinism was evident in his conviction that reason must keep stern control over the passions – a conviction which hardly fitted well with Benthamite hedonism. Cadre men are notorious puritans, and Mill puritanically disliked and distrusted drama or art. The actor, he charged, was 'the slave of the most irregular appetites and passions of his species', and Mill was hardly the one to delight in sensuous beauty for its own sake. Painting and sculpture Mill scorned as the lowest of the arts, only there to gratify a frivolous love of ostentation. Since Mill, in a typically Benthamite utilitarian manner, believed that human action is only 'rational' if done in a prudent, calculating manner, he demonstrated in his *History of British India* a complete inability to understand anyone motivated by mystical religious asceticism or by a drive for military glory or self-sacrifice.

If Emil Kauder is right, and Scottish Calvinism accounts for Smith's introduction of the labour theory of value into economics, then Scottish Calvinism even more accounts for James Mill's forceful and determined crusade for the labour theory of value and perhaps for its playing a central role in the Ricardian system. It also might explain the devoted adherence to the labour theory by Mill's fellow Scot and student of Dugald Stewart, John R. McCulloch.

A prime, and particularly successful example of Mill the cadre man at work was his role in driving through Parliament the great Reform Bill of 1832. The centrepiece of Mill's political theory was his devotion to democracy and universal suffrage; but he was sensibly willing to settle, temporarily, for the Reform Bill, which decisively expanded British suffrage from an aristocratic and gerrymandered to a large middle-class base. Mill was the behind-the-scenes 'Lenin' and master manipulator of the drive for the Reform Bill. His strategy was to play on the fear of the timorous and centrist Whig government that the masses would erupt in violent revolution if the bill were not passed. Mill and his radicals knew full well that no such revolution was in the offing; but Mill, through friends and allies placed strategically in the press, was able to orchestrate a deliberate campaign of press deception that fooled and panicked the Whigs into passing the bill. The campaign of lies was engaged in by important sectors of the press: by the *Examiner*, a leading weekly owned and edited by the Benthamite radical Albany Fonblanque: by the widely read *Morning Chronicle*, a Whig daily edited by Mill's old friend John Black, who made the paper a vehicle for the utilitarian radicals; and by the *Spectator*, edited by the Benthamite S. Rintoul. The *Times* was also friendly to the radicals at this point, and the leading Birmingham radical, Joseph Parkes, was owner and editor of the *Birmingham Journal*. Not only that; Parkes was able to have his mendacious stories on the allegedly revolutionary public opinion of Birmingham printed as factual reports in the *Morning Chronicle* and the *Times*. So well did Mill accomplish his task that most later historians have been taken in as well.

Ever the unifier of theory and praxis, James Mill paved the way for this organized campaign of deception by writing in justification of lying for a worthy end. While truth was important, Mill conceded, there are special circumstances 'in which another man is not entitled to the truth'. Men, he wrote, should not be told the truth 'when they make bad use of it'. Ever the utilitarian! Of course, as usual, it was the utilitarian who was to decide whether the other man's use was going to be 'good' or 'bad'.

Mill then escalated his defence of lying in politics. In politics, he claimed, disseminating 'wrong information' (or, as we would now say, 'disinformation') is 'not a breach of morality, but on the contrary a meritorious act ... when it is conducive to the prevention of misrule. In no instance is any man less entitled to right information, than when he would employ it for the perpetuation of misrule'.

A decade and a half later, John Arthur Roebuck, one of Mill's top aides in the campaign, and later a radical MP and historian of the drive for reform, admitted that

> to attain our end, much was said that no one really believed; much was done that no one would like to own ... often, when there was no danger, the cry of alarm was raised to keep the House of Lords and the aristocracy generally in what was termed a state of wholesome terror.

In contrast to the 'noisy orators who appeared important' in the campaign, Roebuck recalled, were the 'cool-headed, retiring, sagacious determined men ... who pulled the strings in this strange puppet-show'. 'One or two ruling minds, to the public unknown', manipulated and stage-managed the entire movement. They 'use[d] the others as their instruments ...'. And the most cool-headed, sagacious and determined was the master puppeteer of them all, James Mill.

Although he worked as a high official for the East India Company and could not run for parliament himself, James Mill was the unquestioned cadre leader of the group of 10–20 philosophic radicals who enjoyed a brief day in the sun in Parliament during the 1830s. Mill continued to be their leader until he died in 1836, and then the others attempted to continue in his spirit. While the philosophic radicals proclaimed themselves Benthamites, the aging Bentham had little to do personally with this Millian group. Most of the parliamentary philosophic radicals had been converted personally by Mill, beginning with Ricardo over a decade earlier, and also including his son John Stuart, who for a while succeeded his father as radical leader. Mill, along with Ricardo, also converted the official leader of the radicals in Parliament, the banker and later classical historian George Grote (1794–1871). Grote, a self-educated and humourless man, soon became an abject tool of James Mill, whom he greatly admired as 'a very profound thinking man'. As Mill's most faithful disciple, Grote, in the words of Professor Joseph Hamburger, was 'so inoculated, as it were' that for him all of Mill's dicta 'assumed the force and sanction of duties'.

The Millian circle also had a fiery cadre lady, Mrs Harriet Lewin Grote (1792–1873), an imperious and assertive militant whose home became the salon and social centre for the parliamentary radicals. She was widely known as 'the Queen of the Radicals', of whom Cobden wrote that 'had she been a man, she would have been the leader of a party'. Harriet testified to Mill's eloquence and charismatic effect on his young disciples, most of whom were brought into the Millian circle by his son, John Stuart. A typical testimony was that of William Ellis, a young friend of John, who wrote in later years of his experience of James Mill: 'He worked a complete change in me. He taught me how to think and what to live for.'

3.2 Mill and libertarian class analysis

The theory of class conflict as a key to political history did not begin with Karl Marx. It began, as we shall see further below, with two leading French libertarians inspired by J.B. Say, Charles Comte (Say's son-in-law), and Charles Dunoyer, in the 1810s after the restoration of the Bourbon monarchy. In contrast to the later Marxist degeneration of class theory, the Comte–Dunoyer view held the inherent class struggle to focus on *which classes* managed to gain control of the state apparatus. The *ruling* class is whichever group has managed to seize state power; the *ruled* are those groups who are taxed and regulated by those in command. Class interest, then, is defined as a group's relation to the state. State rule, with its taxation and exercise of power, controls, and conferring of subsidies and privileges, is the instrument that creates conflicts between the rulers and the ruled. What we have, then, is a 'two-class' theory of class conflict, based on whether a group rules or is ruled by the state. On the free market, on the other hand, there is no class conflict, but a harmony of interest between all individuals in society cooperating in and through production and exchange.

James Mill developed a similar theory in the 1820s and 1830s. It is not known whether he arrived at it independently or was influenced by the French libertarians; it is clear, however, that Mill's analysis was devoid of the rich applications to the history of western Europe that Comte, Dunoyer, and their young associate, the historian Augustin Thierry, had worked out. All government, Mill pointed out, was run by the ruling class, the few who dominated and exploited the ruled, the many. Since all groups tend to act for their selfish interests, he noted, it is absurd to expect the ruling clique to act altruistically for the 'public good'. Like everyone else, they will use their opportunities for their own gain, which means to loot the many, and to favour their own or allied special interests as against those of the public. Hence Mill's habitual use of the term 'sinister' interests as against the good of the public. For Mill and the radicals, we should note, the public good meant specifically *laissez-faire*–government confined to the minimal functions of police, defence and the administration of justice.

Hence Mill, the pre-eminent political theorist of the radicals, harked back to the libertarian Commonwealthmen of the eighteenth century in stressing the need always to treat government with suspicion and to provide checks to suppress state power. Mill agreed with Bentham that 'If not deterred, a ruling elite would be predatory'. The pursuit of sinister interests leads to endemic 'corruption' in politics, to sinecures, bureaucratic 'places' and subsidies. Mill lamented: 'Think of the end [of government] as it really is, in its own nature. Think next of the facility of the means – justice, police, and security from foreign invaders. And then think of the oppression practised upon the people of England under the pretext of providing them.'

Never has libertarian ruling-class theory been put more clearly or forcefully than in the words of Mill: there are two classes, Mill declared, 'The first class, those who plunder, are the small number. They are the ruling Few. The second class, those who are plundered, are the great number. They are the subject Many'. Or, as Professor Hamburger summed up Mill's position: 'Politics was a struggle between two classes – the avaricious rulers and their intended victims.'[2]

The great conundrum of government, concluded Mill, was how to eliminate this plunder: to take away the power 'by which the class that plunder succeed in carrying on their vocation, has ever been the great problem of government'.

The 'subject Many' Mill accurately termed 'the people', and it was prob-ably Mill who inaugurated the type of analysis that pits 'the people' as a ruled class in opposition to the 'special interests'. How, then, is the power of the ruling class to be curbed? Mill thought he saw the answer: 'The people must appoint watchmen. Who are to watch the watchmen? The people them-selves. There is no other resource; and without this ultimate safeguard, the ruling Few will be forever the scourge and oppression of the subject Many.'

But how are the people themselves to be the watchmen? To this ancient problem Mill provided what is by now a standard answer in the western world, but still not very satisfactory: by all the people electing representa-tives to do the watching.

Unlike the French libertarian analysts, James Mill was not interested in the history and development of state power; he was interested only in the here and now. And in the here and now of the England of his day, the ruling Few were the aristocracy, who ruled by means of a highly limited suffrage and controlled 'rotten boroughs' picking representatives to Parliament. The Eng-lish aristocracy was the ruling class; the government of England, Mill charged, was 'an aristocratical engine, wielded by the aristocracy for their own ben-efit'. Mill's son and ardent disciple (at that time), John Stuart, argued in a Millian manner in debating societies in London that England did *not* enjoy a 'mixed government', since a great majority of the House of Lords was chosen by '200 families'. These few aristocratic families 'therefore possess absolute control over the government ... and if a government controlled by 200 families is not an aristocracy, then such a thing as an aristocracy cannot be said to exist'. And since such a government is controlled and run by a few, it is therefore 'conducted wholly for the benefit of a few'.

It is this analysis that led James Mill to place at the centre of his formidable political activity the attainment of radical democracy, the universal suffrage of the people in frequent elections by secret ballot. This was Mill's long-run goal, although he was willing to settle temporarily – in what the Marxists would later call a 'transition demand' – for the Reform Bill of 1832, which greatly widened the suffrage to the middle class. To Mill, the extension of democracy was more important than *laissez-faire*, for to Mill the *process* of dethroning the aristo-cratic class was more fundamental, since *laissez-faire* was one of the happy consequences expected to flow from the replacement of aristocracy by the rule of all the people. (In the modern American context, Mill's position would aptly be called 'right-wing populism'.) Placing democracy as their central demand led the Millian radicals in the 1840s to stumble and lose political significance by refusing to ally themselves with the Anti-Corn Law League, despite their agreement with its free trade and *laissez-faire*. For the Millians felt that free trade was too much of a middle-class movement and detracted from an overrid-ing concentration on democratic reform.

Granted that the people would displace aristocratic rule, did Mill have any reason for thinking that the people would then exert their will on behalf of *laissez-faire*? Yes, and here his reasoning was ingenious: while the ruling class had the fruits of their exploitative rule in common, the people were a different kind of class: their only interest in common was getting rid of the rule of special privilege. Apart from that, the mass of the people have no common class interest that they could ever actively pursue by means of the state. Furthermore, this interest in eliminating special privilege is the common interest of all, and is therefore the 'public interest' as opposed to the special or sinister interests of the few. The interest of the people coincides with universal interest and with *laissez-faire* and liberty for all.

But how then explain that no one can claim that the masses have always championed *laissez-faire*? – and that the masses have all too often loyally supported the exploitative rule of the few? Clearly, because the people, in this complex field of government and public policy, have suffered from what the Marxists would later call 'false consciousness', an ignorance of where their interests truly lie. It was then up to the intellectual vanguard, to Mill and his philosophic radicals, to educate and organize the masses so that their consciousness would become correct and they would then exert their irresistible strength to bring about their own democratic rule and install *laissez-faire*. Even if we can accept this general argument, the Millian radicals were unfortunately highly over-optimistic about the time span for such consciousness-raising, and political setbacks in the early 1840s led to their disillusionment in radical politics and to the rapid disintegration of the radical movement. Curiously enough, their leaders, such as John Stuart Mill and George and Harriet Grote, while proclaiming their weary abandonment of political action or political enthusiasm, in reality gravitated with astonishing rapidity toward the cosy Whig centre that they had formerly scorned. Their proclaimed loss of interest in politics was in reality a mask for loss of interest in *radical* politics.

3.3   Mill and the Ricardian system

Much has been recently revealed about James Mill's formative and shaping role over his friend Ricardo's system. How much of Ricardianism is really Mill's creation? Apparently a great deal. One thing is certain: it was Mill who took from J.B. Say the great Say's law and converted Ricardo to that stand. Mill had developed Say's law in his important early book, *Commerce Defended* (1808), written shortly before he met Ricardo. Ricardo faithfully followed Say's law, and, while in Parliament, consistently opposed expenditure on public works during the depressed year of 1819. And we have seen that Mill and Ricardo together managed to kill the publication of Bentham's 'pre-Keynesian' *True Alarm* in 1811.

In expounding Say's law, Mill was carrying on and developing the important Turgot–Smith insights on saving and investment. But most of the rest of Mill's economic legacy was a disaster. Much of it was the heart and soul of the Ricardian system. Thus, in a forgotten early work, *The Impolicy of a Bounty on the Exportation of Grain* (1804), Mill sets forth the essence of Ricardianism, from the actual content, to the characteristic disastrous methodology of brutal and unrealistic oversimplification, and to a holistic concentration of unsound macro-aggregates unrelated to the actions of the individual, whether consumer or businessman, in the real world. Mill churns out chunks of alleged interrelations between these macro-aggregates, all *seeming* to be about the real world, but actually relevant only to deeply fallacious assumptions about the never-never land of long-run equilibrium. The methodology is essentially 'verbal mathematics', since the statements are only the implicit churning out of what are really mathematical relations but are never admitted as such. The use of the vernacular language adds a patina of pretend realism that mathematics can never convey. An open use of mathematics might at least have revealed the fallacious assumptions of the model.

Ricardo's exclusive concern with long-run equilibria may be seen from his own declaration of method: 'I put those immediate and temporary effects quite aside, and fixed my whole attention on the permanent state of things which will result from them.'

Unrealistic oversimplification compounded upon itself is the 'Ricardian Vice'. Both the Ricardian and the Say–Austrian methodology have been termed 'deductive', but they are really poles apart. The Austrian methodology ('praxeology') sticks close in its axioms to universally realistic common insights into the essence of human action, and deduces truths only from such evidently true propositions or axioms. The Ricardian methodology introduces numerous false assumptions, compounded and multiplied, into the initial axioms, so that deductions made from these assumptions – whether verbal in the case of Ricardo or mathematical in the case of the modern Walrasians or a blend of both as in the Keynesians – are all necessarily false, useless and misleading.

Thus, in his essay on a bounty on grain, James Mill introduces the typically 'Ricardian' error of melding all agricultural commodities into one, 'corn' (wheat), and claiming corn to be *the* basic commodity. With corn now adopted as a surrogate for all food, Mill makes the sweeping statement that the most scientific principle of political economy is 'that the money price of corn, regulates the money price of everything else'. Why? Here, Mill introduces a typically and brutally drastic variant of Malthusianism. Not just that there is a long-run *tendency* for population to press on the means of subsistence so that wage rates are pushed down to the cost of subsistence. But more, in a typically Ricardian confusion of the non-existent long-run equilibrium with constant, everyday reality, that wage rates are always set by the price of corn (a surrogate for food, or subsistence, in general). Mill lays down the proposition that wage rates are always set directly by the price of corn as 'so obviously necessary, that we need spend no more time proving it'. That takes care of *that*! He concludes therefore that the wage rate is 'entirely regulated by the money price of corn'.

Mill's extreme version of Malthusianism can be seen in his statement that 'no one ... will hesitate to allow ... that the tendency of the species to multiply is much greater than the rapidity with which there is any chance that the fruits of the earth will be multiplied'. Mill even goes so far in wild extremes as to say that 'raise corn as fast as you please, mouths are producing still faster to eat it. Population is invariably pressing close upon the heels of subsistence; and in whatever quantity food be produced, a demand will always be produced greater than the supply'.

Another unfortunate notion contributed to Ricardo by Mill in his 1804 essay is an overriding focus on the behaviour of a few aggregate macro-shares. Labour was assumed to be of uniform quality; therefore, all 'wages' were pushed down to subsistence level by the price of corn. There are only three macro-distributive shares: 'wages', 'profits' and 'rents' in the Ricardian scheme. There is no discussion whatever of *individual* prices or wage rates – the proper concern of economic analysis – and no hint of the existence of or the need for the entrepreneur. Say's brilliant analysis of the entrepreneur's central role is completely forgotten; there is no role for a risk-bearing entrepreneur if all is frozen into a few aggregative chunks in long-run equilibrium, where change is slow or non-existent, and knowledge is perfect rather than uncertain. 'Profits', therefore, are the net returns aggregatively received by capitalists, which could well be called 'interest' or 'long-run profits'.

If wages, profits and rents exhaust the product, then, tautologically and virtually by definition, if one of the three increases, and the *total is frozen*, one or both of the other shares must fall. Hence, the implicit Ricardian assumption of inherent class conflict between the receivers of the three blocs of distributive shares. In the Mill–Ricardian system, wages are fixed by the price of corn, or the cost of food. The cost of food, for its part, is always increasing because of the fixed supply of land and the alleged Malthusian necessity to move to ever less productive land as the population increases and presses on the food supply. Thus: rents are always slowly but inexorably increasing, and money wage rates are always rising in order to maintain the real wage at subsistence level. Therefore – hey presto! – aggregate 'profits' must always be falling.

Schumpeter's blistering critique of the Ricardian system is highly perceptive and perfectly apt:

...he [Ricardo] cut that general system [of economic interdependence in the market] to pieces, bundled up as large parts of it as possible in cold storage – so that as many things as possible should be frozen and 'given'. He then piled one simplifying assumption upon another until, having really settled everything by these assumptions, he was left with only a few aggregative variables between which, given these assumptions, he set up simple one-way relations so that, in the end, the desired results emerged almost as tautologies. For example, a famous Ricardian theory is that profits 'depend upon' the price of wheat. And upon his implicit assumptions, and in the particular sense in which the terms of the proposition are to be understood, that is not only true, but undeniably, in fact trivially, so. Profits could not possibly depend upon anything else, since everything else is 'given', that is, frozen. It is an excellent theory that can never be refuted and lacks nothing save sense.[3]

3.4 Ricardo and the Ricardian system, I: macro-income distribution

While much of the Ricardian system turns out to be the creation of James Mill, perhaps most of it was due to Ricardo himself, who of course must, in any case, bear major responsibility for his own work. To continue the Marxian metaphor, in many ways the Mill–Ricardo relationship might be more of a Marx–Engels than a Lenin–Marx connection.

Ricardo was born in London into a prosperous family of Spanish–Portuguese Jews who had settled in Holland after having been expelled from Spain at the end of the fifteenth century. Ricardo's father had moved to London, where he prospered as a stockbroker, and had 17 children, of whom David was the third. At the age of 11, David was sent by his father to Amsterdam, to attend Orthodox Hebrew school for two years. At the age of 14, with only an elementary education, Ricardo began his business career, employed by his father's 'stockbroker' house. It must be emphasized that, with the exception of the quasi-governmental Bank of England, there were no corporations or corporate stocks in that era. Government bonds were then called 'stocks', and so 'stockbrokers' were what would now be called government bond dealers.

Seven years later, however, David married a Quaker girl, and left the Jewish faith, whereupon he was disowned by his parents. Eventually, he became a confirmed Quaker. A London bank, already impressed with young Ricardo, lent him enough money to set himself up in his own business as a stockbroker. Within a few years, Ricardo made an enormous amount of money in the bond business, until he was ready to retire to the country in his early 40s. In 1799, at the age of 27, Ricardo, bored while whiling away time at a health resort, chanced upon a copy of *The Wealth of Nations*, and devoured it, becoming, like so many others of that era, a dedicated Smithian.

As Schumpeter points out, Ricardo's *Principles* can only be understood as a dialogue with, and reaction to, *The Wealth of Nations*. Ricardo's logical bent was offended at the basic confusion of mind, the chaos that J.B. Say also saw in the Smithian canon, and he, like Say before him, set out to clarify the Smithian system. Unfortunately, and in deep contrast to Say, Ricardo simplified by taking all the most egregious errors in Smith, throwing out all qualifications and contradictions, then building his system upon what was left. The worst of Smith was magnified and intensified. In his basic method, all of Smith's historical and empirical points were tossed out. This was not bad in itself, but it left a deductive system built on deep fallacy and incorrect macro-models. In addition, while Ricardo's theoretical system might have been brutally oversimplified in relation to Smith, his writing style was inordinately crabbed and obtuse. The methodology of verbal mathematics is almost bound to be difficult and obscurantist, with blocks of words spelling out equilibrium mathematical relations in a highly cumbersome manner. But on top of that, Ricardo, in contrast to his mentor Mill, was undoubtedly one of the worst and most turgid literary stylists in the history of economic thought.

In contrast to Adam Smith, for whom the output, or wealth, of nations was of supreme importance, Ricardo neglected total output to place overriding emphasis on the alleged distribution of a given product into macro-classes. Specifically, into the three macro-classes of landlords, labourers and capitalists. Thus, in a letter to Malthus, who on this question at least was an orthodox Smithian, Ricardo made the distinction clear: 'Political economy, you think, is an enquiry into the nature and causes of wealth; I think it should rather be called an enquiry into the laws which determine the division of the produce of industry amongst the classes who concur in its formation.'

Since entrepreneurship could not exist in Ricardo's world of long-run equilibrium, he was left with the classical triad of factors. His analysis was strictly holistic, in terms of allegedly homogeneous but actually varied and diverse classes. Ricardo avoided any Say-type emphasis on the individual, whether he be the consumer, worker, producer or businessman.

In Ricardo's world of verbal mathematics there were, as Schumpeter has astutely pointed out, four variables: total output or income, and shares of income to landlords, capitalists, and workers, i.e. rent, profits (long-run interest) and wages. Ricardo was stuck with a hopeless problem: he had four variables, but only one equation with which to solve them:

$$\text{Total output (or income)} = \text{rent} + \text{profits} + \text{wages}$$

To solve, or rather pretend to solve, this equation, Ricardo had to 'determine' one or more of these entities from outside his equation, and in such a way as to leave others as residuals. He began by neglecting total output, i.e. by assuming it to be a *given*, thereby 'determining' output by freezing it on his own arbitrary assumptions. This procedure enabled him to get rid of one variable – to his own satisfaction.

Next, on to wages. Here, Ricardo took from Mill the hard-core, or ultra-Malthusian, view that 'wages' – all wages – are always and everywhere pressing on the food supply to such an extent that they are always set, and determined, precisely at the level of the cost of subsistence. Labour is assumed to be homogeneous and of equal quality, so that all wages can be assumed to be at subsistence cost. While briefly and dimly acknowledging that labour can have different qualities or grades, Ricardo, like Marx after him, drastically assumed away the problem by blithely postulating that they can all be incorporated into a weighted quantity of 'labour hours'. As a result, Ricardo could maintain that wage rates were uniform throughout the economy. In the meanwhile, as we have seen, food, or subsistence generally, was assumed to be incorporated into one commodity, 'corn', so that the price of corn can serve as a surrogate for subsistence cost in general.

Given these heroic and fallacious assumptions, then, 'the' wage rate is determined instantly and totally by the price of corn, since the wage rate can neither rise above the subsistence level (as determined by the price of corn) nor sink below it.

The price of corn, in its turn, is determined according to Ricardo's famous theory of rent. Rent served as the linchpin of the Ricardian system. For, according to Ricardo's rather bizarre theory, *only* land differed in quality. Labour, as we have seen, was assumed to be uniform, and therefore wage rates are uniform, and, as we shall see, profits are also assumed to be uniform because of the crucial postulate of the economy's always being in long-run equilibrium. Land is the only factor which miraculously is allowed to differ in quality. Next, Ricardo assumes away any discovery of new lands or improvements in agricultural productivity. His theory of history therefore concludes that people always begin by cultivating the most fertile lands, and, as population increases, the Malthusian pressure on the food supply forces the producers to use ever more inferior lands. In short, as population and food production rise, the cost of growing corn must inexorably rise over time.

Rent, in Ricardo's phrase, is payment for the 'use of the original and indestructible powers of the soil'. This hints at a productivity theory, and indeed Ricardo did see that more fertile and productive lands earned a higher rent. But unfortunately, as Schumpeter put it, Ricardo then 'embarks upon his detour'. In the first place, Ricardo made the assumption that at any moment the poorest land in cultivation yields a zero rent. He concluded from that alleged fact that a given piece of land earns rent not because of *its own* productivity, but merely because its productivity is greater than the poorest, zero-rent, land under cultivation. Remember that, for Ricardo, labour is homogeneous and hence wages uniform and equal, and, as we shall see, profits are also uniform and equal. Land is unique in its permanent, long-run structure of differential fertility and productivity. Hence, to Ricardo, rent is *purely* a differential, and Land *A* earns rent solely because of its differential productivity compared to Land *B*, the zero-rent land in cultivation.

To Ricardo, several important points followed from these assumptions. First, as population inexorably increases, and poorer and poorer lands are used, *all the differentials keep increasing*. Thus, say that, at one point of time, corn lands (which sums up all land) range in productivity from the highest, Land *A*, through a spectrum down to Land *J*, which, being marginal, earns a zero rent. But now population increases and farmers have to cultivate more and poorer lands, say *K*, *L*, and *M*. *M* now becomes the zero-rent land, and Land *J* now earns a positive rent, equal to the differential between *its* productivity and that of *M*. And all the previous infra-marginal lands have their differential rents raised as well. It becomes ineluctably true, therefore, that over time, as population increases, rents, and the proportion of income going to rent, increase as well.

Yet, though rent keeps increasing, *at the margin* it always remains zero, and, as Ricardo put it in a crucial part of his theory, being zero rent *does not enter into cost*.

Put another way: quantity of labour cost, being allegedly homogeneous, is uniform for each product, and profits, being uniform and fairly small throughout the economy, form a part of cost that can be basically neglected. Since the price of every product is uniform, this means that the quantity of labour cost on the highest-cost, or zero-rent, land, uniquely determines the price of corn and of every other agricultural product. Rent, being infra-marginal in Ricardo's assumptions, cannot enter into cost. Total rental income is a passive residual determined by selling prices and total income, and selling prices are determined by quantity of labour cost and (to a small extent) the uniform rate of profit. And since the quantity of labour needed to produce corn keeps rising as more and more inferior lands are put into production, this means that the cost of producing corn and hence the price of corn keep rising over time. And, paradoxically, while rent keeps rising over time, it remains zero at the margin, and therefore without any impact on costs.

There are many flaws in this doctrine. In the first place, even the poorest land in cultivation never earns a zero rent, just as the least productive piece of machinery or worker never earns a zero price or wage. It does not benefit any resource owner to keep his resource or factor in production unless it earns a positive rent. The marginal land, or other resource, will indeed earn less of a rent than more productive factors, but even the marginal land will always earn *some* positive rent, however small.

Second, apart from the zero-rent problem, it is simply wrong to think that rent, or any other factor return, is *caused* by differentials. Each piece of land, or unit of any factor, earns whatever *it* produces; differentials are simple arithmetic subtractions between two lands, or other factors, *each of which* earns a positive rent of its own. The assumption of zero rent at the margin allows Ricardo to obscure the fact that *every* piece of land earns a productive rent, and allows him to slip into the differential *as cause*.

We might just as well turn Ricardo on his head and apply the differential theory to wages, and say, with Schumpeter, that 'one pays more for good than for bad land exactly as one pays more for a good than a bad workman'.[4]

Third, in discussing the rise in cost of producing corn, Ricardo reverses cause and effect. Ricardo states that increasing population 'obliges' farmers to work land of inferior quality and *then* causes a rise in its price. But as any utility theory analyst would realize, the causal chain is precisely the reverse: when the *demand* for corn increases, its price would rise, and the higher price would lead farmers to grow corn on higher-cost land. But this realization, of course, eliminates the Ricardian theory of value and with it the entire Ricardian system.

And fourth, as numerous critics have pointed out, it is certainly not true historically that people always start using the highest-quality land and then sink gradually and inevitably down to more and more inferior land. Historically, there have always been advances, and enormous ones, in the productivity of agriculture, in the discovery and creation of new lands, and in the discovery and application of new and more productive agricultural techniques and types of products. Defenders of Ricardo counter that this is a purely historical argument, ignoring the logical beauty of the Ricardian theory. But the whole point is that Ricardo was, after all, advancing a *historical* theory, a law of history, and he certainly claimed historical accuracy for past and future predictions for his theory. And yet it is all a purely arbitrary, and hence largely untrue, assumption of his logical doctrine in the guise of a theory of history. Ricardo's basic problem throughout was making cavalier and untrue historical or empirical generalizations the building blocks of his logical system, from which he drew self-confident and seemingly apodictically true empirical and political conclusions. Yet from false assumptions only false conclusions can be drawn, regardless how imposing the logical structure may or may not be.

Ricardo's differential rent theory has been widely hailed as the precursor of the neoclassical law of diminishing returns, which the neoclassicals were supposed to have generalized from land to all factors of production. But this is wrong, since the law of diminishing returns applies to increasing doses of a factor to *homogeneous* units of other, logically fixed, factors – in this case land. But the whole point of Ricardo's differential rent theory is that his areas of land are not homogeneous at all, but varying in a spectrum from superiority to inferiority. Therefore the law of diminishing returns – as grasped by Turgot and rediscovered by the neoclassicals – simply does not apply.[5]

Rent, though increasing, is then effectively zero and not part of expenses or costs. Rent is disposed of in the Ricardian equation. But we have not yet finished the determination of wages, which so far we have said is precisely fixed at the subsistence level. What will happen to the costs of subsistence over time? They will rise as the cost of the production of corn rises with the increasing population, forcing the cultivation of ever more inferior lands. Over time, in the slow-moving long-run Ricardian equilibria, the cost of food will rise, and since wages must *always* be at the subsistence level, wages will *have* to rise to maintain *real* wage rates equal to the cost of subsistence. Now we begin to close the Ricardian circle. Rents are in effect zero, and wage rates, always at subsistence, must rise over time as the cost of food increases, in order to keep precise pace with the rising cost of subsistence. But, then – voilà! – we have finally determined all the variables except profits (at least to Ricardo's satisfaction), and, since total income is 'given' or kept frozen, this means that profits are the residual from total income. With rents out of the picture, if wage rates have to keep rising over time, this necessarily means that profits, or profit rates, have to keep falling. Hence the Ricardian doctrine of the ever-falling rate of profit (i.e. long-term rate of interest). Note that this is not the same as Adam Smith's view that the profit rate falls over time because and in so far as capital continues to accumulate; profit was supposed to be an inverse function of the stock of capital. Ricardo's doctrine of the falling rate of profit follows by triumphant tautology from his attempt to determine the other factor shares of total income. When profits fall to zero, or at any rate to a low level, capital will cease to accumulate and we arrive at Ricardo's 'stationary state'.

Ricardo, even more than Smith, totally leaves out the entrepreneur. There can be no role for the entrepreneur, after all, if everyone is always in long-run equilibrium and there is never risk or uncertainty. His 'profits', as in Smith, are the long-run rate of return, i.e. the rate of interest. In long-run equilibrium, furthermore, all profits are uniform, since firms rapidly move out of low-profit industries and into high-profit ones until equalization takes place. We then have 'profits' at a uniform rate throughout the economy at any given time.

A plausible insight into Ricardo's habitual confusion of long-run equilibrium and instantaneous adjustments with the real world has been offered by Professor F.W. Fetter. Fetter points out that Ricardo's practical familiarity was not with business and industry (as was, we might note, J.B. Say) but with the bond and foreign exchange markets. Ricardo 'usually assumed that even in industry and agriculture, adjustment took place on the basis of as small price differences, and almost as quickly, as did arbitrage in government securities and in foreign exchange'.[6]

To return to the Ricardian world: note that Ricardo does *not* say that the cost of corn rises over time because rents keep rising on corn land. He must get rid of the rent variable, and he can only do so by assuming that rent is zero at the margin, and therefore never forms any part of costs. Rent, then, is effectively zero. Why then does the cost of corn rise? As we have indicated, because the quantity of labour needed to produce corn, and hence the cost of producing corn, rises over time. This brings us to Ricardo's theory of cost and value. Rents are now out of it. Wages are not costs either, because a key to Ricardo's system is that rising wages lead only to lower profits, and *not* to higher prices. If rising wages meant that costs increased, then Ricardo, who as we shall see had a cost-theory of value and price, would have to say that prices rose rather than that profits would necessarily fall. Wages he treated as uniform, since Ricardo, like Marx after him, maintained that labour was homogeneous in quality. Not only did that mean that wages were uniform; but Ricardo could then treat, as the crucial part of its labour cost, the quantity of labour embodied in any product. Differences in quality or productivity of labour could then be dismissed as simply trivial and as a slightly more complex version of the quantity of labour hours. Quality has been quickly and magically transformed into quantity.

We have reached the edge of the Ricardian – and Marxian – labour theory of value. So far we just have a labour-quantity theory of cost. Ricardo vacillated at this point, between a strict labour theory of cost, and a labour-quantity theory plus the uniform rate of profit. But, since the uniform rate of profit, presumably around 3–6 per cent, is small compared to the quantity of labour hours, Ricardo may be pardoned for dismissing the profit-rate part of cost as of trivial importance. And, since all profit rates are assumed to be uniform, and, as we shall see, Ricardo had a cost theory of value or price, he could easily dismiss the uniform and small proportion, profit, as of no account in explaining relative prices.

It is, of course, peculiar to consider profits, even profits as long-run interest, as part of the 'costs' of production. Again, this usage stems from eliminating any consideration of entrepreneurial profits and losses, and focusing on interest as a long-run 'cost' of inducing savings and the accumulation of capital.

If profits for Ricardo are always uniform, how is this uniform profit determined? Curiously, profits are *in no way* related to savings or capital accumulation; for Ricardo, they are only a residual left over after paying wages. In short, to hark back to our original equation of Ricardian distribution: total output (or income) = rent + profits + wages. Remarkably, Ricardo has attempted to determine all the variables with *only* one variable explicitly determined. Output, as we have seen, was assumed as mysteriously given, from outside the Ricardian system. Wages ('the' uniform wage throughout the economy) is the only explicitly determined variable, determined completely to equal the cost of subsistence, embodied in the cost of producing corn. But that leaves *two* residuals, rents and profits, to be determined. The way Ricardo tries to get around that problem is to dispose of rents. Rents are the differential between the lands in cultivation and the least productive, zero-rent, land in use. The cost of producing corn is equal to the quantity of labour hours embodied in its production. Since rents are zero at the margin, they do not enter into costs, and are passively determined; at the no-rent margin, labour and capital's shares exhaust output. And since wages are supposedly determined by the cost of raising corn, this means that profit *can only* be a truistic residual of wages, otherwise the variable would be overdetermined, and the system would evidently collapse.

The alleged historical laws follow from the model. Since increasing population forces more and more inferior land into cultivation, the cost of labour in producing corn (i.e. the quantity of labour hours needed to produce it), must keep rising. And since price is determined by cost, supposedly boiled down into the quantity of labour hours to produce the good, this means that the price of corn must keep rising over time. But since *real* wage rates are fixed always at the cost of subsistence, and this is assumed to be the price of corn, money wage rates must keep rising over time (while workers remain at the subsistence level), and therefore profits must keep falling in the course of history.

Adam Smith believed that the rate of profit, or the long-run rate of interest return, is determined by the quantity of accumulated capital, so that more capital will lead to a falling rate of profit. While this theory is not fully correct, it at least understands that there is *some* connection between saving, capital accumulation, and long-run interest or profit. But to Ricardo there is no connection whatever. Interest on capital is only a residual. By a series of fallacies, and holistic, locked-in assumptions, trivial conclusions are at last ground out, all with a portentous air, allegedly telling us conclusive insights about the real world. As Schumpeter scornfully puts it: propositions such as 'profits depend upon wages', and the falling rate of profit, are excellent examples of 'that Art of Triviality that, ultimately connected with the Ricardian Vice, leads the victim, step by step, into a situation where he has got either to surrender or to allow himself to be laughed at for denying what, by the time that situation is reached, is *really* a triviality'.[7]

3.5   Ricardo and the Ricardian system, II: the theory of value

This brings us to Ricardo's theory of value, or price. While Ricardo formally admitted that supply and demand determine day-to-day market pricing, he tossed that aside as of no consequence, and concentrated solely on long-run equilibrium, i.e. 'natural' price and the alleged macro-distribution of income in that equilibrium. Utility Ricardo brusquely disposed of as ultimately necessary to production but of no influence whatever on value or price; in the 'value paradox' he embraced exchange value and abandoned utility completely. Not only that: he frankly and boldly discarded any attempt to explain the prices of goods that are not reproducible, that could not be increased in supply by the employment of labour. Hence Ricardo simply gave up any attempt to explain the prices of such goods as paintings, which are fixed in supply and cannot be increased. In short, Ricardo abandoned any attempt at a *general* explanation of consumer prices. We have arrived at the full-fledged Ricardian – and Marxian – labour theory of value.

The Ricardian system is now complete. Prices of goods are determined by their costs, i.e. by the quantity of labour hours embodied in them, trivially plus the uniform rate of profit. Specifically, since the price of each good is uniform, it will equal the cost of production on the highest-cost (i.e. zero-rent) or marginal land in cultivation. In short, price will be determined by cost, i.e. the quantity of labour hours on the zero-rent land used to work on the product. As time goes on, then, and population increases, poorer and poorer soils must be brought into use, so that the cost of producing corn continues to increase. It does so because the quantity of labour hours needed to produce corn keeps increasing, since labour must be employed on ever poorer soil. As a result, the price of corn keeps increasing. Since wage rates are always kept precisely at the subsistence level (the cost of growing corn) by population pressure, this means that money wage rates must continue to increase over time in order to keep *real* wage rates in pace with the ever-rising price of corn. Wage rates must increase over time, and hence profits must keep falling until they are so low that the stationary state is reached.

To return to the idea of rent as not entering into cost: if we focus, as we should on the 'micro' – on the individual farmer or capitalist – it should be clear that the individual *must* pay rent in order to gain use of any particular plot of land in the productive process. To do so, he must outbid other firms in his own as well as other industries. Ricardo's refusal to even consider the individual firm, and his focus on holistic aggregates, enables him to overlook the fact that rents, even if differentials, enter into costs the way *every* expense on factors of production enters into them. This is the only way that is real and that counts in the real world: the point of view of the individual firm or entrepreneur. There is, in fact, no 'social' point of view, since 'society' as an entity does not exist.

Ricardo's system is both gloomy and rife with allegedly inherent class conflict on the free market. First, there is tautological conflict because, given the fixed total, the income shares of one macro-group can only increase at the expense of another. But the point of the free market in the real world is that generally production increases, so that the total pie tends to keep rising. And, second, if we focus on individual factors and on how much they earn, as does the later marginal productivity theory (and as did J.B. Say), then each factor tends to earn its marginal product, and we need not even concern ourselves with the alleged but non-existent laws and conflicts of macro-class income distribution. Ricardo kept his eye unerringly on the radically wrong problem – or rather, problems.

But there is even more class conflict here than implied by Ricardo's tautological macro-approach. For if value is the product solely of labour hours, then it becomes easy for Marx, who was after all a neo-Ricardian, to call all returns to capital exploitative deductions from the whole of 'labour's' product. The Ricardian socialist call for turning over all of the product to labour follows directly from the Ricardian system – although Ricardo and the other orthodox Ricardians did not of course make that leap. Ricardo would have countered that capital represents embodied or frozen labour; but Marx accepted that point and simply riposted that all labour producers of capital, or frozen labour, should obtain their full return. In fact, *neither* was right; if we wish to consider capital goods as frozen *anything*, we would have to say, with the great Austrian Böhm-Bawerk, that capital is frozen labour and *land* and *time*. Labour, then, would be earning wages, land would earn rent, and interest (or long-run profits) would be the price of time.

Recent analysts, in an attempt to mitigate the crude fallacy of Ricardo's labour theory of value, have maintained, as in the case of Smith but even more so, that he was attempting not so much to explain the cause of value and price but to *measure* values over time, and labour was considered an invariable measure of value. But this hardly mitigates Ricardo's flaws; instead, it adds to the general fallacies and vagaries of the Ricardian system *another important* one: the vain search for a non-existent chimera of invariability. For values always fluctuate, and there is no invariable, fixed base of value from which other value changes can be measured.

Thus, in rejecting Say's definition of the value of a good as its purchasing power of other goods in exchange, Ricardo sought the invariable entity, the unmoved power:

> A franc is not a measure of value for any thing, but for a quantity of the same metal of which francs are made, unless francs, and the thing to be measured, can be referred to some other measure which is common to both. This, I think, they can be, for they are both the result of labour; and, therefore, labour is a common measure, by which their real as well as their relative value may be estimated.

It might be noted that both products are the result of capital, land, savings, and entrepreneurship, as well as labour, and that, in any case, their values are incommensurable except in terms of relative purchasing power, as Say had in fact maintained.

Part of Ricardo's impassioned quest for an invariable measure of values undoubtedly stemmed from his deep-dyed scientism. Ricardo was almost as interested in the natural sciences as in economics. From his early youth,

Ricardo was keenly interested in the natural sciences, in mathematics, chemistry, mineralogy and geology. He joined the Geological Society in his 30s shortly after it was founded. It is probable that Ricardo's quest for an invariable measure of values was based on the physical science model; if 'scientific' in the physical sciences meant measurement, then surely this would be required in the human sciences as well. As Emil Kauder wrote, 'I venture to say that Ricardo and his contemporaries believed that economics could only reach the dignity of a science if it could be based on objective measures like the Newtonian Physics'.[8]

An even stronger and more direct class struggle than that implied by the labour theory of value stemmed from Ricardo's approach toward landlords and land rent. Landlords are simply obtaining payment for the powers of the soil, which, at least in the hands of many of Ricardo's followers, meant an unjust return. Furthermore, Ricardo's gloomy vision of the future held that labour must be kept at subsistence level, capitalists must see their profits inevitably falling – these two classes doing as badly as ever (labour) or always worse (capital) while the idle and useless landlords keep inexorably adding to their share of worldly goods. The productive classes suffer, while the idle landlords, charging for the powers of nature, benefit at the expense of the producers.[9] If Ricardo implies Marx, he implies Henry George far more directly. The spectre of land nationalization or the single tax absorbing all land rent follows straight from Ricardo.

One of the greatest fallacies of the Ricardian theory of rent is that it ignores the fact that landlords *do* perform a vital economic function: they allocate land to its best and most productive use. Land does not allocate itself; it must *be* allocated, and only those who earn a return from such service have the incentive, or the ability, to allocate various parcels of land to their most profitable, and hence most productive and economic uses.

Ricardo himself did not go all the way to government expropriation of land rent. His short-run solution was to call for lowering of the tariff on corn, or even repeal of the Corn Laws entirely. The tariff on corn kept the price of corn high and ensured that inferior, high-cost domestic corn land would be cultivated. Repeal of the Corn Laws would enable England to import cheap corn, and thereby postpone for a time the use of inferior and high-cost land. Corn prices would for a while be lower, money wage rates would therefore immediately be lower, and profits would rise, adding to the accumulation of capital. The dread stationary state would be put further off on to the horizon.

Ricardo's other anti-landlord action was political: by entering Parliament by joining Mill and the other Benthamite radicals in calling for democratic reform, Ricardo hoped to swing political power from the grip of the aristocracy, which meant in practice the landlord oligarchy, to the mass of the people.

But if Ricardo was too individualistic or too timorous to embrace the full logical consequence of the Ricardian system, James Mill characteristically was not. James Mill was the first prominent 'Georgist', calling frankly and enthusiastically for a single tax on land rent. In his high office in the East India Company, Mill felt able to influence Indian government policies.

Before obtaining this post, Mill had characteristically presumed to write and publish a massive *History of British India* (1817) without ever having been in that country or knowing any of the Indian languages. Steeped in the contemptuous view that India was thoroughly uncivilized, Mill advocated a 'scientific' single tax on land rent. Mill was convinced as a Ricardian that a tax on land rent was not a tax on cost and *therefore* would not reduce the incentive to supply any productive good or service. Hence a tax on land rent would have no bad effect on production – it would only have the effect of eliminating the ill-gotten gains of the landlords. In effect, a tax on land rent would be no tax at all! The land tax could be up to and including 100 per cent of the social product caused by the differential fertility of the soil. The state, according to Mill, could then use this costless tax for public improvement, and largely for the function of maintaining law and order in India.

We see now the pernicious implications of the fallacious view that any part of the expense of production is in some way, from a holistic or social point of view, 'really' not a part of cost. For if an expense is not part of cost, it is in some sense not necessary to the factor's contribution to production. And therefore this income can be confiscated by the government with no ill effect. Despite the deep pessimism of Ricardo about the nature and consequences of the free market, he oddly enough cleaved strongly, and more firmly than Adam Smith, to *laissez-faire*. Probably the reason was his strong conviction that virtually any kind of government intervention could only make matters worse. Taxation should be at a minimum, for all of it cripples the accumulation of capital and diverts it from its best uses, as do tariffs on imports. Poor laws – welfare systems – only worsen the Malthusian population pressures on wage rates. And as an adherent of Say's law, he opposed government measures to stimulate consumption, as well as the national debt. In general, Ricardo declared that the best thing that government can do to stimulate the greatest development of industry was to remove the obstacles to growth which government itself created.

While Adam Smith's free market views concentrated on the sinister nature of predatory government action, Ricardo was particularly struck by government's pervasive ineptness and counterproductivity. A typical and charming note was struck in a letter from Germany by Ricardo to James Mill in 1817: 'We were very much delayed by the dilatoriness of the German Post, which being a monopoly, is of course very much mismanaged...'.

The paradox of Ricardo's gloom about the alleged class conflict on the free market and his determined opposition to virtually all government intervention was best and most wittily described by Alexander Gray:

> Such is the Ricardian scheme of distribution; in place of the old harmony of interest, he has placed dissension and antagonism at the heart of things. 'The interest of the landlord is always opposed to that of the consumer and manufacturer;' So also the interests of the worker and the employer are eternally and irreconcilably opposed; when one gains, the other loses. Further, the outlook for all, except the landlord, is a process of continual pejoration. ...Yet Ricardo remains immovably non-interventionist. 'These, then', he says, 'are the laws by which wages are regulated'; and he adds inconsequently, 'like all other contracts, wages should be left to the fair and free competition of the market, and should never be controlled by the interference of the legislature'. In a world of Ricardian gloom one might ask, and did in effect ask, why there should not be interference. An optimist carolling that God's in his Heaven, and that all's right with enlightened self-interest has a right to nail the *laissez-faire* flag to the mast, but a pessimist who merely looks forward to bad days and worse times ought not in principle to be opposed to intervention, unless his pessimism is so thorough-going as to lead to the conviction that, bad as all diseases are, all remedies for all diseases are even worse.[10]

Finally, a fundamental and fatal flaw in Ricardo's whole approach in his system was that he started at the wrong end. He began with his overriding focus on the laws of macro-income distribution; his theory of value and price was only a subsidiary appendage, enabling him to maintain that wages are not a part of cost, and therefore that the only influence of rising wages was to cause profits to fall. Ricardo, in short, never grasped the crucial point understood by his continental counterpart, J.B. Say: that there *are no* laws of macro income distribution. Economics only establishes 'micro'-laws determining price, including the prices of the various factors of production. In a sense, of course, the distribution of income in practice is a spin-off of market-determined factor prices; but this 'distribution' also depends on entrepreneurial profits and losses, in short on entrepreneurial responses to risk and uncertainty, and on the supplies at any time of the respective factors. None of the latter can be determined by economic theory. Once again, David Ricardo was pursuing a chimera, and in doing so took British economic theory off on a detour, or rather into a dead end.

Put another way, the French (Cantillon–Turgot–Say) analysis of the free market demonstrated that on the market there *is no* separate 'distribution' of income process, as there indeed would be under a state-controlled, or socialist economy. 'Distribution' is the indirect consequence of free production, exchange, and price determination.[11]

All of this escaped David Ricardo, who had little or no conception of the economy as a web of 'micro'-relations linking together individual utilities, exchanges and prices. As Frank Knight has pointed out, Ricardo, in a letter to his disciple McCulloch, denied that 'the great questions' of macro-income distribution were 'essentially connected' with the theory of value. And further, Ricardo and his followers gave 'practically no hint of a system of economic organization worked out and directed by price forces'.[12]

There is another point that needs to be made about Ricardo's basic economic goal. Chiding Adam Smith for being primarily interested in the total wealth of the nation rather than in the macro-distribution of income, Ricardo pursues his Malthusian hostility to population growth by asking what is the point of looking at gross rather than net income. As Ricardo puts it, in a famous and astonishing passage:

> what would be the advantage resulting to a country from the employment of a great quantity of productive labour, if, whether it employed that quantity or a smaller, its net rent and profits together would be the same... To an individual with a capital of £20,000, whose profits were £2000 per annum, it would be a matter quite indifferent whether his capital would employ a hundred or a thousand men...provided, in all cases, his profits were not diminished below £2000. Is not the real interest of the nation similar? Provided its net real income, its rent and profits be the same, it is of no importance whether the nation consists of ten or of twelve millions of inhabitants.

The difference between ten and twelve million may not make any difference to David Ricardo, but it makes a considerable difference, I should think, to the two million who would not have been around, and to their parents, friends and relations. There is no better example of the aggregative utilitarian economist looking upon the economy from the holistic viewpoint of a social slavemaster, rather than from the point of view of individuals on the market. As Alexander Gray, in his witty and perceptive way, puts it:

> [Ricardo's] logic would lead to the desirability of the population being reduced to one, and that last remnant producing a vast net surplus with the aid of sorcery and mechanical contrivances. The repellent doctrine that man exists for the production of wealth, rather than that wealth exists for the use of man, here finds its classical utterance.[13]

3.6   The law of comparative advantage

Even the most hostile critics of the Ricardian system have granted that at least David Ricardo made one vital contribution to economic thought and to the case for freedom of trade: the law of comparative advantage. In emphasizing the great importance of the voluntary interplay of the international division of labour, free traders of the eighteenth century, including Adam Smith, based their doctrines on the law of 'absolute advantage'. That is, countries should specialize in what they are best or most efficient at, and then exchange these products, for in that case the people of both countries will be better off. This is a relatively easy case to argue. It takes little persuasion to realize that the United States should not bother to grow bananas (or, rather, to put it in basic micro-terms, that individuals and firms in the United States should not bother to do so), but rather produce something else (e.g. wheat, manufactured goods) and exchange them for bananas grown in Honduras. There are, after all, precious few banana growers in the US demanding a protective tariff. But what if the case is *not* that clear-cut, and American steel or semi-conductor firms are demanding such protection?

The law of comparative advantage tackles such hard cases, and is therefore indispensable to the case for free trade. It shows that *even if*, for example, Country A is more efficient than Country B at producing *both* commodities X and Y, it will pay the citizens of Country A to specialize in producing X, which it is *most* best at producing, and buy all of commodity Y from Country B, which it is better at producing but does not have as great a comparative advantage as in making commodity X. In other words, each country should produce not just what it has an absolute advantage in making, but what it is *most* best at, or even least worst at, i.e. what it has a *comparative* advantage in producing.

If, then, the government of Country A imposes a protective tariff on imports of commodity Y, and it forcibly maintains an industry producing that commodity, this special privilege will injure the consumers in Country A as well as obviously injuring the people in Country B. For Country A, as well as the rest of the world, loses the advantage of specializing in the production of what it is most best at, since many of its scarce resources are compulsorily and inefficiently tied up in the production of commodity Y. The law of comparative advantage highlights the important fact that a protective tariff in Country A wreaks injury on the efficient industries in that country, and the consumers in that country, as well as on Country B and the rest of the world.

Another implication of the law of comparative advantage is that no country or region of the earth is going to be left out of the international division of labour under free trade. For the law means that *even if* a country is in such poor shape that it has no absolute advantage in producing *anything*, it still pays for its trading partners, the people of other countries, to allow it to produce what it is *least worst* at.

In this way, the citizens of every country benefit from international trade. No country is too poor or inefficient to be left out of international trade, and everyone benefits from countries specializing in what they are most best or least bad at – in other words, in whatever they have a comparative advantage.

Until recently, it has been universally believed by historians of economic thought that David Ricardo first set forth the law of comparative advantage in his *Principles of Political Economy* in 1817. Recent researches by Professor

Thweatt, however, have demonstrated, not only that Ricardo did not originate this law, but that he did not understand and had little interest in the law, and that it played virtually no part in his system. Ricardo devoted only a few paragraphs to the law in his *Principles*, the discussion was meagre, and it was unrelated to the rest of his work and to the rest of his discussion of international trade.

The discovery of the law of comparative advantage came considerably earlier. The problem of international trade sprang into public consciousness in Britain when Napoleon imposed his Berlin decrees in 1806, ordering the blockade of his enemy England from all trade with the continent of Europe. Immediately, young William Spence (1783–1860), an English physiocrat and underconsumptionist who detested industry, published his *Britain Independent of Commerce* in 1807, advising Englishmen not to worry about the blockade, since only agriculture was economically important; and if English landlords would only spend all their incomes on consumption all would be well.

Spence's tract caused a storm of controversy, stimulating early works by two noteworthy British economists. One was James Mill, who critically reviewed Spence's work in the *Eclectic Review* for December 1807, and then expanded the article into his book, *Commerce Defended*, the following year. It was in rebuttal of Spence that Mill attacked underconsumptionist fallacies by bringing Say's law to England. The other work was the first book of young Robert Torrens (1780–1864), an Anglo-Irish officer in the Royal Marines, in his *The Economists Refuted* (1808).[14] It has long been held that Torrens first enunciated the law of comparative advantage, and that then, as Schumpeter phrased it, while Torrens 'baptized the theorem', Ricardo 'elaborated it and fought for it victoriously'.[15] It turns out, however, that this standard viewpoint is wrong in both its crucial parts, i.e., Torrens did *not* baptize the law, and Ricardo scarcely elaborated or fought for it. For, first, James Mill had a far better presentation of the law – though scarcely a complete one – in his *Commerce Defended* than did Torrens later the same year. Moreover, in his treatment, Torrens, and not Mill, committed several egregious errors. First, he claimed that trade yields greater benefits to a nation that imports durable goods and necessities as against perishables or luxuries. Second, he claimed also that advantages of home trade are more permanent than those of foreign trade, and also that *all* advantages of domestic trade remain at home, whereas part of the advantages of foreign trade are siphoned off for the benefit of foreigners. And finally, following Smith, and anticipating Marx and Lenin, Torrens asserted that *foreign* trade, by extending the division of labour, creates a surplus over domestic requirements that must then be 'vented' in foreign exports.

Six years later, James Mill led Robert Torrens again in presenting the rudiments of the law of comparative advantage. In the July 1814 issue of the

Eclectic Review, Mill defended free trade against Malthus's support for the Corn Laws in his *Observations*. Mill pointed out that labour at home will, by engaging in foreign trade, procure more by buying imports than by producing all goods themselves. Mill's discussion was largely repeated by Torrens in his *Essay on the External Corn Trade*, published in February of the following year. Furthermore, in this work, Torrens explicitly hailed Mill's essay.

Meanwhile, at the very time when this comparative cost ferment was taking place among his friends and colleagues, David Ricardo displayed no interest whatever in this important line of thought. To be sure, Ricardo weighed in to second his mentor Mill's attack on Malthus's support for the Corn Laws, in his *Essay on ... Profits*, published in February 1815. But Ricardo's line of argument was exclusively 'Ricardian', that is, based solely on the distinctive Ricardian system. In fact, Ricardo displayed no interest in free trade in general, or in the arguments for it; his reasoning was solely devoted to the importance of lowering or abolishing the tariff on corn. This conclusion, as we have noted, was deduced from the distinctive Ricardian system, which was to be fully set forth two years later in his *Principles*. For Ricardo the key to the stifling of economic growth in any country, and especially in developed Britain, was the 'land shortage', the contention that poorer and poorer lands were necessarily being pressed into use in Britain. In consequence, the cost of subsistence kept increasing, and hence the prevailing (which must be the subsistence) money wage kept increasing as well. But this inevitable secular increase of wages must lower profits in agriculture, which in turn brings down all profits. In that way, capital accumulation is increasingly dampened, finally to disappear altogether. Lowering or abolishing the tariff on corn (or other food) was, for Ricardo, an ideal way of postponing the inevitable doom. By importing corn from abroad, diminishing fertility from corn land is deferred. The cost of corn, and therefore of subsistence, will fall sharply, and therefore money wage rates will fall *pari passu*, thereby raising profits and stimulating capital investment and economic growth. There is no hint in any of this discussion of the doctrine of comparative cost or anything like it.

But how about the mature Ricardo, the Ricardo of the *Principles*? Once again, except for the three paragraphs on comparative advantage, Ricardo displays no interest in it, and he instead repeats the Ricardian system argument for repeal of the Corn Laws. Indeed, his discussion in the rest of the chapter on international trade is couched in terms of the Smithian theory of absolute advantage rather than of the comparative advantage found in Torrens and especially in Mill.

The three paragraphs on comparative advantage, furthermore, were not only carelessly worded and confused; they were the only account, brief as they were, that Ricardo would ever write on comparative advantage. Indeed, this was his only mention at any time of this doctrine. Even Ricardo's sudden reference to Portugal and his absurd hypothesis that the Portuguese had an absolute advantage over Britain in the production of cloth, seem to indicate his lack of serious interest in the theory of comparative cost.

Furthermore, Ricardo's views on foreign trade in the *Principles* received almost no comment at that time; writers concentrated on his labour theory of value, and his view that wage rates and profits always move inversely, with the former determining the latter.

If Ricardo had no interest in the theory of comparative advantage, and never wrote about it except in this single passage in the *Principles*, what was it doing in the *Principles* at all? Professor Thweatt's convincing hypothesis is that the law was injected into the *Principles* by Ricardo's mentor James Mill, whom we know wrote the original draft, as well as the revisions, for many parts of Ricardo's *magnum opus*. We know also that Mill prodded Ricardo on including a discussion of comparative cost ratios. As we have seen, Mill originated the doctrine of comparative cost, and led in developing it eight years later. Not only that: while Ricardo dropped the theory as soon as he enunciated it in the *Principles*, Mill fully developed the analysis of comparative advantage further, first in his article on 'Colonies' for the *Encyclopedia Britannica* (1818), and then in his textbook, *The Elements of Political Economy* (1821). Once again, Robert Torrens tailed after Mill, repeating his discussion with no additional insights in 1827, in the fourth edition of his 1815 *Essay on the External Corn Trade*.[16] Meanwhile, George Grote, a devoted Millian disciple, wrote in 1819 an important, unpublished essay setting forth the Millian view on comparative advantage.

And so, once again, James Mill, by the force of his mind as well as his personal charisma, was able to foist an original analysis of his own on to the 'Ricardian system'.[17] It is true that Mill was every bit a fan of the Ricardian system as Ricardo himself; but Mill was a man of far broader scope and erudition than his friend, and was interested in far more aspects of the disciplines of human action. It seems possible that Mill, the inveterate disciple and Number 2 man, was Number 1 man far more often than anyone has suspected.

3.7   Notes

1.   William E.C. Thomas, *The Philosophic Radicals: Nine Studies in Theory and Practice 1817–1841* (Oxford: The Clarendon Press, 1979), p. 100.
2.   Joseph Hamburger, *Intellectuals in Politics: John Stuart Mill and the Philosophic Radicals* (New Haven: Yale University Press, 1965), p. 44.
3.   J.A. Schumpeter, *History of Economic Analysis* (New York: Oxford University Press, 1954), pp. 472–3. Compare Walter Bagehot on Ricardo: 'He dealt with abstractions without knowing they were such: he thoroughly believed that he was dealing with real things. He thought that he was considering actual human nature in its actual circumstances, when he was really considering a fictitious nature in fictitious circumstances. And James Mill,

his instructor on general subjects, had on this point as little true knowledge as he had himself.' Quoted in T.W. Hutchison, 'James Mill and Ricardian Economics: a Methodological Revolution?' in Hutchison, *On Revolutions and Progress in Economic Knowledge* (Cambridge: Cambridge University Press, 1978), p. 57; also see ibid., pp. 26–57.

4. Schumpeter, op. cit., note 3, p. 676n.
5. As Schumpeter points out, Ricardo has been falsely credited with anticipating marginal productivity analysis, particularly since some later marginal productivity theorists, such as J.B. Clark, 'represented their theory as an outgrowth of Ricardo's theory of rent'. Yet they didn't realize that 'they were not generalizing Ricardo's schema but upsetting it'. Schumpeter, op. cit., note 3, pp. 674n, 675–6.
6. Frank W. Fetter, 'The Rise and Decline of Ricardian Economics', *History of Political Economy*, 1 (Spring 1969), p. 73.
7. Schumpeter, op. cit., note 3, p. 653n.
8. Emil Kauder, 'The Retarded Acceptance of the Marginal Utility Theory', *Quarterly Journal of Economics*, 67 (Nov. 1953), p. 574.
9. As St Clair sums up Ricardo's view: landlords, 'though contributing nothing in the way of work or personal sacrifice, will nevertheless receive an ever-increasing portion of the wealth annually created by the community'. Oswald St Clair, *A Key to Ricardo* (New York: A.M. Kelley, 1965), p. 3.
10. Alexander Gray, *The Development of Economic Doctrine* (London: Longmans, Green and Co., 1931), pp. 186–7.
11. Schumpeter, op. cit., note 3, pp. 567–8.
12. Frank H. Knight, 'The Ricardian Theory of Production and Distribution', in *On the History and Method of Economics* (Chicago: University of Chicago Press, 1956), p. 41. Also see ibid., pp. 61–3.
13. Gray, op. cit., note 10, pp. 188–9.
14. Torrens served in the Royal Marines from 1797 to 1834.
15. Schumpeter, op. cit., note 3, p. 607.
16. Torrens, furthermore, was scarcely in a position to take the leadership of the free trade forces, since he had abandoned his previously radical defence of unilateral free trade on behalf of reciprocal trade agreements between countries. As for Mill's fellow leading Ricardian and Scotsman, John Ramsey McCulloch, he stuck to the Smithian line, and publicly repudiated the doctrine of comparative cost.
17. See William O. Thweatt, 'James Mill and the Early Development of Comparative Advantage', *History of Political Economy*, 8 (Summer 1976), pp. 207–34.

4 The decline of the Ricardian system, 1820–48

4.1 The conundrum of Ricardo's popularity

What accounts for the popularity of Ricardo's *Principles*, and for the enduring dominance of the Ricardian system? The marginal utility 'revolutionary',
W. Stanley Jevons, writing the preface to the second edition of his great
Theory of Political Economy in 1879, was forced to complain of the continuing dominance of the Ricardian doctrine, and to lament that 'when at length a
true system of Economics comes to be established, it will be seen that that
able but wrong-headed man, David Ricardo, shunted the car of Economic
science on to a wrong line...'. Indeed. And Ricardo won the day with a
theory that was not only far from self-evident but in many ways bizarre (such
as the labour theory of value), and he wrote his work in a crabbed and
obscurantist style that would hardly be expected to sweep the field, either
among laymen or in those more particularly interested in economics.

Part of the explanation, as Schumpeter pointed out, is that Ricardo was
politically in tune with the *Zeitgeist*. Even though his methodology was so
abstract as to be divorced from and to falsify reality, Ricardo's motivation
was not abstract theory but its use in advancing politico-economic conclusions. Ricardo, like Mill, was devoted to free trade and *laissez-faire*, and, as
we shall see, to hard money, and he applied his abstract system like a hammer
in their service. This ideology was fast becoming the wave of the future in
England, in the circles of businessmen and intellectuals.[1]

But what of Ricardo's abysmal writing, in style and in organization? Alexander Gray's heartfelt critique is on the mark:

> As to the form rather than the substance of Ricardo's writings, it is perhaps
> sufficient to say that he was no writer. He himself dimly realized that he was a bad
> writer, but it is doubtful whether he can have known the whole truth. It is
> undiscerning flattery to regard his chief work, *The Principles of Political Economy
> and Taxation*, as a book at all. Rather does it suggest the sweepings of a busy
> man's study – chapters of very varying length, which he clearly found it difficult
> to arrange in the right order, brusque notes and memoranda on points which
> interested the author. In defence, it may be admitted that Ricardo ... did not mean
> to write a book. These were indeed memoranda written for himself and his
> friends, published on his friends' [actually Mill's] incitement. But this is a poor
> consolation to the lonely traveller befogged in the Ricardian jungle.[2]

It is very possible, however, that it was precisely Ricardo's obscurantism
that accounted for his success. For all too many people, laymen and profes-
sionals alike, obscurity and bad writing equal profundity. If they can't understand it, and they hear at every hand that so-and-so is a great man and his
theories the current light, their belief in his profundity will be redoubled.[3,4]
There are great charms to obscurity. Moreover, there are particular charms
for the adepts who cluster around the great man, the circle of initiates who
claim – probably correctly – that only *they* can truly understand his work.

Only they can penetrate the fog caused by the depth of the great man's wisdom. Schumpeter notes that 'quickly his circle developed the attitude – so amusing but also, alas!, so melancholy to behold – of children who have been presented with a new toy. They thought the world of it. To them it was of incalculable value that only he could fail to appreciate who was too stupid to rise to Ricardian heights.'[5] Its murkiness and difficulty only heightened the enjoyment and pride of the adepts over their new toy. Nowadays, this effect is considerably heightened by the fact that obscurity gives disciples and critics more to talk and write about, and thus greatly multiplies the career opportunities for scholars in the current age of publish-or-perish.

Another reason for the popularity of Ricardianism was the persistent cadre activity of the indefatigable James Mill. One of Mill's important actions was to help found the Political Economy Club in London in 1821, a club that quickly became for many years the centre of economic discussion and learning in Great Britain. It is characteristic of the early nineteenth century shift of the locus of economics from Scotland to England that this transfer was one of occupation as well as location. In Scotland, economic thought had centred in the two great universities of Edinburgh and Glasgow, with influence spread through academic, literary and business circles, and members of social clubs in the two cities. In England, on the contrary, there was almost no academic economics in the fossilized university courses of the day. Of the 30 founding members of the Political Economy Club, only one – Thomas Robert Malthus – was an academic, teaching political economy at the East India Company's College at Haileybury. The other leading English economists in the club included David Ricardo, businessman and financier Thomas Tooke (1774–1858), with Colonel Robert Torrens of the Royal Marines chairing the first meeting. Others were businessmen, publicists, and government officials.

A few years later, academic opportunities began to open up. Mill's Scottish friend and fellow leading Ricardian, John Ramsay McCulloch, who had been lecturing for several years, became professor of political economy in 1828 at the University College, London, and joined the Political Economy Club shortly thereafter. But after four years of teaching he had to spend the rest of his life as a financial controller. The first economics post at Oxford was a chair founded by the banker and evangelist Henry Drummond in 1825, but the term of the chair was only five years. The first chair-holder was the attorney and important young economist Nassau William Senior (1790–1864), son of an Anglican vicar in Berkshire, who had studied at Oxford and had joined the Political Economy Club two years earlier.[6] The new King's College, London, established in the same year as University College (1828) as a Tory and Anglican haven to offset its non-denominational neighbour, appointed Senior to its own political economy post in 1831. But Senior was kicked out unceremoniously for publishing a pamphlet urging a reduction in the budget of the Anglican establishment in Ireland, and he spent the rest of his career as a real-property attorney and government lawyer, with the exception of another Drummond professorship at Oxford in 1847–52.

Cambridge treated economics with such disdain that its only contribution was to have a young lawyer of no distinction in the field, George Pryme, teach economics without pay and at unpopular hours. Pryme taught under those conditions for over 40 years from 1816 on, remarkably becoming professor of political economy in 1828. Apparently he wrote nothing in economics and contributed to no important discussions.

4.2 The rapid decline of Ricardian economics

Before setting out to explain a problem one must be quite sure that the problem really exists. Surely, a partial answer to the conundrum of Ricardo's popularity and dominance over English economics is that that dominance was largely a myth. Until recently, the orthodox view in the history of economic thought was that Ricardianism dominated British thought from the date of Ricardo's *Principles* through Jevons's abortive revolution in 1871, and until the 1890s when Alfred Marshall's neo-Ricardianism supposedly integrated marginal utility into a basically Ricardian framework. One of the last expressions of this orthodoxy came in 1949, when Professor Sydney G. Checkland, from an anti-Ricardian perspective, bewailed the manner in which the two Scotsmen, James Mill and McCulloch, like Ricardo – the Spanish–Portuguese Jew – expatriates from their native culture, and therefore presumably alienated from mainstream English life, used brilliant cadre tactics to acquire their hegemony over English thought. Checkland saw that Mill was the cadre leader of the Ricardians, cleverly advising Ricardo not to give publicity to his critics by deigning to reply to them in the third, 1821 edition of his *Principles*. Mill wrote his *Elements of Political Economy* as a Ricardian textbook in 1821, but since it lacked popular appeal, the younger McCulloch, a charismatic, enormously strong, booming, burly, Scotch whisky-drinking figure of a man, took over as the popularizer and propagator of Ricardianism.

The first important revision of the myth of Ricardian triumph came with the Marxist Ronald Meek's rebuttal of Checkland the following year.[7] Checkland, he points out, made the crucial mistake – following J.M. Keynes – of treating Say's law as equivalent to the Ricardian system. While Ricardo and McCulloch followed Mill in considering Say's law to be very important, they did not regard it as crucial to the Ricardian system, which actually comprised the Ricardian theories of value and distribution. While Say's law indeed triumphed early, with only Malthus temporarily opposing it, the Ricardian system proper met a very different fate.

In fact, as he managed to do in other areas of the history of economic thought, John Maynard Keynes, in his *General Theory*, skewed and distorted

Ricardian development. It was only Keynes, in his preoccupation with promoting government deficits and inflationism and attacking Say's law, who made that law the central feature of the Ricardian system. It was also Keynes who distorted the facts by holding up Malthus as the proto-Keynesian hero, stubbornly calling for an anti-Say and anti-Ricardian alternative to the Ricardian system. On the contrary, Malthus, despite various differences, considered himself a Smithian and was generally friendly to Ricardianism as well as to Ricardo personally. Malthus's interest in the alleged 'general glut' and in denouncing Say's law, was an ephemeral product of the post-Napoleonic War depression in England. When England's prosperity returned after 1823, Malthus totally lost interest in the general glut question, and wrote no more about it. Say's law had triumphed except among a few radical fringe people in the economic underworld; and Malthus steadfastly refused to be drawn into alliance with them. These fringe persons, who continued their worn-out cries of a general glut into the 1830s, included the prolific left Tory statist poet and essayist Robert Southey (1774–1843), who had attacked deflation after the Napoleonic War, and MP, geologist, and authority on volcanoes George Poulett Scrope (1797–1876). Raising the fallacious cry of underconsumption, Scrope, in his *Principles of Political Economy* (1833), charged that any decline in consumption in favour of a 'general increase in the propensity to save' would necessarily and 'proportionately diminish the demand as compared with the supply, and occasion a *general glut*'. In this old proto-Keynesian fallacy, savings apparently 'leak' out of the economy, and result in permanent(?) depression. Apparently, investment, since it is transitional and not 'final', is not considered spending at all. And then, as in all varieties of crank economic analysis, the price system, and the relationship of selling prices to costs, is somehow not considered worthy of mention at all.[8]

George Poulett Scrope was originally named George Thomson, son of John Poulett Thomson, head of a firm of Russia merchants. He took the name Scrope after marrying an heiress of the Scrope family. Born in London, Scrope studied at Oxford and Cambridge, and was a member of the House of Commons for 35 years. A champion of free trade, he wrote so many pamphlets on economic issues (about 70) that he was commonly dubbed 'Pamphlet Scrope'.

In contrast to the triumph of Say's law, the Ricardian system proper was rapidly repudiated in the world of English economics. In January 1831, eight years after Ricardo's death, Colonel Robert Torrens addressed the Political Economy Club that Ricardo had helped to found. Torrens raised the crucial question: how many of the Ricardian principles were still held to be correct? His answer: all the great principles of Ricardian system had been abandoned, especially the critical ones of value, rent and profits. Samuel Bailey, in his great espousal of the utility theory of value in 1825, had smashed the labour theory; Thomas Perronet Thompson had disposed of the Ricardian theory of rent; the theory of profit is unsound because Ricardo ignored the replacement of capital; and the Malthusian subsistence theory of wages had been generally abandoned.

To the Marxian Ronald Meek, this wholesale desertion of Ricardianism comprised a capitalist plot against the labour theory of value, whose socialistic implications had been drawn out during the 1820s by the Ricardian socialists. At any rate, by 1829–31, there were no adherents of the labour theory of value left in mainstream British economics; to Meek, the only exception was McCulloch, who in turn had abandoned Ricardo on many other issues, including the idea of productive *vs* unproductive labour, the theory of profit, and the theory of class conflict on the market implicit in the Ricardian theory of distribution.[9] Only Say's law, with its strong *laissez-faire* implications, had survived what Meek laments as 'the purge'.

But the 'purge' or abandonment came even earlier, antedating the Ricardian socialists. Professor Frank W. Fetter, in his classic article,[10] points out that upon Ricardo's death in 1823, James Mill wrote despairingly to McCulloch and noted that they were 'the two and only genuine disciples' of Ricardo in existence and McCulloch did not stay one for long. Fetter notes that economic opinion in the 1820s was diverse and unsettled, except for a general adherence to free trade. Everyone dismissed the portentous Ricardian conclusion that profits varied inversely to wages, except as a banal arithmetic truism. Furthermore, even Ricardo himself had pointed the way to abandoning his own crucial permanent subsistence theory of wages (which the German socialist Ferdinand Lassalle was later to call 'the Iron Law of Wages'). Ricardo had adopted the subsistence wage theory, taken from the hard-core Malthusian first edition of Malthus's *Essay on Population* (1798). But many of his statements apart from this rigid formal model were really adopted from the much weaker, indeed contradictory, second edition of the *Essay* (1803). These were qualifications which Marx would correctly note amounted to a desertion of the 'iron law'. Criticism of Malthusian doctrine prevailed in the journals by the late 1820s. Thus, in early 1826, a writer noted in the *Monthly Review* that the law of relentless increase in population operates only in poor societies. It moves

> in an inverse proportion to the acquisition of wealth; ... it is only when people become more luxuriant, when those engagements which form the principal charm in humble life lose their attractions by the substitution of habits of refinement, that the increase [in population] becomes progressively less.[11]

Finally, in 1829, Nassau W. Senior's letters to Malthus effectively put the boots to the iron law. In this published exchange of correspondence, following the delivery of his lectures on population (*Two Lectures on Population, to*

*which is added A Correspondence between the Author and the Rev. T.R.
Malthus* (London, 1829)), Senior dealt a devastating blow to the Malthusian
doctrine. In the first place, while agreeing that excessive population growth
could conceivably one day constitute a problem, Senior in effect stood Malthus
on his head by pointing out that while population indeed pressed on the food
supply in undeveloped countries, the history of the prosperous countries of
the West had been marked by an increase in the food supply outstripping the
rise in population. Indeed, this fact is simply demonstrated by the rising
living standards of the western countries over the centuries. And this economic growth must be due to a general tendency of agricultural and other
productivity to rise, as well as people devoting themselves to safeguarding
their higher living standards. As a result, population does not grow enough to
reduce the living standards of the public to the subsistence level. And while
Malthus would not verbally go so far as Senior in speaking of a general
'tendency for food to increase faster than population', it was clear from
Malthus's reply that the mellower Malthus of the second edition had triumphed. That Senior saw the full implications of the changes of the second
edition is also demonstrated by his own formulation of the population principle: 'that the population of the world ... is limited only by moral or physical
evil, *or* by fear of the deficiency of those articles of wealth which the habits
of individuals of each class of its inhabitants lead them to acquire'. (Italics
added.)

But while the iron law of wages was in fact finished *de facto*, it still
continued to reign, as it were, *de jure*. For Nassau Senior, suffering from
excessive piety toward Malthus, lacked the instinct for the jugular that would
have stripped the veil of evasions from the grave fallacies of the Malthusian
doctrine. Instead, Senior collaborated in the sham, insisting, though he knew
better, on continuing to hail the Malthusian principle of population as a
cornerstone of economic science. As Joseph Schumpeter, ever alive to the
follies of economists, lamented:

> [Senior] always treated Malthus with infinite respect – he even called him a
> benefactor of humanity (sic!) – and did all in his power to minimize his deviation
> from what he evidently considered to be established doctrine. All the less justifi-
> cation is there for the practice of some later writers who, with nauseating
> pontificality, treated Senior as a none too intelligent pupil who needed to be set
> right by Malthus. As a matter of fact, it is perfectly clear that Senior realized the
> extent to which Malthus' qualifications ought to have spelled recantation and to
> what degree his adherence to some of his former opinions spelled contradiction.[12]

4.3   The theory of rent
The Ricardian theory of rent was effectively demolished by Thomas Perronet
Thompson (1783–1869) in his pamphlet, *The True Theory of Rent* (1826).

Thompson weighed in against this fallacious capstone to the Ricardian system: 'The celebrated Theory of Rent', Thompson charged, 'is founded on a fallacy', for demand is the key to the price of corn and to rent.

> The fallacy lies, in assuming to be the cause what in reality is only a consequence... [I]t is the rise in the price of produce ... that enables and causes inferior land to be brought into cultivation; and not the cultivation of inferior land that causes the rise of rent.

Thompson goes on to note in wonder that Ricardo perceived the fallacy in the view that corn sells for a high price because rent is paid, and not vice versa, and *yet* pressed on to adopt a similar cost theory of price. Here Ricardo reversed cause and effect by maintaining that the cultivation of inferior land causes the price of corn to rise, instead of the other way round.

During the same year, Colonel Robert Torrens himself destroyed the Ricardian theory of rent even more effectively, zeroing in on the crucial fallacy of rent-as-a-differential. Characteristically Torrens, who was involved in all the economic controversies of the day and changed his mind significantly on nearly all of them, delivered his *coup de grace* in the third edition of a work in which he had originally predated Ricardo in the discovery and championing of the theory of differential rent. This work was the *Essay on the External Trade*, originally published in 1815. But now Torrens honed in on the critical point that the rent of land, A, does *not* depend on its being more fertile or productive than some other piece of land, B; that, on the contrary, the rent on each land stems from *its own* productivity, period, in turn partially determined by the scarcity of that particular land and by the demand for its product. The existence of a return on a piece of land is by no means dependent on the existence of inferior lands. As Torrens puts it:

> Neither the gradations of soil, nor the successive applications of capital to land, with decreasing returns, are in any way essential to the appearance or the rise of rents. If all soils were of one uniform quality, and if land, after having been adequately stocked, could yield no additional produce ... still the rise in the value of raw produce ... would cause a portion of the surplus produce of the soil to assume the form of rent.

In the very same year, 1831, that Colonel Torrens was thus pronouncing the death of the Ricardian system, the Rev. Richard Jones (1790–1855), a Cambridge graduate, put the final boots to the Ricardian theory in his discourse 'On Rent', in his *Essay on the Distribution of Wealth*. A Baconian inductivist, historicist, and anti-theorist who paradoxically first succeeded Senior as professor of political economy at King's College, London, and then followed Malthus as professor at the East India College of Haileybury, Jones stressed the error of Ricardo's historical dictum that the most fertile lands are always cultivated first in every country, which then moved successively to less and less fertile lands. For Schumpeter and others to dismiss Jones's case as confusing historical fact with an abstract theoretical model, misses the real point. Fallacious anti-theorist Richard Jones undoubtedly was; but from his own point of view, David Ricardo was *not* simply setting up an abstract and totally unrealistic theoretical model. Ricardo was interested above all in political applications, and he was deluded enough to believe that his model was spewing forth accurate laws of past and future historical trends. For Ricardo, inexorable rises in rent, crippling future economic development, were a predictable empirical consequence of his own theory. Specific empirical facts cannot give rise to or test theory, but a theoretical law that attempts to predict past and future *can* be validly countered by examining the course of actual history. Empirical facts can properly be used to refute empirical generalizations.

The various demolitions of Ricardo's theory of rent, especially that of Perronet Thompson, quickly triumphed in the economic literature. The Thompson critique had been anticipated in the influential journals, in the *British Critic* as early as 1821, and by Nassau W. Senior in the *Quarterly Review* in the same year. By the early 1830s, Thompson's view had triumphed in the journals, including an article by Samuel Mountifort Longfield, the first Irish professor of political economy at Trinity College, Dublin. By the 1840s, the Ricardian theory of rent was dead in the water, and almost beneath discussion; apart from McCulloch, the only one willing to defend it was the ardent and emotional Ricardian, the poet and writer Thomas De Quincey (1785–1859).

David Ricardo, as he himself acknowledged, did not originate his differential theory of rent. It began in 1777, on the publication of *An Enquiry into the Nature of the Corn Laws*, by the Scottish farmer, James Anderson (1739–1808). An Aberdeenshire farmer, Anderson founded and edited the weekly *Bee*, and later moved to London, where he edited publications in agricultural science and the arts. Anderson's theory, however, remained forgotten, until independently replicated by three writers in 1815: Thomas Robert Malthus, in his *Inquiry into the Nature and Progress of Rent*; Sir Edward West's (1782–1828), *Essay on the Application of Capital to Land*; and the first edition of Torrens's *Essay on the External Corn Trade*. Malthus did not integrate his theory into anything like the Ricardian system, and, furthermore, he was scarcely an opponent of the landlords or of land rent. To the contrary, Malthus defended the Corn Laws. On the other hand, West, an attorney and fellow of University College, Oxford, who later served as supreme court justice in India and died early of disease, so closely anticipated the Ricardian system that Schumpeter habitually refers to the 'West–Ricardian' theory.

The interesting question is: what gave rise, in a very short period of time (1815–17) to such intense concern, or at least attention to, the alleged problems of rising rents? For apart from the relatively unknown James Anderson, attention to rising rents occurs within a very few years shortly after the end of Napoleonic Wars. The answer was brilliantly supplied by the early twentieth century American 'Austrian' economist Frank Albert Fetter: the Napoleonic Wars of the first fifteen years of the nineteenth century were marked by high taxation, blockages of food imports, currency inflation, and consequently unprecedentedly high prices for 'corn' in England and hence highly inflated agricultural rents. It is surely no accident, as Fetter notes, that 'the so-called Ricardian doctrine of rent was independently formulated by several other writers – West, Malthus, Torrens and others between 1813 and 1815 – when wheat prices were at their peak'.[13]

4.4 Colonel Perronet Thompson: anti-Ricardian Benthamite

We must pause a moment to consider the fascinating character of Colonel Perronet Thompson, an ardent Benthamite radical, and a champion of free trade and opponent of the Corn Laws. Thompson, the son of a prosperous merchant and banker from Sussex, and MP for a decade, spent the first part of his adult life in the military, retiring from active service in 1922 at the age of 39 with the rank of lieutenant. Despite this relatively low rank, Thompson had been made the first royal governor of the colony of Sierra Leone in 1808, but got himself recalled quickly by clamouring for the abolition of the slave trade. His removal by the Tory British government over the issue of slavery radicalized young Thompson, whose education in classical liberalism was further advanced by reading Adam Smith and Turgot. After retiring from active service, Thompson was compensated for his low rank in important work over a long military career by being repeatedly promoted while inactive. By the time of his death, Thompson had risen to the rank of full general.

Before going into military service, Thompson had graduated from Queen's College, Cambridge, and been made a fellow of that college. On retiring from the military life, he joined Bentham's circle of admirers and plunged into Benthamite utilitarianism and radicalism. Thompson's first published work appeared in the very first issue of Bentham's own periodical, the *Westminster Review* (1824). His *True Theory of Rent*, designed to uphold Adam Smith's views on rent as against Ricardo, followed; and the next year, Perronet Thompson published his well-known *Catechism on the Corn Laws* (1827), generally considered the most important work in the entire anti-Corn Law literature. Later, Thompson became one of the most effective members of the Anti-Corn Law League. In 1829, only half a decade since his plunge into politics, the now Lieutenant Colonel Thomas Perronet Thompson became the sole owner of the Benthamite *Westminster Review*, and contributed articles to every issue until relinquishing ownership seven years later. After being defeated for Parliament in 1834, Thompson won election a year later, taking his stand with George Grote and the philosophic radicals in Parliament. Losing his seat two years later, he ran several times unsuccessfully, serving in Parliament from 1847 to 1852, and again from 1857 to 1859.

Thompson's writings were prolific, and in many areas. At the age of 59, a six-volume collection of his writings to date was published, *Exercises, Political and Others* (1842), and he kept writing pamphlets and newspaper articles on democratic reform until the day before his death, at the age of 86. In addition to his widespread political and economic concerns, Thompson wrote and published works on mathematics, the science of acoustics, and the theory of musical harmony. An organ built on the lines of Thompson's harmonic theory received honourable mention at the Great Exhibition of 1851.

Thompson contributed more to economics than his attack on rent. His first article in the *Westminster Review*, 'On the Instrument of Exchange', followed Bentham's own inflationist views by advocating an inconvertible paper currency. Another, equally dubious, contribution of Thompson's in the same essay followed up a hint made ten years before by Malthus. Malthus, who had been trained in mathematics at Cambridge, had observed, in a pamphlet in 1814, that differential calculus might prove useful in the theory of morals, economics and politics, since many questions in these disciplines centre around the pursuit of maxima and minima. By the time of the publication of his *Principles of Political Economy* in 1820, however, Malthus had wisely grown sceptical of the possibilities of maths in economics as well as in ethics and politics. Thompson, however, also trained in mathematics at Cambridge, had no such scruples, and his 1824 article opened a fateful door by using the differential calculus in defining a maximum gain. The perfect Benthamite, steeped in looking at maxima of pleasure and minima of pain, had struck a fateful chord; Pandora's Box had been opened.

Thompson's sympathy for mathematical economics, however, did not keep him from denouncing the Smith–Ricardo search for a fixed and invariable measure of value, which he wisely dismissed as a chimera. Furthermore, in the *Westminster Review* in 1832, Thompson trenchantly criticized all cost theories of value, pointing out that cost and price almost always differ. And these differences, he added, are not accidental and ephemeral, as Smith and especially Ricardo assumed in their focus on the long-run 'natural' price; on the contrary, these 'short-run' differences are the essence of the dynamic real world: 'This perpetual oscillation on both sides of the cost price, instead of being an inconsiderable accident, is in reality the great agent by which the commercial world is kept in motion'.

4.5   Samuel Bailey and the subjective utility theory of value

In 1825, Samuel Bailey (1791–1870), a rising young merchant from Sheffield, published a thorough demolition of Ricardian value theory, in his *A
Critical Dissertation on the Nature, Measures, and Causes of Value*. Bailey at
last brought into English economics the subjective utility theory of the French
tradition; unfortunately, he was not gracious enough to acknowledge that
fact. While his essay was clearly in the Say tradition, for example, his brief
and brusque references to Say's *Treatise* gave no hints of acknowledging his
indebtedness. But in any case, Bailey's demolition of Ricardo was devastating. Beginning with Ricardo's definition of value as the relative price, or
purchasing power, of particular goods, Bailey went on to show the absurdity
and inner contradiction of Ricardo's claim that each good acquires an absolute and invarying value from the quantity of labour hours embodied in its
production. For one thing, if the quantity of labour needed to produce good *A*
remains the same, its value, contra Ricardo, can scarcely be invariable, if the
quantity of labour embodied in other goods, *B*, *C*, *D*, etc. has changed. In
short, value is strictly relational, a ranking among goods, and therefore cannot be absolute or invariant. Furthermore, Bailey demonstrates that value is
not inherent in goods at all, but is rather always a process of subjective
evaluation in the minds of individuals. Value, as Bailey pointed out, 'in its
ultimate sense, appears to mean the esteem in which any object is held. It
denotes strictly speaking, an effect produced on the mind ...'. Value is purely
a 'mental affection'. Furthermore, he profoundly states that value is not only
a subjective estimation, but also that valuation is necessarily *relative* among
various goods or objects; value is a matter of relative preference. Thus
Bailey:

> When we consider objects in themselves, without reference to each other; the
> emotion or pleasure or satisfaction, with which we regard their utility or beauty,
> can scarcely take the appellation of value. It is only when objects are considered
> as subjects of preference or exchange, that the specific feeling of value can arise.
> When they are so considered, our esteem for one object, or our wish to possess it,
> may be equal to, or greater or less than our esteem for another...

But if value is subjective and relative (or relational) valuation, it follows that
it is absurd for Ricardo to hanker after an invariable measure of value.

In a scintillating and telling passage, Bailey displays the inner contradictions and absurdities of any objective, absolute theory of value, and specifically of the Ricardian quantity of labour variant. The Ricardians had lost
sight of

> the relative nature of value, and ... consider it as something positive and absolute;
> so that if there were only two commodities in the world, and they should both

from some circumstance or other come to be produced by double the quantity of labour, they would both rise in real value, although their relation to each other would be undisturbed. According to this doctrine, everything might at once become more valuable, by requiring at once more labour for its production, a position utterly at variance with the truth, that value denotes the relation in which commodities stand to each other as articles of exchange. Real value, in a word, is on this theory considered as being the independent result of labour; and consequently, if under any circumstances the quantity of labour is increased, the real value is increased. Hence, the paradox, [quoting from the devoted Ricardian Thomas De Quincey] 'that it is possible for A continually to increase in value – in real value observe – and yet command a continually decreasing quantity of B'; and this though they were the only commodities in existence.

In sum, as Bailey pungently noted, 'the very term absolute value, implies the same sort of absurdity as absolute distance...'.

Bailey then enters into a penetrating discussion of the theory of measurement, showing the tremendous gulf between genuine measurement of real or physical objects and any concept of 'measuring' something as subjective and relative as human valuation. In the case of physical objects, such concepts as length or weight are measured by fixing an invariant physical measure, such as a foot rule, and then comparing the length of other objects in question with such a rule. In human valuation, 'measurement' is quite different; it is simply the expression of prices or relative purchasing powers of different goods in terms of one money, or medium of exchange. Here there is no physical operation such as measurement of physical objects. In the case of money there is a 'common expression or denominator of value' in money rather than an invariable physical object of comparison. In fact, these prices or quantities are relative and variable, and there is no invariability involved. Indeed, Bailey would have done still better to abandon the term 'measure' altogether, and to confine it strictly to the invariant standards used to compare physical objects, simply confining the idea of comparing relative prices in terms of money to the term 'common expression' or common denominator'. A great deal of confusion in economic theory might have been avoided.

In the course of demolishing the idea of an invariable measure of value, Bailey took deadly aim at the notion that the value of money is invariant over time, and therefore can be used to compare general prices over time. While the money commodity is not more fixed in value than any other, one of its attributes, and one of the reasons it is chosen as money on the market, is its 'comparative steadiness of value', as Bailey sensibly termed it in a later work on money and its value (*Money and its Vicissitudes in Value*, 1837). But its value is not constant, and therefore there is no way of measuring value over time. But commodities only have value relations to each other at the same time; a commodity has no value relation to itself at different times. As Bailey puts it:

We cannot ascertain the relation of cloth at one time to cloth at another, as we ascertain the relation to cloth in the present day. All that we can do is to compare the relation in which cloth stood at each period to some other commodity ... We cannot say, that a pair of stockings in James the First's reign would exchange for six pair in our own day; and we therefore cannot say, that a pair in James the First's reign was equal in value to six pair now, without reference to some other article. Value is a relation between contemporary commodities, because such only admit of being exchanged for each other; and if we compare the value of a commodity at one time with its value at another, it is only a comparison of the relation in which it stood at these different times to some other commodity.

Until recently, historians have believed that Bailey's work made no impact on the Ricardian world of British economics, and fell into obscurity, only to be resurrected at the end of the nineteenth century by economists looking for forerunners of the marginal utility theory. Actually, we now know that, despite a vicious personal assault (probably by James Mill) on Bailey in the *Westminster Review*, Bailey's *Critical Dissertation* was widely read among economists and virtually swept the field. In his January 1831 funeral rites for the Ricardian system before the Political Economy Club, Colonel Robert Torrens declared that 'as to value', Bailey's *Dissertation* 'has settled that question'. Indeed, the year after Bailey's work was published, Torrens praised it highly in the third edition of his *Essay on the External Corn Trade*, calling it in his preface 'a masterly specimen of perspicuous and accurate logic', spearing 'that vague and ambiguous language in which some of our most eminent economists have indulged'. And remarkably, the changeable Torrens stuck to that estimate throughout his life. In the lengthy introduction to his *The Budget* (1844), in which he revised and retracted many of his earlier views, Colonel Torrens went out of his way to affirm that 'the gifted author of "A Dissertation on the Nature, Causes, and Measures of Value", has set finally at rest the long agitated question, whether value should be regarded as an absolute or positive quality inhering in commodities, or as a relation existing between them'.

Samuel Bailey wrote an effective reply to the *Westminster* critic (*A Letter to a Political Economist*, 1826), but apart from this and his *Money* tract, most of his numerous writings dealt with philosophy and with political reform. For this prosperous Sheffield merchant, born into a mercantile family, founder and four-time president of the Sheffield Literary and Philosophical Society, was in intellectual matters an ardent Benthamite. He devoted the bulk of his intellectual resources to Benthamite writings on philosophy and on radical reform, and twice ran unsuccessfully on a reform ticket for Parliament. Bailey made a considerable philosophical impact with his first book, his *Essay on the Formation and Publication of Public Opinion* (1821). The *Essay's* emphasis on the utilitarian value of free discussion greatly influenced James Mill, John Stuart Mill's *On Liberty*, and Francis Place. In economic matters, Bailey's *Essay* grounded economic activity in subjective, mental phenomena, and explicitly rejected the emphasis on British classical economics on physical material objects. The methodology of economics, Bailey maintained, was introspective of one's empirical surroundings. Bailey saw economics as a 'science of mind' rather than as technology. Clearly, his methodology and philosophy of economics were far more 'Austrian' than has been realized.[14]

Bailey's later works were non-economic, including *Essays on the Pursuit of Truth* (1844), *The Theory of Reasoning* (1851, 1852), and three series of *Letters on the Philosophy of the Human Mind* (1855–62). His final publication was a two-volume book using etymology to rearrange and reinterpret some of Shakespeare's plays (*On the Received Text of Shakespeare's Dramatic Writings and its Improvement* (1862–66)).

Samuel Bailey was the most important and influential subjective value theorist; but he was not the first to bring subjective utility theory to nineteenth century Britain. That honour belongs to the virtually unknown Scotsman, John Craig (c. 1780–c. 1850). All that we know about Craig is that he was a citizen of Glasgow, and was a member of the fellowship of the Royal Society of Edinburgh, and yet nothing else is known about his occupation or background. After writing a three-volume work on the *Elements of Political Science* (1814), Craig made his striking if unnoticed contribution to economics, in his *Remarks on Some Fundamental Doctrines of Political Economy* (1821).

Craig not only brought utility into a British economics dominated by discussions of cost and 'natural price'; for the first time in Great Britain, he brought value theory to the verge of the concept of marginal utility. Starting with the axiom that utility is the basis of all value, Craig proceeds to the influence of supply: 'relative values of commodities may change, and those persons who happen to be possessed of articles which are produced in larger quantities than formerly, or which from other circumstances becomes less in demand, may find themselves poorer...'. In short, greater quantity leads to a lesser value. More abundance leading to lower value had once been a commonplace of economic thought; but precisely why is this true? Craig first notes that an increased quantity of, say, broadcloth will lower its price. He then goes on to explain, in a truly notable passage, that

> All of the broadcloth, that, in the estimation of purchasers, was worth the former price, had been formerly brought to market, and if more is now to be disposed of, it must be to those who did not reckon its utility equivalent to its former cost. New purchasers indeed will appear in proportion to the reduction of price; because at every step of the decline it is brought down to the estimate, which an additional number of persons had formed of its power of producing gratification, or in other words, to their estimate of its value in use.

Thus, John Craig not only explicitly refuted the dominant Smithian view of the separation of value in use from value in exchange, showing that the latter depended strictly on the former. Even more important, Craig had captured the essence of the marginal utility doctrine without the label: showing that as the quantity of a good increases, its price or value must fall in order to tap a new group of purchases whose utility estimate of the good had been too low to allow them to purchase the good at the original higher price for the smaller product. In short, purchasers previously sub-marginal now become marginal for the additional product as the price falls. As Professor Thor Bruce declares,

> Craig appears on the very verge of expressing the idea of marginal utility. He broke away from the theory held by his contemporaries, which was based on the cost idea, and became the first exponent of the idea of the connection between utility and value. In thus emphasizing the utility theory he was the forerunner of the Austrian School of the latter half of the nineteenth century.[15]

Craig doesn't stop there. If more broadcloth, for example, has been produced and its price has therefore fallen, the previous purchasers now have surplus revenue, which they will use to increase the demand and therefore the price of other products. Hence the fall in value of broadcloth will increase the demand and the price of other goods. Therefore, an increased supply of some goods does not necessarily lead to a fall in general values, but rather to a restructuring of prices and to additional real income to consumers.

Craig concludes from his value analysis that exchange-value not only depends on use-value, but is also an accurate measure of that value. Craig points out in his introduction to the *Remarks* that only after the body of his tract was written did he come across J.B. Say's *Treatise* and see the similarity in approach. He adds, however, that Say's proper concentration on exchange-value should have been amended to point out that it is also the embodiment or expression of value in use.

Attacking the Ricardian labour or cost theory of value, Craig points out that the value of any good is determined not by its cost of production, but by its demand and supply, the demand varying continually in accordance with consumer desires, and the supply changing according to the scarcity or abundance of its factors of production, as well as the fertility of agriculture. Or, as Craig put it:

> even if the cost were ascertained, it would not enable us to judge of the exchangeable value. Exchange value depends entirely on the proportion in the market which the demand for an article may bear to the supply, a proportion ever varying, on the one hand, according to the plenty or scarcity of capital or labour, and the fertility of the season.

If Samuel Bailey was preceded by John Craig, he was succeeded, six years after his *Dissertation*, by Charles Foster Cotterill, in his *an Examination of the Doctrine of Value...* (1831). Cotterill not only generally endorsed Bailey's subjective utility theory; he also pronounced, the same year as Torrens, the demise of the Ricardian movement, noting bemusedly that 'there are some Ricardians still remaining'.

4.6   Nassau Senior, the Whately connection, and utility theory

During the late 1820s, Nassau W. Senior delivered a series of lectures as Drummond professor at Oxford, some of which were collected in Senior's only published book, his *Outline of the Science of Political Economy* (1836). Senior carried forward Bailey's subjective utility theory; how much he was influenced by Bailey is difficult to say, since, like all too many economists of his era, Senior acknowledged virtually no like-minded colleagues or influences upon his own work.

Senior did acknowledge J.B. Say, however, and began his value analysis by stating that value depends on utility and scarcity, thus returning to the continental tradition. Senior added that utility is relative to human desires and to different persons, and is not intrinsic in objects. Utility, he pointed out:

> denotes no intrinsic quality in the things which we call useful; it merely expresses their relations to the pains and pleasures of mankind. And, as the susceptibility of pain and pleasure from particular objects is created and modified by causes innumerable, and constantly varying, we find an endless diversity in the relative utility of different objects to different persons, a diversity which is the motive of all exchanges.

Scarcity, or the natural limitation of supply, was for Senior the main influence on relative utility. In the course of his discussion, Senior virtually came to formulate the law of diminishing marginal utility:

> Not only are there limits to the pleasure which the commodities of any given class can afford, but the pleasure diminishes in a rapidly increasing ratio long before those limits are reached. Two articles of the same kind will seldom afford twice the pleasure of one, and still less will ten give five times the pleasure of two.

While he was completing his studies at Oxford, young Senior acquired as his tutor a young man, only three years older than himself, recently appointed as a fellow at Oriel College, from which he had graduated several years earlier. The Rev. Richard Whately (1787–1863), philosopher and theologian, and son of an Anglican minister, was to become Senior's close and lifelong friend. Even though Senior became an attorney, he remained a central part of the Oriel College circle clustered around the charismatic Whately. The circle engaged in literary studies and pursuits, with Senior publishing several literary articles and launching a short-lived literary and intellectual quarterly, the *London Review*. Whately published what was to become the standard text on logic, the *Elements of Logic* (1826), in which Senior included an appendix on 'Ambiguous Terms Used in Political Economy'. Indeed, Whately was probably responsible for injecting an unfortunate tendency in Senior towards word-chopping and logomachy, which helped dampen the influence of the great Senior in the world of economics. At any rate, Senior learned philosophy and theology from Whately, and the latter economics from Senior.

In Oxford, the Oriel circle was becoming a highly influential centre for Liberal and Whig views within the Anglican Church, a remarkable influence indeed in that traditionally high Tory and High Church university.[16] When the Drummond professorship in political economy opened up in 1825, Whately secured the post for Nassau Senior, and when Senior's term expired five years later, he recommended and obtained the position for Whately as his successor. Whately's Drummond lectures, the *Introductory Lectures on Political Economy* (1831, 2nd edition, 1832) continued and expanded the Senior tradition, particularly in value theory.

Indeed, methodologically, Whately went further than Senior. His linguistic and philosophical interests led Whately to see that the concept and terminology of 'political economy' tended to confuse and conflate these two distinct fields. This confusion hindered the scientific development of economics; hence Whately proposed substituting a new word, *catallactics*, the science of exchanges, for political economy. Whately defined man as 'an animal that makes exchanges', pointing out that even the animals nearest to human rationality did not have 'to all appearance, the least notion of bartering, or in any way exchanging one thing for another'. Focusing on human acts of exchange rather than on the *things* being exchanged, Whately was led almost immediately to a subjective theory of value, since he saw that 'the same thing is different to different persons', and that differences in subjective value are the foundation of all exchanges. Moreover, Whately pointed out that 'labour [is] not essential to value', and noted that pearls do not 'fetch a high price *because* men have dived for them; but on the contrary, men dive for them because they fetch a high price'.

Whately saw that the economic realm, and particularly exchange activity on the market, deserved its own sphere of analysis and inquiry. Even if integration later takes place, as analysis is applied to the political realm, there must first be a separation to allow the reasoning process its head.

But after separation and analysis, integration; and Richard Whately understood that the very fact that a separate sphere was secured for catallactic analysis meant all the more that integration with moral and theological analysis was required in order to come to policy conclusions. In his Drummond lectures, Whately was concerned to show, first, that, contrary to Oxford

Tories, political economy was not sinful, materialistic, or opposed to Christianity. In the first place, political economy is not to be considered, as had Smith and the classicals, a study of wealth; it is instead a study of human exchanges. But even a study of wealth is not sinful; in the first place, it is not sinful *per se* to examine the means of increasing wealth. There is no need for the political economist to step beyond his role as a scientist or catallactician, and advocate *policy* as a means of acquiring wealth or on any other grounds. Indeed, once he does so, he advocates public policy not as a political economist but in some other capacity. Whately also denounced, in their turn, the attempt to monopolize economics by the aggressively atheistic, secular, and 'anti-Christian' Ricardian circle. Certainly the latter adjective would not be excessive for people like James Mill and the Benthamite radicals. Whately also believed Ricardian teachings to be dangerous and 'anti-Christian' in the sense that they implied inherent class conflict between capital and labour, and between landlords and everyone else, and therefore denied the essential *laissez-faire* insight of a harmonious social order, an order that testifies to the existence of divine wisdom. In short, for Whately *laissez-faire* harmony and Christian insight into a divine order meet on a broad integrative level. Thus, while economic analysis is scientific and value-free, and cannot *directly* imply political conclusions, such analysis will lead to *laissez-faire* conclusions and, as such, is perfectly consistent with Christian insight into a beneficent divine order.

In addition to his subtle exposition on the nature of and distinctions among positive and normative economics, Whately denounced the naive fact-gathering methodology of the Baconian Cambridge inductivists, led by Richard Jones and William Whewell. The role of fact-gathering, Whately perceptively pointed out, was not in framing theory but in applying it to specific conditions. Looking at facts without the guidance of theory in their selection is virtually impossible. Scientific advances, Whately correctly noted, come not from gathering more data, but from looking at old facts in new ways – an example was modern insight into the nature of the circulation of the blood.

In 1832, Richard Whately left his Drummond chair prematurely on getting a surprise appointment to the high post of Anglican archbishop of Dublin, where he scandalized the evangelical faithful by refusing to be anti-Catholic and by insisting on being joyous on the Sabbath. The position of archbishop carried with it being one of the two 'visitors' of Trinity College, Dublin, the two who formed the ultimate appeals court for all intra-College disputes. Whately used his clout at Trinity to drive through, over fierce opposition, the establishment of a new chair of political economy at Trinity, under terms closely modelled on the Drummond chair. For the rest of his life, Whately examined and selected candidates for the post himself, and paid the salary of the professors.

The opposition from the board and the provost of Dublin University was based on a fear of the alleged radicalism of political economy. The provost wanted Whately to guarantee that the holders of the new chair would have 'sound and safe conservative views', to which the archbishop indignantly replied that he was 'appalled at such a suggestion, involving as it did the introduction of party politics into the subject of abstract science...'.

It was a subtle but important distinction that Whately was trying to convey – on an issue that plagues academia to this day. He was saying that it was proper – indeed important – to select a professor with the correct view of the broader implications of his subject as well as of its strictly scientific aspects. Yet it was decidedly not proper to judge the professoriat on the basis of their direct positions on narrow political issues, which Whately lumped together as 'party politics'. Thus, in gaining agreement on the Whately chair, the archbishop closely quizzed and selected the professors on the basis of their commitment to the Christian-liberal view of the harmony of the universe in general, and of the free market in particular; and to the Senior subjective utility theory of value as against the Ricardian labour theory.

Whately himself wrote a bit more on economics, reiterating his ideas in his *Easy Lessons on Money Matters; for the Use of Young People* (1833), an enormously popular work for children, that went into 15 editions in the next 20 years, and was translated into many languages. Remarkably, in this primer Whately hinted at another huge theoretical advance: generalizing the theory of pricing for all factors of production: 'If you consider attentively what is meant by the words Rent, Hire, and Interest, you will perceive that they all, in reality, signify the same sort of payment.'[17] But, unfortunately, Whately did not apply himself further to economics, and insights into value or distribution theory became scattered and fragmentary. From now on, he would have to rely on Whately chair holders to pursue the subjective tradition more systematically.

The first holder of the Whately chair suited the archbishop's requirements admirably. Samuel Mountifort Longfield (1802–84), the son of an Anglican vicar in County Cork, Ireland, had graduated from Trinity College a decade earlier and had won a gold medal in science for particular excellence in mathematics and physics. Longfield later won a coveted fellowship at Trinity, a post concentrating on mathematics and sciences – areas in which Trinity was far stronger than Oxford and Cambridge, which were just now enlarging their exclusively classical curriculum to enter the modern world. While serving as fellow of the college, Longfield entered Dublin Law School, and, graduating in 1831, became assistant to the Dublin professor of feudal and English law. Not only that: Longfield delivered a series of public lectures on the common law that was highly favourably received.

Mountifort Longfield more than fulfilled Whately's expectations. Not only did he use the leisure and the stimulus of the chair to hammer out a remarkably complete subjective and even marginalist theory of value and distribution – a genuine alternative to Ricardianism; he also imparted his stamp and the tradition of a subjective value theory alternative on Dublin University, leaving worthy successors to his chair. The brunt of Longfield's system was presented in his first published series of lectures, *Lectures on Political Economy* (1834). During the rest of his term, Longfield published two more sets of lectures; in 1836, he left the Whately chair to resume his legal career, becoming Regius professor of feudal and English law at Dublin University. Later he became a member of the Queen's Council. Longfield was an expert in real estate law, and in 1849 he was appointed as one of the three land commissioners in Ireland. A decade later, he became the prestigious judge of the landed estates court in Ireland. From then on he was known widely in Great Britain as 'Judge Longfield' for his efforts on behalf of land reform in Ireland. Aside from a few articles on banking, Longfield had no further leisure to pursue economic studies, and so his remarkable contributions to economics were crammed into his four years in the Whately chair. At the end of his life, Longfield returned to his early interest in mathematics, publishing a mathematical text, *An Elementary Treatise on Series*, in 1872.

Longfield's broad perspective of market harmony was quite similar to Whately's. In his *Lectures*, he wrote that the 'laws according to which wealth is created, distributed, and consumed, have been framed by the Great Author of our being, with the same regard to our happiness which is manifested by the laws that govern the material world'. Furthermore, Longfield was disturbed by Ricardo's pessimistic theory of distribution, and his portrayal of inherent class conflict between workers, capitalists, and landlords, with the former two being doomed by an inevitable rising lion's share of the product accruing to the unproductive class of landlords.

In value theory, Longfield worked out the subjective theory of value and price more fully than had been accomplished before in Great Britain. He concentrated firmly on market price as the important consideration rather than long-run price, and also showed that both are in any case determined by supply and demand. Longfield broke important new ground in his detailed marginal analysis of demand. Here he worked out the concept of consumer demand as a schedule, related to sets of prices, and even developed the idea of individual falling demand schedules as the fundamental basis of aggregate market demand. Even more fully than John Craig, Longfield showed that market demand curves are constituted by a spectrum of supramarginal, marginal, and submarginal buyers, each with different intensities of demand. Furthermore, 'the measure of the intensity of any person's demand for any commodity is the amount which he would be willing and able to give for it, rather than remain without it, or forego the gratification which it is calculated to afford him'. Yet, of course, despite the different intensities of demand, all exchanges will be at the same market price. If, then, 'the price is attempted to be raised one degree beyond this sum, the demanders, who by the change cease to be purchasers, must be those the intensity of whose demand was precisely measured by the former price... Thus the market price is measured by the demand, which being of the least intensity, yet leads to actual purchases'. In short, the marginal demand becomes a key to the determination of price.

In his analysis of supply, Longfield showed that the supply relevant to the real, day-to-day market price is a previously produced stock of a good now fixed for the immediate present period (in short, what would now be called a vertical supply curve for the immediate market period). Furthermore, Longfield saw clearly, in contrast to Ricardo, that cost of production in no sense determines price; at most, it contributes indirectly to that determination by affecting the extent of supply. His analysis comes close to the later Austrian theory by brilliantly pointing out that the effect of cost on supply comes from the expectations of producers in deciding how much of a good to make and put on the market. Thus the cost of production acts by its influence on the supply, 'since men will not produce commodities unless with the reasonable expectation of selling them for more than the cost of producing them'.

Professor Laurence Moss, a biographer of Longfield, has deprecated the latter's contribution to value theory as not a marginal utility theory.[18] Moss complains that while Longfield realized that utility was the source of all demand, he did not analyse utility beyond that, and stuck merely to an analysis of marginal demands and the demand schedule. This revisionist view seems merely to quibble over terms; while Longfield did not use the term marginal utility or break 'utility' down into individuals or groups, his doing so for demand and the degrees of demand goes most of the way towards a complete utility theory. Professor Moss is in danger of mistaking the term for the substance. It is true, however, that an unfortunate lingering Ricardianism led Longfield to endorse labour as a measure of value, a concept which is every bit as fallacious as the labour theory of value itself.

In Ireland, as we shall see, Mountifort Longfield, aided by Whately, left an important legacy of subjective value theory and anti-Ricardianism to his successors in the Whately chair at Dublin. But, unfortunately, he had no influence in England, where he was ironically well-known as Judge Longfield the Irish land reformer and unknown as an important and challenging economist. Senior, though closest in doctrine, knew of Longfield but only referred to him once on a trivial point and displayed no signs of being influenced by him. This neglect was intensified by the extreme provinciality of English economics in the nineteenth century. Generally, they would not deign to notice foreign writers, especially 'colonials' like Irishmen and Americans from whom they might have profited.

But Mountifort Longfield did succeed, at least, in establishing a utility-value tradition in Ireland. His successor in the Whately chair, Isaac Butt (1813–79), proudly called himself a disciple of Longfield, and advised his students to read, above all in economics, Longfield, Say and Senior – a worthy trio indeed. Like Longfield, and even more so, Butt's economic contributions were confined to the 1836–40 term of his Whately chair, his most important publications, *Introductory Lecture* (1837) and *Rent, Profits, and Labour* (1838), consisting of lectures delivered at Trinity. As we shall see below, Butt's main contribution was generalizing Longfield's marginal productivity theory of factor pricing and integrating Say's utility analysis with that theory. In utility theory proper, Butt corrected Longfield's Smith-like error in referring to consumption *per se* as 'unproductive'. Butt also noted that the labour theory of value might be in a sense applicable if labour were the only scarce resource, and if, moreover, it were homogeneous and costlessly mobile between industries. But such conditions are of course impossible.

Isaac Butt began as a precocious classical scholar and translator of Virgil. He was named to the Whately chair at the early age of 23, and, while teaching there, he took his bar examinations. After his term was over, Butt became an eminent attorney, and soon became an alderman of the City of Dublin. Later Isaac Butt denounced British policy during the Irish famine, and went on to became a famous and hard-hitting advocate of Irish home rule. Butt defended leaders of the Irish rising of 1848 in court, as he did the Fenian rebels in the late 1860s. Butt was also the founder, leader and chief organizer of the Home Rule Party, serving for a while in Parliament. His published writings after his Trinity period dealt with the Irish land question, where Butt advocated land reform on behalf of the Irish tenantry. As a tenants' advocate, Butt took the poorly paid side of these legal disputes, and hence was never well off and was often deeply in debt. His main publications on the Irish question were *A Voice for Ireland – the Famine in the Land, What Has Been Done and What is to be Done* (1847), and *The Irish People and the Irish Land* (1867).

Isaac Butt's successor in the Whately chair, James Anthony Lawson (1817–87), was also an attorney involved with the Irish question, but he took the opposing route to Butt, becoming a stern advocate of British law and order and suppression of his rebellious countrymen. Lawson also became the holder of the political economy chair at a remarkably early age (24), serving the full term from 1841 to 1846. Lawson entered Parliament, and rose to become solicitor-general and then attorney-general for Ireland, becoming a judge of the Common Pleas in 1868. There he meted out punishment for land rebels and Fenians; while Richard Cantillon remains as the only possibly murdered man in the history of economic thought, Lawson suffered an attempted assassination on the streets of Dublin in 1882.

Lawson's productivity in economics followed the same restricted path as that of his predecessors. His only published book was his *Five Lectures on Political Economy* (1844), consisting of some of his Trinity lectures; in later years, he occasionally printed some of his lectures on legal topics, the best-known being on mercantile law in 1855.

Unfortunately, the series of Lawson's lectures on value have been lost, his only published reference to them being contained in a brief appendix to his *Five Lectures*. We know enough, however, to see that Lawson was decidedly in the Trinity utility tradition, and even made a distinguished contribution to that doctrine. Thus Lawson declared that it was subjective utility and utility alone that determined the price of all goods. Lawson declared that 'It is a proposition always true, and of universal application, *that the exchangeable value of all articles depends upon their utility*, that is, upon their power to gratify the wants and wishes of man'. (Italics in original.) All other attempted explanations of value he saw as only partial. Demand and supply, for example, can only influence price by way of their effect on utility. In dealing with the effect of an increase of supply, Lawson arrived flatly and notably at the law of diminishing marginal utility. Thus, if someone's supply of a good increased,

> this will generally diminish its utility to him, or the degree in which he desires its possession, for as our particular desires are capable of being satisfied, it is obvious that we may have more of an article than we wished to use, therefore retaining the possession of that surplus is less desirable to us.

When coming to the cost-of-production theory of value, Lawson pointed out that the utility of a product, and not its cost, determines how much anyone will pay for it. While price may sometimes equal cost of production, this does not mean that cost determines the price. On the contrary, the coinciding of cost and price, Lawson added, can only come about 'through the medium of a change in supply and when this cannot be brought about, there is no such coincidence and no tendency toward it'. In that way, Lawson arrived at Stanley Jevons's newly hacked-out value position of a generation later.

In his *Five Lectures*, Lawson also developed the Whatelyan idea of economics as catallactics, as the study of exchanging man. In his first lecture, Lawson declared that economics views man 'in connection with his fellow-man, having reference solely to those relations which are the consequences of a particular act, to which his nature leads him, namely, the act of making exchange'. In his second lecture, Lawson failed to continue this line, and fell back on older discussions of political economy as the study of 'wealth'.[19]

The next holder of the Whately chair, William Neilson Hancock (1820–88), a student of Whately at Oxford, taught at Trinity from 1846 to 1851, and was also an attorney. He was a particularly scholarly lawyer, and in the last

two years of his Trinity term he simultaneously held the chairs of jurisprudence and political economy at the new Queen's College, Belfast. Afterwards, Hancock was a secretary to many government commissions on land
and education matters, and held posts as court clerk, ending his career as
clerk of the Crown and Hanaper in Dublin. He was the principal founder of
the Statistical Society of Ireland in 1847, and the Social Inquiry Society of
Belfast four years later.

In contrast to the other Trinity chair holders, Hancock was interested in
statistics and empirical work; he had graduated from Trinity in 1842 with a
first in mathematics. He published a host of articles and pamphlets on empirical questions. Several dealt, almost inevitably, with the Irish land question,
where, like Longfield and Butt but unlike Lawson, he championed the rights
of the Irish tenantry and deplored the effect upon their condition of the
British-imposed system of land tenure: e.g., *The Tenant-right of Ulster* (1845);
Impediments to the Prosperity of Ireland (1850); and *Two Reports for the
Irish Government on the History of the Landlord and Tenant Question in
Ireland* (1859, 1866). Other pamphlets dealt with taxation and local government, in which he advocated a single tax on income, including the inheritance of wealth. A third group of articles advocated stricter control and supervision of the savings banks. Hancock's statistical work was done under the
influence and guidance of Thomas Larcom, a land surveyor and statistician
who filled many government posts, becoming under-secretary for Ireland in
the 1850s.

While better known for applied economics, Hancock did publish a valuable theoretical work consisting of his *Introductory Lecture on Political
Economy, 1848* (1849) delivered at Trinity College. He began by noting the
ambiguity that had pervaded the use of the word 'value', and made clear that
'the word "price" is fortunately free from all ambiguity, and always means
the exchangeable value of a commodity, estimated in the money of the
country where the exchange takes place'. He proposed, then, to use the word
price exclusively instead of exchange value. Price, furthermore, can change
either 'from the side of things', or 'from the side of money'. Treating the
former, he notes that such changes can only take place as a result of one or
both of the following causes: 'either a change in the degree in which its
possession is desired, or in its desirability; or a change in the force of the
causes by which its supply is limited, or, in other words, by which it is made
scarce'. Turning to demand, Hancock added that 'the degree in which the
possession of a commodity is desired, is measured by the number of persons
able and willing to purchase at each amount of price'. Hancock's utility, or
quasi-marginal utility, analysis, emphasized a slightly different aspect than
did that of his predecessors: namely, another aspect of what we would now
call the falling demand curve. For he noted that 'it is observed that for

commodities in general, their desirability increases very rapidly as their prices fall'.

On supply, Hancock again stressed limitations of supply rather than cost; and the limitations, or scarcities, of supply are dependent on the scarcities of the various factors of production. He implied that the returns to these factors is a question of their prices, and that any explanation of the prices of the factors must treat them uniformly, in accordance with the influences upon their demand and supply, i.e., 'by the application of the laws already stated with regard to other prices'.

But while Hancock was clearly in the Trinity utility tradition, we see already a falling-back, a loss of interest and a greater vagueness in the discussion of value or, indeed, of theory in general. And indeed, William Neilson Hancock was destined to be the last of the distinguished line of Irish subjective utility theorists at Trinity College.

4.7   William Forster Lloyd and utility theory in England

Just because Mountifort Longfield and the Trinity connection had no influence in England does not mean that the utility theory of value died out with such prominent economists as Bailey and Senior. Indeed, Nassau Senior's successor in the Drummond chair at Oxford was also a distinguished utility theorist. William Forster Lloyd (1794–1852) was the son of an Anglican rector from Gloucestershire. Lloyd went to Christ Church, Oxford, where he took a first in mathematics and a second in classics. Lloyd was a reader in Greek and then a lecturer in mathematics at Christ Church, and was also ordained as an Anglican minister, but never served a parish. Lloyd held the Drummond chair from 1832 to 1837, and seems to have done little at all after that. A sickly man, Lloyd retired to his county and displayed little interest in economics, in writing, or in politics before dying in middle age.

But for Lloyd as for the other Drummond and Whately chair holders, his term as professor provided him both opportunity and stimulus to compose, deliver and publish lectures in economics. His various lectures, including one delivered on value in 1833, were all published separately, and then collected and republished as *Lectures on Population, Value, Poor-Laws, and Rent* (1837).

One does not have to agree in politics to have similar views of economic theory. We have seen, for example, James Lawson's hard-core attitude against the peasantry. While William Lloyd was a utility theorist, he was far from a Whatelyan at Oxford; on the contrary, at Oxford Lloyd belonged to the high Tory circle at Christ Church that was the main counterweight to the Liberals at Oriel. Leader of the Christ Church Tories was William's elder brother, Charles Lloyd (1774–1829), who tutored future Prime Minister Sir Robert Peel at Christ Church, and soon became a close friend and adviser to Peel. At his untimely death in 1829, Charles Lloyd was Regius professor of divinity and canon of Christ Church, as well as serving as bishop of Oxford. He was widely known as 'the most influential Oxford Professor of his day'. Even though Lloyd taught and inspired many of the leaders of the future ultra-Tory, proto-Catholic Oxford movement, he himself, as well as William Lloyd, was a moderate, Peelite Tory, both theologically and politically. The influence of Peel and of his late brother Charles undoubtedly secured the Drummond chair for William Lloyd.

Most of Lloyd's lectures were devoted to his quasi-statist and paternalistic views on public policy. Of particular interest, however, was his lecture on value. There Lloyd, stumbling through the literature, thinks he discovers in the *Wealth of Nations* inspiration for a subjective theory of value. Value, Lloyd asserts, is 'a feeling of the mind'. It can be understood as belonging to a single object, he added, where the feeling reveals itself 'at the margin of separation between the satisfied and unsatisfied wants'. But value, or even utility, cannot be intrinsic to any object. Utility, points out E.R.A. Seligman of Lloyd's theory, 'is predicated of an object with reference to the wants of mankind. Ice is useful in summer, useless in winter. Still the intrinsic qualities of ice are at all times and in all places the same'.[20]

After treading what was by now familiar ground about an increase in the supply of an object diminishing and eventually satiating demand, William Lloyd suddenly arrives at a great light – a remarkably clear portrayal of the law of diminishing marginal utility. Lloyd points out:

> Let us suppose the case of a hungry man having one ounce, and only one ounce of food at his command. To him this ounce is obviously of very great importance. Suppose him now to have two ounces. These are still of great importance; but the importance of the second is not equal to that of the single ounce. In other words he would not suffer so much from parting with one of his two ounces ... as he would suffer, when he had only one ounce, by parting with that one, and retaining none. The importance of a third ounce is still less than that of the second; so likewise of a fourth, until at length, in the continual increase of the number of ounces, we come to a point when ... the appetite is entirely ... lost; with respect to a single ounce, it is a matter of indifference whether it is parted with or retained. Thus, while he is scantily supplied with food, he holds a given portion of it in great esteem, in other words, he sets a great value on it; when his supply is increased, his esteem for a given quantity is lessened, or, in other words, he sets a less value on it.

Similarly, Lloyd goes on, the utilities of different goods compared with one another and each of their values falls with increase in supply; so a good that may be more valuable than another in an absolute philosophic sense, in the sense of a class of the commodity, can be worth very little if its supply is abundant. Thus, 'Water is more wanted by a man almost dying with thirst than by another who has quenched his thirst, and desires only to wash himself. It is on want, thus estimated, that value depends'

More specifically,

> If, to a man who has already half a dozen coats, you should offer to give another, he might probably reply that he would have no use for it. Here, however, he would speak, not of the abstract utility of the coat, but of its special utility to him under the circumstances of his want of coats being already so far supplied. This, though not quite the same thing as value, approaches very near to it. The coat would be of no use to him; therefore, were he to have it, it would not be valuable in his estimation... But this is very different from the utility of the coat in the general sense of utility...[21]

William Lloyd was also clear that value, being subjective, could not be measured. In a passage reminiscent of and going beyond Bailey, he writes trenchantly that

> It would indeed be difficult to discover any accurate test, by which to measure either the absolute utility of a single object, or the exact ratio of the comparative utilities of different objects. Still it doesn't follow, that the notion of utility has no foundation in the nature of things. It does not follow, that because a thing is incapable of measurement, therefore it has no real existence. The existence of heat was no less undeniable before thermometers were invented, than at present.

Lloyd goes on to point out, quite correctly, that value or valuation is anterior to exchange, and that such valuations also take place in the case of an isolated Robinson Crusoe economy. Unfortunately, Lloyd was so enamoured of the distinction between value and exchange, and of Smith's faulty split between use- and exchange-values, that he failed to complete the task of the theory of demand and link up marginal utility analysis with consumer demand and the determination of market pricing. Such men as Butt, Longfield, Lloyd and Bailey had hammered out many of the building blocks of the marginal utility theory of pricing and even of the marginal productivity theory of factor prices; it required the Austrians, however, to put the pieces together and set forth an integrated whole.

If Lloyd's value theory seems to have had little or no influence in England, the eminent Nassau Senior's utility theory was picked up and lauded a decade after the publication of his *Lectures*. Thomas C. Banfield (c. 1800–60), had spent many years in Germany, and in his 1844 lectures at Cambridge, Banfield brought to England the good news that economic theory on the Continent was not blighted by any Ricardian miasma; instead, he noted that a flexible form of Smithianism was dominant in Europe. In addition to basing his doctrines on Say, von Storch, and Senior, Banfield was the first English economist to refer to the marginal theorist Heinrich von Thünen, and to the advanced Smithian Friedrich von Hermann. In the preface to his lectures, published as *The Organization of Industry* (1845), Thomas Banfield pointed to the enormous changes that had been made in economic theory during the past two decades by the subjective theory of value, 'which demands of producers at least as much attention to the physical and mental improvement of their consuming fellow-citizens as to the mechanical operations' or production. Wages, he noted, will depend on the productivity of labour, i.e., 'the utility of the instrument of which a man understands the use'. In his lectures, Banfield emphasized the relativity and degree of intensity of wants as the function of economic science.

It certainly seems that economics in England, by the later 1840s, was poised for a mighty 'Austrian' breakthrough, for an integrated system elaborating the effect of human purposes and values and their interaction with the scarcity of resources. Yet something happened; and economics, poised for a great breakthrough, sank back into the slough of fallacies constituting the Ricardian system. And the important body of pre-Austrian or anti-Ricardian thought was forgotten as if it never existed, only to be resurrected either a generation later or as late as the twentieth century. How this unfortunate retrogression came about will be treated below.

4.8   A utility theorist in Kentucky

If the Trinity College contributions to subjective utility theory remained unknown outside Ireland, still more obscure was an isolated and amazing contribution in the course of several articles in a Kentucky newspaper. Written by the youngish but influential editor of the *Frankfort (Ky) Argus*, Amos Kendall (1789–1869), later to become a leading brain-truster of Andrew Jackson in his battle against fractional-reserve banking and particularly against the Bank of the United States, the articles remained unread and unknown even in the United States until exhumed by historians in the twentieth century.[22] And yet especially considering that they were written in 1820, antedating Bailey and even Craig, they were phenomenal. Not only did they champion subjective value; they were the first expression of the law of diminishing marginal utility.

Kendall was moved to explore the question of economic value by a fierce dispute in Kentucky during the catastrophic Panic of 1819 on whether or not debtors should receive relief at the hands of the state government. While Kendall was not opposed to all relief measures, he was disturbed by proposals that would have repudiated all existing debt. To explore the subject in depth, Kendall published three articles in the *Argus*, beginning on 27 April, examining the problems of money and more fundamentally, the nature of value. Unfortunately, in his autobiography, arranged and edited posthumously by his son-in-law, Kendall gives no hint on which economists might have inspired his advanced views.

In his first article, Kendall went straight to the basics and examined the question of value *per se*. He begins by saying that there have been many erroneous explanations of value: labour expended, price, even demand. But, he points out,

> All these notions are erroneous. Things have *value*, not because they are produced by labor, nor because they are in general demand, nor because they will sell or exchange for a certain number of dollars, *but simply because men desire to possess them. Desirableness is value.* In exact proportion that a thing is desirable it is valuable. (Italics in original.)

Kendall went on, in dismissing the 'value paradox', to say that water and air have little or no value because of their abundance: 'Were meat and bread as common as air and light they would possess no more value; they would not create desire.' In the Garden of Eden, land, being superabundant, possessed no value. Labour, Kendall went on, conferred no value, for:

> With regard to the produce of labor, value is generally antecedent to the labor of production. It springs from our desire to possess that which labor may produce. Were labor to fix value upon its products, everything on which much has been spent would be very valuable. This notoriously is not the fact... But labor could not make a thing valuable which was not desirable. Labor may be wasted. It may be applied to the production of that which nobody desires, which has no value.

And Kendall sparkingly concludes: 'Things do not become valuable because men spend labor upon them, but men spend their labor upon them because they are valuable.'

The demand for a product, furthermore, stems from men's desire to obtain it. The desire is primary: 'Demand is not, therefore, the cause of value... A thing becomes desirable or valuable before there is a demand for it. The demand follows... But when the desire to possess it cease, it has value no longer, and is no longer in demand.'

The next step, for Kendall, is that desires, being subjective and evanescent, cannot be measured, and that therefore neither can value:

> What standard can be invented for the desires of men? Can the necessities, the comforts, the pleasures, the fashions, the opinions, and the caprices of man be reduced to any standard? Are they not ever changing like the winds of heaven? Measure never varies. A yard is always equal to the length with which it is compared... These lengths, surfaces, and quantities never vary or change. Therefore they may be reduced to a standard which shall be uniform and last forever. But does value never vary? Will that which is now worth a dollar always be worth just the same sum?

Tastes and desires are ever-changing, and so therefore is value; hence it can have no measure or standard. Kendall then concludes his devastating critique – one that we might wish Ricardo and his epigones had read and understood:

To make a standard of value you must first make every acre of ground, every bushel of wheat, and any given quantity of any other article, at all times, in all situations and under all circumstances, sell for precisely the same amount. There must be no such thing as profit or loss, or buying or selling.

We have said enough to show the utter impossibility of a standard of value, and that to talk seriously of any such thing is simply ridiculous. We may as well talk of a standard of hunger, thirst, opinion, fashion, caprice, and all those wants ... which make things desirable.

4.9   Wages and profits

In addition to the labour theory of value, another vital cornerstone of the Ricardian system – the alleged inverse relation of wages and profits – was also riddled quickly by British economists. We have already seen the disappearance of the hard-core Malthus of the first edition of the *Essay on Population*, so necessary to the conclusions of Ricardian theory.

Even more than the explicit rejection of Malthusianism, the periodicals vehemently attacked the Ricardian view that wages and profits move inversely to each other. The *British Critic* denounced this thesis as early as October 1817, and two years later another writer zeroed in on the methodology of what would later be called the 'Ricardian Vice' with proper scorn:

> taking for granted, as usual, that money never changes in value and the proportion between the supply and demand of any given commodity never alters (which is as if the astronomer were to assume as the basis of his calculations, that all the planets stand still and that they all stand still to all eternity), he assigns a specific sum to be divided between the master and the workman, as the unalterable price of the goods which they produce; from which adaptation of hypothetical conditions, it naturally follows, that, if the workmen get more, the master-manufacturer must receive less, there being only a certain sum to divide between them.[23]

Other writers, including Malthus in 1824, made similar critiques, and also noted that, empirically, wages and profits generally increase or decrease in the same direction. Thus, John Craig pointed out that historically wages and profits moved not inversely but together: 'It is rather a startling circumstance attending this theory, that what it represents as the necessary effect produced by high wages upon profits in all branches of industry, is directly contrary to the experience in each particular trade.' Craig went on to explain that 'a new demand for a commodity at first enriched those, who, being in possession of this commodity, are enabled to raise the price; the desire to participate in their gains soon directs new capital to its production, and a rise in wages speedily ensures'.

Once again, it is not legitimate for Ricardian apologists to dismiss this critique as historical rather than analytical in nature, for empirical generalizations meant to apply directly to reality as in the Ricardian system are properly open to empirical rebuttal. Such rebuttal may challenge the conclusions as well as the more familiarly 'theoretical' procedure of challenging the realism of the theory's premises.

By the 1840s, the idea of an inverse relation between wages and profits had been completely discarded. But if the Malthusian subsistence theory did not determine wages themselves, then what *did*? Not many wandered into this unknown territory. But as early as 1821 the unknown but remarkable Scotsman John Craig emphasized that wages are determined by the supply and demand for labour, and not in any sense by the price of food. Two elements in the demand for labour were stated though not analysed in full: the 'capital from which wages are advanced to the workman', and the 'demand for the produce of his labour'. Craig, by the way, neatly demolished Adam Smith's spurious distinction between 'productive' and 'unproductive' labour. He cogently concluded that 'wealth may consist in whatever be the object of man's desire, and every employment which multiplies those objects of desire, or which adds to their property of yielding enjoyment is productive'.

The next important step in the theory of wages came from Samuel Bailey who, in the course of his definitive critique of Ricardian value theory in 1825, pointed to the crucial role of the productivity of labour in determining wages:

> the value of labour does not entirely depend on the proportion of the whole produce which is given to the labourers in exchange for their labour, but also on the productiveness of labour... The proposition, that when labour rises profits must fall, is true only when its rise is not owing to an increase in its productive powers... If the productive power of labour be augmented, that is, if the same labour produce more commodities in the same time, labour may rise in value without a fall, nay, even with a rise of profits.

One of the critical problems in developing the productivity theory of wages was the Ricardian insistence on emphasizing the alleged laws of aggregate distribution, of 'wages' as a whole and as a total share of national product and income, rather than as wage *rates* of individual units of labour. J.B. Say had presented a productivity theory of wages, but had not analysed the determination of particular wage rates in any detail. Nassau Senior, in the early 1830s, while confused on the topic of wages, came out for the productivity theory. He also managed to demolish Adam Smith's 'productive' *vs* 'unproductive' labour doctrine, stressing, as had J.B. Say, 'production' as the flow of *services*, which emanate both from material and immaterial products.

The truly revolutionary step forward in the theory of wages – indeed in the theory of all factor pricing – came with Mountifort Longfield, in his *Lectures on Political Economy*. As we have seen, Longfield was concerned to show, in contrast to the Ricardian class-conflict theory of income distribution, that workers benefit from capitalist development. (Ironically, Longfield's *laissez-faire Harmonielehre* was replaced by a far more statist attitude in later life.)

In the course of doing so, Longfield took J.B. Say's correct but vague productivity theory of factor incomes, and worked out, for the first time, a remarkable marginal productivity theory of the rental prices (i.e. prices per unit time) of capital goods (which Longfield oddly called 'profits', in a typical confusion of returns on capital with the pricing of capital *goods* that has plagued economics since the early nineteenth century). Working out the specifics, Longfield showed that the price of each machine will tend to equal the marginal productivity of the machine, i.e. the productive value (in terms of value of their products) of the least productive machine which it pays to keep employed on the market, i.e. the marginal machine.

Thus, for the first time, in an unknowing echo of Turgot, Longfield used the proper *ceteris paribus* method of analysing productive returns, holding one factor or class of factors constant, varying another set of factors, and analysing the result.

Longfield stopped there in his brilliant pre-Austrian contribution, applying marginal productivity analysis only to capital goods. He was content that the analysis showed that wages – the residual labour income left over after payment to capital – rose as the marginal productivity of capital goods fell with each increase in the amount of capital. In short, the accumulation of capital led to an increase in wages. Furthermore, Longfield demolished any Malthusian fears totally. Not only was hard-core malthusianism long in the discard, but even the soft-core emphasis on the workers' customary level of wages as determining the supply of labour had the causal chain reversed. Instead, custom, he sensibly pointed out, is guided by the actual prevailing market wage rather than the other way round. As an anonymous Irish follower wrote in the *Dublin University Magazine* a decade later (July 1845), custom will render it suitable to be paid whatever the prevailing wage rate may be, while it would be considered disgraceful to be paid below that norm. Hence the demand for labour, rather than its supply, will dominate the determination of the market wage.

Longfield's further demolition of even soft-core Malthusianism pointed out that population growth can have a favourable effect by widening the market for manufactured goods, thereby raising the marginal productivity of capital goods across the board. Hence population can grow, capital can develop, and both capitalists and workers will benefit – a far more realistic picture of capitalist development than the Ricardian.

Longfield's successor and disciple Isaac Butt, however, was not content to stop there, and he provided an outstanding development of the Longfieldian analysis. In the first place, Butt took the crucial step of seeing that Longfield's marginal productivity analysis could be generalized from capital goods to *all* factors of production: to wages, and to land rent. Each of these classes of factors could be analysed in terms of marginal productivity, and the result would be that each of them would obtain the return, or price, of the least productive factor profitable to be employed on the market (the marginal labourer or acre of land). Thus, whatever kernel of sense there was to the Ricardian differential return theory of land rent, was isolated and incorporated into Butt's brilliant pioneering generalized theory of marginal factor pricing.

Not only that: Butt also built on Say's utility analysis and correct but vague productivity analysis, and integrated it at least in outline, with generalized Longfieldian marginal productivity theory. In short, in a prefiguring of the Austrian Menger–Böhm-Bawerk insight, the value of consumer goods, determined by the subjective utility of the goods to consumers, is imputed back on the market to the values of the various factors of production, which will be set equal to the marginal value productivity of each factor. Thus the unit price of every type of factor will tend to be equal to its marginal value productivity as imputed back through the competitive market process from the subjective utility of the final products.

Unfortunately, this excellent Say–Longfield–Butt tradition of productivity theory had no influence and no successors. Although Senior, as a fellow Whatelyan, certainly knew Longfield's work, he never referred to him or to Butt, and even Longfield's Irish successors at Trinity College, Dublin, while continuing the utility theory of value, neglected the corollary theory of imputation and productivity.

It is true that Longfield's marginal productivity analysis gained one faithful follower in England, Joseph Salway Eisdell, whose two-volume work, *A Treatise of the Industry of Nations* (1839), propounded a sophisticated version of the Longfieldian theory. The book by the unknown Eisdell, however, sank without trace, gaining no reviews in the journals, or citations anywhere else.

But if factor pricing had been analysed, what of profits? If profits could not be explained simply as a residual, then they had to be explained directly, and so some economists began to search for a satisfactory theory of what would determine long-run profits or what would later be called long-run interest return. For one thing, it was pointed out that Ricardo erred greatly in assuming instantaneous and total mobility of capital, and there was a harkening back to the more realistic outlook of Adam Smith. A writer in *Monthly Review*, in 1822, for example, stressed 'the impracticability of transferring capital and the personal acquirements of skill from one business to another'.

But if profits were only uniform as a long-run tendency, what explained them? Malthus moved closer to the correct view, in the *Quarterly Review* in 1824, by stressing that whereas rents are determined by productivity, profit, for example, that is earned in keeping wine and selling it when it matures, is due to 'waiting', and the longer the waiting the greater the margin of profit.

A particularly important contribution to the journal literature pointed to the eventually correct theories of profit and interest. This was an article by

William Ellis (1794–1872) in the Benthamite *Westminster Review* for January 1826. In a highly sophisticated analysis of saving and investment, Ellis pointed out that saving is induced by 'the expectation of greater enjoyment from deferred than immediate consumption', while, on the other hand, investment is called forth by the expectation of profit. In the course of analysing investment, Ellis, with great perceptiveness, distinguished between profit as a return to risk taking as against interest as a return on savings that may also carry a risk premium.

Particularly interesting was Ellis's pioneering risk theory of profits. 'The largeness of the profit', he maintained, 'must be proportioned to the risk incurred in drawing treasure from the hoard and employing it in production'. He also keenly stressed the importance of a large expected profit for undertaking technological innovation. New technology is 'untried' and its introduction must overcome 'the loss of superseded machinery, the want of skill and practice, in workmen and the uncertainty of the result, all unite in preventing the adoption and application of that which is untried'. Chiding previous writers for ignoring innovation and its problems, Ellis pointed out that its difficulties 'are only conquered ... by the prospect of the great additional profit, with which the adopted invention is expected to be accompanied'.

Ellis also introduced separating out the elements of 'gross profit' in a business firm, and distinguishing them from long-run normal interest. Where an entrepreneur uses his own capital exclusively, his gross profit, Ellis perceptively pointed out, can be broken down into premium for risk, remuneration for the entrepreneur's labour and supervision, and, finally the 'remuneration for the productive employment of his savings, which is called interest'. Productive loans in business tend to comprise the interest part of gross business profit.

Who was William Ellis who contributed such a startlingly perceptive and advanced article to one of Britain's distinguished journals? Apparently this was Ellis's sole foray into economics. Born in London, Ellis became a nonconformist missionary, and spent his life working and travelling for the London Missionary Society. Sent to Polynesia from 1816 to 1824, Ellis, who had worked as a gardener in his boyhood, acclimatized many tropical fruits and plants in Polynesia, and also set up the first printing press in the South Seas. The fruits of this labour appeared in his two-volume *Polynesian Researches* (1829). His interest in the theory of profits soon upon his return from his first Polynesian sojourn appears to have been a sport in Ellis's busy missionary career.

While he was not as perceptive as Ellis, a similar analytic division of gross and net profits was contributed by the Scottish philosopher Sir George Ramsay (1800–71), in an unknown and unremarked work, *An Essay on the Distribution of Wealth* (1836). While much of the book was Ricardian, Ramsay adopted the concept of entrepreneur from the French, and he too broke down the gross profits of capital into interest on the use of capital, and the 'profits of enterprise', which was in turn divided into wages of management and superintendence, and payment for the risk incurred by the 'masters', or entrepreneurs. Ramsay pointed out that, analytically, entrepreneurs receive the profits of enterprise, while capitalists receive interest or 'profits' on capital. In practice, however, the two returns are generally combined as the gross profits of capitalist entrepreneurs.

Ramsay was also the first Briton to adopt Destutt de Tracy's analysis of the process of production as either change of the form of matter, or the geographical place, to which Ramsay added, a change in time.

4.10   Abstinence and time in the theory of profits

If profit were perhaps related to risk, what then accounts for the long-run 'interest' component of business profits? The dominant explanation for long-run interest in British economics soon became the abstinence theory of interest.

The first presentation of time as the determinant of interest came from a theory related but superior to abstinence: Samuel Bailey's pioneering time-preference theory. Bailey's discussion came in the course of his brilliant demolition of Ricardo's labour theory of value and his championing of an alternative utility theory. Bailey begins his discussion of time and value by noting that if one commodity takes more time than another for its production, even using the same amount of capital and labour, its value will be greater. While Ricardo admits a problem here, James Mill in his *Elements of Political Economy* indefatigably asserts that time, being 'a mere abstract word', could not possibly add to anything's value.

Rebutting Mill, Bailey points out that 'every creation of value' implies a 'mental operation' – in short, a subjective analysis of value. Given a particular pleasure, Bailey went on, 'We generally prefer a present pleasure or enjoyment to a distant one' – in short, the omnipresent fact of time-preference for human life. Thus:

> We are willing, even at some sacrifice of property, to possess ourselves of what would otherwise require time, to procure it, without waiting during the operation ... If any article were offered to us, not otherwise attainable, except after the expiration of a year, we should be willing to give something to enter upon present enjoyment.

Considerations of time-discount influence buyers, sellers and capitalists, as well as both parties who realize, for example, that wine gains value by being kept for longer periods of time. Bailey, interested in rebutting labour and other objective theories of value rather than explaining interest *per se*, did not press on to explain time-preference as the basis of interest nor to discuss the time-discount rate. But his analysis clearly paved the way for the later Austrian time-preference theory, although Böhm-Bawerk, the creator of the theory, remained unaware of Bailey's insights.[24]

Six years later, G. Poulett Scrope – despite his unfortunate fringe views on Say's law – made an important contribution to profit (or interest) theory, by pioneering an abstinence theory of interest. Writing in the *Quarterly Review* for January 1831, Scrope deplored the absence of any genuine theory of profit in Ricardo, and proceeded to set forth an abstinence theory.

Despite Böhm-Bawerk's uncharitable strictures on the more highly developed abstinence theory of Nassau Senior, there is not a great deal of difference between the abstinence view and the later, and more sophisticated, Austrian theory of time-preference. Profit, said Scrope, was 'the compensation for abstinence from immediate gratification' involved in saving and investing rather than consuming. But Scrope did not stop at outlining an abstinence theory; much of profit, he pointed out, is the narrow form of profit identical with interest. What is vulgarly called 'profit', as Scrope called it, is identical with Ellis's 'gross profit'. This consists, Scrope went on, of interest on capital + insurance against the risks of business + wages for the superintendence labour of the capitalist. Scrope also added monopoly rent, in which he lumped the possession of superior soil or location along with the gains from patented inventions or processes.

But the *locus classicus* of the abstinence theory was the lectures of Nassau W. Senior. It is true that they were not published until 1836, when they were published as the *Outline of the Science of Political Economy* (and also as the article on 'Political Economy' for the *Encyclopedia Metropolitana*), but they were delivered earlier as lectures at Oxford in 1827–28.

Senior pointed out that savings and the creation of capital necessarily involve a painful present sacrifice, an abstinence from immediate consumption, which would only be incurred in expectation of an offsetting reward. Unfortunately, Senior lacked the concept of time-preference, so he was fuzzy about the specific motivation that would lead people to prefer present to future consumption. But he came to very similar conclusions, relating the degree of abstinence-pain (or, as the Austrians would later put it, time-preference for the present over the future) to 'the least civilized' peoples and the 'worst educated' classes, who are generally 'the most improvident, and consequently the least abstinent'.

Even more interesting and valuable than Senior's abstinence theory was his developed theory of capital, which strongly anticipated the Austrian doctrine. For Senior saw that factors of production could be divided into two classes: the original, primary ones: land (or natural resources) and labour; and all the secondary, intermediate goods which are produced by the joint efforts of the primary factors (as well as pre-existing intermediate factors). Eventually, the intermediate factors are transformed into consumer goods that are able to satisfy the wants of the consumers. It might be thought that ultimately the intermediate factors, or capital goods, might be reduced to nature and labour, but this cannot be done, because another element is needed to combine the primary factors into more and more capital: abstinence. For again anticipating the Austrians, Senior saw that a crucial aspect of this process of production is that it must take *time*, and therefore an act of abstinence, 'a term' added Senior, 'by which we express the conduct of a person who either abstains..., or designedly prefers the production of remote to that of immediate results'.

Capital, or capital goods, then, taking time, are the result of the combination of land, labour and abstinence, and consists of the application of present resources to future production. Capital goods are *produced* rather than primary, factors of production. And the way in which production and living standards may increase indefinitely is by using the products of labour and nature, 'as the means of further Production'. Capital, Senior sums up,

> is not a simple productive instrument: it is in most cases the result of all the three productive instruments combined. Some natural agent must have afforded the material, some delay of enjoyment must in general have reserved it from unproductive use, and some labour must in general have been employed to prepare and preserve it.

Senior, then, does not simply have a naive productivity theory of profit or interest. While all factors earn their productivity, and therefore labour earns wages, and land or natural agents earn rent, capital goods are not simple productive agents but complex products of other factors; and so, peeling away the influence of land and labour, the ultimate, distinct productive contribution of capital, is interest – the return to abstinence. While not fully arriving at it, Senior was here groping for a distinction between the *gross* return of capital goods, whose productivity is reflected in their market *prices*, and their *net* return (after deducting from the wages, rents, and prices of other intermediate goods in their production), which equals the rate of interest and is payment for abstinence or time-preference.

In his discussion of how increasing provision of capital funds can allow ever increasing extensions of the division of labour and the production of consumer goods, Nassau Senior captured the essence of the Austrian insight that capital, and eventually production, expands with increased saving because of the superior physical productivity of many longer, or more 'roundabout', processes of production. Since it takes more time to invest in these longer processes and intermediate factors, there must be greater willingness to invest in future as opposed to present enjoyment.

Meanwhile, Senior's fellow Whatelyan, Mountifort Longfield, was working along similar lines. Even if capitalists *qua* capitalists and not as labourers, produce nothing tangible, they perform a vital service in saving capital and paying factors to engage in 'time-consuming' processes of production. While most of the British classicists, including Ricardo, spoke perfunctorily of a period of production, they linked it strictly to the one-year harvest cycle in agriculture. Longfield was able to break out of this agricultural framework, moving 'toward making the time dimension of production a variable in his analysis. He did this by linking the period of production directly to the division of labour and identifying increases in one with extensions of the other'.[25]

Longfield accomplished this linkage by repeating Adam Smith's famous discussion of the pin factory and the division of labour, while showing that extending that division will bring more roundabout processes into play. In short, greater capital investment will eventually lower the labour time required to produce a unit of output, but only by increasing the waiting time between the initial point of investment and the eventual unit of consumer goods. During the time of waiting for the eventual product, the workers must be able to live, and this living is precisely what the capitalists provide.

They do so by 'abstaining' from consumption, thereby allowing the worker to 'consume something produced by the toil of others, although nothing produced by him has yet been consumed by anyone'. In short, while the product of labour is off in the future, the capitalist saves money now and hires the worker: 'The person who employs him [the worker] and directs his labour, in general pays him in the first instance, and repays himself by the sale of the articles thus produced.'[26] In this way, Longfield was able to offer a remarkable anticipation of the Böhm-Bawerkian theory of capital.

The capitalists' gross profit, then, consists of two parts: a return for the service of advancing wages to the workers until the product is sold (long-run interest), and returns for the labour of direction and for the assumption of business risk. Longfield made no attempt to stress the latter and concentrated on the former, the return for the service of advancing wages. Hence, as Longfield points out in anticipation of the sophisticated and highly perceptive Austrian *discounted* marginal productivity theory of factor pricing, the worker in effect pays the capitalist a discount from his marginal productivity for the service of supplying money now rather than having to wait for the sale of the product. Again Longfield:

> [The capitalist] pays the wages immediately, and in return receives the value of [the worker's] labour, to be disposed of to the best advantage... Hence the value of the labour fixed in ... any article, is greater than the wages of that labour. The difference is the profit made by the capitalist for his advances; it is, as it were, the discount which the labourer pays for prompt payment.

It is only a slight step from this analysis to the identification of this discount as a payment for time-preference.

Sir George Ramsay, in his work of 1836, also stressed the importance of time in production and capital, though hardly in as sophisticated a manner as Senior. Time, as well as labour, enters into capital, and Ramsay points as an example to two casks of identical wine. The cask that ages several years longer increases in value, so that value therefore depends not only on labour expended, but also 'on the length of time during which any portion of the product of that labour has existed as a fixed capital'. Lastly, in 1839, Joseph S. Eisdell, an unknown English follower of Longfield, generalized marginal productivity theory, also noting the important service of the capitalists in serving the worker by 'advancing his wages immediately on the performance of his work, before the goods are ready for sale, he being too necessitous to wait until the sale, and the receipt of the money for the goods'. Here Eisdell captured the essence of the service the capitalist renders the worker and for which the latter is willing to 'pay' the former his discount or profit return: the service of paying the worker *now*, at present, while the capitalist takes on the burden of waiting for his return until some point in the future.

4.11 John Rae and the 'Austrian' theory of capital and interest

The most remarkable contribution to the theory of capital and interest in the post-Ricardian period was by the drifter and eccentric, John Rae (1796–1872). Rae set forth his theory as part of a tract designed to argue for a protective tariff: *Some New Principles on the Subject of Political Economy* (Boston, 1834). Rae had the most extensive and fully developed analysis, until Böhm-Bawerk and the Austrians, of the crucial role of *time* in the theory of capital and interest. In the theory of capital, Rae saw that a key to production is increasing investment in capital goods, themselves the product of labour and nature, and that capital goods can be ranked on the basis of their rate of return, and the time necessarily involved from their formation until their depletion. Specifically, lengthening the process of production, or the time involved in the process of investing in capital, will enable the use of capital goods of greater physical productivity. But while waiting a longer time will enable one to tap more physically productive processes of production, this benefit must always be weighed against the unwelcome necessity of waiting longer into the future until the return from capital is obtained. And here, John Rae presented the fullest development to date of the time-preference theory of interest. To balance against the greater productivity of waiting longer into the future, the capitalist must charge an interest rate based on the greater desirability of present as against future goods. In short, investors must sacrifice present for future goods, and so they must be compensated for this investment by a return reflecting their degree of time-preference. Investors will be sacrificing a smaller present good for a larger future good, the degree of difference – their interest return – being dependent on people's cultural and psychological willingness to take a long-run view of the future. Those with lower time-preference rates, i.e. those who take a longer view of the future, are particularly looking to raise the standard of living of their children; on the other hand, for Rae, those with higher time-preference possess weak intellectual and moral principles and suffer from a 'defect of the imagination'.

Rae also anticipated Schumpeterian theory in placing great emphasis on the importance of inventions, and stressed that inventions opened up new opportunities for highly profitable capital investment, and that resulting high profits stimulated such investment.

Schumpeter paid high tribute to Rae's achievement, calling his work a 'theory of capital, conceived in unprecedented depth and breadth', although, oddly enough, he doesn't mention Rae's stress on inventions. Schumpeter does add, however, that given 'ten additional years of quiet work, graced by an adequate income', Rae's *New Principles* 'could have grown into another – and more profound – *Wealth of Nations*'. And Böhm-Bawerk, who had not known of Rae's achievement in the first edition of his *History and Critique of Interest Theories*, for once was very generous in his glowing account in later editions, calling Rae's work 'exceedingly original and remarkable'.

John Rae's accomplishment was all the more striking because it did not come from a writer steeped in the economic discussions of the Great Britain of his day. On the contrary, it came from a man who must be described overall as a brilliant drifter, crank and loser. John Rae was a Scotsman, born in Aberdeen, the son of a prosperous self-made merchant and shipbuilder. Interested in invention and the natural sciences, Rae, as a young maths student at the University of Aberdeen, presented some inventions in mechanics to his professor, who pronounced them ingenious but impractical. Dropping the matter so as not to irritate his practical-minded father, Rae decided, upon graduation, to go to the University of Edinburgh to study medicine. But, typical of Rae, while studying for his M.D. dissertation, he became convinced that prevailing physiological theories were false, and so he dropped out of medical school, determined to write a grandiose 'philosophical history' of mankind. Embarking on this ambitious but truly impractical life work, Rae plunged into the study of biology, philology, ethnology, aeronautics, geology, education, and the social sciences, undoubtedly with radical ideas in them all. Very little of this ever got written or published, his published work consisting of a few scattered articles on such matters as emigration, education, Canadian religion, Hawaiian customs and legislation, and Polynesian languages. His extant unpublished papers are on geological topics.

This sort of life plan was scarcely calculated to yield John Rae a secure income, and the bankruptcy of his father, as well as a possible social stigma from his marrying the daughter of a shepherd, drove him to emigrate to the backwoods of Canada, at the age of 25.

It was during this course of self-study that John Rae read the *Wealth of Nations*, and developed an antipathy to that Scotsman's general commitment to free trade and *laissez-faire*. In particular Rae acquired a lifelong interest in protectionism and government subsidies to industry. At least some of that reaction reflected a typically Scottish Calvinist hostility to luxury and consumer indulgence. A strong advocate of thrift and abstinence, Rae lamented any luxurious consumption among the lower classes, which weakens their 'effective desire for accumulation'. Sensual appetites lead the poor to marry and increase their number of children unduly, also weakening their propensity to save and to raise their standard of living. Rae's first interest in the protective tariff came in Scotland in 1819, attacking the desire of the numerous followers of Adam Smith to greatly lower the taxes and tariffs on whisky, and to allow the manufacture of whisky in small stills. Rae reacted angrily, worrying as he did about the 'general morals of the people' resulting from an abundance of cheap whisky.

Arriving in Canada, Rae soon became a schoolmaster at a private school and a physician in the small village of Williamstown, Ontario. Williamstown was a centre of the Scottish Presbyterian settlement in Canada, and Rae, a devout adherent of the Presbyterian Church of Scotland, embroiled himself in the claims of that Church to government support as against the exclusivist claims of the Church of England. Apart from Anglican élitism unsuited to North American conditions, Rae opined, the Presbyterian Church of Scotland insisted on austere morality as against the laxity of the Anglicans. He criticized the United States for not having an established religion, thereby lessening the incomes and tenure of the clergy and weakening the bonds of 'genuine religion'.

After a decade in Williamstown, John Rae felt it was time to move on. In 1831, he resigned his post as schoolmaster and as one of the three coroners of the Eastern District of Ontario, and moved to Montreal. He had decided to begin work on his life project, or at least a subset of it to be devoted to the 'Present State of Canada', which would present his ideas on Canadian geology and economic development, and to make a strong plea for continued Canadian membership in the British Empire. While in Montreal, he petitioned the government of Upper Canada for a travel and research grant to finance this projected work, but the Upper Canada Assembly felt there were more important things to be done and turned down Rae's grant proposal, despite the favourable recommendation of the lieutenant-governor.

Rae was still determined to work on his life project, and he repaired to the lumbering village of Godmanchester, not far from Montreal, where he apparently worked in menial tasks in lumbering while publishing pro-British Empire articles in the *Montreal Gazette*. There he wrote what was supposed to be another subset of his master plan, his great work on the *New Principles of Political Economy*.

The spirit of revolution against the British Empire was abroad in Canada, and Rae's letters to the *Gazette* were vitriolic in denunciation. The criticisms of Britain, he fulminated, were 'gross misrepresentations, infamous false-hoods and horrid blasphemies'. Recalling the horrors of the French Revolu-tion, Rae thundered that 'the banners of imperial justice must be displayed, else in a short time the reign of terror be attempted in Canada, and red ruin ride triumphantly'.

In view of Rae's strong connections in Montreal, it is difficult to see why he languished in Godmanchester. His sister, Ann Cuthbert, a poet and head-mistress of a boarding school, was married to a wealthy dry-goods merchant, James Fleming. Fleming's brother, John, was a prominent writer as well as a leading official of the Bank of Canada and Bank of Montreal, and the family moved in the circle of leading Scottish Presbyterian merchants and ultra-loyalists of the British Empire, surrounded by a Canadian populace of what they took to be French–Canadian insurgents and radicals.

Rae conceived his *New Principles* to be another subset of his life work, this time devoted to the growth of nations and to the necessity for a protec-tive tariff and other forms of government promotion of industry. He finished the book in 1833 and originally meant to publish it in England, but for some reason changed his plans and travelled to Boston to seek aid in publishing the book there. In Boston, Rae met and was taken under the wing of the powerful Alexander Hill Everett (1790–1847), a leading Boston Brahmin, a protégé of ex-President John Quincy Adams, and recently Adams's minister to Spain. An accomplished linguist and classicist as well as an attorney, Everett had left government service to become the editor of the prominent and influential *North American Review*. A decade earlier, Everett had written *New Ideas on Population* (1823), in which he sensibly attacked Malthus for not realizing that population growth can bring abundance, not poverty, by extending the division of labour, expanding markets and cities, and increasing the produc-tion of food and manufactures.

Everett, like the rest of New England, had lately shifted from free trade to the advocacy of a protective tariff, particularly for the region's nascent textile manufacturers. The protectionists were looking around wildly for textbooks and academics who would support their cause, since the works of Adam Smith and J.B. Say were dominant in American universities. Meeting and being impressed with John Rae and hearing of his new protectionist work, Everett was enthusiastic about him and arranged, sight unseen, to publish the book in Boston.

Apparently, Everett had bought a pig in a poke. Reviewing it in the *North American Review*, Everett damned Rae's *New Principles* with faint praise. He had been looking for a hard-hitting protectionist tract; instead, he found the book filled with technical jargon he could barely comprehend. And much of it had little or no bearing on the tariff issue. The bulk of the book dealt with the theory of capital and interest, and the importance of the expansion of capital to the growth of a nation. As Everett shrewdly pointed out, these views were not really at variance with those of Adam Smith. And none of it bore directly on the protectionist issue.

To Rae himself the connections were clear, if too remote for those interested in public policy. He believed that economic development depended jointly on new inventions and their application in capital investment, and most of his proposed government policies were subsidies and bounties to new inventions and industries, to be financed by heavy tariffs on the imports of 'luxuries'. In that way, Rae's Calvinist soul would be satisfied, for the government would be imposing moral principles by promoting thrift, invention and industry, while discouraging sinful luxuries, especially, in a prefigurement of Thorstein Veblen, where 'consumption is ... conspicuous' and therefore particularly wasteful. Rae's denunciation of luxurious consumption, which Rae boldly called 'a loss to the society, in proportion to their amount', did not sit very well with Everett, but his main criticism was that the country needed a 'well-written and well-reasoned essay on this [protectionist] question', a work of 'sufficient compass and authority to serve as a textbook'. Clearly, John Rae's work did not fill the bill.

The book was a commercial failure, and was quickly forgotten. The understandably chagrined and embittered Rae wrote in a letter, years later, that 'unfortunately, I was induced to publish in Boston, under the assurance from A.H. Everett that it would be appreciated there. He was, however, I believe scared of it. Could not make up his mind, nor could anyone there, if I was right or wrong, and so passed it by with praise of its style, etc. This damned it'. In addition, the free traders and the worshippers at the shrine of Adam Smith – who came in for considerable direct criticism in the book – attacked Rae's work. But possibly more fatal than any of these factors was the timing of the book. For after the tariff of 1833, lowering tariffs considerably, tariff agitation in the United States began to subside, and the tariff was repeatedly lowered throughout the 1840s. Free trade had apparently triumphed, at least until the Civil War.

In Canada, furthermore, there were scarcely any economists or academics fit to appraise Rae's work, and in Britain there was a general scorn for 'colonials', and failure to take North Americans seriously. In England, however, Nassau Senior, whose work on capital and interest was not far from Rae's, read the *New Principles* by the mid-1840s and admired it greatly, and traces of Rae can be found in Senior's later writings. Senior passed the book on to John Stuart Mill, who commended it warmly in his overwhelmingly popular 1848 treatise, the *Principles of Political Economy*. Rae heard of Mill's praise five years later, through a Canadian friend, and wrote warmly if mournfully to Mill that 'it is the only thing connected with that publication which has afforded me any gratification'.

Here a mystery arises for the history of economic thought. Despite Mill's warm commendation of Rae's book in what was the dominant treatise on economics for a generation, no economist anywhere picked up on the reference, and knowledge of Rae virtually disappeared. The only exception was the great Italian classical economist Francesco Ferrara (1810–1900), who translated Rae's *New Principles* into Italian in the mid-1850s. Apart from that, nothing. W. Stanley Jevons, devoted to the history of economic thought, apparently never heard of the book, and even the great Böhm-Bawerk had never read John Rae when in the 1880s he wrote the first edition of his *History and Critique of Interest Theories*. Rae remained unknown to economists until his memory was revived, and his work reprinted, by Professor Charles Whitney Mixter at the turn of the twentieth century. Perhaps a clue to the puzzle is in Böhm-Bawerk's later editions, where he points out that Mill's encomiums to Rae, while warm, were general and even banal, and scarcely conveyed the brilliance and originality of his work on capital and interest. As Böhm-Bawerk explains it:

> But it is a strange fact that in all his numerous quotations [from Rae] John Stuart Mill never included any of the material which constitutes the essence of Rae's original ideas. He quotes, instead, merely ornamental incidentals, and even among those only the sort of thing that could be used to illustrate the traditional doctrines that Mill himself was presenting. And since Rae's book seems to have been read in the original by only extremely few persons, just the most interesting part of its contents remained unknown to his contemporaries. There was little likelihood that they, and even less that subsequent generations would be apprised by Mill's quotations of the importance of the book, or impelled to conduct any research into his quickly forgotten work.[27]

Disappointed in the reception of his book, unemployed and destitute, Rae won an appointment as headmaster of a government district grammar school in what was then the brawling frontier town of Hamilton, Ontario. There he lived in genteel poverty on a low salary and was continually in debt, but he was apparently beloved by his students and was known in Hamilton as a graceful and elegant ice skater as well as president of the Hamilton Literary Society. There he played a prominent role in the first contingent of Hamilton militia which, in 1837 and 1838, helped put down an armed rebellion by Canadian nationalists anxious to cut the ties with the empire. Rae engaged in aeronautical experiments with balloons, and wrote increasingly on geological topics. He also continued to work on the economic geography of Canada, and finally in 1840, completed his *magnum opus,* a lengthy book on the 'Outlines of the natural History and Statutes of Canada'.

Unfortunately, however, the decade of the 1840s saw fate land a series of hammer blows against John Rae. First, the manuscript of his book on Canada was irretrievably lost en route to possible publishers in New York. Second, after teaching in Hamilton for 14 years, Rae was summarily fired in 1848. The problem was that Rae became inevitably embroiled in educational political struggles, particularly over getting Presbyterians appointed to teaching and administrative posts in the Anglican-dominated Ontario school system. Furthermore, in 1843, in the Disruption, the Church of Scotland (and hence its affiliated Presbyterian Church in Canada) split in irretrievable schism, with hard-core Calvinists opposed to secular state domination of the Church splitting off from the established Church of Scotland and forming the Free Church. As we might expect from his character, Rae, along with his friends, joined the Free Church, which lost him the political support of the established Presbyterian officials dominant in his school district. Rae's stay in Hamilton was doomed.

Rae then left Canada and did some school teaching in Boston and New York, where, a year after his dismissal, he received another staggering blow – news of the death of his wife, Eliza. Discouraged, restless, penniless and uprooted at the age of 53, John Rae began a new life of wandering and drift. Attracted by the gold rush, he sailed to California, where he did a little school teaching and carpentry; in ill-health in California, Rae was soon off to the Hawaiian Islands, where he was to spend the rest of his days. There, on the island of Maui, Rae prospered economically for the first time, teaching English to Hawaiian natives, farming, and functioning as medical agent for the board of health. Rae began to blossom politically because of his new friendship with a fellow Scottish expatriate, Robert Crichton Wyllie, a surgeon from Glasgow University, wealthy businessman, and now minister of foreign relations of the Hawaiian Kingdom. With Wyllie's patronage, Rae became coroner, notary public, medical attendant and district judge in Maui.

His favourable circumstances now led Rae to resume his various scientific interests: he wrote articles and papers on geology, particularly on volcanoes, ocean tides, and Hawaiian geology; on the Polynesian language; and tried to revive interest in marketing his long-neglected navigational inventions.

But John Rae was incapable of holding onto money, and so perpetually reverted to destitution. With his patron Wyllie dead, and in ill-health, Rae accepted the offer of an old friend and former student to pay for his trip from Hawaii to live with him permanently at his home in Staten Island. But Rae died on Staten Island the following year.

Restless and eccentric, John Rae in a sense wrote a suitable and poignant epitaph for himself in *New Principles*, in his sensitive appreciation of the lone role of the inventor or innovator in society:

> Pursuing objects not to be perceived by others, or if perceived, whose importance is beyond the reach of their conceptions, the motives of their conduct are necessarily misapprehended. They are esteemed either idlers, culpably negligent in turning account the talents they have got, dullards deficient in the common parts necessary to discharge the common offices of life, or madmen unfit to be trusted with their performance; shut out from the esteem or fellowship of those whose regard they might prize, they are brought into contact with those with whom they can have nothing in common, knaves who laugh at them as their prey, fools who pity them as their fellows. Their characters misunderstood, debarred from all sympathy, uncheered by any approbations, the 'eternal war', they have to wage with fortune, is doubly trying, because they are aware, that, if they succumb, they will be borne off the field, not only unknown, but misconceived.[28]

4.12 Nassau Senior, praxeology, and John Stuart Mill

There are few economists in any age who are self-conscious about the methodology of their craft. Even more was this true during the alleged heyday of the British classical school which, as we have seen, was an era of disintegration rather than triumph of the Ricardian paradigm. But an excellent methodologist was one of the finest economists of that epoch, Nassau W. Senior. Senior indeed took up the torch of the praxeological method that had been expounded and used by the great French economist of the early nineteenth century, Jean-Baptiste Say.

Senior began to spell out his views on methodology in his very first, introductory lecture at Oxford in 1826. With exceptional clarity, he began by stating that economic theory rests on the broadest general insights about human nature, insights that are self-evident in the sense that once stated they command universal assent. Economic theory, says Senior, 'will be found to rest on a very few general propositions, which are the result of observation, or consciousness, and which almost every man, as soon as he hears them, admits, as familiar to his thoughts, or at least, as included in his previous knowledge'. But if these premises, or axioms, rest on general knowledge of man and the world, then conclusions deduced from them must possess equal generality: 'Its conclusions are also nearly as general as its premises – those which relate to the nature and production of wealth, are universally true.' It is then the task of the economist to narrow down the conclusions to those areas which are directly relevant to the problem at hand. Thus:

> those [conclusions] which relate to the distribution of wealth, are liable to be affected by peculiar institutions of particular countries – in the cases, for instance, of slavery, corn laws or poor-laws – the natural state of things can be laid down as

a general rule, and the anomalies produced by particular disturbing causes can be afterwards accounted for.

As specifically part of his apodictic conclusions, Nassau Senior generalized laws that other economists had been approaching or groping for. For example, Senior defined 'wealth' as all goods and services that possess utility and which therefore will be purchased in exchange. He then stated in his first 'fundamental proposition': 'That every person is desirous to obtain, with as little sacrifice as possible, as much as possible of the articles of wealth.' Not only did Senior thus ably generalize some important insights of universal human action: he also in that way dismissed Adam Smith's unfortunate distinction between 'productive' (material) and 'unproductive' (immaterial) labour; everything which people desired and were willing to buy was 'productive'. It is because Ricardo at least implicitly adopted this distinction that he was able to dismiss cavalierly any explanation of the pricing of immaterial services and hence to move toward a cost theory of value.

In elaborating on this first fundamental proposition, Senior moved on to an eloquent summation of the relationship between desire, individual diversity, choice, and human effort:

> In stating that every man desires to obtain additional wealth with as little sacrifice as possible, we must not be supposed to mean that everybody, or indeed anybody, wishes for an indefinite quantity of everything... What we mean to state is, that no person feels his whole wants to be adequately supplied; that every person has some unsatisfied desires which he believes that additional wealth would gratify. The nature and urgency of each individual's wants are as various as the differences in individual character. Some may wish for power, others for distinction, others for leisure... Money seems to be the only object for which the desire is universal; and it is so because money is abstract wealth...
>
> As equal diversity exists in the amount and the kind of the sacrifice which different individuals, or even the same individual, will encounter in the pursuit of wealth.[29]

Two decades later, on returning to the Drummond chair at Oxford, Nassau Senior, in his introductory lectures in 1847, returned to the problem of the methodology of economics (published in 1852 in his *Four Introductory Lectures on Political Economy*). He now defined economic science as expounding 'the laws regulating the production and distribution of wealth, so far as they depend on the action of the human mind' – the latter clause emphasizing that economics was a 'mental' rather than 'physical' science. Indeed, Senior saw clearly that the proper scientific method was dualistic, the physical sciences treating the properties of matter, while the mental ones study 'the sensations, faculties, and habits of the human mind, and regard in matter only the qualities which produce them'. The methods of the two sciences must necessarily differ, for the physical sciences 'being only secondarily conversant with mind, draw their premises almost exclusively from observation or hypothesis'. Observation may guide such strictly empirical sciences as technology, but such sciences as physics, 'those which treat only of magnitude and number. ... draw them altogether from hypothesis'. The physical sciences must rest on tentative hypotheses, precisely because they are 'only secondarily conversant with mind'. On the other hand, 'the mental sciences and the mental arts draw their premises principally from consciousness. The subjects with which they are chiefly conversant are the working of the human mind. And the only mind whose workings a man really knows is his own'. And of course economics was one of the mental sciences.

In this way, Nassau Senior, with brilliant clarity, developed the essentials of what Ludwig von Mises, a century later, would call 'praxeology'. As in the case of other mental sciences, economics cannot, like the physical sciences, conduct experiments. It is true, Senior noted, that economics deals with such material matters as production, productivity and diminishing returns, but the 'political economist dwells on them only with reference to the mental phenomena which they serve to explain', as among the motives or sources or capital, rent, profit, etc. In short, wrote Senior,

> All the technical terms, therefore, of Political Economy, represent either purely mental ideas, such as *demand, utility, value,* and *abstinence,* or objects which, though some of them may be material, are considered by the Political Economist so far only as they are the causes of certain affectations of the human mind, such as *wealth, capital, rent, wages,* and *profits.*

It is important to consider the once famous battle between Nassau Senior and John Stuart Mill on economic method, for Mill was soon to become the undeservedly towering economist for the next half-century. Mill agreed that economics, as a mental science, cannot conduct experiments; but he did not conclude, with Senior, that its premises or axioms should be complete, general and apodictic. Instead, he asserted that the foundations and premises of economics can only be 'hypothetical', that is, they must make assumptions that abstract from, and hence distort, reality. The axioms of economics are only partially, or hypothetically, true. In short, for Mill, since economics focuses on man's desire for wealth, it must *assume,* even though admittedly falsely, that man's *only* desire is for wealth. Thus, as Mill stated in his *Essays on Some Unsettled Questions in Political Economy* in 1844:

> Political Economy ... does not treat of the whole of man's nature as modified by the social state, nor of the whole conduct of man in society. It is concerned with him solely as a being who desires to possess wealth, and who is capable of

judging the comparative efficacy of means for obtaining that end. It predicts only such of the phenomena of the social state as take place in consequence of the pursuit of wealth. It makes entire abstraction of every other human passion or motive… Political Economy considers mankind as occupied solely in acquiring and consuming wealth; and aims at showing what is the course of action into which mankind living in a state of society, would be impelled, if that motive … were absolute ruler of all their actions… Not that any political economist was ever so absurd as to suppose that mankind are really thus constituted, but because this is the mode in which science must necessarily proceed.[30]

Mill conceded that the founding assumption of his economics was 'an arbitrary definition of man'. For it reasoned from 'assumed premises – from premises which might be totally without foundation in fact, and which are not pretended to be universally in accordance with it…'.

And thus, John Stuart Mill, in this adumbration of the methodology of the deliberate creation of the fallacious 'economic man' – the man who is only interested in pursuing wealth – elaborated what might be called the orthodox, or dominant, 'positivist' methodology in economics. The positivist method, set down with such fallacious and fateful clarity by Mill, after a struggle with alternative praxeological (as well as other) methods, finally triumphed in the mid-twentieth century with the unfortunate rise to dominance of the positivism of Vilfredo Pareto and Milton Friedman.

Part of the motivation of Senior's thoughtful lectures on method in 1847 was precisely to engage in a critique and demolition of Millian positivism. Since Mill, like Smith and Ricardo before him, returned to their fallacious limitation of 'wealth' to material goods, the resulting distortion of value and production theory made Senior's task all the more important. Senior's assault on Mill, as well as on Ricardo, was formidable and devastating. He made their essential differences clear:

neither the reasoning of Mr. Mill, nor the example of Mr. Ricardo, induce me to treat Political Economy as a hypothetical science. I do not think it necessary, and, if unnecessary, I do not think it desirable.

It appears to me, that if we substitute for Mr. Mill's hypothesis, that wealth and costly enjoyment are the *only* object of human desire, the statement that they are universal and constant objects of desire, that they are desired by all men and at all times, we shall have laid an equally firm foundation for our subsequent reasoning, *and have put a truth in the place of an arbitrary assumption.* (Italics added.)

Senior goes on to concede that indeed we shall not now be able to infer, from the fact that a labourer may so act as to obtain higher wages, or a capitalist higher profits, that 'they will certainly act in that manner'. But, at least 'we shall be able to infer that they will do so in the absence of disturbing causes. And if we are able, as will frequently be the case, to state the cases in which these causes may be expected to exist, and the force with which they are likely to operate, we shall have removed all objection to the positive as opposed to the hypothetical treatment of the science'.[31]

One danger of the hypothetical method, Senior wisely and prophetically points out, is the perpetual danger of forgetting that the premises are not complete and are only partial and even false assumptions. Another and even deeper flaw is that, since the assumptions are false from the very beginning, there is no way to bring in experience or observation to correct or even check on the conclusions of the abstract analysis. In this way, positivists, who always trumpet their method as being the only truly scientific and 'empirical' one, turn out to be resting on runaway and uncorrectable false premises. On the other hand, and ironically, the praxeological method, which has long been accused of *a priori* mysticism, is the only one that bases theory on broadly known and deeply empirical – indeed universally true – premises!

Being universally true, the praxeological method provides *complete* and general laws rather than partial, and hence generally false, ones. As Marian Bowley astutely sees the difference:

> Thus in the question of the definition of the desire for wealth: if it is stated in Mill's form that everyone always prefers wealth to anything else [the 'economic man'], with the added warning that it is only a hypothesis, the constant relation between the desire for wealth and all other conflicting motives is not defined completely by the general law. It remains necessary to introduce a further premise in each individual stating the general relation of other motives to that of the desire for wealth, as well as evaluating the actual variables. Now Senior's explanation of the desire for wealth includes information as to the interconnections between the variables.

Or, as Miss Bowley explains further:

> Senior's substitution of net advantages for earnings is equivalent to defining in general terms the relation between all the variables which influence the distribution of resources between occupations, instead of leaving that relation to be considered afresh in each use.[32]

Thus, a positivist, assuming that businessmen are always and only interested in maximizing money profits, might well overlook and ignore instances of businessmen placing other motives (such as giving an executive post to one's relative) higher than profits. Or, worse still, if acknowledging such instances, he would be tempted to dismiss these cases contemptuously as 'irrational behaviour'. Similarly, Charles Dickens, who repeatedly spoofed and attacked classical economics in his novels, had a utilitarian son refuse to help his impoverished mother on the ground that the science of political economy told him that to be rational a man must always buy in the cheapest market and sell in the dearest. And since Smith–Ricardo–Mill classical economics solely emphasized cost of production and therefore was totally blocked from even talking about the consumer, it was especially open to this Dickensian misconception.

4.13 Notes

1. J.A. Schumpeter, *History of Economic Analysis* (New York: Oxford University Press, 1954), p. 473 (italics in original).
2. Alexander Gray, *The Development of Economic Doctrine* (London: Longmans, Green and Co., 1931), pp. 170–71. Noting that Ricardo habitually wrote in sweeping conclusions, followed by mumbled qualifications and backtrackings, enabling his followers to claim that such pursuers of the Ricardian logic as Marx and Henry George 'misrepresented' Ricardo, Gray retorts that 'perhaps the final lesson to be learned from Ricardo is that the literary graces are not merely ornamental but useful, and that he who is deficient in the art of expression has only himself to blame if he is misrepresented'. Amen! Ibid., p. 189.
3. No more delightful passage has been written on the effectiveness of the obscure than in the sparkling essay of H.L. Mencken on the work of Thorstein Veblen: 'What was genuinely remarkable about them [Veblen's ideas] was not their novelty, or their complexity, nor even the fact that a professor should harbor them; it was the astoundingly grandiose and rococo manner of their statement, the almost unbelievable tediousness and flatulence of the gifted headmaster's prose, his unprecedented talent for saying nothing in an august and heroic manner... If one tunneled under his great moraines and stalagmites of words, dug down into his vast kitchen-midden of discordant and raucous polysyllables, blew up the hard, thick shell of his almost theological manner, what one found in his discourse was chiefly a mass of platitudes – the self-evident made horrifying, the obvious in terms of the staggering.
   'Marx, I daresay, had said a good deal of it long before him, and what Marx overlooked had been said over and over again by his heirs and assigns. But Marx, at this business, labored under a technical handicap; he wrote in German, a language he actually understood. Professor Veblen submitted himself to no such disadvantage. Though born, I believe, in these States, and resident here all his life, he achieved the effect, perhaps without employing the means, of thinking in some unearthly foreign language – say Swahili, Sumerian or Old Bulgarian – and then painfully clawing his thought into a copious but uncertain and book-learned English. The result was a style that affected the higher cerebral centers like a constant roll of subway expresses. The second result was a sort of bewildered numbness of the senses, as before some fabulous and unearthly marvel. And the third result, if I make no mistake, was the celebrity of the professor as a Great Thinker.' H.L. Mencken, 'Professor Veblen', *A Mencken Crestomathy* (New York: Knopf, 1949), pp. 269–70.
4. St Clair writes about the poet and ardent Ricardian Thomas De Quincey: 'De Quincey, a great admirer of Ricardo, attributed his obscurity to profundity of thought. It is natural, said the author of the *Opium Eater*, that a man of brilliant intellect should express himself in elliptical language, difficult for less gifted persons to follow...'. Oswald St Clair, *A Key to Ricardo* (1957, New York: M. Kelley, 1965), p. xxiii.
5. Schumpeter, op. cit., note 1, p. 474.
6. Senior's ancestors had been prosperous merchants. His grandfather, Nassau Thomas Senior, had converted from Judaism to Christianity in the mid-eighteenth century. Nassau Thomas's father, Moses Aaron Senior, had emigrated from Hamburg in the 1720s; he had come from a long line of Spanish–Portuguese Jews who had been merchants and financiers in Spain and had emigrated to Amsterdam and Hamburg.
7. S.G. Checkland, 'The Propagation of Ricardian Economics in England', *Economica*, n.s., 16 (Feb. 1949), pp. 40–52; Ronald Meek, 'The Decline of Ricardian Economics in England', *Economica*, n.s. 17 (Feb. 1950), pp. 43–62.
8. Other writers doggedly pushing underconsumptionist fallacies in this period include the protectionist Yorkshire landowner and later MP Edward Stillingfleet Cayley (1802–62);

Captain William R.A. Pettman; and a top royal bureaucrat in India, Sir William Henry Sleeman (1788–1856).

9. Since Meek's article, D.P. O'Brien, in the first comprehensive study of McCulloch, has demonstrated that McCulloch had abandoned the Ricardian labour theory of value for the more qualified Smithian cost-of-production theory. In fact, O'Brien shows that McCulloch was far more Smithian than Ricardian. D.P. O'Brien, *J.R. McCulloch: A Study in Classical Economics* (New York: Barnes & Noble, 1970).

10. Frank W. Fetter, 'The Rise and Decline of Ricardian Economics', *History of Political Economy*, 1 (Spring 1969), pp. 67–84.

11. Quoted in Barry Gordon, 'Criticism of Ricardian Views on Value and Distribution in the British Periodicals, 1820–1850', *History of Political Economy*, 1 (Autumn 1969), p. 380.

12. Schumpeter, op. cit., note 1, p. 580n. Also see Edwin Cannan, *A History of the Theories of Production & Distribution* (3rd ed., London: Staples Press, 1917), pp. 133–4.

13. Frank A. Fetter, 'Rent', *Encyclopedia of the Social Sciences*, reprinted in M. Rothbard (ed.), *Capital, Interest, and Rent: Essays in the Theory of Distribution, by Frank A. Fetter* (Kansas City: Sheed Andrews & McMeel, 1977), p. 368.

14. It has only recently been recognized that Bailey was philosophically Austrian – an insight buried in Robert Rauner's neglected 1956 doctoral dissertation at the University of London, 'Samuel Bailey and Classical Economics'. Denis P. O'Brien, 'Classical Reassessments', in W.O. Thweatt (ed.), *Classical Political Economy: A Survey of Recent Literature* (Boston: Kluwer, 1988), pp. 199–200.

15. Thor W. Bruce, 'The Economic Theories of John Craig, A Forgotten English Economist', *Quarterly Journal of Economics*, 52 (August 1938), p. 699.

16. Whately's biographer noted that Oxford 'was one way, and Richard Whately the other. Oxford had resigned itself to Orthodoxy and Toryism and Whately was an inquirer and a liberal'. In W.J. Fitzpatrick, *Anecdotal Memoirs of Richard Whately ...* (London, 1864), I, p. 56, quoted in Salim Rashid, 'Richard Whately and Christian Political Economy at Oxford and Dublin', *Journal of the History of Ideas*, 38 (Jan.–Mar. 1977), p. 148. In 1826, Whately anonymously published a rousing and controversial pamphlet, *Letters of the Church, by an Episcopalian*, calling for disestablishment of the Anglican Church, and separation of Church and state. Ibid.

17. The Rev. John McVickar, professor of political economy and moral philosophy at Columbia University, was moved to rewrite Whately's *Easy Lessons* for an American audience, in his own primer for children, *First Lessons in Political Economy* (1835).

18. Laurence S. Moss, *Mountifort Longfield: Ireland's First Professor of Political Economy* (Ottawa, Ill.: Green Hill Pubs, 1976), pp. 39–42.

19. One English writer who adopted catallactics during this period was the pseudonymous Patrick Plough who, in the custom of the day, both introduced and explained the term within the title of his tract, *Letters on the Rudiments of a Science, called, formerly, improperly, Political Economy, recently more pertinently, Catallactics* (London, 1842). See Israel Kirzner, *The Economic Point of View: An Essay in the History of Economic Thought* (Princeton, N.J.: Van Nostrand, 1960), pp. 72–5.

20. E.R.A. Seligman, 'On Some Neglected British Economists, I', *Economic Journal*, 13 (Sept. 1903), pp. 360–1.

21. Lloyd's 'special utility' was his term for what would later be called 'marginal utility'; 'abstract' or 'general' utility would later be called 'total utility'. See Seligman, op. cit., note 20, pp. 360–1.

22. Kendall was born to a Massachusetts farm family, and graduated from Dartmouth College in 1811 at the head of his class. He became a lawyer, and emigrated to Kentucky in 1814, where he functioned as attorney, editor and postmaster. He became editor of the important *Frankfort (Ky) Argus* in the capital of Kentucky, in 1814, and later became a leading Jacksonian brain-truster and postmaster-general.

23. Quoted in Gordon, op. cit., note 11, p. 384.

24. Bailey, however, did add a welcome methodological critique of James Mill's clumsy attempt to define away the increase of the value of wine through aging as some sort of mystical, vicarious expenditure of a year's worth of labour. As Bailey sardonically rebut-

ted Mill's assertion that the equivalent 'labour may be correctly considered as having been expended' on the wine: 'a fact may be correctly considered as having taken place only when it really has taken place'. Colonel Torrens also provided a similar critique of Mill's labour theory.

25. Moss, op. cit., note 18, p. 67.
26. Ibid., pp. 68, 201.
27. Eugen von Böhm-Bawerk, *Capital and Interest, Vol. I, History and Critique of Interest Theories* (South Holland, Ill.: Libertarian Press, 1959), p. 208.
28. Quoted in R. Warren James, *John Rae: Political Economist* (Toronto: University of Toronto Press, 1965), I, pp. 191–2.
29. Published in Senior's *Outline of the Science of Political Economy* (1836), cited in Marian Bowley, *Nassau Senior and Classical Economics* (1937, New York: A.M. Kelley, 1949), pp. 47–8.
30. It should be noted that, in this passage, Mill also made two exceptions to his assumed exclusive motivation of the desire for wealth: aversion to labour, and desire to consume at present. But he correctly added while these motives may conflict with the pursuit of wealth, they also 'accompany it always as a drag, or impediment, are therefore inseparably mixed up in the consideration of it'.
31. Senior's use of the term 'positive' we would now say is 'praxeologic', his 'hypothetical' we would now say is broadly 'positivist'.
32. Bowley, op. cit., note 29, pp. 63, 62n.

5 Monetary and banking thought, I: the early bullionist controversy

5.1   The restriction and the emergence of the bullionist controversy

The Bank of England had been the bulwark of the English (and, by serving as bankers' bank, of the Scottish) banking system since its founding in 1694. The bank was the recipient of an enormous amount of monopoly privilege from the British government. Not only was it the receiver of all public funds, but no other corporate banks were allowed to exist, and no partnerships of more than six partners were allowed to issue bank notes. As a result, by the late eighteenth century, the Bank of England was serving as an inflationary engine of bank deposits and especially of paper money, on top of which a flood of small partnership banks ('country banks') were able to pyramid their own notes, using Bank of England notes as their reserve. As if this were not enough privilege, when the bank got into trouble by overinflating, it was permitted to suspend specie payment, that is, refuse to meet its obligation to redeem its notes and deposits in specie. This privilege was granted to the bank several times during the century after it opened its doors. However, each time the suspension, or 'restriction' of specie payment lasted only a few years.

In the 1790s, however, a startlingly new epoch began in the history of the British monetary system. In February 1793, a generation of fierce warfare broke out between revolutionary France and the crowned heads of Europe, led by Great Britain. While not exactly continuous, the war lasted, with slight interruptions, until Napoleon was finally defeated in 1815 and the monarchies of Europe reimposed the Bourbon dynasty upon the French nation. This massive war effort meant a rapid escalation of monetary inflation, government spending, and public debt by the British government.

During the 1780s, the inflationary process of bank credit expansion had managed to double the number of country banks in England, totalling nearly 400 by the outbreak of war. The shock of the war led to a massive financial crisis, including runs on the country banks, as well as numerous bankruptcies among banks and financial houses. One-third of the country banks suspended specie payment during 1793.

For a few years, the bank saved itself by pursuing a cautious and conservative policy. But soon, inflationary war finance, the drain of gold abroad in response to higher purchasing power elsewhere, the alarms of war, and the increased demand for gold upon the banks, all combined to precipitate a massive run on banks, including the Bank of England, in February 1797. The country banks suspended specie payments, and the government brought matters to a head by 'forcing' the bank to suspend specie payments, a 'Restriction' which the Bank of England of course was all too delighted to accept. For the bank could now continue operations, could expand credit, inflate its supply of notes and deposits, and insist that *its* debtors must repay their loans, while it could avoid the bother of redeeming its own obligations in specie. In effect, bank notes were unofficially legal tender, indeed virtually the only legal tender, and they were made official legal tender in 1812 until the resumption of specie payments in 1821.

At the beginning, the general view held the restriction to be strictly temporary, and indeed the decree, at any given time, was only supposed to last for a few years. But the restriction was extended repeatedly, and was eventually continued for 24 years, from 1797 to 1821. Until the end of the eighteenth century, it was unthinkable that Great Britain could be on an irredeemable fiat standard for an entire generation.

Apart from a few years during the continental paper period of the American Revolution, the South Sea and Mississippi bubbles of the early eighteenth century, the hyperinflated *assignats* during the French Revolution, or a few brief suspensions of specie payment, the world had always been on some form of gold or silver standard. All these episodes had been mercifully brief if catastrophic. But now, after a while, it began to dawn on the British public that the era of inflationary fiat paper would continue indefinitely.

Great Britain suspended specie payments indefinitely so as to permit the Bank of England, and the banking system as a whole, to maintain and greatly expand the previously inflated system of fractional reserve banking. Accordingly, the bank was able to greatly inflate credit and the money supply of notes and deposits. Statistics for the period are sparse, but it is clear that from 1797 until the end of the Napoleonic Wars the supply of money approximately doubled. This monetary inflation had several predictable – and generally unwelcome – consequences. Domestic prices skyrocketed, the price of silver and especially of gold bullion vaulted upwards in relation to the official par with the pound, and the pound depreciated in the foreign exchange market.[1] The monetary inflation, as usual, proceeded in fits and starts rather than as a smooth line, and so the various consequences in domestic prices, bullion, and foreign exchanges were themselves scarcely uniform or proportional. But the rough general trend was unmistakeable, with the three latter effects each eventually rising to a peak of approximately 40 or 50 per cent over their pre-restriction levels.

Before 1800, decades of inconvertible paper money in England would have been considered unthinkable, and so previous monetary theorists had scarcely contemplated or analysed such an economy. But now writers were forced to come to grips with fiat paper, and to propose policies to cope with an unwelcome new era.

The political controversies during the restriction period centred on explaining the price inflation and depreciation and on assessing the role of the Bank of England. The 'bullionists' pointed out that the cause of the price inflation, the rise in the price of bullion over par, and the depreciation of the pound was the fiat money expansion. They further maintained that the central role in that inflation was played by the Bank of England, freed of its necessity to redeem in specie. Their opponents, the 'anti-bullionists', tried absurdly to absolve the government and its privileged bank of all blame, and to attribute all unwelcome consequences to specific problems in the particular markets involved. Depreciation in foreign exchange was charged to the outflow of bullion caused by excessive imports or by British war expenditures abroad (presumably unrelated to the increased amount of paper pounds or to the lowered purchasing power of the pound). The rise in the price of bullion was supposedly caused by an increased 'real' demand for gold or silver (again unrelated to the depreciated paper pound). The increases in domestic prices received less attention from the two sides of the debate, but they were attributed by the anti-bullionists to wartime disruptions and shortages in supply. Any *ad hoc* cause could be seized upon, so long as the great integrating cause, the expansion of bank credit and paper money, was carefully ignored and let off the hook. In short, the anti-bullionists reverted to mercantilist worry about *ad hoc* causes and the balance of trade on the market. The previous hard-won analysis of money and overall prices went by the board.

5.2   The bullionist controversy begins

The announcement of the restriction brought a flurry of activity, pro and con, consisting not of extensive theoretical analyses but of general statements of approval or warnings of things to come. The prime minister, William Pitt the Younger (1759–1806), and his followers egregiously maintained that there was no cause for alarm, since unlike the *assignats* of the evil French Revolutionaries, the Bank of England was issuing 'private' rather than government paper. Hence the reluctance of the government to make bank notes legal tender until nearly the end of the war, although its policies made them legal tender *de facto*. The opposition leader, Charles James Fox (1749–1806), denounced the restriction and called for resumption of specie payments, and also pointed out that the war against France bore ultimate responsibility for the plunge into fiat paper. And the distinguished playwright and Whig M.P. Richard Brinsley Sheridan (1751–1816) warned that 'we were doomed to all the horrors of a paper circulation'.

The inflationist economic historian Norman Silberling summed up the Fox–Sheridan position unsympathetically as follows:

Fox and Sheridan constituted themselves the leaders of a persistent tirade against the Bank Suspension, not upon grounds of financial principle, but because the Suspension permitted that institution to support the activities of what they regarded as a militaristic, reactionary, and withal bankrupt administration…[T]hey concentrated their eloquent invective against this alliance of Bank and State which was productive of 'robbery and fraud'; and they urged that the Bank be divorced forthwith from their public responsibilities and their participation in the

War. Let the Ministry repay the debts of the Bank (if it could!) and let the bank
resume the honest payment of their Notes.[2]

For the first few years, however, all seemed well. The initial caution of the
bank and the minimal expansion of government demands on its credit, combined with the inevitable time lag between issue of new money and rise in
prices to lull Britons into a false sense of security. The price of food rose
substantially in 1799, but it was easy for the anti-bullionists and other administration apologists to dismiss this rise in a flurry of pamphlets as the product
of crop failure and wartime disruption in the import of grain. Even the Rev.
Thomas Robert Malthus, afterwards to emerge as at least a partial bullionist,
diffidently raised the monetary question, and then dismissed the increase of
paper money as 'rather...the effect than the cause of the high price of provisions'.[3]

In the Spring of 1800, however, war expenditures and bank financing
government debt accelerated, leading to a depreciation of the pound by 9 per
cent in the main foreign exchange market of Hamburg, and gold bullion
appreciated to 9 per cent above its official par value. In addition, domestic
prices rose even more sharply than before. The depreciation of the pound had
evidently begun.

The first phase of the bullionist controversy (1800–4) started when one of
the best of the bullionists published his remarkable pamphlet on the cause of
the depreciation. Certainly there was little in the previous career of Walter
Boyd (c.1754–1837), a wealthy adventurer and seeker of state privilege, to
prepare one for a pamphlet of keen insight into the calamitous consequences
of irredeemable paper money. Boyd had been a wealthy English banker in
Paris, the chief partner of Boyd, Ker and Co., who had to flee for his life in
1793 from the wrath of the French Revolution, which also confiscated his
property. Back in London, Boyd established the banking firm of Boyd, Benfield
and Co., of which he was principal partner. A close friend of Prime Minister
William Pitt for many years, Boyd rode high in the British Establishment,
becoming an MP in 1796 from his partner Paul Benfield's pocket borough. In
1794, the firm floated an important loan to the Austrian emperor. Furthermore, Boyd, Benfield received the enormous contract of £30 million in
government debt after the beginning of the war with France.

Things began to go sour for Boyd in 1796, however, when the Bank of
England, whose loans had been keeping Boyd, Benfield and Co. afloat, failed
to renew its discounts. Boyd tried desperately to get Parliament to establish a
new board for the issue of a massive amount of notes, and the scheme received
considerable support, but it was ended by the opposition of William Pitt.

The only thing left for Boyd was to try to get more Bank of England loans,
and in Parliament during 1796 and 1797 he denounced the bank for too tight

a credit policy, presumably not mentioning himself as one of the prominent sufferers from its allegedly tight money. Facing 'ruin' Boyd managed to obtain financial aid from friends in the Navy Office, and he finally got the bank to lend Boyd, Benfield & Co. £80 000 in 1798. But Samuel Thornton (1755–1838), deputy governor of the Bank of England, and MP, warned Pitt that Boyd, Benfield & Co. was only being kept alive by bank largesse, and as a result, Pitt refused to let the House of Boyd contract for the 1799 public loan. Finally, Boyd, Benfield & Co. went bankrupt in March 1800, and the result was total financial ruin, so much so that Walter Boyd was reluctant to show his face in Parliament.

As might be expected, Boyd put the blame for his failure not on his own reckless feeding at the public trough, but on the niggardly policies of the Bank of England. In November 1800, Boyd wrote *A Letter to the Rt. Hon. William Pitt* published in 1801, which won quick fame and caused Boyd to publish a second edition later that year. With Boyd's *Letter*, the bullionist controversy was born, Boyd now denouncing the Bank of England not for overly tight credit but to the contrary for generating the inflation and monetary depreciation in the first place.

His new-found fame did Boyd little personal good, however, and he promptly went to France for financial manoeuvring. There he was arrested the following year, and jailed by the French until the end of the Napoleonic Wars. He then returned to England, wrote other financial pamphlets, and once again became an MP.

5.3 Boyd's *Letter to Pitt*

Walter Boyd did not intend his pamphlet, the *Letter to Pitt*, to be a treatise on monetary theory. It was, as one historian put it, a 'tract for the times', written in a 'heated temper', and the tract assumed a generally accepted set of monetary principles on the part of his readers. Nonetheless, since Adam Smith and the other eighteenth century economists could not have addressed their analyses to a non-existent inconvertible fiat money, Boyd felt called upon to extend the conventional analysis to this unwelcome new system that had suddenly come to Great Britain. In the course of doing so, Boyd not only launched the 'bullionist controversy', but also set forth an excellent exposition of what came to be known as the 'bullionist' position in the great controversy.

Boyd pointed to the three new and unwelcome conditions: the premium of gold bullion over the paper pound, the depreciation of the pound on the foreign exchange market, and the 'increase in the prices of almost all articles of necessity, convenients, and luxury, and indeed of almost every species of exchangeable value, which has been gradually taking place during the last two years, and which had recently arrived at so great a height'. He argued

that the cause of all three troublesome phenomena was the same: a depreciation of the value of the pound, brought about by 'the issue of Bank-notes,
uncontrolled by the obligation of paying them, in specie, on demand'. An
increase in the supply of money diminishes its value, whether in the form of a
premium on gold bullion or of a rise in the prices of goods. And 'the same
circumstances which raise the value of Gold in the home market, necessarily
tend to depreciate our currency when compared with currency of other countries'. Boyd summed up the bullionist position clearly in the preface to the
second edition (1801) of his *Letter*: 'The premium on bullion, the low rate of
exchange, and the high prices of commodities in general, are...symptoms
and effects of the superabundance of paper'.

If the supply of money is crucial to the movement of prices, bullion and
exchange rates, it becomes vital to clarify what precisely that supply may be.
Before Adam Smith, the eighteenth century British writers on money, such as
Hume and Harris, muddied the waters by including in the concept of money
virtually all liquid assets, such as bills of exchange and government securities. In the *Wealth of Nations*, however, Smith helped matters by distinguishing clearly between money, the general medium of exchange and the final
means of payment, and other liquid instruments that are exchanged *against*
money. Following Smith, Walter Boyd makes the distinction between money,
or 'ready money', and other assets crystal-clear:

> By the words 'Means of Circulation', 'Circulating Medium', and 'Currency',
> which are used almost as synonymous terms in this letter, I understand always
> *ready money*, whether consisting of Bank Notes or specie, in contradistinction to
> Bills of Exchange, Navy Bills, Exchequer Bills, or any other *negotiable* paper,
> which form no part of the circulating medium, as I have always understood that
> term. The latter is the *Circulator*; the former are merely *objects of circulation*.

Not only that: Boyd proceeded to go beyond Smith and to be the first to
clearly identify bank demand deposits as fully 'ready money' as bank notes.
As he put it: 'Credits in the Books of the Banks...may be considered as Bank
Notes *virtually*, though not *really* in circulation...'. Much grief and error
would have been spared economic thought as well as the development of
money and banking if the currency school – the mid-nineteenth century
successors to the bullionists – had heeded this lesson, and understood that
demand deposits were equivalent to bank notes as a part of the supply of
money.

On another crucial point, too, Boyd proved to be far superior to Adam
Smith. Like Cantillon and Turgot, Boyd objected to the unfortunate doctrine,
propounded by Hume and then by Smith, that an increase in the quantity of
money results in an equiproportional increase in the 'price level'. Considering the essence of the Hume model, of assuming a magically great propor-

tionate increase in the money supply and discussing the consequences, Boyd echoes Cantillon rather than Hume:

> if...this country had acquired, by supernatural means, and thrown into every channel of circulation, the same additional currency in gold and silver, within the same period, this influx, altogether disproportioned to the progress of the industry of the country; within that period, could not have failed to produce a very great rise in the price of every species of *property, not all with equal rapidity, but each by different degrees of celerity, according to the frequency or rarity of its natural contact with money.* (Italics added.)

Internationally, such a magical influx of gold and silver according to Boyd and Smith before him, would ordinarily have rapidly flowed out of the country, thereby limiting the inflationary harm that the inflow might do. Unfortunately, as in Smith, the mechanism for this allegedly rapid outflow is highly obscure. At any rate, Boyd pressed on to be the first to apply mainstream monetary theory to the problem of inconvertible fiat currencies. He begins by showing that since bank notes cannot be exported, there is no mechanism, as there is with specie, for draining off an 'excess' quantity of money to foreign countries. As a result, in the first place, the price rise resulting from an influx of specie would not be 'so great as that which has been occasioned by the introduction of so much paper, destitute of the essential quality of being constantly convertible into specie'.

More specifically, according to Boyd, the depreciation of fiat paper in terms of other currencies would be reflected in a rise in the price of gold or silver bullion, and an appreciation of foreign currencies on the foreign exchange market. This view, as Professor Salerno points out, provides the germ of the purchasing-power-parity theory of exchange rates under inconvertible fiat currencies:

> Specifically, Boyd contends that an increase in the supply of inconvertible paper money effects a general rise in domestic prices or, what is the same thing, a depreciation in the exchange value of the currency in terms of commodities which necessarily drives down the value of domestic currency in terms of foreign currencies whose exchange values have remained unchanged. This fall in the value of the inflated and depreciated domestic currency relative to foreign currencies is manifested in the depreciation of the exchange rate. Contained in Boyd's argument...is the seminal formulation of the purchasing-power-parity of exchange-rate determination which, of course, is the logical outcome of the application of the monetary approach to conditions of inconvertible paper currency.[4]

In addition, Walter Boyd set the tone for the bullionists following him by placing the full blame for the monetary inflation on the Bank of England rather than the country banks. For the country banks could not have expanded their notes in circulation, Boyd pointed out, unless their reserve base had expanded proportionately. And that reserve base was constituted by notes of the Bank of England. For the country banks remain under the same 'salutary control' as the Bank of England had been under before the advent of restriction. Just as the bank's notes had to be redeemed on demand in specie, so do the country banks' notes still have to be redeemed in the notes of the Bank of England. The key to the problem is the escape from redeemability that the government had permitted to the Bank of England. As Boyd put it:

> The circulation of Country Bank-notes must necessarily be proportioned to the sums, in specie or Bank of England notes, requisite to discharge such of them as may be presented for payment: but the paper of the Bank of England has no such limitation. It is itself now become (what the coin of the country only ought to be) the ultimate element into which the whole paper circulation of the country resolves itself. The Bank of England is the great source of all the circulation of the country; and, by the increase or diminution of its paper, the increase or diminution of that of every country-Bank is infallibly regulated...

Walter Boyd specifically cited and patterned himself on Adam Smith, and unfortunately also followed Smith in hailing the expansion of private redeemable bank notes as providing a less costly and more efficient 'highway in the sky' (though Boyd did not use that phrase). But, being an embattled Smithian in a new world of fiat money, Boyd stressed his militant opposition to bank notes in a context of fiat money. Boyd denounced inconvertible or 'forced' paper money as 'that dangerous quack-medicine, which, far from restoring vigour, gives only temporary artificial health, while it secretly undermines the vital powers of the country that has recourse to it'. Boyd concluded that restoring the nation's currency 'to its pristine purity', would be 'not only proper and practical, but indispensably necessary, in order to prevent the numberless calamities which the uncontrolled circulation of paper not convertible into specie, must infallibly produce'.

Boyd was what we may call a 'complete' bullionist, and was therefore a sophisticated one. He fully recognized that partial 'real' factors – such as government expenditures abroad, a sudden scarcity of food, or 'a sudden diminution of the confidence of foreigners, in consequence of any great national disaster' – could influence overall prices or the status of the pound in the foreign exchange market. But he also realized that such influences can only be trivial and temporary. The overriding causes of such price or exchange movements – not just in some remote 'long run' but at *all* times except temporary deviations – are monetary changes in the supply of and demand for money. Changes in 'real' factors can only have an important impact on exchange rates and general prices by altering the composition and the height of the demand for money on the market. But since market demands for money are neither homogeneous nor uniform nor do they ever change equiproportionately, real changes *will* almost always have an impact on the demand for money. As Professor Salerno writes·

> ...since real disturbances are invariably attended by 'distribution effects', i.e. gains and losses of income and wealth by the affected market participants, it is most improbable that initially nonmonetary disturbances would not ultimately entail relative changes in the various national demands for money...[U]nder inconvertible conditions, the relative changes in the demands for the various national currencies, their quantities remaining unchanged, would be reflected in their long-run appreciation or depreciation on the foreign exchange market.[5]

Here we must emphasize a crucial distinction between the proper status of the 'short run' and the 'long run' in economic theory. In price theory proper, the short run should take precedence, because it is the real-world market price, while the long run is the remote, ultimate tendency that never occurs, and could only take place if all the data were frozen for several years. In sum, we could only live in the improbable if not impossible world of long-run general equilibrium – where all profits and losses are zero – if all values, technologies and resources were frozen for years. But in *monetary* theory, the order of precedence should be different. For in monetary theory, the impact of partial 'real' factors on the price level, exchange rates, and on the balance of payments, are all ephemera determined by the general factors: the supply of and demand for money. These monetary influences are not 'long-run' in the sense of far off and remote, but are underlying and dominant every day in the real world. The monetary influence corresponding to the long run of general equilibrium would be a condition where all price levels and all real wage levels in a gold standard world would be identical, or strictly proportionate to the relative currency weights of gold. In a freely fluctuating, fiat money world, this would be the situation where all price levels would be strictly proportionate to the currency ratios at the international market exchange rates. But dominant influences of the supply and demand for money on price levels and exchange rates occur in the real world all the time, and always predominate over the ephemera of 'real' specific price and expenditure changes. Hence real-world analysis, which must always predominate, comprises short-run price analysis and slightly longer-run (but still far from final equilibrium) monetary reasoning.

To put it another way: in the real world, all prices are determined by the interaction of supply and demand. For individual prices, this means consumer valuations and consumer demands for a given stock: supply and demand in the real world. This is 'short-run' micro-analysis. For overall prices or the 'price level', the relevant supply and demand is the supply of and demand for money: the result of individual utility valuations of the given stock of money at any time. And while equally real and dominant in the 'macro-sphere', this is determinant in a slightly longer run than the superficial 'real' factors stressed by anti-bullionists in all ages.

5.4   The storm over Boyd: the anti-bullionist response

The *Letter* by someone of Boyd's renown and stature stung the British banking Establishment to the quick.[6] The Establishment responded with a flurry of pamphlets in opposition to Boyd, some of which were subsidized by the government. The key point was to defend the actions of the Bank of England, and to attribute the undesirable consequences of the inflation and depreciation to a hodge-podge of 'real' rather than monetary factors. The most eminent critic whom Boyd could rebut in the second edition of the *Letter*, published a few months after the original, was Sir Francis Baring (1740–1810), founder of the famous banking house of Baring Brothers and Co.

Baring had been born to a clothing manufacturer in Exeter. After plunging into commerce in London, Baring founded his own mercantile firm and became a multimillionaire, and known as the leading merchant in Europe. In addition to his mercantile and banking prominence, Baring was also a director, and then chairman of the board of the East India Company, as well as a long-time Whig MP. Curiously enough, when the restriction first appeared, Baring, in his first monetary pamphlet, while strongly supporting the suspension as a necessary wartime measure, was worried about the inevitable depreciation that would accompany over-issue of paper and suggested a strict limit on the bank's issue. This pamphlet, *Observations on the Establishment of the Bank of England* (1797) went through two quick editions, followed by a supplementary *Further Observations* later the same year.

Now that the bank was under substantial attack, however, Sir Francis rallied round, his previous qualifications and warnings forgotten. In his *Observations on the Publication of Walter Boyd* (1801), Baring absurdly defended the bank from the charge of causing increases in domestic prices by pointing out that the depreciation of the pound on the foreign exchange market was less than the rise in price. But Boyd had not claimed equiproportional rises in all prices, as he pointed out in his rebuttal. Baring also claimed, conveniently enough, that an increase in the money supply could *only* affect foreign exchange rates and not domestic prices.

Another inveterate defender of the bank and an anti-bullionist who entered the controversy in this period was Henry Boase (1763–1827). Boase joined the fray in 1802, and wrote five anti-bullionist pamphlets between then and 1811. He insisted that, under conditions of inconvertibility, exchange rates had nothing to do with the supply of money, but were only determined by the balance of international payments, which in turn was supposed to be set solely by real rather than monetary factors. As Boase put it dogmatically: 'the rate of exchange is governed by the balance of exchange operations, and (great political convulsions apart) by no other principle whatever. ' In his 1802 tract, *Guineas an Unnecessary and Expensive Incumbrance on Commerce*, Boase, as his title indicates, carried the fallacious Smithian 'highway in the sky' argument to its logical conclusion: the restriction was so beneficial that it should be made permanent, 'a permanent measure of prudence and sound policy'.

Who was this Boase, this point man for inflation and fiat money? Born in Cornwall, he went to live for years in Brittany, and then returned to London, where he became a corresponding clerk in 1788 in the banking firm of Ransom, Morland, and Hammersley. The outbreak of the French Revolution the following year found Boase, with his extensive French connections, in a good spot to obtain considerable funds for support of a number of emigré French clergy and nobility in England. Boase then rose rapidly in the bank, becoming chief clerk and then managing partner in 1799. He was also a distinguished evangelical, being a leading member of the London Missionary Society and founder of the British and Foreign Bible Society. After retiring to Cornwall in 1809, Henry Boase became a partner in the Penzance Union Bank and mayor of Penzance.

5.5 Henry Thornton: anti-bullionist in sheep's clothing

Although the bullionist controversy has been studied at length, historians of economic thought have had great difficulty identifying and analysing the various different doctrines held in the bullionist camp. Generally, they have grouped the bullionists into an 'extreme' or 'rigid' camp, consisting of John Wheatley and David Ricardo (to appear later on), and the others, including Henry Thornton, ranked as more sophisticated 'moderates'. The issue supposedly centres on Wheatley and Ricardo's extreme devotion to long-run factors, leading them to deny any role to real factors in determining prices, exchange rates or balances of payments. On the other hand, all the other bullionists, being 'moderate', are supposed to have believed that real factors can often be dominant, and that it is touch and go which factors will prevail in any given situation.

Professor Joseph T. Salerno has recently made a notable advance by providing a far superior framework of analysis of the various thinkers. He notes that Boyd (as we have seen) and Lord King, another leading bullionist, were really 'extreme' rather than moderate, and that they can be classified as such because they realized that monetary factors were always predominant, even though real factors could exert temporary influence. Thus the 'extreme' bullionist camp now includes (a) Ricardo and Wheatley, who ignore all temporary and real factors, as well as short-term processes, and concentrate exclusively and mechanistically on the long run; and (b) Boyd and later Lord

King, who analyse short-run processes and real factors but realize that long-run monetary factors predominate at all times. Then there are (c) 'moderate' bullionists like Thornton who are agnostic about whether real or monetary factors predominate at any given time; and (d) anti-bullionists who ignore all underlying monetary causes. It is clear that Professor Salerno properly gives the accolade to group (b) as having the correct analysis.[7]

But Salerno, it seems to the present author, does not quite go far enough. While he sees fully and lucidly the crucial differences between groups (a) and (b), it is still confusing to classify these two as dwelling in the same camp. For it would clarify matters further if we totally dropped the 'extreme' *vs* 'moderate' distinction. Let group (b) be termed 'complete' bullionists and group (a) 'rigid' or 'mechanistic' bullionists. As for group (c), men like Henry Thornton do not really deserve the term 'bullionist' at all. They are surely 'moderate', though 'confused' might be a better term. Mired in their *ad hoc* approach they could just as well end up, in any given situation, as 'anti-bullionist' rather than 'bullionist'. And, indeed, Henry Thornton began his career of monetary theorist as a moderate *anti*-bullionist, which was his position in the course of his famous contribution of 1802. Later on, as depreciation and inflation continued, Thornton concluded that the preponderance of forces had moved the other way, and he changed his mind, gaining his undeserved historiographical reputation as a bullionist by signing the famous Bullion Committee Report of 1811, which recommended resumption of the gold standard. But Thornton remained a moderate. Focusing on Thornton's later stance, and conflating it with his theoretical work of a decade earlier, only misled historians into extravagantly overpraising Thornton and into placing him unequivocally in the bullionist camp.

During the twentieth century Thornton revival, it was said that earlier historians were unfair in attributing Henry Thornton's (1760–1815) pro-Bank of England bias to his being a director of the bank. It is true that he himself was not a board member of the bank; but his elder brother, Samuel, was a director and deputy governor of the bank, and his grandfather Robert Thornton, as well as Robert's brother Godfrey, was also a director of the Bank of England.

Henry Thornton was a descendant of a long line of prominent merchants. Great-grandfather John was a merchant in Hull, in what was then Yorkshire, in the late seventeenth and early eighteenth centuries. John's sons moved to London to become important merchants there, particularly engaged in trade with Russia and the Baltic. Henry's father, also named John, continued the line of 'Russia merchant' in London, was a senior partner in the firm of Thornton, Cornwall & Co. and was also a leading member and financial supporter, beginning around 1750, of the first generation of evangelicals, low-church puritan Anglicans under the influence of John Wesley. John gave enormous sums to charity, especially for the distribution of countless Bibles and prayer books abroad. Since the Thornton family and several of the other leaders of the movement resided in the wealthy London suburb of Clapham, they were eventually to become known as the highly influential 'Clapham sect'.

Henry Thornton received only a sparse education; at an early age, he began working in the counting houses of his relatives and then of his father. Soon, in 1784, he left the family firm to become a partner in the banking house of Down, Thornton, and Free, where he remained as an active partner until his death. Thornton was able to build the small banking house into one of the largest in the City of London. In 1788, Thornton joined his father and several other family members as a director of the Russia Company. Meanwhile, in 1782, he had been elected an MP, and was soon joined by his brothers Samuel and Robert. Henry was to remain in Parliament, too, for the rest of his life.

Not only was Henry Thornton a distinguished banker, MP and closely related to Bank of England directors; he was also a dedicated leader and patron of the Clapham sect, and his home at Clapham was to serve as a virtual organizing headquarters for the evangelical movement. One of Henry's closest friends, William Wilberforce III, belonged to a powerful family long friendly to and intermarried with the Thorntons. Wilberforce became an MP at about the same time as Thornton, and it was characteristic of their earnestness, personal austerity and moral fervour that they soon came to form an independent 'party of the saints' in Parliament. There, Wilberforce became the leading force in the eventually successful agitation for the abolition of the slave trade in the British West Indies.

In 1796, Thornton married Marianna Sykes, daughter of another 'Russian merchant' from Hull, and also a lifelong family friend. The couple had nine children. Most of Thornton's intellectual energies were expended on evangelical religion; though considered a distinguished expert on banking and finance, he wrote only his famous work of 1802 on paper credit and participated in writing the Bullion Committee Report. The remainder of his voluminous writings were devoted to family prayers, family commentaries on the Bible, and scores of articles on politics, literature and religion for the Clapham sect journal which he helped to found, the *Christian Observer*.

After Thornton' death in 1815, his place as senior partner in the bank was taken by Sir Peter Pole. The bank prospered greatly for a while, but soon it turned out to be undercapitalized and overexpanded, and in 1825 it, along with lesser country banks, was plunged into crisis. It soon failed, despite a friendly £300 000 emergency loan from the Bank of England. Ironically, in view of Thornton's monetary views, there is some evidence that the two men most responsible for the mismanagement were Sir Peter Pole and Henry

Thornton. In particular, Thornton appears to have led the way in lax practices to induce Yorkshire country banks to keep their deposits in his London bank.

Bank failure was no stranger to Thornton. Indeed, it was the temporary failure of his bank in the crisis of 1793 that turned his thoughts to problems of banking, and led him to conclude that it was necessary for the Bank of England to play a supporting, expansionist role in monetary affairs. As the banking theorist Thomas Joplin was to put it in his *Analysis and History of the Currency Question* (1832), on the financial crises of 1793:

> Mr. Thornton, being a banker – a partner, it is curious to remark, of the house that failed on this occasion – had his attention particularly called to this subject: and a very considerable portion of his work, on public credit, is devoted to show, that, in a period of panic, the Bank ought to lean to the side of enlarging, than contracting its issues.[8]

When the restriction came in early 1797, Henry Thornton was honoured by being the only London banker asked to give testimony before the committees of the Houses of Lords and of Commons investigating the suspension of specie payment. Thornton's influence was magnified by the lifelong friendship of Wilberforce and Prime Minister William Pitt, and Pitt's brother-in-law was the first tenant of one of the houses on Thornton's estate. The results of his pondering are scarcely surprising for someone of Thornton's status and background. Taking an inflationist and Establishment line, Thornton opined that in times of crisis paper money could not be limited or suppressed, since that would constitute a shock to commerce. On the contrary, the Bank of England must suspend specie payment in order to avoid the spectre of monetary contraction and general business failure. Indeed, Thornton undoubtedly gladdened the hearts of the bank by criticizing it for not being expansionist enough!

Thornton's testimony won him the accolade of being the foremost authority on monetary affairs, and he was appointed to several parliamentary committees on money, expenditures and foreign exchange. Thornton, indeed, became one of the leading parliamentary defenders of the restriction and of expanded paper credit.

We can easily imagine Henry Thornton's sentiments towards Walter Boyd's *Letter to Pitt* when that tract hit the world of English opinion like a thunderbolt at the turn of 1800–1. Here was this well-connected fellow banker, but an unsound adventurer, this rogue whom his own brother had brought to ruin by persuading the Bank of England to cut off his credit. And now, only months after this man had met his deserved fate, here was Boyd again, trying to gain revenge by discrediting the noble banking and credit system of England. Thornton was stung to try to refute the dangerous Boyd, and it was in the service of this goal that he published his *An Enquiry into the Nature and Effects of the Paper Credit of Great Britain* a year after Boyd's tract, in February or March of 1802.[9]

But first Thornton hit out at Boyd in Parliament, in December 1800. As in his book, his words exerted all the more impact for the eminence of their author combined with their seeming judiciousness and moderation. For there are always a host of people who will hold firmly that the more qualified and tentative the judgement, the more well-balanced and sound it must therefore be. Mushiness of mind, especially in an eminent man, is all too often mistaken for wisdom.

In this early phase of the bullionist debate, Thorntonian mushiness tended inexorably in the wrong direction. The depreciation of the pound in foreign exchange was caused, he opined in his speech in Parliament, not by the increase of paper money, but by the unfavourable balance of trade and specifically by the heavy imports of provisions. Typical of the anti-bullionist view, imports and exports were assumed to have *ad hoc* lives of their own, and not to be determined by relative prices or by the supply and demand for money. But Thornton's anti-bullionism was nothing if not 'moderate', that is, he conceded the theoretical possibility that increased money supply could bring about higher prices:

> as to the assertion that the increased issue of Bank paper was the cause of the dearness of provisions, he [Thornton] would not deny that it might have some foundation; but he would contend that its effect was far from being as great as was being alleged…

Henry Thornton's book on *Paper Credit* was a considerable expansion of his parliamentary speeches, and it was *Paper Credit* that took its place as not only the leading work on behalf of anti-bullionism, but also the most influential on either side of the debate. The timing was right, since the restriction was in particular need of defence in 1802. A peace with France was signed in March, and yet the British government persisted in extending the restriction another year. Soon after that year was up, war with France broke out again, but in the meantime the seeming end of the wartime emergency had taken away the apparent reason for the suspension of specie payments. Other anti-bullionist tracts appearing in 1802 were scarcely rivals for Thornton, ranging from Jasper Atkinson's anonymous pamphlet (*Consideration on the Propriety of the Bank of England Resuming its Payments in Specie…*) denying that inflation had taken place, to another anonymous tract applying Adam Smith's erroneous theory of an automatic limit to excess bank credit to a situation Smith would never have applied it to: fiat money (*The Utility of Country Banks Considered*).

Thornton disarmed many of his critics by conceding the theoretical *possibility* that excess issues of paper money can cause price increases, outflow of gold, higher prices of gold bullion and depreciation of the pound, but maintaining that the situation did not now apply, and that the problems of the day were due to such particular real factors as unusual demand for gold and for the importation of food, and unusual blockages to exports.

Thornton cleverly loaded the dice by spending the bulk of the book on the alleged horrors of monetary deflation and the contraction of bank credit. Deflation would lead to trade depression, unemployment and bankruptcies. Furthermore, he claimed, deflation would not even accomplish an export surplus or an inflow of gold, since it would 'so exceedingly distress trade and discourage manufacturers as to impair…those sources of returning wealth to which we must chiefly trust for the restoration of our balance'. Thornton neglected to realize that if times were really that bad, Englishmen would scarcely earn enough income to sustain a heavy excess of imports. As in all modern agitation against deflation, he also failed to realize that deflation only causes losses and bankruptcies if it is unexpected, revealing an excessive bidding up of wage rates and other business costs. Deflation, in addition to having the healthy impact of purging unsound investments and unsound banks from the economy, would have strictly limited and temporary effect; first, because while inflation is technically unlimited until the value of the currency is totally destroyed, deflation must necessarily be limited to the amount of bank expansion over specie; and second, deflation will cease having a depressionary effect as soon as excessive costs are brought down to pre-inflated levels.

In fact, Thornton acknowledged that the fall in price and the depression brought about by monetary deflation would be 'unusual' and 'temporary'. But he anticipated Keynes in focusing on allegedly sticky wage rates, for

> a fall [of prices] arising from temporary distress will be attended probably with no correspondent fall in the rate of wages; for the fall of price, and the distress, will be understood to be temporary, and the rate of wages, we know, is not so variable as the price of goods. There is reason, therefore, to fear that the unnatural and extraordinarily low price arising from the sort of distress of which we now speak, would occasion much discouragement of the fabrication of manufactures.

There are two problems here. First, while the economic distress, due to faulty forecasting and excess bidding up of wage rates and other costs, will indeed be temporary, there is no reason why the fall in prices should not be permanent. Prices had previously been artificially raised by monetary and credit expansion; their decline simply reflects the contraction of credit down to more realistic levels. The knowledge that the decline is permanent should greatly speed up the adjustment mechanism. Second, if workers persist in keeping their wage demands higher than the market, they have only themselves to blame for their unemployment. Keeping any price, including a wage rate, higher than market equilibrium will always lead to an unsold surplus of the good or service: in the case of labour, unsold labour time, or unemployment. If labourers wish to change their unemployed status, they need only lower their wage demands to clear the market and allow themselves to be hired. We should also recognize that, in this situation, with prices falling and wage rates constant, workers are thereby insisting on higher *real* wage rates than they had enjoyed before. Why should workers holding out for higher real wage rates be able to induce an inflationist policy in the central government?

So worried about deflation was Thornton that he actually urged the bank of England to neutralize outflows of gold so as to obstruct the price-specie-flow mechanism from bringing about equilibrium in the balance of payments. Instead, he would have the bank inflate bank notes to replace gold outflows, and then hope that his vague long-run real principles of 'economy' and 'exertion', of expenditure and income, would eventually work to equilibrate imports and exports. Thus, Thornton writes that

> ...it may be true policy and duty of the bank to permit for a time, and to a certain extent, the continuance of that unfavourable exchange which causes gold to leave the country, and to be drawn out of its own coffers: and it must, in that case, necessarily increase its loans to the same extent to which its gold is diminished.

Thornton's work has been excessively hailed by von Hayek and other historians as being theoretically excellent if unfortunate in its political anti-bullionist conclusions. But his theoretical weakness did not only consist of his excessive horror of deflation and his stress on the alleged empirical dominance of real factors in his analysis of inflation and depreciation. For this stress itself reflected a grave if subtle theoretical flaw in Thornton's entire monetary and balance of payments analysis. His entire analysis lingered disproportionately on the real and short-term factors, to the almost complete neglect of the tendency of the economy towards long-run equilibrium. And even Thornton's perfunctory discussion of long-run equilibrium is divorced from short-run processes and also from its *monetary* nature. It goes without saying that Thornton therefore also neglects the monetary supply and demand nature of the short-run processes leading towards that equilibrium. Thus Professor Salerno, who has given us a notable critique of Thornton, writes:

> Without the conception of international monetary equilibrium at his disposal, he is forced to explain the tendency to balance-of-payments equilibrium by a hazy reference to an alleged disposition amongst people to 'adapt their individual expenditure to their income'. This is in sharp contrast to the extreme bullionists and their eighteenth-century forebears who invariably began their analyses of

balance-of-payments phenomena with a discussion of the nature and necessity of international monetary equilibrium and *then* explained the tendency to balance-of-payments equilibrium as a logical implication of the necessary tendency to an equilibrium distribution of the world stock of money.[10]

Indeed the entire structure and organization of the book tilted Thornton heavily towards short-term real factors and away from any monetary approach towards analysing inflation or the balance of payments.[11]

To sum up: the correct analysis of complete bullionism (such as presented by Boyd and later by Lord King) stresses monetary factors leading to monetary equilibrium, while showing that real factors can only have temporary effects. The analysis of real factors is integrated with, and at all times subordinated to, the monetary factors, and short-run and long-run monetary processes are integrated as well. In Thornton's moderate anti-bullionist position (often miscalled 'moderate bullionist'), however, both real and monetary causal factors and processes are presented as separate and independent of each other, with real factors presented as empirically more important. Short-run factors are similarly stressed, to the neglect of long-run forces.

Henry Thornton has been extravagantly praised by Schumpeter and other historians for adding velocity of circulation to the quantity of money as a determinant of overall prices. But, in the first place, we have seen that ever since the scholastics, the demand for money – the inverse of the 'velocity' – had always been integrated with the supply of money in analysing the determination of general prices. It is true that Thornton analysed the different influences on, and different variabilities of, velocity in considerable and pioneering detail: e.g. frequency of payments, development of clearing systems, confidence in the money, and variations of the same stock of money over time. But unfortunately, Thornton ruined this contribution by not realizing that velocity of circulation is simply the inverse of the demand for money and by treating the velocity as somehow different, and independent of, demand in helping determine the money relation of supply, demand and price.

Thornton has been lauded by von Hayek and others for including bank deposits as well as bank notes in the supply of money. True enough; but, as we have seen, Walter Boyd preceded him in this insight by a year. But not only that: Boyd also demonstrated that bills of exchange and Treasury bills are decidedly *not* part of the money supply, that they are objects of circulation rather than the 'circulator'. But Thornton restored the older error of lumping bills of exchange in with notes and deposits as part of the supply of money.

Henry Thornton did make some important contributions in the last two chapters of *Paper Credit*, particularly in the long-deferred paper money-as-cause of inflation sections that rested uneasily with the separate and contrary earlier chapters. Most of the anti-bullionist writers applied Adam Smith's dictum that bank credit cannot inflate the currency if confined to short-term, self-liquidating, 'real bills'. The difference is that Smith had applied it only to a specie standard, whereas the anti-bullionists extended it to a fiat money system. Thornton replied that this criterion will not work, since an increased quantity of bank notes will also indefinitely inflate the monetary value of the real bills. So that the Smith–anti-bullionist 'limit' is an indefinitely elastic one that will in practice only provide an open channel for bank credit inflation. Thornton further pointed out that the current usury law in Britain of 5 per cent will aggravate the problem. For the free market interest rate or profit rate will rise higher than that in wartime (or in any boom situation). Consequently, the artificial holding down of the bank loan rate below the profit rate will stimulate an excessive borrowing, artificially high levels of investment, and a continuing monetary and price inflation. Thus, holding the bank rate of interest below the profit rate stimulates an increase in the demand for borrowing, and the continuing increase in the supply of money allows that demand to be fulfilled.

In setting forth the inflationary consequences of artificially lowering the rate of interest on bank loans, Henry Thornton anticipated the later Austrian theory of the business cycle, set forth by Ludwig von Mises and F.A. von Hayek and in turn based on the analysis of the Swedish–Austrian economist Knut Wicksell at the end of the nineteenth century. Thornton also hinted at the Austrian analysis of 'forced saving', pointing out that if excessive issues of paper money raise prices of goods more rapidly than wage rates, there will be some increase of capital investment, but that this increase will be at the expense of the labouring classes, and will therefore 'be attended with a proportionate hardship and injustice'. Unfortunately, Thornton did not press on to the Austrian business cycle point: that since the public's time- and saving-preferences are not sufficient to sustain these 'forced' investments, a recession is bound to liquidate those investments when the artificial credit expansion stops and the true savings-consumption preferences of the public are thereby revealed.

It is very possible that, despite the author's prominence in the world of banking, *Paper Credit* might have sunk quickly into obscurity. It was very long (several hundred pages), badly written and organized, unsystematic, muddled, and what its greatest admirers have called 'prolix'. Even von Hayek, Thornton's biggest modern booster, concedes that his 'exposition lacks system and in places is even obscure'. Even his greatest disciple and popularizer, Francis Horner, admitted that Thornton had 'little management in the disposition of his materials'; that he 'frequently...was much embarrassed in the explanation of arguments', that his 'reasonings are not to be trusted' and are sometimes 'defective', that he was not trained in theorizing, that his style was poor, and that 'the various discussions are so unskillfully arranged, that they throw no light on each other, and we can never seize a full view of the plan'. In short, the 'prolixity' and 'the obscurity' of the work 'oppress the reader'.

And yet, ironically, it was this very Francis Horner who rescued *Paper Credit* from these grave defects, and put the work on the map. The form Horner used was a great stroke of luck for granting Thornton's work its maximum impact. We have noted in an earlier chapter on the influence of the Smithian movement (Chapter 17, Volume 1) that Francis Horner was one of a scintillating group of young Scotsmen who studied under Dugald Stewart at the turn of the nineteenth century, and went on to conquer the British intellectual climate for Smithian doctrine. It was in 1802 that these young pupils of Stewart founded the *Edinburgh Review*, which struck the British intellectual world with enormous impact and quickly vaulted to the status of one of the leading journals. And it was precisely in the first, October 1802 issue of the *Edinburgh Review* that Francis Horner wrote his famous review-essay of Thornton's *Paper Credit*. In this 30-page *tour de force* Horner systematized Thornton's work, made as much sense of it as was possible and, as von Hayek admits, 'gave an exposition of the main argument of the book in a form which was considerably more systematic and coherent than the original version'. Horner beat the drums for *Paper Credit*, trumpeted it as 'the most valuable unquestionably of all the publications which the momentous event of the Bank Restriction had produced'. The great fame and influence of *Paper Credit* was unquestionably Thornton mediated through Francis Horner. It was also important to realize that Horner, though chairman of the later Bullion Committee of 1810–11 which recommended resumption of the gold standard, agreed with Thornton in his anti-bullionist stance of 1802.

While Horner hailed Thornton's work as decisive, he paved the way for his (and Thornton's) later change of mind politically by writing that he was not sure which factors – the monetary or the real – had been more decisive in the inflation and the depreciation of the pound. He expressed his fundamental theoretical confusion (along with Thornton's) by declaring himself agnostic on the causal issue, the matter to be decided later by more empirical data. In short, while Thornton, in his *Paper Credit*, carved out the new moderate anti-bullionist position, his follower Horner was what might be called a moderate moderate, squarely in the middle of the issue.

We might also note that Horner took his stand squarely with Thornton against Boyd on the issue of defining the money supply. Rejecting Boyd's lucid 'circulator' *vs* 'objects of circulation', Horner perpetuated Thornton's unfortunate and fuzzy view that there is no definite boundary between commodities and means of exchange, so that everything is a mish-mash of degrees of convertibility.

5.6 Lord King: the culmination of bullionism

When the British government asked Parliament for a year's extension of the bank restriction in April 1802, it had to justify the renewal of suspension on some ground other than the war with France, since the Treaty of Amiens had been signed the previous month. Prime minister Henry Addington (1757–1844) argued that since the balance of payments remained unfavourable to Britain, the suspension of specie payments should be extended – presumably until the balance of trade reversed itself. When the renewal came up again in February of the following year, Addington again argued for an extension of the fiat system on the same grounds. He was answered trenchantly by the great opposition leader, Charles James Fox, who pointed out that 'perhaps even it might happen that the unfavourable turn of the exchange against this country might be owing to the very restriction on the bank'. Not only that, but Fox saw incisively that the outflow of gold was essentially a Gresham's law situation, where money undervalued by the government flows inexorably out of circulation to be replaced by overvalued (or 'bad') money. He essentially showed that this process applies to paper fully as much as to 'bad gold':

> In 1772 to 1773, when there was a great quantity of bad money in the country, the course of exchange was then also much against us...As long as our currency continued bad, the exchange was against us; so is it now, because paper is not much better than bad gold...May it not therefore be expected that as in the former case, when our currency was ameliorated, the course of exchange turned in our favour, so also if the Bank now resumed its cash payments the same favourable circumstances might attend the change?

During this debate, a new voice entered the bullionist controversy, with Peter Lord King (1776–1833) denouncing the restriction in a speech in the House of Lords on 22 February. Taking the lead of the bullionist forces, Lord King zeroed in on the increase of the quantity of paper money during the restriction as the culprit: 'from the time the restriction was first imposed, the course of exchange began to turn against this country in various proportions to the quantity of paper in circulation.' In May, Lord King repeated these arguments in arguing against a bill to extend bank restriction in Ireland. Later in May of 1803, King elaborated his views in a highly important pamphlet: *Thoughts on the Restriction of Payments in Specie at the Bank of England and Ireland*, and then followed with an enlarged second edition of the pamphlet the following year, under the title, *Thoughts on the Effects of the Bank Restriction*. Lord King's *Thoughts* was widely read and highly influential, and with this pamphlet King took his place as the leader of the bullionist camp, just as Thornton, who continued to support the renewal of restriction, was established as the leader of the moderate anti-bullionists.

Lord King was a young nobleman of distinguished lineage. He was the great-grandson of Peter, the first Lord King, who became Lord Chancellor of the realm. The Whig and classical liberal tradition of the King family was emphasized by the fact that the first Lord King's mother was a cousin of John Locke, and that the first Lord King was a protégé of Locke and a leading Whig and MP. Peter King was educated at Eton and at Trinity College, Cambridge, taking his place as a follower of Charles James Fox and an important Whig in the House of Lords in 1800. In addition to his leadership of the hard-money forces in Britain, Lord King, though a great landlord, was a lifelong militant enemy of the Corn Laws. A critic of the Established Church, King was a principal battler for the unpopular cause of emancipation of the Catholics of England, as well as an opponent of the oppression of the Catholics of Ireland. In 1829, Lord King wrote a *Life of John Locke*, revised and expanded into two volumes in the following year.

Lord King began his *Thoughts* with a chapter on 'Paper Money'. Unfortunately, King accepted Smith's fallacious argument for paper money as providing a highway in the sky, but at least he rejected Smith's idea of an automatic 'reflux' of any excess paper to the banking system. Instead, King applied the quantity theory (or, to put it better, the supply and demand theory) of money to the case of convertible paper. King, in a statement which Nassau Senior later referred to admiringly as 'Lord King's principle', stressed that it was important for paper money not to be issued to any extent greater than its 'exact' replacement of the quantity of gold coin in circulation; and that this equivalence is maintained by the immediate convertibility of paper into gold.

King then moved to rebut, one by one, the pro-restrictionist arguments that the Bank of England notes were not excessive and therefore not depreciated. The idea that the bank had not exceeded some abstract proportion of money to industry, or some arbitrary optimum money supply, was effectively shot down, King demonstrating that 'there is no rule or standard by which the due quantity of circulating medium in any country can be ascertained, except the actual demand of the public'. King then shows trenchantly that the demand for money, like the demand for any product, is variable and uncertain:

> The requisite proportion of currency, like that of every other article of use or consumption, regulates itself entirely by this demand; which differs materially in different countries and states of society, and even in the same country at different times...
>
> It is manifest...that the proportion of circulating medium required in any given state of wealth and industry is not a fixed, but a fluctuating and uncertain quantity; which depends in each case upon a great variety of circumstances, and which is diminished or increased by the greater or less degree of security, or enterprise and of commercial improvement. The causes which influence the demand are evidently too complicated to admit of the quantity being ascertained by previous computation or by any process of theory...

King goes on to conclude that

> If the above reasoning is well founded, it must follow that there is no method of discovering *a priori* the proportion of the circulating medium which the occasions of the community require; that it is a quantity which has no assignable rule or standard; an that its true amount can be ascertained only by the effective demand.

Next, King was the first to see the importance of Thornton's devastating critique of his fellow anti-bullionists' extension of Smithian real-bills doctrine, and he put the critique even more strongly. Putting their discount rates below the free market interest rate can permit unlimited extension of bank credit on real bills. Furthermore, the bank possesses no real means of distinguishing between 'real' and 'fictitious' bills, and merchants can always be induced to borrow far beyond real demands of the public by artificially low interest charged by the banks.

In the case of inconvertible paper money, King concluded, there is no way to discover the real demand for money by the public, or to figure out when paper money is excessive or not. Without convertibility, paper circulation is 'deprived of this natural standard, and is incapable of admitting any other'. Hence, banks or governments entrusted with the task of finding the optimum level of money and credit are doomed to 'committing perpetual mistakes'.

Building on Boyd's pioneering work and the contributions of Thornton, Lord King then set out to develop the culmination of the complete bullionist theory of inconvertible paper money, a theory consisting of a systematic and forceful development of supply and demand analysis. He first notes that inconvertible paper is subject to two distinct but related influences towards depreciation: 'want of confidence on the part of the public, and an undue increase of the quantity of notes'. In every instance of inconvertible currency, he notes, both factors have soon gone to work. How does one know, King went on, when depreciation of inconvertible currency has occurred? Walter Boyd had asserted that one test of depreciation was a rise of the free market bullion price higher than the official mint price. King reinforced Boyd's insight by pointing out that bullion value tends to be stable in the short run, making any deviation of the two the result of a change in the value of the paper. King also provides a rigorous grounding for Boyd's second proffered test: the depreciation of the pound compared to other currencies. For a specie-convertible currency cannot depreciate, since any surplus can be exported. But inconvertible paper cannot be exported, and will there 'remain in that country, and, if multiplied beyond the demand, must be depreciated in the degree of its excess'. Furthermore,

> In the course of commercial dealings this increase of quantity is soon discovered; and prices are increased in proportion. A similar effect takes place in transactions with foreign currencies according to the status of their respective currencies.

King goes on to develop a concise statement of the purchasing-power-parity theory of exchange rates under inconvertible currencies.

While in the above passage, King appeared to adopt the mechanistic proportionality quantity theory, he made it clear later in the pamphlet that this proportionality, if it occurs at all, only does so in the long run. For King, like Boyd, was a complete bullionist, and presented by far the best and most developed statement of this position in this entire period. King demonstrates that the inflation process *necessarily* involves a redistribution of wealth and income. Developing hints of process analysis from Hume, King writes that the proportional effect of an increase of the quantity of paper money on prices is far from immediate, and that 'some time must elapse before the new currency can circulate through the community and affect the prices of all commodities'. But while Hume hailed this interval as spurring business activity, King correctly focused on the coerced advantages that this process gives to the early, as opposed to the later, recipients of the new money:

> It is this interval between the creation of the new paper and the rise of prices which may be a source of advantage to the persons who obtain loans from the Bank. The merchant, to whom the notes are immediately issued, employs them in the purchase of goods at the prices which they then bear. But by the very effect of these notes, when they are afterwards circulated, the price of the goods is enhanced and the merchant has the advantage of this rise in addition to the ordinary profits of trade. If he is an exporting merchant, he will receive, beside the usual profit, the amount of the depreciation which will have taken place in the currency between the time of purchasing the goods and the arrival of the remittance in return.

King also calls the depreciation of central Bank of Ireland notes like 'an income tax which levies not for the benefit of Government, but of the proprietors of Irish Bank stock'. And on the Bank of England, he noted that the 'undue advantage [that] has been obtained by the bank in the exact degree of the excess of their notes' has been more than offset by 'the loss and injury to the public, as in all cases of depreciated currency'. Hence 'An indirect tax is thus imposed upon the community, not for the benefit of the public, but of individuals. It is levied in the most pernicious manner; and is of all taxes the least productive in proportion to the loss and inconvenience sustained'.

In short, King recognizes that the privileged beneficiaries of inflation and depreciation are, largely, the central banks themselves and their stockholders, as well as merchants who borrow from these banks, and exporters who benefit by the depreciation of foreign exchange. All these are bought at the expense of the public. King also perceptively notes that it is precisely these groups who had been the main apologists for the bank restriction. He suggests that these London and Dublin merchants had probably never read

Hume, nor precisely traced the theoretical steps by which they obtained the privilege of bank inflation:

> But their experience has undoubtedly led them to the same conclusions; and there can be no doubt that since the period of the Restriction discounts have been obtained from the Bank by commercial men with less difficulty and that these accommodations together with the profits derived from hence have given their minds a strong bias in favour of the measure.

Furthermore, Lord King's mordant analysis of the advantages accruing to the bank as against the public by inflation of its notes led him to denounce *per se* any 'exclusive privilege' in issuing notes granted to the Bank of England. For such a privilege would be 'as unjust and impolitic as to grant a monopoly of any other branch of skill and industry to any private merchant or company'.

Tied in with his rejection of the mechanistic proportionality approach, Lord King conceded that real factors can have subordinate and temporary effects on depreciation and the exchange rate. Indeed, it is precisely this understanding of the temporary effects of real factors that helped lead King to reject the idea of strict proportionality, and hence of any precise quantitative *measurement* of the degree of depreciation or of the excess of paper money. As King wrote: 'nor will the most careful reference to the two tests of the price of bullion and the state of the exchanges enable us to ascertain in what precise degree a currency is depreciated; though the general fact of a depreciation may be proved beyond dispute.' Indeed, he gently chided Boyd for unduly stressing such a measure of excess, and thereby having 'given an advantage to his opponents by insisting too much on the degree of depreciation…'

Finally, it is unfortunate that King followed Smith's and Thornton's confusion of bills of exchange and other evidences of debt with money, and rejected Walter Boyd's clear-cut distinction between them.

Lord King's contribution immediately vaulted him to the front rank of bullionist theorists; and when David Ricardo entered the fray almost a decade later, he hailed King's booklet as having had a great influence on him. For some reason, however, King's vital contribution has been grievously overlooked by most later historians, and even in Nassau Senior's day, in the mid-1840s, Senior found it necessary to chide posterity for neglecting Lord King's great achievement. Indeed, Senior lauded King's work as 'so full, and in the main so true, an exposition of the Theory of Paper Money, that after more than forty years of discussion, there is little to add to it, or to correct'. Senior's reminder was afterwards echoed by Henry D. MacLeod and by Francis A. Walker, and as late as 1911, Jacob Hollander, in his famous resurrection of monetary theory between Smith and Ricardo, briefly hailed

King's pamphlet as a 'remarkable contrast to the prolix obscurity of Thornton's essay, and the heated temper of Boyd's performance', and 'fitted to become, as it speedily did, the epitome of what had already been written in sound criticism and in reasonable interpretation of the Bank's course no less than the inspiration of future effort in the same direction'.[12] Yet, unaccountably, appreciation of King's contribution promptly dropped completely out of sight once again, only to be resurrected in the seminal dissertation of Professor Salerno.

Perhaps the most important immediate impact of Lord King's *Thoughts* was on Francis Horner, for Horner was promptly converted by the booklet from his previous moderate moderate position to his permanent stance of moderate bullionist. The conversion probably rested not so much on King's theoretical analysis, as on his thorough marshalling of the statistics of the restriction period, which convinced the theoretical agnostic Horner that the facts were on the side of the cause of price inflation and depreciation from an excessive issue of paper money. Reviewing King's *Thoughts* in the July 1803 issue of the *Edinburgh Review*, Horner abandoned his previous policy agnosticism on the restriction to plumb squarely for redeemability. 'From the very first', he now wrote, 'there could be no doubt of the impolicy and injustice of the restriction...'. But whereas before, he felt that the facts were too complicated to decide whether Boyd had been right about the restriction's inflationary impact on prices, Horner was convinced by King that Boyd had been right. He now concluded that 'Throughout all these changes, one uniform effect may be perceived which, with the evidence by which it is proved, and the reasonings by which it is explained, is very ably and perspicuously described by Lord King'.

5.7   The Irish currency question

Much of Lord King's strictures were directed against the central Bank of Ireland as well as of England, and indeed, during 1803, as the restriction was extended into the future with the resurgence of war with France, attention shifted to the rapid depreciation of the currency of Ireland.

When Britain imposed the restriction in 1797, it also suspended specie payment for the Bank of Ireland and for the banking system of its Irish colony. It did so even though the Irish banking system was then in relatively sound and uninflated shape. The Bank of Ireland, however, quickly took advantage of its new-found privileges to inflate the supply of money and credit sharply, quadrupling its note circulation over the next six years. By 1803, therefore, the Irish pound had fallen over 10 per cent below its gold standard parity of 108:100 with the English pound. It was particularly evident that the problem here was the Irish supply of paper money, and nothing else, since Belfast, in the English currency orbit with no central bank of its own, remained at par with the English pound, and since the Dublin pound had depreciated to the same extent in Belfast as it had in London.

When the extension of bank restriction came up in Parliament in February 1803, an extension defended by Thornton, a bullionist critique of the Irish situation was launched by Lord King, who continued the same discussion in May when an extension of Irish restriction arose in Parliament.

With attention turned toward the Irish problem, the House of Commons in March 1804 established an Irish currency committee to investigate the matter (more precisely, the 'Select Committee on the Circulating Paper, the Specie and the Current Coin of Ireland'). The Bank of Ireland officials, desperately trying to defend their record, proclaimed with increasing absurdity that the depreciation of the Irish pound was due not to excessive issue but to the mysteriously 'unfavourable' balance of payments out of Ireland. The committee, of which Henry Thornton was a leading member, issued its report in June and gave short shrift to the anti-bullionist rationalizations. It adopted squarely the bullionist insight that the depreciation of the Irish pound was due to excessive issue of paper and extension of credit by the Bank of Ireland, and that this excessive issue had been made possible by the restriction. The committee report presaged the famous bullion committee report six years later, and was notable also for the virtual conversion of Henry Thornton, following Horner, into the moderate bullionist camp. The report declared that the 'great and effectual remedy' for Irish currency ills was 'Repeal of the Restriction Act from whence all the evils have flowed', but it then drew back from such a radical solution to opt for an intermediary solution: for the Bank of Ireland at least to make its notes redeemable in the far less depreciated Bank of England currency. This, in fact, was also the intermediate solution proffered by Lord King. Above all, the committee warned that the Bank of Ireland must limit its paper issue in all times of unfavourable balances of trade, 'and that all the evils of a high and fluctuating Exchange must be imputable to them if they fail to do so'.

Joining the bullionist camp around the Irish currency question were two important members of the Anglo-Irish Establishment. A month before the appointment of the Irish currency committee, Henry Brooke Parnell (1776–1842), the first Baron Congleton, published his pamphlet of *Observations on the State of Currency in Ireland*. Parnell, the son of Sir John, Chancellor of the Irish Exchequer, was educated at Eton and at Trinity College, Cambridge. An influential MP from 1802 on, Parnell's application of bullionist principles to the Irish question was largely influenced by Lord King. Parnell brought charges against the Bank of England of inundating the country with its paper; of diminishing the value of the greatest portion of the property of the country; of establishing a ruinous rate of exchange; and of bringing upon the state all the calamities attending a depreciated currency. As an intermediate remedy,

Parnell also recommended King's proposal to make Irish paper redeemable in Bank of England notes. So compatible was Parnell's booklet with the Irish currency committee report, that the third edition of Parnell's essay placed a summary of the committee's evidence in its appendix.

The committee report, and the King proposal, were also backed by another member of the Anglo-Irish Establishment, the young Irish attorney in London, John Leslie Foster (d. 1842), in his pamphlet, an *Essay on the Principles of Commercial Exchanges* (1804). Foster, the son of an Anglican bishop, and graduate of Trinity College, Dublin, later became an Irish judge and a Tory MP in England. There is also the curious case of James Maitland, the eighth earl of Lauderdale (1759–1839), a Scottish attorney and first a Whig and then a Tory MP. On the one hand, Lauderdale was a fanatical underconsumptionist and opponent of saving – thereby anticipating Keynes – in his *Inquiry into the Nature and Origins of Public Wealth* (1804) and in his argument against debt repayment and for government expenditure *per se* (*Three Letters to the Duke of Wellington*, 1829). On the other hand, Lord Lauderdale was a sound hard-money man, endorsing the Irish currency report in a hard-hitting pamphlet. Not only did Lauderdale agree that excessive paper issue of the Bank of Ireland had led to the depreciation of the Irish pound and the premium on gold; he went beyond the report to insist that outright contraction of Bank of Ireland paper was the only effective remedy for the existing problem (In his *Thoughts on the Alarming State of the Circulation and on the Means of Redressing the Pecuniary Grievances of Ireland* (1805). It is certainly unusual for one person to be at the same time an arch-underconsumptionist and an ardent hard-money deflationist!

While the King and committee solutions did not triumph, the Irish bank officials apparently understood the situation far better than they had let on. For they soon managed to defuse the problem by pursuing harder monetary policies, and thereby bringing the Irish pound back to par with England.

5.8   The emergence of mechanistic bullionism: John Wheatley

After 1804, the Bank of England dampened its expansionist policy for a few years, and inflation and depreciation abated as well. As a result, the bullionist controversy about England and Ireland died down. Phase 1 of the great bullionist controversy was over. There had appeared on the scene three schools of monetary thought and opinion: first, the anti-bullionist apologists of the British government and the Bank of England, whose views can scarcely be dignified by the name of 'theory' and who simply denied that monetary issue had any relation to the evils of inflation and depreciation. Ranged against them, were, second, the complete bullionists, headed by Lord King and by Walter Boyd, who trenchantly applied supply and demand for money analysis to the new conditions of irredeemable fiat money, and who attacked the

Bank of England's over-issue as the cause of the evils, with 'real' factors also playing a temporary and subordinate role. In the middle were, third, the moderates, consisting largely of Henry Thornton and Francis Horner, theoretical agnostics who claimed that either monetary or real factors might be responsible for any given inflation, and emphasized empirically and *ad hoc* which set of factors might be the culprits in any given situation. Starting as a moderate anti-bullionist, the empirical weight shifted quickly for Horner, at least, to enter the moderate bullionist camp by 1803.

Before Phase 1 had ended, however, a fourth school of thought, and the third strand of bullionism, had emerged: mechanistic bullionism. The great error of mechanistic bullionism was not simply to neglect all real influences, and to insist that monetary factors and monetary factors alone determined price levels and exchange rates. If that had been the only flaw, the error would have been a relatively minor one. The main problem was that the mechanists were also moved to neglect *all other* causal factors than the money supply – many of them of great importance. In brief, they neglected the demand for money, in all its subtle variations, and such vital 'distribution' effects – even in the long run – as changes in relative assets and incomes and changes in relative prices. In sum, the mechanists claimed that, in the short run and in the long, the *only* causal factors on price and exchanges were changes in the quantity of money. Hence their erroneous and distorted view that changes in price 'levels' are exactly quantitatively proportionate to changes in the quantity of money.

The mechanistic bullionist view, presumably emerging in over-reaction to the moderates, was first presented by a man who was neither an MP nor otherwise in the public eye: the attorney John Wheatley (1772–1830). In his first of many contributions to monetary economics, *Remarks on Currency and Commerce* (1803), Wheatley set forth the long-run bullionist and monetary approach in its starkest and most simplistic form. Any discussion of temporary adjustments or even temporal processes was cast aside, in order to linger exclusively on final equilibrium states. To Wheatley, all export or import of gold was exclusively determined by its demand and price, i.e. by monetary factors, and bullion prices and exchange rates were solely determined by monetary considerations. Real factors play no role in these matters even temporarily or in the short run. Hence the effect of the supply of money on price levels or exchange rates is strictly and precisely proportionate. Overall prices move, not only proportionately, but also uniformly in 'levels', with no changes occurring in relative prices. Thus Wheatley:

The increase of currency by paper must cause the same reduction in the value of money, in proportion to the activity of its circulation as an increase of currency by specie. But...if paper depreciate money, it must advance in similar proportion the price of articles of subsistence and luxury.

From these principles, it was easy for Wheatley to deduce that it was impossible for an expansion of the money supply *ever* to stimulate the economy, since by definition, 'the wages of labour are augmented only in porportion to the increase [of currency]'. And since wages rise proportionately to the money supply and to all other prices, they can 'purchase no greater quantity of products after the addition than before it', and therefore 'no greater stimulus can in reality exist, and therefore no greater effect is likely to be produced by the deception...'. A heroic conclusion, no doubt, and surely true in the long run; but such blithely dogmatic statements omit the whole point of monetary inflation and its short-run stimulus: e.g. making prices rise faster than wage rates.

Moreover, since Wheatley had an exclusively long-run, and therefore monetary, theory of exchange rates under inconvertibility, he again blithely assumed that the value of any given money was always and everywhere equal, i.e. in the long-run equilibrium, and that fiat money exchange rates always trade at precisely their purchasing-power-parities to their respective monetary purchasing powers. Hence, for Wheatley, not only was a depreciated exchange rate and a premium on specie bullion, an 'unmistakable system' of currency depreciation; it also provided an exact 'measure' of that depreciation. In contrast, King and Boyd, let alone Thornton, only saw currency depreciation when such phenomena existed for 'any considerable time' (Boyd) or were 'long continued' (King). And neither of the latter claimed that such premia or discounted exchange rates provide a precise measure of depreciation.

While John Wheatley did not enjoy anything like the prominence of his fellow debaters on bullionism, he was by no means an insignificant figure. He was born in Kent to a prominent landed and military family of the county. His father William was a high sheriff and deputy lieutenant of Kent; an older brother, William, served as a major-general in the French wars; and a younger brother, Sir Henry Wheatley, was attached for many years to the royal court. Wheatley received a BA from the aristocratic Christ Church, Oxford in 1793, and was then admitted to the bar. His wife, Georgiana, was the daughter of William Lushington, prominent London merchant and an MP for the City of London, and brother of Sir Stephen Lushington, formerly president of the great East India Company. Oddly enough, William Lushington, as chairman of the committee of the merchants of London, had petitioned the Bank of England in March 1797 to be more expansionist in its discount policy.

Wheatley's *Remarks* were attacked in the *Edinburgh Review* by the prominent Whig leader Henry Brougham, on familiar Thorntonian grounds. But while Wheatley followed up his pamphlet with the first volume of *An Essay on the Theory of Money and Principles of Commerce* (1807), his timing was poor, since there was little interest in the bullionist controversy at that time. Wheatley compounded his tactical problems by writing nothing on money for the next nine years, during a time when the bullionist controversy was at its height. For all these reasons, Wheatley's stance was largely overlooked, until in 1809 David Ricardo assumed the leadership of the mechanistic bullionist camp. Wheatley's influence, furthermore, was scarcely helped by his being in chronic financial difficulties virtually all his life. He acted from time to time as agent for the Lushington family in their West India dealings, but financial troubles sent him wandering abroad, and the publication of the second volume of his *Essay* in 1822 was followed promptly by migration to India, where he continued in financial distress, and thence to South Africa with similar problems. But throughout these problems and wanderings, he continued to publish pamphlets calling ardently for freedom of trade.

John Wheatley's exclusive emphasis on the money supply and unitary price levels foreshadowed the modern severe monetarist and macroeconomic split between the monetary and real realms. More pointedly, his mechanistic emphasis on the price level also foreshadowed the unfortunate Fisherine, Chicagoite and later monetarist preoccupation with stabilizing the 'price level' and with fanatically opposing any and all changes in such 'levels'. Even in his early books of 1803 and 1807, Wheatley denounced the alleged evils of falling prices as well as of inflation, and indeed claimed that falling prices were even more damaging. Indeed, the influence of Wheatley's early tracts was gravely weakened by his being soft-core and timid in drawing any policy conclusions from his hard-core analysis. Instead of returning to the gold standard, Wheatley could only suggest the withdrawal of note issue powers from the country banks and the redemption of all small bank notes under £5.

In his 1807 work, he urged that long-term contracts be made in accordance with an index number of price levels and, in his later works, when this plea went unheeded, he began to grow hysterical about the alleged evils of price declines and their injury to the poor. By his 1822 volume Wheatley had gone so far as to urge the postponement of resumption of specie payments until more supplies might enter the country to prevent prices from falling. Indeed, by this point, Wheatley was ready to abandon the gold standard, in his frenzied opposition to falling prices. Yearning for fiat paper stabilized in value by the government, Wheatley wrote: 'if paper were kept without increase or decrease it would be a better measure of value and medium of exchange than gold.' And by the time of his last work, in 1828, written in South Africa, Wheatley called only for fiat paper expansion of the money supply, else 'irremediable poverty is fixed upon as our eternal fate'.

In this way, as in the case of all too many monetarists and mechanistic quantity theorists, Wheatley began as an ardent hard-money bullionist, and was driven over the years by his frenetic hatred of deflation to wind up as a fiat money inflationist.

5.9   Notes

1. During the seventeenth and eighteenth centuries, England had been on a bimetallic stand-ard, but the official rate consistently overvalued gold and undervalued silver in relation to the world market price. As a result, Britain had long been on a *de facto* gold standard. The discussion during the restriction period was complicated by the fact that during those two centuries, it was illegal for Britons to export British gold or silver coins, or bullion melted from such coin. It was legal to export foreign coin or bullion, but more important is the fact that substantial smuggling habitually nullified the export prohibition.

2. Norman J. Silberling, 'Financial and Monetary Policy of Great Britain during the Napo-leonic Wars', *Quarterly Journal of Economics* 38 (1924), p. 420; quoted in Joseph Salerno, 'The Doctrinal Antecedents of the Monetary Approach to the Balance of Payments' (doctoral dissertation, Rutgers University, 1980), pp. 283–4.

3. In his pamphlet, *An Investigation of the Cause of the Present High Price of Provisions* (1800).

4. Salerno, op. cit., note 2, p. 294.

5. Ibid., pp. 299–300.

6. Heightening the impact of the *Letter* was Boyd's ability to point out in the Preface that in the few months since the writing of the body of the text, depreciation of the pound at Hamburg had risen from 9 to 14 per cent, and the premium on gold bullion over the pound had increased to $10^{1}/_{2}$ per cent. He further noted that in the same interval, the bank had at last been forced to disclose to Parliament statistics on the amount of its notes in circula-tion, confirming Boyd's strong hunch of a huge increase in Bank of England notes (from £8.6 million outstanding in February 1798 to £15.45 million in December 1800).

7. See the enlightening historiographical discussion of the bullionist controversy by Salerno, op. cit. note 2, pp. 266–82.

8. Quoted in F.A. von Hayek, 'Introduction', in Henry Thornton, *An Enquiry into the Nature and Effects of the Paper Credit of Great Britain* (1802) (New York: Rinehart & Co. 1939), p. 36n.

9. Thornton's biographer is surely right in rejecting von Hayek's claim that Thornton had been working on *Paper Credit* since 1796. Thornton himself, as von Hayek concedes, states the opposite in his introduction: 'The first intention of the writer of the following pages was merely to expose some popular errors which related chiefly to the suspension of the cash payments of the Bank of England, and to the influence of our paper currency on the price of provisions'. Von Hayek also admits that the book 'was intended partly as a reply to Boyd'. See von Hayek, op. cit., note 8, pp. 42–6; Thornton, op. cit., note 8, p. 67; Standish Meacham, *Henry Thornton of Clapham, 1760–1815* (Cambridge: Harvard Uni-versity Press, 1964), p. 186.

10. Salerno, op. cit., note 2, pp. 364–5.

11. For a thorough critique of Thornton, see Salerno, op. cit., note 2, pp. 357–400.

12. Jacob Hollander, 'The Development of the Theory of Money from Adam Smith to David Ricardo', *Quarterly Journal of Economics*, 25 (May 1911), p. 456.

6 Monetary and banking thought, II: the bullion *Report* and the return to gold

6.1 Ricardo enters the fray

The bullionist controversy sank into oblivion for five years after 1804, largely because a cautious policy on the part of the Banks of England and Ireland temporarily abated the monetary inflation and its unwelcome consequences. Then, during 1809, the heating up of the war with Napoleon rekindled the inflation, bank note circulation increasing from £17.5 million in November 1808 to £19.8 million the following August. Consequently, the pound rapidly depreciated by the Summer, to a discount of 20 per cent on foreign exchange at Hamburg, and to a 20 per cent rise in the market price of gold (at 93 shillings/ounce) over the official mint par of 77s. 10^1/2d. per ounce. It was time for the bullionist controversy to heat up again.

David Ricardo was first and foremost a monetary economist, and, as Professor Peake has reminded us, his focus on money remained a key to the entire body of his economic thought.[1] Ricardo had come upon *The Wealth of Nations* in 1799, and had steeped himself in political economy ever since, his practical life as a wealthy young stock- and bond-broker naturally leading him to emphasize monetary affairs. The rapidly growing depreciation of the pound in 1809 led Ricardo to his first published works on economics, beginning with a letter on the 'Price of Gold' in the *Morning Chronicle* (29 August).

Ricardo's letter made a great impact, particularly by his unique blend of hard core theorizing and impressive command of the empirical and institutional facts of the monetary scene. His first letter to the *Morning Chronicle* was followed by two more, with the letters being shortly expanded into a renowned and highly influential work – Ricardo's first book – *The High Price of Bullion, a Proof of the Depreciation of Banknotes* (the point is summarized in the title), published at the beginning of 1810. The *High Price* went into no less than four editions by the following year.

The various positions in the bullionist controversy had been set during the first phase of the debate (1800–4). It was Ricardo's intention to revive and establish the bullionist position, not only against the anti-bullionists, but more importantly against the more respected and influential moderate anti-bullionist doctrine of Henry Thornton. Thornton was the most important theoretical opponent of bullionism, and so Ricardo set out to take up the cudgels for Lord King, although, in doing so, he unfortunately – as we shall see – reverted to and elaborated the rigid and mechanistic approach of John Wheatley.

It was Thornton, however, who was his leading opponent, and Ricardo set out to convert him; as he wrote in *High Price*:

Mr. Thornton must, therefore, according to his own principles, attribute it [the premium on gold bullion] to some more permanent cause than an unfavourable balance of trade, and will, I doubt not, whatever his opinion may formerly have been, now agree that it is to be accounted for only by the depreciation of the circulating medium.

In the course of the *High Price*, Ricardo set forth clearly the important point that there is no such thing as a shortage of specie or a great need for more of it: that, in effect, *any* level of the money supply is optimal:

> If the quantity of gold or silver in the world employed as money were exceedingly small, or abundantly great…the variation in their quantity would have produced no other effect than to make the commodities for which they were exchanged comparatively dear or cheap. The smaller quantity of money would perform the functions of circulating medium as well as the larger.

As soon as the *High Price* was published in January 1810, Ricardo, hitting on the right tactic to spread his views, sent a copy to that leading moderate and influential MP, on monetary questions, Francis Horner. The effect on Horner was electric, and he was moved, the following month, to introduce – and get passed – a resolution in the House of Commons setting up a select committee to enquire into the cause of the high price of bullion. The justly famed 'bullion committee' of 22 illustrious MPs, chaired by Horner, issued its report in June 1810, recommending the bullionist policy of a return to the gold standard in two years' time. The bullion committee *Report* touched off an intense controversy, within Parliament and in the general pamphlet litera-ture over the following year.

David Ricardo had partially accomplished his objective of converting Henry Thornton, who was perhaps the most influential member of the bullion com-mittee and who co-wrote its *Report*, along with Horner and William Huskisson. Characteristically, it was not Ricardo's bullionist *theory* that had swayed Thornton, but the impressive marshalling of evidence that convinced him at long last that this particular inflation and depreciation were being caused by over-issue of Bank of England notes. Thornton, in short, had joined his disciple Horner before him in remaining a moderate, but in being converted from anti-bullionist to bullionist on empirical grounds.[2] In the parliamentary debate on the bullion *Report* in May 1811, Thornton conceded that the idea of poor harvests and subsidies to foreigners being the cause of the deprecia-tion 'was an error to which he himself had once inclined, but he stood corrected after a fuller consideration of the subject'.

Thornton's conversion was all the more remarkable because his own bank was financially tied to the fiat expansion of bank credit; and the mere issu-ance of the *Report*, even though it did not carry the day in Parliament, was enough to cause a minor run on Thornton's bank. Furthermore, a period of difficulties that were never fully overcome now set in for the bank until it finally failed in 1825, ten years after Thornton's death.

Thornton's conversion, however, was only empirical. Thus, in the course of the debates on the bullion *Report*, he still brought up the bogy of deflation, and suggested that the pound be devalued to its existing market levels in order to ward off a deflation when resumption finally arrived.

Since Ricardo's main focus was combating the views of Henry Thornton, it is not surprising that he overreacted, and, instead of adopting the complete, sophisticated bullionism of Lord King, went on to the rigid and mechanistic doctrines of John Wheatley. In particular, in order to rebut Thornton completely, Ricardo believed that the dispute had to be elevated totally to the theoretical plane, so that he felt forced to maintain that *only* monetary factors, even in the short run, could ever have any influence whatever on prices or exchange rates. Money, Ricardo felt obliged to maintain, is ever and always, even in the short run, totally neutral to the rest of the economy, to everything, that is, except overall prices. As Professor Peake puts it:

> In large part, Ricardo's early works represented a reaction to Henry Thornton's non-neutral monetary economics, and in challenging Thornton's views, Ricardo committed himself to an explanation of output, value, and distribution in real terms consistent with neutral money.[3]

To accomplish his impressive if unbalanced task, David Ricardo had to concentrate exclusively on long-run equilibrium states, and to ignore the market processes towards them. In that way, Ricardo set the stage for his later approach to all economic questions.[4] Ricardo summarized his methodology in the course of his famous correspondence with Thomas Robert Malthus on monetary questions from 1811 to 1813: 'You always have in mind the immediate and temporary effects...[I] fix my whole attention on the permanent state of things which will result from them'.[5]

For money to be strictly neutral to everything except a general level of prices, Ricardo had to assert a strict, radical dichotomization between the monetary and the real worlds, with values, relative prices, production and incomes determined only in the 'real' sphere, while overall prices were set exclusively in the monetary sphere. And never the two spheres could meet. And here began the fateful and all-pervasive modern fallacy of a severe split between two hermetically sealed worlds: the 'micro' and the 'macro', each with its own determinants and laws. Furthermore, as Salerno writes, 'it was Ricardo's strong affirmation of the neutral-money doctrine in his bullionist writings that was to serve as the source of the classical conception of money as merely a "veil" hiding the "real" phenomena and processes of the economy'.[6] In particular, if money is neutral, then value, or relative prices, had to have only 'real' determinants, which Ricardo discovered in embodied quantities of labour.

In the macro area, in contrast, Ricardo set forth a mechanistic, strictly proportional causal relation between the quantity of money and the level of prices, a strictly proportionate 'quantity theory of money'. Again, Peake summed it up very well:

> Theoretically, Ricardo challenged Thornton by developing a strict quantity-theory, neutral-money analysis which resulted in his well-known dichotomization of the economy into goods and money sectors, with no role for money other than to determine the general level of prices. Analytically, this required him to convert Thornton's model into a dichotomized model...by demonstrating real-market equilibrium independent of the money market. A fundamental theme linking all of Ricardo's later works is the continuing search for neutral money.[7]

Thus Ricardo writes that

> The value of the circulating medium of every country bears some proportion to the value of the commodities which it circulates...No increase or decrease of its quantity, whether consisting of gold, silver, of paper-money, can increase or decrease its value above or below this proportion. If the mines cease to supply the annual consumption of the precious metals, money will become more valuable, and a smaller quantity will be employed as a circulating medium. The diminution in the quantity will be proportioned to the increase of its value.

The value of inconvertible paper money, declared Ricardo, becomes determined in the same way. Hence, under any restriction of specie payment,

> any excess of [Bank]...notes would depreciate the value of the circulating medium in proportion to the excess. If twenty millions had been the circulation of England before the restriction...and if the bank were successively to increase it to fifty, or a hundred millions, the increased quantity would be all absorbed in the circulation of England, but would be in all cases, depreciated to the value of the twenty millions.

Under inconvertible currency, furthermore, strict proportionality then gets carried over to the determination of exchange rates. Like Wheatley, Ricardo concluded that only monetary factors ever determine the exchange rate and hence that the depreciation of the exchange rate must precisely measure the extent of monetary inflation and of the over-issue of paper money. In the same way, and to the same precise proportion, the rise in the price of bullion, and the rise in prices of commodities, will also reflect the selfsame over-issue and depreciation.

David Ricardo's arrival on the monetary scene brought him into the first rank of bullionist champions, not because of anything original he had to say, but because of his empirical knowledge of money, his grasp of the literature, and his willingness to refute in detail the arguments of the numerous distinguished men of the anti-bullionist Establishment ranks. Thus, in the course of the storm over the bullion *Report* (see below), Charles Bosanquet (1769–1850), a London merchant governor of the South Seas Company, as well as a son of a former governor of the Bank of England, wrote a pamphlet attacking the *Report*, sneering at it from the point of view of a 'practical man' scoffing at wild and irrelevant theorists (in his *Practical Observations on the Report of the Bullion Committee*, two editions in 1810). Bosanquet's pamphlet drew a famous *Reply to Mr. Bosanquet's Practical Observations* (1811) by Ricardo the following year. Ricardo's pamphlet was a brilliant and effective polemic, in which he marshalled an impressive array of empirical data in the course of a lofty defence of high (and mechanistic) theory as against the dim-wittedness of self-proclaimed 'practical men'. The *Reply* was particularly effective because Ricardo could match Bosanquet in realistic, practical knowledge, a ploy which led many people to overlook the strident unrealism of his theoretical apparatus.

In sum, Jacob Hollander rightly explained Ricardo's influence on behalf of bullionism, not as the result of any original contributions, but

> because, not content with restating a positive theory, Ricardo set up in succession and demolished in turn, sometimes completely, always plausibly, every opposed argument in a written criticism or current opinion…A theory which had a dignified parentage was refurbished, defended from doctrinal attacks, justified by contemporary events, vitalized by urgent timeliness, and vindicated against current criticism. A standard was planted, the field cleared, and an alert and resourceful champion held the lists.[8]

But even at this early date, the hard-money champion was beginning to buckle and if not abandon at least to flounder in the cause. For in his reply to Malthus's review of *The High Price* in the *Edinburgh Review*, reprinted as an appendix to the fourth edition, Ricardo advanced a plan for ending the restriction that abandoned the heart of the gold standard. Specifically, he proposed that the pound sterling be redeemable in gold bullion rather than in coin. But a gold bullion standard means that the average person cannot redeem paper money in a commodity medium of payment, and that gold redemption is confined to a handful of wealthy international financiers. Ricardo's desertion of the gold coin standard was motivated, first, by a Smithian desire to 'economize' on the gold metal, and more prominently, by a fear of deflation that was conspicuously inconsistent with his dismissal of all non-price-level effects of changes in the supply of money. In this phobia about deflation, and in this inconsistency, Ricardo followed his mentor in mechanistic bullionism, John Wheatley.

In addition to Francis Horner, another person inspired by Ricardo's reawakening of the bullion controversy was Robert Mushet (1782–1818). A

Scotsman born near Edinburgh, young Mushet had entered the service of the Royal Mint in 1804, and by the time of the new controversy, had risen to the post of first clerk to the master of the Mint. Mushet's *An Enquiry into the Effects Produced on the National Currency and Rates of Exchange, by the Bank Restriction Bill*, came out early in 1810, before the appointment of the bullion committee, and went quickly into three editions. Mushet was able to add his expertise at the Royal Mint to the hard-core bullionist cause.

6.2   The storm over the bullion *Report*

Although Francis Horner, who formed and chaired the famed bullion committee, was a Whig, the committee itself was scarcely stacked against the Tory government. On the contrary, the committee's 22 members included seven Whigs, seven clear-cut Tories, including even the prime minister and chancellor of the exchequer Spencer Perceval,[9] and eight, including Thornton and Alexander Baring of the renowned banking family, who were independents friendly to the Tory administration. Of the co-authors of the *Report*, Thornton was still considered at the time of appointment of the committee perhaps the leading defender of bank restriction, and William Huskisson (1770–1830) was a leading Tory MP of the Canning wing of the party, who had been a member of the Tory government for several years until 1809.[10] The modal committee member may be summed up as a thoughtful Tory, a supporter of the restriction now troubled by the developing inflation and depreciation of the pound. While David Ricardo was acquainted with Thornton – both had been co-founders of the London Institution and its library in 1805 – his only close friend on the bullion committee was another London Institution co-founder Richard Sharp (1759–1835), a Whig and West Indies merchant.[11] The only member of the committee who shared Ricardo's bullionist hostility to the Bank of England was Henry Brooke Parnell. Indeed, Thornton's presence on the committee and support for the *Report* in Parliament shocked the anti-bullionists and led his wife to offer embarrassed explanations to their friends.[12] Frank W. Fetter summed it up clearly when he wrote that

> The position of Thornton and Huskisson in the Bullion Committee and in their subsequent defence of its Report was taken more in sorrow than in partisanship. It was the outgrowth of their increasing concern over the apathy of the Government and the Bank about the condition of the foreign exchanges and the bullion market, and over the support by the Bank and the Government spokesmen for the 'real bills' doctrine in its most extreme form, i.e., that as long as the Bank's advances were made only on sound commercial assets the amount of the advances could have no effect on prices or the foreign exchanges.[13]

Most important, the bullion *Report* itself was neither Kingian nor Ricardian, but squarely in the Thornton–Horner moderate bullionist camp. Its support for bullionism, in short, was empirical rather than theoretical, concluding reluctantly but firmly that the facts were such that the bank restriction and the bank's monetary inflation had played a large role in the existing inflation and depreciation of the pound sterling. Thornton himself only supported the committee's call for resumption of specie payment in protest at the failure of the bank and government to be chastised and to agree to restricting further issuance of money. As for Ricardo, he only became the leading champion of the committee after the policy conclusions of its *Report* supported his call for resumption of payment in specie.[14] Indeed, Malthus, in his defence of the *Report*, hailed the committee for taking his own moderate stance rather than adopting the Ricardian 'error' of holding a solely monetary explanation of the depreciation.[15]

The *Report* was approved in the full bullion committee by a vote of 13 to 6, and was submitted to Parliament on 8 June 1810.[16] While Prime Minister Perceval was one of the six voting nay – along with his paymaster-general and deputy governor of the bank – there was at first no indication of deep hostility on the part of the administration. Indeed, the Tory press commented favourably on the *Report* when it was first issued. In a few months, however, the administration reversed its course. The best evidence suggests that a command decision was made by the government and the Bank of England in late August or early September to launch an all-out assault upon the bullion *Report*. Leading the battle in Parliament for the government was Nicholas Vansittart (1766–1851), many times secretary to the treasury and soon to be chancellor of the exchequer.[17] In the 1809 debate on resumption of specie payment, Vansittart had coined the patriotic if irrelevant and absurd argument that the 'national resources' of the country sufficed for backing the currency so that there was no need for gold. In the bullion *Report* debate, Vansittart pushed a spectrum of anti-bullionist arguments: first, that immediate resumption was, as usual, inexpedient: second, that the restriction had nothing whatsoever to do with the depreciation of the pound; and third, that Bank of England notes were esteemed every bit as highly as gold coin – an assertion so preposterous and so out of tune with the facts as to bring down upon him open ridicule by George Canning, the leader of a Tory faction out of power.

Masterminding and orchestrating the campaign against the bullion *Report* for Perceval and Vansittart were four shadowy aides and advisers. One was John Charles Herries (1778–1855), son of a London merchant and long-time treasury official, at this time private secretary to the chancellor of the exchequer, and a past and future top financial adviser of Tory leaders. He was himself to be a chancellor of the exchequer in later years. A second figure was Henry Beeke, professor of modern history at Oxford, friend of Vansittart, and prominent advisor of Tory politicians. A particularly mysterious but influential colleague was Jasper Atkinson (1761–1844), about whom little is known except that he was for a quarter-century an official adviser to the government and to the bank, and wrote 13 pamphlets from 1802 to the late 1820s in support of governmental and bank policy. It seems that he was a country banker and active in trade with Holland. He of course published a pamphlet in opposition to the bullion *Report*. Atkinson prepared the pamphlet at the instigation of Herries, and was assisted by his old friend and advisor Henry Beeke.

Perhaps even more curious was the leading role of a Genevan refugee, Sir Francis D'Ivernois, friend of Vansittart, who had been a British secret agent in Europe, and had been a confidential advisor to the British government on relations with France. It was D'Ivernois who first waved the bloody shirt against the bullion *Report* by dragging into the debate the palpably false charge that the *Report* had given aid and comfort to the Napoleonic enemy, had stimulated Napoleon to strengthen his embargo measures against Great Britain, and had emboldened the United States to take a nasty turn toward England. This effective if mendacious red herring was taken up in Parliament by Vansittart and by a leader of the Anglo-Irish Establishment, Robert Stewart, Viscount Castlereagh, the marquis of Londonderry (1769–1822).

Indeed, the major parliamentary motif of the critics of the *Report* was that the restriction was vital for pursuing the war effort against France. Prime Minister Perceval charged that adopting the *Report* 'would be tantamount to a declaration that they would no longer continue those foreign exertions which they had hitherto considered indispensable to the security of the country...'. If Parliament should adopt the *Report* and its policies, Perceval thundered, they 'would disgrace themselves forever, by becoming the voluntary instruments of their country's ruin'. Ringing changes on this wartime necessity, stab-in-the-back theme were Viscount Castlereagh; the High Tory foreign secretary and war secretary Robert Banks Jenkinson, the earl of Liverpool (1770–1828); and the treasurer of the navy and former secretary to the treasury, George Rose (1744–1818), who also contributed two pamphlets to the controversy. Rose was the highest of High Tories, a friend of King George III, an opponent of parliamentary reform, an extreme pro-war advocate, a supporter of the Corn Laws, and an adversary of the abolition of slavery.

In late 1810 and early 1811, a host of pamphlets were published attacking the bullion *Report*, and many of them, both signed and anonymous, were products of the behind-the-scenes campaign of the governmental and bank circles. In addition to Atkinson's pamphlet, Herries weighed in with an anonymous tract, *A Review of the Controversy Respecting the High Price of Bullion, and the State of our Currency*. Charles Bosanquet's *Practical Observations*, rebutted by Ricardo, was another product of this campaign. Particularly important in this effort was the publication of a speech by a prominent attorney, Randle Jackson (1757–1837), which purported to be the views of a concerned bank stockholder.[18] In reality, Jackson was apparently hired by the bank to present its case *sub rosa* against the *Report*. Jackson presented the state-of-the-art critiques by the government: the *Report* had greatly injured commercial credit, the committee was dominated by chronic oppositionists to the government, and it is impossible for bank notes ever to be excessive or to have higher prices than par because they were issued only against 'value received' – a *non sequitur* if there ever was one.

Indeed, the main economic arguments of bank spokesman before the bullion committee and in the parliamentary debates, by men such as Governor John Whitmore and Deputy Governor John Pearse, were an extreme, almost absurd, version of the real bills doctrine: namely, that if bank loans were issued on short-term 'bills of real value, representing real transactions', then bank note issue can never be excessive, and never have any inflationary or depreciating effect on the pound. Walter Bagehot was later to call these arguments 'almost classical by their nonsense'

Perhaps the acme of this nonsense was the pamphlet of the Tory commissioner of audit, Francis Perceval Eliot (c. 1756–1818), who went so far as to maintain that the problem with Huskisson's argument was that he considered the gold guinea to be the standard of value, whereas it is actually the pound sterling. According to Eliot, the pound, precisely because it is fiat money, is the ideal money of account *because* it is by definition 'invariable' in value. On the other hand, Eliot opined, gold or silver, being made of a substantial commodity, must be variable in value.

Meanwhile, a different kind of critic of the *Report* appeared prominently in the pamphlet literature and in Parliament. The eccentric Sir John Sinclair (1754–1835), first and also current president of the board of agriculture, was born to a Scottish noble family and was educated at the universities of Edinburgh and Glasgow, graduating from Trinity College, Oxford in 1775. An MP from 1780 until 1811, Sinclair was a man of great energy and enthusiasm, and a prolific writer in the causes he held dear. In his lifetime, Sinclair published no less than 367 tracts and pamphlets. An advocate of parliamentary reform, Sinclair championed the cause of peace and wrote several pamphlets attacking Pitt's war policy, and calling for peace with England's enemies. He even went so far as to publish a booklet calling for Britain's surrender of Gibraltar to Spain during the American revolutionary war. Sinclair's prime enthusiasm was for agriculture, an art he learned from managing his Scottish estates. Not only was he the first president of the board of agriculture, but he also founded the British Wool Society.

Sinclair was also engrossed in statistical and monetary and fiscal questions. An indefatigable collector of statistics, Sinclair actually introduced the words 'statistics' and 'statistical' into the English language, and during the decade of the 1790s, he collected and published, in 21 volumes, a *Statistical Account of Scotland*. More relevant to our concerns, Sinclair had published, from 1785–90, a three-volume *History of the Public Revenues of the British Empire*. In this work, Sinclair had displayed a determined and all-out zeal for monetary inflation and government spending. As soon as the bullion *Report* was issued, Sinclair wrote to Prime Minister Perceval, asking help for re-printing his work, as part of the task of rebutting the bullion committee. 'You know my sentiments regarding the importance of paper Circulation', he wrote to Perceval, 'which is in fact the basis of our prosperity'. In fact, Sinclair's *Observations on the Report of the Bullion Committee*, published in September 1810, was the very first of many pamphlet attacks on the bullion *Report*.

A storm of pamphlets raged over the bullion *Report*, hoping to influence the parliamentary decision as well as the tides of public opinion. David Ricardo was a host unto himself; in the month of September 1810 alone Ricardo, in the *Morning Chronicle*, defended the conclusions of the *Report*, taking of course the hard-core Ricardian line, attacked the pamphlet of Sir John Sinclair, and also denounced the speech of Randle Jackson, which Ricardo, as a bank stockholder, had heard delivered in person. Malthus wrote two effective articles in the *Edinburgh Review* the following year, taking the Thornton–Horner moderate bullionist position.

Particularly effective defending the *Report* was the Canning–Huskisson faction of Tories, centred in their journal the *Quarterly Review*. As firm Tories, the support of this faction shielded the bullion committee from charges of Whig partisanship. The most widely circulated and one of the most influ-ential pamphlets supporting the *Report* was written by its eminent co-author, William Huskisson. Huskisson's *The Question Concerning the Depreciation of our Currency Stated and Examined* was published in late October 1810 and went into no less than eight editions in rapid succession – the ninth appearing in 1819. The *Quarterly Review* carried on a coordinated campaign on behalf of the *Report*, with contributions by high Tory George Ellis (1753–1815)[19], Huskisson, and even the great George Canning himself. It is not without charm that William Huskisson contributed some passages to Ellis's laudatory review of Huskisson's own pamphlet in the *Quarterly Review*.

All in all, about 90 pamphlets were published in a short period on both sides of the great Bullion controversy. The climax came in May 1811, when Parliament finally got around to debating the *Report*. After four days of debate, all Francis Horner's resolutions incorporating the essence of the *Report* went down to a ringing defeat. The most important resolutions were his first and his last. The first outlined the responsibility of the bank's over-issue for the price inflation and the depreciation of the pound; this resolution was defeated by a vote of 151–75. Horner's final resolution, providing for resumption of the gold standard in two years, lost by a far wider margin, 180–45. Nicholas Vansittart then rubbed it in for the government, getting Parliament to pass resolutions defending the government's and the bank's view of the controversy. Most characteristic was Vansittart's third resolution, restating the 'classic nonsense' in a declaration almost as fatuous as King Canute's command to the tides or a state legislature's redefinition of *pi*. Parliament declared that 'the promissory notes of the said Company [the Bank of England] have hitherto been, and are at this time held in public estimation to be equivalent to the legal coin of the realm and generally accepted as such in all pecuniary transactions…'.

Even though the inflation and the depreciation proceeded apace, the monetary controversy died out for the duration of the Napoleonic wars. In despair, and perhaps to reveal the absurdity of Vansittart's case, the great Peter Lord King now decided to take direct, personal action in protest against the depreciating paper pound. While the pound was not officially legal tender, it was treated as such by government and public alike. To dramatize the true situation, Lord King, in 1811, proclaimed that henceforth he would only accept rent from his tenants either in gold coin, or in bank notes at their market discount – in short, he would insist on the gold equivalent in pounds. King's heroic action forced the government to impose legal tender for payment of rent, at the official par of 21 shillings to the gold guinea. And the following year, Parliament completed the coup by extending legal tender coercion to all payments of every type.

6.3 Deflation and the return to gold

Needless to say, the selfsame Establishment politicians who had used war as their supreme excuse for continuing the restriction, failed to jump with alacrity to go back to the gold standard when the war finally ended in 1815. And yet, conditions were certainly ripe. In a pattern that would set the tone for over a century, the inflationary credit boom of wartime was quickly succeeded by a postwar deflation of money, credit and prices. The wartime inflation was succeeded by a postwar deflationary recession. There is no evidence whatever that the Bank of England deliberately contracted the money supply to pave the way for a return to gold at the prewar par. It was simply the beginning of the classic pattern of fractional-reserve banking powered by a central bank: the creation of boom and bust. Total Bank of England credit fell from £44.9 million on 31 August 1815 to £34.4 million a year later, a drop of 24 per cent. Bank deposits fell by about 15 per cent in the same period, while bank notes fell by 11 per cent.

The bank contraction exerted a powerful leverage effect on the country banks; many country banks failed from 1814 to 1816 and country bank note circulation fell from £22.7 million in 1814 to £19.0 million in 1815 and then to £15.1 million in 1816. In short, country bank notes outstanding fell by 33.5 per cent over the two-year period, and by 20.5 per cent from 1815 to 1816. We may now arrive at a rough estimate of the total contraction of the money supply from August 1815 to August 1816. Total money supply (bank notes + bank deposits + country bank notes) amounted to approximately £60.7 million in 1815; it fell to £50.4 million the following year, a drop of 17 per cent in one year.

The monetary contraction, combined with general public expectations of a return to gold, drove the market gold premium over the official par down nearly to the par price. The monetary inflation had driven the market gold price up to £5.10 at the end of 1813, which was 145 per cent of the old official pre-restriction par of £3 17s. 10^1/2d. After Napoleon's retirement to Elba, the gold price fell to £4 5s. 0d., a premium of only 8 per cent; then, on Napoleon's return to France, the gold price of the pound shot up nearly to its 1813 peak. After Waterloo, once again, the gold price fell sharply and steadily, reaching £3 18s. 6d. in October 1816, a premium of less than 1 per cent. Similarly the market price of silver fell from a peak premium of 38 per cent in 1813 to a premium of only a little over 2 per cent in the first postwar year of 1816. And the price of foreign exchange at Hamburg fell from a premium of 44 per cent in 1813 down to par in 1816. Price deflation accompanied the monetary contraction, British prices falling from a peak of 198 in 1814 (1790 being equal to 100), to 135 in 1816.

Conditions were now perfect to return to gold, and immediate resumption could have been achieved with no further transition problems. But the British Establishment dithered, its only constructive step in 1816 being Parliament's dropping of the formal bimetallic standard, which had only resulted in a *de facto* gold standard in the eighteenth century, and the adoption of a formal gold standard. Silver, from then on, would only be subsidiary coin. But apart from stating that when Britain *did* go back to a specie standard it would be going back to gold, nothing else was done.

The problem was a pervasive desire in the Establishment to resume cheap credit and inflation, as well as an even more widespread phobia about deflation that marred the analysis and policy conclusions of even the most influential champions of a return to gold payments. The bulk of anti-bullionists displayed their hypocrisy and intellectual bankruptcy by reversing their supposed analytical stance. In short, those who stoutly denied, all during the era of inflation, that over-issue of bank notes had any impact on domestic prices or foreign exchange rates, now reversed their course and blamed the fall in prices, as well as the postwar depression, squarely on the contraction of the money supply and the eventual resumption of specie payments. What they wanted, therefore, was easy money and inflation, and they were willing to use any arguments at hand, however inconsistent, to achieve their goal. What they seemed unwilling to realize is that any inflationary boom, especially that of a lengthy and major war, will collapse at war's end into depression and deflation. Much of the deflation was the result of the postwar depression and bankruptcies, for the initial post-war deflation occurred years before the actual return to gold or even the passage of the Resumption Act. The postwar depression was the market's way of readjusting the economy to the enormous distortions of production and investment brought about by the skewed demands of wartime and the inflationary credit boom. In short, the postwar depression was the painful but necessary process of liquidating the distortions of the wartime inflation and of returning to a healthy peacetime economy efficiently serving the consumers.

Another cause of the deflation was industrial and economic progress. The end of the war liberated England to launch one of the greatest periods of economic growth in its history. The Industrial Revolution could at last develop freely and raise the standard of living of the mass of Englishmen – something it could not do when the industrial engine had been diverted to the unproductive waste of war. As a result of the great increase of production, prices kept falling in Britain throughout the 1820s – long past the time when this welcome drop in the cost of living, this 'deflation', could plausibly be blamed on the return to gold in 1821.

The anti-deflation hysteria and the desire to keep inflating delayed the return to gold for five years after 1816. When it became clear that there would be no immediate resumption, the pound began to depreciate again, the price of silver bullion rising from 2 per cent above par in 1816 to 12 per cent premium on 1818. Similarly, the foreign exchange rate at Hamburg rose from par to 5 per cent above. And domestic prices rose from 135 in 1816 to 150 two years later. The weakening of the pound by disappointed expectations of immediate resumption was also greatly compounded by an expansion of bank advances and note issues.

When the restriction came up for one of its periodic renewals in the Spring of 1816, Chancellor of the Exchequer Vansittart pleaded for two more years of renewal so that business could acquire more needed cheap credit. Vansittart was easily able to defeat Francis Horner's resolution for resumption of specie payment in two years. Agriculturists, as usual, had overexpanded and went heavily into debt during the wartime inflation, and then complained heavily when the bubble burst and turned to the government to inflate or expand spending on their behalf. The *Quarterly Review*, reflecting Tory devotion to the interests of aristocratic large landlords, shifted gears from favouring the bullion *Report* to bitterly denouncing deflation.

The most extreme of the inflationists now emerged in the form of two banker brothers from Birmingham, Thomas (1783–1856) and Matthias Attwood (1779–1851), who also served as the spokesmen for the iron and brass industry of the city. Birmingham, as the centre of armaments manufacture, had been a major beneficiary of the war boom. Thomas Robert Malthus, as we have seen, for a few years urged the government to increase deficits to cure the alleged ills of underconsumption, but abandoned this line of thought as soon as the postwar agricultural and economic depression was over. But the prolific Attwoods were to make inflation and permanent incovertible fiat paper money a lifelong crusade. Nothing, for example, could be more starkly opposed to Say's crucial law of markets than the unabashed assertion of Thomas Attwood, in an 1817 open letter to Vansittart, that 'It is the chief purpose of this letter to show that the issue of money will create markets, and that it is upon the abundance or scarcity of money that the extent of all markets principally depends...'.

Along with fiat money and monetary inflation, the Attwoods and their counterparts in the northern industrial city of Liverpool were able to persuade the government to embark on a large-scale programme of deficits, relief and public works to try to generate another inflationary boom. James Mill warned Ricardo in the Autumn of 1816 that 'some villainous schemes of finance' were afoot, and sure enough, the government proposed a deficit bond issue to finance public works, and also loaned out three-quarters of a million pounds during 1817. The temporary resurgence of inflation and prosperity in 1818 was the result, according to the fiery, erratic hard-money radical journalist William Cobbett, of the prodding by Matthias Attwood upon Vansittart, who 'caused bales of paper money to be poured out...', via Bank of England loans to the government.

Indeed, it was undoubtedly the weakening of the pound in 1817–18 that tipped the scales and led to Parliament's passing the act of resuming payments in gold in May, 1819. Resumption in gold coin was supposed to begin four years hence, but actually gold coin payments were launched on the banner day of 8 May 1821. Even though the resultant gold coin standard served as the cornerstone of Britain's economic growth and prosperity for nearly a century, the fierce opposition, confusion, and vacillating of the government made arriving at the proper result seem almost a miracle. The bank opposed resumption down to the very passage of the law in 1819, and it was the government's temporarily cooling relations with the bank that allowed room for the resumption law. Yet, even though a determined effort was launched by men such as Alexander Baring (1774–1848), the Attwoods and the Birmingham manufacturing interests, and the landed aristocrats to overturn resumption, the gold standard held and was even resumed earlier than scheduled, in 1821.[20] Thus the earl of Carnarvon, in mid-1821, denouncing the resumption act for lowering agricultural prices, and calling for monetary expansion and greater government expenditures, openly raised the standard of the landed aristocracy as against the cosmopolitan money men and financiers:

He called upon the House to consider the consequences...of destroying by its means the aristocracy of the country – the gentlemen and the yeomanry of England, on whose existence our institutions alone could rest. The monied interest had been formed by the calls of our finances; they could be removed: they were inhabitants of this or of any other country; but the stability of our institutions, and the safety of the throne itself, depended on our agricultural population...

And yet the gold coin standard held. It held even though two of the most influential champions of resumption were weak reeds when it came to resisting the anti-deflation hysteria. At the end of the war, Ricardo, in his *Proposals for an Economical and Secure Currency* (1816), reverted to his 1811 gold bullion proposal, in which resumption would take place not in coin but in large ingots or gold bars, thereby limiting the gold standard to a few wealthy traders. Gold would not then be the true standard currency of the realm, and would be but a flimsy check against the propensity of government and the banking system to inflate money and credit.

After the publication of his *Principles of Political Economy* in 1817, David Ricardo was the most celebrated economist in England, and his views on currency as well as other economic problems carried great weight. At the urging of his mentor James Mill, Ricardo then entered Parliament in 1819 to battle for his economic views until his death in 1823. He particularly lent his great prestige to urging resumption of gold payments, and somehow his bullion plan lost out rapidly to the more consistent and thoroughgoing gold coin standard.

The most important single politician responsible for the return to gold was the remarkable Tory statesman Robert Peel the Younger (1788–1859), who gave his name ('Peel's Act') to the resumption law. Peel was later, as prime minister, to be responsible, during the mid-1840s, for the repeal of the notorious Corn Laws, as well as the attempt to establish the currency principle into law in Peel's Act of 1844. Peel's accomplishments were particularly remarkable for being bred to the political purple by his distinguished High Tory father. Peel was the eldest son of Sir Robert Peel the Elder, a leading Lancashire cotton manufacturer, whose own father had established the first calico-cotton factory in Lancashire. Sir Robert was a dyed-in-the-wool Tory statist, a fervent supporter of William Pitt, who had written a pamphlet in 1780 praising the *National Debt Productive of National Prosperity*. As an MP the elder Peel had ardently backed the war against France, had put through the first Factory Act, and had opposed the bullion *Report* in 1811.

When young Robert was born, Sir Robert dedicated his first-born son to the world of politics. The brilliant youth went to Harrow, where he was a friend and classmate of Lord Byron, and entered Christ Church College in Oxford, in 1805. In 1808, Peel graduated with high honours, and his doting father promptly purchased him a seat in Parliament the following year. The precocious 21-year-old MP soon became under secretary for war and the colonies, whose ministry conducted the war against France, and in 1812 he became for six years the chief secretary for Ireland. There he followed his father's High Tory principles by fiercely repressing the Irish and taking the lead in opposing the emancipation of Catholics in Great Britain. In 1811, young Peel joined his father in bitter opposition to the bullion *Report.*

In 1819, when the House of Commons named a committee to study the resumption of specie payments, young Robert Peel was chosen chairman over far more experienced members such as Huskisson, Canning, and the ardent bullionist and member of the bullion committee, the Whig George Tierney. Yet Robert Peel orchestrated the report favourable to resumption, and it was Peel who shepherded the resumption law through Parliament. Peel thereby displayed the beginning of his memorable life-long series of shifts away from High Tory statism and towards classical liberalism. Towards, in short, hard money, free trade, and emancipation of the Roman Catholics of Britain. George Canning was in awe at Peel's achievement in attaining the gold coin standard, calling this feat 'the greatest wonder he had witnessed in the political world'. It was particularly piquant that, in effecting this notable change of heart, the younger Peel had to break with his father, who not only opposed resumption, but also signed the petition of several hundred 'Merchants, Bankers, Traders and others' of the City of London, warning of great distress should the committee's recommendation ever become law.

A crucial question, then, is how Robert Peel came to change his mind. Professor Rashid has performed the service of unearthing as the likely instrument of Peel's conversion his former tutor at Oriel College, Oxford, the Rev. Edward Copleston (1776–1849).[21] Copleston was the son of a rector in Devonshire, and was descended from an ancient landed Devon family. Graduating from Corpus Christi College, Oxford in 1795, Copleston became a fellow at Oriel College, getting his MA from there in 1797, and becoming a tutor at Oriel, and professor of poetry at Oxford. Copleston later became dean at Oriel, and by 1814 had risen to provost of Oriel College. He was highly influential at Oxford, and one of the main persons responsible for the raising of academic standards and the subsequent rise of Oxford to its once high estate. Although a staunch Tory and an influential clerical counsellor to the Tory leadership, Copleston was a moderate liberal in the Anglican church and an advocate of Catholic emancipation.

As early as 1811, Copleston had become a determined opponent of inflation and depreciation, especially criticizing its destructive effect on creditors and holders of fixed incomes. In 1819, he decided to intervene in the new bullionist struggle by publishing two pamphlets directed to his former pupil. The first *Letter to the Rt. Hon. Robert Peel...On the Pernicious Effects of a Variable Standard of Value* was published on 19 January 1819, and it was quickly recommended on the floor of the House of Commons by the fiery Whig and proponent of immediate resumption, George Tierney. The pamphlet was also praised in an editorial in the *Times*. The first edition of the *Letter* was sold out immediately, and within a month, three editions had been printed. In March, Copleston published a *Second Letter...* elaborating on the arguments of the first, particularly on the ill effects that inflation and a depreciating pound had on the poor. The large printing of the *Second Letter* was quickly sold out, and a second edition was issued in May.

Evidence of Copleston's influence on Peel comes from the latter's correspondence with his favourite tutor at Oxford, his close friend, the Rev. Charles Lloyd. Lloyd, who was indeed a rival Anglo-Catholic force to Copleston at Oxford, wrote to Peel recommending Copleston's *Letter* at the same time that Peel was recommending it to him. Peel notes that the pamphlet 'has made a great impression' in Parliament, including among its admirers Canning and Huskisson. In fact, it seems likely from Peel's remarks that Copleston's clear-cut restatement of bullionist principle was the first pamphlet he had ever read on the subject.

Matthias Attwood, indeed, went so far as to claim that Peel and Huskisson were followers of Copleston's ideas. If Copleston was crucially influential, then his violent attack in the pamphlet on what Peel referred to as the 'imbecility' of Nicholas Vansittart might have played a large role in reducing Vansittart's influence and getting government policy on resumption changed.

Yet, in the post-resumption debate, even Copleston floundered, claiming in the *Quarterly Review* in 1821 that, while he had upheld the principle of specie payments, he had been opposed to immediate resumption. Complaining about the agricultural distress, he blamed the immediate resumption on the influence of Ricardo, ignoring the latter's own phobia about deflation. Thus the two most influential writers pushing Parliament into resumption, Ricardo and Edward Copelston, each was uncertain about the gold coin standard in the face of deflation. Robert Peel's achievement appears, then, all the more miraculous.

Of particular interest is Copleston's brilliance and possible originality in his challenge to Ricardo by reviving, perhaps unwittingly, the 'complete bullionist' or 'pre-Austrian' monetary tradition of Cantillon and Lord King. Copleston, in the first place, attacked Ricardo's mechanistic assertion that exchange rates *measure* the degree of depreciation, this doctrine resting on the equally mechanistic view that 'a variation in price caused by an altered value of money is common *at once* to all commodities'. (Emphasis Ricardo's.) Copleston countered that it was precisely because prices do *not* adjust smoothly, instantly, and uniformly to inflation that the inflation process is so painful and destructive:

The fact undoubtedly is, that the altered value of money does not affect all prices at the same time: but that wide intervals occur, during which one class is compelled to buy dear while they sell cheap, and others have no prospect whatever of indemnity, or of regaining the relative position they once occupied.

In short, Copleston pointed out the profound truth that in a transition period to a new monetary equilibrium there are always gains by those whose selling prices rise faster than their buying prices, and losses by those whose costs rise faster than selling prices, and who are late in receiving the new money. But, even further, Copleston points out that some of these changes in relative income and wealth will be permanent. In short, changes in the money supply are never neutral to the economy, and their effects are never confined to the 'level' of prices.

Taking issue with David Hume's famous assertion that an increase of the quantity of money in a country generates prosperity, Copleston pointed to the impoverishment of the Spanish and English peasantry from the monetary and price inflation of the sixteenth century. He noted shrewdly, in a lesson that could well be heeded today, that while 'pure theory inculcates the neutral and necessary tendency towards an equitable adjustment', it also 'leaves the intermediate difficulties and delays out of the question, as frictions in a mechanical problem…'.

On the other hand, Copleston was perceptive enough to point out that the path toward equilibrium is faster in monetary than in real matters. In monetary affairs, he noted,

the level is found *almost immediately*. Other commodities require some time to produce them – and the fortunate holder of large quantities may make great profits before an adequate competition can grow up: but in these [money] the time and labour required for the production count for nothing. The commodity is always afloat, waiting only the impulse of profit to determine its direction to the best market.

6.4   Questioning fractional-reserve banking: Britain and the US
Great Britain had now experienced the pain and deprivation of what would become a classic 'business cycle', i.e. the expansion of money, the rise in prices, the euphoric boom, all fuelled by the monetary inflation of a fractional-reserve banking system, succeeded by a monetary contraction, with attendant depression, fall in prices, bankruptcies, unemployment and dislocations. And behind this boom and bust, guiding, organizing, centralizing, and directing the monetary expansion and contraction, was the powerful central bank created and privileged by the central government. In short, it was forcefully impressed upon the public that fractional-reserve banks, especially when organized under a central bank, can and do create and then destroy money, distorting and impoverishing the public and the economy in their

wake. It is no wonder that severe critics of fractional-reserve banking quickly arose, indicting the banks' actions and the system itself, and noting their responsibility for the boom–bust cycle.

Professor Frank W. Fetter notes the 'groundswell of criticism of all banks', but he describes the 'invective' against banks as 'exploiters' of the common people with an air of bemusement at the public's irrationality. But surely this 'populist' invective was well justified: the banks were indeed privileged by the government, enabled to inflate, and thus to set in motion a two-fold great injury upon the public: an inflationary boom dislocating production and investment and wiping out the savings of the thrifty, followed by a painful contractionary bust necessary to correcting the distortions of the boom. All of this could properly be laid to the door of the privileged, central bank-run, fractional-reserve banking system. Looked at in that light, the radical denunciations of banks 'without benefit of economic analysis' look more like a deeper level of analysis than Fetter realizes. Fetter describes these opponents of banking as follows:

> The idea appeared increasingly that banks deprived the public of its natural metallic money and had created paper money as an instrument of oppression...Men who were far apart on most points were in agreement that somebody was making too much money from the paper money system: the restrained criticism of Ricardo, under James Mill's urgings, of the Bank's profits; the strictures of obscure pamphleteers that bankers 'appear to be infinitely more mischievous than the coiners of base money [i.e. counterfeiters of coin]', and that both the Bank of England and the country banks had made 'unfair gains from the restriction measure'; the wholesale invective of Cobbett against bankers as a class; and the denunciations in Jonathan Wooler's *Black Dwarf*, in Leigh Hunt's *Examiner*, and in *Sherwin's Political Register*, where without benefit of economic analysis these radical journals reiterated that the paper money system was one of the oppressors of the people. In 1819, when Parliament was considering resumption, *Sherwin's Political Register* offered this advice: 'Let our tyrants turn their infamous paper into coin of the same weight and fineness, as that of which the people have been deprived...'.[22]

Fetter indicts the radical hard-money journalist William Cobbett[23] for alleged inconsistency in bitterly denouncing the restriction and the bank's inflation, and then attacking the bank for deflating after the war and causing further distress. Yet there is no real inconsistency in attacking the central bank and the fractional-reserve banks for first inflating and then contracting, for that is precisely what they had done, and the entire distress of the boom–bust cycle can thus be laid at their doors.

Knowingly or not, these radical critics of fractional-reserve banking were simply revising and applying the great tradition of hostility to fractional-reserve banking and devotion to 100 per cent reserve in eighteenth century Britain (e.g. Hume, Harris, Vanderlint), a tradition that had been unfortunately derailed by Adam Smith's apologetics for bank paper. In France, the

100 per cent reserve anti-bank tradition had already been revived, as we have seen, by J.B. Say and Destutt de Tracy.

In the United States, meanwhile, similar conditions were bringing about similar results. The United States, too, had entered the Napoleonic Wars in 1812, and subsequently experienced wartime boom, inconvertible bank notes, and comparable grievous inflation. The difference was that the United States had managed to get rid of its central bank (the First Bank of the United States) in 1811, so it achieved inflationary results by the federal government's permitting the private banks to suspend specie payments in August 1814, allowing them to continue in operation and expand credit without having to redeem their notes or deposits. This intolerable situation was allowed to continue for two years after the end of the war, until February 1817, at which point the Madison administration made an inflationary compact with the nation's banks. The compact provided that the US would re-establish a privileged Second Bank of the United States, which would then proceed to inflate credit by at least an agreed-upon amount, in return for the banks graciously consenting to resume meeting their contractual obligations to pay their debts in specie. An inflationary boom, fuelled by an expanding Second Bank ensued, to be followed by the catastrophic panic of 1819, in which the Second Bank was forced to contract suddenly in order to save itself.

The panic of 1819 confirmed Thomas Jefferson's hostility to fractional-reserve banking, and we have seen how he and his friend and old opponent John Adams both declared their enthusiasm for Destutt de Tracy's ultra hard-money treatise on economics. Jefferson was moved by the panic to draw up a remedial 'Plan for Reducing the Circulating Medium', which he asked his friend William Cabell Rives to introduce into the Virginia legislature without disclosing his authorship. The goal of the plan was bluntly stated as 'the eternal suppression of bank paper'. The method was to reduce the circulating medium to the level of specie proportionately over a five-year period, until paper money was withdrawn completely and totally redeemed in specie. After that, the money in circulation would consist solely of specie.

John Adams agreed wholeheartedly. In a letter to his old opponent, the great libertarian Jeffersonian anti-bank and anti-tariff theoretician John Taylor of Caroline, Adams blamed the banks for the 1819–20 depression. He attacked any issue of paper money beyond specie in the bank as 'theft', a position he had elaborated years earlier: 'Every dollar of a bank bill that is issued beyond the quantity of gold and silver in the vaults represents nothing, and is therefore a cheat upon somebody.'[24]

Jefferson's close friend and son-in-law, Governor Thomas Randolph of Virginia, summed up in his inaugural address of December 1820 the predominant Virginia attitude towards banks. Randolph pointed out that specie, in universal demand, had a relatively stable value, whereas banks caused great fluctuations in the supply and value of paper money, with attendant distress. Randolph endorsed not only the collection of all taxes in specie (which later, on the federal level, became the 'Independent Treasury' plan) but also envisioned a currency backed 100 per cent in specie.

But the most important impact of the panic of 1819 on American thought was not simply to reconfirm the hard-money advocates of the older generation. It was to generate and stimulate a new, mighty ultra-hard-money movement, which would later become the Jacksonian movement of the 1830s and 1840s. The goal of the great Jacksonian movement was a monetary system consisting wholly of gold or of 100 per cent gold-backed notes or deposits. Its first goal, achieved after great struggle in the 1830s, was to eliminate the Second Bank of the United States; its second, largely achieved a decade later, was to separate the federal government totally from the banking system by confining its receipts and monetary transactions solely to specie (the 'Independent Treasury'). Its final goal, only partially achieved, was to outlaw fractional-reserve banking altogether, a goal that might well have succeeded if the Democratic Party had not been fatally sundered by the slavery issue.[25]

A remarkably large number of future Jacksonian leaders learned their anti-bank hard-money views from experiencing the panic of 1819. General Andrew Jackson (1767–1845) himself, a wealthy Nashville, Tennessee cotton planter, adopted his lifelong anti-bank views as a result of the panic: indeed, he quickly became the fervent leader of the opposition to inconvertible state paper in Tennessee, as well as to laws for relief of debtors. Top Jacksonian Senator Thomas Hart Benton (1782–1858) of Missouri, affectionately termed 'Old Bullion' for his devotion to gold and hard money, and who was slated to be Martin van Buren's Jacksonian successor in the presidency, was converted from his previous inflationist views by the panic of 1819.[26] And young future Jacksonian and eventual president, James K. Polk (1795–1849), a wealthy cotton planter, began his political career in the Tennessee legislature in 1820 by advocating a speedy return to specie payments.

Historians have had great difficulty interpreting the essential nature of the Jacksonian movement, or for that matter, the economic views of Thomas Jefferson and the Jeffersonians. Jefferson, for example, has been generally perceived as a devoted 'agrarian', opposed to commerce and manufacturing, and Jeffersonian John Taylor of Caroline has been labelled in the same way. In reality, it is hard to see how any 'agrarian' can be opposed to a commerce essential to exporting farm products as well as importing manufactured and other goods to the farmers. It is true that Jefferson, Taylor and others were devoted farmers and personally disliked cities. But they were not opposed to either commerce or industry. What they were opposed to was governmental subsidy and artificial force-feeding of industrial or urban growth. The Jeffersonians favoured *laissez-faire*, private property rights, and the free market, and were therefore opposed to governmental subsidies, protective tariffs, and cheap, inflationary bank credit.

The Jacksonians, too, had strict *laissez-faire* views, except that there were naturally proportionately more who lived in cities or worked in industry. Jacksonians have been variously and even chaotically interpreted by historians as being (a) wild-eyed agrarian hillbillies opposed to commerce and capitalism (historians at the turn of the twentieth century); (b) pre-New Dealers interested in forging a worker-farmer uprising against National Republican-Whig capitalism (Arthur Schlesinger, Jr): and (c) spokesmen for rising entrepreneurs and private, state-chartered banks, trying to throw off central bank shackles upon state bank inflation (Bray Hammond). The wild inconsistencies of these interpretations stem from most historians conflating the free market and state capitalism. The Jeffersonians and Jacksonians were not anti-capitalist but ardently in favour, but to them, in contrast to their enemies the federalists and Whigs, genuine capitalism occurs only when commerce and manufacturing are free, free of both subsidies and constricting controls. Whereas federalists and Whigs were mercantilists who favoured state capitalism, cheap credit, protective tariff, a national debt, and Big Government, the Jeffersonians and Jacksonians were free market or *laissez-faire* capitalists who wanted capitalism and economic growth to develop only under freedom and free markets, i.e. under a system of free trade, free enterprise, ultra-minimal government, and ultra-hard money.

Neither was Jefferson or Jacksonian leadership in any way ignorant or hillbilly. Jefferson himself, as well as most of the other leaders, was thoroughly familiar with the literature of the bullionist controversy, as well as the economic classics. And most of the younger generation of bright economic thinkers and writers were in the Jacksonian camp.

Thus Amos Kendall, influential editor of the *Frankfort (Ky) Argus*, and later to be one of the leading brain-trusters in President Jackson's kitchen cabinet, and his main adviser in the bank war, became a bitter opponent of the banking system as a result of the panic of 1819. The very thought of banks he now found 'disgusting'. The best method of rendering them harmless, he concluded, was simply to prohibit them by constitutional amendment. If this were not feasible, then the banks should be required to post security with the courts enabling them to redeem all their paper.

One of America's first economists, Condy Raguet (1784–1842), found his economic outlook totally transformed by the Panic of 1819. A Philadelphia merchant and attorney of French descent, Raguet had published, in 1815, an inflationist and protectionist tract, an *Inquiry into the Causes of the Present State of the Circulating Medium*. But, in the midst of the panic, Raguet, as state senator from Philadelphia, headed a committee in 1820–21 that looked closely into the causes of and possible remedies for the unprecedented economic depression. Raguet concluded that the depression had been caused by bank credit expansion in the boom, followed by a subsequent contraction when the boom caused specie to drain out of the bank vaults. As a result, Raguet emerged from the depression a dedicated opponent of fractional-reserve banking, and a convinced partisan of free trade. He was impressed that, out of the leading citizens and legislators of 19 counties to whom the Raguet committee sent a questionnaire, 16 counties replied flatly that 'the advantages of the banking system' did not 'outweigh its evils'. From then on, Raguet favoured 100 per cent reserve banking to specie, and, while not a Jacksonian politically, staunchly supported the Jacksonian 'Independent Treasury' plan that divorced the treasury from banks or bank paper. Raguet later expanded his views in his *Of the Principles of Banking* (1830), *A Treatise on Currency and Banking* (1839, 1840), *Principles of Free Trade* (1835), and in a series of journals which he launched in the late 1830s, which included a documentary history of the current commercial crisis as well as reprints of Ricardo and other monetary theorists, and of the bullion *Report*.

Raguet explained, in his *Treatise on Money and Banking*, how expansion of bank credit brought about a boom, higher prices, a demand to export specie and a consequent call upon the banks for specie contraction and crisis. Remarkably, he also anticipated James Wilson of *The Economist* by almost a decade in demonstrating, in a pre-Austrian treatment of the business cycle, how the boom brought about overinvestment in fixed capital goods. Thus Raguet wrote:

> At the winding up of the catastrophe, it is discovered that during the whole of this operation *consumption* has been increasing faster than *production* – that the community is poorer in the end than when it began – that instead of food and clothing it has railroads and canals adequate for the transportation of double the quantity of produce and merchandise than there is to be transported – and that the whole of the appearance of prosperity which was exhibited while the currency was gradually increasing in quantity was like the appearance of wealth and affluence which the spendthrift exhibits while running through his estate, and like it, destined to be followed by a period of distress and inactivity.[27]

The difference is that the more celebrated Wilson, a leader of the so-called banking school of Britain, never realized that the overinvestment was caused by monetary and credit expansion. In short, he never caught up with Raguet and the Jacksonians in the US.

The panic of 1819 also inspired the publication of the first systematic treatise on political economy in the United States, *Thoughts on Political Economy* (1820), by the Baltimore lawyer, Daniel Raymond (1786–1849).[28] Raymond was born into a conservative Connecticut federalist family, and his book was a paean to protective tariffs, and to the nationalist Alexander

Hamilton, whom Raymond considered the only truly sound political econo-mist. But even Hamilton nodded, according to Raymond, on the bank ques-tion, and Raymond, too, came out in opposition to bank credit expansion and in favour of 100 per cent specie banking. Criticizing Hamilton's, and Adam Smith's, assertion that bank notes add to the national capital by economizing on specie, Raymond cited David Hume's statement that 'in proportion as money is increased in quantity, it must be depreciated in value'. Bank credit also promotes extravagant speculation, raises prices of domestic goods in export markets, and brings about a deficit in the balance of trade. To Raymond, the issuing of any bank notes beyond specie was, quite simply, a 'stupendous fraud'. Ideally, he believed that the federal government should eliminate bank paper entirely, and supply the country with a national paper backed 100 per cent by specie.

As can be seen from the case of Raymond, it was not only the Jacksonians who came to a staunch anti-fractional-reserve bank position during the 1819–21 depression. Young frontier state representative from western Tennessee, Davy Crockett (1786–1836), future Whig leader and enemy of the Jacksonians, stated that he 'considered the whole Banking system a species of swindling on a large scale'. Protectionist and future Whig president, General William Henry Harrison (1773–1841), ran successfully for the Ohio state senate in the Autumn of 1819. When attacked at a local pre-election citizens' meeting for being a director of a local branch of the Bank of the United States, Harrison, in a lengthy reply, insisted that he was a sworn enemy of all banks, and especially of the Bank of the United States, and that he was unalterably opposed to its establishment and continuation. And, finally, at least at this time, secretary of state and future president John Quincy Adams fully shared his father's hostility to all fractional-reserve banking. To a Frenchman who had sent him a plan for federal government paper money, Adams commended the famous Bank of Amsterdam, where paper 'was always a representative and nothing more', of specie in its vaults.

6.5   Monetary and banking thought on the Continent
Monetary thought on the European continent often paralleled the richer and more developed controversy in Great Britain. In Sweden, notably enough, a 'bullionist' controversy developed a half-century before the more famous one in Great Britain. Since few Britons were versed in the Swedish language, the controversy and its significance went unremarked outside Sweden.

In the mid-eighteenth century, Sweden experienced four decades (specifi-cally, 1739–72) of roughly democratic government, with political power in the hands of the parliament, or Riksdag, and with representatives chosen from four estates (nobility, clergy, middle class and peasants). Two political parties battling for power in this era, in the nomenclature reminiscent of

Gulliver's Travels, were the 'Hats' and the 'Caps'. The Hats, who were in power from the beginning of the grandiloquently named 'Age of Freedom' until 1765, were mercantilists who believed in using inflation for economic development. Export subsidies, direct subsidies, cheap loans, and high protective tariffs were all used to build internal improvements and to foster favoured industries, especially textile manufacturing (a favourite motto of the Hats was 'Swedish men in Swedish clothing').

The choice method of financing these lavish expenditures was inflationary credit expansion by the central Bank of Sweden. The convenient proto-Keynesian Hat theory was that an increased money supply would all go into increased development and output rather than higher prices. As for the nagging thought that deficits might ensue in the balance of payments, there was no need to worry, since imports would be held down by direct government controls, while increased national income would, in some odd way, promote increased exports.

After several years of inflationary bank credit expansion, the Swedish government went off the silver standard in 1745, and from then on was free to inflate, ad libitum. Thus, total inconvertible bank notes in circulation in 1745 were 6.9 million *daler*, doubling until 1754, when total circulation was 13.7 million *daler*. Monetary inflation accelerated after that, more than doubling in the next four years, reaching 33.1 million *daler* in 1758. Finally, the supply of bank notes reached a peak in 1762 at 44.5 million *daler*, a 545 per cent increase over 1745, or an average of 32.1 per cent per year.

In response to the monetary expansion, prices remained stable for a few years and then rose from 1749 to 1756, the general price index rising 23 per cent in the seven years. After that, as usually happens, the price rise accelerated, doubling in the next eight years, and reaching a peak in 1764. The biggest concern was the foreign exchange rate, which rose even more precipitately. Thus, after remaining only 5 or 6 per cent above par from 1752 to 1755, the rate of Hamburg *mark bancos* in terms of *dalers* rose to 247 per cent above par in 1765.

The fall in the foreign exchange value of the *daler* led the Hat government to attempt direct control of foreign exchange rates. A foreign exchange office was established in 1747 to try to push rates down, using massive French government subsidies to prop up *dalers* in the foreign exchange market. The exchange office succeeded for a few years, bringing the price of Hamburg *mark bancos* down, for example, from 24 per cent above par in 1748 to 5 or 6 per cent above par from 1752 to 1755. But an artificially falling foreign exchange rate combined with rising domestic prices amounted to an enormous subsidy of imports into Sweden. The resulting huge deficit in the balance of payments raised the increasing problem of how a country on inconvertible paper is going to finance the deficits. Finally, loans and subsidies from abroad ceased, the house of cards collapsed, and foreign exchange rates spiralled upward.

It is interesting to see how the Hat theoreticians, led by one Edward Runeberg, explained the mounting crisis. Like the anti-bullionists and the later banking school theorists in Britain, they – even more starkly – reversed the causal chain. The problem, the Hats declared, originated in the deficit in the balance of payments. Where the deficit came from was far more murky; presumably it was a wilful act of greedy consumers and importers. The deficit then caused the price of foreign exchange to rise, which in turn raised the prices of domestic goods in export markets, which in turn pulled up all the prices of domestic goods. Hence the entire domestic inflation was *really* due to the mysterious deficit in the balance of payments. The policy conclusion was clear to the Hats: restrict imports by coercion.

Not once did the Hat theoreticians admit that there could be a causal chain running from increased bank note issue to prices and exchange rates. On the contrary, the Hats advocated further issues in bank money to raise domestic production, which would in turn somehow increase exports, and thereby increase foreign exchange earnings and, along with a coerced restriction of imports, cure the deficit.

In addition to massive private credits, the inflation of money and credit by the Bank of Sweden financed government deficits, many of which were used for heavy Swedish military expenses to fight in the multinational Seven Years' War (1756–63).

As the inflation began to accelerate in 1756, Cap political strength grew steadily, in reaction not only to the inflationary spiral, but also to participation in a widely unpopular war. The Caps, who found their constituency among small merchants and civil servants injured by inflation, were in favour of free trade and *laissez-faire*, and opposed to mercantilism and government controls. As the inflation proceeded, the Caps were able to show how the government-engineered inflation aided privileged manufacturers with cheap bank loans. They also demonstrated how Hat privileges and subsidies aided certain privileged commercial capitalists, especially iron exporters. Smaller industrialists, merchants, and importers opposed to special privilege, were the backbone of the Cap party.

Worried by rising Cap power, the Hats finally stopped the monetary inflation in 1762, but prices and exchange rates continued to rise as expectations of further inflation still held sway. Finally, the Caps toppled the Hats in 1765, and promptly ended the inflation by a heroic policy of monetary deflation, lowering the total supply of bank notes to 33.5 million *daler* in 1768, or a 25 per cent drop in seven years, most of it since 1765. The result was, of course, a sharp deflation in prices and foreign exchange, the *marc banco* rate falling from 247 per cent of par in 1765 to 117 per cent of par three years later. Output and unemployment declined sharply as well.

Throughout this boom–bust cycle, the Caps firmly took what would later be called the bullionist position. The excess issue of bank notes, especially with an inconvertible currency, brought about rises in price and in foreign exchange rates. As we have indicated, the Caps were wisely not content with simply pointing out the economic flaws in the Hats' reasoning. They also attacked the special privileges enjoyed by the Hats, and showed how the Hat constituency benefited by inflation and mercantilism.

The deflationary course taken by the Caps in power may be economically justified by pointing out that drastic measures were necessary to reverse inflationary expectations. But the Caps stressed another attractive political argument: retribution. Why shouldn't the wealthy Hat merchants and industrialist profiteers from inflation pay the major price for a return to the silver standard and sound money? In this way, deflation would reward those who had suffered from inflation, and the profiteers from the previous inflation would, in a sense, pay reparations to compensate the previous victims of inflation. This was far from an absurd programme. And so the Caps set out, quite frankly, to deflate prices and exchange rates down to the pre-1745 Hat inflation and to the old silver par with the *daler*.

Economically, too, the Caps had an important argument: since bank notes received their true value from their silver reserves, the *daler* should always designate the same quantity, or weight, of specie.

Two of the leading Cap economists, however, argued against the deflation and instead suggested going back to silver at the existing rate of twice the old par. One was the Rev. Anders Chydenius (1729–1803), a Lutheran pastor from a small city on the western coast of Finland. Coming from a coastal city in a Finland colonized by Sweden (the Kingdom of Sweden and Finland), and whose trade suffered from state privileges to Stockholm and other Swedish interests, Chydenius early spoke and wrote numerous pamphlets against mercantilism and in favour of free trade. He also propounded a philosophy of natural law and natural rights of every individual. In 1766, as a representative of the Finnish clergy in the *Riksdag*, Chydenius was censured and removed from Parliament for the flagrant crime (in the 'Age of Freedom') of writing a tract, *The Succour of the Realm by a Natural Finance System*, attacking the policy of deflation to the old par after he had voted for it. Apparently changing one's mind after a vote was not permissible. In the pamphlet, Chydenius, without benefit of having read or heard of Adam Smith, worked out some 'real bills' notions of permissible banking in a convertible monetary system.

The other Cap opponent of deflation was a teacher of economics at the University of Uppsala, Pehr Niclas Christiernin. Chirstiernin began at Uppsala as an adjunct in law and economics in 1761, then rose to professor in the same field, then held a chair in philosophy, and finally ended as chancellor of the university. In contrast to the poorly read Chydenius, Chistiernin was steeped in such foreign economic literature as Cantillon, Hume, Justi, Locke and Malynes. In a pamphlet published in 1761 (*Summary of Lectures on the High Price of Foreign Exchange in Sweden*), Christiernin presented a theory of flexible exchange rates as an equilibrating mechanism in inconvertible currency that anticipated the bullionists and was superior to anything written up to that time. Unfortunately, Christiernin remained untranslated into English, and therefore unread there, until 1971. Christiernin pointed out that the continuing increase in the supply of bank notes led to the fall in value of the *daler*, both in raising foreign exchange rates as well as prices of goods at home. The increase in the issue of bank notes, in turn, stemmed from the bank's more liberal lending policy, which lowered the rate of interest sharply by the mid-1750s, and also increased inflation by creating money to redeem all extant government bonds.

Christiernin, however, was far from a hard-core hard-money man. He defended bank notes as useful, increasing activity and employment, and opposed deflation because, he pointed out, prices and wages were sticky downward. It is doubtful, however, that downward stickiness could last for long in the eighteenth century. But Christiernin's main objection to deflation was that his ideal was not sound, metallic money but a pre-Friedmanite desire to stabilize the value of the *daler* and make the price level constant. In pursuit of that goal, he urged open market operations by the central bank. Furthermore, again in anticipation of the monetarists, he admittedly preferred inflation to deflation, if that was the choice.

Unfortunately, the heroic deflationary measures led to temporary Cap reverses. The Hats came back to power in 1769, but although they promptly reinflated, they began to prepare seriously for restoration of the silver standard. When the Caps returned in 1772, however, the powerful merchant capitalists of the Hat party collaborated with the Crown and the nobility to seize power; in a *coup d'état*, overthrowing parliamentary democracy, and installing King Gustav III as absolute monarch. King Gustav returned Sweden to the silver standard in 1777 at the existing market price.

Later, British bullionist views spread to more intellectually accessible parts of the Continent. Thus, in 1816, Johann Georg Busch (1728–1800), a mathematics teacher at the Hamburg Gymnasium, economist and founder of the Academy of Commerce at Hamburg, denounced inflationary banking propelled by government. Busch noted that, as a result,

> The customary abuse has been that too many paper symbols have been produced measured against the needs of the citizens. As a consequence there are too many who want to change back their paper money into the commodity which is and can

be the true symbol of value. Since the bank cannot produce this commodity [gold or silver] out of nature like the paper with letters and figures on it, and since she must then confess that she cannot fulfill her promise [to convert to specie], the deceived citizen must become reluctant to take one [the paper] for the other [specie] money.[29]

Busch identified the financing of war as the main reason for the emergency of governmental bank credit inflation since the beginning of the eighteenth century.

Meanwhile, in Russia, the Baltic German professor of political economy, the Smithian Heinrich Friedrich Freiherr von Storch, denounced government instigation of bank credit and paper money in a lengthy monetary appendix to the 1823 edition of his *Cours d'économie politique*. Storch, like Busch, zeroed in on war as the main reason for continuing inflation:

the principal motive for introducing this calamitous invention [of paper money] in nearly all states of Europe, have been [sic] the financial disorders caused by wars, which have been sometimes just and necessary but mostly useless... How many wars could have been prevented without this unhappy expedient? How many tears and how much blood could have been saved.

The best remedy for this evil, declared Storch, would be return to a pure, 100 per cent gold or silver standard in all nations. Failing that, however, Storch was willing to settle for free private, competing banks which, he was perhaps the first to point out, would be much less inflationary than governmentally privileged banking. As Storch put it:

private banks are those presenting most advantages and least dangers... Great Britain is the only country in Europe where private banks exist; in all other states banking business is concentrated in one institution, if not founded then at least approved and privileged by government. Nevertheless, public banks are much more prone to degenerate than are private banks. As long as banking companies exist in isolation their operations seem to be insignificant: as soon as they form one sole and great institution they excite the attention of the government, their profits being more considerable; and because of this the special protection they enjoy or the privileges which they solicit have to be bought by favours which change their nature and subtly undermine their credit.[30]

6.6   Notes

1. Charles F. Peake, 'Henry Thornton and the Development of Ricardo's Economic Thought', *History of Political Economy*, 10 (Summer 1978), pp. 193–212.
2. Horner's starting point, as we have seen, was a bit different: he had been converted from a moderate neutral to moderate bullionist by Lord King's booklet in 1804.
3. Peake, op. cit., note 1, p. 193.
4. As Peake writes, 'Ricardo's total productive output was dominated by monetary questions, and a full understanding of Ricardo requires an interpretation that includes his monetary works'. Ibid.

5. Malthus, formerly a moderate anti-bullionist, had now become a Thorntonian, and expressed his views in two articles on the bullion controversy in 1811 in the *Edinburgh Review*. See the critique of Malthus in Frank W. Fetter, *Development of British Monetary Orthodoxy, 1797–1875* (Cambridge, Mass.: Harvard University Press, 1965), p. 48.

    On Ricardo's exclusive emphasis on long-run equilibrium in his monetary analysis, see J.A. Schumpeter, *History of Economic Analysis* (New York: Oxford University Press, 1954), pp. 494–5, and Jacob Viner, *Studies in the Theory of International Trade* (New York: Harper & Bros, 1937), pp. 139–40.

6. Joseph Salerno, 'The Doctrinal Antecedents of the Monetary Approach to the Balance of Payments' (doctoral dissertation, Rutgers University, 1980), p. 447. Salerno goes on to point out that Ricardo's strict, mechanistic split between the money and the real, leading to the doctrine that money is a 'veil', led also to the seeming paradox of Ricardo, in his *Principles*, flip-flopping to a highly misleading purely real, non-monetary, 'barter' analysis of the balance of payments. The paradox is only seeming, for a severe split enables someone to leap back and forth between the purely monetary and the purely real. It was the barter analysis of Ricardo's *Principles*, Salerno notes, 'which served as the foundation for the classical theory of the balance of payments'. Ibid., p. 449.

7. Peake, op. cit., note 1, p. 203.

8. Jacob H. Hollander, 'The Development of the Theory of Money from Adam Smith to David Ricardo', *Quarterly Journal of Economics*, 25 (May 1911), p. 470.

9. Spencer Perceval (1762–1812), the son of the earl of Egmont, received an MA from Trinity College, Cambridge in 1781, then became an attorney and king's counsel. An MP from 1796 on, Perceval was an ardent war hawk, and a defender of Pitt's repressive crackdown on anti-war dissidents at home. Rising to solicitor-general and attorney-general, Perceval, as a leading follower of Pitt, became chancellor of the exchequer in 1807, and then added the post of prime minister in 1809. He was assassinated in 1812.

10. Huskisson, though a respected and leading Tory, was all his life a classical liberal and devoted to freedom of trade. Raised by a great-uncle who was a well-known physician to the British embassy at Paris, Huskisson lived with leading French liberals as a youth, and knew Franklin and Jefferson. After the fall of the Bastille, at which he was present, Huskisson joined the Club of 1789 (a group of eminent constitutional monarchist classical liberals). At the age of 20, Huskisson read before the club in 1790, and then printed, a much applauded discourse on the currency.

    Huskisson became a close friend and private secretary to the British ambassador, Lord Gower, and returned with him to England when recalled in 1792. Three years later, he gained a key post as Secretary to the administration in 1795, and became an MP the following year. As a young Pittite, Huskisson rose as secretary to the treasury from 1804 until 1809, and in 1808 played a large share in arranging relations between the Treasury and the Bank of England.

11. Sharp, a great conversationalist known as 'Conversation Sharp', was the son of an English officer, born in Newfoundland, who rose to become a leading West Indies merchant in London as well as head of the hat manufacturing firm of Richard Sharp & Co. This wealthy businessman became a leading Whig, devoted to parliamentary and other liberal reforms. Sharp was a member of many leading London clubs, and was a friend of John Adams, Ricardo and James Mill. He long wanted to write a history of the attainment of American independence. Sharp was also a poet very interested in literature, and a friend of Byron, Coleridge and Wordsworth. He was an MP intermittently from 1806 to 1827.

12. A decade later, Huskisson, during a parliamentary debate on monetary policy, mentioned his 'misfortune' in 1810, 'to differ from some distinguished members of this House to whom I was personally attached, and in whose political views I had generally concurred'. See Frank W. Fetter, 'The Politics of the Bullion Report', *Economica*, n.s. 26 (May 1959), pp. 106–7.

13. Ibid., p. 106.

14. As Frank W. Fetter put it, 'Only after the Bullion Committee had issued a Report...that differed substantially from Ricardo in its analysis of the causes of depreciation but agreed in part with Ricardo's criticisms of the Bank of England and with his view that the

Restriction should stop, regardless of the war, did Ricardo become the champion of the doctrines of the Bullion Report. Its conclusions as to policy were close enough to his so that he, as a pamphleteer and a propagandist, became their defender, thereby achieving a wide reputation'. Frank W. Fetter, 'The Bullion Report Reexamined', (1942) in T.S. Ashton and R.S. Sayers (eds.), *Papers in English Monetary History* (Oxford: The Clarendon Press, 1953), p. 67.

15. Ibid., p. 67.
16. Here we should note the courage of Pascoe Grenfell (1761–1838), Whig merchant and mine promoter, who voted for the bullion *Report* even though a large stockholder in the Bank of England, as well as the timorousness of Alexander Baring, who spoke for the doctrines of the *Report*, but who voted against out of reluctance to return to the gold standard during the war. Grenfell was a Cornishman, whose father was a leading London merchant, and large dealer in tin and copper. Grenfell joined his father's firm, and then became principal managing partner of firms connected with Thomas Williams, the largest manufacturer in Cornwall and Anglesey. Grenfell was an MP from 1802 to 1826.
17. Vansittart, son of Henry Vansittart, a governor of Bengal, received a BA from Christ Church, Oxford, in 1781 and an MA four years later. Vansittart became an attorney and frequent pamphleteer, dedicated to the pro-war and the pro-restriction policies of William Pitt. An MP from 1796 on, Vansittart became a co-secretary to the treasury, the secretary for Ireland, and again secretary to the treasury in various Tory governments. In 1809, Vansittart had led the debate for extending the restriction. He became chancellor of the exchequer in 1812, and remained in that post for ten years.
18. Jackson, who had received an MA from Exeter College, Oxford, in 1793, was a prominent parliamentary counsel, also parliamentary counsel to the East India Co., and counsel to the Corporation of London.
19. George Ellis, whose father was a member of the House of Assembly of St George in the West Indies, had briefly been an MP in the 1790s, but was even more a poet, historian and *littérateur*. A clever poet, who edited and published an anthology of poetry, and the author of a history of the Dutch Revolution of the mid-1780s, George Ellis had been a diplomat, and then became a frequent contributor to the *Anti-Jacobin Review*. He was a close friend of George Canning and of the Scottish Tory writer Sir Walter Scott.
20. Alexander Baring, son of Sir Francis of the great banking family, had been a member of the bullion committee of 1810 who voted against the *Report*. Trained from early life to work in his father's banking house, he married the daughter of the wealthy federalist associate of Robert Morris of Philadelphia, US Senator William Bingham. Baring became head of his family bank in 1810, and was an MP for 30 years from 1806 on.
21. Salim Rashid, 'Edward Copleston. Robert Peel, and Cash Payments', *History of Political Economy*, 15 (Summer 1983), pp. 249–59.
22. Frank W. Fetter, *Development of British Monetary Orthodoxy 1797–1875* (Cambridge, Mass.: Harvard University Press, 1965), pp. 69–70.
23. Cobbett (1762–1835) was one of the few political writers to come from a lower-class background. Son of a peasant family in Surrey, Cobbett became a copying clerk to a lawyer in London, enlisted in the ranks of the army, becoming an NCO in Nova Scotia in 1791, and married a soldier's daughter. Wandering to France and thence to the United States, Cobbett became an English teacher to French refugees and a translator in Philadelphia, where he made his mark in the mid-1790s as a virulently pro-English Tory and federalist and opponent of Jacobinism. He became a newspaper writer, editor, and publisher in Philadelphia in the late 1790s.
    Returning to England in 1800, Cobbett began his highly influential *Cobbett's Weekly Political Register* in 1802, continuing its publication until his death. He also published the parliamentary debates and a multi-volume parliamentary history of England. In 1804, Cobbett shifted sharply and permanently to an all-out radical position, praising parliamentary reform, denouncing paper money, and repeatedly being charged with sedition.
24. Cited in Mark Skousen, *The 100% Gold Standard: Economics of a Pure Money Commodity* (Washington, DC: University Press of America, 1977), p. 45.
25. The corollary goals of the Jacksonian movement were all consistent with the aim of

achieving a free market, *laissez-faire* economy and polity: free trade (accomplished in the 1840s), repayment of the entire national debt (achieved in the 1830s), no federal and precious little state 'internal improvements' (public works), and generally, an ultra-minimal budget or governmental power, certainly on the federal and even on the state and local levels.

26. The plan was two terms of Benton as president, to follow two terms of Van Buren, Jackson's selected heir. But Van Buren never gained his second term, the great split amongst the Jacksonians, symbolically including a split between Van Buren and Jackson himself, coming in 1844 over the crucial question of whether or not the Republic of Texas should be admitted to the Union as a slave state.

27. Condy Raguet, *Treatise on Money and Banking* (1839), p. 137, quoted in Vera Smith, *The Rationale of Central Banking* (1936, Indianapolis, Ind.: Liberty Press, 1990), p. 84.

28. The second, more widely known, edition of this book was published as *The Elements of Political Economy* (2 vols, 1823, 1836, 1840).

29. Quoted in Peter Bernholz, 'Inflation and Monetary Constitutions in Historical Perspective', *Kyklos*, 36, no. 3 (1983), pp. 407–8.

30. Ibid., pp. 408–9.

7 Monetary and banking thought, III: the struggle over the currency school

7.1 The trauma of 1825

In 1823, the British economy finally recovered from the post-Napoleonic War and post-1819 agricultural depression. In fact, an expansionary boom got under way, so much so as to quieten the vociferous agricultural advocates of higher prices and the opponents of the return to gold. Unsurprisingly, Bank of England credit expansion led the way in this new inflationary boom, its total credit rising from £17.5 million in August 1823 to £25.1 million two years later, a huge increase of 43 per cent or 21.7 per cent uncompounded per annum. Much of the monetary and credit boom came through investment in highly speculative Latin American mining stocks. The great hard-money radical William Cobbett kept up a drumfire of attack on this inflation but, significantly, he was also joined, if more privately, by such moderate hard-money men as William Huskisson, who worried that 'this universal Jobbery in Foreign Stock will turn out the most tremendous Bubble ever known'.

By late 1824, the exchanges turned unfavourable, and gold began to flow abroad; by the following year, Britons began to demand gold from the banks in increasing numbers. Huskisson repeatedly warned the Cabinet in the Spring of 1825 that 'the Bank, in its greedy folly, was playing over again the game of 1817'. In late June, a bank in Bristol refused outright to give gold to a noteholder who spurned payments in Bank of England notes, and this ominous incident was widely publicized by Cobbett. Bank of England cash reserves were at their lowest in five years at the end of February, at £8.86 million; and from that low point they fell alarmingly to no more than £3.0 million at the end of October. Bank runs and a bank panic ensued and at the height of that panic, in mid-December, a noteholder of the recalcitrant Bristol bank distributed a leaflet warning the citizens of the city: 'As there is no knowing what may happen, get Gold, for if Restriction come it will be too late'. During the panic, the late Henry Thornton's important bank, Pole, Thornton & Co. went under, despite last-minute borrowing from the Bank of England and despite the fact that Sir Peter Pole, head of the bank, was connected by marriage with the governor of the Bank of England, Cornelius Buller.

After a week of hysteria in mid-December, the Bank of England, pursuing a highly risky policy of massive loans to the banks and rediscounting of bills, managed to stem the run, even though its cash reserves had been reduced to £1.0 million by the end of the year.

The country was saved by a hair's breadth from another suspension of specie payments by the Bank of England. The bank pleaded with the government to order such a suspension, but the Tory government, largely due to the ardent pressure of Huskisson and Canning, resisted the bank's demands. The prime minister, Robert Banks Jenkinson, the earl of Liverpool, much to the disgust of his fellow High Tories of the duke of Wellington faction, agreed with Huskisson that, in the words of one prominent Wellington man, 'if the

[Bank] stopped payment, it would be a good opportunity of taking their Charter from them,...for letting the Bank break'.

The boom and crisis of 1825 dealt a traumatic lesson to thoughtful analysts of the monetary and economic scene. For these dramatic events demonstrated that the gold standard, important as it was as a check on monetary and banking inflation, *was not enough*;: bank failures, and boom and bust cycles, could and would still occur. Something further, then, was needed to fulfil the promise of the bullionists; something more than the gold standard was needed to counter the ills of boom-and-bust and of fractional-reserve banking.

The most concrete and immediate response to the panic of 1825 was a decision of the government to outlaw small denomination (under £5) bank notes, a measure that even the pro-bank credit Adam Smith had favoured. In that way, at least for these popular and widely used small denominations, the public would be using only specie as money. On 22 March 1826, Parliament forbade banks in England and Wales to issue new small notes, or to reissue any old ones after April 1829. After June 1826, the Bank of England continued to obey this edict for a little over a century. In another banking reform, Parliament ended the system that had prevailed since the turn of the eighteenth century: the Bank of England had a monopoly of all commercial banking except for partnerships of less than six persons. This monopoly was now shaken. Corporate and large partnership banks were now permitted in England, by an act of 26 May 1826. Unfortunately, this liberalization was greatly weakened by the act's preserving the bank's monopoly of corporate and large-scale banking inside a 65-mile radius of London. In short, corporate or joint-stock banking was permitted only to the 'country' banks.

Political pressure by Scottish Tories gained an exemption from these reforms for Scotland. In the first place, Scotland already had joint-stock banking and, more importantly, Scotland had long been a swamp of small-bank note inflationism. Even after resumption of the gold standard in 1821, Scotland did not have a gold standard in practice. Frank Fetter discloses the solution as follows:

> Even after the resumption of payments in 1821 little coin had circulated; and to a large degree there was a tradition, almost with the force of law, that banks should not be required to redeem their notes in coin. Redemption in London drafts was the usual form of paying noteholders. There was a core of truth in the remark of an anonymous pamphleteer (1826): Any southern fool who had the temerity to ask for a hundred sovereigns [gold coins], might, if his nerves supported him through the cross examination at the bank counter, think himself in luck to be hunted to the border.[1]

To work, a gold standard must, of course, be truly in effect – in practice as well as in the official statutes.

The Scottish Tories, led by the eminent novelist Sir Walter Scott, successfully blocked application of the anti-small-note reform to Scotland. The mouthpiece for Scottish High Toryism, *Blackwood's Edinburgh Magazine*, after hailing Scott's campaign, published two articles on 'The Country Banks and the Bank of England', in 1827–28, in which it wove together two major strains of ultra-inflationism: going off the gold standard, and praising the country banks. *Blackwood's* also attacked the Bank of England as overly restrictionist, thus helping to launch the legend that the bank was too restrictive instead of being itself the main engine of inflation. In contrast, the *Westminster Review*, mouthpiece for the philosophical radicals, scoffed at the Scots for threatening 'a civil war in defence of the privilege of being plundered' by the bank credit system.

It was also in this period in 1827, that Henry Burgess founded the powerful committee of country bankers, and edited for over 20 years the committee's influential periodical, *Circular to Bankers*. For that entire period, Burgess kept up a drumfire of inflationist vilification of the gold standard, of 'those ignorant, vain, and obstinate, projectors – Huskisson, Peel, and Ricardo', and of the Bank of England for being too restrictive of bank credit. He also denounced the 'Political Economists' as being 'the curse of the country' because of their generally hard-money views. For its part, *Blackwood's Edinburgh Magazine* pursued a similar unwavering line for nearly three decades, denouncing the return to gold in 1819 as having given 'the Jews, stockbrokers, and attorneys of the country, an enormous advantage, at the expense of classes connected with land...'.

On the other hand, William Cobbett continued his hard-hitting anti-bank paper stance, proclaiming in 1828 that 'Ever since that hellish compound Paper-money was understood by me, I have wished for the destruction of the accursed thing: I have applauded every measure that tended to produce its destruction, and censured every measure having a tendency to preserve it'. Blasting the inflationist and privileged Scottish country banks as 'the Scottish monopolists', Cobbett also denounced the Scotsman John Ramsay McCulloch for defending bank paper – 'this Scotch stupidity, conceit, pertinacity and impudence'. Cobbett escalated the attack by asserting that 'these ravenous Rooks of Scotland have been a pestilence to England for more than two hundred years'. It might be commented, of course, that one simple way for England to cast off that 'pestilence' was for England to give Scotland back its independence, a solution that Cobbett and the other nationalist English radicals somehow failed to consider.

Despite the continuing inflationism of the High Tories and of the Birmingham Attwoods, and despite the imminent clash of economic opinion over banking reform, the bulk of economists stood foursquare, from the mid-1820s on, in defence of the gold standard. That much had been agreed upon, and accomplished. Their differences on banking did not prevent unity on this fundamental monetary question. John Ramsay McCulloch, James Mill and Nassau W. Senior, stood solidly in favour of gold. Even the alleged radical, and for a time, pre-Keynesian Malthus expressed complete support for return to the gold standard in 1823 and thereafter. Archbishop Whately, Mountifort Longfield, Thomas Perronet Thompson, even the arch inductivist and historicist Richard Jones of Cambridge, were all staunch supporters of gold. Even the often confused and irenic John Stuart Mill was hard-hitting in defence of gold. The younger Mill, upon reading the testimony, in 1821, of Thomas Attwood in favour of a combined silver and inconvertible fiat paper standard, denounced the idea of depreciating the standard as a 'gigantic plan of confiscation'. Mill thundered 'that men who are not knaves in their private dealings should understand what the word "depreciation" means, and yet support it, speaks but ill for the existing state of morality on such subjects'.[2]

7.2   The emergence of the currency principle

The prohibition of small notes, however, scarcely tackled the main problem. The first to go beyond this minor aspect of banking and go straight to the heart of the matter was a brilliant and influential thinker who has remained as little known to historians as he was obscure in his own day. It is with justice that Lionel Robbins has wittily referred to James Pennington (1777–1862) as the 'Mycroft Holmes' of the later monetary controversy of the classical period.[3]

James Pennington was born into a prominent Quaker family in the town of Kendal, in Westmorland; his father, William, was a bookseller, printer and architect, who eventually became mayor of Kendal. Graduating from a first-rate Quaker school at Kendal, Pennington moved to London. Little is known of his personal life thereafter, except that he lived in Clapham, and that he and his large family of seven children were parishioners, and James a trustee, of the famous Clapham Anglican parish church, obviously abandoning the Quakerism of his youth. Apart from that, we know that he was a merchant, 'gentleman' and accountant, and briefly became a member of the board of control for India in 1832. From then on, retired from commerce, he would be consulted repeatedly in technical financial matters by the government.

In the wake of the great banking crisis of December 1825, London was agog with discussions of money and banking, the august Political Economy Club dealing with this topic in its meetings of 9 January and 6 February, 1826. At the latter occasion, Pennington was present as a guest and, stimulated by the discussion, he sat down to write a memorandum on the subject to the powerful president of the board of trade, the liberal Tory William Huskisson. Huskisson did not request the memo, but he was known to be receptive to intelligent memoranda on crucial topics, and this method of promoting his views may have been suggested to Pennington by his long-time friend, and one of the original founders of the Political Economy Club, the merchant and economist Thomas Tooke. In this first memo to Huskisson on 13 February 'On the Private Banking Establishments of the Metropolis', Pennington outlined with crystal clarity how private banks, by expanding loans, create demand deposits which function as part of the money supply. Walter Boyd and others had pointed this out, but Pennington's exposition was unmatched in its lucidity and, when published as an appendix to Tooke's *Letter to Grenville* (1829), greatly influenced the banking controversies of the era. Unfortunately, the *Letter* did not sufficiently influence Pennington's own camp, the currency school, who stubbornly and tragically failed to realize that bank demand deposits formed part of the supply of money, equivalent to bank notes.

Without any encouragement from Huskisson, Pennington followed up his first memorandum with another, a year later (16 May 1827) on 'Observations on the Coinage'. After explaining the technical procedures of the gold standard, Pennington detailed the dangers to gold of the existence of a paper currency, and then added a tantalizing hint: 'It is possible to regulate an extensive paper circulation...to render its contraction and expansion...subject to the same Law as that which determines the expansion and contraction of a currency wholly and exclusively metallic'. Here was the first indication in Great Britain of the 'Currency Principle': that more than simple gold redeemability was needed to transform bank money into a mere surrogate of gold.

William Huskisson finally sat up and took notice, writing to Pennington that:

> I perceive that towards the end of your Paper on Coinage, you state an opinion that means may be found of preventing those alternations of excitement and depression which have been attended with such alarming consequences to this Country. This, for a long time, has appeared to me to be one of the most important matters which can engage the attention...[T]he too great facility of expansion at one time, and the too rapid contraction of paper credit...at another, is unquestionably an evil of the greatest magnitude.

In short, bank credit and paper money were perceived by Huskisson as responsible for the business cycle; what, then, could be done about it? He urged Pennington to elaborate on his tantalizing suggestion.

The upshot was an ironic one: while James Pennington's third memorandum, in reply, 'On the management of the Bank of England', 23 June, was the first fateful elaboration of the justly famous currency principle, it was scarcely action-oriented enough to suit the minister. At any rate, monetary matters faded temporarily, and Huskisson himself resigned his post the following year, to die three years later. But Pennington's memorandum, nevertheless, was very important, for it declared that to make bank paper currency stable and tied to gold, it must be regulated to conform to the movements of the gold supply. If the Bank of England were the monopoly issuer of notes, Pennington prophetically counselled, it would be easy for it to control the total supply; in lieu of that, the private banks, London and country, could in some way be totally and immediately controlled by the bank. In either case, the bank could then be compelled to keep its securities (i.e. its earning assets) fixed in total amount; if so, its note issues would move in the same direction, and to the same extent, as its stock of gold. While the bank would not have 100 per cent gold reserves to its notes, the legally fixed gap between them would mean that bank notes (and by extension, the total money supply) would move in the same way and to the same extent as the gold supply – thus arriving at the equivalent of 100 per cent specie money for all *further* operations of the bank. Here was the seed of Peel's great Act of 1844, the embodiment of the currency principle.

But Huskisson could not seize on this point, because of Pennington's hesitations and qualifications; in particular, Pennington, of all people, knew full well that bank deposits are just as much creatures of bank credit as bank notes, and that to 'regulate them [deposits] properly will be no easy task'.

It becomes a mystery that Pennington, the founder of the currency principle, should have been so alert to bank deposits' role as money, while the currency school concentrated with such fierce insistence on bank notes alone. They applied this variant of 100 per cent gold money to notes exclusively, leaving deposits to go unchecked and unregulated on their own. Some historians speculate that the currency school made the conscious decision to avoid applying their principle to deposits, because of an alleged difficulty in practical application, and because they believed that note-holders – presumably being a broader or less wealthy section of the population – were more likely to cash in for gold than deposit-holders.[4] If so, then this 'practical' decision to forget about deposits proved, in the long run, to be the height of *im*practicality – indeed, fatal to the currency, or 100 per cent gold, cause. For Peel's Act's prohibitions on further fractional-reserve note issue simply induced the banking system, led by the Bank of England, to shift their inflationary and expansionary attentions to deposits alone – a condition that still prevails throughout the world.

Currency school myopia on demand deposits scarcely extended to their cousins in the United States. On the contrary, such 100 per cent gold leaders and Jacksonian theorists as Condy Raguet, Amos Kendall and the magnificent Jacksonian William M. Gouge of Philadelphia (1796–1863), were perfectly aware of deposits' equivalent role to notes in the issue of bank money. A Philadelphia editor, Gouge became a treasury official in the 1830s, and remained there from that point on. Gouge held firmly that deposits are in all cases equal to notes, that they may be created by bank lending, and that they have the same inflationary effect on prices as bank notes. He called for a return to the 100 per cent gold reserves backing the deposits of the original banks of Hamburg and Amsterdam. Gouge was also the main theoretician of the Van Buren Polk independent treasury system, in which the federal government would separate itself totally from banking, first by keeping no deposits in any banks, spending its funds directly in specie, and second, by accepting in taxes only specie and no bank notes or deposits. In that way, the American banking system would be free, not only of a central bank (as ensured by President Jackson in the early 1830s), but also of any link to or support by the federal government.[5]

Other influential expressions of the currency principle emerged from the panic of 1825. The highly influential Sir Henry Drummond (1786–1860)[6], banker and MP, in the fourth edition (1826) of his *Elementary Propositions on the Currency*, was driven by the crisis to the realization that mere specie convertibility was not enough to avoid boom–bust crises in money and in prices. He therefore concluded that the quantity of paper money should be kept constant, so that variations in the money supply would only reflect changes in the stock of specie. In the same year, Richard Page, writing as 'Daniel Hardcastle', state the currency principle in crystal-clear form: 'That only is a sound and well-regulated state of things, when no greater numerical amount of paper is in circulation than would have circulated of the precious metals if no paper had existed'.[7]

After the crisis of 1825, then, a consensus began to form, beginning with James Pennington and spreading through knowledgeable circles in Britain, that the gold standard is not enough; and that bank credit must not be allowed to expand unduly. At the ultimate pole were the currency school, who believed that commercial banks must be restricted to 100 per cent of gold, at least for any further note issues. Most of the school unfortunately left demand deposits out of their reckoning as not part of the money supply. Other established leaders, such as bank governor John Horsley Palmer, developed the far more qualified view advocating more control by the Bank of England: bank money should pyramid on top of a fixed ratio of reserves to liabilities maintained by the Bank of England.

But if bank credit was to be confined to movements of gold, and thereby to end the threat of inflation and the business cycle, *by what mechanism* was this to be accomplished? In most cases, and certainly among virtually all adherents of the currency school, the answer was to be the Bank of England itself: the very institution which bullionists and their successors had long seen to be the central agent of inflation and credit expansion. The idea was that the bank would either ride herd over the private banks, or, in the developing consensus, to assume a monopoly over all issue of bank notes –

leaving banks to issue demand deposits in a way that tied them inexorably to the Bank of England. In short, the modern banking system, with all its deep inflationary flaws, was what was envisioned and brought forth by the currency school. In the name of ultra-hard money, they unwittingly imposed upon Great Britain, and later the world, the modern, centralized inflationary, fractional-reserve and central bank-dominated banking system. The theory was that the bank would control the private banks through monopoly of note issue and other measures, while the government would rigidly control the bank itself.

The other main instrument of bank control over private banks was to centralize gold in the hands of the bank, and to make Bank of England notes legal tender for all citizens and banks. In that way, the banks would be induced to surrender their gold to the Bank, and to happily pyramid their loans and deposits on top of their bank reserves. Their demand deposits at the bank could always be cashed in for legal tender currency. In short, as this proposed structure came to be established in Britain and then elsewhere, the world was saddled with the modern banking system.

It is still a mystery how men so keenly aware and critical of the cartellizing and inflationary role of the Bank of England should have proposed centralizing control into the hands of the very same bank, and all in the name of stopping inflation and tying the monetary system closely and one-to-one to gold. It was truly putting the fox in charge of the proverbial chicken coop. A minority of currency men, it is true, favoured another variant, first recommended by the spiritual father of the currency school, David Ricardo himself. Already, at the end of his 1816 pamphlet on *Economical and Scarce Currency*, Ricardo had hinted at this solution, influenced by an unpublished proposal of J.B. Say in 1814. In his last, posthumous work, published in 1824, *The Plan for the Establishment of a National Bank*, Ricardo put forward and elaborated the new plan: the appointment of a government board to be in charge of a national note issue monopoly, with the Bank of England essentially confined to credit and deposit banking. The idea was that since the bank could not be trusted to be in charge of monopoly note issue, that function should be trusted to the central government. But, surely, here was even more of a fox, if not a wolf, to be placed in command. Government is just as much, if not more, inclined toward monetary and credit inflation as any private central bank. Government can always use inflation to finance the deficits it desires and to subsidize credit to its political allies.

There were other far more effective ways to restrict bank credit expansion. During the Jackson–Van Buren era in the United States (approximately 1828–40s), which roughly coincided with the period of the currency–banking school controversies in Britain, the programme of the hard-money Jacksonian movement was far more thoroughgoing, and ultimately far more realistic, than their spiritual cousins of the currency school. Both groups aimed at achieving hard money, tied very closely to specie, in order to end inflation and the boom–bust cycle. But, instead of maintaining and strengthening the central bank, the Jacksonians, far more logically, made it their first order of business to destroy it. The next step, for Gouge, Kendall, Raguet and their followers, who included Presidents Jackson and Van Buren, was to separate the federal government totally from money, by establishing an independent treasury system, passed by the Van Buren administration in 1840, repealed by the Whigs, and then permanently re-established by the Jacksonian Polk administration in 1846. The idea of the independent treasury was, first for the treasury to keep its own funds, without depositing them in any banks; and second, for the treasury to accept in taxes and other fees only *specie*, and not even notes of specie-redeeming banks. In that way, the federal government would give no encouragement whatever to the circulation of bank notes or deposits. Another plank in the Van Buren programme, considered but never passed, as being too hard-hitting, was a federal bankruptcy law which would have forced any bank to close its doors whenever it failed to meet its contractual obligations to redeem its notes or deposits in specie on demand. Other parts of the Jacksonian programme were state enforcement of bankruptcy the moment a bank should fail to pay in specie, and even the outlawing of all fractional-reserve banking as inherently fraudulent, as promising something that could not possibly be fulfilled: instantaneous redemption of all demand liabilities in specie.[8]

Less thoroughgoing than the Jacksonian proposals but better than the currency school's reliance on the central bank were the proposals of a free banking group that arose after 1825, calling for elimination of the Bank of England. The free banking proponents, however, were scarcely united in their theoretical outlook or in their goals; some wanted free banking in order to eliminate what they considered to be Bank of England restraint on bank credit expansion; while others wanted it for the opposite reason: to approach the currency school goal of pure specie money.

In the former category, for example, was the veteran inflationist and anti-bullionist, Sir John Sinclair. On the other hand, a particularly important example of the latter, hard-money, category was the long-time bullionist and clerk at the Royal Mint, Robert Mushet. In his substantial book, *An Attempt to Explain from Facts the Effect of the Issues of the Bank of England...* (1826), Mushet set forth a currency principle type of business cycle theory. The Bank of England, he pointed out, set into motion an expansionary policy that created an inflationary boom, and that later had to be reversed into a contractionary depression. Like the later currency school, Mushet's aim was to arrive at a purely metallic currency or its equivalent, but he saw that free banking rather than central banking was a better way to achieve it. Thus,

Mushet hailed the act of 1826, allowing joint-stock banking outside of the environs of London, as an improvement on the previous system, but still leaving intact the 'main evil', 'because they do not take the power from the Bank of England of adding extensively to the currency'. But 'when the monopoly of the Bank expires [in 1833], and the trade in money is perfectly free, a better order of things may arise'. The better order included stability, a currency not suffering from over-expansion, and an end to the boom–bust cycle.[9]

But by far the most important hard-money free banking advocate was the veteran bullionist Sir Henry Brooke Parnell, a leading MP who had taken the bullionist side in the Irish money question in 1804, was a prominent member of the bullion committee, and had supported resumption in 1819. As early as 1824, Parnell had moved in Parliament for an investigation of the Bank of England's charter. In 1826, he denounced the bank's 'exclusive and mischievous privilege'. In 1826 and again the following year, Parnell organized a discussion at the Political Economy Club, on the theme, 'Might not a proper Currency be secured by leaving the business of Banking wholly free from legislative interference?' He left no doubt that his own answer was, Yes.

Parnell set forth his free banking views in his 1827 tract *Observations on Paper Money, Banking, and Overtrading* (1827, 2nd ed., 1829). He began, following Mushet, by placing the blame for the panic of 1825 on the Bank of England's over-issues of 1824–25. The problem was that the law had taken away from the bank 'the great check over abuses in issuing paper money, namely, the competition of rival banks'. Going beyond Mushet, Parnell was not willing to wait for the bank's charter to expire in six years; no, the power of the bank over money, and thereby over prices and the general state of business, was 'so entirely repugnant…that it ought not be tolerated any longer'. Parnell concluded that the remedy was 'a free system of banking', and, overlooking a few pages at the end of Mushet's work, proclaimed that he himself was the first man in England to raise the banner of free banking.[10]

It is hardly surprising, on the other hand, that George Poulett Scrope, the inveterate underconsumptionist, should also have been an inflationist advocate of free banking in this period. In several books and in an article in the *Quarterly Review*, heralded by articles of other like-minded men in that leading Tory journal, Scrope called for the legalizing of small bank notes and an end to the London note issue monopoly of the Bank of England. His programme was designed to fit inflationist ends. Thus the competing banks would be able to redeem their notes in bullion rather than coin. The proclaimed goal of this banking programme was, in Scrope's words, to 'everywhere lower the values of the metals, and with them that of money'.[11]

7.3 Rechartering the Bank of England

The Bank of England's charter expired in 1833, and this seemed to offer critics of the existing system a golden opportunity to effect a fundamental reform. A bank charter committee was selected by the House of Commons in 1832 to engage in a detailed enquiry into the banking system, focusing on the question of the bank's existing monopoly of bank note issue in London and environs. The committee's hearings and inquiry was the most thorough examination of British banking to date, but Parnell, the only member of the committee to vote against rechartering the bank, complained with some justice that the roster of witnesses was stacked against the proponents of free banking by the manoeuvres of the chancellor of the exchequer in Lord Grey's Whig government, the Viscount Althorp.[12]

It was clear that a consensus of witnesses was building towards centralizing note issue in the hands of a strengthened Bank of England, a policy both the currency school, in its misguided way, and the moderately inflationist Establishment, could support. Only a few witnesses favoured bank competition in note issue in London, and only one, the Manchester merchant and joint-stock banker Joseph Chesborough Dyer, opposed the fateful proposal to invest Bank of England notes with legal tender power.

Based on the committee inquiry, Viscount Althorp presented Parliament in 1833 with his legislative programme: to keep the status quo of bank charter and bank note-issue monopoly in London and a 65-mile radius, and to centralize banking further by granting bank notes legal tender power. This meant that, from then on, private and joint-stock banks need not keep any of their reserves in gold, since depositors and note-holders would be compelled by law to accept bank notes in payment; and that only the Bank of England itself would have to meet its contractual obligations to redeem its notes or deposits in gold. This measure of 1833 went a long way to reduce the role of gold coin in everyday life, and to encourage its replacement by bank notes and bank deposits. In presenting his programme, Althorp noted that since the committee hearings, 'the public have been more inclined to look favourably on the management of the Bank of England...'. In short, the loaded committee had done its work well. He further provided a harbinger of the future by stating that his goal was to have all bank notes issued by the Bank of England – which of course is the modern centralized banking system.

The powerful country banking lobby, however, rose up in high dudgeon at this threat to its note-issue privileges, and the Cabinet was forced to back down on its goal of note-issue monopoly for the Bank of England. Lord Althorp was so chagrined at this successful pressure that he almost resigned from the government.

Although there was only one witness against it, the legal tender provision for Bank of England notes only carried in Commons by virtue of support from arch-inflationists opposed to the gold standard; the vote for legal tender was 214 to 156, with hard-money stalwarts Sir Henry Parnell and Sir Robert Peel, the leader of the Tory opposition, voting against.

Outrage against the legal tender law among the public was led, as might be expected, by the country bankers. The committee of country bankers, led by Henry William Hobhouse, pointed out that the law would 'violate private rights, and secure to the Bank of England an unjust and perpetual monopoly'. The committee's memorial justly pointed out that the government had taken measures against the expansionary tendencies of the country banks, but had ignored the 'operation of the same principle' at work in the Bank of England, in its case unchecked by the competition of other banks.

Leading the public reaction against legal tender was the prolific free banking advocate, the Scottish attorney Alexander Mundell. Mundell warned that the 1833 law would lead to the centralization of specie reserves in the country into the hands of the Bank of England. He charged that 'Your [English] industry, which has been already taxed by the exclusive privileges of the Bank of England as it now exists, is thus to be taxed still more by extension of it'.[13]

7.4   The crisis of 1837 and the currency school controversy

For the first time, the law of 1826 had allowed joint-stock banking (except for the Bank of England) to exist in England. But various remaining restrictions had held the number of joint-stock banks down to 14; the act of 1833 had removed these restrictions, and the result was a veritable orgy of joint-stock banks formed in England. Forty-four new banks were added from 1831 to 1835, topped by no less than 59 in 1836 alone, 15 of them established between 1 May and 15 June of that year. A powerful joint-stock bank, the London and Westminster Bank, was even established in London itself in 1834, although of course it was banned from issuing notes.

Along with the increase in the number of banks came an expansion in bank money. Thus the circulation of country bank notes rose from £10 million at the end of 1833 to over £12 million in mid-1836. Of this growth, almost all came from the issue of the new joint-stock banks: from £1.3 million to £3.6 million in the same period.

Although the Bank of England and the private country banks complained at the new competition, the expansion of credit by the bank fuelled this new burgeoning of banks and bank notes. Discounts of the bank expanded from £1.0 million in April 1833 to £3.4 million in July 1835, and rose to over £11 million by the end of the latter year. Total bank credit, in turn, rose from £24 million in 1833 to over £35 million at the beginning of 1837. This expansion took place in the teeth of the bank's loss of specie reserves from £11 million in 1822 to less than £4 million at the end of 1836. So much for the currency principle, and for its modified 'Palmer rule', which the bank's governor, John Horsley Palmer, had explained to the bank charter committee in 1832 that the Bank of England had been following. There is no way that such a practice – of expanding credit while specie reserves were falling – could be tortured into even an approximation of the currency ideal that the money supply should move as if it were the stock of specie in the country.

To top it off, the bank credit expansion led, in what was becoming the usual way, to a financial crisis and panic at the end of 1836 and the beginning of 1837, replete with bank runs, especially in Ireland. There followed the typical signs of recession: contraction of bank credit, decline of production, collapse of stock prices, numerous bankruptcies of banks and other businesses, and a swelling of unemployment.

It is not surprising that the new boom–bust cycle gave rise to parliamentary inquiries – by committees on joint-stock banks in 1836, 1837, and 1838, and even more so to vigorous debates on the banking situation in pamphlets and in the press. Indeed, more than 40 pamphlets were published on the banking system in 1837 alone, and a large number continued the following year.

The pamphlet war was touched off by a remarkable pamphlet by Colonel Robert Torrens,[14] remarkable not only for being the best presentation of the currency school, but also because it signified a sudden conversion of Torrens into the currency ranks. For Torrens, though a distinguished political economist, a friend of Ricardo, and a founder and leading member of the Political Economy Club, had been an ardent, almost wild, inflationist and anti-bullionist during the bullion *Report* struggles. Indeed, Torrens's inflationism had continued at least into 1830.

Then, in the course of confused and bewildering speeches in Parliament in the critical year of 1833, Torrens continued his old bitter anti-deflationist attacks on the resumption act of 1819, but in the midst of them, also inconsistently enunciated the currency principle in clear form:

> Extensive and calamitous experience had established the fact, that a currency, consisting of precious metals, and of paper convertible into these metals on demand, was liable to sudden and very considerable fluctuation, between the extremes of excess and of deficiency…A mixed currency…would suffer a much more considerable contraction…than a purely metallic…Unless our present system of currency were amended by the timely interference of the Legislature, it would go on to occasion periodical and aggravated distress, until, in a national bankruptcy it would find its euthanasia.[15]

In another speech on rechartering the Bank of England, Torrens warned that 'the adoption of the measures proposed by Government for continuing and increasing the exclusive privileges of the Bank of England would inflict upon the country a periodic recurrence in aggravated forms of revulsions of trade, and of panics in the money market...'.

In his notable *Letter to Lord Melbourne*, all hesitation finally fell away, and Colonel Torrens joined the leadership of the currency school ranks. He began by pointing out, in contrast to most of his currency colleagues, that bank deposits were money equally with bank notes, paying tribute to James Pennington for pointing this out. Torrens explained the nature of deposits as money very clearly, showing that a shift of bank liabilities from notes to deposits or vice versa would not change the amount of bank money by which merchants and others can make purchases. He also noted that while most people have learned how an increase in coin and bank notes raises prices and depreciates foreign exchanges, neither the government nor the directors of the Bank of England understand how loans and deposits do the same thing. But tragically, Torrens then inconsistently dismissed deposits as unimportant, apparently on the ground that the bank, not the public, decides whether to keep its liabilities in notes or deposits, and on the further erroneous assumption that country and joint-stock banks pyramid at a fixed ratio upon bank notes as their reserves but not upon bank deposits. From then on, Torrens wrote and acted as if deposits were irrelevant to the money supply.

Torrens also unfortunately conceded that the bank must function as a lender of last resort to banks in distress, but then confined his attack on the bank to its stoking the fires of inflationary credit and not conforming to the currency principle from the beginning. In order to force the currency principle upon the bank, Torrens, for the first time in print, urged that Parliament rigidly separate the bank into an issue department and a banking department. The issue department would be forced to limit its note issues to its actual supply of gold, so that bank notes could only fluctuate to the extent that the bank's stock of gold increases or decreases. In that way, wrote Torrens, 'the circulation [of bank notes] would always remain in the same state, both with respect to amount and to value, in which it would exist were it wholly metallic'.

The problem is that the banking department, in Torrens's and hence the currency plan, would be left totally free and unregulated, on the assumption that the bank could issue credits and deposits, and that those loans and demand deposits would be totally irrelevant to the money supply. The neglect of deposits was the tragic flaw in the currency plan.

Colonel Torrens's assault on the bank was in effect, though not by name, answered in a pamphlet by bank director and former governor John Horsley Palmer.[16] As in the case of bank apologists for decades, Palmer put the blame for the inflation and recession on every institution *but* the bank: on shipments of funds abroad, on bank runs, and on reckless credit expansion by private and joint-stock English and Irish banks. He concluded that the solution – a particular favourite of the bank – was that the bank must have a monopoly of all note issue. Ironically, the currency school, so hostile to the bank, proposed the same plan for different reasons: so that the government could have but one central bank to regulate.

In his *Letter to Lord Melbourne*, Torrens had given credit to the banker Samuel Jones Loyd for originating the idea of the separation of the Bank of England into issue and banking departments. Loyd now weighed in with a pamphlet attack on Palmer, in which he assumed the leadership of the currency camp.[17] Far more simplistic than Torrens, Loyd dogmatically but fatally asserted that notes and deposits are forever absolutely different and therefore can and must be treated totally differently. Professor Fetter offers an amusing and accurate explanation of the triumph of Loyd's simple-minded stance:

> He [Loyd] stated as a fundamental that no man in his right mind could question that note issuing and deposit business were completely separate and that a mixed circulation of coin and notes should fluctuate exactly as would an all-metallic circulation. Despite its theoretical vacuity, there was no denying the effectiveness of Loyd's argument...Loyd's prestige as a successful banker undoubtedly made his words carry conviction to many who...felt that something ought to be done about the Bank of England and that a man who made money in banking must understand banking.[18]

Throughout 1837 and 1838, the currency principle was advocated in highly influential pamphlets – again by Loyd, by David Ricardo's brother Samson, and – in a particularly important pronouncement – by long-time Bank of England director George Warde Norman. Like Loyd, Torrens and Pennington, Norman was a member of the Political Economy Club. His pamphlet of 1838 was a revision of a pamphlet that he had privately printed five years earlier.[19] Norman agreed with Loyd that notes and deposits are totally different, and also suggested granting to the Bank of England a monopoly of all bank notes. Since Norman was a powerful bank director, it would seem that his adoption of the allegedly 'anti-bank' currency principle was akin to B'rer Rabbit urging not to be thrown into the briar patch!

Another economist lending his prestige as one of the last of the Ricardians to the currency principle was the prolific John Ramsay McCulloch, both in a review of some of the year's pamphlets in the *Edinburgh Review* for April 1837, and again in a new edition of Smith's *Wealth of Nations*, which he published the following year. In 1840, at the next stage of the debate, another leading economist joined the fray on behalf of the currency principle: S. Mountifort Longfield, in a notable four-part article, 'Banking and Currency', in *Dublin University Magazine*, an article influenced heavily by McCulloch's writings.

7.5   The crisis of 1839 and the escalation of the currency school controversy

A mild boom in 1837 and 1838 was followed by another economic crisis towards the end of 1838 and during 1839. Bankruptcies and bank runs ensued, and the Bank of England's gold reserve fell from £9.8 million in December 1838 to an extremely low £2.4 million by September 1839. Not only that; but in the teeth of shrinking reserves, the bank, instead of following anything like its own Palmer rule, let alone the more rigorous currency principle, expanded credit still further, thus precipitating an even greater drain of gold from the bank. By July and August 1839, the chancellor of the Exchequer was beginning to contemplate another restriction, another suspension of specie payment on behalf of the bank. The bank was saved only by massive credits from the Bank of France and from Hamburg.

Clearly, the banking situation was becoming intolerable, and something had to be done. Parliament appointed a select committee on banks of issue on 1840 and again in 1841, and massive hearings were held on the question. Disputes in parliamentary testimony and pamphlet controversy were redoubled, and were made more urgent by Horsley Palmer's concession that the bank was finding it almost impossible to adhere to his rule.

Several other groups now arose to challenge the growing currency school consensus. The free banking adherents took a lead from the currency school in lashing out at the Bank of England's responsibility for inflation and for the business cycle. But the force of their opposition to the bank was vitiated by their uniform apologia for the country and joint-stock banks. While it is true that those banks were largely governed by the actions of the bank, it was egregious for them to claim that the private banks were totally passive and blameless in the entire process. The free banking school was particularly discredited by the fact that virtually all of its spokesmen – with the exception of Sir Henry Parnell, who died in 1842, in the middle of the controversy – were themselves joint-stock or country bankers, so that the special pleading in their stance was all too evident. If this group had confined their advocacy of free banking to the largely *political* point that the bank would inevitably be *more* inflationary and dangerous than competitive banking, they would have been far more persuasive. But such restraint is not the usual practice of special pleaders.

The only distinguished economist to take up the free banking cause was Samuel Bailey, the subjective value theorist. But Bailey had founded and was now chairman of the Sheffield Banking Company, and his fervent apologia was all too suspect. Bailey, indeed, was one of the worst offenders in insisting on the passivity of the country and joint-stock banks, and in attacking the very idea that there is something wrong with worrying about changes in the quantity of the money supply. By assuring his readers that competitive banking would always provide 'nice adjustment of the currency to the wants of the people', Bailey overlooked the fundamental Ricardian truth that there is never any social value to increasing the money supply, once the commodity is established, and that inflationary increases in bank credit take place as a process of fraudulent issue of fake warehouse receipts to standard money.

Another school of thought arising in this period was the banking school, at this early point consisting solely of one prominent man, Thomas Tooke. Tooke (1774–1858) was by now an elderly merchant in the Russian trade who, born the son of a chaplain, had started working in St Petersburg at the age of 15, and had become a partner in a mercantile firm in London. Long interested in economic matters, Tooke had been one of the founders of the Political Economy Club, and continued to attend meetings of the club until his death. In the bullion controversy, Tooke was a staunch bullionist, and he strongly supported the resumption of specie payments in 1819. At best, however, Tooke was a confused and inchoate thinker, and whatever theoretical acumen he had was apparently warped beyond repair by decades of immersion in his life-work, a four-volume *History of Prices and of the State of the Circulation from 1792*, published from 1838 to 1848.[20] Inductive play with his statistics was able to convince Tooke, for example, as early as his 1838 volumes, first that high and rising prices during the Napoleonic periods were solely due to bad harvests, lowering the supply of farm products, as well as obstructions of foreign trade, while, second, *falling* prices after the war were caused by better harvests and the resumption of trade. Having concluded that, Tooke was able to press on, in his third volume of the *History of Prices* in 1840, and in his parliamentary testimony the same year, to launch the banking school with the absurd proposition – to quote from a crystal-clear formulation of Tooke four years later – that: 'the prices of commodities do not depend upon the quantity of money indicated by the amount of bank notes, nor upon the amount of the whole of the circulating medium: but that, on the contrary, the amount of the circulating medium is the consequence of prices'.

To be fair to Tooke and his banking school colleagues, they did not mean – or profess to mean – to apply this old fallacy to *inconvertible* currency, as their anti-bullionist forbears had done, but only to convertible currency. But this did not make their analysis or conclusion one whit less absurd. The masterful critique by Torrens deserves to be quoted at some length: Torrens first points out that Tooke has 'the deserved reputation, which even he himself cannot destroy' of having shown by 'an extensive induction from existing and from historical facts...that the value of everything declines as its quantity is increased in relation to the demand'. But then, Torrens notes, Tooke 'turns his back upon himself by affirming that the value of money does not decline, as its quantity is increased in relation to the demand'. Or at least he affirms this for a convertible money standard. But Torrens concludes incisively that the effects of an increase are the same, for convertible or inconvertible currency. The only difference is that there are limits to increases imposed by a convertible currency. Thus: 'Mr. Tooke falls into the misconception of imagining that the limitation to a further decline of value which convertibility imposes, prevents the previous existence of the decline which it subsequently arrests.' Like Adam Smith, the banking school was blithely assuming that the adjustments and restraints of redeemability were instantaneous, and therefore that no problems would be created in the actual processes of the real world.

A particular rapier thrust against Tooke by Torrens four years later cannot be resisted: 'Throughout interminable pages of inconsistent affirmation [in the multi-volume *History of Prices*], he reiterates the inference, that the value of commodities has fluctuated in relation to money and that, therefore, the value of money has not fluctuated in relation to commodities'.

The corollary proposition of the banking school, taken from the anti-bullionists and now brought again to the fore by Tooke, is that the Bank of England *cannot* increase the supply of money (as Tooke put it starkly, 'The Bank of England has not the Power to add to the Circulation'). Even applying this claim only to convertible currency, as the banking school did, it is difficult to hold such a manifest absurdity at length. In practice, therefore, Tooke and the other banking school adherents usually modified this blunt statement to apply only to bank notes issued in loans to private borrowers, and not to purchases of government securities. To the question: what's the difference?, the main contribution to Tooke's doctrine was made in 1844 by John Fullarton: namely, that notes issued in purchase of government securities are 'paid away' and remain permanently in circulation, thus adding to the quantity of money, whereas bank notes 'are only *lent* and *are returnable to the issuers*',[21] and presumably therefore do not add to the money supply. This was what Fullarton dubbed the 'principle of reflux' of notes returning to the banks. Once again, the incisive refutation came from Colonel Torrens, who pointed out that to carry any weight, the 'vaunted principle of reflux' requires *instantaneous* repayment of all loans: 'Allow any interval to elapse between the loan and the repayment and no regularity of reflux can prevent redundancy from being increased to any conceivable extent.'[22]

The same, as well as many other, strictures apply to a variant of Fullarton's and others in the banking school, which, again stemming from the anti-bullionists, held that banks can never over-issue notes provided that their notes are only issued in the course of making short-term, self-liquidating loans matched by inventories of goods in process – the so-called 'real bills' doctrine.

Torrens's role in the currency *vs* banking controversy has a fascinating reverse symmetry with the path taken by Tooke. Whereas Torrens began as an anti-bullionist and apologist for the Bank of England, and now ended as a currency schoolman and opponent of bank credit inflation, Tooke began as a solid bullionist yet ended his days as a pro-bank, anti-bullionist.

Among the various grave inconsistencies in the banking school approach, one particularly stands out: if it is true that banks can do no wrong (at least in a convertible currency), that they cannot over-issue notes or over-expand credit, and that even if they did it could have no effect in raising prices or causing a business cycle, then why not adopt free banking? Why have a privileged monopoly like the Bank of England? Yet the banking school remained a determined enemy of free banking and devoted apologists for the bank. Thomas Tooke's most famous *dictum* was the striking: 'Free trade in banking is synonymous with free trade in swindling.' Fair enough. But, if we analyse this pronouncement logically and we find that banking is synonymous with swindling, then what is the rationale for placing the power of state privilege behind a monopoly 'swindler'? Even if banking is swindling, isn't 'competitive swindling' better than a state-privileged and dominant monopoly swindler? And yet Tooke fiercely fought to preserve the bank and its exclusive privileges in London and environs; his only proposed reform was to induce the bank to hold a higher reserve of specie to liabilities.

The one contribution of the banking school was to continue to emphasize – what Torrens knew but Loyd and Norman did not – that bank notes and bank demand deposits were equal and coordinate parts of the supply of money. Because of their grave error on this point (in Torrens's case to dismiss deposits as always in a fixed ratio to notes), the currency school, and its embodiment in Peel's Act, left deposits as the big hole in their attempt to make the money supply conform to movements in gold. As we have noted, the currency school counterparts in the United States did not make that error.

Free trade and *laissez-faire* thought was growing in dominance in Great Britain during this era, led by the intrepid merchants, manufacturers and publicists from Manchester. But where to stand on the vexed question of banking? Should banking be free or is fractional reserve banking really 'swindling' and therefore different from normal honest enterprise? Was Chancellor of the Exchequer Thomas Spring Rice correct when he stated in Parliament in 1839 'I deny the applicability of the general principle of freedom of trade to the question of making money?'

Of one thing the men of Manchester were certain: there was no quarter to be given the Bank of England. Thus, John Benjamin Smith, the powerful president of the Manchester Chamber of Commerce, reported to the chamber in 1840 that the crisis of 1839 was caused by the Bank of England's contraction, following inexorably from its own earlier 'undue expansion of the currency'. Smith denounced the 'undue privileges' of the bank as the source of its control over the nation's economic life. Testifying before Parliament that year, Smith endorsed the currency school by criticizing the fluctuations of note issues by all the banks as well as the Bank of England, and went on to state: 'it is desirable in any change in our existing system to approximate as nearly as possible to the operation of a metallic currency; it is desirable also to divest the plan of all mystery, and to make it so plain and simple that it may be easily understood by all.' Not only did he thus endorse the currency principle; he went further to endorse Ricardo's scheme of creating a governmental national bank for the purpose of issuing bank notes.[23]

A similar course was taken by Richard Cobden, the shining prince of the Manchester *laissez-faire* movement. Attacking the Bank of England, and any idea of discretionary control over the currency, Cobden fervently declared:

> I hold all idea of regulating the currency to be an absurdity; the very terms of regulating the currency and managing the currency I look upon to be an absurdity; the currency should regulate itself; it must be regulated by the trade and commerce of the world; I would neither allow the Bank of England nor any private banks to have what is called the management of the currency...I should never contemplate any remedial measure, which left it to the discretion of individuals to regulate the amount of currency by any principle or standard whatever...

Rejecting both private and central bank management, Cobden was perceptive enough to see that the goal was not free banking *per se*, but to have a currency that mirrors genuine market forces of supply and demand: i.e. the fortunes of gold or silver money. He saw that the currency principle aimed to do just that, and hence his endorsement. And while his support for a government national bank of issue was too much like leaping out of the frying pan into the fire, it was understandable in the light of his refusal to trust the Bank of England to cleave to the currency path: 'I should be sorry to trust the Bank of England again, having violated their principle [the Palmer rule]; for I never trust the same parties twice on an affair of such magnitude.'

7.6   The renewed threat to the gold standard

Thus a consensus was building rapidly after the crisis of 1839 on behalf of the currency principle. But perhaps the precipitating factor in bringing Sir Robert Peel and the Establishment to enact the principle was a renewed threat to the gold standard. The gold standard had been the agreed-upon consensus of all parties since the 1820s and since the return to gold the assaults of inveterate statists and inflationists like Birmingham's Attwood brothers had faded away. But now, under the stimulus of economic crisis, fiat paper agitation and other inflationist threats to the gold standard surfaced once again.

If Manchester was the home of *laissez-faire* and sound money, Birmingham, its sister manufacturing town in the North, had long been the home of state-sponsored inflationism. Economic recession struck the Birmingham area in 1841, and Birmingham moved once more to a powerful attack upon gold. Thomas Attwood himself had retired from Parliament two years before, but Birmingham's representatives were more than willing to take up the old cause. Attwood had been replaced by merchant and manufacturer George Frederick Muntz, who agreed with the former's currency views; and Richard Spooner, the Tory whom Muntz had defeated for the seat, was an inflationist and a banking partner of Attwood's.

The following year, the Birmingham Chamber of Commerce, presided over by Richard Spooner, launched a furious campaign pressuring the prime minister, Sir Robert Peel, into going off gold. Muntz put out a new edition of an old anti-gold tract and, roaring back to the wars, Thomas Attwood, as might be expected, published articles and wrote numerous letters on his currency nostrums.

The most influential of this outpouring of Birmingham inflationism was the *Gemini Letters*, published anonymously by Thomas B. Wright and John Harlow of Birmingham, first as 35 letters in a country newspaper during 1843, and then in book form the following year as *The Currency Question: The Gemini Letters*. The *Gemini* plea was straight, proto-Keynesian, inflationism: inconvertible paper money should be issued by the government, in sufficient amount to stimulate consumer purchasing power and ensure full employment. In addition, the public debt should be inflated away. Thus, as Wright and Harlow put it:

> The proper plan, it appears to us, is to raise the capacity of the consumer, by securing high wages and ample profits, and by these means making light the fixed national obligations of the people...The only limit they would affix to the issue of paper money would be the degrees of prosperity which the different amount of issues would produce...

There is every reason to believe that the *Gemini Letters* and the Birmingham agitation were influential throughout the country. Henry Burgess and his committee of country bankers used the interchanges between the Birmingham Chamber and Robert Peel to denounce the gold standard. Both the *Times* and the new weekly *Economist* were forced to expend a great deal of energy in defending the gold standard from its 'unsound' enemies. At any rate, it is known that Peel owned a copy of *The Currency Question* and marked key passages in the book.

The threat to gold was reinforced by a renewed agitation to dump gold for a bimetallic gold–silver standard. Heedless of the fact that bimetallism never works in practice (since Gresham's law pushes the undervalued metal out of circulation and encourages the overvalued), the pro-silver forces found in bimetallism a way to support monetary inflation while remaining respectably in favour of precious metals as money. Silver supporters therefore began with a core from the fiat paper group, including Spooner, Matthias Attwood, George Muntz and Henry Burgess, and added numerous bankers and businessmen, such as Richard Page, Henry W. Hobhouse, chairman of the committee of country bankers, William D. Haggard, and the eminent banker Alexander Baring, now Lord Ashburton.

7.7   Triumph of the currency school: Peel's Act of 1844

At the heart of the triumph of the currency principle in Peel's Act of 1844 was one man: the statesman and political genius Sir Robert Peel.[24] Peel has been habitually derided by historians as a confused middle-of-the-roader, a 'flexible' political opportunist, at best a transitional figure unwittingly performing the historical function of ushering in the Conservative and Liberal party system in England. But, as Professor Boyd Hilton has helped to point out, Peel was a far different figure: a statesman in the best sense, a Tory liberal who was consistent and even unyielding in principle and purpose, and flexible and 'entrepreneurial' only in attaining the best tactics to arrive at his fixed ideological goals. As Hilton has demonstrated, in every important sense, economic, financial and moral, Robert Peel was the John the Baptist, the founder, the 'progenitor of Gladstonian liberalism'.[25]

During the 1820s, Peel was for most years head of the Home Office in Tory governments. He had long been opposed to Catholic emancipation, and had even resigned his Cabinet post in 1827 in protest at the accession to the prime ministry of George Canning, head of Tory liberalism and champion of Catholic rights. Two years later, however, after the death of Canning, Peel, back as home secretary, was converted to Catholic emancipation as part of his ever-increasing devotion to the classical liberal, *laissez-faire* cause. At his conversion, Peel had the good grace to honour the prophets and warriors for Catholic emancipation whom he had opposed for so long: Fox, Grattan and Canning himself.

From 1831 on, Peel headed the Tory, now Conservative party, and also was the heart and soul of the liberal faction of the party. Peel's great prime ministry took place in 1841–46. Here he fought vigorously for a peaceful foreign policy, battling against the pro-war, imperialist Palmerston wing of the Liberal party, and managed to conclude peace with the United States in the menacing Oregon boundary controversy. Peel also managed to lower tariffs, but lost in his fight for all-out free trade. His great accomplishment on that front was victory over the furious opposition of the Tory agriculturalists led by Benjamin Disraeli, in the complete repeal of the infamous Corn Laws which had for decades established an enormous import tariff on wheat. In this fight against the artificially high price of food, Peel was spurred by the growing famine in Ireland. Again gracious in victory, Peel hailed his political opponent, the *laissez-faire* Liberal Richard Cobden, as the true architect of the repeal of the Corn Laws. For his success, Peel's government was toppled by Disraeli, and he died in a hunting accident four years later, in 1850.

Robert Peel's proudest achievement, however, was his banking reform, his Act of 1844. The Bank Charter Act of 1833 had provided for possible change in the charter during 1844, so that was the year of potential banking reform. As recent research has revealed, Peel's Act did not originate as a hostile 'strait-jacket, fastened on a reluctant (though subsequently complacent) Bank by the efforts of the Currency School'. Rather the Act came from within the bank itself, 'as an attempt by the Bank to find for itself a short-cut to currency management', as well as a means of obtaining its long-sought monopoly over bank note issue.[26] First, the ardent currency school leader, George Warde Norman, had, as a bank director, been promoting the plan since 1838. Although Norman lost within the bank on his currency proposal in 1840, he persisted, and the following year he became part of a five-man standing committee of the bank to discuss the scheme. By January 1844, William Cotton, the governor of the Bank of England, and a member of the standing committee, had been converted to the currency plan, and when, in early January, Peel asked Cotton and the deputy governor, J.B. Heath (also a member of the standing committee) to confer with him and Chancellor of the Exchequer Henry Coulburn about fundamental banking reform, Cotton was ready.[27] In response to these discussions, Cotton and Heath, on 2 February, submitted to Peel the complete outline of what was soon to become Peel's Act.

In essence, Peel's Act established the currency principle. It divided the Bank of England into an issue department, issuing bank notes, and a banking department, lending and issuing demand deposits. True to the rigid currency school separation of notes and deposits, deposits would be totally free and unregulated, while notes would be limited to a ceiling of £14 million matched by assets of government securities (roughly the extent of existing note issue.) Any further notes could only be issued on the basis of 100 per cent reserve in gold. The second main provision was to grant the Bank of England its long-sought monopoly of the note issue. This was not done immediately, but to be phased in over a period of time. Specifically: no new banks were to issue any bank notes, existing banks were to issue no further notes, and the Bank of England might contract with bankers to buy out their existing notes and replace them with the bank's own. In this way, private bank notes were 'grandfathered' in, and the private (that is, joint-stock plus country) banks were neatly cartellized, under the direction of the bank, with the private banks able to keep out all further competition. This 'grandfather' cartel clause was not only designed to make the transition to the new order gradual; its main effect, and presumably its intent as well, was to bring the private banks – which might be expected to be the chief opponents of the new bill – around to become enthusiastic supporters.

In his manoeuvring within the Cabinet before publicly presenting Peel's Act, the prime minister made it clear that 'if we were about to establish in a new state of society a new system of currency', he would have preferred the Ricardian plan of government notes, with no Bank of England or any other bank notes allowed; but that this plan would be impracticable in the existing state of the real world, where a coalition must be built among such contending forces as the bank itself, Ricardians, free bankers and country bankers. The desideratum, Peel shrewdly advised, was to 'determine to propose the course which they may conscientiously believe to reconcile in the greatest degree the qualities of being consistent with sound principle and suited to the present condition of society'.

News of Peel's coming bank charter bill had spread by the end of February, and the country banks, as expected, vigorously protested the bill during March and April. Finally, Peel introduced the bill to Parliament on 6 May. Shrewdly splitting his opposition, he applied the bill fully only to England. The ban on new banks issuing notes was extended to Scotland and Ireland, but the limitations on existing banks were applied to England alone. For the rest, Scotland and Ireland were left alone for the time being.

The introduction of Peel's bill touched off a flurry of controversy, including a pamphlet war over the Act. In particular, the new controversy gave rise to the banking school, which beforehand had been represented only by Tooke. Tooke weighed in with an *Inquiry into the Currency Principle*, and John Fullarton entered the fray with his aforementioned pamphlet, *On the Regulation of Currencies*, a widely circulated and influential tract even though it was published in August 1844, after the passage of Peel's Act. S.J. Loyd published a defence of the bill, while the formidable Colonel Torrens blasted Tooke in another pamphlet.

The new banking school was noteworthy for being more royalist than the king, more favourable to the Bank of England than the bank itself. In short, the banking school, along with most of the London bankers, favoured the vesting of a monopoly of bank note issue in the Bank of England. Its quarrel was solely with currency principle restrictions on the bank's issue of notes. This was surely the kind of opposition that the Bank of England could live with. While the banking school correctly spotted the main weakness of the currency school in not treating notes and deposits alike, this objection was scarcely directed to extending any sort of reserve requirements to bank deposits as well as notes. On the contrary, they would have been all the more outraged by, say, a consistent Peel's Act that would have placed a 100 per cent reserve requirement on all further bank liabilities, deposits as well as notes.

One bit of *curiosa* about the emergence of the banking school is the lateness of its arrival; coming as it did almost when the fight over Peel's Act was over, and flourishing for a while after, its importance was more for raising theoretical issues and for raising the interest of historians of economic thought than in actually influencing the political battle.

Another noteworthy aspect of the fray was the advent of a new and important star in the economic firmament: John Stuart Mill (1806–73), who joined the banking school side of the debate in an anonymous article, 'The Currency Question', in the radical *Westminster Review*. Actually, Mill had foreshadowed the banking school in an article written at the age of 20, 'Paper Currency and Commercial Distress', in the short-lived radical *Parliamentary Review*. Like so many others, Mill was first moved to turn his attention to banking and business cycles by the economic and financial crisis of 1825–26. But in contrast to many others, he abandoned instead of extending his basic Ricardianism in this area.[28] Instead of seeing the new phenomenon of business cycles as created by monetary disturbances, he saw them as caused by waves of 'speculation', presumably generated by over-optimism. Money and banks were purely passive respondents to fluctuations in the economy. From this there followed his conclusion that movements in the money supply, at least under a gold standard, had no effect on prices or trade. Within the framework of a gold standard, prices rose first, dragging the money supply upwards, and later fell, pulling the money supply down.

How could Mill square this odd doctrine with his overall Ricardianism and its thesis of the influence of the supply of money upon its value? He did so by an ingenious, though bizarre and fallacious, theory of what constitutes the supply of money. The money supply was made up, not only of coin, notes and demand deposits, Mill opined, but also of the 'credit-worthiness' of every member of the public. When a bank made loans to some member of the public, then, it might increase notes or deposits outstanding, but that increase is exactly compensated by a decrease in the 'credit-worthiness' of the borrowing citizens. Therefore, when banks lend money to individuals and businesses, the money supply does not increase at all. On the contrary, when banks purchase government securities or finance its deficit, they add directly to the total money supply by the same amount. In fact, they even add to the money supply when they lend to private citizens beyond the degree of their genuine credit-worthiness. How is such 'credit-worthiness' to be determined? By banks confining their loans to sound borrowers, and to the discounting of 'real bills', that are short-term, matched by inventories of goods in process, and are therefore self-liquidating in a short period of time. Bank credit then happily follows the 'needs of trade' upwards or downwards, and cannot raise prices. While completely fallacious, Mill's theory at least had the merit of providing *some* plausible, logical explanation for the banking school creed – one that was scarcely matched by any of his colleagues.

Furthermore, Mill's doctrine provided a good reason for his devotion to the gold standard, and for his bullionist denunciation of inconvertible fiat money.

Within his theory, if government or the central bank issues inconvertible fiat paper, that paper adds directly to the money supply and to inflation rather than being neutralized by subtracting from credit-worthiness. And devoted to the gold standard he remained. We have already seen Mill's denunciation of Thomas Attwood's inflationary fiat paper scheme in 1833.

And what of the alleged free banking school, which Professor White has put forward as equally strong and vibrant to, and strictly separate from, the rival currency and banking schools? As White himself ruefully admits, they were nowhere to be found, their alleged devotion to free banking failing the most acid of all tests, when Peel's Act was about to bring all commercial banks under Bank of England control. For not only would the bank now have a virtual monopoly of note issue, but in order to obtain notes in exchange for cashed-in deposits, the other banks would now be obliged to keep the great bulk of their reserves at the Bank of England. White tries to explain away the defection of the free bankers as having been bought out by Peel's cartellization-'grandfather' clause: for the banks could continue to issue at their current level and no new competing banks would be permitted. But while this explanation is true enough, it raises the crucial question: how devoted were Professor White's heroes to free banking to begin with? Wasn't the free banking school simply a group devoted to the economic interests of the private commercial banks?

Take, for example, the newly founded *The Bankers' Magazine*, which had supposedly been a leading mouthpiece for free banking for the previous year. A writer in the June 1844 issue, while critical of the currency principle and the move towards monopoly issues for the bank, frankly approved the Peel Act as a whole for aiding profits of existing banks by prohibiting all new banks of issue.

And let us take in particular James William Gilbart (1794–1863), leading spokesman for the country bankers, manager of the London & Westminster Bank, and, according to Professor White, one of the main theoreticians of the free banking school. Gilbart, born in London and descended from a Cornish family, had worked all his life as a bank official and had written works on banking since the late 1820s. Since 1834, he had been manager of the London & Westminster Bank, continually clashing with the Bank of England. Despite Professor White's assurance that the free banking school men were even more fervent than the currency men in attributing the cause of the business cycle to monetary inflation, Gilbart held, typically of the banking school, that bank notes simply expand and contract according to the 'wants of trade', and therefore such notes, being matched by the production of goods, could not raise prices. Furthermore, the active factor goes from 'trade' to prices to the 'requirement' for more bank notes to flow in the economy. Thus Gilbart: 'if there is an increase of trade without an increase of prices, I consider that more notes will be required to circulate that increased quantity of commodities; if there is an increase of commodities and an increase of prices also, of course you would require a still greater amount of notes.' In short, whether prices rise or not, the supply of money must always increase! One wonders who the 'you' is who would have such requirements. On the free market, on the contrary, if there is an increase in the production of commodities, prices will tend to fall and *not* rise; furthermore, increased production of trade does not 'require' or call forth an increase in bank money. The causal chain is the other way round: increased bank note issue raises the money supply and prices, and *also* the nominal money value of the goods being produced.

All historians of economic thought except for Professor White have placed Gilbart squarely in the banking school camp as one of its leaders. Since White seems to agree with Gilbart's fallacious 'wants of trade' analysis, and since he admits that this creed is similar to that of the banking school, his creation of an important new school of 'free banking', challenging both of the others, appears all the more tenuous and artificial. The main difference seems to be marginal and political: while *all* the banking school hailed the banking system as useful and harmless, *most* of them laid special honours on the Bank of England, while Gilbart, as a joint-stock banker himself, placed most approval upon the commercial banks.[29]

When it came to the test, then, Gilbart, like his colleagues on *The Bankers' Magazine*, caved in on what Professor White alleges to be his free banking principles. Thus White concedes:

He [Gilbart] was relieved that the act did not extinguish the joint-stock banks' right of issue and was frankly pleased with its cartellizing provisions: 'Our rights are acknowledged – our privileges are extended – our circulation guaranteed – and we are saved from conflicts with reckless competitors'.[30]

James Gilbart's open status as a banking school inflationist and Robert Peel's staunch devotion to hard money were both revealed in Peel's questioning of Gilbart when the latter testified that country bank notes are only issued in response to the wants of trade, and therefore that they could never be over-issued. He *also* claimed that the Bank of England could never over-issue so long as it only discounted commercial loans and did not buy government bonds.[31] At this point, Sir Robert Peel unerringly zeroed in and drew forth Gilbart's apologia for the banking system. Peel: 'Do you think, then that the legitimate demands of commerce may always be trusted to, as a safe test of the amount of circulation under all circumstances?' To which Gilbart admitted: 'I think they may.' (Nothing about exempting the Bank of England from that trust.) Peel then asked the critical question. The banking school all claimed to be devoted to the gold standard, so that the 'needs of trade' justification for bank credit did *not* apply to inconvertible currency. Peel, suspicious of that devotion to gold, then asked: in the bank restriction days, 'do you think that the legitimate demands of commerce constituted a test that might be safely relied upon?' To which Gilbert evasively replied: 'That is a period of which I have no personal knowledge.' This was a particularly disingenuous point coming from the author of *The History and Principles of Banking* (1834). Moreover, the issue is of course a theoretical one, and no 'personal knowledge' is necessary to make a reply – a point made immediately by Peel. At which point Gilbart threw in the towel on the gold standard: 'I think the legitimate demands of commerce, even then, would be a sufficient guide to go by...'. When Peel pressed Gilbart on the point, Gilbart began to vacillate, changing his views, returning to them, and then again falling back on his lack of personal experience.[32]

Peel was right in being suspicious of the strength of the banking school's devotion to gold. Apart from Gilbart's damaging revelations, his colleague at the London & Westminster Bank, J.W. Bosanquet, kept urging bank suspensions of specie payment whenever times became difficult. And while Thomas Tooke often proclaimed his abhorrence of the Birmingham school, he wrote in 1844 that a crucial limit on any over-issue of bank notes was the needs of trade *in addition to* gold convertibility. The opening was sufficient to allow Robert Torrens to score a palpable hit:

> After a careful examination of Mr. Tooke's recent publication, [1844] I cannot discover any very essential or practical difference between his principles and those of the Birmingham economists. Once deviate from the gold rule of causing the fluctuations of our mixed circulation to conform to what would be the fluctuations of a purely metallic currency and the flood-gates are opened, and the landmarks removed. Between the abandonment of a metallic standard as recommended by the Birmingham economists, and the adoption of arrangements hazarding the maintenance of a metallic standard recommended by Mr. Tooke, the difference in the practicable result might ultimately be nothing.[33]

John Fullarton's admission was even more damaging than Tooke's, avowing, in his popular 1844 tract, that he wholeheartedly agreed with the 'decried doctrine of the old Bank Directors of 1810' – namely, the anti-bullionist position that so long as any bank sticks to short-term real bills 'It cannot go wrong in issuing as many [notes] as the public will receive from it'. And of course 1810 was a year of inconvertible money. It is no wonder that Robert Peel considered all opponents of the currency principle as essentially Birmingham men.

Thus the opposition to Peel's Act, while theoretically important, was politically scattered and ineffective. The bill sailed through overwhelmingly, and became law on 19 July. A second Peel bill, designed to make it more difficult to establish new joint-stock banks, sailed through in September. The result of this tightening of bank control and monopoly as well as cartel privileges to existing banks, was, indeed, the creation of virtually no new joint-stock banks in England for the next eight years.

At this point, Peel completed his currency task by extending its sway to Scotland and Ireland in two bills that became law on 21 July 1845. Cautious in the face of regional traditions, Peel was not as tough on the Scottish and Irish banks as he had been on the English. Whereas the English commercial banks could issue no more bank notes period, the Scottish and Irish banks were treated as Peel's Act of 1844 treated the Bank of England: their *further* bank note issues were limited to 100 per cent gold reserves. Scotland had never had its banking restricted, having been free to establish joint-stock banks and issue notes and deposits throughout Scotland. The Scottish bankers, however, like Gilbart and the English bankers, were easily bought off by cartel privileges even more lucrative than in England. As White admits, 'Peel in essence bought the support of all existing banks by suppressing potential entrants and competition for market shares'.[34] In addition, Peel shrewdly permitted the Scottish banks to keep the privilege, denied to English banks (including the Bank of England) since the 1820s, of continuing to issue their cherished small (£1) notes.

The only important development in the year between the two Peel's Acts was the highly belated entry into the great debate of a new leader of the banking school, James Wilson, founder and editor of the notable new journal, *The Economist*. Wilson (1805–60)[35] had founded *The Economist* for the express purpose of battling for free trade and *laissez-faire*. He criticized Peel's Act when it came up in 1844, but devoted most of his energies to free trade. Finally, in the Spring of 1845, Wilson wrote a famous series of nine articles on 'Currency and Banking' in *The Economist*, attacking the extension of Peel's Act to Scotland and Ireland. Wilson took an orthodox banking school approach, except that each of his positions was so emphatic that the inner inconsistencies and contradictions of the banking school were brought out particularly starkly. Thus Wilson was far more emphatic and militant than Tooke or Fullarton about the importance of preserving the gold standard, so much so that Torrens was later to call Wilson 'the most able of the opponents of the act of 1844'.[36] And yet, of the Big Four of the banking school (Tooke, Fullarton, Mill and Wilson), Wilson was the only one who stated flatly and clearly that short-term, self-liquidating real bills would be sufficient to protect the banks from over-issue, even *without* specie convertibility. Thus, Wilson declared that

inconvertible paper notes might be issued to any extent that legitimate transactions required them, provided such issues were confined to the discount of good bills of exchange, and to loans for short periods, without any risk of depreciation, because a larger quantity never could be so issued than was again shortly returnable to the bank in payment of such loans.[37]

In addition, of all the Big Four Wilson was the friendliest to free banking and desirous of saving the alleged free banking system in Scotland.[38] And yet he also claimed that the Bank of England could never over-issue in a convertible money system, which was quite the opposite of the free banking approach.

7.8   Tragedy in triumph for the currency school: the aftermath

As the Jacksonians and other currency counterparts in the US might have predicted, the currency school harboured a tragic flaw, an Achilles' heel that laid them low and turned their triumph into ashes: the neglect of bank deposits as a coordinate part of the money supply. And so, no sooner had Peel's Act been passed, when the Bank of England, happily ensconced in its briar patch of monopoly, central control, and note restriction but deposit freedom, began to expand its loans and deposits ad libitum. At the end of 1844, bank discounts had been £2.1 million and total bank credit £21.8 million. By the end of February 1846, however, bank credit expansion had been so intense that its discounts totalled £13.1 million and total credits £35.8 million. In short, in only a little over a year, total bank credits had risen by 64 per cent, and discounts by a phenomenal 424 per cent. This expansion was aided by the bank's drastically reducing its discount rate from 4 per cent to $2^1/2$ per cent, not only a huge quantitative reduction, but also a lowering of the rate from its traditional 'penalty rate' above the market, to the market interest rate, thereby greatly stimulating borrowing from the bank by banks and other debtors.

Notes of the Bank of England increased only mildly during this period; the huge rise, as we might expect, took place in bank deposits. In September, 1844, bank deposits totalled £12.2 million; by the end of February, 1846, they had doubled to £24.9 million. In the course of this enormous expansion, bank gold reserves fell sharply.

Most of this expanded bank credit poured into a speculative mania of investing in questionable new domestic railroads. In the years 1845 and 1846, over £180 million of new railroad construction was authorized, about double the total of the entire previous decade. Looking back on the period a few years later, *The Economist* referred to the 'mad scenes' of 1845 and 1846, and to

the folly, the avarice, the insufferable arrogance, the headlong, desperate, and unprincipled gambling and jobbing, which disgraced nobility and aristocracy, polluted senators and senate houses, contaminated merchants, manufacturers, and traders of all kinds, and threw a chilling blight for a time over honest plod and fair industry.

The bank tried feebly to stem the tide during the first half of 1846, but no sooner did bank reserves increase, than the bank, which had raised its discount rate to 3¹/₂ per cent in November 1845, dropped it back to 3 per cent the following August. Bank reserves then resumed their steep decline, falling from £10 million in August 1846, a ratio of specie to notes and bank deposits of 58 per cent, to only £3.0 million in April 1847, a ratio of only 20 per cent.

Again, the bank tried to check the tide it had created and continued to generate, but too little and too late. Interest rates rose with the inflationary boom, so that an increase of the bank discount rate to 4 per cent in January 1847 left the rate still under the market, and between 9 January and 10 April, total bank credits rose by £4.5 million and discounts by £3.8 million.

By April 1847, the Bank of England, as well as the entire financial and economic system, was in deep crisis: it increased its rate to 5 per cent, but market rates were now up to 7 per cent. Rejecting efforts by a minority of bank directors to raise the rate to 7 per cent, or even to 6, the bank made things much worse by keeping its rate at 5 and then rationing credit, suddenly cutting off discounts, calling in loans, and refusing to increase loans regardless of the credit quality of the borrower. The bank's refusal to raise rates and instead discriminate in favour of certain borrowers did not, however, save the commercial bank owned by the bank's own governor, W.R. Robinson, from stopping payments in July, or the bank of two other directors from going under in September.

The bank's sudden contraction, cessation of loans and credit rationing caused a severe business and financial panic in April and May of 1847. This drastic therapy finally eased the bank's own condition by the end of May, with the gold outflow temporarily reversing. By the beginning of July, the bank's reserves had doubled from £3.0 million to £6.0 million, a reserve ratio to deposits of 32 per cent. But no sooner had the pressure eased than the bank began to expand again, in the meanwhile making things worse by keeping its discount rate below the market and indulging in selective credit rationing. In September, the second great crisis of 1847 broke, and mercantile failures spread throughout September and October. Thomas Tooke lamented that 'These *mercantile* failures, in number and in the amount of property involved in them, were unprecedented in the commercial history of this country'. In October, the banks began to break, and bank runs began to spread through the provinces. As a result, the frightened banks began to contract their credit and deposits drastically, in order to increase greatly their percentage of reserves. The reserves of the Bank of England were down sharply once again, to less than 14 per cent of deposits. At that point, the Bank of England threw in the towel, and, for the first of many crises, requested the government to suspend the 100 per cent gold reserve restriction on notes imposed by Peel's Act. Delegations from Liverpool and the North, London private bankers, and members from Scotland also pressed hard for suspension of Peel's Act. The country bank organ, *Circular to Bankers*, charged that the London bankers were considering breaking the Bank of England by redeeming all their deposits. One wonders, in that case, how the commercial banks themselves could have avoided being broken in turn. At that point, the government predictably, and, for the first of many crises, itself threw in the towel by suspending the Peel Act provision of 100 per cent gold reserve restrictions on the issue of Bank of England notes.

The government saved the fractional-reserve system by obediently suspending Peel's Act on 25 October, thereby of course saving the day for the banks and alleviating the immediate crisis – at the expense of, in effect, giving up the currency principle and any attempt to tie the monetary and banking system directly to, and to the same extent as, the behaviour of gold. From then on, Great Britain, and eventually the rest of the world, was stuck with a fractional-reserve banking system issuing demand deposits, pyramiding on top of a central bank monopolizing the issue of notes and centralizing the nation's gold, and generating an endless round of boom–bust cycles of inflation and recession. Furthermore, with gold essentially centralized into the reserves of the central banks, it became easy for all these nations, even though allegedly committed to the gold standard, to go off that standard and on to fiat paper whenever any crisis – such as World War I – presented an alleged need for the rapid inflation of money to finance the war effort.

The heart and soul of the currency principle was a rigid tie of Bank of England note issue to 100 per cent gold reserve; but if this restriction was to be suspended whenever banks or businesses got into trouble, then the currency principle lay in shambles. As the prominent London banker George Carr Glynn correctly prophesied after the 1847 suspension, the public would expect another suspension in every future crisis. And sure enough, that is precisely what happened. In response to the 1847 crisis, there were committees of parliamentary inquiry in 1847 and 1848. The suspension of Peel's Act during the crisis of 1857 was easier, and while there were parliamentary committees in 1857 and 1858, there was, in contrast to the 1847 crisis, no debate on the floor of Parliament. And the suspension of Peel's Act in 1866 was considered so routine that there was not even the bother of a parliamentary committee of inquiry.

It is therefore remarkable that, from the time of the first suspension in 1847, the currency school, without exception, defended the suspension of Peel's Act, giving no sign of realizing that they were thereby abandoning their entire doctrine.[39] For not only did suspension in crises weaken the point of the Act, but also the knowledge that suspension would come to the rescue in any crisis emboldened the bank and banking system to expand credit as if the restrictions of Peel's Act did not exist at all. As a result, all that was left of the currency principle was the monopolization of notes by the Bank of England.

7.9 *De facto* victory for the banking school

It is a cliché that people are often appalled at the consequences of achieving their long-cherished goals. Because of the neglect of deposits, the enactment of the currency principle in Peel's Act in no way moderated bank credit expansion or the boom–bust cycle. Given the dashing of their dreams, the currency school, as in the case of all ideologues whose god has failed, could take several alternative courses of action. The most courageous would have been to admit that their principle was deeply flawed, to concede defeat, and to go back to the drawing board. Unfortunately, human beings are so constituted that they rarely opt for this noble course. Certainly none of the currency school distinguished themselves in this crisis. Instead, they took the route that all too many schools of thought, including the Marxists, have travelled: stoutly proclaiming that their theory is in excellent shape, while subtly but vitally redefining what the theory is all about.

For example, before 1844, the currency school, especially Colonel Torrens, adopted a monetary theory of the business cycle. Economic fluctuations were generated by bank credit expansion, led by the Bank of England, which led to inflation and booms, after which the inevitable contraction brought about bankruptcies and recessions. No sooner did the cycle of 1844–47 occur, however, when the currency men backtracked, virtually joining their old enemies of the banking school. The banking school had always proclaimed that banks and the money supply were merely passive respondents to boom– bust cycles generated by non-monetary forces in the 'real' economy. Usually the culprit was mysterious waves of 'speculation', presumably driven by waves of over-optimism and over-pessimism. Now, the currency school, even Colonel Torrens, proclaimed that they had never, ever promised an end to the business cycle, which is, after all, governed by such non-monetary forces as speculation and over-optimism and pessimism. The most that regulation of the currency could do, the currency school now opined, is to eliminate whatever part of the business fluctuations were caused by movements of the money supply. And this, they staunchly affirmed, Peel's Act had indeed accomplished. The business cycle of 1844–47 might have been severe, but it would have been far worse if Peel's Act and the currency principle had not been in effect.

Thus Colonel Torrens, in numerous apologies for Peel's Act, put the blame for the boom of 1844–46 on 'overtrading' and railway speculation, as if this speculation had come out of the blue and was not the consequence of cheap, expanding bank credit. He also mentioned that one aspect of the inflationary boom was 'rapid conversion of floating to fixed capital', that is, a sinking of liquid capital into an excessive amount of fixed, long-range investment. Again, there was no hint that it was excessive bank credit that had generated this over-investment.

It is revealing to compare two critiques by Torrens of Mill's contention that the currency school claimed to be able to cure all business cycles and 'commercial revulsions'. In 1844, in reply to Mill's essay in *Westminster Review*, Torrens pointed out that the currency school claimed to eliminate *not* all revulsions but only those originating 'in a currency fluctuating alternately above and below the level to which a purely metallic currency would perform'. But in his point-by-point 1857 critique of the banking chapter in Mill's *Principles*, Torrens shifted the emphasis. Instead of paring down monetary-based fluctuations to gold currency, Torrens now claimed that most fluctuations began, not in over-issue by banks, but in disturbances not caused by money, which left the money supply out of harmony with the gold supply. Furthermore, Torrens was now easily able to cite Loyd and Norman in support. Loyd, too, now focused on the alleged non-monetary causes of fluctuations. Focusing, as the banking school had long done, on optimism and speculation, Loyd declared that 'So long as human nature remains what it is, and hope springs eternal in the human breast, speculations will occasionally occur, and bring their attendant train of alternate periods of excitement and depression'.

Thus, with the currency school coming to agree with the banking school on the primacy of non-monetary, and the passive dependence of monetary, causes of the cycle, the way was paved for a *de facto* consensus between the two schools. Since the currency school seemed content with the existing system so long as it enjoyed the *label* of the currency principle, the money supply was now deemed passive enough. At the same time, the Bank of England had enough real discretion and flexibility to satisfy the banking school and reconcile it rather easily to the *status quo*. Thus James Wilson, a leading banking school critic of Peel's Act, was readily able to vote for its continuance in the parliamentary committee of 1857–58. The banking school was content, in the British banking system of 1844–1914, to achieve the *substance* of their own creed while allowing the proud currency men to bask in the *name*. For their part, the currency men enjoyed the laurels of an empty victory: Norman, Torrens and Loyd (after 1850 made Baron Overstone), enjoyed great prestige while proclaiming the *status quo* a triumphant embodiment of their principles. The Bank of England's directors were happy to embrace the supposedly restrictive currency creed, and new currency epigones relayed what had become standard doctrine: misinterpreting the existing system as currency-like, and ignoring the entrenching of the boom–bust cycle in economic life.[40]

With the currency school now committed to the banking school's non-monetary, 'overtrading' theory of the business cycle, and with such hard-money and free-banking writers as Robert Mushet and Henry Parnell gone from the scene, the currency analysis of the business cycle disappeared by default. Of the banking school analysts, the most important elaboration of the non-monetary cycle theory was that of James Wilson, in his *Capital, Currency, and Banking* (1847).[41] Wilson developed what might be called a non-monetary over-investment theory, which foreshadowed the later Austrian cycle theory but lacked the crucial monetary causal element. He focused on railroad over-investment as the cause of the 1844–47 cycle, and persistently predicted a crisis based on his analysis from 1845 until the time of the crash.

In Wilson's brilliant analysis, the boom begins with the excessive investment of savings in fixed capital. Savings are 'floating' or circulating capital, the wages fund that goes into the hiring of workers and buying of raw materials. But because of a sometime propensity to overtrade, businesses may invest in fixed capital beyond the annual supply of savings. Too many money savings are poured into the production of fixed capital, whereas too few are used to produce consumer goods. In short, the boom is characterized by an undue shift of resources from consumption goods to capital goods. The increased expenditure on fixed investment of capital – in the 1845 case heavy railroad investment – on the other hand, increases wages in the hands of consumers. But as the consumers come to spend their wages on a lower supply of consumer goods, the price of consumer goods will inevitably rise. In short, consumption and investment have become excessive in relation to the savings available. In response to the rising prices of consumer goods, consumer goods producers will attempt to expand output and thereby increase their demand for capital, i.e. their demand for loans. But the dearth of savings in relation to the demand for capital will bring about a rise in the rate of interest, and the sharp rise in interest rates will precipitate a recession. In short, the fixed investment-boom producers, in this case, the railways and suppliers of railway material, would be forced into a sharp scramble with the producers of consumer goods for suddenly scarce capital, and the resulting crisis and depression causes the abandonment or indefinite postponement of the excessive fixed investments. During the depression, excessive investment is abandoned, resulting eventually in recovery to a sound and normal condition.

Thus Wilson, in addition to seeing the unwise and excessive investment as well as the overconsumption and undersavings of the boom, demonstrated how the boom is the economic distortion that necessarily generates the unhappy but curative depression that finally restores a sound economy. He also saw how a rise in interest rates, as a signal of overconsumption and undersaving, brings about the restorative recession. In addition, he realized that a lack of savings was a key to the recession and concluded that greater savings would help speed the recovery.

While there is surely over-investment in the higher orders of capital goods during a boom, Wilson misfired when making his sharp distinction between floating and fixed capital. To Wilson, money savings going into fixed capital are somehow lost or 'sunk', and thus disappear from the payment of wages. The problem is not in fixed *vs* floating capital, however, but consumption as against over-investment of all types in the higher orders of capital – whether in fixed plant or greater inventory of raw materials.

But the greatest problem in Wilson's discussion was his neglect of money. Money, he believed, was merely a device for facilitating exchanges, and therefore could never be a cause of economic fluctuations, but only an effect. And yet, if money was not involved, where do the railway firms *get* the new money to spend, even though savings have not risen? The only answer, which Wilson neglects, is an increase in money and bank credit loaned to those firms. And, if the money supply has not increased, why are the increases of wage payments by railway firms and other capital producers not offset by *declines* of wage payments in consumer industries? In short, why does the general level of prices increase from the beginning of the boom? Why don't consumer prices at least initially fall? The answer, once again, is the increase in the supply of money and credit that generates and fuels the boom. And finally, why can't the general run of businessmen, including the railway magnates, realize that their investments are outrunning savings, and why does the eventual critical rise in interest rates come as a shock? The answer, once more, is that the expansion of bank credit artificially lowers the interest rate, and lures business firms into the fatal over-investment.

Despite the fact that Wilson insisted that a quantity of money must not be confused with capital, he yet fell into the old Smithian trap of considering the supply of gold as 'idle and unproductive' capital, and so he believed that capital could be increased, and the depression greatly eased, by government issue of £20 million of small, £1 notes, which would replace the 'idle and unproductive' £20 million of gold in circulation. This huge issue, Wilson assured his readers, would not be inflationary because it would simply add to capital; and besides, he added smugly, no inflation could exist since the paper notes would continue to be convertible into gold. But what sort of gold convertibility, what sort of gold standard, exists when gold is supposed to disappear from circulation? The lesson is that, regardless how much devotion is professed to *laissez-faire* or the gold standard, at the heart of every banking school man, including those professing a free banking position, lies an unreconstructed inflationist.

In his *Principles of Political Economy* (1848), John Stuart Mill set forth a cycle theory that blended Wilson's analysis with a Tookean emphasis on commodity speculation, and unfortunately brought in the Ricardian gloom about the alleged inevitable tendency toward a falling rate of profit as agriculture yields ever lower returns. Mill, in short, fused the standard Tooke–banking school emphasis on speculation, over-optimism, and overtrading with Wilson's analysis of the conversion of circulating into fixed capital. Once again, the doctrine was *non*-monetary, with money playing a passive, non-essential, and at best secondary role. Thus Mill adopted Wilson's railroad investment theory of the cause of the recent 1845–47 cycle. The Ricardian motif led Mill to anticipate Schumpeter and hail the inflationary boom as necessary and vital to the achievement of economic growth, by enabling a periodic escape from the falling rate of profit. As a result, Mill was among the first to develop the idea that business fluctuations tend to repeat as recurring cycles, a process which he considered beneficial. He was not worried about recessions, since the contraction and Say's law ensured a rapid return to full employment and prosperity.

There was another important reason for the effective fusion of the currency and banking schools after the enactment of Peel's Act. Both these groups, after all, were dedicated to retention of the gold standard as their top monetary priority, even though the banking school version tended to be highly attenuated. But as soon as the great crisis of 1847 occurred and brought monetary and banking controversy back to Britain, the ultra-inflationist opponents of the gold standard came on the attack, calling either for fiat money inflation or, at best, a bimetallic gold/silver standard. In the face of this onslaught, the currency and banking schools closed ranks, which largely accounts, for example, for James Wilson's voting to retain Peel's Act in 1858.

In fact, it took no more than the crisis of 1847 to encourage the men of Birmingham to resume their assault on gold. Matthias Attwood's old fiat money pamphlet was promptly reprinted, a Birmingham delegation headed by George Frederick Muntz called upon the prime minister, and the Birmingham Currency Reform Association sent a memorial to the queen. The *Times* felt called upon to denounce the Birmingham men in an editorial and T. Perronet Thompson warned a friend of an increasing flow of 'half-mad pamphlets from Birmingham'. And other sectors in the north of Britain joined in the cry. The Liverpool Currency Reform Association was active enough to be denounced in two issues of *The Economist*, and Scotland revealed its inflationist bent by an anti-gold article in the Tory *Blackwood's Edinburgh Magazine*. Furthermore, an organizing convention of the National Anti-Gold Law League was held in Glasgow and was attended by 3 000 people.

The threat of silver bimetallism also surfaced during the crisis of 1847. Particularly important was the powerful banker, Alexander Baring, now Lord Ashburton, always ready to ride his hobby horse of bimetallism, and a petition of a number of influential 'Merchants, Bankers, and Traders of London against the Bank Act'. Wilson denounced the bimetallist doctrine of Ashburton and the London petitioners as 'extraordinary', and 'most inexplicable and unreasonable'. So serious was the bimetallic threat considered that the two stalwarts of the currency school, Loyd and Torrens, collaborated in writing an anonymous pamphlet in a point-by-point rebuttal of the London petition.[42] The telling thrust in the Torrens–Loyd polemic was to show that the logic of the bimetallist position pointed straight to the far more consistent, though far more dangerous, policy of Birmingham fiat money:

> The Birmingham philosophers are consistent reasoners, and have the sagacity to perceive that an arbitrary extension of the paper circulation is incompatible with the maintenance of a metallic standard. The inferior logicians who have signed the London petition, while demanding the establishment of a double metallic standard, are unable to perceive that an extension of paper money through the exercise...of the relaxing power for which they pray would render impracticable the maintenance of any metallic standard.[43]

The high-water mark of the assault on gold came in votes in Parliament in 1848. In the Commons committee, the veteran radical leader Joseph Hume's motion denouncing Peel's Act for aggravating the crisis of 1847 was defeated by a vote of 13 to 11. The 11 supporters included a coalition of free banking remnants like Hume, inflationists and protectionists like the Birmingham Tory Richard Spooner, and bimetallists like Thomas Baring and Lord Bentinck. Furthermore, the report of the House of Lords committee criticized Peel's Act and recommended watering down the restrictive provisions on bank notes. While the committees were deliberating, the veteran anti-bullionist John Charles Herries moved to repeal the limitations on bank notes of the Act of 1844 and all the Acts of 1845. Here was a rallying-point for all soft currency men of whatever stripe – Birmingham men, bimetallists, or soft gold men. Herries's motion lost rather narrowly, by a vote of 163 to 142. The major speeches for the motion came not from the moderates, but from Birmingham men like Richard Spooner. In answer to Spooner, the great Robert Peel rose and pointed out that although Birmingham doctrine was in 'a small minority' within the House of Commons, outside the House 'of those who talk about the currency, and write about the currency, the vast majority', indeed 'nine tenths', agree with Spooner, that is, want 'issues of paper without the check of convertibility'.

Whether Peel was over-reacting to what he considered expressions of evil, or whether his raising the spectre of Birmingham was a ploy to rally the troops, that tactic was successful, and Herries's motion to consider the reports of the Lords and Commons committees, was defeated without even coming to a formal vote. From then on, for a decade, the spectre of Birmingham was enough to win the moderate gold men and the banking school to an all-out defence of the Peel Act *status quo*. During the mid-1850s, Wilson's *Economist* followed this path, and the veteran currency man James Pennington wrote a worried letter to a friend that 'There is just now a widespread clamour calling for repeal of that Act [the Bank Act of 1844] which clamour, if it prevails, will I think, be followed by a clamour, equally loud, for doing away altogether with the obligation of specie payments'.[44]

We may fittingly close our discussion of the aftermath of Peel's Act by focusing on two important contributions, after the passage of the Act, by the wisest of the currency school, Colonel Robert Torrens. In the course of his critique in 1857 of the banking school chapter of Mill's *Principles*, Torrens added another vital point in criticizing the view that banks, being passive, can have no power to increase their liabilities, and hence have no power to raise prices. Torrens trenchantly pointed out that Mill

> excludes from his consideration the important fact, that banks possess in them- selves the power of increasing and diminishing the demand for banking accom- modation when they raise the rate of discount, the demand for accommodation contracts, and when they lower the rate it expands…and unless he is prepared to disprove the fact that banks can lower the rate of discount, he cannot consistently maintain that their power of increasing the issue is limited…

Amidst all the assaults on the Peel's Act system, by Birmingham fiat money men, bimetallists, remnants of free bankers, and banking school ad- herents, it is remarkable that apparently not a single writer, parliamentarian, or man of affairs called for a tougher policy of plugging up the enormous hole in the currency system by extending the 100 per cent reserve principle to deposits as well as notes. Not a single currency man admitted any flaw in his previous position, nor advocated, like Jacksonians in the United States, pressing on to a full 100 per cent reserve position on all bank demand liabilities, including deposits. The closest that anyone came to this view was Colonel Torrens. In a poignant moment in the history of economic thought, in his last published work at the age of 77, Torrens wrote a review in the January 1858 issue of *Edinburgh Review*, of the collected *Tracts and Other Publications on Metallic and Paper Currency* by his old friend and ally Samuel Loyd, Lord Overstone, edited by John R. McCulloch. After eulogizing the contributions of Lord Overstone, and once again defending Peel's Act, Torrens went on to try to explain the business cycle culminating in the recent crisis of 1857. In sharp contrast to his surrender a decade earlier to the banking school in blaming 'overtrading' for the crisis of 1847, Torrens now strongly affirmed that 'Were there no overbanking, there could not be (except for brief periods) overtrading and excessive speculation'. And the overbanking, since Peel's Act, clearly meant deposits. For Torrens could scarcely ignore the fluctuations that were occurring in the amount of bank deposits. Discussing deposit banking, Torrens emphasized that by creating new demand deposits through loans, the banks exerted 'the same influence upon the markets as an increase in the numerical amount of the circulation [of notes]'. Torrens had always been the only currency man to understand the true monetary importance of deposits; now he pressed on to a vigorous condemnation of the commercial bankers and their expansion of deposits in the recent boom as well as their contraction and bankruptcy during the crisis. Thus, Torrens bitterly inquired:

> Are the scales of justice held even, when a petty thief, or the forger of a five-pound note, is treated as a felon, and when the speculating banker...obtains from the Court of Bankruptcy a full liquidation of his debts, and receives from sympathising friends and half-ruined creditors the means of recommencing his disreputable and mischievous career?

Torrens went on to show how additional loans 'from deposits produce effects upon prices, upon commercial credit and upon the exchanges, results analogous to those produced by additional issues of bank notes'. Virtually conceding that Peel's Act suffered from not being applied to deposits, Robert Torrens now conceded that 'even under a currency exclusively metallic [i.e. coins without notes] overbanking and the insolvency of discount-houses may occasion disasters as formidable as those which can result from an unrestricted use of bank notes and a suspension of cash payments'.

In his conclusion, Torrens expressed strong doubt whether 'the advantages of discount [deposit] banking, even when conducted under a metallic currency, balance the evils it inflicts'. It seems that Torrens was on the brink of advocating the extension of the currency system to deposits, and perhaps if he had lived to write more on money and banking, he would have done so.

7.10 Currency and banking school thought on the Continent

The flowering of the currency and banking school debates in Britain, coupled with the later burgeoning of central banking on the Continent, led to similar controversies in France and Germany in the 1850s and 1860s. Generally, the results were the same: pseudo-currency triumph in the sense that the central bank acquired a monopoly of note issue, and *de facto* banking school victory in elastic, fractional-reserve banking and repeated increases and declines in the supply of money.

In France, *laissez-faire* thought flowered among economists, who proved themselves the true heirs of J.B. Say. Professors, journalists, the long-lasting Société d'Économie Politique, the Société's *Journal des Économistes*, both launched in 1842, and several other scholarly and popular periodicals were dedicated to the free trade and *laissez-faire* cause. In that atmosphere, the French economists naturally plumped for free rather than central banking.

Most of them, unfortunately, felt constrained to adopt banking school doctrine so as to maintain that freely competitive banking, like banks in general,
can never issue excessive notes or bring about a business cycle. They were a
far more genuine free banking group than the British who, as we have seen,
were special pleaders for commercial banking interests rather than consistent
advocates of free banking. Indeed, in this as in other areas, the French, in
contrast to the hesitant, muddled and pragmatic British, were not afraid to be
consistent, rigorous, militant, and therefore 'extremist' advocates of individual liberty and free exchange.

One of the leading, and one of the most interesting, of the French free
banking theorists was Jean Gustave Courcelle-Seneuil (1813–92). Courcelle,
as one historian writes: 'was in favour of absolute freedom and unlimited
competition and was the most uncompromising of all free bankers in France.
The sole permissible regulation, in his view, was one aimed simply at the
prevention of fraud'.[45]

I. Edward Horn (1825–75) was another notable French free banking theorist. In his *La Liberté des Banques* (1866), Horn went so far as to challenge
the idea that the state must have a monopoly on coinage. He pointed out that
private investment bankers could easily gain as much public confidence in
the circulation of their coins as has the state. Horn noted that the state is far
more likely to suspend the obligation of a central bank to redeem in specie
than grant such a boon to the smaller, individual banks. In the paraphrase of
Vera Smith:

> Horn called attention to the greater possibility that the liability of such a [Central]
> bank to pay out specie on demand would be revoked with its consequence of pure
> paper money in place of notes convertible into coin. A bank under State patronage
> always counted on the Government to relieve of its obligation to pay when
> nearing insolvency, and its bankruptcy became legalised instead of its having to
> go into liquidation and suffer the usual penalties of insolvency. This history of
> privileged banks had undeniably been full of bankruptcies.

Horn went on to insist that, under free banking, any refusal whatever to pay
in specie on demand must mean instant liquidation for the errant bank. Only
then could a free banking system work. Horn notes: 'If banks of issue were
given to understand, however, that they were positively and irremediably
responsible for their acts, and had themselves to bear the consequences, they
would be as prudent in their policy as any other business concern'.[46] The
problem is how could government be trusted to enforce prompt specie payment on the banks, especially if many or most banks get into trouble at the
same time?

Courcelle and Horn were both heavily influenced by James Wilson's circulation into fixed capital analysis of the boom. But both men, while stressing

with the banking school that banks cannot over-issue their notes, did admit, in contrast to Wilson, that banks could and did err in fuelling over-investment in fixed capital during the boom. Interestingly enough, Horn, Courcelle, and many of the French free bankers felt they had to deny, by legalistic quibbles, that even bank notes were 'money', since money, in the legalistic though not economic sense, must be strictly confined to the standard specie in which notes were convertible.

But the most fascinating theorists were the tiny intrepid band of Frenchmen who believed in free banking and at the same time were rigorous currency school *ultras*, who despised as fraudulent and inflationary all fiduciary media, all bank liabilities beyond 100 per cent specie reserve. They believed, quite plausibly, that neither a monopoly privileged bank, nor the government that backed it, could be long trusted to maintain 100 per cent gold reserve banking. The leader of this little band was Henri Cernuschi, who, writing two tracts in 1865, declared that the important question was not monopoly note issue *vs* plural or free banking, but whether bank notes should be issued at all. His answer was no, since 'they had the effect of despoiling the holders of metallic money by depreciating its value'. If they were at all useful, they should no more than represent metallic money by 100 per cent; any uncovered notes, any fiduciary media, should be ended totally. Cernuschi favoured free banking because he held that, lacking any special privilege, encouragement, or acceptance by the state, and forced to close the minute banks refused any payment of liabilities, nobody would wish to hold bank notes. As Ludwig von Mises approvingly quoted from Cernuschi: 'I want to give everybody the right to issue banknotes so that nobody should take banknotes any longer'.[47]

A follower of Cernuschi was Victor Modeste, whose policy conclusions were rather different, and brought him close to the hard-core Jacksonians in the United States. Modeste was a dedicated libertarian, who believed that the state is 'the master..., the obstacle, the enemy', and whose announced goal was to replace government by 'self-government'. Modeste agreed with Courcelle and the banking school free bankers that commerce and trade must remain free. He also agreed with them that central monopoly banking was far worse and more damaging than freely competitive banking, and was also opposed to administrative control or regulation of banks. On the other hand, what is to be done about bank notes? In this category, Modeste explicitly included demand deposits, which he saw to be illicit, fraudulent, inflationary, generators of the business cycle, and bearers of 'false money'. His answer was to point out that 'false' demand liabilities which pretend to but cannot be converted into gold, since they go beyond the value of the gold stock, are in reality equivalent to fraud and theft. Modeste concluded that false titles and values are at all times 'equivalent to theft; that theft in all its forms everywhere deserves its penalties…, that every bank administrator…must be warned that to pass as value where there is no value,…to subscribe to an engagement that cannot be accomplished…are criminal acts which should be relieved under the criminal law'. The answer, then, is not administrative regulation but prohibition of tort and fraud under general law.[48]

In Germany, there were few writers influenced by the banking school; most were currency men. In the rigorous currency tradition was Philip Joseph Geyer. Writing in his tract *Banken und Krisen* (Banks and Crises) in 1865, and in another book two years later, Geyer declared that ideally the amount of money in circulation should always remain constant. The money supply is not in fact constant largely because continuing issues of bank notes are not covered by specie. At this point, Geyer contributed one of the first outlines of the Austrian theory of the business cycle, as he pointed out that uncovered bank note issues inject an 'artificial capital' (*kunstliches Kapital*) into the economy, and when this artificial capital exceeds the amount of available 'real' (*naturliches*) capital, over-investment and over-production bring about a crisis. However, Geyer then blundered into an inconsistent underconsumption theory while trying to develop his analysis.

An academic hard-line currency man in Germany was Johann Louis Tellkampf (1808–76). A young Prussian with a doctorate from the University of Göttingen, Tellkampf emigrated to the United States, where he taught first at Union College in law and political economy, as well as history, German language and literature. Then, in 1843, he moved to Columbia College as professor of German language and literature. Three years later, Tellkampf returned to Prussia and became professor of political economy at the University of Breslau. He was later elected to the Prussian senate, where he took a leading part in bank legislation.

Tellkampf's observations on the problems of decentralized banking in the United States led him to argue for strict 100 per cent specie reserves to bank notes, and for one monopoly central bank to put this plan into effect. Tellkampf aided in disseminating the currency principle by co-translating McCulloch's defence of the principle into German in 1859. On the other hand, failing the adoption of his 100 per cent specie plan, Tellkampf was very willing to consider free banking as a second best.

The free bankers in Germany tended to be smaller in number than in France, and currency school rather than banking school men. A notable writer in this camp was Otto Hübner, a leader of the German Free Trade Party. His multi-volume work, *Die Banken* (1854), was largely an empirical survey of banks throughout the world, and argued that banks were soundest and least in danger where they were freest and least controlled. Privileged central banks tend to be wildly run and are in danger of insolvency, as note the suspension of specie payment of the Austrian national Bank, which had financed large deficits of the Austrian government. Hübner's goal, like Cernuschi's in France and like that of Geyer and Tellkampf in Germany, was 100 per cent specie reserve to bank notes. His ideal preference would have been for a state-run monopoly 100 per cent reserve in the bank, like the old banks of Amsterdam and Hamburg, but he recognized the problem of inherent mistrust of state banking. As Vera Smith paraphrases Hübner:

> If it were true that the State could be trusted always only to issue notes to the amount of its specie holdings, a State-controlled note issue would be the best system, but as things were, a far nearer approach to the ideal system was to be expected from free banks, who for reasons of self-interest would aim at the fulfillment of their obligations.[49]

7.11   Notes

1. Frank W. Fetter, *Development of British Monetary Orthodoxy 1797–1875* (Cambridge, Mass.: Harvard University Press, 1965), p. 122.
2. In 'Currency Juggle', *Tait's Edinburgh Magazine* (Jan. 1833). See Fetter, op. cit., note 1, pp. 140–41.
3. Lionel Robbins, *Robert Torrens and the Evolution of Classical Economics* (London: Macmillan, 1958), pp. 245–6.
4. As we shall see below, the currency school was split on the issue of deposits as money: the simplistic insistence on notes as the only bank money being held by the majority led by George Warde Norman and Samuel J. Loyd (Lord Overstone), while the contrary and correct position was held by Sir William Clay and Colonel Robert Torrens.
5. William Gouge's main work was first published as *A Short History of Paper Money and Banking* (1833) in two separate parts, theoretical and historical. Most of the latter was reprinted in England, under the title *The Curse of Paper Money and Banking*, with an introduction, appropriately enough, by the great anti-bank radical, William Cobbett. Both parts were reprinted, virtually intact, in Gouge's own *Journal of Banking* (1841–42).
6. Henry Drummond was the eldest son of the banker Henry Drummond, and was born in Hampshire. He was raised by his maternal grandfather, Henry Dudas, Viscount Melville, and, during his childhood, became a favourite of William Pitt. Educated at Harrow and at Christ Church, Oxford, Drummond left college to become a partner at his father's bank in London. The aristocratic Drummond was a Member of Parliament from 1810 until he retired for ill health three years later. In the meanwhile, Drummond was able to put through Parliament an act outlawing the embezzlement by bankers of securities kept in their safe-keeping. Drummond founded the chair of political economy as Oxford in 1825, and at about the same time became the main leader, prophet and evangelist of the rising movement of pre-millennial millenarianism in Protestant Christianity. Drummond returned to Parliament from 1847 until the end of his life, there serving as a highly independent Tory, favouring war, government, and the ecclesiastical establishment. Drummond wrote many pamphlets on financial and on evangelical themes.
7. In his *Letters to the Editor of the Times' Journal on the Affairs and Conduct of the Bank of England* (1826), cited in Elmer Wood, *English Theories of Central Banking Control 1819–1858* (Cambridge Mass.: Harvard University Press, 1939), p. 110. Another hard-money writer in 1826 was the pseudonymous 'Benjamin Bullion', *Letters on the Currency Question*.
8. For an excellent discussion of the independent treasury programme and its two crucial parts, as well as of the Van Buren bankruptcy proposal, see Major L. Wilson, *The Presidency of Martin Van Buren* (Lawrence, Kan.: The University Press of Kansas, 1984), p. 73 and passim.

9. For Mushet, see Lawrence H. White, *Free Banking in Britain: Theory, Experience, and Debate, 1800–1845* (Cambridge: Cambridge University Press, 1984), p. 62.

10. On Parnell, who has been neglected by most historians, see ibid., pp. 62–3, and Jacob Viner, *Studies in the Theory of International Trade* (New York: Harper & Bros., 1937), pp. 24–241.

11. George Poulett Scrope, *An Examination of the Bank Charter Question* (1833), p. 456. Also see Scrope, *The Currency Question Freed from Money* (1830), *On Credit Currency* (1830). The other articles in 1830 in the *Quarterly Review* were by Edward Edwards and H.A. Nilan. On Scrope, see Fetter, op. cit., note 1, pp. 137–8. White characteristically neglects the vital difference between Scrope's inflationism and hard-money writers in the free banking camp. White, op. cit., note 9, passim.

12. John Charles Spencer, Viscount Althorp (1782–1845), was born in London to an aristocratic family, the son of Earl Spencer. After studying at Harrow and Trinity College, Cambridge, Althorp received an MA from Trinity in 1802. Althorp was an MP for 30 years after 1804. First a supporter of Pitt, Althorp took a generally radical position in Parliament, battling against the leather tax and in favour of Catholic emancipation, and took his stand with the Whig opposition after 1815 in favour of reform, lower taxation, and cutting the budget. In 1830, Althorp refused the prime ministership, and took his place in the Grey ministry as chancellor of the Exchequer and leader of the House of Commons.

   After his father's death in 1833, Althorp succeeded to his father's earldom as Lord Spencer, and withdrew from direct politics in the House of Commons. He continued to be influential, however, in favour of peace with France and repeal of the Corn Laws in the 1840s.

   A Yorkshire landowner and cattleman, Althorp loved agriculture and hunting. He founded or helped to found the Yorkshire Agriculture Society, and the English Agricultural Society (1828), which later became the Royal Agricultural Society.

13. In Alexander Mundell, *The Danger of the Resolutions Relative to the Bank Charter...* (London, 1833). Cited in White, op. cit., note 9, pp. 67–8.

14. Robert Torrens, *A Letter to the Right Honourable Lord Viscount Melbourne on the Causes of the Recent Derangement in the Money Market and on Bank Reform* (London, 1837).

15. Cited in Lionel Robbins, *Robert Torrens and the Evolution of Classical Economics* (London: Macmillan, 1958), p. 89. Robbins, Torrens's biographer, admits his inability to explain Torrens's complete about-face on money and inflationism. Ibid., pp. 73–4.

16. *The Causes and Consequences of the Pressure upon the Money-Market* (London, 1837). Palmer (1779–1858), was the son of William Palmer of Essex, a London merchant, and mayor and high sheriff of Essex. An East India merchant and shipowner, John Horsley Palmer went into partnership with his brother in 1802. He was a director of the Bank of England from 1811 on.

17. In his *Reflections Suggested by a Perusal of Mr. J. Horsley Palmer's Pamphlet* (London, 1837). Loyd (1796–1883), later the first Baron Overstone, was the only son of a dissenting Welsh minister, the Rev. Lewis Loyd. Loyd's mother was a daughter of a Manchester banker, John Jones. Educated at Eton, and then receiving a BA at Trinity College, Cambridge, at the top of the list, in 1818, Loyd gained an MA from Trinity in 1822. By this time, the Rev. Loyd had left the ministry to become a partner in his father-in-law's bank, and then proceeded to found the London branch of Jones, Loyd & Co. In 1834, the bank merged into the new London & Westminster Bank. A successful banker, Samuel Loyd succeeded to his father's leadership in London & Westminster in 1844. Loyd died one of the richest men in England. He was made Lord Overstone in 1850.

18. Fetter, op. cit., note 1, p. 171.

19. Norman, *Remarks Upon Some Prevalent Errors with Respect to Currency and Banking* (London, 1838). Norman (1793–1882) was born in Kent; his father, George Norman, was a merchant in the Norway timber trade, and a sheriff of Kent. George Warde was educated at Eton, and joined his father in the Norway trade, spending many years in Norway. After his father's retirement in 1824, George Warde became sole owner of the business, until it was merged with another mercantile firm in 1830. George Warde Norman was a director

of the Bank of England from 1821 until 1872, and was a member of the bank's treasury committee during the 1840s. Norman was founding member of the Political Economy Club, and was its last surviving original member.

Norman was a liberal devoted to free trade, and a close friend of the great philosophical radical, banker, and classicist George Grote. Norman was widely read in English, continental, Latin, and Norwegian literature.

20.   The first two volumes were published in 1838, the third in 1840, and the fourth in 1848. Two later volumes appeared in 1857, near the end of Tooke's life, but they were largely written by his co-author William Newmarch.

21.   John Fullarton, *On the Regulation of Currencies* (1844). Fullarton (1780–1849), son of a physician, went to India as a medical officer for the East India Company, and rose to become an assistant surgeon in Bengal for over a decade. While in India, he became a partner in the Calcutta banking house of Alexander and Co., and amassed a huge fortune, returning to London in the early 1820s. A founder of the Carlton Club, and author of several pro-Tory articles in the early 1830s, Fullarton, retired, now entered the fray on behalf of the banking school.

22.   For Torrens's role in this and other economic discussions, including a full annotation of each one of his writings, see the delightful work by Lionel Robbins, *Robert Torrens and the Evolution of Classical Economics* (London: Macmillan, 1958), esp. Chapters IV, V, and the bibliographical appendix.

23.   Oddly, Professor White chides Marion Daugherty for putting Smith in the ranks of the currency school rather than of the free bankers, even though White himself concedes four pages later that 'The testimony of Manchesterites J.B. Smith and Richard Cobden [1840] revealed the developing tendency for adherents of laissez-faire, who wished to free the currency school from discretionary management, to look not to free banking but to restricting the right of issue to a rigidly rule-bound state bank as the solution'. White, op. cit., note 9, pp. 71, 75. See Marion R. Daugherty, 'The Currency–Banking Controversy, Part I', *Southern Economic Journal*, 9 (October 1942), p. 147. In particular, see Fetter, op. cit., note 1, pp. 175–6.

24.   Years later, S.J. Loyd, the leader of the currency school, testified that he had never had any personal or political connection with Robert Peel. 'I knew nothing whatever of the provisions of the Act until they were laid before the public. The Act is entirely so far as I know the Act of Sir Robert Peel.' Torrens had no contact with Peel either, and indeed Peel turned down Torrens's request for office based on his leadership in the currency school. Only after Peel's death did Torrens receive a government pension 'in consideration of his valuable contributions to the Science of Political Economy'. As for the veteran adviser James Pennington, his advice was only sought for technical details after the main provisions of Peel's Act had already been determined. Fetter, op. cit., note 1, p. 182n.

25.   Boyd Hilton, 'Peel: A Reappraisal', *Historical Journal*, 22 (Sept. 1979), p. 614. Not that Hilton is sympathetic to Peel's determined role on the behalf of *laissez-faire* and hard money. On the contrary, he is appalled at Peel's 'doctrinaire' stance, an assessment unfortunately echoed by Professor White in his reference to Peel's 'little-recognized dogmatism'. White, op. cit., note 9, p. 77n.

26.   J.K. Horsefield, 'The Origins of the Bank Charter Act, 1844', in T.S. Ashton and R.S. Sayers (eds.), *Papers in English Monetary History* (Oxford: The Clarendon Press, 1953), pp. 110–11.

27.   William Cotton (1786–1866) was the son of a naval captain, merchant, and director of the East India Company. At the age of 15, young William entered the counting house of his father's friend. By 1807, he had become partner in a London mercantile firm, and become general manager in that firm's cordage manufacturing plant. Cotton was a director of the Bank of England for 45 years, from 1821 until his death, and eventually became known as 'the father of the Bank of England'. Cotton was governor of the bank from 1843 to 1845, and was succeeded by Heath. Cotton also invented a successful automatic machine for weighing gold sovereigns, and was a distinguished philanthropist in the Church of England. Cotton was born, and lived most of his life, in the county of Essex, where he became justice of the peace, judge and sheriff.

28. Morris Perlman has pointed out that James Mill, in a book review in 1808, developed an extreme version of the real bills banking school doctrine. In that case, James Mill was never a Ricardian in this area, and John Stuart may have been exercising his filio pietism in bringing back his father's monetary views, as well as Ricardianism in the rest of economics. Morris Perlman, 'Adam Smith and the Paternity of the Real Bills Doctrine', *History of Political Economy*, 21 (Spring 1989), pp. 88–90.

29. See White, op. cit., note 9, pp. 122–6.

30. Ibid., p. 79.

31. So much for James Gilbart's alleged devotion to free banking, years before his surrender to Peel's Act.

32. See the interchange in Hilton, op. cit., note 25, pp. 593–4. It is characteristic of Professor Hilton's lack of insight into economic theory that he brands Peel's questioning as 'inept' and faults him for scoffing at the importance of Gilbart's 'personal knowledge' when judging inconvertible fiat money.

33. Cited in Fetter, op. cit., note 1, p. 193.

34. White, op. cit., note 9, p. 80. Thus the Scottish devotion to their vaunted free banking system turned out to be mainly special pleading. Much of White's book is devoted to the thesis (a) that until Peel's Act of 1845, Scotland enjoyed a regime of free banking uncontrolled by the Bank of England, with liabilities convertible into gold; and (b) that this free system worked far better than England's central bank-dominated one.

    But both parts of this thesis are deeply flawed. On (b) White confines his evidence of superiority to the lower bank failure rate in Scotland. But bank failure is a minor way to gauge the workings of a banking system. White presents no data whatever on whether Scotland suffered any less economic inflation or recession than England. One suspects, then, in the absence of data, that the economic record was about the same for the two parts of the United Kingdom. On (a), the problem is that Scottish banking was scarcely 'free'. Most Scottish bank reserves were kept, not in gold, but in deposits at the Bank of England, or in its surrogate, bills on London. Scottish banks, then, far from being free and independent of the Bank of England, pyramided on top of bank liabilities. Furthermore, the bank habitually bailed Scottish banks out in time of trouble. To top off the argument, the realities were that it was very difficult, both socially and legally, for anyone to actually obtain gold from the Scottish banks in exchange for their liabilities – especially in times of trouble when the gold, of course, was in particularly great demand.

    On Scottish banking in this era, see in particular the definitive work of Sydney G Checkland, *Scottish Banking: A History, 1695–1973* (Glasgow: Collins, 1975). Checkland writes that 'Requests for specie met with disapproval and almost with charges of disloyalty', and 'the Scottish system was one of continuous partial suspension of specie payments. No one really expected to be able to enter a Scots bank...with a large holding of notes and receive the equivalent immediately in gold or silver. They expected, rather, an argument, or even a rebuff. At best they would get a little specie and perhaps bills on London. If they made serious trouble, the matter would be noted and they would find the obtaining of credit more difficult in the future'. And finally, 'This legally impermissible limitation of convertibility, though never mentioned in public inquiries, contributed greatly to Scottish banking success'. Ibid., pp. 184–6. Also: 'the principal and ultimate source of liquidity lay in London, and in particular in the Bank of England'. Ibid., p. 432. Also see Charles W. Munn, *The Scottish Provincial Banking Companies 1747–1864* (Edinburgh: John Donald, 1981), and Charles A. Malcolm, *The Bank of Scotland, 1695–1945* (Edinburgh: R. & R. Clark, n.d.). On the Scottish free banking question, see Murray N. Rothbard, 'The Myth of Free Banking in Scotland', *The Review of Austrian Economics*, 2 (1988), pp. 229–45; Larry J. Sechrest, 'White's Free-Banking Thesis: A Case of Mistaken Identity', Ibid., pp. 247–57.

35. Wilson, son of William Wilson, a prosperous woollen manufacturer, was educated in a Friends' school and, at the age of 16, was apprenticed to a hat manufacturer. Soon, his father bought the firm for James and his brother. In 1824, Wilson came to London, and became a partner in a mercantile firm which, after 1831, became James Wilson & Co. After losing a great deal of money in indigo speculation, Wilson retired from business in

1844. In the meanwhile, he had become interested in economics and free trade, and had published several tracts on commerce and the Corn Laws. Wilson's writings strongly influenced such later free trade stalwarts as Peel and Gladstone. Finally, Wilson founded *The Economist* in 1843, writing almost all of the copy himself, and forged it rapidly into a highly influential journal. Wilson became an MP from 1847 to 1859, and was also financial secretary to the Treasury during the 1850s. Under the Palmerston regime in 1859, Wilson became vice-president of the Board of Trade, paymaster-general, and a Privy Councillor, and then, just before his death, was sent to India as finance minister, where he proceeded, ironically enough, to increase taxes and to issue a great quantity of government paper.

36.   Fetter asserts that Torrens 'never could have said of Wilson's ideas, as he did of Tooke's, 'that the flood-gates are opened, and the landmarks removed'.' Fetter, op. cit., note 1, p. 200.

37.   See Lloyd Mints, *A History of Banking Theory in Great Britain and the United States* (Chicago: University of Chicago Press, 1945), p. 90.

38.   A few years later, in his *Principles of Political Economy*, Mill became sympathetic to freedom of bank note issue, but on general *laissez-faire* rather than specific monetary and banking grounds.

39.   William Cotton, of the Bank of England, thought that the suspension came too soon, and John R. McCulloch thought it of doubtful value, but no currency man attacked the suspension, or even gave any sign of comprehending the significance of the suspension question.

40.   These epigones included Charles Neate, a professor at Cambridge who published his lectures, *Two Lectures on the Currency* (1850); R.H. Mills, a professor at Trinity College, Dublin, in his *The Principles of Currency and Banking*, in the mid-1850s; John Inchbald's *The Price of Money* (1862), and the popular tract by George Combe, *The Currency Question Considered* (1856), which was hailed by the London *Times* and went through six editions within one year.

41.   The book consisted of the nine 1845 articles on Peel's Act, plus later essays.

42.   *The Petition of the Merchants, Bankers and Traders of London Against the Bank Charter Act: with Comments on Each Clause* (London, 1847).

43.   Quoted in Fetter, op. cit., note 1, p. 208.

44.   Ibid., p. 216. Fetter wittily describes the feelings of the Banking School and the other anti-Peel Act gold men *vis-à-vis* the threat from the Birmingham school: 'The situation is suggestive of the attitude that tradition associates with the Duke of Wellington – he had no fear of the enemy, but the very thought of his allies filled him with terror'. Ibid.

45.   Vera C. Smith, *The Rationale of Central Banking* (1936, Indianapolis: Liberty Press, 1990), p. 94.

46.   Ibid., p. 108.

47.   From Henri Cernuschi, *Contre le Billet de Banque* (1866), Cernuschi's testimony before the massive French government's bank inquiry of 1865–66. Translated by Ludwig von Mises, *Human Action* (New Haven: Yale University Press, 1949), p. 443.

48.   Victor Modeste, 'Le Billet Des Banques D'Émission Est-Il Fausse Monnaie?' ('Are Bank Notes False Money?'), *Journal des Économistes*, 4 (Oct. 1866), pp. 77–8. (Translation mine.)

49.   Smith, op. cit., note 45, pp. 115–16.

8 John Stuart Mill and the reimposition of Ricardian economics

8.1 Mill's importance

The Mills, father and son, had a fateful impact upon the history of economic thought. If James Mill played a crucial and neglected role in developing Ricardian economics and its philosophical ally, Benthamite utilitarianism, and in foisting them upon the British intellectual world, his son John was by far the most important force in reimposing Ricardian dominance two decades after it had fallen into decline. It is ironic that the fate of British intellectual life in the nineteenth century should depend so closely on the psychological interplay between famous father and son, ironic since both purported to be austere 'scientists' above all. The two men could not have been more different in character and quality of intellect. James Mill, as we have seen, was a hard-nosed, hard-hitting, self-confident hard-core 'cadre' type, in intellect and action, original in carving out an architectonic system of economics, philosophy and political theory, and then supremely energetic in organizing people and institutions around him to try to put them into effect. James tried to educate John Stuart (1806–73) to follow him in leadership of this philosophic radical cadre, but the education didn't take. After John's famous nervous breakdown at the age of 20, the younger Mill emerged as almost the opposite to his father in temperament and quality of intellect. Instead of possessing a hard-nosed cadre intellect, John Stuart was the quintessence of soft rather than hardcore, a woolly minded man of mush in striking contrast to his steel-edged father. John Stuart Mill was the sort of man who, hearing or reading some view seemingly at utter variance with his own, would say, 'Yes, there is something in that', and proceed to incorporate this new inconsistent strand into his capacious and muddled world-view. Hence Mill's ever-expanding intellectual 'synthesis' was rather a vast kitchen midden of diverse and contradictory positions. As a result, Mill has ever since provided a field day for young Ph.D's caught in the game of publish or perish. Dispute over 'what Mill *really* believed' has become an unending cottage industry. Was Mill a *laissez-faire* liberal? A socialist? A romantic? A classicist? A civil libertarian? A believer in state-coerced morality? The answer is yes, every time. There is endless fodder for dispute because, in his long and prolific life, Mill was all of these and none, an ever-changing kaleidoscope of alteration, transformation and contradiction.

John Mill's enormous popularity and stature in the British intellectual world was partially due to his very mush-headedness. Here was this person of undoubted intellectual parts, an erudite man growing up in a circle of distinguished scholars and political activists, and yet here is this eminent man who sees good in all conceivable positions, even the reader's, whoever he may be. Add to this another unusual note: Mill's felicitous style. For in the history of thought, the style very much reflects the quality of mind; clear-headed thinkers are usually lucid writers, and confused and inchoate thinkers usually write in the same way. Ricardo's crabbed and tortured style reflected the muddled complexities of his doctrine. But Mill was unusual in possessing a graceful and lucid style that served to mask the vast muddle of his intellectual furniture. Ricardo won at least brief popularity for his very obscurity, though he had the invaluable aid in spreading his doctrine of such clear writers as James Mill and John McCulloch. But John Mill won fame and influence partly through the grace of his writing.

If he had known the full extent of his son's defection of character and intellect, the elder Mill would surely have despaired. But he never really found out, for John learned early to dissemble, playing a double game throughout his 20s while his father was still alive. Thus he was perfectly capable of publishing an article praising his father's philosophical favourite, Jeremy Bentham, while at the same time writing an anonymous article elsewhere highly critical of Bentham. Mill's intellectual duplicity proved a sharp contrast to his father's candour.

Oddly enough, however, and weighing the totality of John's career, James might in a sense have been truly pleased. For through all the mush, through all the flabby and soggy 'moderation' that marked the adult John Mill and still attracts moderate liberals of every generation, in the last analysis filiopietism triumphed. When push at long last came to shove in the mind of John Stuart Mill, he came down, albeit of course 'moderately', on the side of his father's two idols, Bentham and Ricardo. In philosophy, he abandoned hard-core cadre Benthamism, for soft-core 'moderate' Benthamite utilitarianism. And in economics, he not only was basically and proclaimedly a Ricardian; he also gladdened his father's ghost by re-establishing Ricardianism on the throne of British economics, a feat he accomplished through the enormous popularity and dominance of his *Principles of Political Economy* (1848). So even though John Stuart substituted moderate for full-fledged democracy, and, still more disturbingly, moderate statism and socialism for his father's *laissez-faire*, James Mill might have been gladdened by his son's ability to reimpose Ricardianism upon the world of economics. Indeed, the great advances of the anti-Ricardians of the 1820s, 1830s, and 1840s were truly forgotten in Mill's re-establishment of the cost, and indeed the labour, theory of value, the Ricardian rent theory, Malthusian wage and population theory and the remainder of the Ricardian apparatus. For not the first or last time in the history of economic and social thought, error displaced truth from the post of dominance in the intellectual world. In placing Ricardo back upon the throne of economics, John Stuart was fulfilling perhaps the most cherished, although one of the most fallacious, of his father's goals and principles.

It should be realized that John Stuart's life in the shadow of his father was not only psychological or organizational. At the age of 16, John entered his father's office in the East India Company, and assisted him for many years, succeeding to his father's high position on James's death in 1836. Mill, indeed, worked full-time at the East India Company until the liquidation of that company in 1858 bestowed upon Mill a handsome pension for the remaining 15 years of his life.

8.2 Mill's strategy and the success of the *Principles*

The proximate reason for the enormous success and influence of the *Principles* was the remarkable best-selling triumph of Mill's first book, *A System of Logic* (1843), which caught on with intellectuals and general readers of the age in a way that no tome on logic and epistemology has done before or since.[1] Mill's *Principles* was shrewdly designed as a comprehensive, massive two-volume treatise in the *Wealth of Nations* mould, accessible to economists and laymen alike. It went through no less than seven editions in Mill's lifetime, as well as a cheap 'people's' edition, and an abridged version for the American market. The *Principles* continued to serve as the standard British text in economics through the early twentieth century.

In a fascinating article, Professor de Marchi contends that much of the seeming confusion, muddle and moderation permeating Mill's *Principles* was a deliberate strategy designed to soften up and conciliate the numerous enemies of Ricardianism and thereby to win their support for a covert re-establishment of Ricardian dominance. To put it far more bluntly than does Professor de Marchi, Mill engaged in a strategy of duplicity to confuse the enemy and to win their support for at least the essentials of the true Ricardian doctrine. If de Marchi is correct, there is far more Machiavelli in Mill's dithering 'openness' to all points of view than has been supposed.[2] De Marchi notes that Mill had consciously adopted, since 1829, what Mill called the strategy of 'practical eclecticism', which amounts to lulling and disarming the opposition and, by seeming conciliation, to manipulate them into believing that they had 'spontaneously' arrived at what Mill held to be the truth – in short, a strategy of deception and duplicity.[3]

It is impossible to estimate how much of John Stuart Mill's inveterate and eternal contradictions, qualifications and alterations were due to honest muddle-headedness and how much to devious and evasive intellectual bro-ken-field running. Did Mill himself always know? At any rate, the tactic seems to have worked, as enemies from all sides of economic theory in general and of Ricardianism in particular, were charmed by Mill's middle-of-the-road benevolence to all and sundry. They might not have been con-verted to hard- or even soft-core Ricardianism, but they were virtually all impressed by Mill's conceding one point after another to themselves or others. (All, of course, except Marx, who, as a pre-eminent cadre type, poured out a proper vial of scorn upon Mill's 'shallow syncretism' and 'attempt to reconcile the irreconcilable.') One by one, Tories, romantics, socialists and 'practical men' warmed up to Mill himself and to his alleged achievements.

Thus we have seen how Mill introduced into economics, and managed to make dominant, the unfortunate hypothetical methodology of positivism, as contrasted to the praxeological system of deduction from true and complete axioms advocated and employed by Say and Senior. (Ricardo had expressed no methodological views, although his method in practice was deduction from a few unreal and deeply flawed axioms.) In the course of pursuing this method, Mill introduced the disastrous and fallacious hypothesis of the 'economic man', which left economics deservedly open to ridicule as false to the nature of man. But Mill's substitution of hypothetical, of at least professedly tentative and humble, positivism, charmed the enemies of deductive praxeology.

For example, there had grown up at Cambridge University a group of militant Baconian inductivists, men who angrily rejected as 'unscientific' any sort of abstract theory in the social sciences. These belligerent anti-theorists, who held that proper theory can only be a patient enumeration and collection of countless empirical 'facts', were the ancestors of American institutionalism and of the German historical school. The Cambridge group of four, who were originally friends as undergraduates, was headed by William Whewell (1794–1866), who became a fellow and then master of Trinity College, an eminent mathematician, a professor of mineralogy and then of moral philosophy at Trinity, and twice vice-chancellor of the University. Another powerful figure in this group was Richard Jones (1790–1855), who succeeded Nassau Senior as professor of political economy at King's College, London, and then succeeded Malthus as professor of political economy and history at Haileybury.[4] Author of a three-volume *History of the Inductive Sciences* (1837) and the *Philosophy of the Inductive Sciences* (1840), Whewell had gushed over Bacon as 'the supreme Legislator of the modern Republic of Science', and 'the Hercules' and 'Hero of the revolution' in scientific method.

In the end, however, Whewell was forced to admit that the inductivist method in economics did not seem able to go beyond destructive criticism to the constructing of any sort of body of economic law. Perhaps that is why Whewell, at least, ended by toying with mathematical Ricardian models, flirting with the kind of abstract economics he had long professed to despise.[5]

William Whewell was not converted from inductivism to positivism by Mill, but he was moved to express approval of Mill's *Principles* as a whole. Others whom Mill charmed were Tory writers long hostile to political economy and to its free trade conclusions. Thus *Blackwood's Magazine* gave the *Principles* a generally favourable review for its author's 'perpetual, earnest, never-forgotten interest,...in the great questions at present mooted with respect to the social condition of man'. And G.F. Young, in the course of a virulent protectionist attack on economics in the Tory *Quarterly Review*, hailed Mill as 'one of the most philosophical and candid of the modern school of economists' – specifically for Mill's positivist admission that political economy was grounded not on correct but only on *partially* true assumptions.

Mill's most conspicuous defection from classical political economy in general, and from Ricardianism in particular, was his numerous concessions to socialism and his apostasy from *laissez-faire*. In general, the British classical economists had not exactly been consistent *laissez-faire* stalwarts, in contrast to J.B. Say and his school in France, including such people as Charles Comte, Charles Dunoyer, Frederic Bastiat, Gustave de Molinari, and their numerous followers. In Britain, consistent *laissez-faire* advocates were to be found rather among writers, intellectuals, and businessmen in Manchester, such as Richard Cobden, John Bright and the recently successful Anti-Corn Law League. They were also to be found in *The Economist*, edited by James Wilson, particularly in its editorial staff writers, Thomas Hodgskin (1787–1869) and young Herbert Spencer (1820–1903). But while the classical economists were not hard-core free market men, they at least tended strongly in that direction; if not a principle, *laissez-faire* was for them at least a guide or tendency to which they could at least partially orient their position. But Mill sharply broke with all that. Steeped in a high moral tone at all times, Mill originated the unfortunate intellectual tradition of conceding that socialism and indeed communism was the 'ideal' social system, and then drawing back by lamenting that it probably could not be attained in this cruel practical world. Pro-capitalists who begin by conceding the moral ground to their opponents are bound to lose the long-run war, if not the short-run battle, to socialism.

Small wonder, then, that various wings of socialists hailed Mill's *Principles*. The Owenite socialists, then the leading socialist group in Great Britain, were highly approving. In addition to words of commendation from Robert Owen (1771–1858) himself, the Owenite writer and lecturer George Jacob Holyoake (1817–1906) was particularly enchanted. The editor of *The Reasoner*, Holyoake hailed Mill's *Principles* with enthusiasm. 'It had been held', he proclaimed, 'that the people were made for political economy' but now, with Mill's *Principles*, 'at length political economy [is] being made for the people'. Holyoake also praised Mill for having spoken of communism 'with more geniality than any political economist had done before', and he gave his working-class readers the benefit of much of that high-priced tome by printing lengthy extracts in the *Reasoner*. No doubt Holyoake was also happy with Mill's proclaimed ideal of a commonwealth of cooperatives, Holyoake being one of the founders and long-term agitators for the cooperative movement in Britain.

Also delighted with the *Principles* was the socialist Thornton Hunt (1810–73), editor of the weekly *Leader*, the main socialist paper in England after

1850. Hunt, a believer in communal ownership and control, particularly welcomed Mill's claim that communism was the ideal state.

But even more important a boost to statism and socialism in Mill's *Principles* was his most un-Ricardian proclamation that while the processes of production were subject to the iron laws of political economy, distribution, on the other hand, was up for grabs, subject to human will and man-made arrangements. Ricardo, whose system rested on allegedly iron laws of distribution, must have turned over rapidly in his grave at that remark. This separation between 'production' and 'distribution' was wholly artificial and totally invalid, since people earn incomes on the market precisely for participating in production, and the two are intimately intertwined. But in making this distinction, Mill gave birth to the calamitous and still prevalent notion that distribution can be changed virtually at will through tax, subsidy or other statist schemes, while the market would still continue to function and produce undisturbed.

It is certainly not surprising that Mill's moral obeisances to cooperatives and communism met warm applause at the hands of the newly burgeoning Christian socialist movement. Of the *troika* of young Anglicans who led the Christian socialists, the Rev. Charles Kingsley (1819–1875) hailed the *Principles*, as did another of the leaders, the attorney John Malcolm Ludlow, in *Fraser's Magazine*.[6] *Fraser's* had been purchased in 1847 by John William Parker, who became its *de facto* editor; Parker was a friend of Kingsley and a Christian socialist sympathizer. The fact that he also happened to be the publisher of Mill's *Principles* scarcely made the paean of *Fraser's* reviewer any less lavish.

8.3 The theory of value and distribution

Mill's handling of the theory of value was characteristic of the man: a hard core of filio-pietism wrapped in layers of enigma and muddle. And so the labour theory/cost-of-production theory of value was restored to a dominant place in classical economics, but hedged about with Mill's usual string of evasive and self-protective qualifications. Thus Mill accepted Bailey's demolition of Ricardo's search for an impossible invariable measure of value. But, on the other hand, Mill displayed his contempt for even the idea that consumption and utility could have any influence upon value by removing consumption from its traditional niche as a basic part of the economics text. Instead, Mill's *Principles* was divided into 'Production', 'Distribution', 'Exchange' and 'Government', with nary a mention of consumption.

Yet, despite Mill's inconsistency and muddle, his stance of humility suddenly dissolved into his astonishingly arrogant claim that his pronouncements would be the last word for all time on the theory of value. In a famous *faux pas*, Mill proclaimed that 'happily, there is nothing in the laws of value which remains for the present or any future writer to clear up: the theory of the subject is complete'. Now, it is true that Mill had the bad luck to be writing these words only two decades before the 'marginalist revolution' completely overturned value theory. But, even so, it was inexcusable for anyone as knowledgeable as Mill was supposed to be in scientific method and the history of science to be caught writing this sort of statement. And Schumpeter tells us that the same sort of *hubris* had marked Mill's *System of Logic*.[7] It is an odd paradox indeed to see a thinker habitually changing course and qualifying every thought and deed, and *yet* insisting that his is the last conceivable word on any particular subject!

Upholding and restoring the dominance of Ricardo's theory of profit, Mill insisted on returning to the Ricardian *dictum* that profits are dependent on, and inversely proportionate to, wages. Cleverly paying obeisance to his friend Nassau Senior's concept of 'abstinence', and agreeing with Senior that profits (interest) were 'the remuneration of abstinence', Mill managed to weaken the concept and to return somehow to insisting on labour as the sole *cause* of profits.[8]

On wages, too, Mill returned squarely to Malthus, differing only by holding out the hope of ameliorating the alleged problem of population growth by enthusiastic and determined use of birth control. The change over the half-century was the difference between the stern preacher and the 'progressive' feminist. Alexander Gray's comment on Mill's passion against what he considered to be excessive births is both witty and apposite:

> In writing on the population question, his [Mill's] voice quivers with a righteous indignation which leads him to a violence of language nowhere to be found in Malthus. Excessive procreation is for Mill on the same level as drunkenness or any other physical excess, and those who are guilty should be discountenanced and despised accordingly.[9]

One of John Stuart Mill's most famous moves in economic theory was his typically dramatic, emotional, and yet carefully hedged 'recantation' of the wages fund doctrine. In company with other classical economists, having explained the supply of labour by the quantity of population, Mill then went on to explain the demand for labour, rather sensibly, as the sum of gross savings, or circulating capital, available for paying workers until the product was produced and sold: this available amount he called the 'wages fund'. This concept was used, again quite intelligently, to demonstrate that should labour unions be able to raise wages for one part of the labour force, this rise could only be at the expense of lowering wages somewhere else.

The wages fund analysis of the demand for labour was, in one important sense, a retreat from Say and others who emphasized that the demand for and prices of factors of production are determined by their productivity in producing consumer goods desired and demanded by the public. For Mill, this retreat was part and parcel of his orchestrated shift back to Ricardo. On the other hand, the wages fund doctrine was correct as far as it went: at any given time, there is a certain amount of gross savings to be invested in paying factors of production. Therefore, paying more in one place because of pressure by suppliers of labour will necessarily reduce demand and payment elsewhere. On the other hand, the wages fund is clearly only a first approximation: for the fund of circulating capital at any given time is not only used to pay wages, but also to pay rent to landlords and interest (profit) to capitalists.

In 1869, Mill's friend and fellow high official at the East India Company, William Thomas Thornton (1813–80), wrote a book entitled *On Labour* critical of Mill's wages fund doctrine. Partly this came as a needed attempt to bring consumer demand, and notably *expected* consumer demand, back into the analysis. But Thornton's main thrust was that the capital fund was not only a fund for wages but also a fund out of which to pay profits to capitalists (and, he might have added, rents on land).

Mill's review of Thornton's book in the *Fortnightly Review* was overly dramatic enough to be seized upon as a 'recantation', and as an indication that unions could indeed raise the average level of wages for workers. Actually Mill, as Schumpeter points out, was simply explaining the doctrine more carefully, and pointing out what should have been obvious: that yes, wages could conceivably increase at the expense of driving profits to zero, but that in the not too long run the result would be failure to maintain as well as to expand capital, and hence the impoverishment of everyone, not least of all the working class. There is nothing here contradictory to the wages fund doctrine. It should be added that Colonel Robert Torrens had made the very same 'concession' on the wages fund 35 years before, and had received none of the attention and noise.[10] The essence of the misnamed 'wages fund' theory was simply a fundamental part of the solidly grounded and established Turgot–Smith theory of capital.[11] How little real significance Mill attached to his 'recantation' is demonstrated by his failure to alter any of his discussion of the wages fund in the seventh and last edition of the *Principles* published during his lifetime (1871), explaining in his new preface that the discussion had not ripened sufficiently to make such a change.

As Professor Hutt has pointed out in his classic work, the prevalent idea that modifying the wages fund theory led straight to economists justifying unionism and collective bargaining was a canard and a red herring created for the occasion by Mill. Adam Smith and McCulloch had justified collective bargaining on the vague notion of labour's alleged 'disadvantage' in bargaining in the labour market. Indeed, Mill himself in the *Principles*, while continuing to hold his original wages fund view, offered the same justification, plus the Ricardian theme that without such collective bargaining wages would be driven down to subsistence level (the iron law of wages once more!). And indeed, Henry Fawcett (1833–84), professor of political economy at Cambridge and a devoted Millian, continued to cling to the original version of the wages fund theory as well as labour's 'disadvantage' argument for trade unions. On the other hand, for example, Mountifort Longfield, a proto-marginal productivity theorist, took the hard line in opposing unions as never being able to effect a general wage increase.[12]

Mill's persistent adherence to the Turgot–Smith–Ricardo theory of savings and capital is demonstrated by one of his famous 'fundamental propositions' on capital, that 'the demand for commodities is not the demand for labour'. Mill was correct on the fundamental nature of this proposition, on the failure of most economists to grasp it, and in hailing Ricardo and Say as two of the economists to stress it particularly. It is no wonder that modern economists, steeped in the fallacies of Keynes, find the proposition 'puzzling'. What it means is that at least the proximate demand for labour is supplied by savings, even though the ultimate demand may be supplied by consumers. More than that: Mill here had hold of the basic Turgot discovery of the time-structure of capital, the fact that savings pays for the factors ahead of production and sale, and that the consumers are last down the line of production. Furthermore, savings builds up a capital structure and increases funds paid to wages and other factors, which cannot get paid unless savings are first taken out of income previously supplied to producers by consumers. This theory of capital provided the building-block for the developed Austrian theory of the time-structure of capital.

It is then not surprising that Mill also supported Say's law, to which his father had contributed so much.[13] In monetary theory, Mill stood squarely in the Ricardian tradition in fervent opposition to irredeemable paper money. However, he deserted that tradition, as we have seen, in favour of the banking school. And while from his banking school mentor, James Wilson, Mill learned of the malinvestments, especially in fixed capital, that occur in business cycle booms, he also adopted the disastrous Wilsonian belief that money plays a passive and unimportant role in these cyclical booms and busts. In this belief, significantly, he harked back to his father's only difference from Ricardo. Indeed, he also adopted a pre-Schumpeterian view that these overinvestment booms, followed by corrective recessions, were necessary to economic growth.

8.4 The shift to imperialism
Classical liberalism, whether natural rights or utilitarian, whether English, French or German, was devoted to a foreign policy of peace. Its firm opposi-

tion to war and imperialism was the libertarian, minimal-government corollary in foreign affairs to its minimal-government stance at home. Opposition to big government, high taxes and interventionism abroad was the corollary of the same opposition at home. Even when the classical liberals were not totally consistent exponents of *laissez-faire* in either domestic or foreign affairs, their basic thrust was in that direction. Peace and free trade were twin policies – reaching the acme of consistency on both counts in the policy positions and agitation of Richard Cobden, John Bright, the Manchester school, and the Anti-Corn Law League.

Among the British classical liberals, non-intervention and anti-imperialism were the dominant tradition. Colonialism and special privileges to investment abroad were properly seen as part of the monopoly privileges and controls imposed by mercantilism, none of which confers advantage – in fact, imposes considerable disadvantage – on the home population. Jeremy Bentham, James Mill and the others were generally solidly anti-imperialist, and advocated that Britain give up its colonies and grant them independence. Bentham originally included India in this emancipation, but was talked out of it by James Mill, a high official in the governing organization of India, the British East India Company. The James Mill exception for India was based on a utilitarian 'white man's burden' argument that, even though England was losing economically from governing India, it must continue doing so for the sake of the Indians, who were too savage to be able to govern themselves. In that way, James Mill was able to cast an altruist–utilitarian patina over England's often bloody repression in India and over his own role in that oppression.

Mill also was able to propound his own Ricardian assault on the landlord class. Following the Ricardian doctrine that landlords were useless and non-productive Mill advocated special taxes on ground rent; being a high official in India, he believed that he was more likely to influence the tax and legal system there. Hence he advocated British nationalization of Indian land, with the state then renting out the land to Indian peasants as long-term tenants; thus, in a pre-George Georgism, the state would absorb all revenues from land rent. In his turn, John Stuart Mill was happy to advocate the same scheme.

Bentham and James Mill also made an exception to their overall anti-imperialism for Ireland, here not indulging in attacks on 'savagery' but simply asserting that freeing Ireland would be politically impossible. A strange position to take by two theorists usually fearless in advocating unpopular policies! We may speculate, however, an alternative explanation: the English liberal and radical masses, throughout the late eighteenth and nineteenth centuries, were generally *laissez-faire*-oriented, *until* the Tories were able to stir up the rabid anti-Catholicism of these dissenter and non-conformist Protestant evangelicals, and thereby split the liberal ranks. Anti-Catholicism long served as the scourge of British liberalism.

But John Stuart Mill, in this crucial area not very filio-pietistic, was able to help change the face of nineteenth century British liberalism. He was able to take a liberal doctrine generally anti-war and anti-imperialist, though with a few glaring exceptions, and transform it into an apologia for imperialism and foreign conquest. Rather than abandon the empire, as his father and other liberals had urged, John Stuart Mill called for its expansion. Indeed, Mill became the leading force in destroying the philosophic radical party in Parliament in 1838, by splitting their ranks and supporting the violent suppression of the Canadian rebellion of that year.

The younger Mill continued the altruistic argument of his father on India, and expanded it to all other peoples of the Third World. They were all barbarous and needed to be subject to a 'benevolent' despotism. He also expanded this hard line to Ireland, lamenting that Ireland could not be entirely crushed under heel because it was legally a part of the United Kingdom. 'I myself have always been for a good stout despotism, for governing Ireland alike India', Mill proclaimed. Himself a high official of the East India Company, John Stuart Mill argued that rule over barbarous colonies like India was best entrusted to autonomous public/private bodies of 'experts' such as the East India Company, rather than to the vagaries of Parliament and the English public. After the dissolution of the company in 1854, however, Mill saw no problem in Parliament appointing commissions of experts such as himself and delegating rule over India to them.

While John Mill grudgingly agreed that the advanced, white settler colonies had to be allowed their independence, he hoped that they would continue to be governed by Great Britain. For, in contrast to his father and other liberals, Mill believed that colonies conferred positive economic advantages on the home country. For a while, Bentham had succumbed to worries about 'surplus' capital at home, to be relieved by imperial expansion, but James Mill had succeeded in persuading Bentham otherwise. As an adherent and virtual co-founder of Say's law, the elder Mill had realized that Say's law meant that there would be no 'gluts' from overproduction or excess capital; therefore, no colonial or imperial safety valve was necessary. John Stuart Mill, however, was converted to the idea of surplus capital by his old friend Edward Gibbon Wakefield (1796–1862), son of Edward Wakefield, a philosophical radical friend of Bentham and James Mill.

Young Wakefield began the heretical pro-imperialist movement with his *Letter from Sydney* (1829), written not from Australia, but from an English prison, where he had been convicted for the fraudulent kidnapping of a young heiress. With this tract, Wakefield launched the 'colonial reformer' movement, and John Mill proudly proclaimed himself Wakefield's first convert. Mill was much too committed to Say's law to buy the idea of surplus production desperately needing foreign markets, but he was committed enough to the Ricardian fears of a falling rate of profit to advocate postponing this day by subsidizing the investment of British capital abroad. The worry about 'surplus capital' that could not be invested at home, should have been put to rest if Mill had been truly committed to Say's law. As for the falling rate of profit, Mill couldn't transcend the Ricardian framework to realize, first, that there is nothing inevitable about a falling rate of profit (i.e. interest), since wages do not inevitably press upon profits; and second, to the extent that profit rates fall over time it is due to falling time-preference rates, and then it is scarcely a tragedy, nor does it cause a depression or stagnation, since this interest or profit rate only reflects the desires and values of the participants in the market. And also, since interest rates are not determined by nor are they inverse to, the stock of capital, there is no guarantee that these rates will be higher abroad than in home countries such as England.

Thus, by being converted to Wakefield's fallacy of the inevitable accumulation of surplus capital in advanced capitalist countries, John Stuart Mill lent his great prestige to the notion that capitalism economically requires empire in order to invest, to get rid of, allegedly surplus savings or capital. In short, Mill was one of the ultimate founders of the Leninist theory of imperialism.

8.5   The Millians

If Mill was able to disarm much of the opposition from the original enemies of Ricardian economics, he was able to establish the dominance of his own muddled version by converting the youth – always the first group to adopt an important new trend or system of thought, for good or ill. At Cambridge the powerful secret Society of Apostles immediately took up the *Principles* for extensive study and discussion. The Apostles of 1848 included: James Fitzjames Stephen (1829–94), later an eminent journalist and attorney; E.H. Stanley (later Lord Derby) (1826–93), a conservative who would twice become foreign secretary; and Vernon Harcourt (1827–1904), later a Liberal MP and Whewell professor of international law at Cambridge. A little later in the early 1850s there came to Cambridge such young Millians as Stephen's brother Leslie (1832–1904), who would later teach at Cambridge and then retire to write works of history and philosophy, including his three volume masterwork, *The English Utilitarians* (1900). This Millian group also included Henry Fawcett who, although blinded in a hunting accident in his mid-20s, went on to become professor of political economy at Cambridge, and to write his *Manual of Political Economy* (1856) as a way of making Mill's *Principles* easier for students and laymen. Fawcett's *Manual* was used as a textbook in British and American Colleges for many years, and went through six editions. Fawcett later became an MP and postmaster general.

While Mill did not have quite the impact on Oxford as he did on Cambridge, we are assured that by the early 1850s, Mill was already 'a classic, both as a logician and as a political economist'.[14]

Two young economists who hailed the *Principles* in book reviews, became strongly influenced by Mill. One was insurance executive William Newmarch (1820–82), who collaborated in the last volume of Thomas Tooke's *History of Prices*; and the other was Walter Bagehot (1826–77), who would become an extremely influential journalist and financial economist. Bagehot was particularly happy to see Mill weaken the *laissez-faire* precepts of political economy by making his mischievous distinction between 'production' and 'distribution'. It is particularly unfortunate that this cynical semi-statist, an attorney who joined the business of his banker-father, became the son-in-law of James Wilson, and succeeded Wilson as editor of *The Economist* shortly before he died in 1860. This change meant a fateful shift from a militant *laissez-faire* policy to a statist advocacy of, among other things, the aggrandizement of the Bank of England over the monetary system. Along with the abandonment of *laissez-faire* by Bagehot came an increasing abandonment on his part of even Millian economic theory, and a shift toward a nihilistic and historicist institutionalism.

Unfortunately, Millianism came to hold sway, not only over Cambridge and Oxford, but even over Trinity College, Dublin. For almost two decades the Whately chair at Trinity had been the great stronghold of utility theory as against Ricardianism. But first, succeeding William N. Hancock in the five-year Whately chair, in 1851, was Richard Hussey Walsh (1825–62), who returned to a cost-of-production theory of value while pursuing his interest in monetary problems. Walsh had graduated from Trinity in 1846, and his lectures were published as *An Elementary Treatise on Metallic Currency* (1853). Being a Roman Catholic, Walsh was legally barred from a permanent academic career at home, and so after his term as Whately professor was over, he went to the colony of Mauritius as an administrative and census official.

The important successor to Walsh was John Elliott Cairnes (1824–75), who became by far the most important Millian in academia. Born in Ireland, Cairnes studied at Trinity College, and, after graduation, was admitted to the bar. He acceded to the Whately chair in 1856, and the following year Cairns won his spurs by publishing his most important work in economics, *The Character and Logical Method of Political Economy*. So far he followed the pattern of Whately chair-holders, but then he broke the mould by being the first of the Whately professors to follow with a lifelong career in university teaching. In 1859, Cairnes was appointed professor of political economy and jurisprudence at Queen's College, Galway; seven years later, he moved to University College, London until forced to resign by ill health in 1872.

J.E. Cairnes has been known as 'the last of the classical economists'; after Mill's death he assumed the mantle of outstanding British economist in the minds of the public, and in 1874 he lashed out in incomprehension at the revolutionary marginal utility theory of William Stanley Jevons (in Cairnes's *Some Leading Principles of Political Economy*). Cairnes was a determined cost-of-production theorist, granting his only significant exception in his well-known 'theory of non-competing groups'. This theory recognized that where factors of production, in particular labour, did not immediately and fully compete with each other, the prices of the factors are determined by demand rather than by cost. Unfortunately, Cairnes lifted the theory from Longfield's *Lectures on Political Economy* without giving him credit; we know that this was not a case of ignorance of a distinguished predecessor, since Cairnes assigned Longfield's work in his own classes.[15]

Cairnes's work of most lasting value, his *Character and Logical Method*, while including some Millian positivism, was essentially a methodological work in the great Nassau Senior–praxeological tradition. Thus Cairnes, after agreeing with Mill that there can be no controlled experiments in the social sciences, adds the important point that the social sciences, nevertheless, have a crucial advantage over the physical sciences. For, in the latter, '*mankind have no direct knowledge of ultimate physical principles*'. The laws of physics are not themselves evident to our consciousness nor are they directly apparent; their truth rests on the fact that they account for natural phenomena. But, in contrast, Cairnes goes on, '*The economist starts with a knowledge of ultimate causes*'. How? Because the economist realizes that the 'ultimate principles governing economic phenomena' are 'certain mental feelings and certain animal propensities in human beings; [and] the physical conditions under which production takes place'. To arrive at these premises of economics 'no elaborate process of induction is needed'. For all we need to do is 'to turn our attention to the subject', and we obtain 'direct knowledge of these causes in our consciousness of what passes in our own minds, and in the information which our senses convey...to us of external facts'. Such broad and basic knowledge of motives for action includes the desire for wealth; and everyone knows 'that, according to his lights, he will proceed toward his end in the shortest way open to him...'.[16]

Cairnes also demonstrates that the economist uses mental experiments as replacements for laboratory experiments of the physical scientist. He shows too, that deduced economic laws are 'tendency', or 'if–then', laws, and furthermore that they are necessarily qualitative and not quantitative, and therefore cannot admit of mathematical or statistical expression. Thus the extent of a rise in price due to a drop in supply cannot be determined, since subjective values and preferences cannot be precisely measured. In his preface to the second edition of the *Character*, written two decades later in 1875,

Cairnes warns against the growing use of the mathematical method of economics, in this case levelling a just criticism at writers like Jevons. For mathematics, in contrast to its use in the physical sciences, cannot yield new truths in economics; and, further, 'unless it can be shown either that mental feelings admit of being expressed in precise quantitative forms, or, on the other hand, that economic phenomena do not depend upon mental feelings, I am unable to see how this conclusion can be avoided'. In the course of his methodological inquiries, and in his battles against Jevons, John Cairnes moved closer to subjective value theory and further from Mill than perhaps he realized.

8.6 Cairnes and the gold discoveries

Cairnes's main contribution to positive economic analysis has been neglected by recent historians, though it was once considered a particularly 'admirable illustration of economic thought and inquiry'. The sudden gold discoveries in California in the late 1840s, followed rapidly by Australia in 1851, and the consequent enormous increase in gold production, raised important questions on their economic consequences in Britain, as well as whether or not the gold pound would depreciate in terms of commodities. Politically, gold standard anti-inflationists tried to minimize the impact of this increased supply on prices, while the inflationists chortled that at least prices would rise greatly. Among economists, men such as Mill and Torrens, previously in the forefront of currency and banking school struggles, displayed remarkably little interest in the entire process. Most of the interested economists took a primitive, proto-Keynesian position that the new gold money would increase capital and employment and therefore would have little effect on prices. If was as if monetary theory had never been discovered!

Perhaps the most banal and absurd paean to the new gold discoveries was emitted by William Newmarch, the disciple of Thomas Tooke. In an address delivered to the British Association for the Advancement of Science in 1853, Newmarch exulted that in Australia 'the effect of the new gold has been to add the stimulus of a very low rate of interest, and of an abundance of capital, to the other great and manifold causes of rapid development'.

Newmarch concluded that

> generally, we are justified in describing the effects of the new gold as almost wholly beneficial. It has led to the development of new branches of enterprise, to new discoveries...In our own country it has already elevated the condition of the working and poorer classes; it has quickened and extended trade; and exerted an influence which thus far is beneficial wherever it has been felt.[17]

Newmarch's inflationist (i.e. monetary inflationist) twaddle was echoed in the Tory *Blackwood's Magazine* by Sir Archibald Alison (1792–1867), a leading Scottish attorney, protectionist and arch-inflationist. Even Professor Henry Fawcett continued the same line, managing to use the wages fund theory for inflationist conclusions. Blithely assuming that the new gold constitutes new capital, Fawcett concluded that therefore the wages fund will increase, raising wages. In fact, it was Fawcett's paper on this question in 1859, his biographer Leslie Stephen tells us, that led 'to the discovery of Fawcett'. From his own perspective, Marx agreed with Fawcett's article, lamenting that the new gold discoveries in California and Australia had lengthened the viability of capitalism, and delayed its revolutionary crisis. Also excited about Fawcett's 'discovery' was the now Bagehot-run *Economist*, which extravagantly hailed the paper as one of those 'very rare occasions' when 'an absolutely new truth can be propounded to such a body'.[18]

On the other hand, there was still a corps of economists pointing out the home truths of the 'quantity theory', namely that the effect of the new gold discoveries would be a rise in prices roughly proportionate to the increase in gold production, accompanied by unfortunate distribution effects, as well as a waste of resources in mining an increased amount of gold.[19] The most important voice, warning of the price-inflationary consequences of the gold discoveries, was the prominent French economist and free trader Michel Chevalier (1806–79). Chevalier raised his voice on the issue throughout the 1850s, his book *On the Probable Fall in the Value of Gold* being translated by Richard Cobden and published in 1859. The veteran and devoted Ricardian essayist and poet, Thomas De Quincey (1785–1859) denounced 'California and the Gold-Digging Mania', in 1852, charging that 'every ounce of Australian gold...should locally be so much more than is wanted'. Bonamy Price, a banking school theorist who had succeeded Senior to the chair of political economy at Oxford, denounced 'The Great City Apostasy on Gold', in 1863, noting that the dominant financial opinion hailing the gold discoveries constituted an aberrant reversion to mercantilist–inflationist fallacy.

The most important response to the gold discoveries was that of John Cairnes, whose interest in the problem was piqued in 1856 by the 'ignorant and preposterous assertion(s)' by William Newmarch and other inflationists. In a series of articles published between 1857 and 1863, Cairnes set forth the quantity analysis, but he also brilliantly went beyond it to resurrect the scholastic–Cantillon process analysis, realizing that the 'distribution' effects of the monetary change process were important parts of the picture that should not be swept under the rug. Cairnes pointed out that the country with new gold mines will be the first to feel their bad effects – the price increases and the waste of resources – after which, as the new gold flows abroad in return for goods, these bad effects become gradually 'exported' to the other countries of the world. In contrast to the gushing of the inflationists, Cairnes showed that the first country to suffer waste of resources from the new gold was Australia, where previously flourishing agriculture was virtually ruined.

The British public and press, however, lost interest in the entire issue by the end of the 1850s. The reason was that prices, after the financial panic of 1857, fell back to being only a little bit higher than ten years earlier. Cairnes pointed out quite correctly, however, that this slight rise in prices masked what amounted to a considerable depreciation of the gold pound, perhaps 20 or 25 per cent. For he noted that 'considering the propitiousness of the seasons, the action of free trade, the absence of war, the contraction of credit [after the crisis of 1857], and the general tendencies to a reduction of cost proceeding from the progress of knowledge, were there no other causes in operation', there would have been a 'very considerable fall of prices at the present time, as compared with, say eight or ten years ago'. In short, without the gold inflation, there would have ben a substantial *fall* in prices, and the slight rise reflected instead a substantial inflationary depreciation of the gold pound. Profound and correct, indeed; but far too theoretical a consideration for the British public, who were content to let the problem go, so long as the effects of depreciation were not starkly visible.

8.7 The Millian supremacy

Thus, by the intellectual authority derived from decades of personal and family prominence and by his work on logic, by force of personality, and by clever strategems employed in his book, John Stuart Mill was able to make his *Principles of Political Economy* the dominant force in British economics from the time of initial publication in 1848. For three decades, Mill and his *Principles* bestrode British economics like a colossus, and, as we shall see in a later volume, England managed to repulse the marginalist Jevonian revolution in the 1870s, at least in its original, undiluted form. Mill had managed to fasten upon Great Britain: a watered-down labour or at least cost-of-production theory of value; a muddled positivist method that gave hostage to inductivist or even organicist critics; a devotion to the gold standard offset by an inflationist, banking school theory of crises and cycles and of gold production, and an adherence to the *status quo* of inflationist Bank of England control and manipulation of the British monetary system. In fact, in every area, John Stuart Mill reimposed the system of Ricardo and his father, but in a far more muddled and diluted manner. In public policy, too, the old Ricardian devotion to *laissez-faire* was replaced by a vague free market presumption to which Mill and his followers were always willing to make extensive exceptions, so free were they of the earlier classical and Ricardian 'dogmatism'. Intellectually, however wrong-headed most of the Ricardianism had been, its positions were at least consistent and clear – even if the reasoning supporting those conclusions was generally tangled and incoherent. But the new Millian neo-Ricardianism had no such virtues; instead, this system was essentially an elusive and self-contradictory jumble. There were no clear-cut positions, only vague tendencies, hedged around by backsliding and qualifications. But British economics was now slowly becoming more centred in academics rather than in businessmen, bankers, or eccentric army officers, and academics and their constituencies all too often confuse contradictory wavering with complexity, wisdom, and judiciousness of mind.

8.8   Notes

1. Schumpeter writes that Mill's *Logic* was 'one of the great books of the century, representative of one of the leading components of its *Zeitgeist*, influential with the general reading public as no other Logic has ever been'. It was due to the *Logic* even more than the *Principles*, adds Schumpeter, that 'one speaks of Mill's sway over the generation of English intellectuals that entered upon their careers in the 1850s and 1860s'. Schumpeter adds that even abroad enthusiasm for Mill's logic was intense. 'The book was found in the house of a peasant in Ireland. It was called the "book of books" by an accomplished Viennese woman (a Fabian and suffragist) who felt herself to be progress incarnate.' Schumpeter adds, with characteristic wit, that these instances show not only the great influence of Mill's *Logic* in the nineteenth century, but also 'that the correlation between individuals' enthusiasm for it, and their competence to judge it was not quite satisfactory'. Schumpeter, *The History of Economic Analysis* (New York: Oxford University Press, 1954), pp. 449, 449n.
2. Cf. Neil B. de Marchi, 'The Success of Mill's *Principles*', *History of Political Economy*, 6 (Summer 1974), pp. 119–57.
3. Ibid., pp. 122, 143.
4. The other two influential inductivists were John Herschel (1792–1871), a distinguished mathematician and astronomer, who gained a knighthood; and Charles Babbage (1792–1871), professor of mathematics at Cambridge, and renowned father of the computer. Another inductivist associated with the Cambridge group was John Cazenove (1788–1879), of a stockbroking family. A long-time member of the Political Economy Club, Cazenove had joined in Malthus's assault on Say's law.
5. See S.G. Checkland, 'The Advent of Academic Economics in England', *The Manchester School of Economic and Social Studies*, 19 (Jan. 1951), pp. 59–66.
6. The third kingpin of the Christian socialists was the Rev. John Frederick Denison Maurice (1805–72).
7. Schumpeter, op. cit., note 1, pp. 451, 530. These strictures of Schumpeter's carry all the more weight coming from a book that is, oddly, highly sympathetic towards Mill.
8. Marx, who seems to have had Mill's number, notes that trying to combine Ricardo's theory of profit and Senior' abstinence theory, Mill is obviously 'at home in absurd contradictions'. Bela Balassa, trying to save the day for Mill, sternly counters that Mill's is a 'synthesis' of the two theories. Bela Balassa, 'Karl Marx and John Stuart Mill', *Weltwirtschaftliches Archiv*, 82 (1959, no. 2), pp. 149ff.
9. Alexander Gray, *The Development of Economic Doctrine* (London: Longmans, Green, 1931), p. 283. For confirmation, note Mill: 'Who meets with the smallest condemnation, or rather, who does not meet with sympathy and benevolence, for any amount of evil which he may have brought upon himself and those dependent upon him, by this species of incontinence? While a man who is intemperate in drink, is discountenanced and despised by all who profess to be moral people, it is one of the chief grounds made use of in appeals to the benevolent, that the applicant has a large family…Little improvement can be expected in morality until the producing of large families is regarded with the same feelings as drunkenness or any other physical excess. But while the aristocracy and clergy are foremost to set the example of this kind of incontinence, what can be expected from

the poor?' John Stuart Mill, *Principles of Political Economy* (5th ed., New York: D. Appleton & Co., 1901), I, 459, 459n.

10. In Torrens, *On Wages and Combinations* (1834).
11. Cf. Schumpeter, op. cit., note 1, pp. 667–71.
12. See W.H. Hutt, *The Theory of Collective Bargaining, 1930–1975* (San Francisco: Cato Institute, 1980), pp. 1–6.
13. On the other hand, Mill's depiction of Say's Law in the *Principles* was relatively weak, and left room for Keynes's calamitous misinterpretation a century later. See W.H. Hutt, *A Rehabilitation of Say's Law* (Athens, Ohio: Ohio University Press, 1974), pp. 24–6.
14. Cf. de Marchi, op. cit., note 2, p. 154.
15. Cairnes's successor to the Whately chair in 1861, and the last holder of that chair in the archbishop's lifetime, was Arthur Houston (1833–1914), who continued in the new Mill–Cairnes cost of production tradition. In his *Principles of Value in Exchange* (1864), Houston held that the 'net cost of production' was the dominent causal force in determining value, and even tried to arrive at a mathematically expressed 'unit of sacrifice' that could measure that cost. 'Criticism' of this theory, as Black noted, 'would be superfluous'. R.D.C. Black, 'Trinity College, Dublin, and the Theory of Value, 1832–1863', *Economica*, n.s. 12 (August 1945), p. 148. Houston wrote other books on comparative law and the English drama. J.G. Smith, 'Some Nineteenth Century Irish Economists', *Economica* n.s. 2 (Feb. 1935), pp. 30–31.
16. J.E. Cairnes, *The Character and Logical Method of Political Economy* (2nd ed., London: Macmillan, 1875) pp. 83–7, 88.
17. Quoted in Crauford D. Goodwin, 'British Economists and Australian Gold', *Journal of Economic History*, 30 (June 1970), p. 412.
18. Cited in ibid., p. 414, 414n.
19. There is no 'waste', however, from the *non*-monetary viewpoint of increasing the supply of gold for industrial and consumption uses, a point which should not be overlooked. Also, there is no 'waste' within the overall framework of maintaining the most useful commodity standard (gold) as a money produced by the market instead of the state.

9 Roots of Marxism: messianic communism

9.1 Early communism

For centuries the alleged ideal of communism had come to the world as a messianic and millennial creed. Various seers, notably Joachim of Fiore, had prophesied the final state of mankind as one of perfect harmony and equality, one where all things are owned in common, where there is no necessity for work or need for the division of labour. In the case of Joachim, of course, problems of production and property, indeed of scarcity in general, were 'solved' by man no longer possessing a physical body. As pure spirits, men as equal and harmonious psychic entities spending all their time chanting praise to God, might make a certain amount of sense. But the communist idea applied to a physical mankind still needing to produce and consume is a very different matter. In any case, the communist ideal continued to be put forward as a religious, millennial doctrine. We have seen in Volume I its enormous influence on the Anabaptist wing of the Reformation in the sixteenth century. Millennial and communist dreams also inspired various fringe Protestant sects during the English Civil War of the mid seventeenth century, particularly the Diggers, the Ranters, and the Fifth Monarchy Men.

The most important forerunner of Marxian communism among these Civil War Protestant sectarians was Gerrard Winstanley (1609–60), the founder of the Digger movement and a man much admired by Marxist historians. Winstanley's father was a textile merchant, and young Gerrard became an apprentice in the cloth trade, rising up to become a cloth merchant in his own right. Winstanley's business failed, however, and he found himself downwardly mobile, an employed agricultural labourer from 1643 to 1648. As the Protestant Revolution escalated in the late 1640s, Winstanley turned to writing pamphlets espousing mystical messianism. By the end of 1648, Winstanley had expanded his chiliastic doctrine to embrace egalitarian world communism, in which all goods are owned in common. His theological groundwork was the heretical, pantheistic view that God is within every man and woman, and is not a personal deity external to man. This pantheistic God has decreed 'cooperation', which for Winstanley meant compulsory communism rather than the market economy, whereas the antithetical creed of the Devil glorified individual selfishness. In Winstanley's schema, God, meaning Reason, cre ated the earth, but the Devil later originated selfishness and the institution of private property. Winstanley added the absurd view that England enjoyed communist property before the Norman Conquest in 1066, and that this conquest created the institution of private property. His call, then, was to return to the supposedly original communist system.[1]

In the final, most fully developed version of his system, *The Law of Freedom in a Platform, or True Magistracy Restored* (1652), Winstanley envisioned a largely agrarian society, in which all goods would be communally owned, and where all wage labour and all commerce or trade would be outlawed. In fact, all sale or purchase of goods would be punishable by death as treasonous to the communist system. Money would be clearly unnecessary since there would be no trade, and presumably it would be outlawed as well. The government would establish storehouses to collect and distribute all goods, and severe penalties would be levied on 'idlers'. By this time, Winstanley's pantheism had begun to shade into atheism, for all professional clergy would be outlawed, there would be no Sabbath observation, and 'ministers' would be elected by the voters to give what would be essentially secular sermons, teaching everyone the virtues of the communist system. Education would be free and compulsory, and most of the children would be channelled into useful crafts – a foreshadowing of the progressive educational creed. Book-learning, which the uneducated Winstanley felt to be far inferior to practical vocational skill, would be discouraged.

Winstanley's strategic recipe for communist victory was for various groups of his followers, or Diggers, to move peacefully into waste or common lands, and to set up communist societies upon them. The first Digger group, led by Winstanley, moved on to waste lands near south London in April 1649, and ten Digger settlements were thereby established over the next year. Only 30 Diggers moved into the first commune, and only a few hundred set up communes across the country. The notion was that these egalitarian communist settlements would so inspire the masses that they would abandon wage work or private property and move on to Digger settlements, thus bringing about the withering away of the market and of private property. In reality, the masses treated the Digger communes with great hostility, causing their suppression in a short period of time. By the time of his *magnum opus* in 1652, Winstanley was vainly appealing to the dictator, Oliver Cromwell, to impose his cherished system from above. The idea of mass direct action to establish his system was rapidly abandoned in the face of reality.

Another more mystical communist sect during the English Civil War was the half-crazed Ranters. The Ranters were classic antinomians, that is, they believed that all human beings were automatically saved by the existence of Jesus, and that therefore all men are free to disobey all laws and to flout all moral rules. Indeed, it was supposed to be good and desirable to commit as many sins as possible in order to demonstrate one's automatic freedom from sin, and to purge oneself of false guilt about committing sins. To the pure at heart, the Ranters opined, all things are pure. The Ranters, like Joachim of Fiore and the Anabaptists of the Reformation, proclaimed the coming age of the Holy Spirit, which moved in every man. The key difference from orthodox Calvinism or Puritanism is that in those more orthodox creeds, the workings of the Holy Spirit were closely tied to the Holy Word – that is, the Bible. For the Ranters and other Inner Light Groups, however, all deuces were literally wild. The Ranters pursued this path, too, to pantheism: as one of their leaders declared: 'The essence of God was as much in the Ivie leaf as in the most glorious Angel.'

The Ranters, then, combined their belief in communism with total sexual licence, including the practice of communism of women, and communal homosexual and heterosexual orgies.[2]

9.2 Secularized millennial communism: Mably and Morelly

During the havoc and upheaval of the French Revolution, the communist creed, as well as millennial prophecies, again popped up as a glorious goal for mankind, but this time the major emphasis was a secular context. But the new secular communist prophets were faced with a grave problem: what will be the agency for this social change? In short, religious chiliasts never had problems about agency, i.e. how this mighty change would come about. The agent would be the hand of Providence, specifically either the Second Advent of Jesus Christ (for pre-millennialists), or designated prophets or vanguard groups who would establish the millennium in anticipation of Jesus's eventual return (for post-millennialists). King Bockelson and Thomas Müntzer were examples of the latter. But if the Christian millennialists possessed the assurance of the hand of Divine Providence inevitably achieving their goal, how could secularists command the same certainty and self-confidence? It looked as if they would have to fall back on mere education and exhortation

The secularist task was made more difficult by the fact that religious millennialists looked to the end of history and the achievement of their goal by means of a bloody Apocalypse. The final reign of millennial peace and harmony could only be achieved in the course of a period known as 'the tribulation', the final war of good against evil, the final triumph over the Antichrist.[3] All of which meant that if the secular communists wished to emulate their Christian forbears, they would have to achieve their goal by bloody revolution – always difficult at best. It is no accident, therefore, that the heady days of the French Revolution would give rise to such revolutionary hopes and aspirations.

The first secularized communists appeared in the shape of two isolated individuals in mid-eighteenth century France. The works of these two men would later burgeon into an activist revolutionary movement amidst the hothouse atmosphere and the sudden upheavals of the French Revolution. One was the aristocrat Gabriel Bonnot de Mably (1709–85), the elder brother of the *laissez-faire* liberal philosopher Etienne Bonnot de Condillac. In contrast to his brother the distinguished philosopher, Mably devoted himself to being a lifelong writer on a large variety of subjects.[4] A man whose works, as Alexander Gray wittily writes, 'are deplorably numerous and extensive'. Mably's prolix and confused writings were astoundingly popular in his day, his entire collected works, ranging from 12 to 26 volumes, being published in four different editions within a few years of his death.

Mably's main focus was to insist that all men are 'perfectly' equal and uniform, that all men are one and the same everywhere. He professed to discern this alleged truth in the laws of nature. Thus, in his chief work *Doutes proposés* (1786), an attack on the libertarian natural rights theory of Mercier de la Rivière, Mably presumes to interpret the voice of Nature: 'Nature says to us...I love you equally'.[5]

As in the case of most communists after him, Mably found himself confronted with one of the great problems of communism: if all property is owned in common and each person is equal, then the incentive to work is negative, since only the common store will benefit and not the individual worker in question. Mably in particular had to confront this problem, since he also maintained that man's natural and original state was communism, and that private property arose to spoil matters precisely because of the indolence of some who wished to live at the expense of others.[6]

Mably's proposed solutions to this grave problem were scarcely adequate. One was to urge everyone to tighten their belts, to want less, to be content with Spartan austerity. His other answer was to come up with what Che Guevara and Mao tse-Tung would later call 'moral incentives': to substitute for crass monetary rewards the recognition of one's merits by one's brothers – in the form of ribbons, medals, etc. Alexander Gray notes that Mably makes use of such 'distinctions' or 'Birthday Honours Lists', to stimulate everyone to work. He goes on to point out that the more 'distinctions' are handed out as incentives, the less they will truly distinguish, and the less influence they will therefore exert. Furthermore, Mably 'does not say how or by whom his distinctions are to be conferred'.

Gray adds that in a communist society in reality, many people who *don't* receive honours may and probably will be disgruntled and resentful at the supposed injustice involved, yet their 'zeal doesn't flag'.[7]

Thus, in his two proffered solutions, Gabriel de Mably was resting his hope on a miraculous transformation of human nature, what the Marxists would later see as the advent of the New Socialist Man, willing to bend his desires and his incentives to the requirements of, and baubles conferred by, the collective. But for all his devotion to communism, Mably was at bottom a realist, and so he held out no hope for its triumph. On the contrary, man is so steeped in the sin of selfishness and private property that only the palliatives of coerced redistribution and prohibitions of trade are even possible. It is no wonder that Mably was not equipped to inspire and stimulate the birth and growth of a revolutionary communist movement.

If Gabriel de Mably was a pessimist, the same cannot be said of the highly influential work of the unknown Morelly, author of *Le Code de la Nature* (*The Code of Nature*), published in 1755, and going into five further editions by 1773. Morelly had no doubts of the workability of communism: for him there was no problem of laziness or negative incentives. There was no need, in short, for any change in human nature or the creation of a New Socialist Man. In a vulgarization of Rousseau, man is everywhere good, altruistic, and dedicated to work: it is only institutions that are degrading and corrupt, specifically the institution of private property. Abolish that, and man's natural goodness would easily triumph. (Query: where did these corrupt institutions come from, if not from man?) Banish property, and crime would disappear.

For Morelly, the administration of the communist utopia would also be easy. Assigning every person his task in life, and also deciding what material goods and services would fulfil his needs, would apparently be a trivial problem for the ministry of labour or of consumption. For Morelly, all this was merely a matter of trivial enumeration, of listing things and persons. Here is the ancestor of Marx and Lenin's dismissal of the gigantic problems of socialist administration and allocation as merely a question of book-keeping.

But things, after all, are not going to be that easy. Mably, the pessimist on human nature, was apparently willing to leave matters to voluntary actions of individuals. But Morelly, the alleged optimist, was cheerfully prepared to employ brutally coercive methods to keep all the 'good' citizens in line. Once again, as in Mably, the edicts of the proposed state would be written clearly by Nature, as revealed to the founder Morelly. Morelly worked out an intricate design for his proposed government and society, all allegedly based on the clear dictates of natural law, and most of which were to be changeless and eternal – to Morelly, a vital part of the scheme.

In particular, there is to be no private property, except for daily needs: every person is to be maintained and employed by the collective, every man is to be forced to work, to contribute to the communal storehouse according to his talents, and will then be assigned goods from these stores according to his needs, to be brought up communally, and absolutely identically in food, clothing and training. Philosophic and religious doctrines are to be absolutely prescribed; no differences are to be tolerated; and children are not to be corrupted by any 'fable, story, or ridiculous fictions'. All buildings must be the same, and grouped in equal blocks; all clothing is to be made out of the same fabric. Occupations are to be limited and strictly assigned by the state.

Finally, these laws are to be sacred and inviolable, and anyone attempting to change them is to be isolated and incarcerated for life.

As in all the communist utopias, Mably's and Morelly's, as Alexander Gray makes clear, are ones under which 'no sane man would on any conditions consent to live, if he could possibly escape'. The reason, apart from the grave lack of incentives in utopias to produce or innovate, is that 'life has reached a static state...Nothing happens, nothing can happen in any of them'.[8]

It should be added that these utopias were debased, secularized versions of the visions of the Christian millennialists. In the Christian millennium, Jesus

Christ (or, alternatively, his surrogates and predecessors) comes back to earth to put an end to history; and presumably, there will be enough enchantment in glorifying God without worrying about the absence of earthly change. And, as we have seen, this is particularly true in Joachim of Fiore's envisioned millennium of people without earthly bodies. But in the secularized utopias there reigns, at best, gray gloom and stasis totally contrary to man's nature on earth.

Meanwhile, however, Christian millennialism was also revived in these stormy times. Thus, the Swabian German pietist Johann Christoph Otinger, during the mid-eighteenth century, prophesied a coming theocratic world kingdom of saints, living communally, without rank or property, as members of a millennial Christian commonwealth. Particularly influential among later German pietists was the French mystic and theosophist Louis Claude de Saint-Martin (1743–1803), who in his influential *Des Erreurs et la Verité* (*Errors and Truth*) (1773), portrayed an 'inner church of the elect' allegedly existing since the dawn of history, which would take power in the coming age. This 'Martinist' theme was developed by the Rosicrucian movement, concentrated in Bavaria. Originally alchemist mystics during the seventeenth and eighteenth centuries, the Bavarian Rosicrucians began to stress the coming takeover of world power by the inner church of the elect during the dawning millennial age. The most influential Bavarian Rosicrucian author, Carl von Eckartshausen, expounded on this theme in two widely read works, *Information on Magic* (1788–92) and *On Perfectibility* (1797). In the latter work, he developed the idea that the inner church of the elect had existed backwards in time to Abraham and then forwards to a world government to be ruled by these keepers of the divine light. This third and final age of history, the age of the Holy Spirit, was now at hand. The illuminated elect destined to rule the new communal world were, fairly obviously, the Rosicrucian Order itself, since their major evidence for the dawn of the third age was the rapid spread of Martinism and Rosicrucianism itself.

And these movements were indeed spreading during the 1780s and 1790s. The Prussian King Frederick William II and a large portion of his court were converted to Rosicrucianism in the late 1780s, as was the Russian Czar Paul I a decade later, based on his reading of Saint-Martin and Eckartshausen, both of whom he considered to be transmitters of divine revelation. Saint-Martin was also influential through his leadership of Scottish Rite Masonry in Lyons, and was the main figure in what might be called the apocalyptic-Christian wing of the Masonic movement.[9]

9.3   The conspiracy of the Equals

Inspired by the works of Mably and especially Morelly, a young journalist from Picardy decided, amidst the turmoil of the French Revolution, to found a conspiratorial revolutionary organization to establish communism. Strategically, this was an advance on the two founders, who had had no idea but simple education of how to achieve their goal. François Noël ('Caius Gracchus') Babeuf (1764–97), a journalist and commissioner of land deeds in Picardy, came to Paris in 1790, and imbibed the heady revolutionary atmosphere. By 1793, Babeuf was committed to economic equality and communism. Two years later, he founded the secret Conspiracy of the Equals, organizing around his new journal, *The Tribune of the People*. The *Tribune*, like Lenin's *Iskra* a century later, was used to set a coherent line for his cadre as well as for his public followers. As James Billington writes, Babeuf's *Tribune* 'was the first journal in history to be the legal arm of an extralegal revolutionary conspiracy'.[10]

The ultimate ideal of Babeuf and his Conspiracy was absolute equality. Nature, they claimed, calls for perfect equality; all inequality is injustice: therefore community of property was to be established. As the Conspiracy proclaimed emphatically in its *Manifesto of Equals* – written by one of Babeuf's top aides, Sylvain Maréchal – 'We demand real equality, or Death; that is what we must have'. 'For its sake', the *Manifesto* went on, 'we are ready for anything; we are willing to sweep everything away. Let all the arts vanish, if necessary, as long as genuine equality remains for us'.

In the ideal communist society sought by the Conspiracy, private property would be abolished, and all property would be communal, and stored in communal storehouses. From these storehouses, the goods would be distributed 'equitably' by the superiors – apparently, there was to be a cadre of 'superiors' in this oh so 'equal' world! There was to be universal compulsory labour, 'serving the fatherland...by useful labour'. Teachers or scientists 'must submit certifications of loyalty' to the superiors. The *Manifesto* acknowledged that there would be an enormous expansion of government officials and bureaucrats in the communist world, inevitable where 'the fatherland takes control of an individual from his birth till his death'. There would be severe punishments consisting of forced labour against 'persons of either sex who set society a bad example by absence of civic-mindedness, by idleness, a luxurious way of life, licentiousness'. These punishments, described, as one historian notes 'lovingly and in great detail',[11] consisted of deportation to prison islands.

Freedom of speech and the press are treated as one might expect. The press would not be allowed to 'endanger the justice of equality' or to subject the Republic 'to interminable and fatal discussions'. Moreover, 'No one will be allowed to utter views that are in direct contradiction to the sacred principles of equality and the sovereignty of the people'. In point of fact, a work would only be allowed to appear in print 'if the guardians of the will of the nation consider that its publication may benefit the Republic'.

All meals would be eaten in public in every commune, and there would, of course, be compulsory attendance for all community members. Furthermore, everyone could only obtain 'his daily ration' in the district in which he lives: the only exception would be 'when he is traveling with the permission of the administration'. All private entertainment would be 'strictly forbidden', lest 'imagination, released from the supervision of a strict judge should engender abominable vices contrary to the commonweal'. And, as for religion, 'all so-called revelation ought to be banned by law'.

Not only was Babeuf's egalitarian communist goal an important influence on later Marxism–Leninism, but so too was his strategic theory and practice in the concrete organization of revolutionary activity. The unequal, the Babeuvists proclaimed, must be despoiled, the poor must rise up and sack the rich. Above all, the French Revolution must be 'completed' and redone; there must be total upheaval (*bouleversement total*), total destruction of existing institutions so that a new and perfect world can be built from the rubble. As Babeuf called out, at the conclusion of his own *Plebeian Manifesto*: 'May everything return to chaos, and out of chaos may there emerge a new and regenerated world.'[12] Indeed, the *Plebeian Manifesto*, published slightly earlier than the *Manifesto of Equals*, in November 1795, was the first in a line of revolutionary manifestos that would reach a climax in Marx's *Communist Manifesto* a half-century later.

The two manifestos revealed an important difference between Babeuf and Maréchal which might have caused a split had not the Equals been crushed soon afterwards by police repression. For in his *Plebeian Manifesto*, Babeuf had begun to move toward Christian messianism, not only paying tribute to Moses and Joshua, but also particularly to Jesus as his, Babeuf's, 'co-athlete', and in prison Babeuf had written *A New History of the Life of Jesus Christ*. Most of the Equals, however, were militant atheists, spearheaded by Maréchal, who liked to refer to himself with the grandiose acronym l'HSD, *l'homme sans Dieu* (the man without God).

In addition to the idea of a conspiratorial revolution, Babeuf, fascinated by military matters, began to develop the idea of people's guerilla warfare: of a revolution being formed in separate 'phalanxes' by people whose permanent occupation would be making revolution – what Lenin would later call 'professional revolutionaries'. He also toyed with the idea of military phalanxes securing a geographical base, and then working outwards from there: 'advancing by degree, consolidating to the extent that we gain territory, we should be able to organize'.

A secret, conspiratorial inner circle, a phalanx of professional revolutionaries – inevitably this meant that Babeuf's strategic perspective for his revolution involved some fascinating paradoxes. For in the name of a goal of harmony and perfect equality, the revolutionaries were to be led by a hierarchy commanding total obedience; the inner cadre would work its will over the mass. An absolute leader, heading an all-powerful cadre, would, at the proper moment, give the signal to usher in a society of perfect equality. Revolution would be made to end all further revolutions; an all-powerful hierarchy would be necessary allegedly to put an end to hierarchy forever.

But of course, as we have seen, there was no real paradox here, no intention to eliminate hierarchy. The paeans to 'equality' were a flimsy camouflage for the real objective, a permanently entrenched and absolute dictatorship, in Orwell's striking image, 'a boot stamping on a human face – forever'.

After suffering police repression at the end of February 1796, the Conspiracy of the Equals went further underground, and, a month later, constituted themselves as the Secret Directory of Public Safety. The seven secret directors, meeting every evening, reached collective and anonymous decisions, and then each member of this central committee radiated activity outwards to 12 'instructors' each of whom mobilized a broader insurrectionary group in one of the 12 districts of Paris. In this way, the Conspiracy managed to mobilize 17 000 Parisians, but the group was betrayed by the eagerness of the secret directorate to recruit within the army. An informer led to the arrest of Babeuf on 10 May 1796, followed by the destruction of the Conspiracy of the Equals. Babeuf was executed the following year.

Police repression, however, almost always leaves pockets of dissidents to rise again, and the carrier of the torch of revolutionary communism was a Babeuvist arrested with the leader but who managed to avoid execution. Filippo Giuseppe Maria Lodovico Buonarroti (1761–1837) was the eldest son of an aristocratic but impoverished Florentine family, and a direct descendant of the great Michelangelo. Studying law at the University of Pisa in the early 1780s, Buonarroti was converted by disciples of Morelly on the faculty. As a radical journalist and editor, Buonarroti then participated in battles for the French Revolution against Italian troops. In the Spring of 1794, he was put in charge of the French occupation in the Italian town of Oneglia, where he announced to the people that all men must be equal, and that any distinction whatever among men is a violation of natural law. Back in Paris, Buonarroti successfully defended himself in a trial against his use of terror in Oneglia, and finally plunged into Babeuf's Conspiracy of Equals. His friendship with Napoleon allowed him to escape execution, and eventually to be shipped from a prison camp to exile in Geneva.

For the rest of his life, Buonarroti became what his modern biographer calls 'The First Professional Revolutionist', trying to set up revolutions and conspiratorial organizations throughout Europe. Before the execution of Babeuf and others, Buonarroti had pledged his comrades to write their full story, and he fulfilled that pledge when, at the age of 67, he published in Belgium *The*

Conspiracy for Equality of Babeuf (1828). Babeuf and his comrades had been long forgotten, and this massive work now told the first and most thorough-going story of the Babeuvist saga. The book proved to be an inspiration to revolutionary and communist groupings, and it sold extremely well, the English translation of 1836 selling 50 000 copies in a short space of time. For the next decade of his life, the previously obscure Buonarroti was lionized throughout the European ultra-left.

Brooding over previous revolutionary failures, Buonarroti counselled the need for iron élite rule immediately after the coming to power of the revolutionary forces. In short, the power of the revolution must be immediately given over to a 'strong, constant, enlightened immovable will', which will 'direct all the force of the nation against internal and external enemies', and very gradually prepare the people for their sovereignty. The point, for Buonarroti, was that 'the people are incapable either of regeneration by themselves or of designating the people who should direct the regeneration'.

9.4   The burgeoning of communism

The 1830s and 1840s saw the burgeoning of messianic and chiliastic communist and socialist groups throughout Europe; notably in France, Belgium, Germany and England. Owenites, Cabetists, Fourierites, Saint Simonians, and many others sprouted and interacted, and we need not examine them or their nuanced variations in detail.[13] While the Welshman Robert Owen (1771–1858) was the first one to use the word 'socialist' in print in 1827, and also toyed with the word 'communionst', the word 'communist' finally caught on as the most popular label for the new system. It was first used in a popular printed work, Étienne Cabet's utopian novel, *Voyage in Icaria* (1839),[14] and from there the word spread like wildfire across Europe, spurred by the recent development of regular steamboat mail service and the first telegraphy. When Marx and Engels, in the famous opening sentence of their culminating *Communist Manifesto* of 1848, wrote that 'A spectre is haunting Europe – the spectre of Communism', this was a bit of hyperbolic rhetoric, but was still not far off the mark. As Billington writes, the talismanic word 'communism' 'spread throughout the continent with a speed altogether unprecedented in the history of such verbal epidemics'.[15]

In this welter of individuals and groups, there are some interesting ones to focus on. The earliest German exile group of revolutionaries was the League of Outlaws, founded in Paris by Theodore Schuster, under the inspiration of the writings of Buonarroti. Schuster's pamphlet, *Confession of Faith of an Outlaw* (1834) was perhaps the first projection of the coming revolution as a creation of the outlaws and marginal outcasts of society, the ones outside the circuit of production whom Marx would understandably dismiss brusquely as the '*Lumpenproletariat*.' The *Lumpen* were later emphasized in the 1840s by the leading anarcho-communist, the Russian Mikhail Bakunin (1814–76), and by various strains of the New Left of the late 1960s and early 1970s.

The Outlaws was the first international organization of communist revolutionaries, comprised of about 100 members in Paris and nearly 80 in Frankfurt am Main. The League of Outlaws, however, disintegrated about 1838, many, including Schuster, going off into nationalist agitation. But it was succeeded quickly by the larger group of German exiles, the League of the Just, also headquartered in Paris. The German communist groups always tended to be more Christian than the others. Thus, Karl Schapper, leader of the Paris headquarters section of the League of the Just, addressed his followers as 'Brothers in Christ' and hailed the coming social revolution as 'the great resurrection day of the people'. Intensifying the religious tone of the League of the Just was the prominent German communist, the tailor Wilhelm Weitling (1808–71). In his secretly printed manifesto that he wrote for the League of the Just, *Humanity, as it is and as it ought to be* (1838), which though secret was widely disseminated and discussed, Weitling proclaimed himself as a 'social Luther', and denounced money as the source of all corruption and exploitation. All private property and all money was to be abolished and the value of all products to be calculated in 'labour-hours' – the labour theory of value taken all too seriously. For work in public utilities and heavy industry, Weitling proposed to mobilize a centralized 'industrial army', fuelled by the conscription of every man and woman between the ages of 15 and 18.

Expelled from France after revolutionary troubles in 1839, the League of the Just moved to London, where it also established a broader front group, the Educational Society for German Workingmen, in 1840. The three top leaders of the society, Karl Schapper, Bruno Bauer, and Joseph Moll, managed to enlarge the total to over 1 000 members by 1847, including 250 members in other countries in Europe and Latin America.

A fascinating contrast is presented in the persons of two young communists, both leaders of the movement during the 1840s, and both totally forgotten by later generations – even by most historians. Each represented a different side of the communist perspective, and together two different strands in the movement.

One was the English Christian visionary and fantast, John Goodwyn Barmby (1820–?). At the age of 20, Barmby, then an Owenite, arrived in Paris with a proposal to set up an international association of socialists throughout the world; a provisional committee was actually formed, headed by the French Owenite Jules Gay, but nothing came of the scheme. The proposal, however, did prefigure the First International. More importantly, in Paris, Barmby discovered the word 'communist', and adopted and spread it with enormous fervour. To Barmby, 'communist' and 'communitarian' were interchangeable terms, and he helped organize throughout France what he reported to the English Owenites as 'social banquet(s) of the Communist or Communitarian school'. Back in England, Barmby's fervour was undiminished. He founded a communist propaganda society, soon to be called the Universal Communitarian Society, and established a journal, *The Promethean or Communitarian Apostle*, soon renamed *The Communist Chronicle*. Communism, to Barmby, was both the 'societarian science' and the final religion of humanity. His *Credo*, propounded in the first issue of *The Promethean*, avowed that 'the divine is communism, that the demoniac is individualism...'. After that flying start, Barmby wrote communist hymns and prayers, called for the building of communitariums, all directed by a supreme communarchy headed by an elected communarch and communarchess. Barmby repeatedly proclaimed 'the religion of Communism', and made sure to begin things right by naming himself 'Pontifarch of the Communist Church'.

The subtitle of *The Communist Chronicle* revealed its neo-Christian messianism: 'The Apostle of the Communist Church and the Communitive Life: Communion with God, Communion of the Saints. Communion of Suffrages, Communion of Works and Communion of Goods.' The struggle for communism, declared Barmby, was apocalyptic, bound to end with the mystical reunion of Satan into God: 'in the holy Communist Church, the devil will be converted into God...And in this conversion of Satan doth God call people...in the communion of suffrages, of works, and of goods both spiritual and material...for these latter days.'[16] The arrival in London of Wilhelm Weitling in 1844 led him and Barmby to collaborate on promoting Christian communism, but by the end of 1847, they had lost out and the communist movement was shifting decisively toward atheism.

The crucial turn came in June 1847, when the two most atheistical communist groups: the League of the Just in London, and the small 15-man Communist Correspondence Committee of Brussels, led by Karl Marx, merged to form the Communist League. In its second congress in December, ideological struggles within the league were resolved when Marx was asked to write the statement for the new party, to become the famed *Communist Manifesto*.

In any case, Cabet and Weitling each left permanently for the United States in 1848, to try to establish communism there. Both attempts foundered ignominiously amid America's expanding and highly individualistic society. Cabet's Icarians settled in Texas and then in Nauvoo, Illinois, then split and split again, until Cabet, ejected by his former followers in Nauvoo, left for St Louis and died, spurned by nearly everyone, in 1856. As for Weitling, he gave up more rapidly. In New York, he became a follower of Josiah Warren's individualistic though left-Ricardian labour-money scheme, and in 1854 he deviated further to become a bureaucrat with the US immigration service, spending most of his remaining 17 years trying to promote his various inventions. Apparently, Weitling, willy-nilly, had at last 'voted with his feet' to join the capitalist order

Meanwhile, Goodwyn Barmby sequestered himself in one after another of the Channel Islands to try to found a utopian community, and denounced a former follower for setting up a more practical *Communist Journal* as 'an infringement of his copyright' on the word 'communism'. Gradually, however, Barmby abandoned his universalism and began to call himself a 'National Communist', and, in 1848, he went to France, became a unitarian minister and friend of Mazzini and abandoned communism for revolutionary nationalism.

On the other hand, a leading young French communist Théodore Dézamy (1808–50), represented a competing strain of militant atheism and a tough, cadre approach. In his youth the personal secretary of Cabet, Dézamy led the sudden communist boom launched in 1839 and 1840. By the following year, Dézamy became perhaps the founder of the Marxist–Leninist tradition of ideologically and politically excommunicating all deviationists from the correct line. In fact, in 1842, Dézamy, a highly prolific pamphleteer, turned bitterly on his old mentor Cabet, and denounced him, in his *Slanders and Politics of Mr. Cabet*, for chronic vacillations. In *Slanders*, Dézamy, for the first time, argued that ideological as well as political discipline was requisite for the communist movement.

More importantly, Dézamy wanted to purge French communism of the influence of the quasi-religious poetic and moralistic communist code propounded by Cabet in his *Voyage in Icaria* and especially in his *Communist Credo* of 1841. Dézamy attempted to be severely 'scientific' and claimed that communist revolution was both rational and inevitable. It is no wonder that Dézamy was greatly admired by Marx.

Furthermore, pacific or gradual measures must be rejected. Dézamy insisted that a communist revolution must confiscate all private property and all money immediately. Half-measures will satisfy no one, he claimed, and furthermore, as Billington paraphrases it, 'Swift and total change would be less bloody than a slow process, since communism releases the natural goodness of man...'.[17]

Not only would revolutionary communism be immediate and total: it would also be global and universal. In the future communist world, there will be one global 'congress of humanity', a single language, and a single labour service called 'industrial athletes', who perform work in the form of communal youth festivals. Moreover, the new 'universal country' would abolish not only 'narrow' nationalism, but also such divisive loyalties as the family. In stark practical contrast to his own career as ideological excommunicator, Dézamy proclaimed that under communism conflict would be logically impossible: 'there can be no splits among Communists; our struggles among ourselves can only be struggles of harmony, or reasoning...', since 'communitarian principles' constitute 'the solution to all problems'.

Amidst this militant atheism there was, however, a kind of religious fervour and even faith. For Dézamy spoke of 'this sublime devotion which constitutes socialism', and he urged proletarians to re-enter 'the egalitarian church, *outside of which there can be no salvation*'.

Dézamy's arrest and trial in 1844 inspired German communists in Paris such as Arnold Ruge, Moses Hess and Karl Marx, and Hess began to work on a German translation of Dézamy's code, under the encouragement of Marx, who proclaimed the code 'scientific socialist, materialist, and real humanist'.[18]

9.5   Notes

1. Most of the Protestant groups, on the other hand, held the very different, and essentially correct, view that the Norman Conquest imposed state-created feudal-type landed estates on an England which had been much closer to being an idyll of genuine private property.

    Engels and other historians and anthropologists also saw original early communism, or a Golden Age, in primitive, pre-market tribal societies. Modern anthropological research, however, has demonstrated that most primitive and tribal societies were based on private property, money, and market economies. Thus, see Bruce Benson, 'Enforcement of Private Property Rights in Primitive Societies: Law Without Government'. *Journal of Libertarian Studies*, 9 (Winter 1989), pp. 1–26.

2. Something should be said here about the most prominent of these radical groups, the Fifth Monarchists. While not necessarily communists, they were akin to the Anabaptists of the Reformation in that they were post-millennialists who believed that only they, the elect, would be saved. Further, they believed that it was their historical mission to destroy everyone else in the world, so as to liberate the world from sin, and usher in the imminent Second Coming of Jesus and the establishment of the Kingdom of God on earth.

3. We are simplifying here from the often daunting complexities of millennial thought. For example, in the highly developed pre-millennial doctrines of twentieth century 'fundamentalism', the period of the tribulation will be a very hectic seven years, the 'seventieth week' of the *Book of Daniel*, in which not only the Anti-Christ ('The Beast'), but also 'The Dragon" (the Anti-God), the 'False Prophet' (the Anti-Spirit), 'The Scarlet Woman', and many other evil beings will be overcome. Thus, see George M. Marsden, *Fundamentalism and American Culture: The Shaping of Twentieth-Century Evangelicalism: 1870–1925* (New York: Oxford University Press, 1980), pp. 58–9.

4. In his day and later, Mably was often referred to as an 'abbé', but he had left the clergy early in life.

5. Quoted and translated in Alexander Gray, *The Socialist Tradition* (London: Longmans Green, 1946), p. 87.

6. Ibid., p. 88.

7. Ibid., pp. 90–91.

8. Ibid., pp. 62–3.

9. On Saint-Martin, Eckartshausen and their influence, see the revealing article by Paul Gottfried, 'Utopianism of the Right: Maistre and Schlegel', *Modern Age*, 24 (Spring 1980), pp. 150–60.

10. James H. Billington, *Fire in the Minds of Men: Origins of the Revolutionary Faith* (New York: Basic Books, 1980), p. 73.

11. For this phrase and other translated quotes from the *Manifesto*, see Igor Shafarevich, *The Socialist Phenomenon* (New York: Harper & Row, 1980), pp. 121–4. Also see Gray, op. cit., note 5, p. 107.

12. Billington, op. cit., note 10, p. 75. Also see Gray, op. cit., note 5, p. 105n. As Gray comments, 'what is desired is the annihilation of all things, trusting that out of the dust of

destruction a fair city may arise. And buoyed by such a hope, how blithely would Babeuf bide the stour', Ibid. p. 105.

13.   Except that the important 'class struggle' contributions of the Saint Simonians will be dealt with below.

14.   Cabet (1788–1856) had been a distinguished French lawyer and attorney-general of Corsica, but was ousted for radical attitudes toward the French government. After founding a radical journal, Cabet fled into exile in London during the 1830s and virtually became an Owenite. Despite Cabet's nationality, the book was originally written and published in English, and a French translation was published the following year. A peaceful communist rather than a revolutionary, Cabet tried to establish utopian communes in various failed projects in the United States, from 1848 until his death.

15.   Billington, op. cit., note 10, p. 243.

16.   Billington, op. cit., note 10, p. 257.

17.   Billington, op. cit., note 10, p. 251.

18.   See J.L. Talmon, *Political Messianism: the Romantic Phase* (New York: Praeger, 1960), p. 157.

10 Marx's vision of communism

10.1   Millennial communism

The key to the intricate and massive system of thought created by Karl Marx
(1818–83) is at bottom a simple one: *Karl Marx was a communist.* A seemingly banal or trite statement set alongside Marxism's myriad of jargon-
ridden concepts in philosophy, economics, history, culture et al. Yet Marx's
devotion to communism was his crucial point, far more central than the
dialectic, the class struggle, the theory of surplus value, and all the rest.
Communism was the goal, the great end, the desideratum, the ultimate end
that would make the sufferings of mankind throughout history worthwhile.
History is the history of suffering, of class struggle, of the exploitation of
man by man. In the same way as the return of the Messiah, in Christian
theology, would put an end to history and establish a new Heaven and a new
Earth, so the establishment of communism would put an end to human
history. And just as for post-millennial Christians, man, led by God's prophets and saints, would establish a Kingdom of God on Earth (and, for pre-
millennials, Jesus would have many human assistants in establishing such a
Kingdom), so for Marx and other schools of communists, mankind, led by a
vanguard of secular saints, would establish a secularized kingdom of heaven
on earth.

In messianic religious movements, the millennium is invariably established
by a mighty, violent upheaval, an Armageddon, a great apocalyptic war between good and evil. After this titanic conflict, a millennium, a new age, of
peace and harmony, a reign of justice, would be established upon the earth.

Marx emphatically rejected those utopians who aimed to arrive at communism through a gradual and evolutionary process, through a steady advancement of the good. No, Marx harked back to the apocalyptics, the post-
millennial coercive German and Dutch Anabaptists of the sixteenth century,
to the millennial sects during the English Civil War, and to the various groups
of pre-millennial Christians who foresaw a bloody Armageddon at the Last
Days, before the millennium could be established. Indeed, since the immediatist
post-mils refused to wait for gradual goodness and sainthood to permeate
among men, they joined the pre-mils in believing that only a violent apocalyptic final struggle between good and evil, between saints and sinners, could
establish the millennium. Violent, worldwide revolution, in Marx's version
made by the oppressed proletariat, would be the instrument of the advent of
his millennium, communism.

In fact, Marx, like the pre-mils (or 'millenarians') went further to hold that
the reign of evil on earth would reach a peak just before the apocalypse. For
Marx as for the millenarians, writes Ernest Tuveson,

> The evil of the world must proceed to its height before, in one great complete
> root-and-branch upheaval, it would be swept away...

> Millenarian pessimism about the perfectibility of the existing world is crossed by a supreme optimism. History, the millenarian believes, so operates that, when evil has reached its height, the hopeless situation will be reversed. The original, the true harmonious state of society, in some kind of egalitarian order, will be re-established.[1]

In contrast to the various groups of utopian socialists, and in common with religious messianists, Karl Marx did not sketch the features of his future communism in any detail. Not for Marx, for example, to spell out the number of people in his utopia, and the shape and location of their houses, the pattern of their cities. In the first place, there is a quintessentially crazy air to utopias that are mapped by their creators in precise detail. But more importantly, spelling out the details of one's ideal society removes the crucial element of awe and mystery from the allegedly inevitable world of the future. In the same way, science fiction movies lose their glamour and excitement when, in the second half of the film, the mysterious, powerful and previously invisible monsters become concretized into slow-moving green blob-like creatures that have lost their mysterious aura and have become almost commonplace.

But certain features are broadly alike in all visions of communism. Private property is eliminated, individualism goes by the board, individuality is flattened, all property is owned and controlled communally, and the individual units of the new collective organism are in some vague way equal to one another.

This millennialist emphasis on the collective is a long way from the orthodox Christian, Augustinian, stress on the individual soul and his salvation. In orthodox, a-millennial Christianity, the individual does or does not achieve salvation, until Jesus returns and puts an end to history, and ushers in the Day of Judgement. There is no millennium on earth; the Kingdom of God remains safely, and appropriately, in heaven. But millennialism's emphasis on achieving a Kingdom of God *on earth* inevitably stressed – especially in the required human agency of the post-millennialists – the inevitable collective march toward the Kingdom in and through history. In what we may call the 'immediatist' version of post-mil doctrine, as we have seen in Volume I in the Brethren of the Free Spirit, the coercive Anabaptists of the Reformation, in Christian communists and in a secularized version in Marxism, the object is to seize immediate power in a violent revolution, and to purge the world of sinners and heretics, i.e. all who are not followers of the sect in question, so as to establish the millennium, the precondition of Jesus's Second Advent. In contrast, the *gradualist* post-mils, in less violent and precipitate fashion, who would seize control of most of the Protestant churches in the northern United States during the nineteenth century, wanted to use state power to coerce morality and virtue and then establish the Kingdom of God, not only in the US, but throughout the world. As one historian penetratingly concludes about one of the most prominent post-mil economists and social scientists of the late nineteenth century – a passage that could apply to the entire movement:

> In [Richard T.] Ely's eyes, government was the God-given instrument through which we had to work. Its preeminence as a divine instrument was based on the post-Reformation abolition of the division between the sacred and the secular and on the State's power to implement ethical solutions to public problems. The same identification of sacred and secular...enabled Ely to both divinize the state and socialize Christianity: he thought of government as God's major instrument of redemption...[2]

Gradualists or immediatists, all millennialists have caused grave social and political trouble by 'immanentizing the eschaton' – in the political philosopher Eric Voegelin's infelicitously worded but highly perceptive phrase. As an orthodox Christian, Voegelin believed that 'the eschaton' – the Final Days, the Kingdom of God – must be kept strictly out of earthly matters and be confined to the other-worldly realms of Heaven and Hell. But to take the 'eschaton' out of Heaven and bring it down into the processes of human history, is to create grave problems and consequences: consequences which Voegelin saw embodied in such immanent and messianic movements as Marxism and Nazism.

In common with other utopian socialists and communists, Marx sought in communism the apotheosis of the collective species – mankind as one new super-being, in which the only meaning possessed by the individual is as a negligible particle of that collective organism. One incisive portrayal of Marxian collective organicism – what amounts to a celebration of the New Socialist Man to be created during the communizing process – was that of a top Bolshevik theoretician of the early twentieth century, Alexander Alexandrovich Bogdanov (1873–1928). Bogdanov, like Joachim of Fiore, spoke of 'three ages' of human history: first was a religious, authoritarian society and a self-sufficient economy. Next came the 'second age', an exchange economy, marked by diversity and the emergence of 'autonomy' of the 'individual human personality'. But this individualism, at first progressive, later becomes an obstacle to progress as it hampers and 'contradicts the unifying tendencies of the machine age'. But then there will arise the third age, the final stage of history, communism, though not as with Joachim, an age of the Holy Spirit. This last stage will be marked by a collective self-sufficient economy, and by

> the fusion of personal lives into one colossal whole, harmonious in the relations of its parts, systematically grouping all elements for one common struggle – struggle against the endless spontaneity of nature...An enormous mass of creative activity...is necessary in order to solve this task. It demands the forces not of man but of mankind – and only in working at this task does mankind as such emerge.[3]

The acme of messianic communism appears in the frenzied three-volume phantasmagoria by the notable German blend of Christian messianist and Marxist–Leninist–Stalinist, Ernst Bloch (1885–1977). Bloch held that the 'inner truth' of things could only be discovered after 'a complete transformation of the universe, a grand apocalypse, the descent of the Messiah, a new heaven, and a new earth'. As J.P. Stern writes in his review of Bloch's three-volume *Principle of Hope*, the book contains such remarkable declamations as '*Ubi Lenin, ibi Jerusalem*' ('Where Lenin is, there is Jerusalem'), and that 'the Bolshevist fulfillment of Communism' is part and parcel of 'the age-old fight for God'. There is also more than a hint, in Bloch, that disease, nay even death itself, will be abolished upon the advent of communism.[4]

In contrast, there is no more eloquent championing of orthodox Christian individualism and revulsion against collectivism, than G.K. Chesterton's critique of the views of a leading Fabian socialist, Mrs Annie Besant – in which Chesterton swats Mrs Besant's pantheistic Buddhism:

> According to Mrs Besant the universal Church is simply the universal Self. It is the doctrine that we are really all one person; that there are no real walls of individuality between man and man... She does not tell us to love our neighbor; she tells us to be our neighbors...the intellectual abyss between Buddhism and Christianity is that, for the Buddhist or theosophist, personality is the fall of man, for the Christian it is the purpose of God, the whole point of his cosmic idea.[5]

Let us turn to some of the main features of communism. In the typical communal millennial future, an epoch of bliss and harmony, *work*, the necessity to labour, becomes de-emphasized or disappears altogether. Labour, at least labour in order to maintain and advance one's living standards, does not ring true with very many people as a feature of utopia. Thus, in the vision of Joachim of Fiore, perhaps the first medieval millennialist, no work would be required to disturb the endless round of celebration and prayer, because mankind would have achieved the status of immaterial objects. If man were pure spirit, it is true that the economic problem – the problem of production and living standards – would necessarily disappear. Unfortunately, however, Marx, being an atheist and materialist, could not exactly fall back on a Fiore-like communism of pure spirit. How could solidly material human beings solve the problem of production and of maintaining and expanding their living standards?

There was method in Marx's refusal to treat the communist stage in any detail. His utopia was shadowy. On the one hand, Marx assumed and asserted that goods in the future communist society would be superabundant. If so, there would of course be no need to refer to the universal economic problem of scarcity of means and resources as applied to ends. But by assuming away the problem, Marx bequeathed the puzzle to future generations, and Marxists have been split on the question: will communism itself bring about this magical state of superabundance, or should we wait *until* capitalism brings superabundance before we establish communism? Generally, Marxist groups have solved this problem, not in theory but in practice (or 'praxis') by cleaving to whatever path would allow them either to conquer or to maintain their power. Thus Marxist vanguards or parties, on seeing an opportunity to seize power, have been invariably willing to skip the 'stages of history' preordained by their Master and exercise their revolutionary will. On the other hand, Marxist élites already entrenched in power have prudentially put off the ultimate goal of communism ever further into a receding future. And so the Soviets were quick to stress hard work and gradualism in persevering toward the ultimate goal.[6]

There are several other probable reasons for Marx's failure to detail the features of ultimate communism, or, indeed, of the necessary stages to achieve it. First is that Marx had no interest in the economic features of his utopia; a simple question-begging assumption of unlimited abundance was enough. His main interest, as we shall see, was in the philosophic, indeed religious, aspects of communism. Second, communism for Marx was an inverted form of Hegel and his philosophy of history; it was the revolutionary end to Marx's neo-Hegelian version of 'alienation' and of the 'dialectic' process by which the *aufhebung* (transcendence) and negation of one historical stage is replaced by another and opposing one. In this case: the negation of the evil condition of private property and the division of labour, and the establishment of communism, in which man's unity with man and nature is achieved. To Marx, as to Hegel, history necessarily proceeds by this magical dialectic, in which one stage gives rise inevitably to a later and opposing stage. Except that to Marx, the 'dialectic' is material rather than spiritual.[7] Marx never published his neo-Hegelian *Economic and Philosophic Manuscripts of 1844*, in which the philosophic basis of Marxism was set forth, and one essay of which, 'Private Property and Communism', contained Marx's fullest exposition of the communist society. One reason for his refusal to publish was that, in later decades, Hegelian philosophy had gone out of fashion, even in Germany, and Marx's followers were interested more in the economic and revolutionary aspects of Marxism.

10.2 Raw communism

Another important reason for Marx's failure to publish was his candid depiction of the communist society in the essay 'Private Property and Communism'. In addition to its being philosophic and not economic, he portrayed a horrifying but allegedly necessary stage of society immediately *after* the necessary violent world revolution of the proletariat, and before ultimate communism is to be finally achieved. Marx's post-revolutionary society, that of 'unthinking' or 'raw' communism, was not such as to spur the revolutionary energies of the Marxian faithful.

For Marx took to heart two bitter critiques of communism that had become prominent in Europe. One was by the French mutualist anarchist Pierre-Joseph Proudhon, who denounced communism as 'oppression and slavery', and to whom Marx explicitly referred in his essay. The other was a fascinating book by the conservative Hegelian monarchist Lorenz von Stein (1815–1890), who had been assigned by the Prussian government in 1840 to study the unsettling new doctrines of socialism and communism becoming rampant in France. Not only did Marx show a 'minute textual familiarity' with Stein's subsequent book of 1842, but he actually based his concept of the proletariat as the foundation and the engine of the world revolution on Stein's insights into the new revolutionary doctrines as rationalizations of the class interests of the proletariat.[8]

Most remarkably, Marx admittedly agreed with Proudhon's, and particularly Stein's, portrayal of the first stage of the post-revolutionary society, which he agreed with Stein to call 'raw communism'. Stein forecast that raw communism would be an attempt to enforce egalitarianism by wildly and ferociously expropriating and destroying property, confiscating it, and coercively communizing women as well as material wealth. Indeed, Marx's evaluation of raw communism, the stage of the dictatorship of the proletariat, was even more negative than Stein's: 'In the same way as woman is to abandon marriage for general [i.e. universal] prostitution, so the whole world of wealth, that is, the objective being of man, is to abandon the relation of exclusive marriage with the private property owner for the relation of general prostitution with the community.' Not only that, but as Professor Tucker puts it, Marx concedes that 'raw communism is not the real transcendence of private property but only the universalizing of it, not the overcoming of greed but only the generalizing of it, and not the abolition of labour but only its extension to all men. It is merely a new form in which the vileness of private property comes to the surface'. In short, in the stage of communalization of private property, what Marx himself considers the worst features of private property will be maximized. Not only that: but Marx concedes the truth of the charge of anti-communists then and now that communism and communization is but the expression in Marx's words, of 'envy and a desire to reduce all to a common level'. Far from leading to a flowering of human personality as Marx is supposed to claim, he admits that communism will negate it totally. Thus Marx:

> In completely negating the *personality* of men, this type of communism is really nothing but the logical expression of private property. General *envy*, constituting itself as power, is the disguise in which *greed* re-establishes itself and satisfies

itself, only in *another* way ...In the approach to *woman* as the spoil and handmaid of communal lust is pressed the infinite degradation in which man exists for himself.[9]

All in all, Marx's portrayal of raw communism is very like the monstrous regimes imposed by the coercive Anabaptists of the sixteenth century.[10]

Professor Tucker adds, perhaps underlining the obvious, that 'These vivid indications from the Paris manuscripts of the way in which Marx envisaged and evaluated the immediate post-revolutionary period very probably explain the extreme reticence that he always later showed on this topic in his published writings.'[11]

But if this communism is admittedly so monstrous, a regime of 'infinite degradation', why should anyone favour it, much less dedicate one's life and fight a bloody revolution to establish it? Here, as so often in Marx's thought and writings, he falls back on the mystique of the 'dialectic' – that wondrous magic word by which one social system inevitably gives rise to its victorious transcendence and negation. And, in this case, by which total evil – which interestingly enough, turns out to be the post-revolutionary dictatorship of the proletariat and not preceding capitalism – becomes transformed into total good.

To say the least, Marx cannot and does not attempt to explain how a system of total greed becomes transformed into total greedlessness. He leaves it all to the wizardry of the dialectic, now a dialectic fatally shorn of the alleged motor of the class struggle, which yet somehow transforms the monstrosity of raw communism into the paradise of communism's 'higher stage'.

10.3   Higher communism and the eradication of the division of labour
The Hell of the first, or lower, stage of communism has been vividly expressed by Marx. What of the Heaven of the higher stage, of the 'positive humanism' of ultimate communism? Unfortunately, Heaven's features are vague and murky indeed, perhaps too insubstantial, if Marx had published his *Manuscripts*, to overcome the all too palpable horrors of raw communism. The key is that man is supposedly freed from the necessity of labour. The elimination of private property frees him from greed, succeeding the orgiastic culmination of greed achieved during raw communism. In particular, man is freed from the division of labour, from specialization, which prevents him from developing 'all' his faculties for the sheer joy of it, and 'forces' him to work for others – either in the market, or under the despotic power of feudalism, or oriental despotism, or under the dictatorship of the proletariat in the first stage of communism. Without the division of labour, and with the evil of exchange of goods and services at last eliminated, man is now freed from the 'alienation' of not consuming his own product. This alienation is not, as many Marxists seem to believe, the result of the capitalists' alleged

extraction of the 'surplus' produced by the workers. More deeply, this aliena-tion is the product of the division of labour and of specialization itself. That division eliminated, man, in the neo-Hegelian mystique of Marx, will return 'to himself', will be united with 'himself', and alienation will then be ended.

All this makes a kind of sense only if one realizes that, for Marx as for Hegel, 'man' is a collective and not an individual organic entity. For Hegel and for Marx, the history of 'man' is the history, the ups and downs, of what amounts to a single collective organism. If, for Marx, there is a division of labour, specialization and exchange, this means that 'man' is tragically split within 'himself', so that the process of achieving the higher stage of commu-nism, the end of human history in the same way that the Kingdom of God on earth had been an end, is a process by which man is no longer alienated from his collective 'self' and achieves unity with himself. At the same time, 'he' also achieves unity with 'nature', for in the Marxian system the only 'nature' is that which has been created by centuries of man's labour and activity. Thus, as Robert Tucker points out, Friedrich Engels's famous statement about communism has been misinterpreted widely, not least by Marxists unfamiliar with the philosophical nature of their own system. Friedrich Engels (1820–95) wrote, in his *Anti-Dühring*:

> The whole sphere of the conditions of life which environ man, and which have hitherto ruled man, now comes under the dominion and control of man, who for the first time becomes the real, conscious lord of Nature, because he has now become master of his own social organization...Man's own social organisation, hitherto confronting him as a necessity imposed by Nature and history, now becomes the result of his own free action. The extraneous objective forces that have hitherto governed history pass under the control of man himself... It is the ascent of man from the kingdom of necessity to the kingdom of freedom.[12]

As Tucker points out, to the reader unfamiliar with Marxian philosophy, this passage might well be construed as referring to man's mastery of nature via technology. However,

> in actuality, it refers to the mastery of technology as man's own nature outside himself. The kingdom of necessity is the alienated world of history, the realm of object-bondage. The 'extraneous objective forces' over which man is to become lord in the kingdom of freedom are understood as the externalized forces of the species-self. The nature to which man will no longer be subservient is his own nature.[13]

In short, as in many other places in Marx, a passage which at least superfi-cially seems to contain at least a modicum of sense – although fallacious – turns out on deeper study to be but a part of the mumbo-jumbo of Marx's neo-Hegelian philosophy.

Particularly important for Marx is that communism does away with the division of labour. By being free of specialization, the division of labour, and working for others (including the consumers) man as labourer is freed from all limits. Thus liberated, 'man produces in order to realize his nature as a being with manifold creative capacities requiring free outlet in a "totality of human life-activities"'.[14] Or, as Engels put it in his *Anti-Dühring*, the disappearance of the division of labour will mean that productive labour will give 'each individual the opportunity to develop all his faculties, physical and mental, in all directions and exercise them to the full'.

The idea of everyone developing all of their faculties 'in all directions' is mind-boggling, and conjures up the absurd picture of a world of autistic dilettantes, each heedless of social demand for their services or products, and each dabbling whimsically and sporadically in every activity. This image is confirmed by Marx's most famous passage describing the communist system in Part I of his 'The German Ideology', an unpublished essay written in 1845–46. There he writes that communism 'corresponds to the development of individuals into complete individuals and the casting off of all natural limitations'. How are 'all natural limitations' cast off? – a tall order indeed. Let Marx explain. As soon as the division

> of labour comes into being, each man has a particular, exclusive sphere of activity, which is forced upon him...He is a hunter, a fisherman, a shepherd, or a critical critic, and must remain so if he does not want to lose his means of livelihood; while in communist society, where nobody has one exclusive sphere of activity but each can become accomplished in any branch he wishes, society regulates the general production and thus makes it possible for me to do one thing today and another tomorrow, to hunt in the morning, fish in the afternoon, rear cattle in the evening, criticize after dinner, just as I have a mind, without ever becoming hunter, fisherman, shepherd or critic.[15]

One of the most apt comments on this passage is the witty *mot* of Alexander Gray. 'A short weekend on a farm might have convinced Marx that the cattle themselves might have some objection to being reared in this casual manner, in the evening.' More broadly, Gray remarks 'that each individual should have the opportunity of developing *all* his faculties, physical *and* mental in all directions, is a dream which will cheer the vision only of the simple-minded, oblivious of the restrictions imposed by the narrow limits of human life' 'For life', Gray points out, 'is a series of acts of choice, and each choice is at the same time a renunciation...'. The necessity of choice, Gray perceptively reminds us, will exist even under communism:

> Even the inhabitant of Engels' future fairyland will have to decide sooner or later whether he wishes to be Archbishop of Canterbury or First Sea Lord, whether he

should seek to excel as a violinist or as a pugilist, whether he should elect to know all about Chinese literature or about the hidden pages in the life of the mackerel.[16]

The abolition of the division of labour meant also that all differences – and hence 'opposition' – between town and country had to be eliminated, with industry somehow equally diffused throughout the country (the world?). As a result, all large cities would have to be destroyed. As Engels said in *Anti-Dühring*: 'it is true that in the huge towns civilization has bequeathed to us a heritage which it will take much time and trouble to get rid of. But it must and will be got rid of, however protracted a process it may be.'[17]

It is not surprising that the Soviet authorities did not take a very favourable view of Marxian communism. Marxian pieties can go just so far. Thus, the Soviet Communist Party's theoretical journal *Kommunist* referred favourably to the unpublished work of a Soviet economist, V.M. Kriukov, who wrote that

> An unintelligent person and philistine might form his own picture of communism approximately as follows: you rise in the morning and ask yourself, where shall I go to work today – shall I be chief engineer at the factory or go and head the fishing brigade? Or shall I run down to Moscow and hold an urgent meeting of the presidium of the Academy of Science?

Kommunist adds the warning: 'It will not be so.' No doubt, and quite sensibly. But of course the Soviet authorities did not acknowledge the fact that by repudiating this 'unintelligent' notion they were renouncing the key to the whole Marxian system, the point and goal of the entire struggle.[18]

More importantly, the Soviet authorities jettisoned the basic goal of Marxism by abandoning the idea that communism will eliminate the division of labour. The revision began with Stalin's last work in 1952, shortly before his death, and intensified after that. Evading and sometimes falsifying the writings of the Founders, the Soviet revisionists were relatively sound in realism and economics but weak on the Marxian heritage. Sometimes, the Soviet experts simply and sharply stated the facts: 'A man cannot do literally everything'; 'In the system of Communist production relations, the division and specialization of labour will remain essential'; and 'It is absolutely obvious that Communist society would be unthinkable without a constantly developing and intensifying division of labour'. Substitute the words 'modern' or 'industrial' for 'communist' and the Soviet economists were right on the mark. But in what sense is this 'communism' any longer?[19]

Six years before *Anti-Dühring*, moreover, Engels betrayed the entire Marxian vision in the course of a bitter polemic against the anarchists. In defending the idea of authoritarianism under communism, Engels reminded the self-styled anti-authoritarian anarchists that 'a revolution is certainly the most authoritarian thing there is; it is the act whereby one part of the population imposes its will upon the other part by means of rifles, bayonets, and cannon – authoritarian means...'. But more importantly, Engels jeered at the idea that there will be no authoritarianism, and hence no division of labour, in a communist factory. Engels pointed out that factory production requires both, and also demands that the workers subordinate themselves to technological necessity. Thus: 'keeping the machines going requires an engineer to look after the steam engine, mechanics to make the current repairs, and many other labourers whose business it is to transfer the products...'. Moreover, he pointed out, technology and the forces of nature subject man 'to a veritable despotism independent of all social organization'. 'Wanting to abolish authority in large-scale industry', Engels warned, 'is tantamount to wanting to abolish industry itself, to destroy the power loom in order to return to the spinning wheel'.[20]

Refreshingly sober words, no doubt, but totally alien to the spirit of Marxism and certainly to all that Marx said or wrote on the topic, as well as most other writings of Engels. To Marx, all labour in future communism is not economic, but *artistic*, the free and spontaneous creativity allegedly typical of the artist. For Marx in his economic *magnum opus*, *Capital*, communist man has been transformed from an alienated man into an aesthetic man who regards everything in artistic terms. Thus, on the factory, industrial production under communism will have no authoritarian direction but rather unity will be achieved as with musicians in a symphony orchestra.

Engels, however, was an interesting case. A bit more of an economist than Marx, and the man who introduced his friend and partner to British classical economics, Engels was capable of alternating the wildest utopian fantasies of communism with a suddenly perceptive insight into its economic difficulties. Thus, even in *Anti-Dühring* Engels at one point admits that 'the task of economic science', as capitalism moves forward rapidly and inexorably to its collapse, is 'to uncover amid the changes of the economic transition the elements of the future new organisation of production and exchange which will remove the previous malfunctioning (of the capitalist economy)'. It was never a task, however, that either Engels or Marx would ever bother to take up.

Furthermore, in 'The Principles of Communism', an essay written in late 1847 that became the first draft for the *Communist Manifesto*, Engels laid bare one of the crucial, usually implicit, assumptions of the communist society – that superabundance will have eliminated the problem of scarcity:

> Private property can be abolished only when the economy is capable of producing the volume of goods needed to satisfy everyone's requirements...The new rate of industrial growth will produce enough goods to satisfy all the demands of society...Society will achieve an output sufficient for the needs of all members,

This superabundant production somehow will have been achieved by a wondrous technological progress that would eliminate the need for any division of labour.

Engels, however, in the midst of this bold assumption, felt compelled to waffle, and to admit that this communist millennium could not be achieved 'immediately', or 'at one blow'. For 'it would not be possible immediately to expand the existing forces of production to such an extent that enough goods could be made to satisfy all the needs of the community'. During the transition period, at least, says Engels, 'industry will have to be run by society as a whole for everybody's benefit. It must be operated by all members of society in accordance with a common plan...Private property will also have to be abolished and it must be replaced by the sharing of all products in accordance with an agreed plan'.[21]

Any believer in the labour theory of value who tried to set forth a scheme of economic calculation under socialism would likely fasten on the idea of setting prices, and paying wages, in accordance with the labour time expended on production. The issue of labour-time tickets was precisely the plan proposed by Robert Owen, by the Ricardian individualist-anarchist Josiah Warren, and by the German Ricardian socialist Johann Karl Rodbertus (1805–75). One of Friedrich Engels's most penetrating economic insights came in the course of demolishing the labour-ticket money utopian socialism of Rodbertus, a beloved figure in Germany at that time.[22]

Engels denounced the Rodbertus doctrine in a preface to the first German edition of Marx's *The Poverty of Philosophy*, the year after Marx's death (1884). Here Engels had the impudence to condemn Rodbertus's labour money as 'childishly naive', and to press on to scorn Rodbertus for overlooking economic law and the competitive market process:

> To desire in a society of producers who exchange their commodities, to establish the determination of value by labour time, by forbidding competition to establish this determination of value through pressure on prices in the only way in which it can be established, is therefore merely to prove that...one has adopted the usual Utopian disdain of economic laws.

Engels goes on to assert that competition, by 'bringing into operation the laws of value of commodity production in a society of producers who exchange their commodities', creates the only possible organization of social production 'in the circumstances'. Engels goes on to engage in a scornful and perceptive critique of socialist attempts at calculation (at the very least of the Rodbertus variety):

> Only through the undervaluation and overvaluation of products is it forcibly brought home to the individual commodity producers what things and what quan-

tity of them society requires or does not require. But it is just this sole regulator
that the Utopia in which Rodbertus also shares would abolish. And if we have to
ask what guarantee we have that the necessary quantity and not more of each
product will be produced, that we shall not go hungry in regard to corn and meat,
while we are choked in beet sugar and drowned in potato spirit, that we shall not
lack trousers to cover our nakedness while trouser buttons flood us in millions –
Rodbertus triumphantly shows us his famous calculation, according to which the
correct certificate has been handed out for every superfluous pound of sugar, for
every unsold barrel of spirit, for every unusable trouser button, a calculation
which 'works out' exactly, and according to which 'all claims will be satisfied and
the liquidation correctly brought about'.[23]

Engels adds that 'If now competition is to be forbidden to make the individual producers aware, by the rise or fall of prices, how the world market
stands, then their eyes are completely blinded'.

Professor Hutchison's comment on this performance by Engels is all too *à
propos*:

Mises and Hayek could hardly have made the point more forcefully. What is most
extraordinary is the combination of penetrating critical insight regarding the vital
function of the competitive price mechanism as applied to the Utopian notions of
Rodbertus together with the totally uncritical, purblind complacency regarding his
own and Marx's Utopian assumptions (as he himself had earlier revealed them in
his 'Principles of Communism' in such irresponsible vacuities as 'the joint and
planned exploitation of the forces of production by society as a whole')....The
hordes of infallible Prussian officials and 'the Prussian State Socialism', for
relying on which Engels so castigates Rodbertus, would inevitably be required
(and, of course, have been deployed) many times over for Engels's and Marx's
own Utopian 'planning'.[24]

But such few perceptions on the part of Engels come under the category of
what he himself once called 'howlers'. Apart from them, ultimate communism was naively to achieve the transcendence of both work and the division
of labour. But that is not all. Along with the transcendence and negation of
private property will come the negation of virtually all aspects of modern
civilization, which Marx also considered 'subsidiary modes of production'
alienating man from his supposed true nature. Thus:

Religion, the family, the state, law, morality, science, art, etc., are only *particular*
modes of production, and fall under its general law. The positive transcendence of
private property, as the appropriation of *human* living, is, therefore the positive
transcendence of all alienation and thus the return of man from religion, the
family, the state, etc., to his *human*, i.e. *social* existence. (Italics are Marx's)[25]

But if all these cherished institutions are to be rudely stripped from man,
what then remains to this poor, 'liberated' creature? For make no mistake,

these post-Marxian creatures would be deprived of all human interrelations that make up a society. These 'complete' individuals would be deprived of law, family, custom, religion, and, of course, of all exchange of goods and services, i.e. they would be complete, hermetically sealed creatures each isolated from everyone else. Ironically, then, leftists who habitually though falsely denounce individualist thinkers for advocating a world of isolated 'atomistic', hermetically sealed individuals, themselves worship a theorist whose vision of the ideal future is precisely of such a monstrous world. At the same time, of course, each will have the consolation of knowing that they are all trivial particles in a mighty collective organism now united with 'itself' – and that any vagueness or inconsistency in this picture will be resolved by the sorcery of the 'dialectic', in which all contradictions transcend their negations into a higher unity.[26]

What will allegedly be left to man under communism is a new and bizarre form of art or aesthetics. Man will be stripped of wealth and possessions, but he will be far 'richer' in another sense: unalienated, and fulfilling himself in all directions, he will approach his own creations rich in the appreciation of beauty. He will be, in the words of Marx in 'Private Property and Communism', a *'rich man profoundly endowed with all the senses'*, he will realize his natural tendency to arrange all things 'according to the laws of beauty'. Until communism man's appreciation of beauty had been sullied by greed and possession. But, for Marx, *having*, possessing, implies the 'simple alienation of all the [physical and spiritual] human senses...'.

Professor Tucker, who has done much to explicate Marx's vision of communism, concludes that 'economic activity will turn into artistic activity...and the planet itself will become the new man's work of art. The alienated world will give way to the aesthetic world'. But, if ultimate communism abandons and eliminates all sense of having, of ownership, in order to liberate man for purely aesthetic creation and contemplation, then communism *itself* must be transcended, since even communism implies some form of having or possessing. As Tucker points out, 'Consequently, the final condition of man will be beyond all ownership, beyond the property principle, and in this sense *beyond communism'.*[27] Hence Marx ends his fullest discussion of communism (in 'Private Property and Communism') with these faintly ominous sentences:

> Communism is the position as the negation of the negation, and hence the *actual* phase necessary for the next stage of historical development in the process of human emancipation and recovery. *Communism* is the necessary pattern and the dynamic principle of the immediate future, but communism as such is not the goal of human development – the structure of human society.[28]

So what is the final stage *even beyond* communism, the final-final *Aufhebung*, the great transcendence, the ultimate negation? It is a world beyond all ownership and all possession, a world fully liberated for the spontaneous flowering of all faculties in all directions and for the unsullied, totally sensate appreciation of pure beauty. We may be pardoned for concluding that, wittingly or unwittingly – and with Marx it is difficult to know which – the final-final stage is the stage of the graveyard for the human race. After the turmoil and upheaval of all the *Aufhebungs* will come the 'peace' of a universal cemetery. For no possession, no use of resources, means rapid and universal starvation. Deprived of all labour for productive goals and of all possessions, mankind will have precious little time left for the appreciation of pure beauty.

Whether or not they saw the full horror of Marx's ultimate 'positive humanism', there is no doubt that the Soviets were always uneasy at the thought of this abyss. The Soviet editor of a Russian translation of Marx's manuscripts, published in 1956, on analysing the above passage, asserts that by 'communism as such' Marx meant raw communism of the initial stage. But this is almost a wilful misinterpretation of Marx's final words on beyond the ultimate stage. The Soviets had trouble enough with the 'withering away of the State' in the highest stage of communism, which to them meant at most a shift from official state ownership of all resources to ownership by 'social' or 'administrative' organizations, officially proclaimed as non-states.[29] The reason that Marx suppressed the publication of this essay in his lifetime seems similar to the Soviet's burying of their allegedly final-final goal. To say that even the Marxist public is 'not yet ready for it' is a rich understatement; one trusts that they never will be.

In socialist practice, of course, while communist countries never got to the 'highest stage', there seemed to be little evidence of either a notable appreciation of beauty or of great spontaneous or artistic creativity. Perhaps even the relative physical deprivation rather than the rapid and absolute starvation of 'beyond communism' of twentieth century socialist regimes was responsible for the grey and grim cast universally acknowledged to pervade these countries.

But of course all these problems are neatly buried by the pervasive but implicit premise underlying all of Marx's discussions of communism: the unsupported, unquestioned assumption that throughout all these changes, production remains happily abundant, if not superabundant. Hence the economic problem is simply and quietly assumed away.

Some might protest that, in our discussion of communism, we have not mentioned the feature that is generally considered the hallmark of that system: the slogan, 'From each according to his ability, to each according to his needs'. This phrase seems to contradict our view that the essence of the communist society is a secularized religion rather than economics. The *locus classicus*, however, of Marx's proclamation of this well-known slogan of French socialism, was in the course of his vitriolic *Critique of the Gotha Program* in 1875, in which Marx denounced the Lassallean deviationists who were forming the new German Social Democratic Party. And it is clear from the context of his discussion that this slogan is of minor and peripheral importance to Marx. In point 3 of his *Critique*, Marx is denouncing the clause of the programme calling for communization of property and 'equitable distribution of the proceeds of labour'. In the course of his discussion, Marx states that inequality of labour income is 'inevitable in the first stage of communist society,...when it has just emerged after prolonged birth pangs from capitalist society. Right can never be higher than the economic structure of society and the cultural development thereby determined'. On the other hand, Marx goes on,

> In a higher phase of communist society, after the enslaving subordination of individuals under division of labour, and therewith also the antithesis between mental and physical labour, has vanished; after...the productive forces have also increased with the all-round development of the individual, and all the springs of cooperative wealth flow more abundantly – only then can the narrow horizon of bourgeois right be fully left behind and society inscribe on its banners: from each according to his ability, to each according to his needs![30]

It should be evident from this passage and its context that Marx's final sentence, far from being the point and the culmination of his discussion, was stated briefly only to be dismissed. What Marx is saying is that the key to the communist world is not any such principle of the distribution of goods, but the eradication of the division of labour, the all-round development of individual faculties, and the resulting flow of superabundance. In such a world, the famous slogan becomes of only trivial importance. Indeed, Marx proceeds immediately after this passage to denounce talk among socialists of 'equal right' and 'equitable distribution' as 'ideological nonsense about "right" and other trash common among the democrats and French Socialists...'. He then quickly adds that 'it was in general incorrect to make a fuss about so-called "distribution" and put the principal stress on it'.[31,32]

The absolute misery and horror of the ultimate stage (and *a fortiori* of the beyond-ultimate stage) of communism should now be all too apparent. The eradication of the division of labour would quickly bring starvation and economic misery to all. The abolition of all structures of human interrelation would bring enormous social and spiritual deprivation to every person. And, even the alleged 'artistic' intellectual and creative development of all man's faculties in all directions would be totally crippled by the ban on all specialization. How can true intellectual development or creation come without concentrated effort? In short, the terrible economic suffering of mankind under communism would be fully matched by its intellectual and spiritual deprivation. Considering the nature and consequences of communism, to call this horrific dystopia a noble and 'humanist' ideal can at best be considered a grisly joke, in questionable taste. The prevalent notion, for example, that Marxian communism is a glorious ideal for man perverted by the later Engels or by Lenin or Stalin, can now be put into proper perspective. None of the horrors committed by Lenin, Stalin, or other Marxist–Leninist regimes can match the monstrousness of Marx's communist 'ideal'. Perhaps the closest approximation was the short-lived communist regime of Pol Pot in Cambodia which, in attempting to abolish the division of labour, managed to enforce the outlawry of money – so that for their tiny rations the populace was totally dependent upon the niggardly largesse of the communist cadre. Moreover, they attempted to eliminate the 'contradictions between town and country', by following the Engels goal of destroying large cities, and by coercively depopulating the capital, Phnom Penh, overnight. In a few short years, the Pol Pot group managed to exterminate one-third of the Cambodian population, perhaps a record in genocide.[33]

Since under ideal communism everyone could and would have to do everything, it is clear that, even before universal starvation set in, very little could get done. To Marx himself, all differences among individuals were 'contradictions' to be eliminated under communism, so that presumably the mass of individuals would have to be uniform and interchangeable.[34] Whereas Marx apparently postulated normal intellectual capabilities even under communism, to later Marxists, it seems that difficulties could be alleviated by the emergence of superhuman beings. To Karl Kautsky (1854–1938), the German Marxist who assumed the mantle of the top leadership of Marxism upon the death of Engels in 1895, under communism 'a new type of man will arise...a superman...an exalted man'. Leon Trotsky waxed even more lyrical: 'Man will become incomparably stronger, wiser, finer. His body more harmonious, his movements more rhythmical, his voice more musical...The human average will rise to the level of an Aristotle, a Goethe, a Marx. Above these other heights new peaks will arise'. If the beyond ultimate stage of communism ever lasts long enough to breed a new super-race, we may safely leave it to the communist theoreticians of that future day to resolve the problem of whether the 'contradiction' of 'permitting' a super-Aristotle to tower over an Aristotle may be allowed to exist.[35]

Neither should libertarians be taken in by the Marxian goal of the 'withering away of the State' under communism, or in the use of the phrase, borrowed from the cherished aim of the French free market libertarians Charles Comte and Charles Dunoyer: a world where the 'government of persons is replaced by the administration of things'. There are two major flaws in this formulation from the *laissez-faire* libertarian viewpoint. First, of course, as the Russian anarcho-communist Mikhail Bakunin (1814–76) insistently pointed out: it is absurd to try to reach statelessness via the absolute maximization of state power in a totalitarian dictatorship of the proletariat (or more realistically a select vanguard of the said proletariat). The result can only be maximum statism and hence maximum slavery. As perhaps the first of the 'new class' theorists, and anticipating the iron law of oligarchy of Michels and Mosca, Bakunin prophetically warned that a minority ruling class will once again, after the Marxian revolution, rule the majority:

> But the Marxists say, this minority will consist of the workers. Yes, no doubt...of former workers, who, as soon as they become governors or representatives of the people, cease to be workers and start looking down on the working masses from the heights of state authority, so that they represent not the people but themselves and their own claim to rule over others. Anyone who can doubt this knows nothing of human nature...The terms 'scientific socialist' and 'scientific socialism', which we meet incessantly in the works and speeches of the...Marxists, are sufficient to prove that the so-called people's state will be nothing but a despotism over the masses, exercised by a new and quite small aristocracy of real or bogus 'scientists'. ...They [the Marxists] claim that only dictatorship, their own of course, can bring the people freedom; we reply that a dictatorship can have no other aim than to perpetuate itself, and that it can engender and foster nothing but slavery in the people subjected to it. Freedom can be created only by freedom...[36]

Indeed, only a believer in the preposterous necromancy of the 'dialectic' could believe otherwise, that is, could believe that a totalitarian state can inevitably and virtually instantly be transformed into its opposite, and that therefore the way to get rid of the state is to work as hard as possible to maximize its power.

But the problem of the dialectic is not the only, indeed not even the main, problem with Marxian communism. For Marxism shares with the anarchists a grave problem of the higher stage of pure communism, assuming for a moment that it could ever be reached. The crucial point is that, both for anarchists and for Marxists, ideal communism is a world without private property, and that all property and resources will be owned and controlled in common. Indeed, the anarcho-communists' major complaint against the state is that it is allegedly the main enforcer and guarantor of private property and therefore that to abolish private property the state must also be eradicated. The truth, of course, is precisely the opposite: the state, through history, has been the main despoiler and plunderer of private property. With private property mysteriously abolished, then, the elimination of the state under communism (of either the Marxian or anarchist variety) would necessarily be a mere camouflage for a new state that would emerge to control and make decisions for communally owned resources. Except that the state would not be called such, but rather renamed something like a 'people's statistical bureau', as has already been done in Khadafy's Libya, and armed with precisely the same powers It will be small consolation to future victims, incarcerated or shot for committing 'capitalist acts between consenting adults' (to cite a phrase made popular by Robert Nozick), that their oppressors will no longer be the state but only a people's statistical bureau. The state under any other name will smell as acrid. Furthermore, it will be inevitable, under the iron law of oligarchy, that 'world communal decisions' will *have* to be undertaken by a specialized élite, so that the ruling class will inevitably reappear, under Bakuninite as well as any other form of communism.[37]

And, as we have indicated, in the 'beyond-communism' stage, the stage of universal no-ownership and therefore of no action and no use of resources, death for the entire human race would swiftly ensue.

Marx and his followers have never demonstrated any awareness of the vital importance of the problem of allocation of scarce resources. Their vision of communism is that all such economic problems are trivial, requiring neither entrepreneurship nor a price system nor genuine economic calculation – that all problems could be quickly solved by mere accounting or recording. The classic absurdity on this matter was laid down by Lenin, who accurately expressed Marx's view in declaring that the functions of entrepreneurship and of allocation of resources have been '*simplified* by capitalism to the utmost' to mere matters of accounting and to 'the extraordinarily simple operations of watching, recording, and issuing receipts, within the reach of anybody who can read and write and knows the first four rules of arithmetic'. Ludwig von Mises wryly and justly comments that Marxists and other socialists have had 'no greater perception of the essentials of economic life than the errand boy, whose only idea of the work of the entrepreneur is that he covers pieces of paper with letters and figures'.[38]

It is perhaps all too fitting that we now find that the idea of communism as a simple problem of book-keeping and registration was perhaps originated by the French apocalyptic fantast and inspirer of Marx, Théodore Dézamy.[39]

10.4   Arriving at communism

Karl Marx had a crucial problem. He was not interested, as were the scorned 'Utopian' socialists, in merely exhorting everyone to adopt the communist path to a perfect society. He did not propose to leave the attainment of communism to the imperfect free wills of mankind. He demanded a certain, 'inevitable' path, a 'law of history' that would demonstrate the absolute inevitability of history's reaching its final glory in a communist society. But here he was at a disadvantage relative to the various Christian wings of messianic communism: for, unlike them, there was here no inevitable Messiah to arrive and usher in a Kingdom of God on earth. As in the case of the post-mils, however, it was up to mankind, rather than the Messiah, to estab-lish the Kingdom. Even without a Messiah, a vigilant and growing vanguard could establish the Kingdom; and the vanguard could even help in various pre-mil versions of millennialism. So that leadership by a dedicated vanguard was very much in the messianic tradition.

As Professor Tucker points out, Marx was not lacking a moral theory. He was definitely a moralist, but a highly curious one. In his 'mythic vision', the 'good', the 'moral', consists of participating in the inevitable triumph of the proletarian revolution, while the 'bad', or 'immoral', is trying to obstruct it.

> The answer to the question as to what should be done is given in the mythic vision itself, and can be summed up in a single word: 'Participate!'...So Marx...says that it is not a matter of bringing some utopian system or other into being (i.e. of defining a social goal and purposefully endeavoring to realize it) but simply of 'consciously participating in the historical revolutionary process of society which is taking place before our very eyes'.[40]

Thus, to be moral means to be 'progressive', to be in tune with the inevita-ble future workings of the laws of history, whereas the harshest condemna-tion is reserved for those who are 'reactionary', who dare to obstruct, even with partial success, such allegedly predestined turns of events. Thus Marx-ists are particularly vehement in denouncing revolutionary moments in which the existing rule of 'progressives' is replaced by 'reactionaries', and the clock is, miraculously, in the metaphor of historicist inevitability, 'turned back'. For example: the Franco revolution against the Spanish republic, and Pinochet's overthrow of Allende in Chile.

But if a certain change is truly inevitable, *why* is it important for human agency to lend a hand, indeed to struggle mightily on its behalf? Here we turn to the critical matter of *timing*. While a change may be inevitable, the inter-vention of man can and will speed up this most desired of happenings. Man can function, in one of Marx's favourite obstetrical metaphors, as a 'midwife' of history.[41] Man's intervention could give the inevitable a helpful push.

Yet, Marx's obstetrical analogies are only a feeble attempt to evade the self-contradiction between the idea of inevitability and action to achieve the inevitable. For according to Marx, the timing as well as the nature of events is determined by the material dialectic of history. Socialism is brought about, wrote Marx in *Capital*, by the 'operation of the immanent laws of capitalistic production itself'. As von Mises points out, to Marx

> Ideas, political parties, and revolutionary actions are merely superstructural; they can neither delay nor accelerate the march of history. Socialism will come when the material conditions for its appearance will have matured in the womb [obstet-rics again!] of capitalist society, neither sooner or later. If Marx had been consist-

ent, he would not have embarked upon any political activity. He would have waited quietly for the day on which 'the knell of private capitalist property sounds'.[42]

Marx might not have been logical or consistent, but his attitude was squarely in the millennialist tradition. As Professor Tuveson points out:

Several characteristics of historical Communist movements recall millenarian agitations. There is, for one, the well-known fanaticism of millenarian believers...The firm conviction that a sequence of events, leading to universal redemption, is ordained (or 'determined') would seem to lead to passivity on the part of an individual...But, characteristically, there is a vitally important qualification. Although the series of events is prophesied, their *timing* may be retarded by the failure of mankind. To delay the coming of redemption, then, is a great sin, against one's fellow beings, against posterity, against the power that has ordained events. But whole-hearted, zealous participation in the historically determined duties, doing what the old millenarians would call 'doing God's will', gives special *éclat*. In most millenarian groups there is something corresponding to the 'Communist Party'. In Revelation itself there are the hundred and forty-four thousand, 'the first fruits unto God and to the Lamb', who are without guile, for they are 'without fault before the throne of God'. (Revelation XIV:4–5). Thus, the whole proletariat, like the whole body of the saved, is without damning fault, but the specially distinguished group...are chosen from the chosen.[43]

But there was still a remaining problem: *whence comes the inevitability* in the Marxian schema? The proof that his cherished communist ideal would inevitably, 'scientifically' arrive, would occupy Marx for the rest of his life. Certainly, he found the outlines of such proof in the mysterious workings of the Hegelian dialectic, which he bent to his use.

10.5 Marx's character and his path to communism

Karl Marx, as the world knows, was born in Trier, a venerable city in Rhineland Prussia, in 1818, son of a distinguished jurist, and grandson of a rabbi. Indeed, both of Marx's parents were descended from rabbis. Marx's father Heinrich was a liberal rationalist who felt no great qualms about his forced conversion to official Lutheranism in 1816. What is little known is that, in his early years, the baptized Karl was a dedicated Christian. In his graduation essays from the Trier *gymnasium* in 1835, the very young Marx prefigured his later development. His essay on an assigned topic, 'On the Union of the Faithful with Christ' was orthodox evangelical Christian, but it also contained hints of the fundamental 'alienation' theme that he would later find in Hegel. Marx's discussion of the 'necessity for union' with Christ stressed that this union would put an end to the tragedy of God's alleged rejection of man. In a companion essay, 'Reflections of a Young Man on the Choice of a Profession', Marx expressed a worry about his own 'demon of ambition', of the great temptation he felt to 'inveigh against the Deity and curse mankind'.

Going first to the University of Bonn and then off to the prestigious new University of Berlin to study law, Marx soon converted to militant atheism, shifted his major to philosophy, and joined a *Doktorklub* of young (or Left) Hegelians, of which he soon became a leader and general secretary.

The shift to atheism quickly gave Marx's demon of ambition full rein. Particularly revelatory of Marx's adult as well as youthful character are volumes of poems, most of them lost until a few were recovered in recent years.[44] Historians, when they discuss these poems, tend to dismiss them as inchoate romantic yearnings, but they are too congruent with the adult Marx's social and revolutionary doctrines to be casually dismissed. Surely, here seems to be a case where a unified (early plus late) Marx is vividly revealed. Thus in his poem 'Feelings', dedicated to his childhood sweetheart and later wife Jenny von Westphalen, Marx expressed both his megalomania and his enormous thirst for destruction:

> Heaven I would comprehend
>   I would draw the world to me;
> Living, hating, I intend
>   That my star shine brilliantly...

and

> ...Worlds I would destroy forever,
> Since I can create no world;
>   Since my call they notice never...

Here is a classical expression of Satan's supposed reason for hating, and rebelling against, God.

In another poem, Marx writes of his triumph after he shall have destroyed God's created world:

> Then I will be able to walk triumphantly,
>   Like a god, through the ruins of their kingdom.
> Every word of mine is fire and action.
>   My breast is equal to that of the Creator.

And in his poem, 'Invocation of One in Despair', Marx writes:

> I shall build my throne high overhead
>   Cold, tremendous shall its summit be.

> For its bulwark – superstitious dread
> For its marshal – blackest agony.[45]

The Satan theme is most explicitly set forth in Marx's 'The Fiddler', dedicated to his father:

> See this sword?
>   the prince of darkness
> Sold it to me.

And:

> With Satan I have struck my deal,
>   He chalks the signs, beats time for me
> I play the death march fast and free.

Particularly instructive is Marx's lengthy, unfinished poetic drama of this youthful period, *Oulanem, A Tragedy*. In the course of this drama his hero Oulanem, delivers a remarkable soliloquy, pouring out sustained invective, a hatred of the world and of mankind, a hatred of creation and a threat and vision of total world destruction.

Thus Oulanem pours out his vials of wrath.

> ...I shall howl gigantic curses on mankind:
>   Ha! Eternity! She is an eternal grief...
> Ourselves being clockwork, blindly mechanical,
>   Made to be the foul-calendars of Time and Space,
> Having no purpose save to happen, to be ruined,
>   So that there shall be something to ruin...
> If there is a something which devours,
>   I'll leap within it, though I bring the world to ruins–
> The world which bulks between me and the Abyss
>   I will smash to pieces with my enduring curses.
> I'll throw my arms around its harsh reality:
>   Embracing me, the world will dumbly pass away,
> And then sink down to utter nothingness,
>   Perished, with no existence – that would be really living!

And

> ...the leaden world holds us fast,
>   And we are chained, shattered, empty, frightened,

Eternally chained to this marble block of Being...
and we –
We are the apes of a cold God.[46]

All this reveals a spirit that often seems to animate militant atheism. In contrast to the non-militant variety, which expresses a simple disbelief in God's existence, militant atheism seems to believe implicitly in God's existence, but to hate Him and to wage war for His destruction. Such a spirit was all too clearly revealed in the retort of the militant atheist Bakunin to the famous pro-theist remark of the deist Voltaire: 'If God did not exist, it would be necessary to create Him." To which the demented Bakunin retorted: 'If God did exist, it would be necessary to destroy Him." It was this hatred of God as a creator greater than himself that apparently inspired Karl Marx.

Also prefiguring the man was a trait that Marx developed early in his youth and never relinquished: a shameless sponging on friends and relatives. Already in early 1837, Heinrich Marx, castigating his son Karl's wanton spending of the money of others, wrote to him that 'on one point... you have wisely found fit to observe an aristocratic silence; I am referring to the paltry matter of money'. Indeed, Marx took money from any source available: his father, mother, and throughout his adult life, his long-suffering friend and abject disciple, Friedrich Engels, all of whom fuelled Marx's capacity for spending money like water.[47]

An insatiable spender of other people's money, Marx continually complained about a shortage of financial means. While sponging on Engels, Marx perpetually complained to his friend that his largess was never enough. Thus, in 1868, Marx insisted that he could not make do on an annual income of less than £400–£500, a phenomenal sum considering that the *upper tenth* of Englishmen in that period were earning an average income of only £72 a year. Indeed, so profligate was Marx that he quickly ran through an inheritance from a German follower of £824 in 1864, as well as a gift of £350 from Engels in the same year.

In short, Marx was able to run through the munificent sum of almost £1200 in two years, and two years later accept another gift of £210 from Engels to pay off his newly accumulated debts. Finally, in 1868, Engels sold his share of the family cotton mill and settled upon Marx an annual 'pension' of £350 from then on. Yet Marx's continual complaints about money did not abate.[48]

As in the case of many other spongers and cadgers throughout history, Karl Marx affected a hatred and contempt for the very material resource he was so anxious to cadge and use so recklessly. The difference is that Marx created an entire philosophy around his own corrupt attitudes toward money. Man, he thundered, was in the grip of the 'fetishism' of money. The problem was the existence of this evil thing, not the voluntarily adopted attitudes of some people toward it. Money Marx reviled as 'the pander between...human life and the means of sustenance', the 'universal whore'. The utopia of communism was a society where this scourge, money, would be abolished.

Karl Marx, the self-proclaimed enemy of the exploitation of man by man, not only exploited his devoted friend Friedrich Engels financially, but also psychologically. Thus, only three months after Marx's wife, Jenny von Westphalen, gave birth to his daughter Franziska in March 1851, their live-in maid, Helene ('Lenchen') Demuth, whom Marx had 'inherited' from Jenny's aristocratic family, also gave birth to Marx's illegitimate son, Henry Frederick. Desperately anxious to keep up *haute bourgeois* conventions and to hold his marriage together, Karl never acknowledged his son, and, instead, persuaded Engels, a notorious womanizer, to proclaim the baby as his own. Both Marx and Engels treated the hapless Freddy extremely badly, Engels's presumed resentment at being so used providing him a rather better excuse. Marx boarded Freddy out continually, and never allowed him to visit his mother. As Fritz Raddatz, a biographer of Marx, declared, 'if Henry Frederick Demuth was Karl Marx's son, the new mankind's Preacher lived an almost lifelong lie, and scorned, humiliated, and disowned his only surviving son'.[49] Engels, of course, picked up the tab for Freddy's education. Freddy was trained, however, to take his place in the working class, far from the lifestyle of his natural father, the quasi-aristocratic leader of the world's downtrodden revolutionary proletariat.[50,51]

Marx's personal taste for the aristocracy was lifelong. As a young man, he attached himself to his neighbour, Jenny's father Baron Ludwig von Westphalen, and dedicated his doctoral thesis to the baron. Indeed, the snobbish proletarian communist always insisted that Jenny imprint 'née von Westphalen' on her calling card.

10.6   Notes

1. Ernest L. Tuveson, 'The Millenarian Structure of *The Communist Manifesto*', in C.A. Patrides and Joseph Wittreich (eds), *The Apocalypse: in English Renaissance Thought and Literature* (Ithaca: Cornell University Press, 1984), pp. 326–7. Tuveson speculates that Marx and Engels may have been influenced by the outburst of millenarianism in England during the 1840s. On this phenomenon, particularly the flare-up in England and the US of the Millerites, who predicted the end of the world on 22 October 1844, see the classic work on modern millenarianism, Ernest R. Sandeen, *The Roots of Fundamentalism: British and American Millenarianism, 1800–1930* (Chicago: University of Chicago Press, 1970). See Tuveson, ibid., p. 340, n. 5.

2. Jean B. Quandt, 'Religion and Social Thought: The Secularization of Postmillennialism', *American Quarterly*, 25 (Oct. 1973), pp. 402–3. Actually, Ely, in common with many other post-mils, was not all *that* gradual, as he spoke of the New Jerusalem, 'which we are all eagerly awaiting'.

3. Quoted in S.V. Utechin, 'Philosophy and Society: Alexander Bogdanov', in Leopold Labedz (ed.), *Revisionism: Essays on the History of Marxist Ideas* (New York: Praeger, 1962), p. 122.

4. J.P. Stern, 'Marxism on Stilts: Review of Ernst Bloch, *The Principle of Hope*', *The New*

Republic, 196 (9 March 1987), pp. 40, 42; Leszek Kolakowski, *Main Currents of Marxism* (Oxford: Oxford University Press, 1984), III, pp. 423–4.

5. G.K. Chesterton, *Orthodoxy* (New York: 1927), pp. 244–5. Quoted in Thomas Molnar, *Utopia: the Perennial Heresy* (New York: Sheed & Ward, 1964), p. 123.

6. 'The C.P.S.U. [Communist Party of the Soviet Union], being a party of scientific communism, advances and solves the problems of communist construction as the material and spiritual prerequisites for them become ready and mature, being guided by the fact that necessary stages of development must not be skipped over...'. *Fundamentals of Marxism—Leninism* (2nd rev. ed., Moscow: Foreign Languages Publishing House, 1963), p. 662. Also see ibid., pp. 645–6, 666–7, 674–5.

7. On alienation and the dialectic, see Chapter 11.

8. Stein treated French socialism and communism as ideologies of the propertyless proletariat, aiming to destroy the historical foundations of European society based on the principles of individual personality and private property. The difference of course, is that Marx, in contrast to the other 'classless' socialists and communists, embraced this connection to the proletariat, whereas Stein condemned and warned against it. See the excellent and illuminating work by Robert C. Tucker, *Philosophy and Myth in Karl Marx* (Cambridge: Cambridge University Press, 1961), pp. 114–7. Stein's book, Lorenz von Stein, *Der Socialismus und Communismus des Heutigen Frankreichs* (Leipzig: 1842), remains untranslated. (Later editions were entitled *Geschichte des socialen Bewegung in Frankreich*, 1850, 1921). Stein spent his mature years as professor of public finance and public administration at the University of Vienna, 1855–88.

9. Quoted in Tucker, op. cit., note 8, pp. 155. Italics are Marx's.

10. Indeed, it is no accident that Marxian historians, from Engels to Ernst Bloch, have been great admirers of these regimes and movements, first, because of their communism, and second, because they were certainly 'people's movements', bubbling up from the lower classes.

11. Tucker, op. cit., note 8, pp. 155–6.

12. *Anti-Dühring* became the common name for Engels's *Herr Eugen Dühring's Revolution in Science*, which came out in 1878, five years before Marx's death. Three general chapters, not focused on Dühring, came out in French in 1880, as *Socialism: Utopian and Scientific*, which became second to the *Communist Manifesto* as a popular presentation of Marxism in the late nineteenth century. The English translation, authorized by Engels, was published in 1892, and therefore Engels must be held responsible for such a clumsy locution as the verb 'environ'. See R.C. Tucker (ed.), *The Marx-Engels Reader* (2nd ed., New York: W.W. Norton, 1972), pp. 715–6.

13. Tucker, op. cit., note 8, pp. 196–7.

14. Ibid., p. 198.

15. Tucker, op. cit., note 12, p. 160. Similarly, in his *Anti-Dühring*, Engels heaped scorn upon the sort of 'Prussian socialism' which would preserve the division of labour as 'inevitable in the nature of things'. In contrast, Engels proclaimed that in the future communism, 'In time to come there will no longer be any professional porters or architects, and that the man who for half an hour gives instructions as an architect will also push a barrow for a period, until his activity as an architect is once again required'. Ibid., p. 718. In this spirit, Maoist China, during the Cultural Revolution, randomly substituted surgeons and janitors for each other in hospitals.

Finally, in his *Woman and Socialism* (1883), the faithful German Marxist and working-class organizer, August Bebel (1840–1913), paraphrased Marx's passage for the role of women under communism: 'At one moment a practical worker in some industry she is in the next hour educator, teacher, and nurse: in the third part of the day she exercises some art or cultivates a science; and in the fourth part she fulfills some administrative function'. Quoted in Ludwig von Mises, *Socialism: An Economic and Sociological Analysis* (Indianapolis: Liberty Classics, 1981), p. 168n.

16. Alexander Gray, *The Socialist Tradition* (London: Longmans, Green, 1946), p. 328.

17. Tucker, op. cit., note 12, p. 723.

18. Tucker, op. cit., note 8, p. 197n.

19. On the debate within the Soviet Union on this issue, see Herman Akhminov, 'The Prospects for the Division of Labor', *Bulletin of the Institute for the Study of the USSR* (July 1964), pp 3–18.
20. Friedrich Engels, 'On Authority', written in 1872 and first published in an Italian collection in 1874. Tucker, op. cit., note 12, p. 731.
21. English translation by William O. Henderson, *The Life of Friedrich Engels* (London: Frank Cass, 1976) I, pp. 369–76. Cited in T.W. Hutchison, *The Politics and Philosophy of Economics: Marxians, Keynesians and Austrians* (Oxford: Basil Blackwell, 1981), pp. 9–12, 14.
22. On Ricardian socialists, and on Rodbertus's business cycle theory, see Chapter 13 below. Rodbertus was an independently wealthy Prussian politician and civil servant, who lived most of his life as a leisured and erudite Prussian country squire. (He purchased an estate near the town of Jagetzow in East Prussia, and promptly renamed himself Rodbertus von Jagetzow.) His basic thrust was that labour is bound down by the iron or brazen law of wages (so named by Lassalle, as we shall see below), but that justice can be imposed by socialism run by the state, a literally divine, self-creative living organism, best headed by the king (in short, a monarchical socialism). Rodbertus sternly warned, however, that people are not yet moral enough for such socialism – and would not be for another five hundred years. See Gray, op. cit., note 16, pp. 343–51.
23. Hutchison, op. cit., note 21, p. 15. Hutchison points out that 'Engels's warning regarding imbalances in the supply of trousers and trouser buttons has recently acquired embarrassing relevance' in Soviet Russia. In 1980, *Pravda* (Moscow) had complained that, in regard to priority of supply, 'in the clothing industry trousers are on the list of the "most important", but zip-fasteners are not'. Ibid., p. 20n.
24. Ibid., pp. 15–16.
25. 'Private Property and Communism', in Tucker, op. cit., note 12, p. 85.
26. As Tucker puts it, 'Socialized humanity is not only a classless but also a stateless, lawless, family-less, religion-less and generally structure-less collectivity of complete individuals who live in harmony with themselves, with each other, and with the anthropological nature outside them. It hardly needs pointing out that this society without social structure is not a social order in any meaningful sense of that term. Speaking in the younger Marx's vein, it is an un-society'. Tucker, op cit., note 8, p. 201.
27. Ibid., pp. 158–61.
28. Tucker, op. cit., note 12, p. 93.
29. The Soviet version of ultimate communism hardly differed from the first stage, of Soviet life itself. All the central, new, disturbing messianic or bizarre features of communism are played down or buried. Thus, to the Soviets, higher or true communism was *not* the end of history, but merely a society that 'will change and improve continuously'. Communist abundance will emphatically *not* be fabulous lands flowing with milk and honey'. There will simply be 'rapid and continuous advance' of 'socialist science and technology' *Fundamentals of Marxism Leninism*, op. cit., note 6, pp. 698–9, and pp. 698–717.
30. Karl Marx, *Critique of the Gotha Programme* (New York: International Publishers, 1938), p. 10. The critique was first published by Engels in 1891, after Marx's death. The Lassalleans were followers of the late Ferdinand Lasalle (1825 64) a blowhard and dandy who was extremely popular in Germany, especially beloved by the working class, and the pre-eminent organizer of the proletariat. Typically, Lassalle died early in a most unproletarian and aristocratic way – in a duel over a lady. One of Lasalle's two major deviations from Marxism was his ultra-Malthusian devotion to the Malthus–Ricardo subsistence theory of wages as determined by population growth, which he popularized in the most rigid form, and allegedly named the 'iron law of wages', in which form it won widespread fame. In reality, Lassalle dubbed it the 'brazen law of wages' (in the sense of 'made of brass'), and his most common locution was 'the brazen and gruesome law of wages' (*das eherne und grausame Gesetz*).

Lassalle's other and more important deviation was his embrace and worship of the state. Marx saw the state as a tyrannical instrument of mass exploitation which required a violent revolution to overthrow. Lassalle, in Hegelian fashion, on the other hand, worshipped the state as a guide and developer of freedom, as the fusion of man into a spiritual whole, and as an eternal instrument for moral regeneration. The only problem with the state, for Lassalle, was the fact that it was not yet controlled by the workers, but this could be rectified simply by enacting universal suffrage, after which the state would be run by a workers' party and the workers would then *become* the state and all would be well. The state would promptly transfer the control of production to workers' associations which would thus circumvent the brazen law by appropriating to themselves the surplus profits now extracted by the capitalists. See Gray, op. cit., note 16, pp. 332–43.

31. Actually, Marx goes on to make a useful point: that distribution always flows from the 'conditions of production' and cannot be separated from it. One would like to think that this was not only an argument against the 'vulgar socialists' but also an implicit slap at J.S. Mill, who thought that while production was bound by economic law, 'distribution' could be separated from production and reformed by state action.

32. See the excellent discussion of this point in Tucker, op. cit., note 8, p. 200.

33. The Soviet people were spared the full cataclysm of communism when Lenin, a master pragmatist, drew back from the early Soviet attempt (1918–21) to abolish money and leap into communism (later deliberately mislabelled 'war communism'), and went back to the largely capitalist economy of the New Economic Policy. Mao tried to bring about communism in two disastrous surges: the Great Leap Forward, which attempted to eliminate private property and to eliminate the 'contradictions' between town and country by building a steel plant in every backyard; and the Great Proletarian Cultural Revolution, which tried to eliminate the 'contradiction' between intellectual and manual labour by shipping an entire generation of students to forced labour in the wilds of Sinkiang. On the myth of 'war communism', see the illuminating discussion in Paul Craig Roberts, *Alienation and the Soviet Economy* (Alburquerque: University of New Mexico Press, 1971), pp. 20–47.

34. In an amusing note, during the New Left period of the late 1960s, the *Liberated Guardian* broke off from the quasi-Maoist journal, *The Guardian*, in New York City, on the ground that the latter functioned in the same way as any 'bourgeois' periodical, with specialized editors, typists, copy-readers, business staff, etc. The *Liberated Guardian* was run by a 'collective' in which, assertedly, every person performed every task without specialization. The same criticism, followed by the same solution, was applied by the women's caucus which confiscated the property of the New Left weekly, *Rat*. Both periodicals, as one would expect, died a mercifully swift death. See Murray N. Rothbard, *Freedom, Inequality, Primitivism, and the Division of Labor* (Menlo Park, Calif. Institute for Humane Studies, 1971), pp. 15n, 20.

35. See von Mises, op. cit., note 15, p. 143. Also see Rothbard, op. cit., note 34, pp. 8–15.

36. Bakunin, *Statehood and Anarchy*: quoted in Leszek Kolakowski, *Main Currents of Marxism: Its Origins, Growth and Dissolution* (New York: Oxford University Press, 1981), I, pp. 251–2. See also Abram L. Harris, *Economics and Social Reform* (New York: Harper & Bros, 1958), pp. 149–50.

37. On self-ownership and on the impossibility of communal ownership, see Murray N. Rothbard, *The Ethics of Liberty* (2nd ed., Atlantic Highlands, NJ: Humanities Press, 1983), pp. 45–50.

38. Italics are Lenin's. V.I. Lenin, *State and Revolution* (New York: International Publishers, 1932), pp. 83–4; von Mises, op. cit., note 15, p. 189. Also see Harris, op. cit., note 36, pp. 152–3n.

39. See the standard biography of Marx by David McLellan, *Karl Marx: His Life and Thought* (New York: Harper & Row, 1973), p. 118.

40. Tucker, op. cit., note 8, p. 229.

41. On obstetrical metaphors in Marxism, see Gray, op. cit., note 16, p. 299 and 299n.

42. Ludwig von Mises, *Theory and History*, (1957, Auburn, Ala.: Ludwig von Mises Institute, 1985), p. 81.

43. Tuveson, op. cit., note 1, pp. 339–40.

44. The poems were largely written in 1836 and 1837, in his first months in Berlin. Two of the

poems constituted Marx's first published writings, in the *Berlin Atheneum* in 1841. The others have been mainly lost.

45.   Richard Wurmbrand, *Marx and Satan* (Westchester, Ill: Crossway Books, 1986), pp. 12–13

46.   For the complete translated text of *Oulanem*, see Robert Payne, *The Unknown Karl Marx* (New York: New York University Press, 1971), pp. 81–3. Also excellent on the poems and on Marx as fundamentally a messianist is Bruce Mazlish, *The Meaning of Karl Marx* (New York: Oxford University Press, 1984).

Pastor Wurmbrand points out that *Oulanem* is an anagram of Emmanuel, the Biblical name for Jesus, and that such inversions of holy names are standard practice in Satanic cults. There is no real evidence, however, that Marx was a member of such a cult. Wurmbrand, op. cit., note 45, pp. 13–14 and passim.

47.   Friedrich Engels (1820–95) was the son of a leading industrialist and cotton manufacturer, who was also a staunch pietist from the Barmen area of the Rhineland in Germany. Barmen was one of the major centres of pietism in Germany, and Engels received a strict pietist upbringing. An atheist and then a Hegelian by 1839, Engels wound up at the University of Berlin and the Young Hegelians by 1841, and moved in the same circles as Marx, the two becoming fast friends in 1844.

48.   See the enlightening estimates in Gary North, *Marx's Religion of Revolution: The Doctrine of Creative Destruction* (Nutley, NJ: Craig Press, 1968), pp. 26–8. Also see ibid. (2nd ed., Tyler, Texas: Institute for Christian Economics, 1989), pp. 232–56.

49.   Fritz J. Raddatz, *Karl Marx: A Political Biography* (Boston: Little Brown & Co., 1978), p. 134.

50.   Marx's zeal in covering up his indiscretion was at least matched by historians of the Marxist establishment, who managed to suppress the truth about Freddy Demuth until recent years. Although the truth was known to leading Marxists such as Bernstein and Bebel, the news of Marx's illegitimate fatherhood was only disclosed in 1962 in Werner Blumenberg's *Marx*. See in particular W.O. Henderson, *The Life of Friedrich Engels* (London: Frank Cass, 1976), II, pp. 833–4. Some loyal Marxists still refuse to accept the ugly facts. Thus, see the labour of love by the late leader of the 'Draperite' wing of the Trotskyist movement, Hal Draper, *Marx–Engels Cyclopedia* (3 vols, New York: Schocken Books, 1985).

51.   As for Engels, he refused to marry his mistress Mary because she was of 'low' descent. After Mary's death her sister Lizzie became Engels's mistress. Engels magnanimously married Lizzie on her deathbed 'in order to provide her a "last pleasure"'.

11 Alienation, unity, and the dialectic

11.1 Origins of the dialectic: creatology

'Alienation', to Marx, bears no relation to the fashionable prattle of late twentieth century Marxoid intellectuals. It did not mean a psychological feeling, of anxiety or estrangement, which could somehow be blamed on capitalism, or on cultural or sexual 'repression'. Alienation, for Marx, was far more fundamental, more cosmic. It meant, at the very least, as we have seen, the institutions of money, specialization, and the division of labour.[1] The eradication of these evils was necessary to unite the collective organism or species man 'to himself', to heal these splits within 'himself' and between man and 'himself' in the form of man-created nature. But the radical evil of alienation was yet far more cosmic than that. It was metaphysical, a deep part of the philosophy and the world-view that Marx picked up from Hegel, and which, through its allied 'dialectic', brought to Marx the outlines of the engine that would inevitably bring us communism as a law of history, with the ineluctability of a law of nature.

It all started with the third century philosopher Plotinus, a Platonist philosopher and his followers, and with a theological discipline seemingly remote from political and economic affairs: *creatology*, the 'science' of the First Days. We have already seen, in fact, that another allied and almost equally remote branch of theology – *eschatology*, or the science of the Last Days – can have enormous political and economic consequences and ramifications.

The critical question of creatology is: why did God create the universe? The answer of orthodox Augustinian Christianity, and hence the answer of Catholics, Lutherans, and Calvinists alike, is that God, a perfect being, created the universe out of benevolence and love for His creatures. Period. And this seems to be the only politically safe answer as well. The answer given by heretics and mystics from early Christians on, however, is quite different: God created the universe not out of perfection and love, but out of felt need and imperfection. In short, God created the universe out of felt uneasiness, loneliness, or whatever. In the beginning, before the creation of the universe, God and man (the collective organic species, of course, not any particular individual), were united in one, so to speak, cosmic blob. How we can even speak of 'unity' between man and God before man was even created is a conundrum that will have to be cleared up by someone more schooled in the divine mysteries than the present author. At any rate, history then becomes a process, indeed a pre-ordained process, by which God develops *His* potential, and man the collective species develops *its* (or his?) potential. But even as this development takes place, and both God and man develop and render themselves more perfect in and through history, offsetting this 'good' development a terrible and tragic thing has also taken place: man has been separated, cut off, 'alienated' from God, as well as from other men, or from nature. Hence the pervasive concept of alienation.

Alienation is cosmic, irremediable, and metaphysical, inherent in the very process of creation, or rather, irremediable until the great day inevitably arrives: when man and God, having both fully developed themselves, finish the process and history itself by re-merging, by uniting once again in the merger of these two great cosmic blobs into one.

Note, first, how this great historical process comes about. It is the inevitable, pre-ordained 'dialectical' process of history. There are, as usual, three stages. Stage one is the original phase: man and God are in happy and harmonious unity (a unity of pre-creation?) but things, particularly with the human race, are rather undeveloped. Then, the magic dialectic does its work, stage two occurs, and God creates man and the universe, both God and man developing their potentials, with history a record and a process of such development. But creation, as in most dialectics, proves to be a two-edged sword, for man suffers from his cosmic separation and alienation from God. For Plotinus, for example, the Good is unity, or The One, whereas Evil is identified as any sort of diversity or multiplicity. In mankind, evil stems from self-centredness of individual souls, 'deserter[s] from the All'.

But then, finally, at long last, the development process will be completed, and stage two develops its own *Aufhebung*, its own 'lifting up', its own transcendence into its opposite or negation: the reunion of God and man into a glorious unity, an 'ecstasy of union', and end to alienation. In this stage three, the blobs are reunited on a far higher level than in stage one. History is over. And they shall all live(?) happily ever after.

But note the enormous difference between this dialectic of creatology and eschatology, and that of the orthodox Christian scenario. In the first place, the alienation, the tragedy of man in the dialectical saga from Plotinus to Hegel, is metaphysical, inescapable from the act of creation itself. Whereas the estrangement of man from God in the Judeo-Christian saga is not metaphysical but only moral. To orthodox Christians, creation was purely good, and not deeply tainted with evil; trouble came only with Adam's Fall, a moral failure not a metaphysical one.[2] Then, in the orthodox Christian view, through the Incarnation of Jesus, God provided a route by which this alienation could be eliminated, and the individual could achieve salvation. But note again: Christianity is a deeply individualistic creed, since each individual's salvation is what matters. Salvation or the lack of it will be attained by each individual, each individual's fate is the central concern, not the fate of the alleged collective blob or organism, man with a capital M. In the orthodox Christian schema, each individual goes to Heaven or Hell.

But in this allegedly optimistic mystical view (nowadays called 'process theology'), the only salvation, the only happy ending is that of the collective organism, the species, with each individual member of that organism being brusquely annihilated along the way.

This dialectical theology, in particular its creatology, began in full flower with the Plotinus-influenced ninth century Christian mystic John Scotus Erigena (c. 815 – c. 877) an Irish–Scottish philosopher located in France, and continued through a heretical underground of Christian mystics, in particular such as the fourteenth century German, Meister Johannes Eckhart (?1260 – ?1327). The pantheistic outlook of the mystics was similar to the call of the Buddhist–theosophist–socialist Mrs Annie Besant: as Chesterton perceptively and wittily noted, not to love our neighbour but to *be* our neighbour. Pantheist mystics call upon each individual to 'unite' with God, the One, by annihilating his individual, separated, and therefore alienated self. While the means of various mystics may differ from the Joachites, or the Brethren of the Free Spirit, whether through a process of history or through an inevitable Armageddon, the *goal* remains the same: obliteration of the individual through 'reunion' with God, the One, and the ending of cosmic 'alienation', at least on the level of each individual.

Particularly influential for G.W.F. Hegel and other thinkers in this tradition was the early seventeenth century German cobbler and mystic Jacob Boehme (1575–1624), who added to this heady pantheistic brew the alleged mechanism, the force that drives this dialectic through its inevitable course in history. How, Boehme asked, did the world of pre-creation transcend itself into creation? Before creation, he answered, there was a primal source, an eternal unity, an undifferentiated, indistinct, literal Nothing (*Ungrund*). (It was, by the way, typical of Hegel and his Idealist followers to think that they add grandeur and explanation to a lofty but unintelligible concept by capitalizing it.) Oddly enough, to Boehme, this No-thing possessed within itself an inner striving, a *nisus*, a drive for self-realization. It is this drive which creates a transcending and opposing force, the *will*, which creates the universe, transforming the Nothing into Something.

11.2 Hegel and the man–God

The key step in secularizing dialectic theology, and thus in paving the way for Marxism, was taken by the lion of German philosophy, Georg Wilhelm Friedrich Hegel (1770–1831). Born in Stuttgart, Hegel studied theology at the University of Tübingen, and then taught theology and philosophy at the Universities of Jena and Heidelberg before becoming the leading philosopher at the new jewel in the Prussian academic crown, the University of Berlin. Coming to Berlin in 1817, Hegel remained there until his death, ending his days as rector of the university.

In the spirit of the Romantic movement in Germany, Hegel pursued the goal of unifying man and God by virtually identifying God as man, and thereby submerging the former into the latter. Goethe had recently popularized the Faust theme, centring on Faust's intense desire for divine, or absolute knowledge, as well as divine power. In orthodox Christianity, of course, the overweening pride of man in trying to achieve god-like knowledge and power is precisely the root cause of sin and man's Fall. But, on the contrary, Hegel, a most heretical Lutheran indeed, had the temerity to generalize the Faustian urge into a world-philosophy, and into an alleged insight into the inevitable workings of the historical process.

In Professor Tucker's words, Hegelianism was a 'philosophic religion of self in the form of a theory of history. The religion is founded on an identification of the self with God'.[3] It should not be necessary to add at this point that 'the self' here is not the individual, but the collective organic species 'self'. In a youthful essay on 'The Positivity of the Christian Religion', written at the age of 25, Hegel revealingly objects to Christianity for 'separating' man and God except 'in one isolated individual' (Jesus), and placing God in another and higher world, to which man's activity could contribute nothing. Four years later, in 1799, Hegel resolved this problem by offering his own religion, in his 'The Spirit of Christianity'. In contrast to orthodox Christianity, in which God became man in Jesus, for Hegel Jesus's achievement was, *as a man*, to become God! Tucker sums this up neatly. To Hegel, Jesus:

> is not God become man, but man become God. This is the key idea on which the entire edifice of Hegelianism was to be constructed: there is no absolute difference between the human nature and the divine. They are not two separate things with an impassable gulf between them. The absolute self in man, the *homo noumenon*, is not mere godlike..., *it is God*. Consequently, in so far as man strives to become 'like God', he is simply striving to be his own real self. And in deifying himself, he is simply recognizing his own true nature.[4]

If man is really God, what then is history? Why does man, or rather, do men, change and develop? Because the man–God is not perfect, or at least he does not begin in a perfect state. Man–God begins his life in history totally unconscious of his divine status. History, then, for Hegel, is a process by which the man–God increases his knowledge, until he finally reaches the state of absolute knowledge, that is, the full knowledge and realization that he is God. In that case, man–God finally realizes his potential of an infinite being without bounds, possessed of absolute knowledge.

Why then did man–God, also termed by Hegel the 'world-self' (*Weltgeist*) or 'world-spirit', create the universe? Not, as in the Christian account, from overflowing love and benevolence, but out of a felt need to become conscious of itself as a world-self. This process of growing consciousness is achieved through creative activity by which the world-self externalized itself. This externalization occurs first by creating nature or the original world, but second – and here of course is a significant addition to other theologies –

there is a continuing self-externalization through human history. The most important is this second process, for by this means man, the collective organism, expands his building of civilization, his creative externalizing, and *hence* his increasing knowledge of his own divinity, and therefore of the world as his own self-actualization. This latter process: of knowing ever more fully that the world is really man's self, is the process which Hegel terms the gradual putting to an end of man's 'self-alienation', which of course for him was also the alienation of man from God. To Hegel, in short, man perceives the world as hostile *because* it is not himself, because it is alien. All these conflicts are resolved when he realizes at long last that the world really *is* himself. This process of realization is Hegel's *Aufhebung*, by which the world becomes de-alienated and assimilated to man's self.

But why, one might ask, is Hegel's man so odd, so neurotic, that he regards every thing that is not himself as alien and hostile? The answer is crucial to the Hegelian mystique. It is because Hegel, or Hegel's man, cannot stand the idea of himself not being God, and therefore not being of infinite space and without limits. Seeing any other being, or any other object, exist, would mean that he himself is not infinite or divine. In short, Hegel's philosophy is severe and cosmic solipsistic megalomania on a grand and massive scale. Professor Tucker develops the case with characteristic acuity:

> For Hegel alienation is finitude, and finitude in turn is bondage. The experience of self-estrangement in the presence of an apparent objective world is an experience of enslavement...Spirit [or the world self], when confronted with an object or 'other', is *ipso facto* aware of itself as merely finite being, as embracing only so much and no more of reality, as extending only so far and no farther. The object is, therefore, a 'limit'. (*Grenze*.) And a limit, since it contradicts spirit's notion of itself as absolute being, i.e., being-without-limit, is necessarily apprehended as a 'barrier' or 'fetter'. (*Schranke*.) It is a barrier to spirit's awareness of itself as that which it conceives itself truly to be – the whole of reality. In its confrontation with an apparent object, spirit feels imprisoned in limitation. It experiences what Hegel calls the 'sorrow of finitude'.
>
> The transcendence of the object through knowing is spirit's way of rebelling against finitude and making the break for freedom. In Hegel's quite unique conception of it, freedom means the consciousness of self as unbounded: it is the absence of a limiting object or non-self...This consciousness of 'being alone with self'...is precisely what Hegel means by the consciousness of freedom...
>
> Accordingly, the growth of spirit's self-knowledge in history is alternatively describable as a progress of the consciousness of freedom.[5]

11.3 Hegel and politics

Typically, determinist schema leave convenient implicit escape-hatches for their creators and advocates, who are somehow able to rise above the iron determinism that afflicts the rest of us. Hegel was no different, except that his escape-hatches were all too explicit. While God and the absolute refer to man as collective organism rather than to its puny and negligible individual members, every once in a while great individuals arise, 'world-historical' men, who are able to embody attributes of the absolute more than others, and act as significant agents in the next big historical *Aufhebung* – the next great thrust into the man–God or world-soul's advance in its 'self-knowledge'. Thus, during a time when most patriotic Prussians were reacting violently against Napoleon's imperial conquests, and mobilizing their forces against him, Hegel reacted very differently. Hegel wrote to a friend in ecstasy about having personally seen Napoleon riding down the city street: 'The Emperor – this world-soul – riding on horseback through the city to the review of his troops – it is indeed a wonderful feeling to see such a man.'[6]

Hegel was enthusiastic about Napoleon because of his world-historical function of bringing the strong state to Germany and the rest of Europe. Just as Hegel's fundamental eschatology and dialectic prefigured Marxism, so did his more directly political philosophy of history. Thus, following the Romantic writer Friedrich Schiller, Hegel, in an essay in 1795, claimed that the equivalent of early or primitive communism was ancient Greece. Schiller and Hegel lauded Greece for the alleged homogeneity, unity and 'harmony' of its *polis*, which both authors gravely misconceived as being free of all division of labour. The consequent *Aufhebung* disrupted this wonderful unity and fragmented man, but – the good side of the new historical stage – it did lead to the growth of commerce, living standards, and individualism. For Hegel, moreover, the coming stage, heralded by Hegel's philosophy, would bring about a reintegration of man and the state.

Before 1796, Hegel, like many other young intellectuals throughout Europe, was enchanted by the French Revolution, individualism, radical democracy, liberty and the rights of man. Soon, however, again like many European intellectuals, Hegel, disillusioned in the French Revolution, turned toward reactionary state absolutism. In particular, Hegel was greatly influenced by the Scottish statist, Sir James Steuart, a Jacobite exile in Germany for a large part of his life, whose *Inquiry into the Principles of Political Economy* (1767) had been greatly influenced by the ultra-statist German eighteenth century mercantilists, the cameralists. Hegel read the German translation of Steuart's *Principles* (which had been published from 1769–72), from 1797 to 1799, and took extensive notes. Hegel was influenced in particular by two aspects of Steuart's outlook. One held that history proceeded in stages, deterministically 'evolving' from one stage (nomadic, agricultural, exchange, etc.) to the next. The other influential theme was that massive state intervention and control were necessary to maintain an exchange economy.[7] It comes as no surprise that Hegel's main disillusion in the French Revolution came from its individualism and lack of unity under the state. Again foreshadowing Marx, it became particularly important for man (the collective organism) to surmount unconscious blind fate, and 'consciously' to take control of 'his' fate via the state. And so Hegel was a great admirer not only of Napoleon the mighty world-conqueror, but also Napoleon the detailed regulator of the French economy.

Hegel made quite evident that what the new, developing strong state really needed was a comprehensive philosophy, contributed by a Great Philosopher to give its mighty rule coherence and legitimacy. Otherwise, as Professor Plant explains, 'such a state, devoid of philosophical comprehension, would appear as a merely arbitrary and oppressive imposition of the freedom of individuals to pursue their own interest'.

We need make only one guess as to what that philosophy, or who that Great Philosopher, was supposed to be. And then, armed with Hegelian philosophy and Hegel himself as its fountainhead and great leader, 'this alien aspect of the progressive modern state would disappear and would be seen not as an imposition but a development of self-consciousness. By regulating and codifying many aspects of social practice, it gives to the modern world a rationality and a predictability which it would not otherwise possess...'.[8]

Armed with such a philosophy and with such a philosopher, the modern state would take its divinely appointed stand at the height of history and civilization, as God on earth. Thus: 'The modern State, proving the reality of political community, when comprehended philosophically, could therefore be seen as the highest articulation of Spirit, or God in the contemporary world'. The state, then, is 'a supreme manifestation of the activity of God in the world', and, 'the State stands above all; it is Spirit which knows itself as the universal essence and reality'; and, 'The State is the reality of the kingdom of heaven'. And finally: 'The State is God's Will.'[9]

Of the various forms of state, monarchy is best, since it permits 'all' subjects to be 'free' (in the Hegelian sense) by submerging their being into the divine substance, which is the authoritarian, monarchical state. The people are only 'free' when they are insignificant particles of this unitary divine substance. As Tucker writes, 'Hegel's conception of freedom is totalitarian in a literal sense of the word. The world-self must experience itself as the totality of being, or in Hegel's own words must elevate itself to "a self-comprehending totality", in order to achieve the consciousness of freedom. Anything short of this spells alienation and the sorrow of finitude'.[10]

According to Hegel, the final development of the man–God, the final break-through into totality and infinity, was at hand. The most highly developed state in the history of the world was now in place – the existing Prussian monarchy under King Friedrich Wilhelm III.

It so happened that Hegel's apotheosis of the existing Prussian monarchy neatly coincided with the needs of that monarch. When King Friedrich Wilhelm III established the new University of Berlin in 1818 to assist in supporting, and propagandizing for, his absolute power, what better person for the chair of philosophy than Friedrich Hegel the divinizer of state power? The king and his absolutist party needed an official philosopher to defend the state from the hated revolutionary ideals of the French Revolution, and to justify his purge of the reformers and classical liberals who had helped him defeat Napoleon. As Karl Popper puts it:

> Hegel was appointed to meet this demand, and he did so by reviving the ideas of the first great enemies of the open society [especially Heraclitus and Plato] ... Hegel rediscovered the Platonic Ideas which lie behind the perennial revolt against freedom and reason. Hegelianism is the renaissance of tribalism... [Hegel] is the 'missing link', as it were, between Plato and the modern forms of totalitarianism. Most of the modern totalitarians,...know of their indebtedness to Hegel, and all of them have been brought up in the close atmosphere of Hegelianism. They have been taught to worship the state, history, and the nation.[11]

On Hegel's worship of the state, Popper cites chilling and revealing passages:

> The State is the Divine Idea as it exists on earth... We must therefore worship the State as the manifestation of the Divine on earth... The State is the march of God through the world... The State must be comprehended as an organism... To the complete State belongs, essentially, consciousness and thought. The State knows what it wills... The State...exists for its own sake... The State is the actually existing, realized moral life.[12]

All this rant is well characterized by Popper as 'bombastic and hysterical Platonism'.

Much of this was inspired by Hegel's friends and immediate philosophical predecessors, men like the later Fichte, Schelling, Schlegel, Schiller, Herder and Schleiermacher. But it was Hegel's particular task to turn his murky doctrines to the job of weaving apologetics for the absolute power of the extant Prussian state. Thus Hegel's admiring disciple, F.J.C. Schwegler, revealed the following in his *History of Philosophy*:

> The fullness of his [Hegel's] fame and activity, however, properly dates only from his call to Berlin in 1818. Here there rose up around him a numerous, widely extended, and...exceedingly active school; here too, he acquired, from his connections with the Prussian bureaucracy, political recognition of his system as the official philosophy; not always to the advantage of the inner freedom of his philosophy, or of its moral worth.[13]

With Prussia as the central focus, Hegelianism was able to sweep German philosophy during the nineteenth century, dominating in all but the Catholic areas of southern Germany and Austria. As Popper put it, 'having thus become a tremendous success on the continent, Hegelianism could hardly fail to obtain support in Britain from those who [felt] that such a powerful movement must after all have something to offer...' Indeed, the man who first introduced Hegel to English readers, Dr J. Hutchinson Stirling, admiringly remarked, the year after Prussia's lightning victory over Austria, 'Is it not indeed to Hegel, and especially his philosophy of ethics and politics, that Prussia owes that mighty life and organization she is now rapidly developing?'[14] Finally Hegel's contemporary and acquaintance, Arthur Schopenhauer, denounced the state–philosophy alliance that drove Hegelianism into becoming a powerful force in social thought:

> Philosophy is misused, from the side of the state as a tool, from the other side as a means of gain   Who can really believe that truth also will thereby come to light, just as a byproduct?...*Governments made of philosophy a means of serving their state interests, and scholars made of it a trade*...(Italics Schopenhauer's)[15]

In addition to the political influence, Popper offers a complementary explanation for the otherwise puzzling widespread influence of G.W.F. Hegel: the attraction of philosophers to high-sounding jargon and gibberish almost for its own sake, followed by the gullibility of a credulous public. Thus Popper cites a statement by the English Hegelian Stirling: 'The philosophy of Hegel, then, was...a scrutiny of thought so profound that it was for the most part unintelligible'. Profound for its very unintelligibility! Lack of clarity as virtue and proof of profundity! Popper adds:

> philosophers have kept around themselves, even in our day, something of the atmosphere of the magician. Philosophy is considered a strange and abstruse kind of thing, dealing with those things with which religion deals, but not in a way which can be 'revealed unto babes' or to common people; it is considered to be too profound for that, and to be the religion and the theology of the intellectuals, of the learned and wise. Hegelianism fits these views admirably; it is exactly what this popular superstition supposes philosophy to be.[16]

11.4 Hegel and the Romantic Age

G.W.F. Hegel, unfortunately, was not a bizarre aberrant force in European thought. He was only one, if the most influential and the most convoluted and hypertrophic, of what must be considered the dominant paradigm of his age, the celebrated Age of Romanticism. In different variants and in different ways, the Romantic writers of the first half of the nineteenth century, especially in Germany and Great Britain, poets and novelists as well as philosophers, were dominated by a similar creatology and eschatology. It might be termed the 'alienation and return' or 'reabsorption' myth. God created the universe out of imperfection and felt need, thereby tragically cutting man, the organic species, off from his (its?) pre-creation unity with God. While this transcendence, this *Aufhebung*, of creation has permitted God and man, or

God–man, to develop their (its?) faculties and to progress, tragic alienation will continue, until that day, inevitable and determined, in which God and man will be fused into one cosmic blob. Or, rather, being pantheists as was Hegel, until man discovers that he is man–God, and the alienation of man from man, man from nature, and man from God will be ended as all is fused into one big blob, the discovery of the reality of and therefore the merger into, cosmic Oneness. History, which has been predetermined towards this goal, will then come to an end. In the Romantic metaphor, man, the generic 'organism' of course, not the individual, will at last 'return home'. History is therefore an 'upward spiral' towards Man's determined destination, a return home, but on a far higher level than the original unity, or home, with God in the pre-creation epoch.

The domination of the Romantic writers by this paradigm has been expounded brilliantly by the leading literary critic of Romanticism, M.H. Abrams, who points to this leading strain in English literature stretching from Wordsworth to D.H. Lawrence. Wordsworth, Abrams emphasizes, dedicated virtually his entire output to a 'heroic' or 'high Romantic argument', to an attempt to counter and transcend Milton's epochal poem of an orthodox Christian view of man and God. To counter Milton's Christian view of Heaven and Hell as alternatives for individual souls, and of Jesus's Second Advent as putting an end to history and returning man to paradise, Wordsworth, in his own 'argument', counterpoises his pantheist vision of the upward spiral of history into cosmic unification and man's consequent return home from alienation.[17] The eventual eschaton, the Kingdom of God, is taken from its Christian placement in Heaven and brought down to earth, thereby as always when the eschaton is immanentized, creating spectacularly grave ideological social, and political problems. Or, to use a concept of Abrams, the Romantic vision constituted the secularization of theology.

Greek and Roman epics, Wordsworth asserted, sang of 'arms and the man', 'hitherto the only Argument heroic deemed'. In contrast, at the beginning of his great *Paradise Lost*, Milton declares:

> 'That to the height of this great Argument
> I may assert Eternal Providence
> And justify the ways of God to man'.

Wordsworth now proclaimed that his own Argument surpassing Milton's was instilled in him by God's 'holy powers and faculties', enabling him (presaging Marx's yearnings) to create his own world, even though he realized, in an unwonted flash of realism, that 'some call'd it madness'. For there 'passed within' him 'Genius, Power, Creation, and Divinity itself'. Wordsworth concluded that 'This is, in truth, heroic argument', an 'argument/Not less but more Heroic than the wrath/Of stern Achilles'. Other Englishmen steeped in the Wordsworthian paradigm were his worshipful follower Coleridge, Shelley, Keats, and even Blake, who, however, tried to blend Christianity and pantheism.

All these writers had been steeped in Christian doctrine, from which they could spin off on their own heretical, pantheistic version of millennialism. Wordsworth himself had been trained to become an Anglican priest. Coleridge was a philosopher and a lay preacher, who had been on the edge of becoming a unitarian minister, and was steeped in neoplatonism and the works of Jacob Boehme, Keats was an explicit disciple of the Wordsworthian programme, which he called a means toward secular salvation. And Shelley, though an explicit atheist, idolized the 'sacred' Milton above all other poets, and was constantly steeped in study of the Bible.

It should also be noted that Wordsworth, like Hegel, was a youthful enthusiast for the French Revolution and its liberal ideals and later, disillusioned, turned to conservative statism and the pantheist version of inevitable redemption through history.

The German Romantics were even more immersed in religion and mysticism than were their English counterparts. Hegel, Friedrich von Schelling, Friedrich von Schiller, Friedrich Hölderlin, Johann Gottlieb Fichte, were all theology students, most of them with Hegel at the University of Tübingen. All of them tried explicitly to apply religious doctrine to their philosophy. Novalis was immersed in the Bible. Furthermore, Hegel devoted a great deal of favourable attention to Boehme in his *Lectures on the History of Philosophy*, and Schelling called Boehme a 'miraculous phenomenon in the history of mankind'.

Moreover, it was Friedrich Schiller, Hegel's mentor, who was influenced by the Scot Adam Ferguson to denounce specialization and the division of labour as alienating and fragmenting man, and it was Schiller who influenced Hegel in the 1790s by coining the explicit concept of *Aufhebung* and the dialectic.[18]

In England, several decades later, the tempestuous conservative statist writer Thomas Carlyle paid tribute to Friedrich Schiller by writing a biography of that Romantic writer in 1825. From then on, Carlyle's writings were permeated with the Hegelian vision. Unity is good, and diversity or separateness is evil and diseased. Science as well as individualism is division and dismemberment. Selfhood, Carlyle ranted, is alienation from nature, from others, and from oneself. But one day there will come the breakthrough, the spiritual rebirth, led by world-historical figures ('great men') by which man will return home to a friendly world by means of the utter cancellation, the 'annihilation of self' (*Selbst-tödtung*).

Finally, in *Past and Present* (1843), Carlyle applied his profoundly anti-individualist (and, one might add, anti-human) vision to economic affairs. He denounced egoism, material greed and *laissez-faire*, which, by fostering the severance of men from each other, had led to a world 'which has become a lifeless other, and in severance also from other human beings within a social order in which 'cash payment is...the sole nexus of man with man".'. In opposition to this metaphysically evil 'cash nexus' lay the familial relation with nature and fellow-men, the relation of 'love'. The stage was set for Karl Marx.[19]

11.5   Marx and Left revolutionary Hegelianism

Hegel's death in 1831 inevitably ushered in a new and very different era in the history of Hegelianism. Hegel was supposed to bring about the end of history, but now Hegel was dead, and history continued to march on. So if Hegel himself was not the final culmination of history, then perhaps the Prussian state of Friedrich Wilhelm III was not the final stage of history either. But if it was not the final phase of history, then mightn't the dialectic of history be getting ready for yet another twist, another *Aufhebung*?

So reasoned groups of radical youth, who, during the last 1830s and 1840s in Germany and elsewhere, formed the movement of Young, or Left, Hegelians. Disillusioned in the Prussian state, the Young Hegelians proclaimed the inevitable coming apocalyptic revolution to destroy and transcend that state, a revolution that would *really* bring about the end of history in the form of national, or world, communism.

One of the first and most influential of the Left Hegelians was a Pole, Count August Cieszkowski (1814–94) who wrote in German and published in 1838 his *Prolegomena to a Historiosophy*. Cieszkowski brought to Hegelianism a new dialectic of history, a new variant of the three ages of man. The first age, the age of antiquity, was, for some reason, the age of emotion, the epoch of pure feeling, of no reflective thought, of elemental immediacy and unity with nature. The 'spirit' was 'in itself' (*an sich*). The second age of mankind, the Christian era, stretching from the birth of Jesus to the death of the great Hegel, was the age of thought, of reflection, in which the 'spirit' moved 'toward itself', in the direction of abstraction and universality. But Christianity, the age of thought, was also an era of intolerable duality, of man separated from God, of spirit separated from matter, and thought from action. Finally, the third and culminating age, the coming age, heralded by Count Cieszkowski, was to be the age of action. In short, the third post-Hegelian age would be an age of practical action, in which the thought of both Christianity and of Hegel would be transcended and embodied into an act of will, a final revolution to overthrow and transcend existing institutions. For the term 'practical action', Cieszkowski borrowed the Greek word *praxis* to summarize the new age, a term that would soon come to acquire virtually talismanic influence in Marxism. This final age of action would bring about, at long last, a blessed unity of thought and action, theory and praxis, spirit and matter, God and earth, and total 'freedom'. Along with Hegel and the mystics, Cieszkowski stressed that *all* past events, even those seemingly evil, were necessary to the ultimate and culminating salvation.

In a work published in French in Paris in 1844, Cieszkowski also heralded the new class destined to become the leaders of the revolutionary society: the *intelligentsia*, a word that had recently been coined by a German-educated Pole, B.F. Trentowski, who had published his work in Prussian-occupied Poznan.[20] Cieszkowski thus heralded and glorified a development that would at least be implicit in the Marxist movement (after all, the great Marxists, including Marx, Engels and Lenin, were all bourgeois intellectuals rather than children of the proletariat). If not in theory, this dominance of Marxist movements and governments by a 'new class' of *intelligentsia* has certainly been the history of Marxism in 'praxis'. This dominance by a new class has been noted and attacked from the beginnings of Marxism unto the present day: notably by the anarcho-communist Bakunin, and by the Polish revolutionary Jan Waclaw Machajski (1866–1926), during and after the 1890s.[21] It was also a similar insight into the German Social Democratic Party that prompted Robert Michels to abandon Marxism and develop his famous 'iron law of oligarchy' – that all organizations, whether private, governmental, or Marxist parties, will inevitably end up being dominated by a power élite.

Cieszkowski, however, was not destined to ride the wave of the future of revolutionary socialism. For he took the Christian messianic, rather than atheistic, path to the new society. In his massive unfinished work of 1848, *Our Father (Ojcze nasz)*, Cieszkowski maintained that the new age of revolutionary communism would be a third age, an age of the Holy Spirit (shades of Joachism!), an era that would bring a Kingdom of God on earth 'as it is in heaven'. Thus, the final Kingdom of God on earth would reintegrate all of 'organic humanity', and would erase all national identities, with the world governed by a Central Government of All Mankind, headed by a Universal Council of the People.

But at the time, the path of Christian messianism was not clearly destined to be a loser in the intra-socialist debate. Thus, Alexander Ivanovich Herzen (1812–70), a founder of the Russian revolutionary tradition, was entranced by Cieszkowski's brand of Left Hegelianism, writing that 'the future society is to be the work not of the heart, but of the concrete. Hegel is the new Christ bringing the word of truth to men...'[22] And soon, Bruno Bauer, friend and mentor of Karl Marx and the leader of the *Doktorklub* of Young Hegelians at the University of Berlin, hailed the new philosophy of action in late 1841 as 'The Trumpet Call of the Last Judgment'.[23]

But the winning strand in the European socialist movement, as we have indicated, was eventually to be Karl Marx's atheism. If Hegel had pantheized and elaborated the dialectic of Christian messianics, Marx now 'stood Hegel on his head' by atheizing the dialectic, and resting it, not on mysticism or religion or 'spirit' or the absolute idea or the world-mind, but on the supposedly solid and 'scientific' foundation of philosophical materialism. Marx adopted his materialism from the Left Hegelian Ludwig Feuerbach, particularly his work on *The Essence of Christianity* (1843). In contrast to the Hegelian emphasis on 'spirit', Marx would study the allegedly scientific laws of matter in some way operating through history. Marx, in short, took the dialectic and made it what we can call a 'materialist dialectic of history'.

A lot of unnecessary pother has been made about terminology here. Many Marxist apologists have fiercely maintained that Marx himself never used the term 'dialectical materialism' – as if mere non-use of the *terms* lets Marx off the hook – and also that the concept only appeared in such later works of Engels as the *Anti-Dühring*. But the *Anti-Dühring*, published before Marx's death, was, like all other such writings of Engels, cleared with Marx first, and so we have to assume that Marx approved.[24]

The fuss stems from the fact that the term 'dialectical materialism' was widely stressed by the Marxist–Leninist movement of the 1930s and 1940s, these days generally discredited. The concept was applied by Engels, who of the two founders was particularly interested in the natural sciences, to biology. Applied to biology, as Engels did in the *Anti-Dühring*, dialectical materialism has an unmistakably crazy air. In an ultra-Hegelian manner, logic and logical contradictions, or 'negations', are hopelessly confused with the processes of reality. Thus: butterflies 'come into existence from the egg through negation [or transcendence] of the egg...they are negated again as they die'. And 'the barleycorn...is negated and is supplanted by the barley plant, the negation of the corn...The plant grows...is fructified and produces again barleycorns and as soon as these are ripe, the ear withers away, is negated. As a result of this negation of the negation we have gained the original barleycorn...in a quantity ten, twenty, or thirty times larger'.[25]

Furthermore, Marx himself, and not only Engels, was also very interested in Darwin and in biological science. Marx wrote to Engels that Darwin's work 'serves me as a basis in natural science for the class struggle in history' and that 'this is the book which contains the basis in natural history for our view'.[26]

By recasting the dialectic in materialist and atheist terms, however, Marx gave up the powerful motor of the dialectic as it operated throughout history: either Christian messianism or providence or the growing self-consciousness of the world spirit. How could Marx find a 'scientific' materialist replacement, newly grounded in the ineluctable 'laws of history' that would explain the inevitability of the imminent apocalyptic transformation of the world into communism? It is one thing to base the prediction of a forthcoming Armageddon upon the Bible; it is quite another to deduce this event from allegedly scientific laws. Setting forth the specifics of this engine of history was to occupy Karl Marx for the rest of his life.

Although Marx found Feuerbach indispensable for adopting a thoroughgoing atheist and materialist positions, Marx soon found that Feuerbach had not gone nearly far enough. Even though Feuerbach was a philosophical communist, he basically believed that if man forswore religion, then his alienation from his self would be over. To Marx, religion was only one of the problems. The entire world of man (the *Menschenwelt*) was alienating, and had to be radically overthrown, root and branch. Only apocalyptic destruction of this world of man would permit true human nature to be realized. Only then would the existing 'un-man' (*Unmensch*) truly become man (*Mensch*). As Marx thundered in the fourth of his 'theses on Feuerbach', 'one must proceed to destroy [the] 'earthly family' [as it is] 'both in theory and in practice'.[27]

In particular, declared Marx, true man, as Feuerbach had argued, is a 'communal being' (*Gemeinwesen*) or 'species being' (*Gattungswesen*). Although the state as it exists must be negated or transcended, man's participation in the state operates as such a communal being. The main problem comes in the private sphere, the market, or 'civil society', in which un-man acts as an egoist, as a private person, treating others as means, and not collectively as masters of their fate. And in existing society, unfortunately, civil society is primary, while the state, or 'political community', is secondary. What must be done to realize the full nature of mankind is to transcend the state and civil society by politicizing all of life, by making all of man's actions collective. Then real individual man will become a true and full 'species being'.[28]

But only a revolution, an orgy of destruction, can accomplish this task. And here, Marx harkened back to the call for total destruction that had animated his vision of the world in poems of his youth. Indeed, in a speech in London in 1856, Marx was to give graphic and loving expression to this goal of his 'praxis'. He mentioned that in Germany in the Middle Ages there existed a secret tribunal called the *Vehmgericht*. He then explained: 'If a red cross was seen marked on a house, people knew that its owner was doomed by the *Vehm*. All the houses of Europe are now marked with the mysterious red cross. History is the judge – its executioner the proletarian'.[29]

Marx, in fact, was not satisfied with the philosophical communism to which he and Engels had separately been converted by the slightly older Left Hegelian Moses Hess (1812–75) in the early 1840s. To Hess's communism, Marx, by the end of 1843, added the crucial emphasis on the *proletariat*, not simply as an economic class, but as destined to become the 'universal class' when communism was achieved. As we have indicated above, Marx actually acquired his vision of the proletariat as the key to the communist revolution from the 1842 work of Lorenz von Stein, an enemy of socialism, who interpreted the socialist and communist movements as rationalizations of the class interests of the proletariat. Marx discovered in Stein's attack the 'scientific' engine for the inevitable coming of the communist revolution. The proletariat, the most 'alienated' and allegedly 'propertyless' class, would be the key.

Marx had now worked out the outline of his secular messianic vision: a material dialectic of history, with the final apocalyptic revolution to be achieved by the proletariat. But how specifically was this to be accomplished? Vision was not enough. What scientific laws of history could bring about this cherished goal? Fortunately, Marx had a crucial ingredient for his attempted solution close at hand: in the Saint-Simonian concept of human history as driven by an inherent struggle among economic classes. The class struggle along with historical materialism was to be an essential ingredient for the Marxian material dialectic.

11.6   Marx as utopian

Despite Marx's claim to be a 'scientific socialist', scorning all other socialists whom he dismissed as moralistic and 'utopian', it should be clear that Marx himself was even more in the messianic utopian tradition than were the competing 'utopians'. For Marx not only sought a future society that would put an end to history: he claimed to have found the path towards that utopia inevitably determined by the 'laws of history'.

But a utopian, and a fierce one, Marx certainly was. A hallmark of every utopia is a militant desire to put an end to history, to freeze mankind in a static state, to put an end to diversity and man's free will, and to order everyone's life in accordance with the utopian's totalitarian plan. Many early communists and socialists set forth their fixed utopias in great and absurd detail, determining the size of everyone's living quarters, the food they would eat, etc. Marx was not silly enough to do that, but his entire system, as Thomas Molnar points out, is 'the search of the utopian mind for the definitive stabilization of mankind or, in gnostic terms, its reabsorption in the timeless'. For Marx, his quest for utopia was, as we have seen, an explicit attack on God's creation and a ferocious desire to destroy it. The idea of crushing the many, the diverse facets of creation, and of returning to an allegedly lost unity with God began, as we have seen, with Plotinus. As Molnar sums up:

> In this view, existence itself is a wound on nonbeing. Philosophers from Plotinus to Fichte and beyond have held that the reabsorption of the polichrome universe in the eternal One would be preferable to creation. Short of this solution, they propose to arrange a world in which change is brought under control so as to put

an end to a disturbingly free will and to society's uncharted moves. They aspire to return from the linear Hebrew–Christian concept to the Greco-Hindu cycle – that is, to a changeless, timeless permanence.

The triumph of unity over diversity means that, for the utopians, including Marx, 'civil society, with its disturbing diversity, can be abolished'. Molnar then makes the interesting point that when Hayek and Popper rebut Marxism by demonstrating

> that no mind – not even that of a Politburo equipped with supercomputers – can overview the changes of the marketplace and its myriad components of individuals and their interactions, they miss the mark. Marx agrees with them. But, he wants to abolish the marketplace and its economic as well as intellectual ('legal, political, philosophical, religious, aesthetic') components, so as to restore a simple world – a monochrome landscape. His economics is not economics but an instrument of total control.[30]

All well and good, but, as the history of communist countries has shown, there are not many followers of Marx who are willing to settle for a world where no economic calculation is possible, and therefore where production collapses and universal starvation ensues.

Substituting in Marx for God's will or the Hegelian dialectic of the world-spirit or the absolute idea, is monist materialism, in its central assumption, as Molnar puts it, 'that the universe consists of matter plus some sort of one-dimensional law immanent in matter'. In that case, 'man himself is reduced to a complex but manipulable material aggregate, living in the company of other aggregates, and forming increasingly complex super aggregates called societies, political bodies, churches'. The alleged laws of history, then, are derived by scientific Marxists as supposedly evident and immanent within this matter itself.

The Marxian process towards utopia, then, is man acquiring insights into his own true nature, and then rearranging the world to accord with that true nature. Engels, in fact, explicitly proclaimed the Hegelian concept of the man–God: 'Hitherto the question has always stood: What is God? – and German [Hegelian] philosophy has resolved it as follows: God is man…Man must now arrange the world in a *truly* human way, according to the demands of his *nature*'.[31]

But this process is rife with self-contradictions; for example, and centrally, how can mere matter gain insights into his (its?) nature? As Molnar puts it: 'for how can matter gather insights? And if it has insights, it is not entirely matter, but matter *plus*'.

In this allegedly inevitable process, of arriving at the proletarian communist utopia after the proletarian class becomes conscious of its true nature, what is supposed to be Karl Marx's own role? In Hegelian theory, Hegel himself is the final and greatest world-historical figure, the man–God of man–Gods. Similarly, Marx in his view stands at a focal point of history as the man who brought to the world the crucial knowledge of man's true nature and of the laws of history, thereby serving as the 'midwife' of the process that would put an end to history. Thus Molnar:

> Like other utopian and gnostic writers, Marx is much less interested in the stages of history up to the present (the egotistic *now* of all utopian writers) than in the final stages when the stuff of time becomes more concentrated, when the drama approaches its denouement. In fact, the utopian writer conceives of history as a process leading to himself since he, the ultimate *comprehensor*, stands in the center of history. It is natural that things accelerate during his own lifetime and come to a watershed: *he* looms large between the Before and the After.[32]

The achievement of the Marxist utopia is, moreover, dependent upon leadership and rule by the Marxian cadre, the possessors of the special knowledge of the laws of history, who will proceed to transform mankind into the new socialist man by the use of force. In the Judeo-Christian tradition, the existence of evil is accounted for by the free will of the individual. In monist, determinist systems, on the other hand, all history is supposed to be determined by fixed laws, and therefore evil can only be *apparent*, while really acting in a deeper sense as a servant of the higher good. All apparent evil must be truly good, and serve some sort of determined plan, whether it be the unfolding of the God–man or an atheistic version thereof. Coercing people by a cadre in order to create a new socialist man cannot be evil or unacceptable in a just society. On the contrary, it is the duty of the Marxist vanguard, they who are the servants of the next inevitable stage of history, to impose such a regime. This is a duty to history, that alleged entity to which the cadre are in service, and who (which?) is destined to judge the actions of the past, to judge them as moral or immoral, as either advancing the birth of the allegedly inevitable historical future, or of thwarting such birth. In short, history or the cadre has the privilege and duty of judging any person or movement as being either 'progressive' (i.e. advancing the determined march of history) or 'reactionary' (retarding that inevitable march).

11.7 Notes

1. On alienation in Marx as rooted in exchange and the division of labour, and not simply in the capitalist wage-relation, see Paul Craig Roberts, *Alienation and the Soviet Economy* (Alburquerque, NM: University of New Mexico Press, 1971); and Paul Craig Roberts and Matthew A. Stephenson, *Marx's Theory of Exchange, Alienation, and Crisis* (2nd ed., New York: Praeger, 1983).
2. In extreme variants, such as the gnostic heretics of the early Christian era, the creation of matter was itself pure evil, an act by the Devil, or Demiurge, with spirit remaining divine.
3. Robert C. Tucker, *Philosophy and Myth in Karl Marx* (Cambridge: Cambridge University Press, 1961), p. 39.

4. Ibid., p. 41. These and other early essays by Hegel were first published as a collection of *Early Theological Writings* in 1907.
5. Ibid., pp. 53–4.
6. Quoted in Raymond Plant, *Hegel* (Bloomington, Ind.: Indiana University Press, 1973), p. 120.
7. Hegel was also influenced by Steuart's great rival, Adam Smith, but unfortunately in the wrong direction. From the *Wealth of Nations* Hegel concluded that the division of labour had brought man the misery of specialization, alienation, etc. More interestingly, from Smith's friend the Rev. Adam Ferguson's famous line on events that are 'the product of human action but not of human design', Hegel got the idea of each individual agent of the world-soul's pursuing the world-soul's purposes without conscious intent. This is Hegel's famous concept of the 'cunning of reason' at work through history.

   Ferguson, in turn, arrived at his famous phrase, not by analysis of the free market, as Hayek implies, but from an attempt to show that the revolt in Scotland in 1745, which almost succeeded in bringing the dread Catholic Jacobites to power, was unconsciously pursuing God's benevolent purpose of shaking Scottish Presbyterians – assumed of course to be God's true Church – out of their religious apathy. In short, the Scottish Catholics, though consciously pursuing evil ends, were unwittingly carrying out God's designs. Out of apparent evil, good. Similarly, when Hegel later hailed Napoleon as the 'world-histori-cal' man, he saw Napoleon as intending to pursue evil but unconsciously furthering God's benevolent design. See Richard B. Sher, *Church and University in the Scottish Enlighten-ment* (Princeton, NJ. Princeton University Press, 1985), pp. 40–44.
8. Plant, op. cit., note 6, p. 96.
9. See ibid., pp. 122, 123, 181.
10. Tucker, op. cit., note 3, pp. 54–5. E.F. Carritt points out that, for Hegel, 'freedom' is 'desiring above all things to serve the success and glory of their State. In desiring this they are desiring that the will of God should be done...'. If an individual thinks he should do something which is *not* for the success and glory of the state, then, for Hegel, 'he should be "forced to be free".' How does a person *know* what action will redound to the glory of the state? To Hegel, the answer was easy. Whatever the state rulers demand, since 'the very fact of their being rulers is the surest sign of God's will that they should be'. Impeccable logic, indeed! See E.F. Carritt, 'Reply' (1940), reprinted in W. Kaufmann, (ed.), *Hegel's Political Philosophy* (New York: Atherton Press, 1970), pp. 38–9.
11. Karl R. Popper, *The Open Society and its Enemies* (5th ed., Princeton, NJ: Princeton University Press, 1966), II, pp. 30–31.
12. Ibid., p. 31.
13. Ibid., p. 33.
14. In 1867. See ibid., p. 34.
15. Ibid., p. 33.
16. Ibid., pp. 27, 30. For an explanation of what Popper refers to as the 'scherzo-style' of his chapter on Hegel, see ibid., pp. 393–5.
17. M.H. Abrams, *Natural Supernaturalism: Tradition and Revolution in Romantic Literature* (New York: Norton, 1971). Milton's depiction of the Fall and the Second Advent is truly eloquent and stirring. On the loss of Eden: 'Farewell happy Fields/Where Joy forever dwells...'. And on the Second Advent: 'Time will run back and fetch the age of gold', 'And then at last our bliss/Full and perfect is,/But now begins...'
18. On the influence of Schiller's views of organicism and alienation on Hegel, Marx and later sociology, see Leon Bramson, *The Political Context of Sociology* (Princeton, NJ: Princeton University Press, 1961), p. 30n.
19. See Abrams, op. cit., note 17, p. 311.
20. B.F. Trentowski, *The Relationship of Philosophy to Cybernetics* (Poznan, 1843), in which the author also coined the word 'cybernetics' for the new, emerging form of rational social technology which would transform mankind. See James H. Billington, *Fire in the Minds of Men: Origins of the Revolutionary Faith* (New York: Basic Books, 1980), p. 231.
21. On Machajski, see Paul Avrich, *The Russian Anarchists* (Princeton, NJ: Princeton Univer-

sity Press, 1967), pp. 102–6. Machajski's preferred solution to the problem of domination by the intellectuals was scarcely convincing. Machajski called for a secret organization of revolutionary workers, The Workers' Conspiracy, presumably headed by himself, which would lead the proletarian revolution, and establish a 'classless' society shorn of the evil distinctions between mental and manual labour.

22. Billington, op. cit., note 20, p. 225.

23. It is to Bauer that the world owes the terms 'critical' and 'criticism', which Marxists have long employed as endlessly repeated slogans ever since; e.g., 'Critique of Critical Theory', 'Critical Legal Studies', etc.

24. According to Schumpeter, moreover, Marx was virtually a co-author of the *Anti-Dühring*. Joseph A. Schumpeter, *Capitalism, Socialism, and Democracy* (New York: Harper & Bros., 1942), p. 39n.

25. Engels, *Anti-Dühring*, cited in Ludwig von Mises, *Theory and History* (3rd ed., Auburn, Ala.: Ludwig von Mises Institute, 1985), p. 105. Also see the sardonic commentary on this passage by Alexander Gray, *The Socialist Tradition* (London: Longmans, Green, 1946), p. 300n. Gray also notes Marx's summary of the dialectic in the *Poverty of Philosophy*, which he comments is 'not without entertainment value': 'The yes becomes no, the no becomes yes, the yes becomes at the same time yes and no, the no becomes at the same time no and yes, the contraries balance, neutralize, and paralyze each other'. (My own translation from Gray's French quote.)

26. Marx to Engels, 16 Jan. 1861 and 19 Dec. 1860. See Gary North, *Marx's Religion of Revolution: Regeneration Through Chaos* (2nd ed., Tyler, Texas: Institute for Christian Economics, 1989), pp. 89n–90n.

27. Tucker, op. cit., note 3, p. 101.

28. Ibid., p. 105.

29. Ibid., p. 15.

30. Thomas Molnar, 'Marxism and the Utopian Theme', *Marxist Perspectives* (Winter 1978), pp. 153–4. The economist David McCord Wright, while not delving to the religious roots of the problem, stressed that one group in society, the statists, seek 'the achievement of a fixed ideal static pattern of technical social organization. Once this ideal is reached, or closely approximated, it need only be repeated endlessly thereafter'. David McCord Wright, *Democracy and Progress* (New York: Macmillan, 1948), p. 21.

31. Molnar, op. cit., note 30, pp. 149, 150–51.

32. Ibid., pp. 151–2.

12 The Marxian system, I: historical materialism and the class struggle

12.1 The Marxian strategy

Marx desperately sought a materialistic dialectic of history, a dialectic that would account for all basic historical change and would lead inevitably to communist revolution. Lacking a Boehmeian 'nisus' or mystical inner drive to serve as motor of the dialectic, Marx had to fall back on class conflict embedded in historical materialism. But it was characteristic of Marx that this crucial area of the Marxian system, along with other important discussions, was presented, not systematically, but in the course of fugitive paragraphs or even passages, here and there throughout the writings of Marx and Engels. The system has to be constructed out of these widely separated passages. As a result, or perhaps from the inherently grave weakness of the argument, Marx's terminology is invariably vague and fuzzy, and his allegedly law-like linkages of the dialectic virtually non-existent. Often they are mere unsupported assertion. As a result, the Marxian system is not only a tissue of fallacies, but of flimsy fallacies and linkages as well.

No economic or social theory is obliged to come up with correct predictions, in the sense of forecasts of the future. But the Marxian doctrine is different. Like pre-millennial pietists who are forever predicting an imminent Armageddon, Marx claims to come up with 'laws of history' which, according to him, are 'scientific' rather than mystical. Well, if he knows the laws of history, then Marx had better come up with correct predictions of such allegedly determined laws. Yet all his predictions have proved utterly wrong. At this point, Marxists invariably fall back on changing the prediction, or pointing to some offsetting factor (seen only in hindsight) that temporarily delayed the prediction from coming true. Thus, as we shall see further below, one of Marx's predictions, crucial to the inevitable workings of the road to socialism, was that the working class would suffer increasing poverty and immizeration. When the working classes, in contrast, obviously continued to gain spectacularly in living standards in the western world, Marxian apologists fell back on the assertion that Marx meant only poverty 'relative to' the capitalist class. It is doubtful, however, whether bloody revolution will be waged by a proletariat for having only one yacht while capitalists have a dozen each. 'Relative' misery is a very different kettle of fish. The Marxists then came up with the view that western workers' standards of living were rising because of a 'temporary' delay brought about by western imperialism, enabling western workers to be 'capitalists' relative to the exploited Third World. The fact that Marx and Engels were themselves in favour of western, particularly German, imperialism, as a progressive force, is usually passed over in silence by Marxian writers.

On theoretical matters, the strategy of Marxists is similar. Increasingly, as crucial Marxian doctrines become evidently too absurd to be held seriously, e.g. technological determinism of all life, or the labour theory of value, they are abandoned by the Marxist, who then proceeds to maintain stubbornly that he is still a 'Marxist', and that Marxism essentially still holds true. But this is the attitude of a mystical religious adept rather than of a scientific or even a rational thinker.

One crucial weapon wielded often by Marxists and by Marx himself was 'the dialectic'. Since the dialectic allegedly means that the world and human society consist of conflicting or 'contradictory' tendencies side by side or even within the same set of circumstances, *any* prediction can then be justified as the result of one's deep insight into whichever part of the contradictory dialectic might be prevailing at any given time.[1] In short, since either *A* or non-*A* can occur, Marxians can safely hedge their bets so that no prediction of theirs can ever be falsified. It has been said that Gerry Healy, the absolute leader of the left-wing British Trotskyite movement until scandal brought him down in recent years, was able to maintain his power by claiming the power of exclusive insight into the mysterious workings of the dialectic. And an outstanding example of hedging one's bets by Marx himself was described in a letter to Engels. Marx writes to Engels that he has just forecast something in his column for the *New York Tribune*. He adds cynically and revealingly: 'It is possible that I may be discredited. But in that case it will still be possible to pull through with the help of a bit of dialectic. It goes without saying that I phrased my forecasts in such a way that I would prove to be right also in the opposite case'.[2]

12.2   Historical materialism

There is no place in his system where Marx is fuzzier or shakier than at its base: the concept of historical materialism, the key to the inevitable dialectic of history.

At the base of historical materialism and of Marx's view of history is the concept of the 'material productive forces'. These 'forces' are the driving power that creates all historical events and changes. So what are these 'material productive forces'? This is never made clear. The best that can be said is that material productive forces mean 'technological methods'. On the other hand, we are also faced with the term 'mode of production', which seems to be the same thing as material productive forces, or the sum of, or systems of, technological methods.

At any rate, these material productive forces, these technologies and 'modes of production', uniquely and monocausally create all 'relations of production' or 'social relations of production' independently of people's wills. These 'relations of production', also extremely vaguely defined, seem to be essentially legal and property relations. The sum of these relations of production somehow make up the 'economic structure of society'. This economic structure is the 'base' which causally determines the 'superstructure', which includes natural science, legal doctrines, religion, philosophies, and all other forms of 'consciousness'. In short, at the bottom of the base is technology which in turn constitutes or determines modes of production, which in turn determines relations of production, or institutions of law or property, and which finally in turn determine ideas, religious values, art, etc.

How, then, do historical changes take place in the Marxian schema? They can *only* take place in technological methods, since everything else in society is determined by the state of technology at any one time. In short, if the state of technology is T and everything else is the determined superstructure, S, then to Marx,

$$T_n \rightarrow S_n$$

where n is any point of time. But then, the only way in which social change can take place is via change in technology, in which case

$$T_{n+1} \rightarrow S_{n+1}$$

As Marx put it in the clearest and starkest statement of his technological determinist view of history, in his *Poverty of Philosophy*:

> In acquiring new productive forces men change their mode of production, and in changing their mode of production, their means of gaining a living, they change all their social relations. The hand mill gives you society with the feudal lord; the steam mill society with the industrial capitalist.

The first grave fallacy in this farrago is right at the beginning: Where does this technology come from? And how do technologies change or improve? Who puts them into effect? A key to the tissue of fallacies that constitute the Marxian system is that Marx never attempts to provide an answer. Indeed he cannot, since if he attributes the state of technology or technological change to the actions of man, of individual men, his whole system falls apart. For human consciousness, and individual consciousness at that, would then be determining material productive forces rather than the other way round. As von Mises points out:

> We may summarize the Marxian doctrine in this way: In the beginning there are the 'material productive forces', i.e., the technological equipment of human productive efforts, the tools and machines. No question concerning their origin is permitted; they are, that is all; we must assume that they are dropped from heaven.[3]

And, we may add, any changes in that technology must therefore be dropped from heaven as well.

Furthermore, as von Mises also demonstrated, consciousness, rather than matter, is predominant in technology:

> a technological invention is not something material. It is the product of a mental process, of reasoning and conceiving new ideas. The tools and machines may be called material, but the operation of the mind which created them is certainly spiritual. Marxian materialism does not trace back 'superstructural' and 'ideological' phenomena to 'material' roots. It explains these phenomena as caused by an essentially mental process, viz. invention.[4]

Machines are embodied ideas. In addition, technological processes do not only require inventions. They must be brought forth from the invention stage and be embodied in concrete machines and processes. But that requires savings and capital investment as well as invention. But, granting this fact, then the 'relations of production', the legal and property rights system in a society, help determine whether or not saving and investment will be encouraged and discouraged. Once again, the proper causal path is *from* ideas, principles, and the legal and property rights 'superstructure' *to* the alleged 'base'.

Similarly, machines will not be invested in, unless there is a division of labour of sufficient extent in a society. Once again, the social relations, the cooperative division of labour and exchange in society, determine the extent and development of technology, and not the other way round.[5]

In addition to these logical flaws, the materialist doctrine is factually absurd. Obviously, the hand mill, which ruled in ancient Sumer, did *not* 'give you' a feudal society there: furthermore, there were capitalist relations long before the steam mill. His technological determinism led Marx to hail each important new invention as *the* magical 'material productive force' that would inevitably bring about the socialist revolution. Wilhelm Liebknecht, a leading German Marxist and friend of Marx, reported that Marx once attended an exhibition of electric locomotives in London, and delightedly concluded that electricity would give rise to the inevitable communist revolution.[6]

Engels carried technological determinism so far as to declare that it was the invention of fire that separated man from the animals. Presumably the group of animals to whom fire somehow arrived were thereupon determined to evolve upward; the emergence of man himself was simply a part of the superstructure.

Even granting Marx's thesis momentarily for the sake of argument, his theory of historical change still faces insuperable difficulties. For why can't technology, which somehow develops as an automatic given, simply and smoothly change the 'relations of production' and the 'superstructure' above it? Indeed, if the base at each moment of time determines the rest of the superstructure, how can a change in the base *not* smoothly determine an appropriate change in the rest of the structure? But, again, a mysterious element enters the Marxian system. Periodically, as technology and the modes of production advance, they come into conflict, or, in the peculiar Hegelian–Marxian jargon, in 'contradiction' to the relations of production, which continue in the conditions appropriate to the past time period and past technology. These relations therefore become 'fetters' blocking technological development. Since they become fetters on growth, the new technology gives rise to an inevitable social revolution that overthrows the old production relations and the superstructure and creates new ones that have been blocked or fettered. In this way, feudalism gives rise to capitalism, which in turn will give way to socialism.

But if technology determines social production relations, what is the mysterious force that delays the change in those relations? It couldn't be human stubbornness or habit or culture, since we have already been informed by Marx that modes of production impel men to enter into social relations apart from their mere wills.

As Professor Plamenatz points out, we are merely *told* that the relations of production become fetters on the productive forces. Marx merely asserts this point, and never even attempts to offer a cause, material or otherwise. As Plamenatz puts the entire problem:

> then, all of a sudden, without warning and without explanation, he [Marx] tells us that there nevertheless arises inevitably from time to time an incompatibility between them [the productive forces and the relations of production] which only social revolution can resolve. This incompatibility apparently arises because the dependent variable [the relations] begins to impede the free operation of the variable on which it depends. [The material productive forces.] This is an astounding statement, and yet Marx can make it without even being aware that it requires explanation.[7]

Professor Plamenatz has shown that part of the deep confusion is both generated, and camouflaged, by Marx's failure to define 'relations of production' adequately. This concept apparently includes legal property relations. But if legal property relations were at fault in this dialectical delay in adjustment, thus setting up the 'fetters', then Marx would be conceding that the problem is really legal or political rather than economic. But he wanted the determining base to be *purely economic*; the political and the ideological had to be merely part of the determined superstructure. So 'social relations of production', allegedly economic, were the fetters; but this can only makes sense if this means the property rights or legal system. And so Marx got out of his dilemma by being so fuzzy and ambivalent about the 'relations of production' that these relations could be taken either as *including* the property structure, as *identical* with that structure, or else the two might be totally *separate* entities.

In particular, Marx accomplished his obscurantist purpose by asserting that the property rights system was part of the 'legal expression of' the 'relations of production' – thus somehow being able to be part of the superstructure and yet of the economic 'relations of production' at the same time. 'Legal expression', needless to say, was not defined either. As Plamenatz summed up, the entire concept of 'relations of production', so necessary to the Marxian thesis of material or economic determinism, serves Marx as a 'ghost battalion closing a vital gap in the front of Marxian theory'.[8] Yet in all this there is no way that the concept of 'relations of production' can make economic determinism intelligible, and there is no way by which these relations can either be determined by the modes of production *or* can in themselves determine the property rights system.

The only possible coherent chain of causation, in contrast, is the other way round: from ideas to property rights systems to the fostering or crippling the growth of saving and investment, and of technological development.

Twentieth century Marxists, from Lukacs to Genovese, have often tried to save the day from the embarrassment of the technological determinism of Marx and his immediate followers. They maintain that all sophisticated Marxists know that the causation is not unilinear, that the base and the superstructure really influence each other. Sometimes, they try to torture the data to claim that Marx himself took such a sophisticated position. Either way, they are characteristically obfuscating the fact that they have in reality abandoned Marxism. Marxism is monocausal technological determinism, along with all the rest of the fallacies we have depicted, or it is nothing, and it has demonstrated no inevitable or even likely dialectic mechanism.[9]

12.3   The class struggle

Even assuming that the unexplained incompatibility between the productive forces and the relations of production exists, why shouldn't this incompatibility continue forever? Why doesn't the economy simply lapse into permanent stagnation of the technological forces? This 'contradiction', so to speak, was scarcely enough to generate Marx's goal of the inevitable proletarian communist revolution.

The answer that Marx supplies, the motor of the inevitable revolutions in history, is inherent class conflict, inherent struggles between economic classes. For, in addition to the property rights system, one of the consequences of the relations of production, as determined by the productive forces, is the 'class structure' of society. For Marx, the fetters are invariably applied by the privileged 'ruling classes', who somehow serve as surrogates for, or living embodiments of, the social relations of production and the legal property system. In contrast, another, inevitably 'rising' economic class somehow embodies the oppressed, or fettered, technologies and modes of production.

The 'contradiction' between the fettered material productive forces and the fettering social relations of production thus becomes embodied in a determined class struggle between the 'rising' and the 'ruling' classes, which are bound, by the inevitable (material) dialectic of history to result in a triumphant revolution by the rising class. The successful revolution at last brings the relations of production and the material productive forces, or technological system, into harmony. All is then peaceful and harmonious until later, when further technological development gives rise to new 'contradictions', new fetters, and a new class struggle to be won by the rising economic class. In that way, feudalism, determined by the hand mill, gives rise to middle classes when the steam mill develops, and the rising middle classes, the living surrogates of the steam mill, overthrow fetters imposed by the feudal landlord class. Thus, the material dialectic takes one socio-economic system, say feudalism, and claims that it 'gives rise' to its opposite, or 'negation', and its inevitable replacement by 'capitalism', which thus 'negates' and transcends feudalism. And in the same way electricity (or whatever) will inevitably give rise to a proletarian revolution which will permit electricity to triumph over the fetters that capitalists place upon it.

It is difficult to state this position without rejecting it immediately as drivel. In addition to all the flaws in historical materialism we have seen above, there is no causal chain that links a technology to a class, or that permits economic classes to embody either technology or its 'production relations' fetters. There is no proffered reason why such classes must, or even plausibly might, act as determined puppets for or against new technologies. Why must feudal landlords try to suppress the steam mill? Why can't feudal landlords invest in steam mills? And why can't capitalists cheerfully invest in electricity as they already have in steam? Indeed, they have in fact happily invested in electricity, and in all other successful and economical technologies (as well as bringing them about in the first place). Why are capitalists inevitably oppressed under feudalism, and why are the proletariat equally inevitably oppressed under capitalism? (On Marx's attempt to answer the latter question, see below.)

If, finally, class struggle and the material dialectic bring about an inevitable proletarian revolution, why does the dialectic, as Marx of course maintains, at that point come to an end? For crucial to Marxism, as to other millennial and apocalyptic creeds, is that the dialectic can by no means roll on forever. On the contrary, the chiliast, whether pre- or post-millennial, invariably sees the end of the dialectic, or the end of history, as imminent. Very soon, imminently, the third age, or the return of Jesus, or the Kingdom of God on earth, or the total self-knowledge of the man–God, will effectively put an end to history. Marx's atheist dialectic, too, envisioned the imminent proletarian revolution, which would, after the 'raw communist' stage, bring about a 'higher communism' or perhaps a 'beyond communist' stage, which would be a classless society, a society of total equality, of no division of labour, a society without rulers. But since history is a 'history of class struggles' for Marx, the ultimate communist stage would be the final one, so that, in effect, history would then come to an end.

Critics of Marx, from Bakunin to Machajski to Milovan Djilas, have of course pointed out, both prophetically and in retrospect, that the proletarian revolution, whichever its stage, would not eliminate classes, but, on the contrary, would set up a new ruling class and a new ruled. There would be no equality, but another inequality of power and inevitably of wealth: the oligarchic élite, the vanguard, as rulers, and the rest of society as the ruled.

In order to round out his system, Marx was interested in the dialectical workings of the past, the passages from oriental despotism or the 'Asiatic mode of production' to the ancient world, thence to feudalism, and from feudalism to capitalism. But his main interest, understandably, was in demonstrating the precise mechanism by which capitalism was supposed to give way, imminently, to the proletarian revolution. After working out this broad system, the rest of Marx's life was largely devoted to demonstrating and developing these alleged mechanisms.

12.4   The Marxian doctrine of 'ideology'

Even Marx must dimly recognize that not 'material productive forces', not even 'classes', act in the real world, but only individual consciousness and individual choice. Even in the Marxian analysis, each class, or the individuals within it, must become conscious of its 'true' class interests in order to act upon pursuing or achieving them. To Marx, each individual's thinking, his values and theories, are all determined, *not* by his personal self-interest, but by the interest of the class to which he supposedly belongs. This is the first fatal flaw in the argument; why in the world should each individual ever hold his class higher than himself? Second, according to Marx, this class interest determines his thoughts and viewpoints, and *must* do so, because each person is only capable of 'ideology' or false consciousness in the interest of his class. He is not capable of a disinterested, objective search for truth, nor of pursuit of his own interest or of that of all mankind. But, as von Mises has pointed out, Marx's doctrine pretends to be pure, non-ideological science, and yet written expressly to advance the class interest of the proletariat. But, while all 'bourgeois' economics and all other disciplines of thought were interpreted by Marx as false by definition, as 'ideological' rationalizations of bourgeois class interest, the Marxists

> were not consistent enough to assign to their own doctrines merely ideological character. The Marxian tenets, they implied, are not ideologies. They are a fore-

taste of the knowledge of the future classless society which, freed from the fetters of class conflicts, will be in a position to conceive pure knowledge, untainted by ideological blemishes.[10]

Dr David Gordon has aptly summed up this point:

If all thought about social and economic matters is determined by class position, what about the Marxist system itself? If, as Marx proudly proclaimed, he aimed at providing a science for the working class, why should any of his views be accepted as true? Mises rightly notes that Marx's view is self-refuting: if all social thought is ideological, then *this* proposition is itself ideological and the grounds for believing it have been undercut. In his *Theories of Surplus Value*, Marx cannot contain his sneering at the 'apologetics' of various bourgeois economists. He did not realize that in his constant jibes at the class bias of his fellow economists, he was but digging the grave of his own giant work of propaganda on behalf of the proletariat.[11]

Von Mises also raises the point that it is absurd to believe that the interests of any class, including the capitalists, could ever be served better by a false than by a correct doctrine.[12] To Marx, the point of philosophy was only the achievement of some practical goal. But if, as in pragmatism, truth is only 'what works', then surely the interests of the bourgeoisie would not be served by clinging to a false theory of society. If the Marxian answer holds, as it has, that false theory is necessary to justify the existence of capitalist rule, then, as von Mises points out, from the Marxian point of view itself the theory should not be necessary. Since each class ruthlessly pursues its own interest, there is no need for the capitalists to justify their rule and their alleged exploitation to *themselves*. There is also no need to use these false doctrines to keep the proletariat subservient, since, to Marxists, the rule or the overthrow of a given social system depends on the material productive forces, and there is no way by which consciousness can delay this development or speed it up. Or, if there are such ways, and the Marxists often implicitly concede this fact, then there is a grave and self-defeating flaw in the heart of Marxian theory itself.

It is a well-known irony and another deep flaw in the Marxian system that, for all the Marxian exaltation of the proletariat and the 'proletarian mind', all leading Marxists, beginning with Marx and Engels, were emphatically bourgeois themselves. Marx was the son of a wealthy lawyer, his wife was a member of the Prussian nobility and his brother-in-law Prussian minister of the interior. Friedrich Engels, his lifelong benefactor and collaborator, was the son of a wealthy manufacturer, and himself a manufacturer. Why were not *their* views and doctrines also determined by bourgeois class interests? What permitted *their* consciousness to rise above a system so powerful that it determines the views of everyone else?

In this way, every determinist system attempts to provide an escape-hatch for its own believers, who are somehow able to escape the determinist laws that afflict everyone else. Unwittingly, these systems become in that way self-contradictory and self-refuting. In the twentieth century, Marxists such as the German sociologist Karl Mannheim attempted to elevate this escape-hatch into High Theory: that somehow, 'intellectuals' are able to 'float free', to levitate above the laws that determine all other classes.

12.5   The inner contradiction in the concept of 'class'

A 'class' is a set of entities with one identifiable thing in common. Thus there is a class of 'bald eagles' or of 'geraniums', and such a class can be widened or narrowed: e.g., the class of 'geraniums growing in New Jersey'. A 'social class' is a class of human beings with one thing in common. The number of identifiable social classes is virtually infinite. Thus: there is the 'class of people over 6 feet 4 inches in height', the 'class of people named Smith', the 'class of people weighing under 160 pounds', etc. *ad infinitum*. Some of these classes will be useful for certain types of social analysis (e.g. the 'class of people over 65 years of age with diabetes'), for medical or insurance or demographic purposes. But from our point of view, in a study of the Marxian theory of class, these classes are all worthless because there is no inherent conflict between them. In the market economy, in the international division of labour and exchange of products, there is no inherent conflict between short and tall people, people of various weights and names, etc. All classes live in harmony through the voluntary exchange of goods and services that mutually benefits them all. Furthermore, there is no reason for an individual in a free society, or in a market economy, to act on behalf of 'the interests of his class' rather than, or even as a surrogate for, his own individual interest. Will a person, when deciding at what job to work, or what investment to make, first and foremost consult his 'class interest' as the member of a 'class over 6 feet tall'? The very idea is absurd.

Is there no time, then, when social classes are in inherent conflict? Yes, there are such times, but only when some classes are privileged by state coercion, while other classes are restricted or burdened by state coercion. Ludwig von Mises perceptively used the term 'caste' to identify groups either privileged or burdened by the state, as distinguished from 'classes', which are simply groups of people on the free market in no sense in inherent conflict. The caste system in India was a classic case. The privileged or 'ruling' castes acquired power, income, and status by state coercion; the submerged or 'ruled' castes, for example, were prevented by coercion from leaving the lowly occupations of their ancestors. Other ruling and ruled 'castes' or classes are not as rigid as the Indian caste system, but still they partake of the same coercively determined status. Thus, the Brahmin caste, privileged by the state, was in inherent conflict with the Untouchables, who were submerged as a class by the state. These castes then have conflicting class (or 'caste') interest: the Brahmins to maintain their privileges, the Untouchable or other submerged castes to break out of their burdens. The point is that, by the use of state power, each individual Brahmin has a common or 'class' interest in maintaining his privileges; while each Untouchable has a common class interest in freeing himself from oppression.

Thus, even in less rigid cases than in an absolute caste system, the class of short and tall people, or the class of people named Smith, normally living in peace and harmony, could *become* classes in inherent conflict. Suppose, for example, the state decrees a large subsidy for all people over 6 feet tall, or a special heavy tax on all those under 5 feet 5 inches. If special privileges were heaped on people named Smith, then this would be a privileged class at the expense of everyone else, and there would be an economic incentive to try to join the 'ruling class', people named Smith, as quickly as possible.

Even in such situations, as Marx in practice could not deny, there were and are individuals who, for various reasons of ideology or opportunism, fail to follow their own common class-interest. There were and are Brahmins who put the demands of justice (that is, ideas or principles) higher than their class interest, or Untouchables who, for personal interest, willingly submit to the existing order.

There is a grave inner contradiction at the heart of the Marxian system, in Marx's crucial concept of class. In the Marxian dialectic, two mighty social classes face each other in inherent conflict, the ruling and the ruled. In the first two of history's major conflicts: 'oriental despotism', and 'feudalism', the social classes are defined by Marx in what we have seen to be the libertarian, or Misesian, manner: as classes privileged or burdened by the state. Thus, in 'oriental despotism', or the 'Asiatic mode of production', the emperor and his technocratic bureaucracy run the state, and constitute its 'ruling class'. This class acquires privileges from the state, and taxes and controls the 'ruled' classes, that is, everyone else, largely the peasantry but also craftsmen and merchants. Here Marx adopts the libertarian (as we have seen advanced by James Mill) definition of a two-class system, the ruling Few who have gained control of the state, who are governing and exploiting the ruled Many. Under feudalism, a similar concept applies. The landlord class has acquired territory through war and conquest, and has settled down to oppress the peasantry and the merchants and craftsmen via coerced rents, taxes, controls and serfdom. Once again, Marx's class categories are 'caste' categories: the ruling class is such by virtue of its having gained control of the state, the main social apparatus of coercion.

All well and good. But then, suddenly, when Marx gets to capitalism, the class categories change, without acknowledgement. Now the ruling class is not simply defined as the class that runs the state apparatus. Now, suddenly, the original act of rule or 'exploitation' is the voluntary market wage contract, the very act of a capitalist hiring a worker and a worker agreeing to be hired. This in itself, to Marx, establishes a common 'class-interest' among capitalists, exploiting a 'common class' of workers. It is true that Marx also believed that this 'capitalist class' runs the state, but only as 'the executive committee of the ruling class', that is, of a ruling class that *previously existed* on the free market, because of the wage system. So that what Marx, as analyst of oriental despotism or feudalism, would consider ruling-class exploitation still exists under capitalism, but only as an *addendum* to the pre-existing capitalist exploitation of the workers through the wage system. Ruling-class exploitation under capitalism is unique in exercising a *double* exploitation: *first*, on the market as part of the wage contract, and *second*, the alleged exploitation by the state as executive committee of the ruling class.

It should be evident that Marx's analysis of class is by this point a mishmash, in total disarray; two contradictory definitions of class are jammed together, unfused and unacknowledged. Why should capitalism, of all systems, be able to levy a 'double' exploitation that no other ruling class in Marx's historical schema can ever enjoy?

But the crucial point is that Marx's definition of class and class conflict under capitalism is hopelessly muddled and totally wrong. How can 'capitalists', even in the same industry let alone in the entire social system, have any thing crucial in common? Brahmins and slaves, in a caste system, certainly enjoy a common class-interest, in conflict with other castes. But what is the common 'class-interest' of the 'capitalist class'? On the contrary, capitalist firms are in continual competition and rivalry with each other. They compete for raw material, for labour, for sales and customers. They compete in price and quality, and in seeking new products and new ways to get ahead of their competitors. Marx, of course, did not deny the reality of this competition. So how can all capitalists, or even 'the steel industry', be considered a class with common interests? Again, in only one way: the steel industry only enjoys common interests if it can induce the state to create such interests through special privilege. State intervention to impose a steel tariff, or a steel cartel with restricted output and higher price, would indeed *create* a privileged 'ruling class' of steel industrialists. But no such class having common interests pre-exists on the market before such intervention comes about. Only the state can create a privileged class (or a subordinate and burdened class) by acts of intervention into the economy or society. There can be no 'capitalist ruling class' on the free market.

Similarly, there can be no 'working class' with common class-interests on the free market. Workers compete with each other, just as capitalists or entrepreneurs compete with each other. Once again, if groups of workers can use the state to exclude other groups, they can become a ruling class as against the excluded groups. Thus, if government immigration restrictions keep out new workers, the native workers can benefit (at least in the short run) at the expense of incomes of immigrants; or if white workers can keep black workers out of skilled jobs by state coercion (as was done in South Africa), the former becomes a privileged or ruling class at the expense of the latter.

An important point here is that *any* group that can manage to control, or gain privileges from, the state can take its place among the exploiters: this can be specific groups of workers, or businessmen, or Communist Party members, or whatever. There is no reason to assume that only 'capitalists' can acquire such privileges.

In his class analysis, Marx constantly had to struggle with the fact that neither capitalists nor workers act in practice as if they are each members of monolithic, conflicting classes. On the contrary, capitalists persist in competing with each other, and workers likewise. Even in their rousing *Communist Manifesto*, Marx and Engels had to admit that 'The organization of the proletarians into a class, and consequently into a political party, is continually being upset again by the competition among the workers themselves'. Indeed.

But there are more grave problems. For Marx had his two-class analysis; the essence of each titanic struggle in history is between two great social classes: the ruling *vs* the ruled, the rising class in tune with the new material productive forces, the declining one out of tune. But it is one thing to employ a two-class ruler *vs* ruled analysis according to libertarian or Millian definitions; since there are indeed common caste interests and conflicts, this concept is here a simplification, but an important and workable one. But what are we to do in the complex, multi-class world of the capitalist market economy? How can we employ a two-class model there, either for market or political action?

And there is no question that Marx is committed to the two-class model: capitalists *vs* proletarians. All other classes fade away, so that the mighty, exploited immizerated class can and will rise up as a monolith to overthrow 'the capitalist class'. As Marx and Engels say in the *Communist Manifesto*: 'Our epoch, the epoch of the bourgeoisie, possesses, however, this distinctive feature: it has simplified the class antagonisms: Society as a whole is more and more splitting up into two great hostile camps, into two great classes directly facing each other: Bourgeoisie and Proletariat'.[13]

But in practice, in analysing recent history or current events, Marx and Engels were forced to talk about many classes and groups, and their interactions – thereby implicitly but definitely betraying their own absurd two-class model. And so we have the problem that Marx's two classes are far from monoliths, that their members compete with each other constantly and collaborate very rarely, and also that in capitalist society in particular it is impossible to analyse historical action by squeezing all human actors into two classes.

In practice, however, Marx and other Marxists happily use a multi-class model in analysing historical events: 'steel capital', 'textile capital', 'armament capital', 'finance capital', etc. But they do not seem to realize that while they are being far more realistic than when prating about 'capitalists' *vs* 'workers' as two-class monoliths, they are totally betraying the Marxian dialectic itself. No inevitable revolution, for example, will ever follow from multi-class squabbling – certainly not Marx's cherished proletarian one.

Marx himself, and Marxists generally, have devoted many millions of words to the concept and use of the term 'class'. Yet in all his writings, Marx never once defined it. For if he had attempted a definition, the stark inner contradiction in the concept, the slippage between state creation and mere market action, would have become starkly clear, and something would have had to give.

Thus, in Marx's theoretical *magnum opus, Capital*, there is no attempt at a definition of class. Only an incomplete Volume I was published in Marx's lifetime (1867), at which point he had substantially finished working on the book. After Marx's death in 1883, Engels worked up, edited and published the remaining manuscript in two further volumes (1885, 1894).[14] Only in the famous very last chapter of the third volume does Marx finally arrive at an attempt to define what he and Engels had been talking and writing about for four decades. It is an unfinished chapter of startling brevity – five short paragraphs. In this chapter, 'Classes', Marx begins with the classical Ricardian triad: that the sources of income in the market economy are wages, profits and rents, and that the receivers of such income constitute the 'three big classes of modern society' – labourers, capitalists and landlords.[15] So far, so good. But then Marx adds that even England, 'the most highly and classically developed' capitalist country, contains 'middle and intermediate strata [which] even here obliterate lines of demarcation everywhere'. But, he quickly hastens to assure his readers that this problem is irrelevant, since the concentration and polarization of classes is proceeding apace.

Marx then begins the third paragraph of this seemingly climactic chapter. 'The first question to be answered is this: What constitutes a class?' Indeed. He then adds that the reply to this question 'follows naturally' from the reply to a second, related question: 'What makes wage-labourers, capitalists, and landlords constitute the three great social classes?' We are now primed for the answer, first to the latter Ricardian question and then to the first, critical query, 'What constitutes a class?'

On the second question, Marx states that 'at first glance' the identity of incomes with their sources constitutes the answer. After all, workers earn wages from their labour, capitalists make profits from their capital, and landlords obtain rent from their land. But Marx quickly warns us that this simple answer will not do. For:

> However, from that standpoint, physicians and officials, e.g., would also constitute two classes, for they belong to two distinct social groups, the members of each of these groups receiving their revenues from one and the same source. The same would also be true of the infinite fragmentation of interest and rank into which the division of social labour splits labourers as well as capitalists and landlords – the latter, e.g. into owners of vineyards, farm owners, owners of forests, mine owners and owners of fisheries.

Precisely. Marx has said it very well; his cherished two-class monolith model (or three-class, if we throw in the allegedly declining 'feudal remnant' – the landlord class) lies totally in ruins.[16]

Thus Marxian class theory, and therefore Marxism, lay destroyed by its creator's own hand. But if it is always darkest before the dawn, if the suffering of the oppressed class is greatest just before the apocalyptic revolutionary moment, we would expect Karl Marx to step in and triumphantly save the day. How does he do it? How does the drama unfold? In one of the great anti-climactic moments in the history of social thought, the manuscript ends with the lines we have just quoted. There is just a cryptic footnote from Engels: 'Here the manuscript breaks off'.

The way Engels puts it implies that the Master was struck down just as his pen was ready to wield the Answer that would rescue the crumbling Marxian theory of class and place it on solid foundations. But we know this was not true, for the 'breaking off' occurred 16 years before Marx's death. Marx had ample time for his dramatic and conclusive answer. Why didn't he pursue it? We can only conclude that he couldn't, that he was stopped, that he realized that there *was* no answer, and that Marxism would henceforth have to rely on repetition and bluster to carry it through.

12.6   The origin of the concept of class

We have seen above that James Mill, in the early decades of the nineteenth century, worked out a simple but cogent and effective two-class theory of class; the ruling class that ran the state, and the remainder of society, who constituted the ruled. At about the same time, during the Restoration period in France after the fall of Napoleon in 1814, a group of *laissez-faire* libertarian theorists were working out a far more sophisticated version of the same model, a model that contained a historical and sociological dimension absent in James Mill. This group were the spiritual and physical descendants of the ideologues of the Napoleonic era, and the major link was J.B. Say. Say was the inspirer and elder statesman of this Restoration group, which was led by his son-in-law Charles Comte (François Charles Louis Comte, 1782–1837) and Charles Dunoyer (Barthélemy Charles Pierre Joseph Dunoyer, 1786–1862). An important follower of Comte and Dunoyer was the young Augustin Thierry (1795–1856), soon to become to most notable of French historians. At the beginning of the Restoration and until 1820, Comte and Dunoyer founded and edited *Le Censeur* followed by *Le Censeur Européen*, periodicals that became the centre for the new *laissez-faire* movement.

Like Mill, Comte and Dunoyer defined conflicting classes as those who gained control of the state apparatus as against those who were controlled by the state. But they also pointed out that history had been a history of such class (or 'caste') struggles. Under oriental despotism, the emperor and his bureaucracy constituted the ruling class; in early Europe, conquering tribes settled down among the conquered to constitute a state with a ruling class; historically, then, another component of such a ruling class is that, at least initially, it was of a different ethnic group from the ruled. In this way, ethnic oppression reinforced political–economic class oppression by the state.

But to Comte and Dunoyer, the new element, the factor that would bring about the inevitable emergence and triumph of a classless (in the sense of 'casteless') society, was what they called *industrielisme*. The emergence of an industrial society required an international free market economy to enable it to work; hence Comte and Dunoyer saw it as inevitable that a free market economy would spread throughout Europe and eventually the world, dissolving the ruling classes, and bringing about a libertarian region and world, a world free of the oppression of the state. Thus the state, in this vision, would wither away, to be dissolved into the market exchange economy, and in the explicit language of Comte and Dunoyer, 'the government of men would be replaced by the administration of things'.

Thus Comte and Dunoyer saw the world as being split into the productive classes (workers, entrepreneurs, producers of all kinds), crippled and oppressed by the 'non-productive' classes, using the state to levy tribute upon the producers. The 'non-producers' were, in particular, politicians, government officials, and *rentiers* living off government bonds, as well as subsidized businessmen or receivers of government privilege. The 'peak of perfection', which Comte and Dunoyer saw as eventually arriving, 'would be reached if all the world worked, and no one governed'.

In their analysis, Comte and Dunoyer went beyond their mentor, J.B. Say, with his blessing, to add the historical, sociological, and political philosophic dimensions to the strictly economic.

The Comte–Dunoyer movement were firm and militant believers in individual liberty and in property rights. Thus Dunoyer's attack on egalitarianism: 'Equality would be the reversal of that fundamental law of humanity and of society' which provides that the income and the position of each man 'depends above all on his conduct, and is proportionate to the activity, the intelligence and the morality and the persistence of his efforts'. And on liberty, Dunoyer wrote that for 40 years, 'I have defended the same principles: liberty in everything, in religion, in philosophy, in literature, industry, in politics. And by liberty I mean the triumph of individuality...'.[17]

The worm in the apple, the way in which libertarian social class analysis got transmuted into a mixture of itself and its opposite, was provided by a garrulous French aristocrat Henri, Comte de Saint-Simon (Claude Henri de Rouvroy, Comte de Saint-Simon 1760–1825). Saint-Simon, a hopelessly muddled thinker, was not aided in his existential confusion by his penchant for picking up ideas orally, at salons, instead of by systematic reading.[18] For a while, during the *Censeur* period, Saint-Simon, who had picked up the Comte–Dunoyer ideas at salons, was what could best be described as a fellow-traveller of theirs, and pushed their ideas in his own periodical, *l'Industrie* (1816–18). After that, however, Saint-Simon grew increasingly authoritarian and hostile to *laissez-faire* liberalism. Having imbibed libertarian class analysis from Comte and Dunoyer, he characteristically got the concepts confused, and introduced the fateful and unacknowledged contradiction: between conflicting classes in the sense of those who govern, or are governed by, the state *versus* employers *vis-à-vis* wage earners on the free market. The Marxian jumble was Saint-Simon's dubious contribution to social thought. After Saint-Simon's death in 1825, his disciple Olinde Rodrigues, an engineer and son of a bureaucrat, joined by Enfantin and Bazard, founded the Saint-Simonian journal *Le Producteur* which, followed by conferences and tracts for the remainder of the 1820s, converted their deceased master's confused social philosophy into a militant proposal for a totalitarian socialist system. This system was to be run by what the Saint-Simonians considered the true class representatives of *industrielisme*: an alliance of engineers and other technocratic intellectuals with investment bankers, coordinated and led by a banker-dominated central bank.

In short, in contrast to communist socialism, which was at least ostensibly egalitarian, Saint-Simonianism was frankly élitist, to be run by the 'good' and allegedly modern classes. Thus the Saint-Simonians, who were the first users of the word 'socialism', repudiated capitalists and entrepreneurs, on behalf of their favoured bankers and intellectual classes, representing the worker–producers. It is perhaps not coincidental that, of the two maximum co-leaders of Saint-Simonianism, Enfantin and Bazard, Barthélemy Prosper Enfantin was the son of a banker, was trained as a banker and engineer, and had been a mathematics student of Olinde Rodrigues. Nor is it surprising that Saint-Simonianism appealed hugely to the investment bankers, the *Producteur* being financed by the prominent banker, Jacques Laffitte. The Saint-Simonian culture reached the peak of its remarkable influence in France from 1830–32, after which the dual popes of this political–religious cult, Enfantin and Saint-Amand Bazard (1791–1832) had a fiery split on the free love question on which every disciple was required to take immediate sides. Unfortunately, the destructive split between the two popes came too late, and the Saint-Simonian socialist movement had already become astoundingly influential throughout Europe. In France, artists and writers became Saint-Simonians, including George Sand, Balzac, Hugo, and Eugène Sue, while in music Berlioz attempted to apply Saint-Simonian principles by composing a *Song on the Installation of Railroads*, and Franz Liszt played the piano at Saint-Simonian meetings.

In England, the reactionary romantic pantheist Thomas Carlyle took to Saint-Simonian socialism immediately, and became its leading spokesman in England, going so far as to translate and attempting to publish the master's final work, *The New Christianity*, in which he foreshadowed the development of his movement into the cult of a new religion. Of more lasting importance was the deep influence that Saint-Simonianism had on John Stuart Mill. For it was the Saint-Simonians who were initially and largely responsible for Mill's quasi-conversion from his father's hard-core free market views to semi-socialism. In his *Autobiography*, Mill explains that he read every Saint-Simonian tract and how it was 'partly by their writings that [his] eyes were opened to the very limited and temporary value of the old political economy, which assumes private property and inheritance as indefeasible facts and freedom of production and exchange as the *dernier mot* of social improvement'. Indeed, in a letter to a leading French Saint-Simonian, Gustave d'Eichtal, a friend of Rodrigues, Mill went so far as to concede that some form of Saint-Simonian socialism 'is likely to be the final and permanent condition of our race', although he differed with them in believing that it would take a long time for mankind to become capable of achieving that happy state.[19]

There is no country, however, that took to Saint-Simonianism with more gusto than Germany. In the early 1830s, Saint-Simonianism 'went like wild-fire through the German literary world'.[20] Its enthusiastic adepts included the eminent political writer, Friedrich Buchholz and the famous poet Heinrich Heine, while the Young German school of poets became Saint-Simonian adepts. But the most important influence of Saint-Simonianism in Germany was on the Young Hegelians, Young German poets such as T. Mundt and G. Kuehne were Hegelian university lecturers on philosophy. More directly, Saint-Simonianism exercised a formative influence on Marx. In the first place, Marx's home town of Trier had been part of the German Rhineland occupied by France for two decades of the French revolutionary wars. Hence the town had become greatly susceptible to French intellectual influences. As a result, Trier was rife with Saint-Simonian agitation when Marx was a young adolescent; so much so that the archbishop felt obliged to condemn Saint-Simonian doctrines from the pulpit. Ludwig Gall, former secretary to the Trier city council, was a prominent and prolific Saint-Simonian writer. There is little doubt that Marx read Gall's writings.

Another powerful influence on Marx was one of his favourite teachers at the University of Berlin, Eduard Gans, one of Hegel's favourite disciples, who taught criminal law. Gans was both a Hegelian and a Saint-Simonian, and the interpenetration of the two doctrines in Germany deeply shaped the views of the Young Hegelians, of whom Marx became a leader. As Billington notes, 'The entire phenomenon of left Hegelianism has indeed been described as "nothing more than a Hegelianized Saint-Simonianism or a Saint-Simonianized Hegelianism".'[21] Steeped in Saint-Simon as well as Hegel, Marx found the concept of class struggle, as strained through the defective lenses of the Saint-Simonians, ready to hand and suited for incorporation into his own Grand Design. In addition to the class struggle between proletarians and capitalists, Marx also adopted the Saint Simonian version of industry and its embodiment (among the Saint-Simonians and in Marx, the workers) as inevitably victorious, along with the future goal of history as the withering away of the state and the 'replacement of the government of men by the administration of things'. There was, of course, a crucial difference between this abortive concept and its original. Among Comte and Dunoyer, the utopian state was to be a purely free society of individual property-holders and free market exchangers; for Marx it was to be a communal collective 'self' ownership of all goods by 'man', with no extant division of labour, specialization, money or exchange.

Marx himself has testified to a particularly powerful Saint-Simonian influence over him, as conveyed by his beloved mentor, surrogate father, and future father-in-law, Baron Ludwig von Westphalen. Towards the end of his life, Marx told his close friend and admirer, the Russian liberal aristocrat Maxim Kovalevsky, that he had imbibed Saint-Simonianism from von Westphalen, who was apparently an ardent admirer of Saint-Simonian doctrine.

We have already seen that in the *Communist Manifesto*, Marx and Engels slipped into the original libertarian, rather than the Saint-Simonian–Marxian theory of class, confusing the state-privileged with capitalists who hire workers on the market. In a penetrating discussion, Professor Ralph Raico has pointed out that the term 'bourgeois' as used on the Continent provided the basis for that confusion. As Raico notes:

> When Marx says that the *bourgeoisie* is the main exploiting and parasitic class in modern society, '*bourgeoisie*' may be understood in two different ways. In England and the United States, it has tended to suggest the class of capitalists and entrepreneurs who make their living by buying and selling on the (more or less)

free market...On the Continent, however, the term '*bourgeoisie*' has no such necessary connection with the market: it can just as easily mean the class of 'civil servants' and *rentiers* off the public debt as the class of businessmen involved in the process of social production.[22]

Raico goes on to state that the systematic exploitation of other classes by bureaucrats and public debt-holders 'was a commonplace of 19th century social thought'; Tocqueville, for example, denounces the 'middle class' rule under the '*bourgeois* monarchy' of Louis Phillippe (1830–48) as follows: 'It settled into every office, prodigiously increased the number of offices, and made a habit of living off the public Treasury almost as much as from its own industry.'[23]

But this is far from all. Professor Raico shows that, in analysing specific historical events, particularly in contemporary French history, Marx and Engels kept slipping into the state-bound two-class, libertarian-type analysis. Thus, consider Marx's *Eighteenth Brumaire of Louis Bonaparte* (1852), analysing the events leading up to Bonaparte's *coup* of 2 December 1851, which Marx himself portrayed as a 'demonstration how the *class struggle* in France created circumstances and relationships that made it possible for a grotesque mediocrity to play a hero's part'. In the *Eighteenth Brumaire*, Marx writes indignantly of:

> This executive power, with its enormous bureaucracy and military organization, with its ingenious state machinery, embracing wide strata, with a host of officials numbering half a million, this appalling parasitic body, which enmeshes the body of French society like a net and chokes all its pores, sprang up in the days of the absolute monarchy...Every *common* interest was straightway severed from society, counterpoised to it as a higher general *interest*, snatched from the activity of society's members themselves and made an object of government activity, from a bridge, a schoolhouse and the communal property of a village community to the railways, the national wealth and the national university of France... All revolutions perfected this machine instead of smashing it. The parties that contended in turn regarded the possession of this huge state edifice as the principal spoils of the victor... [U]nder the second Bonaparte...the state seems to have made itself completely independent. As against civil society, the state machine has consolidated its position...[24]

Not only is Marx using here a two-class state-bound analysis of class conflict, but he foreshadows the libertarian development of the idea of the state as an anti-social instrument, as in Herbert Spencer and in Franz Oppenheimer, and even Albert Jay Nock's advanced twentieth century libertarian analysis of 'state power' as being an interest inherently opposed to, and exploitative of, 'social power'.

Fine. But *where* in all of this are the capitalists and their use of the state as their 'executive committee' to redouble their exploitation of the proletariat?

Where, in fact, are capitalists and proletariat *at all*? As Raico points out, there is a delicious irony here. For sophisticated libertarian analysts speak not only of state power, but also of various groups in history – Asiatic bureaucratic despotism, feudal landlords, Communist Parties, or whatever – who have managed to gain control of the state and use its coercive apparatus of exploitative rule over the rest of society. Thus, as Raico notes, the Marxian analysis 'here completely ignores the massive use of state-power by *segments of the capitalist class*, and limits itself to the exploitative activities of those directly in control of the state apparatus'. Why Marx and Engels 'should care to whitewash the capitalists in this way', Raico concludes ironically, 'I cannot say'.[25]

Marx repeated a similar analysis 20 years later in his *The Civil War in France* (1871) on the rise and fall of the Paris Commune. That Commune, he wrote, aimed at restoring 'to the social body all the forces hitherto absorbed by the State parasite feeding upon, and clogging the free movement of society'. In particular, the Commune was able to succeed, at least for a while, 'by destroying the two greatest sources of [government] expenditure – the standing army and State functionarism'.

Finally, Engels in his 1891 preface to the *Civil War in France*, applied this same libertarian, and very un-Marxian, analysis to the existing political situation in the United States:

Nowhere do 'politicians' form a more separate and powerful section [class?] of the nation than precisely in North America. There, each of the two major parties which alternately succeed each other in power is itself in turn controlled by people who make a business of politics... It is in America that we see best how there takes place this process of the state power making itself independent in relation to society... we find two great gangs of political speculators, who alternately take possession of the state power and exploit it by the most corrupt means and for the most corrupt ends – the nation is powerless against these two great cartels of politicians who are ostensibly its servants, but in reality dominate and plunder it.[26]

Professor Raico concludes his analysis as follows:

It seems, therefore, that there are *two* theories of the state (as well as, correspondingly, two theories of exploitation) within Marxism: there is the customarily discussed and very familiar one [and the one which Marx himself proclaimed], of the state as the instrument of the ruling class (and the concomitant theory which locates exploitation within the production process); and there is the theory of the state which pits it against 'society' and 'nation' (two surprising and significant terms to find in this context...). Moreover, it would seem suggestive that it is this *second* theory that predominates in those writings of Marx which, because of their nuanced and sophisticated treatment of concrete and immediate political reality, many commentators have found to be the best expositions of the Marxian historical analysis.[27]

12.7   The legacy of Ricardo

As Karl Marx plunged into the economics of capitalism that would occupy the rest of his life, he found ready at hand a marvellous weapon: Ricardian economics. In contrast to J.B. Say and the French tradition, Ricardo concentrated not on market exchange and its inevitable focus on individual actors and enchangers benefiting from exchange, but on 'production' followed by 'distribution' of income as a distinct and separate process. Ricardo's main focus was on how this social income from production is 'distributed'. Whereas Say or Turgot looked at individual factors of production and how their income emerges from production and exchange, Ricardo focused only on entire, allegedly homogeneous, 'classes' of producers: workers earning wages, capitalists earning 'profits' and landlords acquiring rent. As von Mises pointed out: 'On the market there are always only single individuals...Even Marx had to make a point of explaining that as purchases and sales are made only between single individuals, it is not admissible to look to them for relations between social classes'.[28]

For Ricardo, then, tautologically, *given* total production, which was mysteriously *there* and not explained, more of the fixed total pie obtained by one class must mean less for other classes. There are, as we remember, no entrepreneurs in Ricardo, because the Ricardians had their eyes firmly fixed on long-run equilibrium, which is supposed to describe living reality, and in such equilibrium, devoid of change or uncertainty, there is no room for entrepreneurship. Thus, for Ricardo, the conditions were already there for a class-struggle theory of the capitalist economy.

Not only that. For the delighted Marx found that Ricardian doctrine was, in effect, a quantity of labour theory of value. Utility dropped out, and since only reproducible goods and not non-reproducible goods such as Rembrandt paintings were considered explainable, only the cost of production was considered a determinant of the embodied value of goods. And since Ricardo finessed 'rent' as allegedly not a part of cost, the only possible cost except labour hours was profit (interest) or cost of capital, and this was so small as to be readily neglected. Besides, profits are allegedly only a declining residual after the payment of wages, which are doomed to keep rising in money but not in real terms as population continues to press upon the food supply.

In the gloomy Ricardian perspective, there are two logical paths towards a call for change in the *status quo*. For Marx the labour theory of value, the view that labour is the sole producer of value, meant that the capitalist's return, profit, constituted the exploitative extraction of 'surplus value' from the workers. The workers produce all value, but the capitalists are able somehow to coerce the workers into accepting wages that are below the full product. In fact, adopting the Malthusian–Ricardian view of population, the workers are paid a subsistence wage, while the capitalists extract the remainder of the workers' product as their surplus value, or profit. To the old Malthusian problem: wouldn't the same problem of overpopulation foil a socialist economy? the Marxian answer was that such an iron law of wages (to adopt the term of Lassalle) would not apply under socialism.

Oddly, neither Marx nor his critics ever realized that there is one place in the economy where the Marxian theory of exploitation and surplus value *does* apply: not to the capitalist–worker relation in the market, but to the relation of master and slave under slavery. Since the masters own the slaves, they indeed only pay them their subsistence wage: enough to live on and reproduce, while the masters pocket the surplus of the slaves' marginal product over their cost of subsistence. This surplus value extracted from the slave constitutes the profits of the masters from slave-ownership. In the free society, in contrast, the workers, owning their own bodies and their own labour, pocket their full marginal product (discounted, as an Austrian would add, by the interest return the labourers freely and willingly pay to the capitalists for advancing them the value of their production now rather than wait until after the product is produced and sold).

Yet, such is the process of capitalization in the market that, in a system of slavery in the midst of a general market economy (as in the American South), the surplus value will be capitalized (by bidding up the value, and therefore the selling or buying price of the slaves). The long-run tendency will be for the business of slavery to yield a return equal to that of any other industry. The surplus profits will be bid away into the general rate of return on capital.

To return to Marx, he also found very handy the Smithian concept (not, to the latter's credit, much employed by Ricardo) that only *material commodities*, and not immaterial services, constitute production or value. Material goods are frozen labour, whereas immaterial labour services are, in Marxian terms, 'non-productive'. In this area, Marx took a giant step backwards from Ricardo to Adam Smith. All this, however, fitted neatly into Marxian philosophical materialism.

Marx also found that Ricardo had already treated all labour as homogeneous, with any differences in quality simply weighted by some sort of index to reduce them to quantity of labour hours.

One logical path for a radical Ricardian, clearly, was to call for the expropriation of surplus value, and the establishment of a system in which the labourers earn the full value of their product. As we shall see shortly, this was the path taken by the 'Ricardian socialist' writers in Britain. But there was another, more logical path. After all, the Ricardians could and did say that capital earned profits from their supplying workers with capital goods, with 'frozen labour'. Such a service is clear, otherwise the workers would not have had to rely on capitalists for money while working on the product. Marx's reply, that capital goods, being frozen labour, should be owned by the workers misses the point that *something*, some service must have been added by the capitalists – which, as we have already seen, was essentially savings and, if we may put it that way, who were advancing the workers' 'frozen time'.

A very different radical path, much more Ricardian and indeed already trod by James Mill, was to concentrate on the other possible bugbear class in the Ricardian system: the landlords – they who simply extract a return for no service, for simply sitting on the 'original and indestructible powers of the soil'. Furthermore, in their own vision of historical laws, the orthodox Ricardians saw the capitalists losing profit, the workers static at subsistence level, and the social product increasingly eaten up by the parasitic landlord class. The nationalization of land rent, then, the 'pre-Henry Georgist' route, was taken by other disciples, including the last of the consistent, radical Ricardians, Henry George.

But how has Marx managed to dispose of the land question that so agitated Ricardo and Mill? First of all, Marx was the great prophet of man as labourer; in his version of Hegelianism, man *created* nature, indeed the entire universe. Since land is man's creature, there is no room for worry about land or land-created value. Labour is all. Second, land as the basis for technology, the economy, and the social system, was the key to the feudal system, but feudalism was part of the dying 'pre-capitalist' pre-industrial order, a reactionary remnant unworthy of attention. Basically, then, Marx simply assimilated land into 'capital', and returns on land into profits. Thus land – the annoying superfluous third class of factors – can drop out and make way for the mighty two-class polarization and final struggle between the capitalists and the proletariat.

12.8   Ricardian socialism

Marx was hardly the first person to arrive at radical proletarian conclusions from the Ricardian system and the labour theory of value. Mediating between Ricardo and Marx were the 'Ricardian socialists', who greatly influenced Marx, but whose influence has been depreciated by Marxists – including Marx himself – who like to think that the master's unique genius in arriving at neo-Ricardian socialism had no predecessors.

The first Ricardian socialist was William Thompson (1775–1833), a well-to-do Irish landlord from County Cork. Thompson's prolix and repetitious work, *An Inquiry into the Principles of the Distribution of Wealth*, published in 1824, went into three editions in the next half-century. An extreme Benthamite utilitarian, Thompson in his *Inquiry* also simply declared that 'labour is the *sole* parent of wealth'. Neither utility, pleasure, or scarcity had anything to do with it. From this flat assertion, the labour theory of value swiftly followed. As Alexander Gray puts it, with his characteristic wit, 'it should be obvious that if the definition selected gives in advance an assurance labour is the *sole* parent of wealth, this ought to be a considerable aid towards proving that wealth may be attributed entirely to labour' [29]

Thompson advocated a world of free and voluntary exchanges as a way of ensuring that workers will earn their product. But what of the *existing* system of exchange? Anticipating Marx, these exchanges were, according to Thompson, coerced, the capitalists 'seizing the products of their labour [of the labourers] by force'. But here, on the edge of Marxism, Thompson retreated into a libertarian class analysis. For what constitutes such coercion? An entire spectrum of 'bounties, protestations, apprenticeships, guilds, corporations, monopolies' – which sounds very much like Comte, Dunoyer, or James Mill.

But Thompson presses on. Rent and profit are, in particular, 'surplus value' (in Thompson's original phrase) extracted from the exploited workers. But then Thompson retreats again from his full vision, conceding that 'the labourer must pay for the use of these [capital goods], when so unfortunate as not to possess them'. So even though Thompson is full of invective against the greedy and rapacious capitalists, he concedes that they perform a necessary function. How much, then, should they be paid? It is not surprising that Thompson floundered in trying to discover such a principle.

Thompson wound up, then, far from a revolutionary; instead, his mild, pre-John Stuart Mill-like solution was to encourage cooperatives as a means of arriving at inter-class harmony (in his *Labor Rewarded*, 1827). But this scarcely exhausted Thompson's heresies as a pre-Marxian. For, being dedicated to free exchange, Thompson sensibly had to admit that from exchange often emerges accumulation, and from accumulation there arises the dread capitalist class. Thus: 'you cannot abridge the exchanges and consequent accumulations of the capitalist without at the same time abridging all barter'. And, further, admitting the serpent of wages and rent back into Eden: 'Why not permit the labourer to exchange for the use of a house, a horse, a machine, as well as for its possession?[30]

The other founding father of Ricardian socialism in 1820s, John Gray (1799–1883), was possessed, like Thompson, of a most un-Marxian spirit of moderation. As a young Scottish clerk in a wholesale house in London, Gray published his socialistic *Lectures on Human Happiness* in 1825. An arch-utilitarian, and expounder of the Ricardian labour theory of value, Gray fulminated against capitalists as exploiters of the working class, and, like Marx, saw the seeds of such exploitation in trade or barter. If William Thompson's innovation was the phrase 'surplus value', John Gray's particular contribution to the Marxian brew was to bring back, in a heavy way, the physiocratic-Adam Smith notion of productive *vs* unproductive labour, and thus rescue this flawed concept from Ricardian neglect. Not only that: but Gray narrowed the Smithian standard of productive labour considerably. As Gray put it, '*they only* are productive members of society who apply *their own hands* either to the cultivation of the earth itself, or to the preparing and appropriating the produce of the earth to the uses of life'. Having narrowed the definition of productive, Gray then began to make curious concessions, admitting, for example, that some occupations may be to some extent 'useful' although 'unproductive'.

John Gray then proceeded happily to run through the list of British occupations, and to allocate in an obviously purely arbitrary way the percentages of 'productivity' or 'usefulness' in each occupation. Thus, Gray contends that merchants, manufacturers and others who are 'mere distributors of wealth', could still be 'useful' but 'only in a *sufficient* number'. Gray concluded that the productive classes were far short of half the total population.

Harking back, perhaps unconsciously, to the ancient Greeks, Gray reserved some of his choicest venom for the retailers, whom he savaged as 'productive' only of 'deception and falsehood, folly and extravagance, slavery of the corporeal, and prostitution of the intellectual faculties of man'.[31]

It turns out that for Gray, the main sin, the crucial evil, is competition. The competition of labour pushes the wages of labour down to a minimum. Standard Marxian fare, no doubt. But, in addition, even though labour is supposedly the sole creator of value, Gray also worries that competition, with equal perniciousness, also keeps to a minimum the amount of profits and rent.[32]

John Gray concludes with the general principle that every individual in society, except those living on fixed incomes, finds their incomes limited and ground down by competition.

It turns out that the exploitation of labour, indeed of *everyone*, is engineered by competition itself, which 'limits' production. Put an end to competition, then, and not only will the ideal world arrive where the labourer earns his full product, but also wealth will then be multiplied 'without any known limits'. The world is only impoverished because of competition; eliminate it, and wealth will be abundant for all.[33]

Even though Gray maintained that competition could be abolished immediately and with only good effects, he was distressingly vague on how to accomplish this feat. He seemed to favour some sort of all-embracing cooperative, thereby bringing him close to Thompsonian reform. Soon, however, Gray shifted his attention to the 'limitations' on production allegedly imposed by hard money, and so he turned increasingly to a call for accelerating amounts of cheap and easy money.

Thus, in 1831, Gray's book *The Social System* called for cheap and abundant credit to fuel and finance increased production, guided by a governmental national bank. Gray, of course, also advocated irredeemable paper money and the abolition of the gold standard. This analysis was further developed in John Gray's last work, *Lectures on the Nature and Use of Money* (1848).

After 1848, John Gray's social protests ceased completely, and so until recently it was assumed by historians that he had died 'around 1850'. It turns out, however, that Gray, shortly after the publication of his *Lecture of Human Happiness*, founded with his brother James the famous publishing firm of J. & J. Gray of Edinburgh. As the firm flourished, especially after 1850, Gray settled down to a comfortable existence, and died at a ripe old age of 84 in 1883.

A decade and a half after Thompson and Gray, the third leading Ricardian socialist made his appearance: John Francis Bray (1809–97), in his major work, much quoted by Marx, *Labour's Wrongs and Labour's Remedy* (1839). Bray was born in Washington DC, the child of English actors, and, when his mother died, his ailing father brought John Francis back to Leeds in England in 1822. In Leeds, Bray became a compositor, and plunged into the trade-union movement, becoming treasurer of the Leeds Working Men's Association in 1837.

Like the others an extreme utilitarian, Bray, in *Labour's Wrongs*, asserts that God had meant men to be happy, but that unhappiness was injected into the world by the institution of private property, which destroyed the just institution of communal property, particularly in the land. From private property arose the odious division of labour and class conflict, exploitation of labourers and extraction of their surplus value by the capitalist class. Moreover, Bray averred that the root problem is the alleged fact of unequal exchange. Although understanding that, in market exchanges, each party benefits, Bray asserts that, especially in a labour contract, this is not enough, that the exchange and its benefits must be 'equal'.

Not realizing that there is no point in *any* exchange unless the value, for each man, of each of the two exchanged goods is *unequal*, Bray, in a notable pre-Marxian passage, asserts:

> Men have only two things which they can exchange with each other, namely, labour and the product of labour; therefore, let them exchange as they will, they merely give, as it were, labour for labour. If a system of exchanges were acted upon, the value of all others would be determined by the entire cost of production, and equal values would always exchange for equal values.[34]

Here we have packed into one short compass a number of crucial Marxian fallacies: that only commodities are produced or important (in contrast to allegedly non-productive services); the ancient Aristotelian fallacy that exchange *implies* equality of value; the labour theory of value; and the idea that in a just world, prices will all be equal to their costs of production, basically the quantity of labour hours expended in production.

To John Bray, as to Marx after him, the remedy for all this systemic evil is communism, 'the most perfect form of society man can institute'. But in contrast to Marx, Bray saw no inevitable mechanism or law of history to yield that great event. To the contrary, and in contrast to the other communists of his day, John Bray perceived that communism required a New Communist Man to work, but that the advent of this new man was definitely not on the horizon. Any communism would come up against 'the foul and loathsome selfishness which now more or less accompanies every action, clings to every thought, and pollutes every aspiration'.[35]

Instead, Bray focused his vision, not on the impractical and remote ultimate goal, but on his allegedly practical transition, or intermediate, social goal. That happened to be a hypertrophied version of the cooperative schemes that had proved so alluring to Thompson and Gray. Bray proposed that the world be organized into one vast cartellized network of cooperative corporations: that is, cooperatives organized on the principle of one stockholder, one vote. The cartellized network would be achieved by the workers and cooperators *buying out* all existing capitalists. Bray did not seem to see that acquiring the capital to finance this most massive buy out of all time might be even more impractical than organizing Marx's violent proletarian revolution.

Scratch a socialist of this epoch and one will find a money crank. Sure enough, Bray envisioned that the cooperative cartel, once established, would eliminate existing money, and substitute a national bank that would issue notes to each worker based on the quantity of labour-time he had expended in production. The goods the labourer would buy would in their turn be priced at the amount of labour-time embodied within them. Perhaps if Marx had ever been interested in charting his future communist economy, labour-time notes might have been part of his package.

Strictly, there would be no reason for Marxian labour-time notes to increase, but John Bray, as an inflationist, did not of course see it that way. The function of his national bank would be to keep money issued and flowing 'like blood within the living body,...equably through society at large, and infuse universal health and vigor'. The note issue would, of course, always be kept 'within the limits of the actual effective capital existent' – a form of 'needs of trade' argument at least as absurd as the usual variant.[36] For the nominal 'value' of existing capital would of course increase as the money supply kept rising.

A few years after the publication of *Labour's Wrongs*, in 1842, Bray returned to the United States. A second book, *A Voyage from Utopia*, was finished in manuscript, but remained unpublished until the 1950s. For the rest of his life in the United States, Bray wrote sporadically, contributing many letters to labour and socialist periodicals, as well as chapters in the mid-1850s for an unfinished book, *The Coming Age*. Bray's life was as sporadic as his output. He found making a living precarious, working for brief jobs as a printer for newspapers, and complaining, rather inconsistently with his doctrines, that American employers were far more exploitative than British, the 'Yankees', as Professor Dorfman paraphrased Bray, 'appear[ing] more like gamblers and sharpers than honest businessmen'.[37]

Eventually, Bray went west to Michigan, where he had inherited some land, and eked out a living as a newspaperman and small farmer. During the 1870s and 1880s, Bray became vice-president of the American Labor Reform League and was a member of the socialistic Knights of Labor. His later writings, some of which denounced spiritualism, emphasized attacks on the gold standard and a call for an abundance of state paper money that would allegedly drive interest rates down to zero. His communist ideal was now abandoned as utopian.

Two of Bray's later writings are worthy of note. Even though he was opposed to slavery in *Labour's Wrongs*, his opposition to the Civil War in his anonymous anti-war pamphlet, *American Destiny: What Shall it Be, Republican or Cossack?* (1864) led him onward to judge slavery as really no worse than countries cursed by a huge public debt. Moreover, the natural state of the black man, to Bray, is 'nakedness and indolence', so that a South that freed its slaves would decay irremediably, with capital disappearing, and plantations returning to the wilderness.

In his final book, *God and Man a Unity and All Mankind a Unity* (1879), John Bray added to his money crankism the idea of a 'non-theological religion', in which establishing the right social institutions would bring about a this-worldly kind of 'immortality'.

A striking anomaly is a writer of the 1820s and later who is invariably listed by historians as a leading Ricardian socialist, but who was most emphatically neither a Ricardian nor a socialist. Thomas Hodgskin (1787–1869) was a brilliant, innovative and self-educated political theorist who, far from being a socialist, was a *laissez-faire* libertarian to the point of being an individualist anarchist. Hodgskin's father was a storekeeper at the naval dockyard who sent his son to sea at the age of 12. Eventually, Hodgskin's individualist instincts and principles rubbed against naval discipline, and one day, he writes, 'I complained of the injury done me, by a commander-in-chief, to himself, in the language that I thought it merited; he had unjustly deprived me of every chance of promotion from my own exertions, and that was robbing me of every hope'.[38]

As one might expect, Hodgskin's naval commander did not take kindly to his outburst of righteous indignation, and Hodgskin was forcibly retired from the navy, at half-pay, at the comparatively young retirement age of 25. Embittered, Hodgskin promptly took revenge on the navy by publishing his first book, *An Essay on Naval Discipline* (1813), a blistering attack on military tyranny. Eloquently, Hodgskin began his work by setting down the main lesson he had learned: 'Patiently submitting to oppression (because it comes from a superior) is a vice: to surmount your fears of that superior, and resist it, is a virtue'.[39]

Hodgskin's experience left him a bitter enemy of government and government intervention in all its forms; and several years of travelling around

Europe and reading and meeting people strengthened and deepened these convictions. Returning to Great Britain, Hodgskin published a two-volume travel book, *Travels in the North of Germany* (Edinburgh, 1820), in which, as Alexander Gray puts it, 'innocent *Reisebilder* are interlarded with anarchistic digressions, doubtless to the amazement and perturbation of many of his readers'.[40]

Settled in London, Hodgskin was, for the rest of his life, to work as a lecturer and a journalist. He worked for a while with people who seemed to be his natural allies for *laissez-faire*: Francis Place, James Mill, and the philosophic radicals. But very shortly it became clear that there were severe philosophical differences between them. In the first place, Hodgskin abandoned his early Benthamite utilitarianism for a trenchant and militant natural law and natural rights position. In his brilliant and logical work, *The Natural and Artificial Right of Property Contrasted* (1832), Hodgskin presented a radicalized Lockean view of property rights. An ardent defence of the right of private property, including a homesteading defence of private property in land, Hodgskin corrected Locke's various slippages from a consistent 'Lockean' position. To Hodgskin, it was crystal-clear that 'natural' private property rights were sound and just (such as each man in his own person, or in property that he creates or land that he homesteads, or in property which he acquires in an exchange of just property titles). On the other hand, great mischief was performed by 'artificial' property rights, that is, rights created by government artificially, in defiance of natural law and natural rights. Hodgskin's work remains today as one of the best expositions of natural property rights doctrine.

Another difference with the Benthamites was that unfortunately and anomalously, Hodgskin imbibed the labour theory of value from another influential 'Ricardian socialist' of the day, the pseudonymous 'Piercy Ravenstone'.[41] Ravenstone denounced private ownership of land and capital for creating stolen, or 'artificial', property, whereas since labour is the sole creator of production, by rights, or naturally, all income should redound to labour. Rent and profit, asserted Ravenstone, are extracted from the product of labour: this 'fund for the maintenance of the idle is the surplus produce of the labour of the industrious'. Furthermore, Ravenstone put forth a truly bizarre theory of capital, in which 'capital' is a non-existent concept designed to cloak the theft of labour's surplus. Capital, Ravenstone absurdly declared, 'may be increased to any imaginable amount without adding to the real riches of a nation'.[42]

From then on, Hodgskin was afflicted by an anomalous combination of *laissez-faire* anarchism and a Ravenstonian labour theory of value. How square the two? At first, Hodgskin tried to do so by attributing the exploitation, the 'surplus value' of labour, solely to such government intervention as the Combination Laws, which restricted the right to form labour unions. Hence Hodgskin helped found the *Mechanics' Magazine*, and then its affiliate, the London Mechanics' Institute, an institution for lectures to the working classes. During the course of the successful Ricardian–Benthamite agitation for repeal of the Combination Laws in 1824, Hodgskin wrote his Ravenstonian booklet, *Labour Defended Against the Claims of Capital* (1825), followed by Mechanics' Institute lectures published as *Popular Political Economy* (1827).

Particularly bizarre was Hodgskin's development of the Ravenstonian view that capital is unimportant and non-existent. Hodgskin denies that any savings are involved in capital, any advances from foregone consumption. Circulating capital, he says sophistically, are not produced in advance; the bread the worker buys is baked each day rather than being stored in advance by the capitalist. In fact, of course, no one claims that the capitalist actually stores the workers' food and other means of subsistence in advance; but his saved money is advanced ahead of production and sale to the worker, which enables the worker to buy his subsistence now instead of having to wait for years. As for fixed capital, not only is it stored-up labour – a general Ricardian socialist argument – but these machines are only 'inert, decaying and dead matter', unless 'guided, directed and applied by skillful hands'. Hodgskin concludes that 'fixed capital does not derive its utility from previous, but present labour', grotesquely ignoring the fact that just because capital and labour need each other does not make labour the *sole* factor of production. In the crowning absurdity, Hodgskin declares that 'it is a miserable delusion to call capital something saved'.

There is no question that Hodgskin's ultra labourism influenced Karl Marx, but his extreme labour theory of value does not make him a Ricardian, much less a socialist. In fact, Hodgskin was highly critical of Ricardo and the Ricardian system, denounced Ricardo's abstract methodology and his theory of rent, and considered himself a Smithian rather than a Ricardian. Smith's natural law and harmony-of-interest free market doctrine was also far more congenial to Hodgskin.

Although continuing to be a labourist, Hodgskin became increasingly repelled by the English labour movement, and its growing interest in state intervention. Labour unions he no longer saw as much of a remedy, let alone a panacea. Increasingly, he saw that the only way to reconcile labourism and *laissez-faire* was to press for the repeal of all government intervention, indeed of all positive law that was not simply a restatement of natural law and natural rights. For all such law was an invasion of rights of property. In contrast to the Ricardian socialists who extolled cartel-like cooperatives, Hodgskin called for removal of all government restrictions on free and unlimited competition. He enthusiastically joined Cobden and Bright in agitation for repeal of the Corn Laws, and in repealing feudalistic laws restricting and entailing land from free sale outside the family. From 1846–55, Hodgskin served as an editor of the *Economist*, the journalistic champion of *laissez-faire*, with as yet no important incompatibility of views with editor-in-chief James Wilson. There he became a friend and mentor of the young Herbert Spencer, hailing Spencer's anarchistic work, *Social Statics*, with the exception of denouncing the early Spencer's pre-Georgist land socialism on behalf of Lockean individualism.

Furthermore, even at his most labourist in the 1820s, Thomas Hodgskin, in contrast to John Gray, widened rather than narrowed the definition of 'labour'. Mental activity is as much 'labour', he pointed out, as muscular exertion, so he warned against limiting the term 'labour' to the 'operations of the hands'. Not only that: Hodgskin also pointed out cogently that the capitalist is also very often a manager, and therefore also a 'labourer'. So whereas capitalists may be oppressors, businessmen in their capacity as managers or 'masters', 'are labourers as well as their journeymen'. And there is nothing wrong with the wages of management.[43]

In addition, the Hodgskin of the 1820s hailed retailers as 'indispensable agents', and praised wholesalers and merchants in Smithian terms as conferring blessings on society by pursuing their own interests. Even bankers 'are still very important, and have long been very useful labourers'. Banking, 'let us never forget…is altogether a private business, and no more needs to be regulated by meddling statesmen, than the business of paper-making'. Finally, in his *Popular Political Economy*, Hodgskin eulogized the market price system, which, in a deep sense, is 'the finger of Heaven, indicating to all men how they may employ their time and talents most profitably for themselves, and most beneficially for the whole society'.[44]

After his retirement from the *Economist* editorial board, Hodgskin continued to write articles for that journal. There he praised commerce ('We are all merchants…and…trade is only mutual service by mutual dealing'); speculation ('without speculation we should have no railroads, no docks, no great companies…') and competition ('the soul of excellence, and gives to every man his fair reward').[45]

In his final publication, of lectures on criminal law delivered in 1857, Thomas Hodgskin summed up his economic and political philosophy. The people's wants for higher standards of living, he declared, 'can only be satisfied by more freedom, and less taxation'. The free trade principles of the 1840s must be only a stepping-stone towards ever purer and more consistent *laissez-faire*. Ultimately, all government services must be privatized and subjected to the requirements of the free market:

The unrestricted competition, which nature establishes, must be the rule for all our transactions; and by the higgling of the market, which is mutual and free action, the salaries of [government] officials, and the payments of the priesthood must be regulated as well as the profit of the shopkeeper, and the wages of the labourer.

In printing his lectures, Hodgskin announced his intention of completing and publishing a masterwork, *The Absurdity of Legislation Demonstrated*, which would show, 'in a connected didactic form', that 'all legislation, which of course includes Government, is founded on false assumptions'.[46]

Unfortunately, Hodgskin never completed the work, or published anything further, and when he died, in 1869, at the age of 82, this man, once so widely influential, received not a single obituary notice in the London papers. But, at any rate, enough is surely known to dismiss the view that this individualist, despite the labourism that influenced Marx, was in any sense a socialist, or even a Ricardian.

12.9 Notes

1. As Gray wittily puts it, the dialectic often seems 'to the illiterate and ignorant outsider to become a mere toy which enables every swing of every pendulum to be regarded as the embodiment of a great philosophical principle'. Alexander Gray, *The Socialist Tradition* (London: Longmans, Green, 1947), p. 300.
2. In Igor Shafarevich, *The Socialist Phenomenon* (New York: Harper & Row, 1980), p. 210.
3. Ludwig von Mises, *Theory and History* (1957, Auburn, Ala.. Mises Institute, 1985), pp. 111–2.
4. Ibid., pp. 109–10.
5. In the *Poverty of Philosophy*, Marx angrily denounced Proudhon for making this very point, that division of labour precedes machines.
6. See M.M. Bober, *Karl Marx's Interpretation of History* (2nd rev. ed., Cambridge, Mass.: Harvard University Press, 1948), p. 9.
7. John Plamenatz, *German Marxism and Russian Communism* (New York: Longmans, Green & Co., 1954), p. 29.
8. Ibid., p. 27.
9. For a defence of technological monocausality as a key to Marxism by the founder of Russian Marxism, George V. Plekhanov (1857–1918), see Plekhanov, *The Development of the Monist View of History* (New York: International Publishers, 1973). Cf. David Gordon, *Critics of Marxism* (New Brunswick, MJ: Transaction Books, 1986), p. 22. For a critique of Marxism–Plekhanovism, see Leszek Kolakowski, *Main Currents of Marxism* (Oxford: Oxford, University Press, 1981), pp. 340–2.
10. Von Mises, op. cit., note 3, p. 126.
11. David Gordon, 'Mises Contra Marx', *The Free Market*, 5 (July 1987), pp. 2–3.
12. For the refutation of another, allied point in Marx's ideology doctrine, that each economic class has a different logical structure of mind ['polylogism'], see Ludwig von Mises, *Human Action* (New Haven, Conn.: Yale University Press, 1949), pp. 72–91.
13. In the first, 'Bourgeois and Proletarians' section of the *Communist Manifesto*, Marx and Engels continually confuse the concepts of 'caste' and 'class', i.e. class as special privilege vs sets of individuals on the free market. Thus: 'In the earlier epochs of history, we find almost everywhere a complicated arrangement of society into various orders, a manifold gradation of social rank. In ancient Rome we have patricians, knights, plebeians, slaves; in the Middle Ages, feudal lords, vassals, guild-masters, journeymen, apprentices, serfs; in almost all of these classes, again, subordinate gradations, [i.e., classes as castes]'.

Further, 'The modern bourgeois society that has sprouted from the ruins of feudal society has...established new classes, new conditions of oppression...[The unexamined leap from a caste-class to a free-market situation]'.

14. During the 1870s, Marx led Engels to believe that he was working hard and steadily on Volumes II and III of *Capital*. At Marx's death, Engels was astonished to find that Marx had done virtually no work on the manuscript since 1867, in short, that Marx had lied shamelessly to his friend and patron. See W.O. Henderson, *The Life of Friedrich Engels* (London: Frank Cass, 1976), II, p. 563.

15. See below on the Ricardian contribution to the Marxian theory of class.

16. Cf. these insights from Marxism's outstanding twentieth century opponent, Ludwig von Mises: 'The theory of irreconcilable class conflict is illogical when it stops short at dividing society into three or four large classes. Carried to its logical conclusions, the theory would have to go on dissolving society into groups of interests till it reached groups whose members fulfilled precisely the same function. It is not enough to separate owners into landowners and capitalists. The differentiation must proceed until it reaches such groups as cotton spinners who manufacture the same count of yarn, or the manufacturers of black kid leather, or the brewers of light beer....No special common interest unites the owners of arable land, of forests, of vineyards, of mines, or of urban real estate... There are no common interests among labourers either. Homogeneous labour is as non-existent as the universal worker. The work of the spinner is different from the work of the miner and the work of the doctor ... Nor is unskilled labour homogeneous. A scavenger is different from a porter'. Ludwig von Mises, *Socialism: An Economic and Sociological Analysis* (4th ed., Indianapolis: Liberty Classics, 1981), pp. 300–301.

17. See James Bland Briscoe, 'Saint-Simonianism and the Origins of Socialism in France, 1816–32' (doctoral dissertation in history, Columbia University, 1980), p. 59.

18. It is difficult not to agree with Alexander Gray's assessment of Saint-Simon, as quoted from the French social philosopher Émile Faguet: 'Saint-Simon is a rare example of incoherence in his life, incoherence in his character, and incoherence in his detailed ideas, combined with a fixity in his ruling views.' (My translation.) Gray, op. cit., note 1, p. 160n.

19. See F.A. von Hayek, *The Counter-Revolution of Science* (Glencoe, Ill.: The Free Press, 1952), p. 158.

20. Ibid., p. 159.

21. James Billington, *Fire in the Minds of Men: Origins of the Revolutionary Faith* (New York: Basic Books, 1980), p. 225.

22. Ralph Raico, 'Classical Liberal Exploitation Theory: A Comment on Professor Liggio's Paper', *The Journal of Libertarian Studies*, 1 (Summer 1977), p. 179.

23. Alexis de Tocqueville, *Recollections*, ed. by J.P. Mayer and A.P. Kerr (Garden City, New York: Doubleday & Co. 1970), p. 5.

24. Raico, op. cit., note 22, pp. 179–80. Professor Tucker, curiously enough, hails *The Eighteenth Brumaire* as a 'brilliant masterpiece', and an application of class struggle analysis and the materialist conception of history. But isn't this work a demonstration of quite the opposite? See Robert C. Tucker (ed.), *The Marx–Engels Reader* (2nd ed., New York: W.W. Norton, 1978), p. 594.

25. Raico, op. cit., note 22, p. 180.

26. Ibid., p. 180, 183n4.

27. Ibid., p. 180.

28. Von Mises, op. cit., note 16, p. 292; he notes that this passage in Vol I of *Capital* was not in the first 1867 edition, but was added by Marx in the French edition (1873). The insertion was connected to the desperate changes made by Marx in his theory in Volume III of *Capital*, not published until after his death.

29. Gray, op. cit., note 1, p. 271.

30. From *Labour Rewarded*. See Gray, op. cit., note 1, p. 276.

31. Ibid., p. 290n.

32. Ibid., p. 294.

33. Ibid., pp. 294–5.

34. Quoted in G.D.H. Cole, *Socialist Thought: The Forerunners, 1789–1850* (London: Macmillan, 1959), p. 137.
35. Gray, op. cit., note 1, p. 287
36. In Joseph Dorfman, *The Economic Mind in American Civilization, 1606–1865* (New York: Viking Press, 1946), II, p. 688.
37. Ibid., p. 689.
38. Élie Halévy, *Thomas Hodgskin* (London: Ernest Benn, Ltd, 1956), p. 30.
39. Ibid., p. 31.
40. Gray, op. cit., note 1, p. 278.
41. Piercy Ravenstone, *A Few Doubts as to the Correctness of Some Opinions Generally Entertained on the Subjects of Population and Political Economy* (London, 1821).
42. Halévy, op. cit., note 38, pp. 89n–90n. Ravenstone was apparently not a socialist either. Best indications are that he was either the Rev. Edward Edward, a High Tory Anglican clergyman, or Richard Puller, the equally Tory son of a director of the South Sea Company, the Tory speculative banking scheme. Ravenstone's goal was apparently to strike an effective blow against capitalism and free markets by one of their ancient enemies, the High Tory advocates of statism and big government.
43. Gray, op. cit., note 1, p. 282.
44. Ibid., p. 280. Gray, an adherent of the Austrian School, adds a teasing and witty note on his fellow Austrians: 'Even an orthodox economist of these days, brought up on Tales from the Viennese Woods, may well be forgiven if his faith falters when invited to identify the price-system with the finger of Heaven.'
45. In Halévy, op. cit., note 38, pp. 148–9.
46. Ibid., p. 164.

13 The Marxian system, II: the economics of capitalism and its inevitable demise

13.1 The labour theory of value

We have seen that, for the latter half of his life, Karl Marx, exiled in Britain far from the political or possible revolutionary fray, spent the last years of his life searching for the mechanism by which the economics of capitalism would inevitably and ineluctably give rise to its own revolutionary over-throw. In short, the mechanism by which the capitalist class would be expro-priated by the revolutionary proletariat, which would then proceed to usher in the various stages of communism.

Marx found a crucial key to this mechanism in Ricardo's labour theory of value, and in the Ricardian socialist thesis that labour is the sole determinant of value, with capital's share, or profits, being the 'surplus value' extracted by the capitalist from labour's created product. 'Capital' was merely 'frozen labour', so that any possible contribution to the product devolves on labour as well.

But, in order to arrive at the labour, or quantity-of-labour-hours, theory of value, Marx, in his systematic work *Capital*, had to dispose of other, subjec-tive, claimants to determining value. He also had to demonstrate that value was somehow objectively embodied in the product (a material good, of course, since Marx, with Smith, had dismissed immaterial services as 'unpro-ductive'). He attempted to perform this feat at the very beginning of Volume I of *Capital*, and how he did it is highly instructive.

Marx begins *Capital* by concentrating on 'the commodity', an object – as we have seen, a *material substance* – which has utility for satisfying human wants. In this way like Ricardo, he leaves immaterial services out of the picture, and also omits studying the value of non-reproducible products, which have no ongoing costs of production. Like Ricardo, Marx also begins with the necessity of utility, but, like his master, he quickly dismisses this basic fact as of little or no use in explaining 'exchange-value', the proportion in which commodities exchange for one another on the market. As in Smith and Ricardo, therefore, use-value and exchange-value, or price, of commodi-ties are sundered from each other. How, then, explain exchange-value? How, in short, explain the proportions by which commodities exchange for each other on the market?

Marx adds that, superficially, it seems that exchange values are relative, that they fluctuate in relation to each other, and that therefore there is nothing objectively 'intrinsic' in the product that determines its value. Marx then sets out to correct this alleged error. Here is the crucial paragraph:

> Let us take two commodities, *e.g.,* corn and iron. The proportions in which they are exchangeable, whatever these proportions may be, can always be represented by an equation in which a given quantity of corn is equated to some quantity of iron: *e.g.,* 1 quarter corn = x cwt.iron. What does this equation tell us? It tells us

that in two different things – in 1 quarter of corn and x cwt.of iron, there exists in equal quantities something common of both. The two things must therefore be equal to a third, which in itself is neither the one nor the other. Each of them so far as it is exchange-value, must therefore be reducible to this third…of which thing they represent a greater or less quantity.[1]

Thus, Marx inserts his crucial error at the very beginning of his system. The fact that two commodities exchange for each other in some proportion does *not* mean that they are therefore 'equal' in value and can be 'represented by an equation'. As we have learned ever since Buridan and the scholastics, two things exchange for each other only because they are *unequal* in value to the two participants in the exchange. *A* gives up to *x* to *B* in exchange for *y*, because *A* prefers *y* to *x*, and *B*, on the contrary, prefers *x* to *y*. An equals sign falsifies the essential picture. And if the two commodities, *x* and *y*, were really equal in value in the sight of the two exchangers, why in the world did either of them take the time and trouble to make the exchange? Marx's concentration on 'the commodity' threw him off from the very start, for the focus should have been not on the thing, the material object, but in the individuals, the actors, *doing* the exchanging, and deciding whether or not to make the trade.

If there is no equality in value, then there is clearly no third 'something' to which these values must be equal. Marx compounds his original error with another, assuming that if there were an equality of value, there is therefore necessarily some third tangible thing to which they must be equal and by which they can be measured. There is no warrant for this leap from equality of value to measurement of an objective third entity; the implicit, and fallacious, assumption is that 'value' is an objective entity like weight or length which can be scientifically measured against some third, external, standard.

Having made two egregious and fatal mistakes in one paragraph Marx presses on inexorably to his conclusion. Emphasizing by mere assertion that utility can have nothing whatever to do with exchange-values, a point crucial to his case, he claims that use-values have nothing to do with exchange-values or prices. This means that all real attributes of goods, their natures, their varying qualities, etc., are abstracted from, and can have nothing to do with, their values. By tossing out all real-world properties from the discussion, Marx is perforce left with goods as the embodiment of pure, abstract, undifferentiated labour hours, the quantity of allegedly homogeneous labour hours embodied in the product.

Marx of course sees that there are great problems with this approach. What about the scholastic thrust: is the market expected to cover the costs, the enormous number of labour hours, needed to make a product in an obsolete way? If a book is printed, or hand-scripted, is the market going to cover the payment for the enormous number of labour hours needed in the hand-copying process? Is the market expected to pay the labour costs of carrying goods across land, as compared to shipping them by sea? Marx's way of disposing of these awkward questions was to create the concept of 'socially necessary' labour time. The determinant of the value of a good is not any old labour time spent on, or embodied in, its production, but only labour time that is 'socially necessary'. But this is a cop out, and evades the issue by begging the entire question. Market value is determined only by the quantity of 'socially' necessary' labour time. But what is 'socially necessary'? Whatever the market decides. So a crucial ingredient of explaining market value is market decisions, market values, themselves.

To elaborate further: Marx defines 'labour time socially necessary' as 'that required to produce an article under the normal conditions of production, and with the average degree of skill and intensity prevalent at the time'.[2] This brings up a corollary problem: how to meld a myriad of different qualities and skills of labour into one homogeneous, abstract 'labour hour'? Here, taking up a hint from Ricardo, Marx inserts the concepts of 'average' and 'normal'. It all averages out. But how is this average obtained? It is done by weights, with higher quality, unusually productive labour weighted more heavily in quantity labour-time units than is the labour of an unskilled worker. But who decides the weights? Once again, Marx's crucial question-begging methodology comes into play. For Marx acknowledges that it is the *market*, its relative prices and wages, which determines the weights, *i.e.* which labour is more productive or higher in quality and in what degree than some other forms of labour. So market values, prices, and productivities are being used to try to explain the determinants of those same values and prices.[3]

13.2 Profit rates and 'surplus value'

Marx proceeds with his model in a Ricardian socialist manner. In contrast to Ricardo, however, land and rent are simply assimilated into 'capital', since man's labour allegedly created all land anyway, and since the importance of land and feudalism allegedly disappears as capitalism proceeds on its way. Values and prices of land therefore need not be treated or explained. There are, then, two mighty classes under capitalism: the homogeneous labourers, the proletariat; and 'the capitalists' [as in Smith and Ricardo, there are, of course, no entrepreneurs. All is in slowly moving long-run equilibrium]. But the values of goods are the sole creation of quantities of labour-hours. Capitalists, by some sort of coercion, by their imposed set of property relations, extract by force a 'profit' from the product of the 'exploited' workers. This profit is 'surplus value', the value seized by capitalists out of total value produced.

Profit, for Marx, is derived *only* from exploiting labour; it is the surplus value over the wages necessary for the subsistence of labour. Profits, on the other hand, have nothing to do with the amount of capital invested; for capital is only dead matter, stored or frozen labour, and can therefore no longer be 'exploited' to provide current profits.[4] Only 'living' labour, then, can be used to provide profit for the capitalist. But if the amount of profit is extracted solely from labour, this means that any accumulation of capital will necessarily *reduce* the *rate* of profit earned by the capitalist. Thus, suppose no capital or, in Marxian terms, 'constant' capital is used,[5] and investment is made solely in the form of 'variable capital' used to pay wages. Suppose that profits from production of the good are $100, and total variable capital, or wage payment, is $1 000. In that case, the profit rate is 10 per cent. On the other hand, suppose that there is investment in capital goods amounting to, say, another $1 000. Total capital investment is then $2 000, but since profits are only derived from labour they are still the same $100, so that the profit rate has now fallen to 5 per cent.

What determines wages, the amount grudgingly accorded to the workers by the capitalist class? Here Malthus and the iron law of wages make their vital appearance, determining wages at all times at the means of subsistence. Marx, of course, hastens to clear his future communist utopia from any Malthusian problems by asserting that Malthus and the iron law only holds sway under capitalism, and would certainly not apply under communism.

It must be emphasized that the iron law is crucial to Marx's entire system. For Marx, the value and price of every good is determined by its cost, *i.e.,* the quantity of labour hours embodied in its production. Marx believed that, on the market, capitalists pay workers the 'value of their labour-power', by which he meant, of course, *not* their productivity or marginal productivity, but the 'cost' of producing and maintaining the labour, *i.e.*, the cost, or the quantity of labour hours, needed to produce the labourers' means of subsistence.[6]

Professor Conway, in his generally excellent survey and critique of Marxism, claims that Marx's theory of surplus value does not *require* the iron law of wages, since the capitalists could still extract some surplus value even if wages were higher than the subsistence wage. Very true, except that *then* wages in the Marxian system would be undetermined, and indeed there would be no reason to assume that surplus value exists at all, or that it is large enough to have any importance in the economy. Besides, if wages are not locked into the bare means of subsistence, then the plight of the workers under capitalism might not be so pitiable after all. And what if there were then very little substance to spur the workers into the revolutionary overthrow of capitalism that Marx insisted was inevitable? Thus, in the *Communist Manifesto*, Marx and Engels proclaimed emphatically that the average wage is always 'the minimum wage, *i.e.,* that quantum of the means of subsistence [*Lebensmittel*], which is absolutely requisite [*notwendig*] to keep the laborer in bare existence as a laborer. What, therefore, the wage-laborer appropriates by means of his labor, merely suffices to prolong and reproduce a bare existence'.[7,8] And Engels, in his late work *Anti-Dühring* (1878), asserts that large-scale industry 'restricts the consumption of the masses at home to a starvation minimum...'

There are great problems in Marx's model. His theory implies that, since profits are only derived from the exploitation of labour, profit *rates* are necessarily lower in heavily capitalized than in labour-intensive industries. But everyone, including Marx, is forced to acknowledge that this manifestly does *not* hold true on the market. The tendency on the market, as Smith and Ricardo well knew, is for rates of profit to tend toward equality in all industries. But how so, if profit rates are necessarily and systematically higher in the labour-intensive industries?

Here is surely the most glaring single hole in the Marxian model. Marx acknowledged that, in the real world, profit rates clearly tend toward equality (or, as Marx termed it, an 'average rate of profit'), and that real prices or exchange-values in capitalist markets therefore do not exchange at their Marxian quantity-of-labour values. Marx admitted this crucial problem, and promised that he could solve the problem successfully in a later volume of *Capital*. He struggled with this problem for the rest of his life, and never solved it – perhaps one of the main reasons that he stopped working early on *Capital* and never published the later volumes. In the first edition of his great *History of the Theories of Capital and Interest* published in 1884, the year after Marx's death, the outstanding Austrian theorist Eugen von Böhm-Bawerk, in his critique of Marx, pointed out that 'Marx himself became aware of the fact that there was a contradiction here, and found it necessary for the sake of his solution to promise to deal with it later on. But the promise was never kept, and indeed could not be kept'.[9]

Böhm-Bawerk later noted that the growing legion of Marxian adepts continued to maintain their faith that the master would eventually come up with a solution to this grave and apparently ineradicable flaw in the Marxian system.[10] Then, in the preface to Marx's posthumous second volume of *Capital*, Friedrich Engels teasingly and rather childishly declared that in a forthcoming volume Marx would solve the famous profit rate and value problem, and invited all Marxian and other economists to a kind of prize essay contest to guess how Marx was going to solve this seemingly insoluble contradiction. In the ensuing nine years until the publication of the climactic Volume III of *Capital*, a surprisingly large number of economists tried their hands at this little game. In the preface to the long-awaited Volume III, published in 1894, a year before his own death, Engels was able to demonstrate triumphantly that none of these economists had come close to winning the prize.[11] Thus Engels was far less cautious than Marx in being willing to go public and trumpet a 'solution' that Marx had apparently not felt worthy of being published.[12]

Volume III was subjected to detailed, withering, thoroughgoing demolition two years later by Böhm-Bawerk in his extensive review essay, *Karl Marx and the Close of His System*.[13] A century later, Böhm-Bawerk's devastating refutation of the Volume III solution and therefore the Marxian system remains definitive. It swept the boards in professional economics, and has remained dominant ever since, successfully inoculating economists, at least, against the Marxian virus, and certainly against the labour theory of value. Unfortunately, Böhm-Bawerk's point was too technical to have much impact outside the ranks of economists, and, since then, Marxism has held its greatest attraction in the ranks of sociologists, historians, the literati, and others who tend to be economically ignorant.

Böhm-Bawerk, in sum, posed the grave inner contradiction of Marxian theory plainly and starkly: Marx claimed that goods exchanged on the market in proportion to the quantities of labour embodied in them (i.e., that their values are determined by the quantity of labour-hours needed to produce them), and *yet* also conceded that the rates of profit on all goods tended to be equal. And yet, if the first clause is true, the rates of profit would be systematically lower in proportion to the intensity of capital investment, and higher in proportion to their labour-intensiveness of production. Marx promised to resolve this insoluble contradiction in Volume III and to reconcile these two fundamentally contradictory propositions.

In *Karl Marx and the Close of His System*, Böhm-Bawerk demonstrated that Marx's proffered 'solution' was a sham, and that actually what Marx did was to throw in the towel and admit that, on the capitalist market, profit rates were equal and therefore that prices were *not* proportional to or determined by the quantity of labour hours in the production of goods. Instead, Marx in effect embraced standard Ricardian theory and admitted that prices were actually determined by the costs (or, in his terminology, 'prices') of production plus the average rate of profit. In this way, while pretending to have saved his theory by talking grandly about competition transforming 'values into prices of production', Marx had actually abandoned the labour theory of value altogether and had therefore scuttled his entire system.

Böhm-Bawerk then goes into a systematic critique of various Marxian arguments attempting to save the phenomenon, including nonsense about 'total value' being equal to total prices of all products.

It is instructive to note the reaction of Marxists to Volume III and to Böhm-Bawerk's exposure and demolition of their system's grave inner contradictions. Too often, they reacted in the manner of religious cultists and not honest scientists. That is, when their system is caught in egregious fallacies or contradictions, or makes grossly faulty predictions, cultists save their theory *by changing the terms* of the argument. That is, they assert that the theory said something quite different, or that the prediction had really been different. Similarly, the extremely popular Millerite movement in the early 1840s had confidently forecast the exact date of Jesus's Second Advent, in 1843. When Jesus did not arrive on the predicted date, the Millerites characteristically claimed a slight error in their calculations, and postponed the happy date for another few months. When Jesus failed to arrive once more, most Millerites dispersed, but some of the hard-core faithful changed the terms of the argument by insisting that Jesus had indeed arrived on the expected date, but that his advent was invisible, the more visible second part of the Second Coming to arrive at some future date. (This latter group became the Seventh Day Adventists.) And so the fallback position of the Marxian apologists was the outrageously false claim that Marx never *meant* his labour-determined values to determine, or in any way affect, market prices. Marx, they asserted loftily, had no interest in such petty matters as market price; his labour-quantity-created 'values' were simply embodied mystically into market commodities, presumably then to have no relevance whatever to the real world of market capitalism.

Thus Paul Sweezy asserted that Marx was not dealing with prices at all but really in 'what today might be called economic sociology'.[14] G.D.H. Cole tried to claim, in his *What Marx Really Meant*, that for Marx, in contrast to other economists, value had nothing to do with determining prices, but was, essentially *by definition*, the quantity of labour hours embodied in a product. Alexander Gray levelled a witty and devastating critique of Cole:

> But the identity of value and embodied labour was surely something that Marx thought he had *proved* (and which therefore required proof) in the opening pages of *Capital*...If the identity of value and labour is a matter of definition and assumption, then at least we know the meaning Marx attaches to 'value': but in that case the pretended proof in the opening chapter is mere eye-wash; since one states, but does not prove, definitions. Also in that case it is to be feared that the whole of *Capital*, resting on an arbitrary definition which implies the conclusion to be reached, is an example of wandering vainly in a circle, even more than the most critical critics had thought possible. If, on the other hand, the identity of value and labour is a matter of proof and not of definition, we are still left to grope for the meaning Marx attaches to 'value'.[15]

While official Marxists have all taken this escape-hatch – saving the labour theory of value by rendering it irrelevant – the only full-scale Marxist attempt to rebut Böhm-Bawerk was that of the Austrian Marxist Rudolf Hilferding (1877–1941), *Böhm-Bawerk's Critique of Marx*, published in 1904, with the English translation being published in 1920. Hilferding's apologetics, taking the fallback line that Marx never meant values to determine prices, is a clumsy and garbled work. It is interesting that Hilferding's friend and fellow leading Austro-Marxist theoretician, Otto Bauer, dismissed Hilferding as never having truly understood the nature of the problem. Bauer enrolled in

Böhm-Bawerk's great seminar at the University of Vienna in order to learn enough to be able to refute Böhm-Bawerk's celebrated critique. In the end, Bauer gave up the task, virtually admitting that the Marxian labour theory of value was indefensible.[16] Most modern Marxist scholars hold the labour theory of value to be an embarrassment, and sophisticated Marxists have dropped it altogether, unfortunately without also giving up the system of which it is a crucial and necessary part.[17]

A curious case of Marxist apologetics is a book widely and extravagantly touted as the definitive *critique* of Marxism. In his *Marxism*, Professor Thomas Sowell takes the Hilferding line and adds further errors of his own. Thus, he berates Böhm-Bawerk for having 'repeatedly misunderstood' Marx, when the meticulous Böhm-Bawerk understood Marx all too well, and Sowell follows Hilferding in erroneously claiming that Böhm-Bawerk and other critics wrongly held that Marx identified 'values' with prices. On the contrary, Böhm-Bawerk and the others were fully aware that labour-created 'values' were supposed to determine, but not be the same as, exchange-values, or prices. It is also ironic that an author who makes a big point of castigating well-known economists who write on Marxian economics without once citing Marx, should yet make the egregious and pompous claim that Marx referred 'nowhere to a *theory* of value, despite a numerous – and undocumented – interpretive literature to the contrary'. As a reviewer of Sowell points out, such a reference by Marx can easily be found in Volume III of *Capital*.[18]

Although orthodox Marxists of course do not acknowledge it, the Hilferding fallback position, while indeed saving the equalization of profit in the real world, does so at the grave cost of abandoning the labour theory of value. Or, what is the same, leaving it as an empty and meaningless shell. But if there is no labour theory of value, then there is no surplus value, no exploitation and no reason for the proletariat to rebel against a world in which their product is not being systematically confiscated by the capitalist class.

The most interesting and flamboyant case of an ardent Marxist who behaved honourably when confronted with the stark contradiction between Volumes I and III of *Capital* was the Italian economist Achille Loria (1857–1943). For Loria, the first volume of *Capital* had been 'a masterpiece wherein all is great, all alike incomparable and wonderful'. Yet to Loria Volume III was a grievous death-blow to Marx's own system. Loria in fact did not need to wait for Böhm-Bawerk's critique; in his own review of Volume III, Loria attacked the book as a 'mystification' instead of a 'solution'. Loria denounced the book as 'the Russian campaign' [à la Napoleon] of the Marxian system, its 'complete theoretical bankruptcy', a 'scientific suicide', and the 'most explicit surrender of his own teaching'.[19]

Let Alexander Gray have the perceptive and hilarious last word on Marx's value theory:

To witness Böhm-Bawerk or Mr. [H.W.B.] Joseph carving up Marx is but a pedestrian pleasure; for these are but pedestrian writers, who are so pedestrian as to clutch at the plain meaning of words, not realising that what Marx really meant [Cole] has no necessary connection with what Marx undeniably said. To witness Marx surrounded by his friends is, however, a joy of an entirely different order. For it is fairly clear that none of them really knows what Marx really meant; they are even in considerable doubt as to what he was talking about; there are hints that Marx himself did not know what he was doing. In particular, there is no one to tell us what Marx thought he meant by 'value'. And indeed, what all these conjectures reveal is somewhat astounding, and, one would have to think unique. *Capital* is, in one sense, a three-volume treatise, expounding a theory of value and its manifold applications. Yet Marx never condescends to say what he means by 'value', which accordingly is what anyone cares to make it as he follows the unfolding scroll from 1867 to 1894. Nor does anyone know to what world all this applies. Is it to the world in which Marx wrote? Or to an abstract, 'pure' capitalist world existing ideally in the imagination, and nowhere else? [Croce] Or (odd as the suggestion may appear) was Marx (probably unconsciously) thinking in terms of medieval conditions? [Wilbrandt] No one knows. Are we concerned with *Wissenschaft*, slogans, myths, or incantations? Marx, it has been said, was a prophet – and perhaps this suggestion provides the best approach. One does not apply to Jeremiah and Ezekiel the tests to which less inspired men are subjected. Perhaps the mistake the world and most of the critics have made is just that they have not sufficiently regarded Marx as a prophet – a man above logic, uttering cryptic and incomprehensible words, which every man may interpret as he chooses.[20]

13.3   The 'laws of motion', I: the accumulation and centralization of capital

Thus, Karl Marx had established, to his own satisfaction at least, the labour theory of value and the reconciliation of the theory with the tendency of profit rates toward equality. But Marx was not particularly interested in explanatory laws for the workings of the capitalist system. He was interested in pressing on to what he called the 'laws of motion' (a revealingly mechanistic term!) of the capitalist system, that is, in its inevitable march towards the victory of revolutionary communism, a march that would proceed 'with the inexorability of the laws of nature'. How and where, then, was capitalism bound to move?

One crucial aspect of the inevitable doom of capitalism is the inescapable law of the falling rate of profit. The extant uniform equilibrium rate, according to Marx, was doomed to keep falling. Both Smith and Ricardo had theories of a falling rate of profit, each fallacious, and each arrived at in completely different ways. To Smith, the rate of profit (or interest) is determined by the stock of capital; the greater the amount of capital accumulated, the lower the profit rate. Ricardo, in contrast, was worried about the increasing squeeze of the economy by the landlords as inexorable population growth puts ever more inferior lands under cultivation. Labour hours required for production are raised, thereby raising both money wages and rents, hence eating increasingly into profits.[21]

Marx's falling rate of profit follows from the accumulation of capital over time, but in a way different from Smith's or Ricardo's.[22] As we have seen, for Marx capital is deadweight, and provides no profit to the capitalist. All his profit comes from the exploitation of 'living' labour, and therefore amassing more capital necessarily lowers his rate of profit, the ratio of his total profit divided by his total capital invested. And since the hallmark of capitalist development is continuing accumulation of capital, this means that capitalism is doomed to ever-falling rates of profit.

But, one may well ask, if the accumulation of capital necessarily slashes profits, why do capitalists, who are clearly motivated by a search for higher rather than lower profits, insist on continuing to accumulate? Why do they persist in cutting their own throats?

One Marxian answer to this riddle is 'competition', and Leninists in particular like to explain the allegedly later development of 'monopoly capitalism' and of imperialism as attempts by capitalists to form cartels, or find investment outlets abroad, as attempts to stave off the dread consequences of competition.[23] But the mere citation of 'competition' is scarcely an adequate answer. It is true, for example, that a new discovery or a new industry will cause very high profits at the beginning, and that in the pursuit of these profits new, competing firms will eventually bid down the rate of profit in the industry. But, in the short run, at least, and before equilibrium arrives, these capitalists are still making high and above normal profits. But, in contrast, the Marxian businessman who accumulates capital, *loses* profits *at each step of the way,* and not simply in the long run. It is therefore difficult to see why any one capitalist, at any step of the way, would ever be tempted to join in the accumulative parade.

Marx's ultimate answer to this riddle is deceptively simple: capitalists accumulate, despite the immediate and future fall in their profits because, well, they have an irresistible, irrational urge, or 'instinct' to do so. This, of course, is no explanation at all; it abandons any genuine explanation under the cloak of a high-sounding but ultimately meaningless label such as 'drive' or 'instinct'. It makes the same error as the legendary attempt to 'explain' why opium puts people to sleep by solemnly intoning that opium has 'dormitive power'. Note the *Leitmotif* of irrationality in Marx's analysis of why capitalists accumulate in Volume I of *Capital*: 'Accumulate, accumulate! That is Moses and the prophets!...Therefore, save, save, i.e., reconvert the greatest possible of surplus-value, or surplus-product into capital! Accumulation for accumulation's sake, production for production's sake'.[24]

Not for the sake of profits! And a similar theme appears in Marx's earlier essay, *Wage Labor and Capital*': 'That is the law which again and again throws bourgeois production out of its old course and which compels capital to intensify the productive forces of labour, *because* it has intensified them..., the law which gives capital no rest and continually whispers in its ear: "Go on! Go on!"[25]

There was, of course, another way by which Marx and the Marxists could salvage the rationality of the accumulation of capital, and that was to take the fallback Hilfdering route, and abandon the labour theory as a doctrine relevant to the real world. Marx, indeed, took this road as well as claiming a mystical urge to accumulate 'for its own sake'. In this manifestation, or face, of Marx, capitalist innovators do indeed make an initially high profit above the uniform 'average' rate prevailing in the market; these pioneers make high 'surplus profits', followed by imitators and competitors until the profit rate is eventually driven down to the equilibrium, or average rate. All well and good, and in this variant at least, reality again wins out. However, once again, the price of acknowledging reality is prohibitive: for if this sort of thing happens habitually on the market, why does the rate of profit have to fall *at all*, much less present us with an inexorable, continuing tendency? Once again, as in the Böhm-Bawerk–Hilferding imbroglio, Marxists can only embrace reality by abandoning the Marxian system. Unfortunately, they of course do not acknowledge this surrender, and continue to proclaim that reality has only required a slight adjustment to the true doctrine.

Whichever course the Marxists take, it is crucial for them to salvage the continuing accumulation of capital, since it is through such accumulation that increased productivity and particularly technological innovations take place and are instituted in the economy. And we must remember that it is through technological innovation that capitalists dig their own grave, for the capitalist system and capitalist relations become the fetters that block technological development. Some technological method that capitalism cannot encompass, which Marx late in life thought would be electricity, would provide the spark, the necessary and sufficient base for the inevitable overthrow of capitalism and the seizing power by the 'final' historical class, the proletariat.

To Marx, two consequences followed necessarily from the alleged tendency to the accumulation of capital and the advance of technology. The first is the 'concentration of capital', by which Marx meant the inexorable tendency of each firm to grow ever larger in size, for the scale of production to enlarge.[26] Certainly, there is a great amount of expansion of scale of plant and firm in the modern world. On the other hand, the law is scarcely apodictic. Why may not the accumulation of capital be reflected in a growth in the *number* of firms, rather than merely in increasing the size of each? And while many industrial processes grow by increasing the optimal scale, others flourish by being relatively small and flexible in size. Henry Ford's massive automobile factories were economic and profitable for a while; but, later, by the 1920s, they inevitably led to severe losses because such massive investment proved inflexible in meeting changes in the nature and form of consumer demand. And while automobile plants are large-sized, automobile *parts* plants and firms are typically small in size. Furthermore, new and small firms have typically outcompeted large Behemoths in introducing inventions and technological innovations—the very area that most interested Marx. Large-scale firms tend to become bureaucratic, hidebound, and mired in intellectual and financial vested interests in existing plants and ways of production. Time after time, only new, small firms can carry out the cutting-edge of technological innovation.[27]

If Marx's law of the concentration of capital is by no means certain, then his next thesis, the 'law of the centralization of capital', is in even shakier shape. Here Marx asserted an inevitable law by which smaller firms in each industry go to the wall, and are absorbed in fewer and fewer giant firms – in short, a tendency toward the monopolization of industry. For one reason, competition 'always ends in the ruin of many small capitalists, whose capitals partly pass into the hands of their conquerors, and partly vanish completely'. For a second reason for his law, Marx pointed to the recent invention of the joint-stock company, or corporation, and its ability to concentrate masses of small capital into one organization. But this process of centralization or monopolization can be, and has been, counteracted by such developments as the growth of new processes (as we have seen above) and by the spread of geographical competition. Thus, in addition to small innovators we have mentioned, the alleged dominance of the Big Three automobile firms in the US has been eradicated by the growth of foreign (Japanese, West German, etc.) competition. Furthermore, while small 'family' retail groceries were superseded, the alleged monopolization of the retail grocery business by A&P in the 1930s was pulverized by the growth of the new technology of supermarkets. In the meanwhile, the small groceries have returned in the new form of convenience or 24-hour stores. In New York City, in recent years, larger supermarkets have been outcompeted in the quality and variety of fruit and vegetables by small, 24-hour Korean–American family stores. In late nineteenth and early twentieth century America, the Standard Oil monopoly of petroleum refining was rocked by its bureaucratic failure to perceive that the new Texas and Oklahoma oil fields were the wave of the future in crude oil, and by its backwardness in seeing that kerosene would rapidly be giving way to gasoline as the dominant petroleum product. This muscle-bound failure left room for small and vigorous new entrepreneurs such as Gulf and Texaco to leap in and eliminate Standard's dominance in oil.

A final instructive example of excessive scale of firm and unprofitable monopoly, was the result of the vast merger boom of 1899–1901, in which literally scores of industries, following the lure of monopoly profits, merged into one monopoly firm, and almost invariably lost heavily, and were forced to give way to strenuous multi-firm competition.[28]

Thus, no one can predict which way the winds of competition, of creation and decline, of innovation and decay, will blow. Certainly one of the tendencies of capitalism is a greater variety and spectrum of quality of product, and this tendency promotes 'decentralization' rather than Marxian centralization. Suffice it to say that there is no evidence, despite the numerous attempts of the federal government to give artificial impetus to centralization, that American industry is any more centralized now than it was at the turn of the twentieth century.[29]

Finally, there is another side to the rise of corporations that Marx naturally leaves out. The very instrument by which the joint-stock company can raise otherwise unavailable masses of capital, has transformed the economy from one of a small number of capitalists, to a modern world in which every person, be he or she ever so small, can and does become a capitalist. That is, virtually everyone owns a few shares of stock, or owns shares of pension funds invested in stocks or bonds. 'Every man a capitalist' is, in today's world, a pervasive condition rather than a hopeful slogan for the future.

Stressing this point leaves one subject to ridicule by Marxists and left-liberals, who point out, obviously enough, that an individual capitalist owning a few shares of stock exerts little power in the corporate world. But such ridicule is ignorant and misplaced, since the point is that in this sense, stockholders are like consumers. The individual consumer has little say over the types and amounts of goods and services produced, but the mass of consumers together exert total economic power. Similarly, the man who owns one share of stock may have little say in corporate decisions, but the disaffection of even a relatively small minority could have costly consequences for the large shareholders if the disaffected sell their stock and send the values of shares plummeting. Large stockholders will exert direct control of a corporation, but far more indirect power lies in the hands of the mass of small shareholders, just as the ultimate economic power over each firm is wielded by the mass of consumers in their decisions on whether and how much to buy of the firm's product.

To return to Marx and his laws of concentration and centralization of capital. We are now beginning to see the lineaments of why, for Marx, capitalism is inevitably rushing to its appointed doom. First, of course, Marx must rely on his absurd monolithic two-class model, all of society being increasingly squeezed into two uniform classes each with common interests: the capitalists and the proletariat. But the law of the centralization of capital means that the ranks of the capitalists are continually diminishing (as we have seen, running in the teeth of the virtual universalization of the ranks of capitalists from the development of capital markets and corporations). Indeed, the ever-smaller number of ever-wealthier and more powerful capitalists succeed by 'expropriating' their fellow capitalists, and driving them downward into the ranks of the proletariat (since, in Marx's two-class schema, there is no other place for them to go).[30] Before even bringing the workers themselves into the picture, we can see that the ranks of the capitalists, as they dwindle, necessarily become more beleaguered.

The genuine absurdity of this picture was unwittingly revealed by the German Marxist Karl Kautsky, dubbed by Engels, in apostolic succession, the next pope of the Marxian movement. Kautsky simplistically pursued the logic of his master. As Kautsky summed up this process in his book on the Erfurt programme:

> capitalist production tends to unite the means of production, which have become the monopoly of the capitalist class, into fewer hands. This evolution finally makes all the means of production of a nation, indeed of the whole world economy, the private property of a single individual or company, which disposes of them arbitrarily. The whole economy will be drawn into one colossal undertaking, in which every thing has to serve one master. In capitalist society private ownership in the means of production ends with all except one person being propertyless. It thus leads to its own abolition, to the lack of property by all and the enslavement of all.[31]

And what is more, we are advancing toward this state of affairs 'more rapidly than most people believe.'

It's as if Kautsky can now glimpse a bit of the absurdity of the position into which the logic of the Marxian system has placed him. Lest we be tempted to sit back and wait for the one Goldfinger, worth umpteen quadrillion dollars, who holds the entire world of impoverished slaves in his thrall, Kautsky hastens to assure us that the world will not have to wait for the *entire* process to work itself out. Instead, 'the mere approach to this condition must increase the sufferings, conflicts, and contradictions in society to such an extent, that they become intolerable and society bursts its bounds and falls to pieces...'[32] Kautsky, however, did not succeed in drawing back before inadvertently revealing how preposterous the Marxian model really is.

13.4 The 'laws of motion', II: the impoverishment of the working class

The vital corollary for the Marxian system, of the ever-thinning ranks of the centralized capitalists, is the ever-swelling ranks of the proletariat, and their increasing impoverishment and immiseration. The two antagonistic classes engage in a dialectic all their own, the culminating dialectic in the Marxian system. On the one hand: the ever-thinning ranks of the ever-wealthier capitalists, until (or nearly until) one man owns all the wealth in the world; on the other, the ever-swelling ranks of the ever-more impoverished proletariat, until the proletarian masses rise up and take over. But let Marx tell the story, in what amounts to his rousing peroration in the penultimate chapter of Volume I of *Capital*:

Hand in hand with this centralisation, or this expropriation of many capitalists by few, develop, on an ever-extending scale, the cooperative form of the labour-process, the conscious technical application of science, the entanglement of all peoples in the net of the world-market, and with this, the international character of the capitalistic regime. Along with the constantly diminishing number of the magnates of capital, who usurp and monopolise all advantages of this process of transformation, grows the mass of misery, oppression, slavery, degradation, exploitation; but with this too grows the revolt of the working-class, a class always increasing in numbers, and disciplined, united, organized by the very mechanism of the process of capitalist production itself. The monopoly of capital becomes a fetter on the mode of production, which has sprung up and flourished along with, and under it. Centralisation of the means of production and socialisation of labour at last reach a point where they become incompatible with their capitalist integument. This integument is burst asunder. The knell of capitalist private property sounds. The expropriators are expropriated.[33]

Now here is a critical and crucial point in the Marxian argument. The increasing impoverishment of the working class is a key to the Marxian system, because on it rests the allegedly inevitable doom of capitalism and its replacement by the proletariat.[34] If there is no increasing impoverishment, there is no reason for the working class to react against their intensifying exploitation and burst asunder their 'capitalist integument', those fetters on the technological mode of production. So how does Marx demonstrate the increasing poverty of the proletariat?

At this point, Marx seems to grow desperate, and to come up with a number of varied and contrasting arguments, some of which are mutually contradictory. It's as if Marx wildly tries to multiply the arguments, however feeble, in the hope that at least one will stick, and that he will demonstrate the inevitability of the next, proletarian communist, stage of history. But all of these attempts to prove increasing misery come up, first and foremost, against an insuperable obstacle, an obstacle that only Ludwig von Mises has clearly demonstrated.[35] For if workers' wages are already and at all times at the means of subsistence, kept there by the iron law, how can they get any *worse off*? They have been at maximum poverty level, so to speak, for a long time. But if for that reason they cannot get worse off, where is the dynamic that will lead them to rise up and overthrow the system? We can concede, of course, that the new proletarians, so rudely tossed into the ranks of the working class by their triumphant fellow-capitalists, will be particularly edgy and disgruntled at their new lot in life. But surely Marx would not be content to *confine* his revolutionary workers to the relatively limited ranks of recently déclassé capitalists. Especially since the bulk of the workers simply remain where they have always been: at the margin of subsistence.[36]

Setting aside for the moment this grave inner contradiction with the iron law of wages, *how* does Marx propose to establish his alleged law of the increasing impoverishment of the proletariat? In one answer, the eternally falling rate of profits puts a severe pressure on capitalists to find more profit by sweating and exploiting the proletariat more intensively, making them work harder and for longer hours. But aside from the problem of the ever-present iron law, Marx is faced with the problem: why did capitalists allow their rate of exploitation to grow slack until finally spurred on by a falling rate of profit? Don't capitalists always and at all times try to maximize their rates of profit? And if so, and unless we are to assume a sudden intensification of greed, or of eagerness for profit among capitalists, they are never slack or lax in squeezing the greatest possible amount of profit from the workers. But then, how can a falling rate of profit spur them on to ever-greater heights? Surely, it is not simply a desire for profit.

Here Marx falls back on a suggested mechanism for this increased exploitation of labour and falling wage rate: the accelerating growth of a permanent 'industrial reserve army', a growing legion of the unemployed. It is increased competition from the unemployed that forces wage rates downwards, and increasingly continues to do so as capitalism advances.

But how can there be a continuing army of the unemployed, when wages to the unemployed are zero? Why don't the unemployed starve to death before they can ever constitute a competitive threat to the employed proletariat? If Marx answers that the unemployed are rapidly absorbed into the employed ranks, driving down wage rates thereby, then he abandons his requirement for increasing impoverishment: the growth of a permanent, and expanding, army of the unemployed. So how are they supported and how do they continue in existence?

Also, where does the industrial reserve army come from? Market economists know that unemployment quickly eliminates itself by lowering wage rates. Only if wage rates are bolstered above the market equilibrium level does unemployment become permanent; and if, as Marx maintains, the unemployed army *lowers* wage rates through its competition, then it should rapidly disappear and pose no further problems.

But where does the industrial reserve army come from in the first place? For Marx, it is the old bugaboo, technological unemployment. Industry is mechanized, and workers are thrown, presumably permanently, out of jobs. But what of the expansion of quantity demanded and of production brought about by technological innovation? And what of the increased demand for production and resources in *other* industries that are freed by cheaper products in the technologically expanding industry? And what, as we have seen above, of lower wage rates as the free market way of maintaining full employment of labour? Technological unemployment is an old and oft-discredited bogey. When automatic dialling for telephones was established, for example, there was a general piteous wail that the poor, beloved telephone operators would be thrown out of work by this productive, but heartless, innovation. And yet, of course, the lower prices of telephone service resulted in an enormous expansion of telephone's market, *including* a substantial increase in the number of telephone operators. Similarly, the number of workers in the construction industry have been *increased* not slashed, by the development of cranes, electric shovels, and other construction machinery, as compared to the good old days of hand shovels. All in all, for the technological unemployment argument to work as a way of demonstrating increasing impoverishment, not only would each successive technological innovation have to cause permanent unemployment, but the effect would have to accelerate over time, and thereby more than offset any equilibrating tendencies towards greater employment that the market might possess.

In the discussion of the alleged industrial reserve army, we have been dealing with Marx's assertion that there is a permanent, secular increase of that army. Below, we shall deal with another Marxian doctrine, of the recurrence of *cyclical* unemployment, which, along with ever-worsening cyclical depressions, may provide the motor of increasing misery and proletarian revolution.

Another Marxian argument for the inevitability of the impoverishment of the working class is found particularly in the *Communist Manifesto*. As machinery develops and capitalists accumulate capital, Marx and Engels lament, labour loses its variety of skills, and the proletariat gets pushed into ever simpler, more monotonous and unskilled tasks, and this de-skilling lowers the average wage.[37]

This feeble argument rings particularly hollow nowadays, when left-liberal friends of the working class are pushing the exactly *opposite* lament: that, in an age when ever greater numbers of labour are going into high-skilled computer and electronics work, what is to happen to the poor, aging unskilled labourer, left behind in the march of progress?

A related Marxian argument stresses not so much the increasing impoverishment of the working class, but its immiseration through aggravated 'alienation', increasing monotony or repulsiveness of work caused by expanding mechanization. While Marx himself indeed refers to such alleged expanding misery in work of the labouring class, we have seen at length above that for Marx 'alienation' had nothing to do with subjective psychology, or monotony of work, but was cosmically rooted in, and indeed defined as an attribute of, the basic modern system of exchange and the division of labour, and, beyond that, in the separation of individual men from Man and from Nature that was going to be cured, and could only be cured, by communism. Apart from the empirical problem of how more monotonous work was really becoming, and the contrast to the liberating nature of the increasing variety of wants, products and occupations, it is difficult to see how or why any 'alienation' should *increase* significantly over time, much less how this increase is conveyed in some way to the working class. No, the case of increasing misery as a spur to revolution must be a palpable and objective one, evident to the working class, or be no case at all.

We are left with the doctrine of the growing impoverishment of the prole-tariat, a doctrine so crucial in Marx that it can hardly be trivialized as a 'prediction' that somehow went astray. This 'prediction' is absolutely critical to the allegedly inevitable tendency for the workers to rise up and overthrow capitalism, a tendency that is supposed to deepen and accelerate as capitalism progresses. And yet, it has been starkly evident to everyone that one of the vitally significant facts of the century and a half since the birth of Marxism has been the continuing, spectacular growth in real wages and in the standard of living of the working class and of the mass of the population. Indeed what we have seen in this period is the most spectacular growth in industrialization and in living standards in the history of the world. Moreover, and particularly telling in a critique of Marx, that advance of the working class has been particularly striking precisely in the advanced capitalist countries of the West, those that were supposed to herald the growing impoverishment of the proletariat. Here is a stern and unrelenting fact that every Marxist must face, and one that by itself can and should destroy the Marxian system. How have the Marxists dealt with this grave problem?

Some Marxists, of course, have simply abandoned the ship, either noisily proclaiming their defection or quietly slipping from the fold. A few Marxists, as Schumpeter bemusedly notes, 'actually do not mind taking up the ridiculous position that a tendency for the working class's standard of life to fall is in fact observable'.[38] But generally, Marxists have tried to save the phenomenon, salvage the theory, by various fallback positions or forms of evasion. One popular tactic asserts that the underlying *tendency* toward impoverishment still exists, but has been 'temporarily' (one or two centuries?) offset by counteracting factors. A popular but bizarre Leninist variant is that workers in the West have benefited from imperialist western exploitation of, or investment in, the Third World, so that in a sense, western workers become 'capitalists' on an international scale. In the first place, in this transmutation of the oppressed proletariat of the West into exploiting 'capitalists' of the Third World, what ever happened to the inevitable *dwindling* of the capitalist class? Second, the grotesquerie of this doctrine may be gauged by the fact, as P.T. Bauer has demonstrated in many works, that the bulk of the Third World, however poor, has *also* been developing rapidly in recent decades, and the standard of living of their working masses has steadily risen. Not only that; but this development and rise in standards has taken place precisely in those areas and regions of the Third World (e.g. port cities) in closest trading and investment touch with developed western countries. On the other hand, it is the remote areas of the Third World, not yet opened up to trade with the West, that have lagged behind in this economic growth. None of this can be squared with the image of the western world making its tremendous strides over the century at the expense of what would have to be very rapid and deep impoverishment and immiseration of the masses in the Third World.[39]

Apart from imperialism, there have been other intervening factors that various Marxists claim to have temporarily interrupted the working of inevitable impoverishment. A particularly popular choice, at about the turn of the twentieth century, was the closing of the frontier in the western United States. The frontier thesis eventually lost popularity as the event receded in memory and the workers' living standards continued their inexorable advance, although it was curiously revived in the outlandish 'stagnation thesis' of the late 1930s, in which the closing of the frontier (along with other ill-chosen factors) was suddenly supposed to have risen up out of its grave of four decades and smitten the economy with an unexplained delayed immiseration.

But by far the most popular fallback position has been to change the terms of the argument and the prediction. Flying in the face of the evidence, these Marxists contend that Marx 'did not really mean' 'absolute' impoverishment, a continuing fall in the standard of living; he meant a fall in the *relative* income of the workers, relative, of course, to the standard of living of the capitalist class. It was 'relative impoverishment', not 'absolute', that Marx supposedly meant, and that the Marxists were now proclaiming.[40]

As an empirical question, relative impoverishment may or may not be true at various times and places, but its cogency is certainly dubious. It is certainly clear that the degree of inequality, for example, under oriental despotism or in the absolutist France of Louis XIV was far greater than it is under modern capitalism. But more important is the ludicrousness of relying on 'relative impoverishment' as a sufficient motor for the working class to rise up in bloody revolution to overthrow the capitalist class. If a worker has one yacht, will he rise up in rebellion because there are others in the society who have two or three? Or, to put it more realistically, will a worker with two colour TV sets rise up in revolution because Rockefeller or Lee Iacocca or Hugh Hefner has a larger set in each room? We are a long, long way from immiseration. The coming inevitable wrath of the proletariat has turned, at last, to farce.

And yet even the head of official Marxism after Engels, Karl Kautsky, being forced in 1899 to admit that the standard of living of the workers was rising, was compelled to fall back on the view that what Marx really meant was relative, or what Kautsky called 'social', poverty. By 'social poverty' Kautsky frankly meant envy, or 'covetousness', and so he was obliged to fall back on the view that gaining in income but seeing *others* gain more would suffice to rouse the workers into enough envy to rise up and overthrow the entire system.[41] In any case, it is far more plausible that envy would be institutionalized in political drives, say, for a progressive income tax or various subsidies from government, rather than erupt in a revolutionary destruction of the entire system.

All this does not deny that there are indeed passages in Marx which describe only a relative impoverishment of the working class and a growth in their envy at those wealthier than they.[42] The point, however, is that there is *also* another, dominant strain in Marx's writings which forecasts and stresses an increasing *absolute* real, objective impoverishment of the working class.

Finally, there is a glaring inner contradiction at the heart of Marxian economics that is never resolved. If the capitalists suffer over time from a falling rate of profit, and workers suffer from increasing impoverishment, who is *benefiting* in the distribution of the economic pie? At least in the Ricardian system, the capitalists suffer from a falling rate of profit, and the workers are kept at brute subsistence level, but *some* group keeps grabbing all the social benefits – the parasitic landlords and their increasing absorption of the social product by land rent. But in the Marxian system, the landlords have disappeared, increasingly and rapidly assimilated into the capitalist class. So how can *both* mighty classes lose out under developing capitalism?[43]

13.5   The 'laws of motion', III: business cycle crises

A final variant of Marx's attempt to demonstrate the inevitability of the proletarian revolution was closely related to the doctrine of absolute impoverishment. This variant, however, stressed, not a steady secular trend toward growing impoverishment or an industrial reserve army, but rather increasingly destructive business cycle crises and depressions, marked by impoverishment and cyclical unemployment. We turn now to Marx's theory, or rather his various *theories* of cycles and crises, for his writings contain several very different and incompatible theories. Perhaps Marx, in desperation, was willing to come up with a number of theories, hoping that one of them, at least, might stick.

13.5.1   Underconsumptionism

The underconsumption explanation of depression was Marx's dominant variant of cycle theory, as evidenced for example, by his and Engels's repeated attacks on Say's law, and on Ricardo's adherence to that law.[44] The point, as elaborated particularly in Marx's *Theories of Surplus Value* (written 1861–63), is that as capitalist accumulation and production advances, it outstrips the ability of the exploited workers, who earn far less than the value of their product, to consume. The mass of workers cannot consume enough to buy the capitalist product, and the slack is not taken up by the capitalist exploiters, who are far more interested in saving and accumulating than in consuming. Hence, Say is incorrect, and there is systemic general overproduction, with production outstripping the masses' ability to consume.[45] As Marx repeatedly says, 'the majority of the people, the labouring population, can extend their consumption only within very narrow limits'.

Marx returns to this dominant underconsumptionist theme in Volume III of *Capital*. In capitalism, Marx writes, the 'consuming power of society' is determined by 'antagonistic conditions of distribution', which 'reduce the consumption of the great mass of the population to a variable minimum within more or less narrow limits'. Moreover,

> the consuming power is furthermore restricted by the tendency to accumulate, the greed for an expansion of capital and a production of surplus-value on an enlarged scale... The market must, therefore, be continually extended... But to the extent that the productive power develops, it finds itself at variance with the narrow basis on which the conditions of consumption rest.

Also, in Volume III of *Capital*, Marx writes: 'The ultimate reason for all crises always remains the poverty and restricted consumption of the masses, in the face of the drive to develop the productive forces as if only the absolute consumption of society set a limit to them'.[46]

The most obvious and blatant problem with an underconsumptionist theory of economic crises is that it explains too much. For if the consumption of the masses is never enough to buy back the product and keep business profitable, why is there no *permanent* depression? Why are there *booms* as well as busts? Both Marx and Engels apparently sensed this problem, and hence saw the need for at least a supplementary theory. Thus, in Volume III of *Capital*, Marx, in addition to the quote above, conceded that there are at least temporary boom periods before crises, when wages rise and workers obtain a larger share of the product.[47] Engels, too, in *Anti-Dühring*, first states that 'large-scale industry, which hunts all over the world for new consumers, restricts the consumption of the masses at home to a starvation minimum and thereby undermines its own internal market'. But, then, a bit later in the same work, Engels, after asserting that 'the underconsumption of the masses is therefore also a necessary condition of crises', admits the concept cannot explain 'why crises exist today' while 'they did not exist at earlier periods'.

By the time that Engels wrote the preface to the first English edition of Volume I of *Capital* in 1886, however, the problem had been neatly resolved to his own satisfaction. While business cycles of boom and bust had indeed prevailed until 1867, he opined, the English economy was now satisfactorily bogged down in permanent depression. Whatever the subsidiary causes of the booms, they were now ended, and permanent depression would soon usher in the proletarian revolution. Amidst the sea of wreckage of self-assured Marxian 'predictions', this was one of the most absurdly and strikingly wrong. Thus Engels:

The decennial cycle of stagnation, prosperity, over-production, and crisis, ever recurrent from 1825 to 1867, seems indeed to have run its course; but only to land us in the slough of despond of a permanent and chronic depression. The sighed-for period of prosperity will not come; as often as we seem to perceive its heralding symptoms, so often do they vanish into air. Meanwhile, each succeeding winter brings up afresh the great question, 'what to do with the unemployed'; but while the number of the unemployed keeps swelling from year to year, there is nobody to answer that question; and we can almost calculate the moment when the unemployed losing patience will take their own fate into their own hands.[48]

In the event, of course, prosperity came to England long before the proletarian revolution.

In any case, underconsumption is a totally flawed theory, whether used to explain cyclical crises or permanent depressions. In the first place, savings do not 'leak out' of the economy; they are spent, on vitally important investments in resources and capital goods. More importantly, as in the case of every crazy theory, the price system quietly drops out of the picture, and we are left with such aggregative juggernauts as 'production' and 'consumption' facing each other. There is no such thing as overproduction; there is only too much produced for the *price* that consumers are willing to pay, a price which, in crises, does not cover the costs incurred by businessmen. But, once we recognize *that*, we must then also see that, in order to bring production and consumption into balance, in order to eliminate the problem of supply, or stock, being greater than demand, all that need happen is for prices to fall. Let prices fall, and they will soon equilibrate supply and demand, and business losses will only be temporary. And this point leads the analyst to consider the next step: why did businessmen – entrepreneurs with a sterling overall record in forecasting demand and costs – why this time did they bid up costs so excessively high that they suffer losses in trying to sell the product? In short, why did businessmen make this cluster of severe forecasting errors that mark the period of economic crisis? None of this, of course, could be considered by Marx and by the underconsumptionists, who do not bother considering the price system. Moreover, Marx, like Smith and Ricardo before him, has no conception of the entrepreneur or of the function of entrepreneurship.

Finally, it is well known that crises invariably begin, not in the consumer goods industries that underconsumptionism would lead us to expect, but precisely in capital goods industries, and in those industries farthest and most remote from the consumer. The problem it would seem – correctly – is *too much* rather than *too little* consumption.[49]

13.5.2   The falling rate of profit

The second crisis theory, prominent in Volume III of *Capital*, focuses on the Marxian falling rate of profit. The incessant drive of capitalists to accumulate brings about a secular trend of the rate of profit to fall. Finally, when profit falls below 'a certain rate', the growth of capital ceases, and an economic crisis ensues. Just as capitalism leads to an overproduction of goods in relation to consumption, so too it creates an over-accumulation of capital. The cessation of capital investment leads to a recession in the capital goods industries, which then widens into a general depression.

While this second explanation of economic crisis at least has the merit of focusing on capital goods industries rather than consumption, it is scarcely an improvement. In the first place, once again, the falling rate of profit seems to describe a law of secular decline; but why should it lead to a *specific* economic collapse, much less a cyclical series of booms and busts? Even if the profit rate falls, why should businessmen stop investing, especially all of a sudden? What is the mechanism to explain the sudden, sharp upper turning point? Moreover, even if the profit rate falls, the admittedly increasing mass of saved capital might well increase the *absolute amount* of aggregate profits, so that even though the *rate* falls, the process may still stimulate a great deal of further investment.

Furthermore, even if Marx could explain an upper turning point and a sharp crash, why should there ever be a *revival*? Here is a particularly shaky point in Marx: capital *decumulates* greatly during the crisis, so that the capital denominator actually declines, and hence the rate of profit to total investment rises. This process can again create greater investment, and another boom. The likelihood, however, that a depression will be steep enough to actually consume capital and *also* raise profit rates more than the alleged continuing tendency for the profit rate to fall, is very low. And even if a recovery gets under way, why should a lusty boom ensue?

There is, finally, no hint in Marx or Engels why these cycles or depressions are supposed to increase in intensity, universality, and depth over time, finally to result in permanent depression and revolution.

All in all, the falling rate of profit strand of cycle theory is singularly shadowy and unconvincing.

13.5.3 Disproportionality

Here, in the 'disproportionality' theory of Marx, we return, in a deep sense, to where we, or rather Marx himself, began: to communism, and the desire to eradicate the market and the division of labour. Woven into his discussions in *Capital* and *Theories of Surplus Value* (written 1861–63) is the view that cycles and crises inevitably stem from the market process. To Marx, the problem was endemic in the market economy, and particularly in the money, or indirect exchange, economy. Since the market allegedly had no coordinating mechanism, all production and exchange, according to Marx, is chaotic, discoordinated, a regime of what he called 'the anarchy of production'. As Boher sums it up:

This theory is concerned with the maladjustments and disproportionalities traced to the anarchy of competition; to the blundering, incoordinate moves of multitudes of individual capitalists; to the complexities of the many elements which must fit into each other in an enormously complex world, and which will do so by sheer accident if not by planned design; and to the vagaries of wind and weather.[50]

Marx had a telling point against the Ricardians, the British classicists of his day. The world does not indeed bask happily in the never-never land of long-run equilibrium. But what Marx overlooked is precisely what the Ricardians overlooked: if they had shifted their focus out of the cloudland of long-run equilibrium, and back to the real world of the market economy, they would have discovered a very different world. They would have seen what Turgot and the French and Italians and scholastics had seen: the real world of markets is not perfectly, but still harmoniously and dynamically coordinated by two crucial elements: a price system that is free to fluctuate to equate the changing forces of supply and demand; and entrepreneurs who, in their continuing search for increased profits and avoidance of losses, perform this coordinating task. But by focusing on long-run equilibrium, the British classicists had eliminated both the real world price system and the vital entrepreneurial role in the market economy – the successful anticipation of change in a changing and uncertain world. If there is no price system for the exchange of property titles to goods and services, and there are no capitalist–entrepreneurs, then indeed production is in a state of 'anarchy'.

Marx also saw that discoordination might cause over-accumulation of capital, and wove this theme into the preceding variant – the falling rate of profit – in an attempt to explain cycles and crises. Some later economists, notably the Russian Marxist economist Tugan-Baranowsky, elaborated these hints into what has been called a 'non-monetary over-investment theory' of the business cycle.[51]

Marx saw that the monetary and credit system played an important role in cycles and crises: credit is important in the centralization of capital: it encourages speculation, intensifies the crisis, and accelerates overproduction. But to emphasize bank credit as a fundamental cause of the cycle could have been fatal for Marx's attempt to pin the blame for cycles and crises on forces inherent within the capitalist market economy. And so it was necessary for him to repudiate any possible currency school emphases on the causal role of bank credit: 'The superficiality of Political Economy', Marx writes in *Capital*, 'shows itself in the fact that it looks upon the expansion and contraction of credit, which is a mere symptom of the periodic changes of the industrial cycle, as their cause'.[52]

Despite his overt scorn for John Stuart Mill, Marx was thereby driven into implicit support for the Mill–Tooke–banking school theory of the business cycle.[53] As we have seen, the currency school writers themselves were forced into this view after the seeming failure of Peel's Act of 1844 to eradicate business cycles. While all banking school-type theorists on *non* monetary disproportionality and over-investment were obliged to admit that expansion of money and bank credit were necessary conditions to a cycle boom, they all proclaimed that credit cycles were only passive resultants of non-monetary cycles of 'over-' and 'under-' trading or of 'speculation'. Thus Millian non-monetary cycle theory permeated the ranks of economists, and encouraged economists, including Marx, to blame the capitalist market economy for the recurrence of business cycles. The insights of the vanished currency school, the realization that money and credit as a *necessary condition* was close to saying a *cause*, and the original insight that it takes bank credit expansion to distort the market's signals to entrepreneurs and create a boom-bust cycle, remained buried, to be discovered or rediscovered by Ludwig von Mises in 1912.

13.6   Conclusion: the Marxian system

Thus, Karl Marx created what seems to the superficial observer to be an impressive, integrated system of thought, explaining the economy, world history, and even the workings of the universe. In reality, he created a verita-ble tissue of fallacies. Every single nodal point of the theory is wrong and fallacious, and its 'integument' – to use a good Marxian term – is a web of fallacy as well. The Marxian system lies in absolute tatters and ruin; the 'integument' of Marxian theory has 'burst asunder' long before its predicted 'bursting' of the capitalist system. Far from being a structure of 'scientific' laws, furthermore, the jerry-built structure was constructed and shored up in desperate service to the fanatical and crazed messianic goal of destruction of the division of labour, and indeed of man's very individuality, and to the apocalyptic creation of an allegedly inevitable collectivist world order, an atheized variant of a venerable Christian heresy.

During the 1960s, messianic and romantic Marxists liked to make a sharp separation between the earlier lovable, idealistic, 'humanist' Marx, and the later, mean, hard-core, proto-Stalinist 'economist' Marx. But we now know that there is no such division. There is only one Marx, whether early or late, once he adopted Marxism in the 1840s. There is even a good case for seeing one lifelong Marx, including his crazed, demonic poems calling for universal destruction in his still earlier graduate school years at Berlin. In fact, the humanist Marx is scarcely a relief from the later economist – quite the contrary. All Marxes-in-one were in service to his fanatical and destructive messianic vision of communism. A convincing case can be made, indeed, that the well-known horrors of twentieth century communism: of Lenin, Stalin, Mao and Pol Pot, can be considered the logical unfolding, the embodi-ment, of the nineteenth century vision of their master, Karl Marx.

13.7   Notes

1. Karl Marx, *Capital, Vol. I* (New York: International Publishers, 1967), p. 37.
2. Ibid., I, p. 39.
3. Compare the discussion in David Conway, *A Farewell to Marx: An Outline and Appraisal of His Theories* (Harmondsworth, Mddx: Penguin Books, 1987), pp. 83–9.
4. As Böhm-Bawerk was later to point out, even if we choose to adopt this cost-of-production approach, we have to recognize that capital embodies not just labour, and land, but also *time*. Land, as we shall see further, was tossed out by Marx by amalgamating it into capital; but if time had been acknowledged as an important factor, then time-preference would have to be acknowledged, and the entire Marxian system would have collapsed.
5. 'Constant' because, according to Marx, capital goods, being deadweight, cannot generate any profit, or increased value.
6. Professor Conway neatly summarizes Marx's point: '...the labourer is paid in wages per day a sum of value equal in amount to the value of his labour-power for a day. Since the value of a day's labour-power is equal to the amount of labour required to produce that day's labour-power, it follows that the value of a day's labour-power is equal to the amount of labour required to produce the labourer's means of subsistence consumed per day'. Conway, op. cit., note 3, pp. 96–7.
7. In a previous passage of the *Manifesto*, Marx and Engels had written that 'the price of a commodity, and therefore also of labour [later modified to 'labour-power'], is equal to the cost of production'. Furthermore, 'the cost of production of a workman is restricted, almost entirely, to the means of subsistence that he requires for his maintenance, and for the propagation of his race'. See Robert C. Tucker (ed.), *The Marx–Engels Reader* (2nd ed., New York: W.W. Norton, 1972), pp. 479, 485.
8. On the dependence of the Marxian system on the iron law of wages, see Ludwig von Mises, 'The Marxian Theory of Wage Rates', in Eugen von Böhm-Bawerk, *The Exploitation Theory of Socialism–Communism* (3rd ed., South Holland, Ill.: Libertarian Press, 1975), pp. 147–51. Von Mises's essay was originally published in *Christian Economics*, May 1961.

   As von Mises points out, Marx did not like the *name* 'iron law of wages', because it was coined by his great rival in German socialist politics, Ferdinand Lassalle (1825–64), but he adhered strongly to the *concept*.

   Curiously, Lassalle's famous phrase, translated into English as 'the iron law', should have been called, as Alexander Gray points out, 'the brass' or 'brazen' law of wages. As Gray characteristically adds, 'in any case, being metallic, it does not greatly matter. A maniac for accuracy might indeed point out that what he [Lassalle] most frequently called it was *'das eherne* [brazen] *und grausame* [cruel] *Gesetz* [law]' which somehow sounds even more horrible'. Alexander Gray, *The Socialist Tradition* (London: Longmans, Green, 1946), p. 336.
9. Eugen von Böhm-Bawerk, *Capital and Interest* (London: Macmillan, 1890), p. 390.
10. Eugen von Böhm-Bawerk, *Karl Marx and the Close of His System* (New York: A. M. Kelley, 1949), p. 5.
11. Ibid., pp. 5–6. The 'contestants' included the well-known German statistician Wilhelm Lexis (1885), the Marxist Conrad Schmidt (1889, 1892–93), the Italian Marxist Achille Loria (1890), the *laissez-faire* liberal Julius Wolf (1891), and a number of Italian economists during 1894.
12. Remember that, as we have noted in our discussion of the definition of class, Karl Marx was scarcely cut off in midstream from working on *Capital*. He had abandoned work on his *magnum opus* at the time of publication of Volume I, and had spent a decade and a half lying to his doting friend and patron about his continuing to work on *Capital*.
13. First published as *Zum Abschluss des Marxschen Systems* in a *Festschrift* for Karl Knies in 1896, and published as a separate booklet the same year. It was a rapid success, being translated the following year into Russian, and the English translation coming out in 1898. Unfortunately, 'close' is a peculiar and misleading term; a far more accurate title would have been *Karl Marx and the Completion of His System*.

14. Paul M. Sweezy, 'Professor Cole's *History of Socialist Thought'*, *American Economic Review*, 47 (1957), p. 990. Cited in Gary North, *Marx's Religion of Revolution* (Nutley, NJ: The Craig Press, 1968), p. 163. Sweezy also maintained that the German Ladislaus von Bortkiewicz had refuted Böhm-Bawerk's critique of Marx, but Samuelson pointed out that von Bortkiewicz's position was far closer to Böhm-Bawerk than it was to Marx. Paul Samuelson, 'Wages and Interest: A Modern Discussion of Marxian Economic Models', *American Economic Review*, 47 (1957), pp. 890–92.
15. Gray, op. cit., note 8, p. 319.
16. See Ludwig von Mises, *Notes and Recollections* (South Holland, Ill.: Libertarian Press, 1978), pp. 39–40.
17. For a thorough critique of recent attempts by a group of 'analytical Marxists', to jettison the labour theory of value and yet retain Marxism, see David Gordon, *Resurrecting Marx* (New Brunswick, NJ.: Transaction Books, 1990).
18. Sowell's claim is on page 153 of the London: Lawrence and Wishart edition. Sowell also absurdly denies that Marx believed at all in a labour theory of value. Thomas Sowell, *Marxism: Philosophy and Economics*: (London: Unwin Paperbacks, 1986), pp. 3–5, and *passim*. The excellent and devastating review of Sowell is David Ramsay Steele, 'Review of Thomas Sowell, *Marxism: Philosophy and Economics'*, *International Philosophical Quarterly*, 26 (June 1986), pp. 201–3.
19. Böhm-Bawerk, op. cit., note 10, p. 30. Also see Gray, op. cit., note 8, p. 317.
20. Gray, op. cit., note 8, pp. 321–2.
21. *Real wages*, of course, remain at subsistence level.
22. Marx, of course, was not interested in the land question, since land was supposed to be withering away in importance with the decline of the 'feudal-land' remnant as capitalism advanced on its determined course. Furthermore, Marx was anxious to get on to his two-class, capitalists *vs* proletariat model, and so he simply assimilated land into the concept of 'capital'.
23. The Leninist theory depends on the claim that both state monopoly capitalism and imperialism come later than competitive, non imperialist capitalism, the latter condition having prevailed during Marx's lifetime. But imperialism – tribes or nation-states conquering or aggressing against, and robbing, other tribes or nations – is as old as recorded history, and state monopoly capitalism at least as old as the mercantilist era.
24. Marx, op. cit., note 1, I, p. 595.
25. Tucker, op. cit., note 7, p. 213.
26. Thus, Marx wrote, in Volume I of *Capital*, that 'It is a law, springing from the technical character of manufacture, that the minimum amount of capital which the capitalist must possess has to go on increasing', and 'the development of capitalist production makes it necessary constantly to increase the amount of capital laid out in a given industrial undertaking'. Cf. Conway, op. cit., note 3, pp. 126–7.
27. This has been spectacularly true in the computer industry. In the cases of xerography and Polaroid photography, as well, the pathbreaking innovations that founded the industry were met with incomprehension and rejection by the Behemoths in the photography field. For these and other pre-computer examples, see John Jewkes, David Sawers, and Richard Stillerman, *The Sources of Invention* (1959, 2nd ed., New York: Norton, 1968).
28. On the merger movement at the turn of the century and its collapse, see Gabriel Kolko, *The Triumph of Conservatism: A Reinterpretation of American History, 1900–1916* (Glencoe, Ill.: The Free Press, 1963); Arthur S. Dewing, *Corporate Promotion and Reorganizations* (Cambridge, Mass.: Harvard University Press, 1924); idem., *The Financial Policy of Corporations* (5th ed., New York: Ronald Press, 1953), 2 vols; and Naomi R. Lamoreaux, *The Great Merger Movement in American Business, 1895–1904* (New York: Cambridge University Press, 1985).
29. It is unfortunate that Professor Conway, in his generally illuminating work on Marxism, uncritically accepts the Marxian dictum of the tendency of giant firms to dominate each industry. Conway, op. cit., note 3, p. 128.
30. In Marx's colourful language, the centralization of capital consists of 'the expropriation of many capitalists by few', or, in even more vivid rhetoric, 'One capitalist always kills

many'. Marx, op. cit., note 1, I, p. 763.

31. Quoted in Ludwig von Mises, *Socialism: An Economic and Sociological Analysis* (2nd ed., New Haven: Yale University Press, 1951), p. 362.

32. *Ibid.*

33. Marx, op. cit., note 1, I, p. 763.

34. Thus, Marx writes, again in *Capital*: 'The greater the social wealth, the functioning capital, the extent and energy of its growth, and, therefore, also the absolute mass of the proletariat and the productiveness of its labour, the greater is the industrial reserve army... The relative mass of the industrial reserve army increases therefore with the potential energy of wealth. But the greater this reserve-army in proportion to the active labour-army, the greater is the mass of a consolidated surplus population... The more extensive, finally,...the industrial reserve army, the greater is official pauperism. *This is the absolute general law of capitalist accumulation'.* (Italics Marx's.) Marx , op. cit., note 1, I, p. 664.

35. Thus, von Mises writes that Marx tried to demonstrate the inevitability of socialism 'by the famous prognostication that capitalism generates necessarily and unavoidably, a progressive impoverishment of the masses of the wage earners. The more capitalism develops', he says, the more 'grows the mass of misery, oppression, slavery, exploitation. With "the progress of industry" the worker "sinks deeper and deeper", until finally, when his sufferings become unbearable, the exploited masses revolt and establish the everlasting bliss of socialism'.

But von Mises then points out, this crucial argument 'contradicts the whole Marxian theory of the determination of wage rates...[T]his theory asserts that wage rates are under capitalism always and necessarily so low that for physiological reasons they cannot drop any further without wiping out the whole class of wage earners. How is it then possible that capitalism brings forth a progressive impoverishment of the wage earners? Marx in his prediction of the progressive impoverishment of the masses contradicted the essential teachings of his own theory'. Von Mises, op. cit., note 8, pp. 150–51.

36. In a remarkably frenetic and unconvincing whirl of Marxian apologetics, Professor Sowell tries to absolve Marx of this contradiction by denying *both* parts: the Marxian adherence to the iron law of wages, *and* the progressive impoverishment of the working class. On the former, Sowell latches on to anti-Lassalle mutterings by Engels in a footnote, and in correspondence between Marx and Engels, and then comes up with a spectacularly original definition of 'subsistence' which implies not a bare minimum existence, but a rising standard of living! On progressive impoverishment, he dismisses this concept as early *Communist Manifesto* Marx, rejected by the mature Marx of *Capital*, and he clings for support to the Marxist–Leninist economist Ronald Meek. To defend this absurd interpretation, Sowell is forced to write off embarrassingly pro-impoverishment passages in *Capital*, such as we have seen above, as 'lurid' remarks applying only to *particular* groups of workers, and to conveniently ignore the peroration chapter of *Capital*. Sowell, op. cit., note 18, pp. 128–31. Marx also took the impoverishment line in his *Value, Price and Profit* (1865). Cf. North, op. cit., note 14, pp. 140–41.

37. 'Owing to the extensive use of machinery and to division of labour, the...[workman] becomes an appendage of the machine, and it is only the most simple, most monotonous, and most easily acquired knack, that is required of him. Hence, the cost of production of a workman is restricted, almost entirely, to the means of subsistence that he requires for his maintenance, and for the propagation of his race.' Tucker, op. cit., note 7, p. 479.

38. Schumpeter, *History of Economic Analysis* (New York: Oxford University Press, 1954), p. 686n. Many Marxists have claimed, at the least, that the standard for life of the English workers fell at the advent of the Industrial Revolution, say from the middle or late eighteenth century to the mid-nineteenth, but the scholarship of R. Max Hartwell and others have well disposed of this Marxian charge.

39. Cf. Conway, op. cit., note 3, p. 132.

40. Schumpeter, who generally treats Marx excessively gently, pours proper scorn on the relative impoverishment theorists: 'Still other interpreters have made efforts to make Marx's law mean relative misery only, i.e. a fall in the relative share of labor, which, besides being equally untenable, clearly violates Marx's meaning.' Schumpeter, op. cit.,

note 38, p. 686n. On absolute impoverishment, also see M.M. Bober, *Karl Marx's Interpretation of History* (2nd ed., Cambridge Mass.: Harvard University Press, 1948), pp. 213–21.

41. Von Mises, op. cit., note 31, pp 381–4. As von Mises points out, it is at least equally likely that envy of the workers is aroused by an *increase* in egalitarianism and in their relative status, thus causing greater irritation at a gap that is now *smaller*.

42. Cf. Conway, op. cit., note 3, p. 133.

43. See Gottfried Haberler, 'Marxist Economics in Retrospect and Prospect', in M. Drachkovitch (ed.), *Marxist Ideology in the Contemporary World – Its Appeals and Paradoxes* (Hoover Institution, New York: Praeger, 1966), pp. 118, 183.

44. 'If judged by the amount of space it receives, and especially by the persistently repeated references to it early and late in his and Engels' writings, the underconsumption theory seems to dominate over the other theories.' Bober, op. cit., note 40, p. 232. We are indebted to Bober for his classic discussion of Marx's cycle theories, in *ibid.*, pp. 232–57.

45. Thus, Marx in *Theories of Surplus Value*: 'Overproduction has specifically for its condition the general law of the production of capital...while on the other side the mass of producers remains restricted – and on the basis of the capitalist system of production must remain restricted – to an average quantum of wants.' See Bober, op. cit., note 40, p. 240. Also see Tucker, op. cit., note 7, pp. 443–65. It is significant that passages setting forth underconsumption theory in Chapter XVII of the *Theories of Surplus Value* are the *only* discussion of crisis theory in Tucker's *Reader*. In the headnote to the selections, Professor Thomas Ferguson, after pointing out that Marx, curiously, 'left no developed account of his views on crises', adds that Chapter XVII of *Theories* 'contains the best and most systematic discussion by Marx on economic crises'. Tucker, p. 443.

46. Astonishingly, Sowell maintains not only that there is no trace of underconsumptionism in Marx, but that those who assert it only cite each other, not Marx himself. He has, for one thing, apparently never heard of Bober's standard work. Sowell, op. cit., note 18, pp. 78–9, 85–8.

47. Marx and Engels also felt the need to separate themselves as much as they could from straight underconsumption, in view of the fact that two of their great German rivals and opponents were ardent underconsumptionists. These were the Prussian aristocrat and evolutionary state socialist Johann Karl Rodbertus (1805–75), and the University of Berlin economist and social reformer Eugen Karl Dühring (1833–1921).

48. Engels, 'Preface to the English Edition', in Marx, op. cit., note 1, I, p. 6.

49. For a further critique of underconsumptionism, see Murray N. Rothbard, *America's Great Depression* (4th ed., New York: Richardson & Snyder, 1983), pp. 55–8.

50. Bober, op. cit., note 40, pp. 251–2.

51. Mikhail Ivanovich Tugan-Baranowsky (1865–1919). Strictly speaking, Tugan-Baranowsky was a Ukrainian who taught in Russia's St Petersburg. He first enunciated his business cycle theory in his doctoral dissertation, 'The Industrial Crises in England', published in Russian in 1894. Tugan-Baranowsky taught political economy at St Petersburg until 1917, when he became minister of finance and general secretary of the Central Rada of the Ukraine. The following year, Tugan-Baranowsky became head of the Ukrainian Academy's socio-economic department and of its Institute for the Study of Economic Cycles. At his death in 1919, Tugan was economic adviser to the Ukrainian delegation at Versailles. See Sergio Amato, 'Tugan-Baranowsky...' in I.S. Koropeckyj (ed.), *Selected Contributions of Ukrainian Scholars to Economics* (Cambridge, Mass.: Harvard University Press, 1984), pp. 1–59. On non-monetary over-investment cycle theories, see Gottfried Haberler, *Prosperity and Depression* (4th ed., Cambridge, Mass.: Harvard University Press, 1958), pp. 72–85. Amato maintains that the German economist Arthur Spiethoff (1873–1957), who launched his own version of the cycle theory in 1902–3, purloined it from Tugan-Baranowsky's German translation in 1901, then claimed it as his own original discovery. Amato, 'Tugan-Baranowsky', p. 6.

52. See Bober, op. cit., note 40, p. 275. Sowell, on the other hand, claims that Marx held money and credit to be the sole cause of the business cycle. Sowell, op. cit., note 18, pp. 92–5.

53. Indeed, Marx's entire theory of money was profoundly influenced by Thomas Tooke and the banking school. Marx believed, with Tooke, that changes in price levels determined changes in the quantity of money and not *vice versa*, and that balance of payments deficits were determined by real rather than monetary factors. Hence, in his theory of money and its effects, Marx was the opposite of a Ricardian. See Arie Arnon, 'Marx's Theory of Money: the Formative Years', *History of Political Economy*, 16 (Winter 1984), pp. 560–75.

14 After Mill: Bastiat and the French *laissez-faire* tradition

14.1   The French *laissez-faire* school

John Stuart Mill's conquest of British economics by his 1848 treatise, *The Principles of Political Economy*, succeeded in imposing a miasma upon British economics for at least a quarter-century. In some respects, indeed, the subjectivist (or, in its trivialized label, the 'marginalist') revolution against Mill, led abortively by Jevons in the 1870s, never really took hold in Great Britain. The Millian miasma imposed a vague and incoherent adhesion to the labour theory, or at best the cost-of-production theory, of value; to the methodology of positivism, tempered by a confused inductivism; to individualism, muddled by organicism; to a vague, tentative preference for the free market easily overridden by almost any objection, in particular the alleged ability of labour unions to win general wage increases as well as the supposed moral superiority of socialism. Politically, in short, Mill was cleverly positioned to be the patron saint of *laissez-faire* as well of virtually any and all attacks against it – in short, to be the philosopher of the British *status quo* as it existed or as it might become. At the same time, Mill became the modern liberal intellectual's favourite straw-man champion of *laissez-faire*, ever ready to make the most damaging concessions to his modern liberal opponents. In that way, the modern liberal intellectual can sound the triumphal note: 'But even *Mill* admits...' and thus expect to win the day by the invocation of authority alone.

In monetary and banking affairs, indeed, Mill was the guru for precisely the *status quo* as imposed by the Peel Act of 1844 and continuing until World War I: that is, a broad commitment to hard money in the form of the gold standard, but cleverly and fundamentally vitiated by a Bank of England monopoly control of a fractional-reserve banking system that could readily inflate money and credit within that allegedly sound system.

Although of all countries, British economics in the nineteenth century (and down through World War II) managed to accrue the greatest prestige, it was not able to exercise total hegemony over economics abroad. In France, in particular, the legacy of J.B. Say led, in dramatic contrast, to a subjective utility and consistent *laissez-faire* tradition that managed to retain dominance over French economics for nearly a century. We have seen that French *laissez-faire* economics was established in the Restoration period after 1815 by a brilliant group of young economists and social theorists inspired by J.B. Say, and headed by Charles Dunoyer and by Say's son-in-law Charles Comte. Although Comte died in middle age, Dunoyer lived long enough to write his three-volume *magnum opus, De la liberté du Travail (On the Freedom of Labour)*, (1845), and to preside over the founding, in 1842, of the leading Société d'Économie Politique (The Society of Political Economy), which would meet monthly for decades, as well as its scholarly journal, the *Journal des Économistes*, which had been launched a few months before the society.

From then until World War I, an admirable and productive cadre of economists staffed the main French academic posts, edited and wrote for numerous
scholarly journals, formed associations and conferences, and wrote and lectured indefatigably on behalf of harmony of interests and general prosperity
through free markets, free trade, and *laissez-faire*. It is remarkable that at
least three generations of French economists were schooled in, and carried on
and developed, this *laissez-faire* tradition. Despite generations of changing
fashions and enormous temptations from the side of statism and special
privilege, French economists, for nearly a century, stuck to their guns and
remained stalwart champions of *laissez-faire* and enemies of state intervention and special privilege.

Here we might pay special attention to the men who collaborated on the
first encyclopedia of economics, an excellent two-volume work, *Dictionnaire
d'Économie Politique* (Paris: Guillaumin, 1852–53), co-edited and published
by Gilbert Guillaumin (1801–64), an indefatigable publisher of countless
French economic and *laissez-faire* works during the nineteenth century. The
co-editor Charles Coquelin (1805–52), himself a major contributor to the
dictionary, unfortunately died shortly before publication. The dictionary went
through four printings. Another leading light of the dictionary, and founding
secretary of the Société d'Économie Politique, was Joseph Garnier (Clément
Joseph Garnier, 1813–81), for some years editor-in-chief of the *Journal des
Économistes*, and author of several highly successful textbook treatises in
economics including: *Éléments d'économie politique (1845* – many editions),
and *Éléments des Finances* (1858 – many editions).

French *laissez-faire* economists pioneered, not only encyclopedias of economics, but also the study of the history of the discipline. The first history of
economic thought was the *Histoire de l'économie politique en Europe* (1837,
4th edition, 1860, English translation, *History of Political Economy in Europe*
1880), by Jérome-Adolphe Blanqui (1798–1854), who studied political economy
under Say, and succeeded him as professor. Blanqui was also for many years
editor-in-chief of the *Journal des Économistes*. Joseph Garnier had been
Blanqui's student. Blanqui, in turn, was the son-in-law of Michel Chevalier
(1806–79). An engineer and Saint-Simonian socialist in his youth, Chevalier
became a *laissez-faire* liberal, becoming professor of political economy at the
Collège de France, and publishing the three-volume *Cours d'Économie Politique*
(1842–50). Chevalier was also a statesman, negotiating the famous fee trade
treaty with England (England being represented by the great Richard Cobden)
in 1860, a high-water mark of the free trade and free market movement in
nineteenth century Europe. Another prominent student of Chevalier was Henri
(Joseph Léon) Baudrillart (1821–92), who went on to teach political economy
at the Collège de France, and whose *Manuel d'Économie Politique* was published in 1857, and went into numerous editions.

Another prominent economist was the Pole Louis Wolowski (1810–76), a brother-in-law of Michel Chevalier. Born in Warsaw, Wolowski emigrated to France in 1834, founding and editing for many years the *Revue de législation et jurisprudence*. Possessor of a doctorate of law and another in political economy, Wolowski was to become a banker, statesman and professor as well as being associated for many years with the *Journal des Économistes*. Wolowski's nephew, Émile Levasseur (1828–1911) became a prominent economic historian and successor to Baudrillart at the Collège de France. Levasseur published a well-known work on the *Histoire des classes ouvrières en France* (History of the Working Classes in France) (1859) and, in 1867, published a *Précis d'Économie Politique*, which went into many editions. Wolowski and Levasseur, it should be noted, wrote a scintillating joint article in defence of property rights, on 'Property', for Lalor's three-volume *Cyclopedia of Political Science*, published in the United States in 1884.

A worthy successor to Jérome-Adolphe Blanqui as historian of economic thought in the French *laissez-faire* school was Maurice Block (1816–1901). Born in Berlin but emigrating to France, Block worked in the statistical department of the ministry of agriculture, industry and trade. By his 40s, Block was a full-time editor and writer in economics. For 44 years, from 1856 virtually until his death, Block served as editor of the *Annuaire d'économie politique et de la statistique* (Annual of Economics and Statistics), as well as editor of the *Dictionnaire générale de la Politique* (from 1862 and later years), and the *Dictionnaire de l'Administration Française* (1855 and later years), and also wrote several important books on the theory of statistics, on socialism, on French finances, and a *Petit manuel d'économie politique*, published in 1873 and going into many editions. An erudite and indefatigable scholar, Maurice Block served for over 40 years as a reporter on all economic writings in Europe for the *Journal des Économistes*, capping his career with a great two-volume history of economic thought, *Le progrès de la science économique depuis Adam Smith* (1890). In his *Progrès*, Block praised the new Austrian school, and denounced the historicism and opposition to economic law of the German historical school.

Three generations of Says also took a prominent part in the French movement of *laissez-faire* economics. Jean-Baptiste's only son Horace-Émile Say (1794–1860) was merchant for a time in the United States and especially in Brazil, and served as a commercial judge and a councillor of state during the period of the Second Republic, 1859–61. Horace Say wrote a book on the history of commercial relations between France and Brazil. Horace's son, Jean-Baptiste Léon Say (1826–96), became a prominent statesman devoted to free trade and *laissez-faire*. Léon Say wrote many articles for the *Journal des Économistes*, he was the owner of the *laissez-faire*-oriented *Journal des Débats*, and he was the minister of finance from 1872 to 1879, and again in

1882. He was also president of the French Senate in 1882. Léon Say concluded a preliminary free trade treaty with England in 1880, and successfully opposed the introduction of an income tax.

One of the last of the fiery and uncompromising free market and anti-interventionists of the French school was Yves Guyot (1843–1928), a prolific writer who also served as city councillor of Paris (1876–85) and minister of public works (1889–92). Guyot succeeded the venerable Gustave de Molinari after he stepped down as editor of the *Journal des Économistes* in 1909.

So dominant was the *laissez-faire* school in France during the nineteenth century that its teaching permeated the popular culture. Popular writers, journalists and novelists expounded on the harmony of interests, and on the mutual benefit and the general prosperity brought about by the free market. Thus no more lucid and inspiring an economic primer and paean to the workings of the free market has ever been written than the lectures to French workers, formed into the *Handbook of Social Economy: Or the Workers' ABC*, written by the popular novelist Edmond About (1828–85).[1]

Indeed, the very lucidity and popularity of the French writers was turned against them by the British classical economists, generally dense and obscure writers, who could turn their very elegance of style against the French, and denounce them for superficiality of thought and scholarship. This tradition has been redoubled by modern historians, whose intense hostility to the French writers' political conclusions reinforces their brusque dismissal. In particular, modern historians unfairly dismiss the French writers as mere popularizers, lacking theoretical depth.

14.2   Frédéric Bastiat: the central figure

Particularly suffering from historical neglect is the most famous of the French *laissez-faire* economists, Claude Frédéric Bastiat (1801–50), to whom the two-volume *Dictionnaire d'Économie Politique* (1852) was respectfully and affectionately dedicated. Bastiat was indeed a lucid and superb writer, whose brilliant and witty essays and fables to this day are remarkable and devastating demolitions of protectionism and of all forms of government subsidy and control. He was a truly scintillating advocate of an untrammelled free market. Frédéric Bastiat's justly famous 'Petition of the Candlemakers' is still anthologized in books of economic readings; in this satiric petition to the French parliament, the candlemakers' trade association petitions the government to protect their industry, which employs many thousands of men, from the unfair, unjust, invasive competition of a foreign light source: the sun. Bastiat's candlemakers petition the government to shut out the sunlight all over France – a protective device that would give employment to many millions of worthy French candlemakers.

Bastiat's fable of the broken window also brilliantly refuted Keynesianism nearly a century before its birth. Here, he outlines three levels of economic analysis. A mischievous boy hurls a rock at a plate glass store window, and breaks the glass. As a crowd gathers round, the first-level analysis, common sense, comments on the event. Common sense deplores the destruction of property in breaking the window, and sympathizes with the storekeeper for having to spend his money repairing the window. But then, says Bastiat, comes the second-level, sophisticated analyst or what we might call a proto-Keynesian. The Keynesian says: oh, but you people don't realize that the breaking of the window is *really* an economic blessing. For, in having to repair the window, the storekeeper invigorates the economy by his spending, and gives welcome employment to glaziers and their workers. Destruction of property, by compelling spending, therefore stimulates the economy and has an invigorating 'multiplier effect' on production and employment.

But then in steps Bastiat, the third-level analyst, and points out the griev-ous fallacy in the destructionist proto-Keynesian position. The alleged so-phisticated critic, says Bastiat, concentrates on 'what is seen' and neglects 'what is not seen'. The sophisticate *sees* that the storekeeper must give employment to glaziers by spending money to repair his window. But what he doesn't see is the storekeepers's opportunity foregone. If he did not have to spend the money on repairing the window, he could had *added* to his capital, and to everyone's standard of living, and thereby employed people in the act of advancing, rather than merely trying to sustain, the current stock of capital. Or, the storekeeper might have spent the money on his own consump-tion, employing people in *that* form of production.

In this way, the 'economist', Bastiat's third-level observer, vindicates com-mon sense and refutes the apologia for destruction of the pseudo-sophisti-cate. He considers what is not seen as well as what is seen. Bastiat, the economist, is the *truly* sophisticated analyst.[2]

Frédéric Bastiat was also a perceptive political, or politico-economic, theo-rist. Attacking statism as a growing parasitic burden upon producers in the market, he defined the state as 'the great fiction by which everyone tries to live off everyone else'. And in his work on *The Law* (1850), Bastiat insisted that law and government must be strictly limited to defending the persons, the liberty, and the property of people against violence; any going beyond that role would be destructive of liberty and prosperity.

While often praised as a gifted popularizer, Bastiat has been systematically derided and undervalued as a theorist. Criticizing the classical Smithian distinction between 'productive' labour (on material goods) and 'unproduc-tive' labour (in producing immaterial services), Bastiat made an important contribution to economic theory by pointing out that *all* goods, including material ones, are productive and are valued precisely because they produce

immaterial services. Exchange, he pointed out, consists of the mutually beneficial trade of such services. In emphasizing the centrality of immaterial
services in production and consumption, Bastiat built on J.B. Say's insistence
that all market resources were 'productive', and that income to productive
factors were payments for that productivity. Bastiat also built upon Charles
Dunoyer's thesis in his *Nouveau traité d'économie social* (New Treatise on
Social Economy) (1830) that 'value is measured by services rendered, and
that products exchange according to the quality of services stored in them'.[3]

Perhaps most important, in stark contrast to the Smith–Ricardo classical
school's exclusive emphasis on production, and neglect of the goal of economic endeavours – consumption, Bastiat proclaimed once again the continental emphasis on consumption as the goal and hence the determinant of
economic activity. Bastiat's own oft-repeated triad: 'Wants, Efforts,
Satisfactions' summed it up: wants are the goal of economic activity, giving
rise to efforts, and eventually yielding satisfactions. Furthermore, Bastiat
noted that human wants are unlimited, and hierarchically ordered by individuals in their scales of value.[4]

Bastiat's concentration on *exchange*, and on analysis of exchange, was
also a highly important contribution, especially in contrast to the British
classicists' focus on production of material wealth. It was the emphasis on
exchange that led Bastiat and the French school to stress the ways in which
the free market leads to a smooth and harmonious organization of the economy.
Hence the importance of *laissez-faire*.[5]

Frédéric Bastiat was born in 1801 in Bayonne, in south-western France,
the son of a landowner and prominent merchant in the Spanish trade. Or-
phaned at the age of nine, Bastiat entered his uncle's business firm in 1818;
when, seven years later, he inherited his grandfather's landed estate, Bastiat
left the firm and became a gentleman farmer. But his interests were neither in
trade nor in agriculture, but in the study of political economy. Fluent in
English, Italian and Spanish, Bastiat steeped himself in all the extant economic literature in these languages. Apart from an unsuccessful attempt to
establish an insurance firm in Portugal in the early 1840s, as well as being a
member of the district council and his undemanding service as a country
judge, Bastiat spent two decades in quiet study and reflection on economic
problems. He was most heavily influenced by J.B. Say, partially by Adam
Smith, by Destutt de Tracy, and particularly by the great four-volume *laissez-
faire* libertarian work of Charles Comte, *A Treatise on Legislation* (1827).
Indeed, as a teenager, Bastiat had been a subscriber to Comte and Dunoyer's
journal, *Le Censeur*, and he was to become a friend and colleague of Dunoyer's
in the struggle for free trade.

Bastiat entered the economic literature with a sparkling attack on protectionism in France and England in the *Journal des Économistes* in late 1844, an

article which created a sensational impact. Bastiat followed this up with another article in the *Journal*, in early 1845, denouncing socialism and the concept of a 'right to labour'. During the few years he had left on earth, Bastiat poured forth a stream of lucid and influential writings. His two-volume *Economic Sophisms* (1845), a collection of witty essays on protectionism and government controls, sold out quickly, going into several editions, and was swiftly translated into English, Spanish, Italian and German. During the same year, Bastiat published *Cobden et la Ligue*, his tribute to Cobden and the Anti-Corn Law League: a history of the League that included the principal speeches and articles by Cobden, Bright, and other stalwarts of the League.

After setting up a free trade association in Bordeaux in 1846, Bastiat moved to Paris, where he stepped up his literary efforts and organized a national association for free trade. He became the secretary-general of the national association, as well as editor-in-chief of *Le Libre-Échange (Free Trade)*, the periodical of the French free trade association. Even though in frail health, Bastiat also participated in the revolution of 1848, being elected to the constituent and then the legislative assembly, where he served from 1848 until his death.

Bastiat's final political service has been undervalued by most historians. While generally voting in the minority in the assembly as a stalwart of individual liberty and *laissez-faire*, Bastiat was highly influential as vice-president (and often acting president) of the assembly's finance committee. There he fought tirelessly for lower government spending, lower taxes, sound money, and free trade. While he fought ardently in opposition to socialist and communist schemes, Bastiat elected to sit on the Left, as a proponent of *laissez-faire* and the republic, and as an opponent of protectionism, absolute monarchy, and a warlike foreign policy. As a consistent civil libertarian, Bastiat also fought against the jailing of socialists, the outlawry of peaceful trade unionism, or the declaration of martial law. Bastiat also made his mark by at least partially converting the man who would become the president of the provisional republic in 1848, the eminent poet and orator Alphonse Marie Louis Lamartine (1790–1869) from his previous socialism to (an admittedly inconsistent) *laissez-faire* position.[6]

Bastiat died young in 1850, leaving his two-volume theoretical *magnum opus*, *Economic Harmonies*, only partially published; the remainder was published posthumously. It was a fitting memorial to Bastiat that his friend Michel Chevalier, the man whom he had converted to free trade and *laissez-faire*, should have been the one to conclude, with Richard Cobden, the great free trade Anglo-French treaty of 1860.

Bastiat met Cobden on his first trip to England in the summer of 1845, and for the remainder of Bastiat's life the two men were close friends and frequent correspondents, visiting each other frequently. The two influenced each other greatly, Bastiat providing Cobden with broader theoretical insights in his devotion to free trade, and the latter inspiring Bastiat to organize a movement in France similar to the Anti-Corn Law League. In particular, Cobden took from Bastiat a devotion to natural law and natural rights; an emphasis on the harmony of individuals, groups, and nations through the mutual benefits of the free market; and a staunch opposition to war and an interventionist foreign policy, and a devotion to international peace. The two also shared a consistent devotion to *laissez-faire* devoid of the numerous hesitancies and qualifications imposed by the classical economists, or of the gloomy Ricardian hostility to landlords or to land rent.[7]

14.3   The influence of Bastiat in Europe

Inspired by Bastiat's organizing and by his theories, free trade associations rapidly established themselves in various countries in Europe. Belgium formed a free trade association shortly after France, and the Belgian group stayed in constant correspondence with Bastiat and his *Libre-Échange*. Former minister Charles de Brouckère, burgomaster of Brussels, was president of the Belgian association. In Italy an association for free trade established the journal *Contemporaneo* in the Autumn of 1846, and printed a statement hailing the French free trade association. While the statement praised the Anti-Corn Law League, it also lauded the French association as more all-encompassing in its free-market position: 'the British Association has declared war against only one of the evils in its own country [tariffs and the Corn laws], while the French Association has adopted a more general plan that encompasses the entire human race. It wishes to induce all nations to fraternize, and to invite everyone to the banquet of production and consumption.'[8]

One of the prominent signers of the Italian statement was Professor Raffaele Busacca, a vigorous defender of free trade and a prolific writer on statistical, historical and theoretical subjects in economics.

A particularly important follower and admirer of Frédéric Bastiat was the man who became the unquestioned leader and dominant force in economic theory and policy in nineteenth century Italy. He was the Sicilian-born Francesco Ferrara (1810–1900), a stalwart advocate of *laissez-faire*, professor of political economy at the University of Turin, and the teacher and mentor of most Italian economists of the next generation. Ferrara also played an important political role in the unification of Italy and was at one time minister of finance of the new nation. In addition, Ferrara was an eminent historian of economic thought, to which he contributed the editorship of the first two series of the multi-volume translation, *Biblioteca dell'Economista* (Turin, 1850–69), and especially his two-volume *Esame storico-critico di economisti e dottrine economiche* (1889–92). For many years, Ferrara was professor at the University of Turin, and there trained many prominent Italian economists. In addition to Bastiat, upon whom he lavished 100 pages in his great *Esame*, Ferrara particularly hailed the works, of Say, Dunoyer and Chevalier.

Ferrara's theoretical contributions, like Bastiat's, have been systematically underweighted by harsh modern, anti-*laissez-faire* critics who, as in the case of Bastiat, find it difficult to believe that anyone who is ardently and consistently in favour of *laissez-faire* could possibly be an important scholar and economic theorist. Thus, Ferrara's 'cost-of-reproduction' theory of value, often dismissed as a clumsy rewrite of Ricardian 'cost-of-production', has recently been shown instead to be a partial anticipation of subjective, marginal utility theory.[9]

For several decades Francesco Ferrara's exchange-oriented and *laissez-faire* economics held sway among Italian economists. In the 1870s, however, the interconnected statist trends of protectionism and of the German historical school, as well as outright socialism, began to infest Italian economics. Ferrara valiantly combated the new trends. A formal split occurred in 1874, when the younger statists, centred in Padua, formed the Association for the Development of Economic Studies, publishing a journal which soon became the *Giornale degli Economisti*. On the other hand, the Ferraristas, centred in Florence, formed the Adam Smith Society, and published the weekly *L'Economista*. While outnumbered, the Ferrara group produced some notable younger disciples, including Domenico Berardi, who published a critique of government intervention in 1882 and a book on money 30 years later; A. Bertolini, who wrote a critique of socialism in 1889; and Fontanelli, who wrote a critique of unions and strikes. In particular, we might mention Tulio Martello of Bologna, known as the last of the Ferraristas. With the characteristic half-sneer which he tended to reserve for ardent partisans of *laissez-faire*, Schumpeter wrote of Martello's challenging call for polymetallism as the path of complete monetary freedom in *La Moneta* (1883), that 'the value of which is but slightly impaired by some liberalist vagaries on free coinage'.[10]

While seemingly battling a rear-guard action against overwhelming odds, Ferrara and his school actually hung on long enough to turn the tide, by influencing the new 'army of marginalist–liberalists' led by Maffeo Pantaleoni. The group seized control of the dominant economic journal (the *Giornale degli Economisti*) in 1890, and was to remain dominant for years thereafter.[11]

Sweden was a country heavily influenced by Bastiat, who became the major authority in Swedish economics and politics. A young Swede, Johan August Gripenstedt (d. 1874), met Bastiat on a trip to France, and was deeply influenced for the rest of his life by the French *laissez-faire* leader. Gripenstedt became the greatest of the economic liberals in Sweden during the 1860s and 1870s, as well as the most influential politician in Sweden. By 1870, Gripenstedt, almost single-handed, had managed to eliminate all import and export prohibitions in Sweden, to abolish all export duties, to reduce tariffs on manufactured goods, and to bring about free trade in agricultural products.

Shortly after Gripenstedt's death, his followers and disciples formed the Stockholm Economic Society in 1877, dedicated to the principles of Bastiat and Gripenstedt. Some of the leading members were: Johan Walter Arnberg, director of the Bank of Sweden, who warned of the dangers of socialism stemming from businessmen's demands for government subsidies; G.K. Hamilton, professor of economics at the University of Lund, so dedicated to Frédéric Bastiat that he named his son 'Bastiat' in 1865; A.O. Wallenberg, founder of the Stockholm Euskilda Bank; and Johan Henrik Palme, leading banker, dedicated to free trade.

Two prominent *laissez-faire* political leaders in the Economic Society should be mentioned. One was Axel Gustafsson Bennich, director-general of the customs, and right-hand man of Gripenstedt. Bennich was an indefatigable and joyous battler for free trade and *laissez-faire* throughout his long life. Another was the president of the Stockholm Economic Society, Carl Freidrich Waern, a Gothenburg merchant who became minister of finance and head of the board of trade. Waern resigned from the latter post because he refused to sign a law mandating protection of young timber in the forests, a measure he denounced as an egregious invasion of the rights of private property.

As was true of *laissez-faire* thinkers and activists in England and France, Swedish libertarians were split on what to do about banking. Central banker Johan Arnberg and economist Hans Forssell favoured the central Bank of Sweden as a means of abolishing all private bank notes, which they considered inflationary and pernicious. On the other hand, banker A.O. Wallenberg championed free banking.

By the mid-1880s, however, in Sweden as in the rest of Europe, statism began to make a successful comeback and gradually to become dominant. Protectionists began to infiltrate the Economic Society by the mid-1880s, and Sweden adopted a protective tariff system in 1888. In 1893, the symbol of protectionist triumph came with a protectionist being chosen president of the former central nucleus of free trade, the Stockholm Economic Society. During the 1880s, too, despite the bitter attacks of Forssell and other founding stalwarts, the society began to champion social welfare and other *Kathedersozialist* ('socialism of the chair') policies. In this way, Swedish economic theory and policy shifted, during the decade, from its original French *laissez-faire* orientation toward the German historical school and its 'monarchical socialism'. This sharp change was greatly facilitated by German being made the dominant foreign language in the Swedish public schools in 1878.[12]

But even in Prussia, a free trade party was established during the late 1840s dedicated to Bastiat's principles. The Prussian free trade movement was led by John Prince Smith (1809–74), son of an English father and German mother, who corresponded frequently with Bastiat. In one letter Prince Smith wrote to Bastiat:

The friends to whom I have shown your book [*Economic Harmonies*] are enthusiastic about it. I promise you that it will be read eagerly by our best thinkers... We hope to establish a formal league among the democratic parties and the free traders. 'Bring Bastiat here', a leader of the democrats said to me, 'and I promise to lead 10,000 men in a procession to celebrate his visit to our capital'.[13]

John Prince Smith was born in London in 1809, the son of a barrister. On the death of his father, he began working at the age of 13 for a London mercantile firm.[14] Later he turned to journalism, travelling to his mother's country, and in 1831 became a teacher of English and French at a *gymnasium* in the port of Elbing in East Prussia. Learning economics in Germany, Prince Smith, by the 1830s, began writing articles on behalf of the free market, and vigorously defended seven professors who had been fired in 1837 from the University of Göttingen for protesting the despotic revocation of the liberal Hanoverian constitution. His ensuing difficulties with the Prussian educational administration led Prince Smith to leave his teaching post in 1840 and turn to full-time journalism.

Prince Smith not only came out generally for the free market, but also began a vigorous and consistent anti-war and anti-militarist stand, which brought him to advocate the elimination of the Prussian state's bulwark, the standing army, and its replacement by a far cheaper and popularly controlled citizens' militia.

In 1843, Prince Smith launched his lifelong crusade for freedom of trade, putting it in a historical and sociological context reminiscent of the writings of Comte and Dunoyer. Furthermore, Prince Smith made clear that for him 'free trade' meant not simply absence of international trade barriers but also an absolute free market at home, with the state confined only to police protection.[15]

In 1846, Prince Smith, joined by several associates, sent an address to Robert Peel, in which they congratulated the British prime minister for his outstanding achievement in repealing the Corn Laws. Peel's gracious and highly principled reply caused a sensation in Prussia, and Prince Smith was inspired by the response to found, in December of that year, the German Free Trade Union.[16] The union, consisting of business leaders and scholars, held its first, organizing meeting the following March in the hall of the Berlin Stock Exchange. The great majority of the 200 attendees were businessmen.

For the rest of his life, John Prince Smith led the way in Germany in agitating for free markets and free trade. In 1860, he founded the Economic Society as the successor to the Free Trade Union. His home in Berlin (he had married the daughter of a wealthy Berlin banker) became a salon for liberal Prussian politicians, some of whom formed the Progressive Party. In 1858, Prince Smith helped found the annual congress of German economists, which was dedicated to *laissez-faire* until its final meeting in 1885.

At the congress, Prince Smith delivered papers attacking usury laws, criticizing patents, and denouncing irredeemable paper money. In 1863, Prince Smith helped found and co-edited the *Quarterly Journal for Economy, Politics, and Cultural History (Vierteljahrschrift für Volkwirtschaft, Politik, und Kulturgeschichte)*, along with the ultra-individualist Julius Faucher (1820–78), Prince Smith's closest collaborator. The *Quarterly Journal* soon became 'the chief theoretical organ of classical liberalism in Germany',[17] and continued in existence for 30 years. Fluent in French, Prince Smith contributed to the French *Journal des Économistes*, and he also helped organize, and wrote for, a *Concise Dictionary of Economics (Handwörterbuch der Volkwirtschaftslehre*, 1866), modelled after the French *laissez-faire Dictionnaire d'Économie Politique*.

During the 1870s and 1880s, *laissez-faire* views in Prussia and Germany were swiftly replaced by the dominance of the German historical school, statism, and 'socialism of the chair'. This radical change was greatly fostered by the political triumph of Bismarck and Prussian militarism over classical liberalism, and the union of the bulk of the German nation under the Prussian domination of 'blood and iron'.

The high point of the European free trade movement came early, at a famous international congress of economists, organized by the Belgian free trade association at Brussels, from 16–18 September 1847. Inspired by the Anti-Corn Law League victory and the Bastiat movement, and by a triumphal 14 month-long European tour by Cobden in 1846–47, the congress met to decide the free trade question. Presided over by the Belgian de Brouckère, the congress consisted of 170 delegates from 12 countries, and included publicists, manufacturers, agriculturists, merchants and statesmen, as well as economists. While Bastiat was unable to attend, de Brouckère, in his opening address, hailed Bastiat as the 'zealous apostle of our doctrines'. Particularly active at the congress was the French delegation, especially Louis Wolowski, Charles Dunoyer, Jérome-Adolphe Blanqui and Joseph Garnier; also active was John Prince Smith, head of the Prussian delegation. Other prominent attendees were Colonel Thomas Perronet Thompson, of the English parliament, and James Wilson, editor of *The Economist*.

While a small contingent of protectionists spoke at the congress, they were swamped by the free traders, who passed a resounding declaration for freedom of trade. Unfortunately, plans for further meetings of the congress were broken up by the Revolution of 1848, which delivered a grave setback to the movement for economic freedom in Europe, from which it took some years to recover. After a brief Indian Summer of the 1860s, the *laissez-faire* movement for free markets, free trade and international peace, began in the 1870s and 1880s to give way, tragically, to a Europe of protectionism, militarism, welfare states, compulsory cartels and warring international power blocs.

Nationalist and statist economics, an industrial recrudescence of commercial mercantilism, began to dominate Europe.

14.4   Gustave de Molinari, first anarcho-capitalist

Of all the leading libertarian French economists of the mid- and late nineteenth centuries, the most unusual was the Belgian-born Gustave de Molinari (1819–1912). Born in Liège, the son of a Belgian physician and a baron who had been an officer in the Napoleonic army, Molinari spent most of his life in France, where he became a prolific and indefatigable author and editor in lifelong support of pure *laissez-faire*, of international peace, and in determined and intransigent opposition to all forms of statism, governmental control and militarism. In contrast to British soft-core utilitarianism on public policy, Molinari was an unflinching champion of freedom and natural law.

Coming to Paris, the cultural and political centre of the French-speaking world, at the age of 21 in 1840, Molinari joined the Société d'Économie Politique on its inception in 1842, and became the secretary of Bastiat's association for free trade when it was formed in Paris in 1846. He soon became one of the editors of the association's periodical, *Libre-Échange*. Molinari quickly began to publish widely in the free trade and free market press in Paris, becoming an editor of the *Journal des Économistes* in 1847. He published his first of many books in 1846, *Études Economiques: sur l'Organisation de la Liberté industrielle et l'abolition de l'esclavage (Economic Studies: on the Organizaton of Liberty and the Abolition of Slavery)*.

The young Molinari, however, hit the *laissez-faire*-oriented Société d'Économie Politique like a thunderclap in 1849, with his most famous and original work. He delivered a paper expounding, for the first time in history, a pure and consistent *laissez-faire*, to the point of calling for free and unhampered competition in what are generally called uniquely 'public' services: in particular, the sphere of police and judicial protection of person and private property. If free competition is better and more efficient in supplying *all other* goods and services, Molinari reasoned, why not for this last bastion, police and judicial protection – a view that over a century later would come to be called 'anarcho-capitalism'.

Molinari first set forth his view in the *Journal des Économistes*, the periodical of the Société, in February 1849.[18] This article was quickly expanded into book form, *Les Soirées de la Rue Saint-Lazare*, a series of fictional dialogues between three protagonists: the conservative (advocate of high tariffs and state monopoly privilege); the socialist; and the economist (clearly himself). The final, or eleventh, *Soirée* elaborated further on how his concept of free market protective services could work in practice.[19]

A meeting of the Société d'Économie Politique in the Autumn of 1849 was devoted to Molinari's radically new theory as expounded in the *Soirées*. After

Molinari had presented the essence of his proposal in a paper, the assembled libertarian dignitaries engaged in a discussion. Apparently the new theory threw them, because unfortunately no one dealt with the essence of the new doctrine. Charles Coquelin and Frédéric Bastiat could only fulminate that no competition anywhere can exist without a back-up by the supreme authority of the state (Coquelin), and that the force needed to guarantee justice and security can *only* be imposed by a 'supreme power', (Bastiat). Both engaged in pure assertion without argument, and both here chose to ignore what they knew full well in all other contexts: that this 'supreme power' had scarcely proved to be a reliable guarantor of private property in the past or present (to say nothing, alas, of the future).

Of all the leading libertarian minds assembled, only Charles Dunoyer deigned to try to rebut Molinari's argument. He deplored that Molinari had been carried away by the 'illusions of logic', and maintained that 'competition between governmental companies is chimerical, because it leads to violent battles'. Apart from ignoring the *truly* violent battles that have always occurred *between states* in our existing 'international anarchy', Dunoyer failed to grapple with the very real incentives that would exist in an anarcho-capitalist world for defence companies to engage in treaties, contracts and arbitrations.[20] Instead, Dunoyer proposed to rely on the 'competition' of political parties *within* a representative government – hardly a satisfactory solution to the problem of social conflict from a libertarian, anti-statist point of view. Dunoyer also opined that it was most prudent to leave force in the hands of the state, 'where civilization has put it' – this from one of the great founders of the conquest theory of the state!

Unfortunately, except for these few remarks, the libertarian economists assembled failed to deal with Molinari's thesis, their discussion largely criticizing Molinari for allegedly going too far in attacking all use of the power of eminent domain by the state.[21]

Particularly interesting was the general treatment of the maverick Molinari by his fellow French *laissez-faire* libertarian economists. Even though he persisted in advocating his anarcho-capitalist or free market protection views for many decades (e.g. in his *Les Lois Naturelles de l'Économie Politique*, 1887), Molinari was scarcely treated as a pariah for his heretical views. On the contrary, he was treated as he indeed was: the logical culmination of their own *laissez-faire* views which they respected even though they could not fully agree. On the death of Joseph Garnier in 1881, Molinari became the editor of the *Journal des Économistes*, a post which he occupied until his ninetieth year in 1909.[22] Molinari only backtracked on his anarchistic views in his very late works, beginning in his *Esquisse de l'organisation politique et économique de société future* (1899). Here he retreated to the idea of a single monopoly defence and protection company, which service would be contracted out by the central state to a single private corporation.[23]

How Molinari was considered by his colleagues may be seen from the footnote by Joseph Garnier, the editor of the *Journal*, on introducing Molinari's first revolutionary article in 1849. Garnier noted:

> Although this article may appear utopian in its conclusions, we nevertheless believe that we should publish it in order to attract the attention of economists and journalists to a question which has hitherto been treated in only a desultory manner and which should, nevertheless, in our day and age, be approached with greater precision. So many people exaggerate the nature and prerogatives of government that it has become useful to formulate strictly the boundaries outside of which the intervention of authority becomes anarchical and tyrannical rather than protective and profitable.[24]

Fifty-five years later, at the appearance of the first English translation of Molinari's work, his fellow-octogenarian, the *laissez-faire* attorney and economist, Frédéric Passy (1822–1912), wrote a moving tribute to his old friend and colleague Molinari. He wrote of his 'esteem and admiration for the character and talent' of the man 'who is the doyen of our ...liberal economists – of the men with whom, though, alas! few in number, I have been happy to stand side-by-side during more than half a century'. Passy went on to state that these liberal principles had been proclaimed by Cobden, Gladstone and Bright in England, and by Turgot, Say, Chevalier and Bastiat in France. 'And my belief grows yearly stronger that, but for these principles, the societies of the present would be without wealth, peace, material greatness, or moral dignity.' Molinari, Passy added, 'has maintained these principles from his youth', from his *Soirée de la Rue St. Lazare* during the 1848 Revolution, though lectures and writings, to his editorship of the *Journal des Économistes,* where 'month-by-month the important Review of which he is editor-in-chief repeats them in a fresh guise'. And finally, Molinari's books, where: 'annually, so to speak, a further book, as distinguished for clearness of grasp as for admirable literary style, goes out to testify to the constancy of his convictions no less than to the unimpaired vigour of his mental outlook and the virile serenity of his green old age.'[25]

14.5   Vilfredo Pareto, pessimistic follower of Molinari

One prominent person rarely associated by scholars with the Bastiat-Ferrara *laissez-faire* school was the eminent sociologist and economic theorist, Vilfredo Federico Damaso Pareto (1848–1923). Pareto was born in Paris into a noble Genoan family. His father, the Marchese Raffaelle Pareto, a hydraulic engineer, had fled Italy as a republican and supporter of Mazzini. The senior Pareto returned to Italy in the mid-1850s and gained a high rank in the Italian civil service. The young Pareto studied at the Turin Polytechnic where he earned a graduate engineering degree in 1869; his graduate thesis was on the fundamental principle of equilibrium in solid bodies. As we shall see in a later volume, Pareto's thesis led him to the idea that equilibrium in mechanics is the proper paradigm for investigation into economics and the social sciences.[26] After graduation, Pareto became a director of the Florence branch of the Rome Railway Company, and in a few years he became managing director of a Florence firm manufacturing iron and iron products.

Pareto soon plunged into political writing, taking a fiery stand in favour of *laissez-faire* and against all forms of government intervention, defending personal and economic freedom, and attacking plutocratic subsidies and privileges to business with equal fervour to his denunciations of social legislation or proletarian socialist forms of intervention. Pareto was one of the founders of the Adam Smith Society in Italy, and also ran unsuccessfully for Parliament twice during the early 1880s.

Heavily influenced by Molinari, Pareto's writings came to the latter's attention in 1887. Molinari then invited Pareto to submit articles to the *Journal des Économistes*. Pareto met the French liberals, and formed a friendship with Yves Guyot, who was to be Molinari's successor as editor of the *Journal* and who was to write Molinari's obituary in 1912. Shortly after getting in touch with Molinari, Pareto's mother died, and he was able to give up his manufacturing post, become a consulting engineer, get married, and retire to his villa in 1890 to devote the rest of his life to writing, scholarship, and the social sciences. Freed of his business duties, Pareto plunged into a one-man crusade against the state and statism, and formed a close friendship with the *laissez-faire* neoclassical marginalist economist Maffeo Pantaleoni (1857–1924), who drew Pareto into technical economic theory. Having become a Walrasian under Pantaleoni's tutelage, Pareto succeeded Léon Walras as professor of political economy at the University of Lausanne. Pareto continued at Lausanne, also teaching sociology, until 1907, when he fell ill, and retired to a villa on Lake Geneva, where he continued to study and write until his death.

Pareto's shift into technical neoclassical theory did not for a moment abate his ardent battle for freedom and against all forms of statism, including militarism. An idea of his trenchant *laissez-faire* liberalism can be gained from his article on 'Socialism and Freedom' published in 1891:

> So we can group socialists and protectionists under the name of restrictionists, whilst those who want to base the distribution of wealth solely on free competition can be called liberationists...
>
> Thus restrictionists are divided into two types: socialists, who through the intervention of the state, wish to change the distribution of wealth in favour of the less rich; and the others, who, even if they are sometimes not completely con-

scious of what they are doing, favour the rich – these are the supporters of commercial protectionism and social organisation of a military type. We owe to Spencer the demonstration of the close analogy of these two types of protectionism. This similarity between protectionism and socialism was very well understood by the English liberals of the school of Cobden and that of John Bright and was clarified in the writings of Bastiat.[27]

Pareto's writings, furthermore, are studded with appreciative and often lengthy quotes from Molinari. Thus, in the same article on 'Socialism and Freedom', Pareto praises Molinari for advancing a unique and bold system that 'proceed(s) towards the conquest of freedom, using all the knowledge that is offered by modern science'.

In his 'Introduction to Marx's *Capital*' in a book on Marxism (*Marxisme et économie pure*, 1893), Pareto was clearly influenced by the French libertarian Dunoyer–Comte concept of the 'ruling class' as whatever group controls the state. He ended the chapter with a lengthy and admiring quote from Molinari, who carried through this libertarian class doctrine. Pareto ended the Molinari quote with this sentence: 'Everywhere the ruling classes have one thought – their own selfish interests – and they use the government to satisfy them.'[28]

Pareto's first great treatise on economics, the *Cours d'Économie Politique* (1896), was heavily influenced by both Molinari and Herbert Spencer. In every polity, he points out, there is a minority ruling class exploiting the majority who are the ruled. Tariffs Pareto treats as an example of legal spoliation, plunder and theft. Pareto left no doubt that his objective was to eradicate all such legalized plunder. As Placido Bucolo points out, Pareto did *not*, as some analysts claim, adopt a Marxian view of class struggle in his *Cours*. Instead, he adopted the French libertarian class doctrine. Thus, Pareto says in the *Cours*:

> the class struggle assumes two forms at all times. One consists in economic competition which, when it is free, produces the greatest ophelimity [utility] ...[For] every class like every individual, even if it only acts to its own advantage, is indirectly useful to the others... The other form of class struggle is the one whereby every class does its utmost to seize power and make it an instrument to despoil the other classes.[29]

Laissez-faire liberalism had been a genuine mass movement in much of the nineteenth century: certainly in the United States and Great Britain, and partially in France, Italy, Germany, and throughout western Europe. Much of the time in the latter half of the century, the socialist idea was considered less of a threat to liberty, by classical liberals such as Pareto and Spencer, than the existing system of militarist and warlike statism dominated by privileged businessmen and landlords, the system to which Pareto would give the vivid and contemptuous name, 'pluto-democracy'. By the turn of the century, however, it was becoming clear to *laissez-faire* liberals that the masses had been captivated by socialism, and that socialism would pose an even greater threat to freedom and free markets than had the older, neomercantilist, pluto-democratic system.

Laissez-faire liberals throughout Europe had been gloriously optimistic during most of the nineteenth century. It was obvious that liberty provided the most rational, the most prosperous, system, the system most attuned to human nature, the system that works for the harmony and peace of all peoples and nations. Surely, the centuries-long shift from statism to freedom, from 'status to contract' and from the 'military to the industrial' that had brought about the Industrial Revolution and immense improvement for the human race, was destined to continue and expand, ever onward and upward. Surely, freedom and the world market were bound to expand forever, and the state gradually to wither away.

The comeback, first, of aggressive business statism in the 1870s, followed by expanding mass support for socialism in the 1890s, however, put a rude end to the ingrained optimism of *laissez-faire* liberals. The perceptive *laissez-faire* thinkers saw that the twentieth century would bring the shades of night, and put an end to the great civilization – the realm of progress and freedom – that had been the product of nineteenth century liberalism. Pessimism and despair began to grip the slowly vanishing breed of *laissez-faire* liberals, and understandably so. They foresaw the growth everywhere of statism, tyranny, collectivism, massive wars, and social and economic decline.

Each of the aging *laissez-faire* liberals reacted to this momentous and fateful new trend in his own way. Spencer continued to fight on to the end, placing greater emphasis on what he considered the main threat of socialism as against the business statism that he had previously combated. Pareto's path was to change radically into a stance of bitter cynicism. The world, he concluded as he saw the inexorable decline of libertarian ideas and movements, is governed not by reason but by irrationality, and it now became Pareto's role to analyse and chronicle those irrationalities. Thus, in an article in 1901, Pareto notes that everywhere in Europe, both socialism and national-ism–imperialism are on the increase, and that classical liberalism is being ground down between them: 'all over Europe the Liberal party is disappear-ing, as are the moderate parties...The extremists stand face to face: on one side socialism, the great rising religion of our age; on the other side, the old religions, nationalism and imperialism.'[30]

Faced with the failure of his hopes and with the looming statist hell of the twentieth century, Vilfredo Pareto, in the words of his perceptive biographer S.E. Finer, decided to 'retreat to Galapogos', a remote island that, in the argot of Pareto's day, served as a metaphor and a vantage point for a totally detached analysis and critique of the folly looming around him.[31] The final push for Pareto on the road to 'Galapogos' came in 1902, when the Italian Socialist Party abandoned its opposition to the protectionist policy of the 'bourgeois' statist government. The two long-standing enemies of *laissez-faire* liberalism had now joined forces! From that point on, Pareto's retreat to a detached and aristocratic Olympian bitterness was complete.[32]

The first book of Pareto's in which the new pessimistic stance becomes dominant is his *Les Systèmes Socialistes* (2 vols, 1901–2). But his newly detached stance did not at all mean that he had abandoned his libertarian ideals or his method of social analysis. Indeed, Finer writes of Pareto that Molinari was 'a man whom [he] admired till his dying day'.[33] Thus Pareto writes bitterly of how in society, robbery through government is far easier, and hence more attractive, than hard work for the acquisition of wealth. As Pareto mordantly wrote, in a passage that anticipated such twentieth century libertarian theorists as Franz Oppenheimer and Albert Jay Nock:

> Social movements usually follow the line of least resistance. While the direct production of economic goods is often very hard, taking possession of those goods produced by others is very easy. This facility has greatly increased *from the moment when deprivation became possible through the law and not contrary to it.* [Italics Pareto's.] To save, a man must have certain control over himself. Tilling a field to produce grain is hard work. Waiting in the corner of a wood to rob a passer-by is dangerous. On the other hand, going to vote is much easier and if it means that all those who are unadaptable, incapable and idle will be able to obtain board and lodging by it, they will hurry to do so.[34]

Pareto unfortunately championed a positivist methodology in keeping with his reliance on the model of physics and mechanics. But this was more than offset by his supplying us a deathless anecdote in a brilliant defence of natural economic law as against the 'anti-economists' of the German historical school. It is an anecdote that Ludwig von Mises liked to relate in his seminar:

> Once, during a speech which he was making at a statistical congress in Bern, Pareto spoke of 'natural economic laws,' whereupon [Gustav] Schmoller, who was present, said that there was no such thing. Pareto said nothing, but smiled and bowed. Afterward he asked Schmoller, through one of his neighbors, whether he was well acquainted with Bern. When Schmoller said yes, Pareto asked him again whether he knew of an inn where one could eat for nothing. The elegant Schmoller is supposed to have looked half pityingly and half disdainfully at the modestly dressed Pareto – although he was known to be well off – and to have answered that there were plenty of cheap restaurants, but that one had to pay something everywhere. At which Pareto said: 'So there *are* natural laws of political economy!'[35]

14.6   Academic convert in Germany: Karl Heinrich Rau

While John Prince Smith and his colleagues were battling valiantly for *laissez-faire* in the court of business and public opinion, the most prominent academic economist in Germany was becoming a highly influential convert to the cause. Karl Heinrich Rau (1792–1870) was the most important academic economist in Germany in the first half of the nineteenth century, and perhaps down to his death in 1870. Rau was born in Erlangen, a Protestant town in northern Bavaria, and his father was Lutheran pastor and professor of theology at the university there. Graduating from Erlangen in 1812, Rau taught at secondary school, and in 1818 became professor of political economy at the University of Giessen. Four years later, Rau became professor of political economy at the University of Heidelberg and held that post until his death nearly half a century later. In addition to being a widely liked and influential teacher, Rau played an active and influential role in the government of Baden, indeed helping to shape the outlook of Baden officialdom for 50 years.

In addition to being a long-time consultant to the Baden government, Rau became a court councillor upon accession to the chair at Heidelberg, and became a privy councillor at Baden in 1845. Several times, Rau served in the Baden Diet, and in 1848 was elected a member of the Frankfurt Parliament.

Trained in German cameralism, Rau, for the first two decades of his lengthy career, was a temporizing moderate in his views, attempting to balance the Smithian system of natural liberty with cameralism, deductive theory with a compendium of facts and statistics. A cautious moderate, Rau was leery of abolishing the guilds, and defended an organicist view of the state as against Adam Smith.

On the other hand, as time went on, Rau became increasingly *laissez-faire* liberal and less and less statist. The beginning of this gradual but accelerating conversion came in the early 1820s; in 1819–20, Rau translated the six-volume treatise of the moderate Smithian Heinrich Friedrich von Storch, a Baltic German teaching in Russia and writing in French. Rau's German translation of Storch's *Cours d'économie politique* was published in three volumes.

Particularly important, however, was Rau's multi-volume textbook on economics, the *Lehrbuch der politischen Oekonomie*. The first volume of the *Lehrbuch* was published in 1826, and the second in 1828. The *Lehrbuch* promptly became the standard economics text in Germany, going through eight editions in Rau's lifetime, with a ninth edition of Volume I published six years after Rau's death. Moreover, Rau's *Lehrbuch* was translated into no less than eight languages![36]

Rau's increasingly classical liberal views were reflected in the successive editions of the *Lehrbuch*. Still more were they reflected in the pages of the economic journal, the *Archiv der politischen Oekonomie und Polizeiwissenschaft*, which Rau founded in 1835.

The culmination of Karl Rau's conversion to *laissez-faire* came at the height of libertarian economic opinion in Europe, in the years around 1847. In his address to the university community at Heidelberg in November 1847, Rau denounced state intervention as the creation of ever-increasing special privileges to the aid of selfish interest groups; state intervention, then, can only benefit one person or group at the expense of another. Moreover, government intervention, instead of curing social problems, creates many new problems of its own. Rau warned, in his Heidelberg address, of the liberties endangered by government planning and controls, and particularly warned of the spread of socialist and communist 'fantasies'; in the absence of private property and private enterprise, only force could be used to induce people to work.[37]

14.7   The Scottish maverick: Henry Dunning Macleod

Henry Dunning Macleod (1821–1902) was an exuberant and prolific Scottish maverick who, in the teeth of the Millian monolith dominating Britain after 1848, never received his due from British economists or British academics.[38] Macleod was born in Edinburgh, the son of a Scottish landowner, and studied mathematics at Trinity College, Cambridge, graduating in 1843. He became an attorney and was admitted to the bar six years later. Two years afterward, Macleod wrote a report on the administration of poor-relief in several Scottish parishes, and went on to establish the first poor-law union in Scotland. In 1854, Macleod was made a director of the Royal British Bank, and this immediately sparked a lifelong fascination with economics, and specifically with matters of money and banking.

Macleod wrote prolifically on monetary matters, his *Theory and Practice of Banking* (1855) becoming influential and going through five editions. Macleod took a firm gold standard and free banking position, unfortunately adopting also the banking school apologia for inflationary, fractional-reserve banking. Macleod was the one who introduced the term 'Gresham's law' into economics, and also contributed an important analysis of the ways in which fractional-reserve bank credit operates, in particular how bank loans *create* deposits, which then function on the market as money substitutes in the same way as bank notes.

If Macleod had confined his economic work to money and banking, he might have earned considerable respect among British economists; although he differed from the mainstream in favouring free banking, his pro-gold standard and anti-bimetallist views, as well as his banking school orientation, were close enough to the reigning orthodoxy to bring him the acclaim he deserved.[39] But Macleod ran into a wall of opposition in Britain because he

stood squarely against the British Smith–Ricardo–Mill labour theory of value
and material concept of wealth. As a result, Macleod's dream of becoming a
professor never materialized.

Inspired by Archbishop Whately, Macleod went back to the late eighteenth
century and discovered the Abbé de Condillac, whom he exuberantly declared to have been the true founder of economics, in contrast to the labour
theory and materialist doctrine of Adam Smith. Enthusiastically adopting the
Whately concept of 'catallactics' as the genuine method of economics, Macleod
argued that Condillac, with his focus on economics as the science of exchanges, rather than 'wealth', was the founder of the catallactic approach.
Condillac, noted Macleod, like the Italian economists of the eighteenth century, 'places the origin and source of value in the human mind, and not in
labour, which is the ruin of English Economics'. Furthermore, Macleod
asserted, Condillac was correct that exchange value stems from value conferred upon goods by consumers, so that value and demand derive solely
from mental desires by consumers. Contrary to Smith and Ricardo who
believed that the labour of producers confers value on products, 'Value does
not spring from the labour of the producer, but from the desire of the consumer'.[40]

Since value stems from subjective valuation by consumers, it follows,
declared Macleod, that men engage in exchange precisely because each man
values what he gains more than what he gives up, else he would not have
embarked on the exchange. Hence, echoing scholastic and continental theorists from Jean Buridan onwards, both parties to any exchange must gain in
value. Macleod went on, in the proto-Austrian spirit, to declare that *anticipated* market prices determine costs that will be incurred in production rather
than the other way round:

> It is indisputably true that things are not valuable because they are produced at
> great expense, but people spend much money in producing because they expect
> that others will give a great price to obtain them... Buyers do not give high prices
> because sellers have spent much money in producing, but sellers spend much
> money in producing because they hope to find buyers who will give more.[41]

As if Henry D. Macleod did not give enough offence to mainstream nineteenth and twentieth century economics, he capped his crimes by hailing the
great libertarian and catallactician Frédéric Bastiat, whom he saluted as 'the
brightest genius who ever adorned the science of Economics'. Bastiat, Macleod
declared, 'plucked up by the roots the noxious fallacies which are the Economics of Adam Smith and Ricardo... He simply cleared away the stupendous chaos and confusion and mass of contradictions of Adam Smith...'[42]

In his revolutionary work of 1871 which brought marginalism and at least
a semi-Austrian position to England, W. Stanley Jevons issued a cry from the

heart against the 'noxious influence' of the stifling authority of John Stuart Mill over economics in England. Ever eager to find and rediscover neglected forerunners, Jevons hailed Bastiat and Macleod as well as Senior, Cairnes and others. Unfortunately, as is evidenced by his treatment at the hands of the *New Palgrave*, Macleod's reputation clearly needs to be resuscitated once again.[43]

14.8 Plutology: Hearn and Donisthorpe

Another forerunner and contemporary hailed by the revolutionary marginalist Stanley Jevons was the Irish–Australian economist, William Edward Hearn (1826–88). Born in County Cavan, Ireland, Hearn was one of the last students of the great Whatelyite economists at Trinity College, Dublin, entering in 1842 and graduating four years later. There he learned an economics very different from the dominant Millian school in Britain, an economics steeped in subjective utility theory and a catallactic focus upon exchange. Made the first professor of Greek at the new Queen's College, Galway in Ireland at the age of 23, Hearn received an appointment five years later, in 1854, as professor of modern history, logic and political economy as well as temporary professor of classics at the new University of Melbourne, Australia. In a country otherwise devoid of economists, Hearn had little incentive to pursue economic studies; he became dean of the law faculty and chancellor of the university. Most of his scholarship was devoted to such diverse subjects as the condition of Ireland, the government of England, the theory of legal rights and duties, and a study of the Aryan household, on all of which he published books issued in London as well as Melbourne. Hearn also served as a member of the legislative council of the state of Victoria and as leader of the Victoria House.

Hearn wrote only one book in economics from his eyrie in Australia, but it proved highly influential in England. *Plutology, or the Theory of the Efforts to Satisfy Human Wants*, was published in Melbourne in 1863 and reprinted in London the following year.[44] 'Plutology' was a term that Hearn adopted from the French *laissez-faire* economist J.G. Courcelle-Seneuil (1813–92), in his *Traité théorique et pratique d'économie politique* (1858) to mean a pure science of economics, a scientific analysis of human action. There are, indeed, hints in Hearn that he sought a broad science of human action going beyond even the limits of catallactics, or exchange.[45]

Hearn's *Plutology* was patterned after Bastiat. Like Bastiat, Hearn provided a *Harmonielehre*, demonstrating the 'unfailing rule' that the pursuit of self-interest produces a flow of services on the market in the 'order of their social importance'. Like Bastiat, Hearn began with a chapter on human wants, the satisfaction of which is central to the economic system. Human wants, Hearn pointed out, are hierarchically ordered, with the most intense wants satisfied first, and with the value of each want diminishing as the supply of goods to fulfil that want increases. In short, Hearn came very close to a full-fledged theory of diminishing marginal utility. Since each party to every exchange gains from the transaction, this means that each person gains more than he gives up – so that there is an inequality of value, and a mutual gain, in every exchange.

The value of every good, showed Hearn, is determined by the interaction of its utility with its degree of scarcity. Demand and supply thereby interact to determine price, and competition will tend to bring prices down to the minimum cost of production of each product. Thus Providence, through competition, brings about a beneficent social order, a natural harmony, through the free market economy.

In all these doctrines, Hearn anticipated the imminent advent of the Austrian School of economics, as well as echoing and building upon the best utility/scarcity/harmony–mutual benefit analyses of continental economics. Also anticipating the Austrian School, and building upon Turgot and various nineteenth century French and British writers including John Rae, was Hearn's analysis of entrepreneurship. The entrepreneur contracts with labour and 'capital' (i.e. lenders) at a fixed price, attains full title to the eventual output, and then bears the profit or loss incurred by eventual sale to the particular entrepreneur at the next stage of production.

Hearn also showed that capital accumulation increases the amount of capital relative to the supply of labour, and therefore raises the productivity of labour, as well as standards of living in the economy. He saw that capital could accumulate, and therefore living standards could increase in the economy, without limit. In addition, Hearn generalized the law of diminishing returns, expanding it from land to all factors of production, being careful to assume a given technology and supplies of natural resources.

A champion of free trade, William Hearn called for the removal of Catholic disabilities in Britain, the freeing of the Irish wool trade, the abolition of usury laws and entail, and the removal of all restrictions on transactions in land. Opposing government intervention, Hearn declared that government's only function is to preserve order and enforce contracts, and to leave all other matters to individual interest.

Hearn's *Plutology* was used as an economics text in Australia for six decades until 1924 – indeed it was virtually the only work on economics published in Australia until the 1920s. While the book went unnoticed upon its publication in London in 1864, it soon drew high praise from several economists, especially Jevons, who hailed it as the best and most advanced work on economics to date. Jevons featured *Plutology* prominently in his path-breaking *Theory of Political Economy* (1871). Apart from these citations, however, Hearn's work gave rise to only one plutological disciple. The attorney and mine-owner Wordsworth Donisthorpe (1847–?) published his *Principles of Plutology* (London: Williams & Norgate, 1876), which apparently was mentioned by no economic work from that day until the publication of the *New Palgrave* in 1987, either in the literature of the time or in any of the histories or surveys of economic thought. While scarcely an earth-shattering work, Donisthorpe's 206-page book certainly did not deserve to sink without trace.[46]

Most of *Principles of Plutology* was devoted to ground-clearing methodology, discussion of definitions, and attacks on plutology's great methodological rival, 'political economy'. But yet there was much valuable substantive discussion in Donisthorpe, a lucid writer who admirably wanted to forge a scientific economics that would clearly distinguish between analysis and ethical or political advocacy. Defining plutology as the purely scientific investigation of the uniformity or relations between values, Donisthorpe went on to point out that values are all relative; and that these values, including the value of money, vary continually and unpredictably, in contrast to units such as weights which remain fixed and unvarying. There are different intensities of wants, and different degrees of utility, and the interaction of these utilities and relative scarcities determine values.

In a proto-Austrian manner, Donisthorpe also distinguished between directly useful and indirectly useful goods, and showed how the latter had varying degrees of remoteness from the pleasure-giving stage of goods; in short, Donisthorpe engaged in a sophisticated analysis of the time-structure of production. He also had a pioneering analysis of the influence of substitutes and complements ('co-elements') upon values. While Donisthorpe's discussion of demand curves (i.e. schedules), supply, and price was interesting but hopelessly confused (e.g. he denied that an increased desire of consumers for a product would raise their demand for the product), he did present a remarkably clear foreshadowing of Philip Wicksteed's insight of four decades later that withholding the stock of a product by suppliers really amounts to the suppliers' 'reservation demand' for that product. Thus Donisthorpe:

> In the first place sellers and buyers are not two classes, but one class... To refuse a certain price for an article is to give that price for it. A proprietor who refuses to sell a horse for fifty guineas virtually gives fifty guineas for the horse in the hope of getting more for him another day, or else because he obtains more gratification from the horse than from fifty guineas. Proprietors who do not sell must be regarded as virtually buyers of their own goods.[47]

Perhaps from disappointment at the reception of his book, Wordsworth Donisthorpe, like Hearn before him, abandoned economic theory and plutology from then on, and spent the next two decades battling on behalf of libertarianism and individualism in law and political philosophy.[48]

14.9   Bastiat and *laissez-faire* in America

Frédéric Bastiat's writings found a receptive climate in *laissez-faire*-oriented United States. This was particularly true of the distinguished political and social scientist Francis Lieber (1800–72), a young Prussian scholar who had fled a central Europe inhospitable to German nationalism. In 1835, Lieber succeeded the Jeffersonian Thomas Cooper as professor of political economy and history at the University of South Carolina. Lieber's two-volume *Manual of Political Ethics* (1838–39) was a comprehensive defence of the absolute rights of private property, as well as its corollary, the right of free exchange of that property. 'Man yearns', said Lieber, 'to see his individuality represented and reflected in the acts of his exertions – in property'. Property, noted Lieber, existed before society and the state, and the state's function is to defend property rights, the unrestricted right of exchange, accumulations, and bequest, from attack. The role of the independent judiciary, an institution created in the United States, was to be guardian over private property, and to do so by applying the common law, 'a body of rules of action grown up spontaneously and independently of direct legislative or executive action'.

In 1856, Lieber acquired the chair of history and political science (formerly chair of political economy and history), at Columbia University in New York City. In his inaugural address at Columbia, Lieber delivered a paean to free exchange, which is fundamental to civilized life.

Lieber happily taught political economy from the text of Say's *Treatise*, and argued that economics teaches the idea of 'the natural, simple and uninterrupted state of things in which man is allowed to apply his means as best he thinks'. So devoted was Lieber to freedom of trade that he believed that the time would soon come when nations would include free trade in their bills of rights. Indeed, Lieber wrote the introduction to the first English translation of Bastiat's *Sophisms of Political Economy* in 1848. That translation had been made by Lieber's friend, Louisa Cheves McCord (1810–79), daughter of the former head of the Bank of the United States Langdon Cheves, and wife of Colonel David McCord, a protégé of Thomas Cooper and a South Carolina banker, planter, attorney and newspaper publisher. A devoted admirer of Bastiat, Mrs McCord also wrote journal articles denouncing socialism and communism.

But the two outstanding followers of Frédéric Bastiat in the United States were Francis Amasa Walker (1799–1875)[49] and his close friend and younger New Englander, the Rev. Arthur Latham Perry (1830–1905). Amasa Walker was the son of a blacksmith, who soon rose to become a successful shoe manufacturer in Boston as well as a railroad promoter. His earliest economic interest was in money and banking, where he became an ardent Jacksonian. Even though a bank director, Walker endorsed the currency principle, and fervently advocated 100 per cent gold money, with bank notes banned from going beyond the specie in the vaults of the banks. In addition, most notes, especially small denominations, were to be gradually eliminated. Bank credit, Walker pointed out, creates inflation and boom–bust cycles, as the banks face an outflow of gold abroad and are forced to contract their credit and bank notes. Walker also realized that gold discoveries need not create crises and panic, since the gold could make possible a more rapid achievement of 100 per cent specie money.

Amasa Walker retired from industrial activity in 1840, at the age of 41, and from then on devoted himself to economics and to political activity. He lectured on economics at Oberlin and Amherst, and from 1853 to 1860 was an examiner in political economy at Harvard. Walker wrote a number of essays for the New York financial organ, *Merchants' Magazine*, and in 1857 published a book on money and banking, *The Nature and Uses of Money*. He also served in the Massachusetts legislature and as secretary of the state of Massachusetts.

Walker, by then a lecturer at Amherst College, published, at the end of the Civil War, a scintillating general treatise on economics, *The Science of Wealth: A Manual of Political Economy* (Boston: Little, Brown, 1866), which incorporated his monetary views into a general treatise on *laissez-faire*. The book was immensely popular, at home and abroad, going into eight editions in the next eight years.

Walker's money and banking views were the centrepiece of his book. He took the rare position of advocating a system of free banking *within* a firm matrix of legally required 100 per cent reserve.[50] Walker wrote:

> Much has been said...of the desirableness of *free banking*. Of the propriety and rightfulness of allowing any person who chooses to carry on banking, as freely as farming or any other branch of business, there can be no doubt. But it is not, and can never be, expedient or right to authorize by law the universal manufacture of currency...[When] only notes equivalent to certificates of so much coin are issued, banking may be as free as brokerage. The only thing to be secured would be that no issues should be made except upon specie in hand.[51]

In his general economics, Walker emphasized catallactic analysis, and employed the concepts of wealth and value squarely in the Bastiat tradition. In fact, Walker heaped a great deal of praise on Bastiat's theory of value, and proceeded to include several pages of quotes and examples from Bastiat's *Harmonies*. In addition, Walker continued in the French tradition of stressing the entrepreneur as a force in production very different from that of the pure capitalist.[52]

But unquestionably the outstanding disciple of Bastiat in the United States was Arthur Latham Perry. Perry, a graduate of Williams College in 1852, almost immediately accepted the position in which he would spend the bulk of his life teaching history, political economy, and German at his *alma mater*. Perry had ben introduced to Bastiat's works by his friend Amasa Walker, and he reported that 'I had scarcely read a dozen pages in that remarkable book [Bastiat's *Harmonies of Political Economy*] when the Field of the Science, in all its outlines and landmarks, lay before my mind just as it does today [1883]...from that time Political Economy has been to me a new science; and that I experience then and thereafter *a sense of having found something...*'[53]

In the Spring of 1864, Perry wrote a series of articles on 'Papers on Political Economy' for the *Springfield Republican*, which set forth Perry's Bastiat-derived viewpoint on political economy. The proper focus of economic theory, he declared, was value, and value is determined by the mutual services exchanged in any transaction. The crucial axiom and focus of economic analysis, added Perry, is that men exert effort in order to satisfy desires, and trade is a mutual exchange of services to bring about those satisfactions. Both parties gain from every exchange, else they would not engage in the transaction. Workers, Perry pointed out, could only gain if more capital is employed in hiring them, which would increase wage rates per worker.

Encouraged by Walker, Perry expanded his articles into a textbook, published the following year. *Elements of Political Economy*, later called *Political Economy*, became by far the most successful economic textbook in the country, going through no less than 22 editions in 30 years. In his text, Perry not only paid tribute to Bastiat, but also hailed Macleod, and adopted the Macleod vision of the history of economic thought – saluting Condillac, Whately, Bastiat and Macleod as leaders of the correct services, catallactic, or what Perry called the 'All Sales' school.[54] Engaging in a detailed and sophisticated analysis of exchange and its preconditions in values and the division of labour, Perry went beyond Bastiat to purge economics totally of the vague and materialistic Smithian concept of 'wealth' and to focus instead completely on exchange.[55]

Although he did not use the term 'entrepreneur', Perry's concentration on value and exchange as a human *activity* led him to treat the businessman as an active forecasting entrepreneur rather than a robotic participant in a static general equilibrium. Thus: 'your man of business must be a man of brains. The field of production is no dead level of sluggish uniformity like the billowy and heavy sea'; instead, the occupation 'requires foresight, wise courage, and a power of adaptation to varying circumstances'.[56]

True to his focus on the great mutual benefits of exchange, Arthur Perry lauded free exchange and denounced all restrictions and limitations upon that process. Thus Perry points out that

> ...anybody can know that what is rendered in an exchange is thought less of on the whole than what is received. The slightest introspection tells any man *that*. As

this must always be true of each of the parties to any exchange,...each is glad to part with something for the sake of receiving something else... A very little introspection will inform any person, that were this higher estimate wanting in the mind of either of the two parties, the trade would not take place at all... Hence no law or encouragement is needed to induce any persons to trade; trade is natural, as any person can see who stops to ask himself why he has made a given trade; and on the other hand, any law or artificial obstacle that hinders two persons from trading who would otherwise trade, not only interferes with a sacred right, but destroys an inevitable gain that would otherwise accrue to two persons alike.[57]

Perry particularly attacked such virulent interferences in free exchange as minimum wages, labour unions, usury laws, and paper money. While Perry, even more than Walker, failed to realize fully that bank deposits were as much part of the money supply as notes, he went even beyond Walker's 100 per cent reserve proposal for paper money, to calling for the eradication of paper money completely, even if backed 100 per cent by specie. He believed, however, that bank credit and issue of deposits should be totally free within that matrix.

Perry was especially vehement in attacking protectionism, writing numerous articles and delivering hundreds of speeches on behalf of free trade and against protection. The protective tariff, Perry pointed out, was unsound economically; it violated property rights, and it violated the letter and spirit of the Ten Commandments. A protective tariff stole from the western farmer to establish privileges for a few manufacturers. Perry courageously withstood the pressure of powerful Williams alumni, headed by ironmonger George H. Ely, against his free trade teachings. After the assassination of his former student, lifelong friend, and fellow-member of the Cobden Club of Great Britain, President James A. Garfield, Perry took the highly unpopular step in New England of leaving the Republican Party as the 'party of privilege' and corruption, and joining the Democratic Party. Much admired by free trade statesmen, Perry was asked by President Cleveland to be his secretary of the Treasury.

Another *laissez-faire* stalwart, at least for the prime years of his life, was Perry's friend and colleague who taught rhetoric at Williams, the Rev. John Bascom (1827–1911). During the 1850s and 1860s, Walker, Perry and Bascom made a formidable team in New England. Perry persuaded Bascom to write a book on economics, and Bascom's *Political Economy* (1859) extolled the forces of production and competition in seeking profit and in thereby benefiting the commonwealth. Government's only role is to protect the rights of private property, so that production can do its work. Bascom also pointed out that 'monopoly' can only be meaningfully defined as an exclusive grant of privilege by the government; otherwise *all* property could be called 'monopoly'. Bascom also joined Walker in advocating 100 per cent specie reserves to bank notes.

Later, John Bascom became president of the University of Wisconsin, and succeeded Perry in the chair of history and political economy at Williams when the latter retired in the 1890s. Bascom must have become a severe trial to his old friend, however, because by the 1880s, Bascom had begun to abandon the cause and write books in the new statist discipline of 'sociology'. Bascom now shifted drastically to call for the government privileging of labour unions, and for the abolition of the 'excess' of individualism. Bascom had now come to believe that the only danger from socialism and collectivism was 'unreasonable resistance to [this] organic force which is pushing into our lives'. 'Growth' [i.e. collectivism], Bascom smugly concluded, 'must have its way'.[58] Clearly, John Bascom had rapidly made his peace with the new intellectual current that swept Europe and the United States in the 1880s and 1890s.

One of the most unusual – and most advanced – of the American admirers of Frédéric Bastiat was the Boston merchant Charles Holt Carroll (1799–1890). A staunch adherent of free trade and *laissez-faire*, Carroll, in articles in mercantile and financial magazines from 1855 until 1879, concentrated on questions of money and banking. In essence, Charles Carroll was the last Jacksonian, continuing to argue the ultra-hard money cause long past the tremendous setback it received during the Civil War, when greenbackism and the national banking act necessarily led sound money men to concentrate on sheer return to the gold standard. Moreover, Carroll was not content to advocate 100 per cent banking; he perceptively and consistently urged 100 per cent banking for demand deposits as well as notes. Carroll, indeed, was particularly clear in demonstrating that bank demand deposits mainly arise from the extension of loans by the banks. He also pointed out the fallacy of the Smithian 'real bills' justification for fractional-reserve banking. Furthermore, Carroll realized that central banking, epitomized by the Bank of England, allows far more room for the expansion of fractional reserve and 'fictitious' money than would a system of free banking. But in addition, Carroll went beyond most hard-money advocates by calling for the elimination of such potentially dangerous currency *names* as 'the dollar' (which give the illusion that these units are goods-in-themselves), and their replacement as the currency unit by regular, ordinary-language definitions of weight in gold, e.g. in numbers of troy ounces. For international currencies, that is, for currencies not redeemable in a common metal, Carroll worked out the essence of the purchasing-power-parity theory for the underlying determination of exchange rates on the world market.[59]

14.10   Decline of *laissez-faire* thought

By the latter decades of the nineteenth century, *laissez-faire*, in economic thought and in social and political influence, was in decline throughout

Europe and the United States. Pareto was scarcely the only *laissez-faire* thinker in despair. Spearheaded by the welfare–warfare state developed in Prussia, academics and politicians alike scorned the 'old fashioned' tenets of *laissez-faire* and embraced the seemingly modern and 'progressive' advance of statism, state planning and welfare state measures. American academics, trained in Germany, the home of the Ph.D., came back from Europe singing the praises of the 'organic' Big State, scorned the idea of economic law and the market economy, and advocated class 'harmony' through Big Government. It is scarcely a coincidence that this new modern Big Government was desperately in need of academics, scientists, journalists and other opinion-moulding intellectuals, first, to engineer the consent of the public to the new dispensation of statism, and second, to participate in staffing, regulating, and legislating for the new planned economy. In short, the new dispensation meant a huge increase in monetary demand (by the state) for the services of pro-statist intellectuals, an important fact which did not go unnoticed among the ranks of the new progressive intelligentsia.

Throughout Europe, small associations of academics and businessmen dedicated to *laissez-faire* were replaced by larger organizations of mainly academics dedicated to professionalism and the promotion of their academic–economic gild. Not coincidentally, the new organizations were often explicitly statist and devoted to eradicating *laissez-faire*. Richard T. Ely, German-educated academic empire-builder devoted to institutionalism, statism, and Christian socialism, was the main founder of the American Economic Association, specifically excluding *laissez-faire* economists such as William Graham Sumner and Perry who had formed a political economy club; after this exclusionist policy was later rejected by Ely's colleagues as too extreme, Ely resigned from the AEA in a huff, and was only reconciled in later years.

Whereas *laissez-faire* thought was in decline, the tyranny of the British classical model, re-established by Mill in 1848, was ripe for collapse. The precedents for replacement of the classical model had already been worked out by past economists: by the scholastics, Cantillon, Turgot, and Say and the nineteenth century French; by Whately, the Trinity College, Dublin school, and Longfield and Senior, in Britain and Ireland. The next great advance in economic thought was the overthrow of the classical Ricardian paradigm, and the arrival of the subjectivist revolution (generally mis-labelled the marginalist revolution) beginning in the 1870s. The famous marginalist triad of Jevons, Walras and Menger and the Austrian School has been fortunately dehomogenized in recent years, inspired by the classic article of William Jaffé two decades ago,[60] and it is now clear that the revolution against the classical school paradigm went far beyond emphasis on the marginal unit of a good or service, especially in the hands of Carl Menger and his followers. But that is the stuff of another volume.

14.11   Notes

1. About's *Handbook* went into many editions. See the English translation, *Handbook of Social Economy, or the Worker's ABC* (London: Strahan & Co., 1872).
2. A century later, Bastiat's broken window fallacy served as the inspiration and centrepiece of Henry Hazlitt's excellent and best-selling economic primer, *Economics in One Lesson* (New York: Harper & Bros, 1946).
3. Dean Russell, *Frédéric Bastiat: Ideas and Influence* (Irvington-on-Hudson: Foundation for Economic Education, 1965), p. 20.
4. See Joseph T. Salerno, 'The Neglect of the French Liberal School in Anglo-American Economics: A Critique of Received Explanations', *The Review of Austrian Economics*, 2 (1988), p. 127.
5. See the sensitive appreciation of this aspect of Bastiat's contribution in Israel M. Kirzner, *The Economic Point of View* (Princeton, NJ: D. Van Nostrand, 1960), pp. 82–4.
6. On the trials and tribulations which the *laissez-faire* liberals had with the Revolution of 1848, which generally had an unfavourable effect on the *laissez-faire* movement, see David M. Hart, 'Gustave de Molinari and the Anti-Statist Liberal Tradition, Part I', *The Journal of Libertarian Studies*, V (Summer 1981), pp. 273–6.
7. For Cobden's encomiums to Bastiat, see Russell, op. cit., note 3, pp. 73–4.
8. Ibid., p. 90.
9. Thus Piero Barucci writes that Ferrara's value theory 'was meant to be a critical reply to Ricardo's labor theory of value, in which Ferrara did not see any element of subjectiveness. With his reproduction cost he intended to work out a theory of value which took into account both the element of cost and that of utility of goods. The value of a good would be, in this way, the comparison between the utility attributed by a subject to the good itself and the cost he thinks he would have to incur to reproduce the good. Indeed, this theory emphasized the fact of the utility of goods'. Piero Barucci, 'The Spread of Marginalism in Italy, 1871–1890', in R.D.C. Black, A.W. Coats, and C.D.W. Goodwin (eds), *The Marginal Revolution in Economics: Interpretation and Evaluation* (Durham, NC: Duke University Press, 1973), p. 260. Also see the important article by Salerno, op. cit., note 4, p. 121. And see ibid, p. 144n. 10, and F. Caffè, 'Ferrara, Francesco', *The New Palgrave: Dictionary of Economics* (London: Macmillan, 1987), II p. 302.
10. J.A. Schumpeter, *History of Economic Analysis* (New York: Oxford University Press, 1954), p. 1081.
11. See Barucci, op. cit., note 9, p. 264. Achille Loria, the leading Italian socialist and historicist of this period, noted that Ferrara and his school lauded Bastiat, considered Ricardo and Stuart Mill as dangerous and sophistical theorists and abhorred the German economists as 'advocates of interventionism and socialism'. Although a fervent opponent of everything Ferrara stood for, Loria was perceptive – and gracious – enough to refer to Ferrara as 'the greatest Italian economist of the nineteenth century' and 'without doubt the greatest genius of which the economic science of our country boasts'. Salerno, op. cit., note 4, p. 144n8. Also see ibid., pp. 121–2.
12. In Norway, we know that a popular treatise on economics was inspired by Bastiat. (H. Lehmann, *Velstandslaere*, 1874.) On the Swedish Economic Society, see Eli F. Heckscher, 'A Summary of Economic Thought in Sweden, 1875–1950', *The Scandinavian Economic History Review*, 1 (1953), pp. 105–25.
13. Russell, op. cit., note 3, p. 91.
14. It is perhaps significant that Prince Smith's father, John Prince Smith, Senior, wrote tracts in favour of natural law and free trade, for example, *Elements of the Science of Money* (1813). See Donald G. Rohr, *The Origins of Social Liberalism in Germany* (Chicago: University of Chicago Press, 1963), pp. 85ff.
15. 'Prince Smith used the term "free trade" in a wide sense, as in his assertion…that "to the state free trade assigns no other task than just this: *the production of security*".' Ralph Raico, 'John Prince Smith and the German Free Trade Movement', in W. Block and L. Rockwell (eds.), *Man, Economy, and Liberty: Essays in Honor of Murray N. Rothbard* (Auburn, Ala.: The Ludwig von Mises Institute, 1988), p. 349n.8.

16. See W.O. Henderson, 'Prince Smith and Free Trade in Germany', *Economic History Review*, 2nd ser., 2 (1950), p. 297, rprt. in W.O. Henderson, *Britain and Industrial Europe, 1750–1870* (Liverpool, 1954).
17. Raico, op. cit., note 15, p. 346. On the near-individualist anarchism of Julius Faucher, see Andrew R. Carlson, *Anarchism in Germany, Vol. 1: The Early Movement* (Metuchen, NJ: The Scarecrow Press, 1972), pp. 65–6.
18. Gustave de Molinari, 'De la production de la securité', *Journal des Économistes*, XXV (Feb. 1849), pp. 277–90. Translated as Gustave de Molinari, *The Production of Security* (trans. J. McCulloch, New York: Center for Libertarian Studies, May 1977).
19. See the complete translation of the eleventh *soirée* in 'Appendix', David M. Hart, 'Gustave de Molinari and the Anti-statist Liberal Tradition, Part III', *The Journal of Libertarian Studies*, VI (Winter 1982), pp. 88–102.
20. See Murray N. Rothbard, *For a New Liberty: the Libertarian Manifesto* (1973, rev. ed., New York: Libertarian Review Foundation, 1985). For an appreciative discussion of Molinari and of the concept of total privatization of protection from crime, see Bruce L. Benson, 'Guns for Protection and Other Private Sector Responses to the Fear of Rising Crime', in D. Kates (ed.), *Firearms and Violence: Issues of Public Policy* (San Francisco: Pacific Institute for Public Policy Research, 1984), pp. 346–56. Also see Benson, *The Enterprise of Law* (San Francisco: Pacific Institute, 1990).
21. For the discussion around Molinari's thesis, see the *Journal des Économistes*, XXIV (15 October 1849), pp. 315–6. For more on a summary of the discussion, see Murray N. Rothbard, 'Preface', Molinari, op. cit., note 18, pp. i–iii.
22. Molinari lived in Belgium during the decade of the 1850s. He returned to Belgium upon the *coup d'état* of Louis Napoleon in December 1851, which precipitated Bonaparte's despotism in France. With the aid of his friend Charles de Brouckère, Molinari was appointed professor of political economy at the Belgian Royal Museum of Industry in Brussels, and at the Higher Institute of Commerce in Antwerp. His lectures at the museum formed the basis of Molinari's major theoretical work, his *Cours d'Économie Politique* (2 vols, Paris, 1863). Molinari continued to write articles and reviews for the *Journal des Économistes* during his Belgian years, also founding the *Économiste belge* in 1855, an even more frankly radical journal which he continued to edit for another 13 years. Molinari returned to Paris in 1860, becoming editor-in-chief of the *laissez-faire* journal, the *Journal des Débats*, from 1871 to 1876.
23. This book was unfortunately the only one of Molinari's works to be translated into English, as *The Society of Tomorrow* (New York: G.P. Putnam's Sons, 1904). On Molinari's retreat in his later years, and for an elaboration of his views in general, see David M. Hart, 'Gustave de Molinari and the Antistatist Liberal Tradition, Part II', *The Journal of Libertarian Studies*, V (Autumn 1981), pp. 399–434.
24. Molinari, op. cit., note 18, pp. 1–2.
25. Frédéric Passy, 'Prefatory Letter', in Molinari, op. cit., note 23, pp. xxviii–xxix. A prolific author on economics himself, Passy was at one point president of the Société d'Économie Politique, as well as a member of the French Chamber of Deputies, 1881–88. Passy was a co-founder of the International Peace League in 1867, and, for his work on behalf of peace and international arbitration, was awarded the Nobel Peace Prize in 1901.
26. Pareto's role in the development of mathematical neoclassical general equilibrium theory will be treated in a later volume; the present section deals with his political economy. See however, on the Pareto–Croce debate on positivism *vs* praxeology as the proper economic method, Murray N. Rothbard, *Individualism and the Philosophy of the Social Sciences* (San Francisco: Cato Institute, 1979), pp. 54–6.
27. In P. Bucolo (ed.), *The Other Pareto* (London: Scolar Press, 1980), p. 44.
28. From Molinari's *Précis d'économie politique et de la moral* (1893), in Bucolo, op. cit., note 27, p. 68.
29. Quoted in ibid., p. 144.
30. Ibid., p. 141.
31. See the illuminating article by S.E. Finer, 'Pareto and Pluto-Democracy: the Retreat to Galapogos', *American Political Science Review*, 62 (1968), pp. 440–50. Even more im-

portant is Finer's introduction to Vilfredo Pareto, *Sociological Writings* (ed. S.E. Finer, London: Pall Mall Press, 1966).

32. See Bucolo, op. cit., note 27, p. 166.
33. Finer, in Pareto, op. cit., note 31, p. 18.
34. Bucolo, op. cit., note 27, pp. 149–50.
35. Theo Suranyi-Unger, *Economics in the Twentieth Century* (New York: W.W. Norton, 1931), p. 128. My own translation from Pareto's quoted sentence.
36. More specifically, eight editions appeared of Volume I, on theory, in Rau's lifetime, as well as five editions of Volume II, on economic policy, and five editions of Volume III, on public finance, beginning in 1832. A sixth posthumous edition of Volume III was revised by Rau's ex-student, also from Erlangen, Professor Adolph Wagner. Wagner also rewrote and published the ninth edition of Volume I in 1876. See Keith Tribe, *Governing Economy: The Reformation of German Economic Discourse 1750–1840* (Cambridge: Cambridge University Press, 1988), p. 183 and 183n.
37. See Donald G. Rohr, *The Origins of Social Liberalism in Germany* (Chicago: University of Chicago Press, 1963), pp. 78–84. Also see H.C. Recktenwald, 'Rau, Karl Heinrich', *The New Palgrave*, op. cit., note 9, IV, p. 96.
38. This is true of his current treatment by British academics as well, as witness the sustained sneer that permeates the article by Murray Milgate and Alastair Levy, "Henry Dunning Macleod," *The New Palgrave*, op. cit., note 9, III, pp. 268–9.
39. For an appreciative discussion of Macleod by a modern pro-gold standard, banking school French theorist, see Charles Rist, *History of Monetary and Credit Theory* (1940, New York; A.M. Kelley, 1966), pp. 73, 102, 203, 205, 261.
40. Salerno, op. cit., note 9, pp. 130–1. Also see, Murray N. Rothbard, 'Catallactics', *New Palgrave*, op. cit., note 9, II, p. 377.
41. Salerno, op. cit., note 9, p. 131. See Henry Dunning Macleod, *The Elements of Political Economy* (London: Longman, Brown, 1857), pp. 98–100, 111, 127. Also see Macleod, *The History of Economics* (New York: G.P. Putnam's, 1896); and idem., *A Dictionary of Political Economy*, Vol. I (London, 1863).
42. Salerno, op. cit., note 9, p. 132.
43. W. Stanley Jevons, *The Theory of Political Economy* (Baltimore: Penguin Books, 1970), pp. 57, 261. Also see Israel M. Kirzner, *The Economic Point of View* (New York: D. Van Nostrand, 1960), pp. 73, 202–3.
44. J.A. LaNauze writes of the Hearn work that 'It was an innovation in English political economy to begin a treatise with a chapter on human wants, and to make the satisfaction of wants a central theme... But his is an innovation only in English writing. The prominence which Hearn gives to wants is simply a reflection of his reading from French literature. His chapter is in places almost a transcription from Bastiat's *Harmonies*, and his sub-title echoes Bastiat's frequently repeated phrase, "Wants, Efforts, Satisfactions!"' J.A. LaNauze, *Political Economy in Australia* (Carlton, Australia: Melbourne University Press, 1949), pp. 56–8. See also the discussion of Hearn in Salerno, op. cit., note 9, pp. 125–9.
45. Kirzner, op. cit., note 43, pp. 202n7, 212n2.
46. Williams & Norgate was an important publisher of the day, the publisher of Herbert Spencer's works and of the philosophic journal *Mind*. This is not surprising in view of the libertarian individualist philosophy common to both Donisthorpe and Spencer.
47. Wordsworth Donisthorpe, *Principles of Plutology* (London: Williams & Norgate, 1876), p. 132. Also see Peter Newman, 'Donisthorpe, Wordsworth', *New Palgrave*, op. cit., note 9, I, pp. 916–7.
48. On Donisthorpe as libertarian, see W.H. Greenleaf, *The British Political Tradition,* Vol. II, *The Ideological Heritage* (London: Methuen, 1983), pp. 277–80.
49. Not to be confused with his son and namesake, a moderate statist who was to become first president of the American Economic Association. (Francis Amasa Walker, 1840–97.)
50. Walker, squarely in the American tradition, insisted, as against the British currency school, that bank deposits were fully as much part of the money supply as bank notes. And yet, oddly and inconsistently, he failed to include deposits in his 100 per cent reform proposal,

asserting unconvincingly that restriction of notes to their equivalent in specie would exert a sufficient check on the creation of deposits.

51. Amasa Walker, *The Science of Wealth* (3rd ed., Boston: Little, Brown, 1867), p. 230–31.
52. Ibid., pp. 9–13; also see Salerno, op. cit., note 9, pp. 133–5.
53. Arthur Latham Perry, *Political Economy* (1883, 21st ed., New York: Scribner, 1892), p. ix.
54. Despite his devotion to Walker for leading him to Bastiat, and despite his being one of those *laissez-faire* economists to whom Perry dedicated his book, Perry privately reproved Walker for 'being too much in bondage to Adam Smith'. See Sidney Fine, *Laissez-faire and the General Welfare State* (Ann Arbor: University of Michigan Press, 1956), p. 52n16.
55. For an appreciation of Perry's contribution, see Kirzner, op. cit., note 43, pp. 75–7.
56. Joseph Dorfman, *The Economic Mind in American Civilization* (New York: Viking Press, 1949), III, p. 57.
57. Perry, op. cit., note 53, pp. 102–3.
58. Dorfman, op. cit., note 56, III, pp. 178–9.
59. For the collected writings of Charles H. Carroll, see Charles Holt Carroll, *Organization of Debt into Currency* (E. Simmons, ed., Princeton: Van Nostrand, 1964).
60. William Jaffé, 'Menger, Jevons and Walras De-Homogenized', *Economic Inquiry*, 14 (Dec. 1976), pp. 511–24.

Bibliographical essay

As we noted in Volume I, it is impossible for a bibliographical essay in a comprehensive history of economic thought to list, much less to annotate, every source for the history, much less for the important ancillary fields of history of social, political and religious thought, all of which, in addition to economic history proper, impinge on the development and conflicts in economic thought. The best I can do, then, is to describe and annotate those sources, largely secondary ones, which I found most helpful in working on this study. I hope, then, that this bibliographical appendix may serve as a guide to readers who wish to delve into various topics and areas in this vast and complex field.

Overall bibliographies
By far the most comprehensive bibliographical essay in the history of economic thought is the remarkably full treatment in Henry W. Spiegel, *The Growth of Economic Thought* (3rd ed., Duke University Press, 1991), which now stretches to no less than 161 pages, and is by far the most valuable feature of the book. The four-volume *New Palgrave: A Dictionary of Economics* (London: Macmillan, and New York: Stockton Press, 1987), contains a number of excellent essays on particular economists. At the other end of the spectrum, the brief sketches in the unpretentious paperback by Ludwig H. Mai, *Men and Ideas in Economics: A Dictionary of World Economists, Past and Present* (Lanham, MD: Rowman and Littlefield, 1977) are surprisingly useful. Fewer but far more in-depth entries are discussed in Mark Blaug, *Great Economists Before Keynes* (Cambridge: Cambridge University Press, 1986).

J.B. Say
It is truly a scandal that there is not a single biography of the great J.B. Say in English (and only one in French, an old work by Ernest Teilhac). In fact, there is precious little analysis of any aspect of Say's thought except for a mountain of work devoted to the small part of it known as 'Say's law' – and too much of *that* deals with mathematical equations that Say would have properly scorned in any case. Say's *magnum opus* is translated into English as *A Treatise on Political Economy* (ed. Clement C. Biddle, 6th Amer. ed., 1834, New York: A. M. Kelley, 1964), based on the final fifth French edition of 1826. Biddle's excellent notes occasionally correct lapses from *laissez-faire* by the author. Also see J.B. Say, *Letters to Mr. Malthus* (1821, New York: A.M. Kelley, 1967). It is also unfortunate that in the mighty and definitive multi-volume Sraffa edition of Ricardo's works and letters, Say's letters to Ricardo are printed in the original French and not translated into English. Considering the enormous resources that were poured into the Ricardo project, it is difficult to see why these letters were not translated.

On the ideologues and their philosophical and scientific background, see the notable discussion in F.A. von Hayek, *The Counter-Revolution of Science* (Glencoe, Ill.: The Free Press, 1952), pp. 105–16. De Tracy is covered fully in Emmet Kennedy, *Destutt De Tracy and the Origins of 'Ideology'* (Philadelphia: American Philosophical Society, 1978). On Say and the ideologues, see Leonard P. Liggio, 'Charles Dunoyer and French Classical Liberalism', *The Journal of Libertarian Studies*, 1 (Summer 1977), pp. 153–65; and Mark Weinburg, 'The Social Analysis of Three Early 19th Century French Liberals: Say, Comte, and Dunoyer', *The Journal of Libertarian Studies*, 2 (Winter 1978), pp. 45–63. Also see Charles Hunter Van Duzer, *Contribution of the Ideologues to French Revolutionary Thought* (Baltimore: The Johns Hopkins University Press, 1935). Some connections between the Ideologues, and Storch, Brown, and Mill can be found in Cheryl B. Welch, *Liberty and Utility: The French Idéologues and the Transformation of Liberalism* (New York: Columbia University Press, 1984). Welch, however, overstresses the alleged utilitarianism of the French school. On the conflict between the ideologues and Napoleon, see Lewis A. Coser, 'Napoleon and the Idéologues', in George B. de Huszar (ed.), *The Intellectuals* (Glencoe, Ill.: The Free Press, 1960), pp. 80–86.

On Jefferson's monetary views and his plan to eliminate bank paper, see Murray N. Rothbard, *The Panic of 1819: Reactions and Policies* (New York: Columbia University Press, 1962), p. 140. Also see Clifton B. Luttrell, 'Thomas Jefferson on Money and Banking: Disciple of David Hume and Forerunner of Some Modern Monetary Views', *History of Political Economy*, 7 (Spring 1975), pp. 156–73.

On Say as a Smithian, see J. Hollander, 'The Founder of a School', in J.M. Clark et al., *Adam Smith, 1776–1926* (Chicago: University of Chicago Press, 1928) and on the influence of Say's *Treatise* in Europe, see Palyi, 'The Introduction of Adam Smith', in *ibid.*, pp. 180–233. On the influence of the *Treatise* in the United States, see Michael J.L. O'Connor, *Origins of Academic Economics in the United States* (New York: Columbia University Press, 1944), pp. 120–35.

A discussion of Say's critique of statistics is to be found in Claude Ménard, 'Three Forms of Resistance to Statistics: Say, Cournot, Walras', *History of Political Economy*, 12 (Winter, 1980), pp. 524–9. Ménard is incorrect, however, in believing that the last English translation of the *Traité* was the 1821 version based on the 4th French edition. For the currently available translation was based on the 5th French edition of 1826, and therefore includes Say's excellent Introduction presenting his critique of the statistical method.

A trenchant comparison and contrast between Say's and Ricardo's theories of value, and a critique of Say's rebuff of Condillac and Genovesi on the gains of exchange, is to be found in the excellent chapter, 'Ricardo versus

Say. Cost or Utility the Foundation of Value?', in Oswald St Clair, *A Key to Ricardo* (1957, New York: A. M. Kelley, 1965), pp. 260–96.

Say's theory of the entrepreneur is discussed, not totally satisfactorily, in J.A. Schumpeter's *History of Economic Analysis* (New York: Oxford University Press, 1954), and Robert F. Hébert and Albert N. Link, *The Entrepreneur: Mainstream Views and Radical Critiques* (New York: Praeger, 1982), pp. 29–35. For an excellent discussion of Say on the entrepreneur and a contrast with the treatments of Smith and Ricardo, see G. Koolman, 'Say's Conception of the Role of the Entrepreneur', *Economica*, 38 (August 1971), pp. 269–86. On Say's pre-Austrian view of the values of the factors of production being derived from their products instead of vice versa, see the passage in Marian Bowley, *Studies in the History of Economic Theory Before 1870* (London: Macmillan, 1973), p. 127.

The best place to read about Say's law of markets is in the bulk of his *Letters to Malthus* and in his *Treatise*. Most of the voluminous modern literature on Say's law has little to offer; but see Schumpeter, *History of Economic Analysis*, pp. 615–25; Henry Hazlitt, (ed.), *The Critics of Keynesian Economics* (1960, 2nd ed., New Rochelle, NY: Arlington House, 1977), pp. 11–45; and especially the grievously neglected William H. Hutt, *A Rehabilitation of Say's Law* (Athens, Ohio: Ohio University Press, 1974). Keynes's notorious attack on Say's law may be found in John Maynard Keynes, *The General Theory of Employment, Interest, and Money* (New York: Harcourt, Brace, 1936), p. 23.

On Say's unique attitude of implacable hostility toward taxation, see Murray N. Rothbard, 'The Myth of Neutral Taxation', *Cato Journal*, 1 (Autumn, 1981), pp. 551–4. On Say and his followers as libertarians, see Weinburg, 'Social Analysis', pp. 54–63. On Say's methodology, see Murray N. Rothbard, *Individualism and the Philosophy of the Social Sciences* (1973, San Francisco: Cato Institute, 1979), pp. 45–49.

Jeremy Bentham

On Bentham and the Benthamites, see the classic work by Élie Halevy, *The Growth of Philosophic Radicalism* (1928, Boston: Beacon Press, 1955). For an excellent critique of the utilitarians, see John Plamenatz, *The English Utilitarians* (2nd ed., Oxford: Basil Blackwell, 1958); Bentham is discussed in Chapter 4. For a discussion of Bentham, the Benthamite circle, and the radicals, see William E.S. Thomas, *The Philosophic Radicals: Nine Studies in Theory and Practice, 1817–1841* (Oxford: The Clarendon Press, 1979). On Bentham as a weak reed as a *laissez-fairist*, see Ellen Frankel Paul, *Moral Revolution and Economic Science* (Westport, Conn.: Greenwood Press, 1979), pp. 45–80. The classic article on Bentham as a statist economist is T.W. Hutchison, 'Bentham as an Economist', *Economic Journal*, 66 (June 1956), pp. 288–306, reprinted in J. Spengler and W.R. Allen, *Essays in Economic Thought* (Chicago: Rand McNally, 1960), pp 330–48. On Bentham as a pre-Skinnerite, see Douglas C. Long, *Bentham on Liberty* (Toronto: University of Toronto Press, 1977). Gertrude Himmelfarb's blistering critique of Bentham as panopticon planner is in her *Victorian Minds* (1968, Gloucester, Mass.: Peter Smith, 1975), and in her 'Bentham's Utopia', in Himmelfarb, *Marriage and Morals Among the Victorians* (New York: Knopf, 1986), pp. 111–43. For a critique of utilitarianism as a basis for *laissez-faire* , see Murray N. Rothbard, *The Ethics of Liberty* (Atlantic Highlands, NJ: Humanities Press, 1982), pp. 201ff. Also see Rothbard, 'Praxeology, Value Judgments, and Public Policy', in E. Dolan (ed.), *The Foundations of Modern Austrian Economics* (Kansas City: Sheed & Ward, 1976), pp. 89–111.

For Bentham's economic writings, see the definitive three-volume edition by Werner Stark, *Jeremy Bentham's Economic Writings* (London: George Allen & Unwin, 1952–54).

James Mill

A perceptive study of James Mill and his pervasive influence on Ricardo and Ricardian economics is T.W. Hutchison, 'James Mill and Ricardian Economics: A Methodological Revolution?', in *On Revolutions and Progress in Economic Knowledge* (Cambridge: Cambridge University Press, 1978). Also see the earlier version of that article, Hutchison, 'James Mill and the Political Education of Ricardo', *Cambridge Journal*, 7 (Nov. 1953), pp. 81–100. The superb article by William O. Thweatt, 'James Mill and the Early Development of Comparative Advantage', *History of Political Economy*, 8 (Summer 1976), pp. 207–34, shows that Mill originated the important law of comparative advantage and that Ricardo lacked interest in the law for reasons implicit in his own Ricardian system. Also see William O. Thweatt, 'James and John Stuart Mill on Comparative Advantage: Sraffa's Account Corrected', in H. Visser and E. Schoorl (eds), *Trade in Transit* (Doordrecht: Martinus Nijhoff, 1987); Denis P. O'Brien, 'Classical Reassessments', in Thweatt (ed.), *Classical Political Economy*; *A Survey of Recent Literature* (Boston: Kluwer, 1988), pp. 188–93; and Thweatt, 'Introduction', *ibid.*, pp. 8–9.

For James Mill as the first 'Georgist', see William J. Barber, 'James Mill and the Theory of Economic Policy in India', *History of Political Economy*, 1 (Spring 1969), pp. 85–100. Mill's cadre activity and outlook is brilliantly and lucidly portrayed in two works by Joseph Hamburger, *James Mill and the Art of Revolution* (New Haven: Yale University Press, 1963), and *Intellectuals in Politics: John Stuart Mill and the Philosophic Radicals* (New Haven: Yale University Press, 1965). The first book shows how Mill manipulated public and government opinion behind the scenes, using systemic duplicity, to drive through the Reform Bill of 1832. The second, despite its title, deals more with James and his Millians than with John Stuart, and portrays and explains the rise and decline of the Millian radicals as a political force in Parliament in the 1830s. *Intellectuals in Politics* is also unique in setting forth and discussing James Mill's libertarian two-class theory of class conflict based on where a group stands in relation to the state. William Thomas's *Philosophic Radicals* should also be consulted on the Mills and the radicals. The standard, but very old, life is Alexander Bain, *James Mill: A Biography* (1882, New York: A.M. Kelley, 1967). As in so many areas of early nineteenth century social thought, Élie Halévy's *Growth of Philosophic Radicalism,* provides keen insights; indeed, it was this work that inaugurated the modern upward reevaluation of the contributions of James Mill.

On James Mill's central role in founding the highly influential Political Economy Club of London, see James P. Henderson, 'The Oral Tradition in British Economics: Influential Economists in the Political Club of London', *History of Political Economy,* 15 (Summer 1983), pp. 149–79.

For a recent discovery of the central role of James Mill in fostering the unfortunate real bills–banking school doctrine, see Morris Perlman, 'Adam Smith and the Paternity of the Real Bills Doctrine', *History of Political Economy,* 21 (Spring 1989), pp. 88–9.

David Ricardo and the Ricardian system

The literature on Ricardo and Ricardianism is almost as enormous as on Smith, and so it must be winnowed judiciously here. All of Ricardo's works and correspondence are collected in the definitive eleven-volume labour-of-love edition edited by the left–Ricardian neo-Marxist Piero Sraffa, *The Works and Correspondence of David Ricardo* (Cambridge: Cambridge University Press, 1951–55). There are no satisfactory biographies of Ricardo; the only one available is the chatty family history by David Weatherall, *David Ricardo* (The Hague: Martinus Nijhoff, 1976). The best explanation and critique of the Ricardian system is Oswald St Clair, *A Key to Ricardo* (1957, New York: A.M. Kelley, 1965). There are brilliant insights into Ricardo and Ricardianism scattered, in disorganized fashion, throughout Schumpeter's *History of Economic Analysis;* indeed, much of his *History* may be interpreted as a devastating assault on Ricardianism. For a properly acidulous view of Ricardianism, see also Frank H. Knight, 'The Ricardian Theory of Production and Distribution', in *On the History and Method of Economics* (Chicago: University of Chicago Press, 1956), pp. 37–8. Not surprisingly, some of the critiques of Adam Smith's theory apply also to Ricardo; see, in particular, Cannan's subtle *A History of the Theories of Production & Distribution* (3rd ed., London: Staples Press, 1917); Gray's sardonic and delightful *The Development of Economic Doctrine* (London: Longmans, Green, 1931); Douglas's lucid and trenchant 'Smith's Theory of Value and Distribution'; Ellen Paul's forceful and perceptive *Moral Revolu-*

tion and Economic Science (Westport: Conn.: Greenwood Press, 1979); and Richard H. Timberlake Jr's 'The Classical Search for an Invariable Measure of Value', *Quarterly Review of Economics and Business*, 6 (Spring 1966), pp. 37–44. For a demonstration of the crucial importance to the Ricardian system – in contrast to Smith – of the quantity-of-labour theory of value, see L.E. Johnson, 'Ricardo's Labor Theory of the Determinant of Value', *Atlantic Economic Journal*, 12, (March 1984), pp. 50–59.

Unlike Adam Smith, David Ricardo has fortunately not been the recent recipient of a centennial-type boost to his reputation. But the indefatigable Samuel Hollander was of course there, as in the case of Smith, torturing Ricardo into the mould of a modern general-equilibrium theorist. Samuel Hollander, *The Economics of David Ricardo* (Toronto: The University of Toronto Press, 1979).

In recent articles Terry Peach has set forth a masterful defence of the 'traditionalist' view of Ricardo presented in this work, as well as a critique of the 'corn model' interpretation of Ricardo offered by Sraffa, and of the opposing Hollander proto-general equilibrium approach. In particular, Peach shows that Ricardo was marked by an increasingly intensified labour theory of value, an overriding concentration on the long-run equilibrium 'natural price', on very rapid increases of population returning the economy to long-run equilibrium, and by a total neglect of the role of demand in price as well as of the role of scarcity in determining the supply of reproducible goods. See in particular, Terry Peach, 'David Ricardo: A Review of Some Interpretative Issues', in William O. Thweatt, (ed.), *Classical Political Economy: A Survey of Recent Literature* (Boston: Kluwer, 1988) pp. 103–31. Also see Peach, 'David Ricardo's Treatment of Wages', in R.D.C. Black (ed.), *Ideas in Economics* (London: Macmillan, 1986).

The last effusion of the orthodox Keynesian view of the alleged triumph of Ricardianism in Britain is Sydney G. Checkland, 'The Propagation of Ricardian Economics in England', *Economica*, n.s., 16 (Feb. 1949), pp. 40–52. Revisionism of this view began with Ronald L. Meek, 'The Decline of Ricardian Economics in England', *Economica*, n.s. 17 (Feb., 1950), pp. 43–62, continued through Schumpeter's *History* and culminated in two excellent articles: Frank W. Fetter, 'The Rise and Decline of Ricardian Economics', *History of Political Economy*, 1 (Spring 1969), pp. 67–84; and Barry Gordon, 'Criticism of Ricardian Views on Value and Distribution in the British Periodicals, 1820–1850', *History of Political Economy*, 1 (Autumn 1969), pp. 370–87. The anti-Say's law underworld in Britain is explored in Barry J. Gordon, *Non-Ricardian Political Economy: Five Neglected Contributions* (Boston: Harvard Graduate School Baker Library, 1967).

Whenever any hint appears deprecating either the wisdom or the majesty of David Ricardo we can depend upon Samuel Hollander to enter the fray in combat; and, sure enough, Hollander weighs in with the maverick view that simply everyone was a Ricardian. Samuel Hollander, 'The Reception of Ricardian Economics', *Oxford Economic Papers*, 29 (July 1977), pp. 221–57

The anti-Ricardians

Perhaps the best place to begin a study of the host of important non- or anti-Ricardian economists in nineteenth century Britain is with the pioneering article that resurrected them from the oblivion in which they had been cast by the triumph of John Stuart Mill: Edwin R.A. Seligman's 'On Some Neglected British Economists, I', and 'On Some Neglected British Economists, II', in the *Economic Journal*, 13 (Sept. 1903), especially pp. 347–63, and in *Economic Journal*, 13 (Dec. 1903), pp. 511–35, reprinted in his *Essays on Economics* (New York: Macmillan, 1925). Seligman is particularly good on Craig, Longfield, Ramsay and Lloyd. R.C.D. Black's brief but highly important article on the Irish economists is his 'Trinity College, Dublin, and the Theory of Value, 1832–1863', *Economica*, n.s. 12 (August 1945), pp. 140–48. Also see J.G. Smith, 'Some Nineteenth Century Irish Economists', *Economica*, n.s. 2 (Feb. 1935), pp. 20–32. On Richard Whately, see Salim Rashid, 'Richard Whately and Christian Political Economy at Oxford and Dublin', *Journal of the History of Ideas*, 38 (Jan. – March 1977), pp. 147–55. On Whately, Lawson and catallactics, see Israel M. Kirzner, *The Economic Point of View* (Princeton, NJ: Van Nostrand, 1960), pp. 72–5; and Murray N. Rothbard, 'Catallactics', *The New Palgrave. Dictionary of Economics* (London. Macmillan, 1987), I, p. 377.

We are fortunate enough to have some comprehensive works on individual economists of this era. Particularly outstanding is Marian Bowley's *Nassau Senior and Classical Economics* (1937, New York: A.M. Kelley, 1949; Octagon Books, 1967). Miss Bowley deals not only with Senior but also with many of his confrères. S. Leon Levy's chatty and uncomprehending *Nassau W. Senior, 1790–1864* (New York: A.M Kelley, 1970) provides useful information on Senior's life and genealogical background. Unfortunately, Miss Bowley's later collection of essays accomplishes little, reflecting a falling away from the previously perceptive Austrian position of herself and of her mentor Lord Robbins, and a wish to rejoin the Ricardians in the historiographical mainstream of economic thought. Marian Bowley, *Studies in the History of Economic Theory Before 1870* (London: Macmillan, 1973). Also excellent is Robert M. Rauner, *Samuel Bailey and the Classical Theory of Value* (Cambridge, Mass.: Harvard University Press, 1961). Rauner's book, however, unfortunately omits the Austrian orientation of Bailey's philosophy and methodology as expounded in Rauner's preceding doctoral dissertation at the University of London, 'Samuel Bailey and Classical Economics' (1956).

See Denis P. O'Brien, 'Critical Reassessments', in Thweatt (ed.), *Classical Political Economy*, pp. 199–200. Again, Laurence S. Moss, *Mountifort Longfield: Ireland's First Professor of Political Economy* (Ottawa, Ill: Green Hill Publishers, 1976), has the merit of dealing with other economists of the day in addition to Longfield, and contains an up-to-date bibliography. The definitive work on Colonel Torrens is Lionel Robbins, *Robert Torrens and the Evolution of Classical Economics* (London: Macmillan, 1958). The important work demonstrating that even the allegedly arch-Ricardian J.R. McCulloch was not really a Ricardian for very long, is Denis P. O'Brien, *J.R. McCulloch: A Study in Classical Economics* (New York: Barnes & Noble, 1970).

On Nassau Senior's notable exchange on population theory with T. Robert Malthus, see Bowley, *Nassau Senior*, pp. 117–22; Cannan, *History*, pp. 133–4; and Schumpeter, *History*, pp. 580–81.

Primary sources particularly rich in rewards for the reader are: Samuel Bailey's excellent *A Critical Dissertation on the Nature, Measure, and Causes of Value* (1825, New York: A.M. Kelley, 1967); Nassau W. Senior's *Outline of the Science of Political Economy* (1836, New York: A.M. Kelley, 1965); and *The Economic Writings of Mountifort Longfield* (R.D.C. Black, ed., Clifton, NJ: A.M. Kelley, 1972).

Useful journal articles are Thor W. Bruce, 'The Economic Theories of John Craig, a Forgotten English Economist', *Quarterly Journal of Economics*, 52 (August 1938), pp. 697–707; Laurence S. Moss, 'Isaac Butt and the Early Development of the Marginal Utility Theory of Imputation', *History of Political Economy*, 6 (Winter 1974), pp. 405–34; and Richard M. Romano, 'William Forster Lloyd – a Non-Ricardian?' *History of Political Economy*, 9 (Autumn 1977), pp. 412–41. Also on Lloyd, see Emil Kauder, *A History of Marginal Utility Theory* (Princeton, NJ: Princeton University Press, 1965), pp. 38–41.

On the life of Thomas Perronet Thompson, see the account by Norma H. McMullen, 'Thomas Perronet Thompson', in J. Baylen and N. Gossman (eds.), *Biographical Dictionary of Modern British Radicals, Vol I: 1770–1830* (Atlantic Highlands, NJ: Humanities Press, 1979), pp. 475–9. For Thompson on rent, see Robbins, *Robert Torrens*, pp. 43–4; on Thompson's critique of the cost theory of value, see Gordon, 'Criticism', p. 374. Also see Schumpeter, *History*, pp. 672–3, 713–4. On Thompson and the calculus, see Spiegel, *Growth*, pp. 293–4, 507–08.

The definitive study, biography, and collected works of John Rae (all that are still extant except the bulk of his geological papers), are to be found in R. Warren James's two-volume *John Rae: Political Economist* (Toronto: University of Toronto Press, 1965). Also see the discussion of Rae in Joseph Dorfman, *The Economic Mind in American Civilization, 1606–1865* (New

York: Viking Press, 1946), II, pp. 779–89; and Joseph J. Spengler, 'John Rae on Economic Development: A Note', *Quarterly Journal of Economics*, 73 (August 1979), pp. 393–406. The best critique of Rae's *New Principles* is in Eugen von Böhm-Bawerk, *Capital and Interest, Vol. I History and Critique of Interest Theories* (South Holland, Ill.: Libertarian Press, 1959), pp. 208–40.

For the isolated and remarkable case of the American subjective utility theorist Amos Kendall, developing his views in his Kentucky newspaper, see the full text of his articles in the *Autobiography of Amos Kendall*, ed., W. Stickney (1872, New York: Peter Smith, 1949), pp. 227–36. Also see Murray N. Rothbard, *The Panic of 1819: Reactions and Policies* (New York: Columbia University Press, 1962), p. 55.

For Nassau Senior, John Stuart Mill, and the early praxeology *vs* positivism debate, see Marian Bowley, *Nassau Senior*, pp. 27–65. Also see Rothbard, *Individualism*, pp. 49–51. For a contrasting view of the debate, see Fritz Machlup, 'The Universal Bogey', in M. Peston and B. Corry (eds.), *Essays in Honour of Lord Robbins* (White Plains, NY: International Arts & Sciences Press, 1973), pp. 99–117. On Dickens's *Hard Times* and its caricature of economics and utilitarianism, see Ludwig von Mises, *Socialism* (1922, Indianapolis: Liberty Classics, 1981), p. 422.

The bullionist controversy

Despite the importance and renown of the bullionist controversy for the emergence of monetary and banking thought in the early nineteenth century, there is no fully satisfactory account and analysis. A good chronological account can be found in Frank Whitson Fetter, *Development of British Monetary Orthodoxy, 1797–1875* (Cambridge: Mass.: Harvard University Press, 1965), which should be supplemented by the classic analytical discussion in Jacob Viner, *Studies in the Theory of International Trade* (New York: Harper & Bros, 1937), Chapters III–IV. Also see the brief but valuable treatment in Chi-Yuen Wu, *An Outline of International Price Theories* (London: George Routledge & Sons, 1939), still the best published history of theories of international money and prices. Edwin Cannan's 'Introduction' to the Bullion Report, both contained in *The Paper Pound of 1797–1821* (2nd ed., London, P.S. King & Son, 1925), is a classic discussion of the events of the restriction era.

Also useful is Lloyd W. Mints, *A History of Banking Theory in Great Britain and the United States* (Chicago: University of Chicago Press, 1945), which is however marred by his exclusive concentration on the evils of the real bills doctrine; and Charles Rist, *History of Monetary and Credit Theory From John Law to the Present Day* (1940, A.M. Kelley, 1966), which on the contrary, suffers from devotion to the real bills doctrine, at least under a gold standard.

By far the best treatment of the bullionist writers is by Joseph Salerno, 'The Doctrinal Antecedents of the Monetary Approach to the Balance of Payments' (doctoral dissertation, Rutgers University, 1980). Salerno's paradigm of classifying the variants of bullionists is a path-breaking one, from which all future discussion must start. His emphasis is on the international monetary aspect of the controversy.

Jacob H. Hollander's path-breaking article, 'The Development of the Theory of Money from Adam Smith to David Ricardo', *Quarterly Journal of Economics*, 25 (May 1911), pp. 429–70, is still indispensable. *The Dictionary of National Biography's* articles on the various writers and statements involved in the controversy often provide excellent background information.

Henry Thornton's contribution has been well served, perhaps too much so, by later historians. In particular, see F.A. von Hayek's extremely favorable 'Introduction' to the reprint of Thornton's *Inquiry* (New York: Farrar & Rienhart, 1939). Also see David A. Reisman, 'Henry Thornton and Classical Monetary Economics', *Oxford Economic Papers*, n.s. 23 (March 1971), pp. 70–89. For a biography, see Standish Meacham, *Henry Thornton of Clapham, 1760–1815* (Cambridge, Mass.: Harvard University Press, 1964); and on his banking activities, see E.J.T. Acaster, 'Henry Thornton – the Banker, Part I', *The Three Banks Review*, no. 104 (December 1974), pp. 46–57. For an opposing position, see Salerno, 'Doctrinal Antecedents'. On Francis Horner, see Frank W. Fetter, 'Introduction' to Fetter (ed.), *The Economic Writings of Francis Horner* (London: London School of Economics, 1957). And on John Wheatley, see Frank W. Fetter, 'The Life and Writings of John Wheatley', *Journal of Political Economy*, 50 (June 1942), pp. 357–76. Salerno, 'Doctrinal Antecedents', has single-handedly brought back into focus the notable achievements of Peter Lord King, in elaborating the complete bullionist position.

Thornton's crucial role in provoking David Ricardo into a mechanistic bullionism in opposition to the former's muddled approach, is brought out in the excellent and important article by Charles F. Peake, 'Henry Thornton and the Development of Ricardo's Economic Thought', *History of Political Economy*, 10 (Summer 1978), pp. 193–212. Also see Salerno, 'Doctrinal Antecedents'. On Ricardo, see also R.S. Sayers, 'Ricardo's Views on Monetary Questions', *Quarterly Journal of Economics* (1953), in T.S. Ashton and R.S. Sayers (eds.), *Papers in English Monetary History* (Oxford: The Clarendon Press, 1953), pp. 76–95. David Weatherall, *David Ricardo*, has a considerable discussion of Ricardo's monetary views. On the bullion committee report itself, see Fetter, *Development*; Frank W. Fetter, 'The Bullion Report Reexamined' (1942), in Ashton and Sayers, *Papers*, pp. 66–75, and especially the definitive Frank W. Fetter, 'The Politics of the Bullion Report', *Economica*, n.s. 26 (May 1959), pp. 99–120.

On the resumption of specie payment, see, in addition to many of the above sources, Cecil C. Carpenter, 'The English Specie Resumption of 1821', *Southern Economic Journal*, 5 (July 1938), pp. 45 54. Salim Rashid makes a notable contribution in uncovering the important influence of Edward Copleston on the return to gold, in Salim Rashid, 'Edward Copleston, Robert Peel, and Cash Payments', *History of Political Economy*, 15 (Summer 1983), pp. 249–59.

On the response to banking and the panic of 1819 in the United States, see Rothbard, *The Panic of 1819*. Also see Mark Skousen, *Economics of a Pure Gold Standard* (1977, 2nd ed., Auburn, Ala.: Ludwig von Mises Institute of Auburn University, 1988). On Jefferson, also see Luttrell, 'Thomas Jefferson', and on Busch and Storch, see the interesting discovery of Peter Bernholz, 'Inflation and Monetary Constitutions in Historical Perspective', *Kyklos*, 36, no. 3 (1983), pp. 406–9.

We are fortunate to have the Swedish controversy of the mid-eighteenth century era of fiat money brought recently to our notice. For an illuminating survey, see Robert V. Eagly (ed.), *The Swedish Bullionist Controversy* (Philadelphia: American Philosophic Society, 1971), in his 'Introductory Essay'. The remainder of the book translates Pehr Niclas Christiernin's 1761 tract for the first time, *Summary of Lectures on the High Price of Foreign Exchange in Sweden*. Also see the lengthy and fascinating article by Carl G. Uhr, 'Anders Chydenius, 1729–1803, A Finnish Predecessor to Adam Smith', *Western Economic Journal*, 2 (Spring 1964), pp. 85–116.

Currency and banking schools

The best overall summary of the currency and banking school controversy is Marion R. Daugherty, 'The Currency-Banking Controversy, Part I', *Southern Economic Journal*, 9 (Oct. 1942), pp. 140–55; and 'The Currency-Banking Controversy: II', *Southern Economic Journal*, 9 (Jan. 1943), pp. 241–50. The fullest and indispensable account is Frank W. Fetter, *Development of British Monetary Orthodoxy, 1797–1875* (Cambridge, Mass.: Harvard University Press, 1965). Also see Jacob Viner, *Studies in the Theory of International Trade* (New York: Harper & Bros, 1937), Chap. V, and, on the United States as well as Britain, Lloyd Mints, *A History of Banking Theory in Great Britain and the United States* (Chicago: University of Chicago Press, 1945). Elmer Wood, *English Theories of Central Banking Control, 1819–1858* (Cambridge, Mass.: Harvard University Press, 1939), is particularly good on the theoretical controversies in the aftermath of Peel's Act.

On the background of Peel's Act, see J.K. Horsefield, 'The Origins of the Bank Charter Act, 1844', in T.S. Ashton and R.S. Sayers (eds.), *Papers in English Monetary History* (Oxford: The Clarendon Press, 1953), pp. 109–25. Peel himself is re-evaluated in an important article by Boyd Hilton, 'Peel: A

Reappraisal', *Historical Journal*, 22 (Sept. 1979), pp. 585–614. Hilton is responsible for reinterpreting Peel as a statesman with increasingly fixed classical liberal principles, within which he used superb tactics to put his principles into effect. But Hilton, on the other hand, who does not understand economic theory, misconstrues who beats whom in economic argument, and sneers at Peel as being an inflexible dogmatist in contrast to the previous historical interpretation of Peel as unprincipled opportunist.

James Pennington is collected, brought to the fore, and analysed by R.S. Sayers in his edition of the *Economic Writings of James Pennington* (London: London School of Economics, 1963). Robert Torrens, his theories, and his controversies, are annotated and treated in a superb work by Lionel Robbins, *Robert Torrens and the Evolution of Classical Economics* (London: Macmillan, 1958). The best discussion of Thomas Tooke is still T.E. Gregory, 'Introduction', to Thomas Tooke and William Newmarch, *A History of Prices and of the State of the Circulation from 1792 to 1856* (New York: Adelphi Printing Co., 1928). Arie Arnon absurdly tries to make a key to Tooke's thought the latter's non-existent conversion to free banking. Arie Arnon, 'The Transformation in Thomas Tooke's Monetary Theory Reconsidered', *History of Political Economy*, 16 (Summer 1984), pp. 311–26. James Wilson's business cycle theory is illuminated in Robert G. Link, *English Theories of Economic Fluctuations, 1815–1848* (New York: Columbia University Press, 1959), which also has a good discussion of John Stuart Mill's cycle theory. For an elaboration of Wilson's thesis, see H.M. Boot, 'James Wilson and the Commercial Crisis of 1847', *History of Political Economy*, 15 (Winter 1983), pp. 567–83.

Vera C. Smith, *The Rationale of Central Banking* (1936, Indianapolis: Liberty Press, 1990) is a pioneering and excellent work on free and central banking school controversies in Britain, the United States, France and Germany, and is still by far the best work on the subject.

On Johann Louis Tellkampf, see, in addition to Smith, Joseph Dorfman, *The Economic Mind in American Civilization* (New York, 1946), II, pp. 833–5. Smith not only highlights important but otherwise obscure writers such as Cernuschi and Modeste, but also presents a good summary of the history of banking in the four countries in the nineteenth century. Particularly important is Smith's classifying her theorists on a two-dimensional, and therefore four-term, grid, i.e. where they stand on currency principle *vs* banking principle, and free *vs* central banking. Lawrence H. White, *Free Banking in Britain: Theory, Experience, and Debate, 1800–1845* (Cambridge: Cambridge University Press, 1984), performs the service of reviving emphasis on free banking thought, pro and con, after a 50-year hiatus. But while he adds more names to Smith's account for Great Britain, he is seriously misleading in shifting to a three-term classification and category mistake: free banking, banking school, and currency school. This new taxonomy ignores the fact that his free bankers are scarcely a united school, being seriously split into currency and banking men. Furthermore, the free bankers in Britain scarcely deserve being elevated to the dignity of a school of thought, since almost all of them were commercial bankers swaying to their economic interests of the moment, and not interested in consistent free banking. Moreover, White misleads by hailing Scotland in the first half of the nineteenth century as a land of free banking, when Scottish banks merely pyramided on top of the Bank of England, and were often bailed out by the bank. Neither can the Scottish banks be really said to rest on gold convertibility. They kept very little gold reserve, and greatly resisted any attempts by their customers to demand specie. White's attempt to show that the Scottish banks were superior to the English system makes not even a token effort to demonstrate that they were less inflationary; his sole evidence is a lower failure rate, which by no means shows that the banking system was working better for the economy. Sometimes, a truly competitive industry will have a higher failure rate than a privileged one, and so much the better.

For the fascinating debate among the French laissez-faire thinkers on how to apply libertarian principles to the vexed questions of banking, see, among others, Henri Cernuschi, *Contre le Billet de Banque* (Against Bank Notes) (Paris, 1866); Victor Modeste, 'Le Billet Des Banques D'Emmission et la Fausse Monnaie', (Bank Notes and False Money), *Journal des Économistes*, 3 (August 1866), pp. 188–212; Gustave Du Puynode, 'Le Billet de Banque N'est Ni Monnaie Ni Fausse Monnaie', (A Bank Note is Neither Money Nor False Money); ibid., 3 (Sept 1866), pp. 392–5; Léon Wolowski, ibid., pp. 438–41; J.G. Courcelle-Seneuil, 'Le Billet De Banque N'est Pas Fausse Monnie', ('Bank Notes Are Not False Money'), ibid., 342–9; Victor Modeste, 'Le Billet Des Banques D'Emmission Est-Il Fausse Monnaie?' ('Are Bank Notes False Money?'), ibid., 4 (Oct., 1866), pp. 73–86; Gustave Du Puynode, 'Le Billet De Banque N'est Ni Monnaie Ni Fausse Monnaie', ('Bank Notes Are Neither Money Nor False Money'), ibid., 4 (Nov. 1866), pp. 261–7; Th. Mannequin, 'L'Emmission Des Billets de Banque' ('Bank Notes'), ibid., 4 (Dec. 1866), pp. 396–410.

John Stuart Mill

It is difficult to think of anyone in the history of thought who has been more egregiously and systematically overestimated, as an economist, as a political philosopher, as an overall thinker, or as a man, than John Stuart Mill. Unfortunately, historians have tended to follow the example of opinion in Mill's own lifetime. Current historians have continued this tradition, even in economics, where his reputation has unfortunately been making a comeback. As a corollary, the over-investment of 'scholarly resources' in Mill, in trying to track, interpret and render coherent his every word and thought, is enormous.

It is hardly possible, still less worthwhile, to ponder it all, and all the more difficult to find the proper assessment of him as a devious and muddled filiopietist. I can only recommend what I have found the most useful in uncovering the essential Mill.

First, of course, for Mill himself: most important for our purposes is his *Principles of Political Economy,* either in the classic Ashley edition (1909, rprt., Penguin, 1970), or in the edition in his *Collected Works* (2 vols, Toronto: University of Toronto Press, 1965). Also important is Mill's *Essays on Some Unsettled Questions on Political Economy* (1844, rprt., London: London School of Economics, 1948).

The standard biography is Michael St John Packe, *The Life of John Stuart Mill* (London: Secker & Warburg, 1954). Iris Wessel Mueller, *John Stuart Mill and French Thought* (Urbana, Ill: University of Illinois Press, 1956) is interesting on the influence of French socialist theorists on Mill. The quarrel (*cherchez la femme!*) over the extent to which Harriet Taylor influenced Mill in a socialist direction is reflected at length in F.A. von Hayek, *John Stuart Mill and Harriet Taylor* (Chicago: University of Chicago Press, 1951) (yes), and H.O. Pappe, *John Stuart Mill and the Harriet Taylor Myth* (Melbourne: Melbourne University Press, 1960) (no). In any case, there is no doubt that Mill suffered, as Gertrude Himmelfarb amusingly put it, from 'excessive uxoriousness'. The best portrayal of the young Mill as leader of the philosophical radicals is in Joseph Hamburger, *Intellectuals in Politics: John Stuart Mill and the Philosophical Radicals* (New Haven: Yale University Press, 1965).

Probably the best of the breed of recent apologia for Mill's economic policy views is Pedro Schwartz, *The New Political Economy of J.S, Mill* (Durham, NC: Duke University Press, 1972). For a sardonic corrective, see Ellen Frankel Paul, 'John Stuart Mill: 1806–1873', in *Moral Revolution and Economic Science* (Westport, Conn.: Greenwood Press, 1979), pp. 146–99.

The most recent, and by far the most grandiose, of the current glorifications of Mill is Samuel Hollander, *The Economics of John Stuart Mill* (2 vols; Toronto: University of Toronto Press, 1986). This work is Part III of Hollander's massive and bizarre project to transform all the classical economists into perfect little propounders of neoclassical, general equilibrium doctrine. A devastating and most welcome demolition of this entire enterprise is the review of the Mill volumes by Terence W. Hutchison, 'Review of *The Economics of John Stuart Mill*, by Samuel Hollander', *Journal of Economic Literature*, 25 (March 1987), pp. 120–22. Calling 'the whole gigantic operation' a 'reunification wrapped in anachronism', Hutchison asks:

why should 1,037 pages be written – or read – on the economics of J.S. Mill? Why not compile a 1,037-page anthology of Mill's own economic writings with some useful notes and an informative introduction? Mill is not a newly discovered writer, and in any case, Hollander has no new biographical information to offer. Nor did Mill write so obscurely and abstrusely that a lot of space might be required to make his meaning clear. In fact, to this reviewer, Mill seems a rather more lucid and orderly writer than Hollander.

Hutchison points out that, since father James Mill cannot be fitted into the proto-Walrasian mould, his influence on his son is seriously underrated. In fact, Hutchison concludes that Hollander's volumes 'display an extraordinary capacity...for dismissing, disregarding, or devaluing evidence, however plain and unambiguous, that conflicts with the Hollander interpretations'. (Hutchison, pp. 120–21.)

Alexander Gray, *The Development of Economic Doctrine* (London: Longmans, Green, 1931), has an incisive discussion of Mill and Cairnes, pp. 277–92. There is a keen technical critique of Mill amidst the other classical economists, in Edwin Cannan's *A History of the Theories of Production & Distribution* (3rd ed, London: Staples Press, 1917).

One of the most valuable, and also one of the most neglected economists and historians of thought, of our time, is William H. Hutt. Hutt's *The Theory of Collective Bargaining 1930–1985* (San Francisco: Cato Institute, 1980), pp. 1–6, straightens out the century-old confusion about the wages fund theory and economists' attitude towards labour unions. And Hutt's *A Reha bilitation of Say's Law* (Athens, Ohio: Ohio University Press, 1974), should be consulted for Mill's ambivalent role in the advancement of that law.

The neo-conservative historian Gertrude Himmelfarb is almost always worth reading, even if we must dissent from her depiction of two Mills, the conservative compulsory moralist (good) and the libertarian (bad). Gertrude Himmelfarb, *On Liberty and Liberalism: The Case of J.S. Mill* (New York: Knopf, 1974). Mill is scarcely that clear-cut; in a sense, there is only one Mill – multi-faceted, self-contradictory, kaleidic, devious, muddled and filiopietistic.

By far the most useful essay on the strategy, reception, and importance of Mill's *Principles* is N.B. de Marchi, 'The Success of Mill's *Principles*', *History of Political Economy,* 6 (Summer 1974), pp. 119–57. Also on Mill as rehabilitating Ricardo, see Frank W. Fetter, 'The Rise and Decline of Ricardian Economics', *History of Political Economy,* 1 (Spring 1969), pp. 80–81. For the indirect impact of Mill's triumph, see J.G. Smith, 'Some Nineteenth Century Irish Economists', *Economica,* n.s. 2 (Feb. 1935), pp. 25–32; and R.D.C. Black, 'Trinity College, Dublin, and the Theory of Value, 1832–1863', *Economica,* n.s. 12 (August 1945), pp. 146–8.

For an excellent article on John Stuart Mill and the shift of classical liberals towards imperialism, see Eileen P. Sullivan, 'Liberalism and Imperialism: J.S. Mill's Defense of the British Empire', *Journal of the History of Ideas*, 44 (Oct. – Dec. 1983), pp. 599–617. On Wakefield, also see Leonard P. Liggio, 'The Transportation of Criminals: A Brief Political-Economical History', In R. Barnett and J. Hagel III (eds), *Assessing the Criminal: Restitution, Retribution, and the Legal Process* (Cambridge, Mass.: Ballinger Publication Co., 1977), pp. 285–91.

In Mill's shadow: Cairnes and the inductivists

On Cairnes's methodology, see John Elliott Cairnes, *The Character and Logical Method of Political Economy* (2nd ed., London: Macmillan, 1875); and Murray N. Rothbard, *Individualism and Philosophy of the Social Sciences* (1973; San Francisco: Cato Institute, 1979), pp. 49–50, On Cairnes and the Australian gold controversy, see Crauford D. Goodwin, 'British Economists and Australian Gold', *Journal of Economic History*, 30 (June 1970), pp. 405–26; and Frank W. Fetter, *Development of British Monetary Orthodoxy, 1797–1875* (Cambridge, Mass.: Harvard University Press, 1965), pp. 240–9.

On the rise of William Whewell and the Baconian inductivists, see N.B. de Marchi and R.P. Sturges, 'Malthus and Ricardo's Inductivist Critics: Four Letters to William Whewell', *Economica*, n.s. 40 (Nov. 1973), pp. 379–93; I. Bernard Cohen, *Revolution in Science* (Cambridge, Mass.: Belknap Press of Harvard University Press, 1985), p 528; and S.G. Checkland, 'The Advent of Academic Economics in England', *The Manchester School of Economic and Social Studies*, 19 (Jan. 1951), pp. 59–66.

Socialist and Marxist thought

On socialism in general, and on Marx and Marxism in particular, literally millions of words have been written, and out of this vast pot pourri and kitchen-midden I can only select those readings and sources which have proved most helpful. For an overall analysis and critique of socialism, the premier work is Ludwig von Mises, *Socialism* (3rd English ed. Indianapolis: Liberty Classics, 1981).

By far the most useful history of socialist thought is the brilliant, witty, perceptive, and properly mordant work by Alexander Gray, *The Socialist Tradition* (London: Longmans, Green, 1947). Also indispensable is the massive, enormously researched, and exciting work by James H. Billington, *Fire in the Minds of Men: Origins of the Revolutionary Faith* (New York: Basic Books, 1980). While not as strong in analysis of theories as Gray, Billington in unique in tracing all the interrelations of a large number of revolutionary and socialist figures, as well as revealing and stressing the numerous irrationalities of their positions. So deep is Billington's contempt for his subjects, however, that once in a while he mistakenly lumps *all* radical advocates of social change in with socialists, such as his big mistake of treating the *laissez-faire* radical J.B. Say as a socialist. These are minor flaws, however, in a monumental book. Also helpful is Igor Shafarevich, *The Socialist Phenomenon* (New York: Harper & Row, 1980).

On the other hand, the highly touted, multi-volume history of socialist thought by G.D.H Cole, in particular Vol. I, *Socialist Thought: The Forerunners 1789–1850* (London: Macmillan, 1959), and Vol. II, *Socialist Thought: Marxism and Anarchism 1850–1890* (London: Macmillan, 1957), is woefully inadequate, both as history and as analysis.

Unfortunately, Alexander Gray's work omits the vital theme of apocalyptic millennialism in socialist and Marxist thought. On this theme see the amillennial Christian critique in Thomas Molnar, *Utopia: The Perennial Heresy* (New York: Sheed & Ward, 1967), and in the brief but profound article by Molnar, 'Marxism and the Utopian Theme', *Marxist Perspectives* (Winter 1978), pp. 144–58. Also see Molnar's mentor Eric Voegelin, 'The Formation of the Marxian Revolutionary Idea', *Review of Politics*, 12 (July 1950), pp. 275–302; and J.L. Talmon, *Political Messianism: The Romantic Phase* (New York: Praeger, 1960). See also the brief treatment of 'Socialistic Chiliasm', in von Mises, *Socialism*, pp. 249–55.

On the various radical groups during the English Civil War, see the good, up-to-date survey by F.D. Dow, *Radicalism in the English Revolution, 1640–1660* (Oxford: Basil Blackwell, 1985). The Dow book is marred by his taking the egalitarian communist Winstanley as the touchstone for evaluation of the other radical groups.

Theocratic millennialists such as the Rosicrucians are treated in Paul Gottfried, 'Utopianism of the Right: Maistre and Schlegel', *Modern Age*, 24 (Spring 1980), pp. 150–60. See also Gottfried, *Conservative Millenarians; the Romantic Experience in Bavaria* (New York: Fordham University Press, 1979).

The fascinating work by C. Patrides and J. Wittreich (eds.), *The Apocalypse: in English Renaissance Thought and Literature* (Ithaca: Cornell University Press, 1984), far broader than its subtitle, includes two important articles directly relevant to Marxism: Ernest L. Tuveson, 'The Millenarian Structure of *The Communist Manifesto*', pp. 323–41; and M.H. Abrams, 'Apocalypse: Theme and Variations', pp. 342–68.

M.H. Abrams's brilliant book, *Natural Supernaturalism: Tradition and Revolution in Romantic Literature* (New York: W.W. Norton, 1971), demonstrates that Marx's thought is an atheist variant of a pantheistic determinist view of human history. In this view, the collective organism, man, separated and alienated from God–nature–himself by the dialectical act of creation of the universe, is destined some day to return in a mighty cosmic merger into unity with God–nature–himself, thereby putting an end to history. Abrams demonstrates that this bizarre world-view permeated the entire Romantic period, not only in the poetic–philosophic system of Marx's spiritual mentor, Hegel, but also in Hegel's fellow German Romantics, such as Schlegel, Schiller, Schelling, Schleiermacher, Novalis, and in such English Romantics as Wordsworth and Coleridge. Abrams shows that this determined pantheistic–organicist 'upward spiral home' world-outlook continues down into such twentieth century Romantic figures as D.H. Lawrence.

Robert C. Tucker, *Philosophy and Myth in Karl Marx* (New York: Cambridge University Press, 1961) is the crucial, indispensable work in clarifying and illuminating the vital importance of millennial, apocalyptic communism in the Marxian system, as well as explicating Marx's path through Hegelianism to Marxian communism. Tucker's *Philosophy and Myth* is the most important single work on Marx's philosophy of communism, and therefore on Marxism as a whole. Tucker's second edition (Cambridge University Press, 1972), unfortunately adds nothing, even references. All it does is weaken a few of Tucker's anti-Marxian insights in a few passages. The monumental work of Leszek Kolakowski, *Main Currents of Marxism: Its Origins, Growth and Dissolution, I: The Founders* (New York: Oxford University Press, 1981), is particularly significant for its analysis of alienation and the Hegelian-and-Marxian dialectic in Plotinus and the heretical Christian mystics of the Middle Ages. Kolakowski brilliantly traces these concepts to the creatological heresy that God created man and the universe not out of an abundance of love but out of a felt need to remedy God's own imperfections.

The most complete collection of Marx and Engels's work in English is Marx and Engels, *Collected Works* (New York: International Publishers, 1975–), destined to be completed in 51 volumes.

There is also now available a three-volume labour of love by Hal Draper, *The Marx–Engels Cyclopedia* (New York: Schocken Books, 1985), giving every aspect of Marx's and Engels's lives in worshipful and even stupefying detail. Vol. I is the *Marx–Engels Chronicle,* an account of every day in the lives of the two heroes, Vol. II, the *Marx–Engels Register*, and Vol. III, the *Marx–Engels Glossary (and Index).* Unfortunately, Draper's hagiographical approach leads him to deny the recent but accepted revelation that Marx fathered an illegitimate son, Freddie Demuth, by his housemaid, and then pressured his friend, patron, and patsy Engels into acknowledging the child as his own.

Of the numerous anthologies of Marx–Engels's writing, the best and most penetrating is Robert C. Tucker (ed.), *The Marx–Engels Reader* (2nd ed., New York: W.W. Norton, 1972).

Particularly valuable is Dr David Gordon's splendid annotated bibliographical essay, *Critics of Marxism* (New Brunswick, NJ: Transaction Books, 1986).

The best and most penetrating book on Marxism and Marxian economics is David Conway, *A Farewell to Marx: An Outline and Appraisal of His Theories* (Harmondsworth, England: Penguin Books, 1987). On the other hand, the most spectacularly overrated work on Marxism is Thomas Sowell, *Marxism: Philosophy and Economics* (London: Unwin Paperbacks, 1986), which for most of its length is more a work of Marxian apologetics than of critical analysis. For a devastating review of Sowell, see David Ramsay Steele, 'Review of Thomas Sowell, *Marxism: Philosophy and Economics*', *International Philosophical Quarterly*, 26 (June 1986), pp. 201–3.

There is no completely satisfactory biography of Marx. One of the great merits of the rather stodgy David McLellan, *Karl Marx: His Life and Thought* (New York: Harper & Row, 1973) is that it has at last displaced as the standard life of Marx the outdated and hagiographical Franz Mehring, *Karl Marx: The Story of His Life* (Ann Arbor, Michigan: University of Michigan Press, 1962). Robert Payne's excellent but underrated *Marx* (New York: Simon & Schuster, 1968), uncovered the sordid story of Marx's foisting of his illegitimate son upon the hapless Engels. Payne's work was the first time this important disclosure appeared in English. The original revelation was in the German work by Werner Blumenberg, *Karl Marx...*(Hamburg, 1962), but Payne added considerable new evidence, even tracking down the illegitimate son's birth certificate. Leopold Schwarzchild, *The Red Prussian: The Life and Legend of Karl Marx* (New York: Scribner's, 1947), is refreshingly critical of someone who certainly deserves it, but the work is not only out of date, it is short on scholarship and long on fictional 'thoughts' and 'statements' allegedly and without evidence emitted by Marx.

Fortunately, there is now, at long last, an excellent biography available of Engels, the thorough and vivid W.O. Henderson, *The Life of Friedrich Engels* (2 vols, London: Frank Cass, 1976).

In addition to Tucker, extremely valuable on Marx as a philosophico-religious communist, as well as on Marx's youthful path to communism, is Bruce Mazlish, *The Meaning of Karl Marx* (New York: Oxford University Press, 1984). In this work, Mazlish keeps his propensity toward psychoanalytical history under restraint. On Marx as communist, also see Murray N. Rothbard, 'Karl Marx: Communist as Religious Eschatologist', in Yuri Maltsev (ed.), *Requiem for Marx* (Auburn, Ala.: Ludwig von Mises Institute of Auburn University, 1993), pp. 221–94. Also indispensable on the young Marx, including the translated text of his revealing poetic drama, *Oulanem*, is Robert Payne, *The Unknown Karl Marx* (New York: New York University Press, 1971). For other translations of the poems, also see Pastor Richard Wurmbrand, *Marx and Satan* (Westchester, Ill.: Crossway Press, 1986), although Wurmbrand goes beyond the evidence in claiming that Marx was actually a member of a Satanic cult. On Marx, also see Fritz J. Raddatz, *Karl*

Marx: A Political Biography (Boston: Little, Brown, 1978). An excellent but grievously neglected work on Marx and on the Marxian system is Gary North, *Marx's Religion of Revolution: Regeneration Through Chaos* (1968, 2nd ed., Tyler, Texas: Institute for Christian Economics, 1989). North properly stresses the essence of Marxism as a 'religion', and he was also the first to puncture the myth of Marx as 'poverty-stricken' during his years in London. Instead, North demonstrates that Marx lived high off the hog supplied by Engels and other devoted followers, all the while whining about his money problems, demanding new subventions and constantly in debt. And all the time denouncing 'money fetishism' under capitalism! North also helps correct the common underestimation of Engels and overvaluation of Marx, which he shrewdly attributes to Engels's 'traditional Germanic awe of the academic drudge, [which] colored his own self-evaluation right up until his death'. North, 'Preface', *Religion of Revolution*, p. xliii. For an excellent summation of North's findings about Marx's sponging and other unlovely aspects of his character, see Gary North, 'The Marx Nobody Knows', in Maltsev (ed.), *Requiem for Marx*, pp. 75–124.

On Hegel and on Marx's derivation of his world-outlook from Hegel, Tucker's *Philosophy and Myth* is excellent. Kolakowski's *Main Currents* is indispensable on the origins of the dialectic, and Raymond Plant's *Hegel* (Bloomington, Indiana: University of Indiana Press, 1973) has been particularly helpful and lucid in ploughing through the Hegelian morass, especially on his political philosophy. On Hegel's influence from Sir James Steuart see also Paul Chamley, 'Les origines de la pensée économique de Hegel', *Hegel-Studien*, Band 3 (1965), pp. 225–62. On Hegel's political philosophy, also see the anthology in Walter Kaufmann (ed.), *Hegel's Political Philosophy* (New York: Atherton Press, 1970), especially E.F. Carritt, 'Reply', (1940). For a blistering critique of Hegel, see Karl R. Popper, *The Open Society and Its Enemies* (New York: Harper Torchbooks, 1963), Volume II. On Left revolutionary Hegelianism, see Billington, *Fire in the Minds*, and David McLellan, *The Young Hegelians and Karl Marx* (London: Macmillan, 1969).

On historical materialism and the dialectic in Marx, see the lucid and powerful critique by Ludwig von Mises in *Theory and History* (1957, Auburn, Ala.: von Mises Institute, 1985), pp. 102–58; the detailed rebuttal to Marx by John Plamenatz, in *German Marxism and Russian Communism* (New York: Longmans, Green & Co., 1954), pp. 9–54, supplemented by Plamenatz, *Man and Society, II* (London: Longmans, 1963); and the classic work by M.M. Bober, *Karl Marx's Interpretation of History* (2nd rev. ed., Cambridge, Mass.: Harvard University Press, 1948).

On the Marxian concept of class and class struggle, see the profound critique by Ludwig von Mises, in *Socialism: An Economic and Sociological Analysis* (3rd ed., Indianapolis: Liberty Classics, 1981), pp. 292–313. Von

Mises's brilliant juxtaposition of the concepts of 'class' *vs* 'caste' was introduced here, with the term 'estate' being used for the latter concept. 'Caste'
was used, instead, in von Mises, *Theory and History*, pp. 112–47, which also
critically analyses the Marxian doctrine of 'ideology'. For an excellent discussion of class and caste, also see Walter Sulzbach, '"Class" and Class
Struggle', *Journal of Social Philosophy and Jurisprudence*, 6 (1940–41),
pp. 22–34.

On Marx and Engels's occasional confused lapse into the libertarian caste
notion of class, particularly in their analyses of contemporary French events,
see the little gem of an article by Ralph Raico, 'Classical Liberal Exploitation
Theory: A Comment on Professor Liggio's Paper', *The Journal of Libertarian Studies*, 1 (Summer 1977), pp. 179–83. And see in particular the expansion of Raico's analysis in his 'Classical Liberal Roots of the Marxist Doctrine of Classes', in Maltsev (ed.), *Requiem for Marx*, pp. 189–220. On the
confusions in the concept of 'bourgeois' which aggravated this muddle, see
Raico, 'Classical Liberal Exploitation', p. 179; and the illuminating discussion in Raymond Ruyer, 'The New Bourgeois' (unpublished MS, 8 pp.,
translated by R. Raico from Ruyer, *Éloge de la societé de la consommation*,
Paris: Calmann-Levy, 1969).

On the Saint-Simonians as the carrier of the confused version of the class
doctrine, and the relation between Saint-Simon and the libertarians Charles
Comte and Charles Dunoyer, see the *locus classicus* of this history in Élie
Halévy, 'Saint-Simonian Economic Doctrine', (1907), in his *The Era of
Tyrannies* (1938, Garden City, NY. Doubleday Anchor Books, 1965), pp. 21–
104. Also see Leonard P. Liggio, 'Charles Dunoyer and French Classical
Liberalism', *Journal of Libertarian Studies*, 1 (Summer 1977), pp. 153–78.
Mark Weinburg, 'The Social Analysis of Three Early 19th Century French
Liberals: Say, Comte, and Dunoyer', 2 (Winter 1978), pp. 45–63; and James
Bland Briscoe, 'Saint-Simonianism and the Origins of Socialism in France'
(doctoral dissertation in history, Columbia University, 1980). For a modern
translation of a work of a leading member of the Comte–Dunoyer school, see
Augustin Thierry, *Theory of Classical Liberal 'Industrielisme'* (trans. Mark
Weinburg, New York: Center for Libertarian Studies, Feb. 1978).

On the relationship, and contrast, between the *laissez-faire* liberal
ideologues, and the scientistic and technocratic Saint-Simonians, see the
important work of F.A. von Hayek, *The Counter-Revolution of Science* (Glencoe, Ill.: The Free Press, 1952). A major work of the Saint-Simonians is
translated as *The Doctrine of Saint-Simon: An Exposition* (trans. G.G. Iggers,
Boston: Beacon Press, 1958). The totalitarianism of the Saint-Simonians is
denounced in Georg G. Iggers, *The Cult of Authority* (2nd ed., The Hague:
Martinus Nijhoff, 1970); and their follies wittily revealed by Alexander Gray,
The Socialist Tradition, pp. 136–68; and sometimes hilariously portrayed in

J.L. Talmon, *Political Messianism: The Romantic Phase* (New York: Praeger, 1960), pp. 35–124. The movements of the Saint-Simonians, and their influence on Marx, are traced in Billington, *Fire in the Minds*; and for the Kovalevsky revelation of his childhood mentor Baron Ludwig von Westphalen's Saint-Simonian influence on Marx, see Georges Gurvitch, 'Saint-Simon et Karl Marx', *Revue Internationale de Philosophie*, 14 (1960), p. 400.

The best discussion of the Ricardian socialists: William Thompson, John Gray, and John Francis Bray, is in the always scintillating Alexander Gray, *The Socialist Tradition* (London: Longmans, Green, 1947), pp. 269–96. On these three, and especially on Bray, also see G.D.H. Cole, *Socialist Thought: The Forerunners, 1789–1850* (London: Macmillan, 1959), pp. 112–9, 132–9. Also on Bray, see Joseph Dorfman, *The Economic Mind in American Civilization, 1606–1865* (New York: Viking Press, 1946), II, pp. 686–9, 961–2.

On Thomas Hodgskin, we are fortunate enough to have a superbly written biography, by the great Élie Halévy, *Thomas Hodgskin* (1903, London: Ernest Benn Ltd, 1956). It is now all the more true what Alexander Gray first wrote in 1948: 'It is rather extraordinary, and not wholly creditable to us, that we should be indebted to a Frenchman for the only biography of Hodgskin; it is even more extraordinary that we should have to rely for our knowledge of a large part of Hodgskin on such extracts from his unpublished papers as M. Halevy has elected to translate into French.' Gray, *Socialist Tradition*, p. 278n. The great improvement, however, is that the Halevy book is now translated into English.

Also on Hodgskin, see Gray, *Socialist Tradition*, pp. 277–83; Gray, a hard taskmaster, is appreciative of Hodgskin's talents, praising his 'intellectual eminence and distinction', and adding that Hodgskin 'leaves most acutely a feeling that here was one designed for greatness which, owing to the misfits of time and of life, was never attained' (p. 277).

For a valuable article on Hodgskin and the *Economist*, which, however, overrates the influence of Hodgskin on Herbert Spencer, see Scott Gordon, 'The London *Economist* and the High Tide of Laissez Faire', *The Journal of Political Economy*, 63 (Dec. 1955), pp. 461–88.

On Marx and the economics of capitalism, see Conway, *A Farewell to Marx;* and the classic refutation of Marx's theory of value by Eugen von Böhm-Bawerk, *Karl Marx and the Close of His System* (Sweezy ed., New York: Kelley, 1949). On Marx and the iron law of wages, see Ludwig von Mises, 'The Marxian Theory of Wage Rates', in Eugen von Böhm-Bawerk, *The Exploitation Theory of Socialism–Communism* (3rd ed., South Holland, Ill.: Libertarian Press, 1975), pp. 147–51. On Marx's concept of alienation as grounded in the division of labour, and not simply in the wage system, see Paul Craig Roberts, *Alienation and the Soviet Economy* (1971, 2nd ed., New

York: Holmes & Meier, 1990); and Paul Craig Roberts and Matthew A. Stephenson, *Marx's Theory of Exchange, Alienation and Crisis* (2nd ed., New York: Praeger, 1983). On Marx and impoverishment, see Gary North, *Marx's Religion of Revolution* (Nutley, NJ: The Craig Press, 1968), pp. 140–41; Bober, *Karl Marx's Interpretation of History*, pp. 213–21; Mises, *Socialism*, pp. 381–4; and Schumpeter, *History*, p. 686n. On Marx's cycle theory, see Bober, *Marx's Interpretation*. On Tugan-Baranowsky's non-monetary over-investment, or disproportionality, variant of Marxian cycle theory, see Sergio Amato, 'Tugan-Baranowsky...', in I.S. Koropeckyj (ed.), *Selected Contributions of Ukrainian Scholars to Economics* (Cambridge, Mass.: Harvard University Press, 1984), pp. 1–59; and Gottfried Haberler, *Prosperity and Depression* (4th ed., Cambridge, Mass.: Harvard University Press, 1958), pp. 72–85.

The latest group of 'analytical Marxists' in England, headed by John Roemer and Jon Elster, are highly fashionable, possibly because they have virtually abandoned Marxism altogether, having embraced methodological individualism. The analytical Marxists have abandoned the labour theory of value, redefining 'exploitation' as consisting only in income and wealth inequality – a leftist but most un-Marxian doctrine. For a critique of this school by an orthodox Marxist, see Michael A. Lebowitz, 'Is "Analytical Marxism" Marxism?', *Science and Society*, 52 (Summer 1988), pp. 191–214. For a definitive demolition of analytical Marxism, see David Gordon, *Resurrecting Marx: The Analytical Marxists on Freedom, Exploitation, and Justice* (New Brunswick, NJ: Transaction Books, 1990).

The French *laissez-faire* school and its influence
On the French *laissez-faire* school and its influence in Europe and the United States in the nineteenth century, see the seminal article by Joseph T. Salerno, 'The Neglect of the French Liberal School in Anglo-American Economics: A Critique of Received Explanations', *Review of Austrian Economics*, 2 (1988), pp. 113–56. In this important and subtle essay, Salerno corrects the conventional historical deprecation of the theoretical acumen of Bastiat and the French liberals, and demonstrates their considerable influence on nineteenth century economic theory, including the marginalists.

The only satisfactory biography of Bastiat is Dean Russell, *Frédéric Bastiat: Ideas and Influence* (Irvington-on-Hudson: Foundation for Economic Education, 1965). Although Russell is an admirer of Bastiat, he undervalues Bastiat's economic theory, as grossly inferior from the point of view of the Austrian School. Russell fails to take into account that Bastiat's emphasis on immaterial *services* rather than material goods, as well as his emphasis on consumer wants, were great *steps forward* toward Austrian theory as compared to dominant British classicism. More material on Bastiat's career as legislator can be found in George Charles Roche III, *Frédéric Bastiat: A Man Alone* (New Rochelle, NY: Arlington House, 1971), pp. 82–122. See also the discussion of Bastiat in Israel M. Kirzner, *The Economic Point of View* (Princeton, NJ: D. Van Nostrand, 1960), pp. 82–4. Also see Robert F. Hébert, 'Claude Frédéric Bastiat', *New Palgrave Dictionary*, I, pp. 204–5. On the international congress of economists held in Brussels, see Joseph Garnier, 'Économistes (Congrès des)', in C. Coquelin and C. Guillaumin (eds.), *Dictionnaire d'Économie Politique* (Paris: Guillaumin, 1852), I, pp. 671–2. There is no substitute for reading the delightful work of Bastiat directly; see the translations of his volumes *Economic Harmonies, Economic Sophisms,* and *Selected Essays of Political Economy*, all published by Princeton, NJ.: D. Van Nostrand, 1964.

The best discussion of Molinari is the three-part article by David M. Hart, 'Gustave de Molinari and the Anti-statist Liberal Tradition: Part I', *Journal of Libertarian Studies,* V (Summer 1981), pp. 263–90; 'Gustave de Molinari and the Anti-statist Liberal Tradition: Part II', *Journal of Libertarian Studies*, V (Autumn, 1981), pp. 399–434; and 'Gustave de Molinari and the Anti-statist Liberal Tradition: Part III', *Journal of Libertarian Studies*, VI (Winter 1982) pp. 83–104.

There are English translations of Molinari's path-breaking anarcho-capitalist work: *The Production of Security* (New York: Center for Libertarian Studies, May 1977) (with preface by M. Rothbard); and his Eleventh Soirée in Hart, 'Molinari, Part III', pp. 88–104. The only book of Molinari's translated into English came when he had already retreated from anarcho-capitalism: *The Society of Tomorrow* (New York: G.P. Putnam's Sons, 1904).

For an appreciative discussion of Molinari and private protection by a modern economist, see Bruce L. Benson, 'Guns for Protection and Other Private Sector Responses to the Fear of Rising Crime', in D. Kates (ed.), *Firearms and Violence: Issues of Public Policy* (San Francisco: Pacific Institute for Public Policy Research, 1984), pp. 346–56.

On the influence of Bastiat and Francesco Ferrara in Italy, and on the spread of historicism and socialism in the 1870s, see Luigi Cossa, *An Introduction to the Study of Political Economy* (London: Macmillan, 1893).

For an overall discussion of French academic economics in the nineteenth century, see Alain Alcouffe, 'The Institutionalization of Political Economy in French Universities, 1819–1896', *History of Political Economy*, 21 (Summer 1989), pp. 313–44.

On Francesco Ferrara and the Italian *laissez-faire* school, also see Ugo Rabbeno, 'The Present Condition of Political Economy in Italy', *Political Science Quarterly*, 6 (Sept. 1891), pp. 439–73; and Piero Barucci, 'The Spread of Marginalism in Italy, 1871–1890', in R.D.C. Black, A.W. Coats, C.D.W.

Goodwin (eds.), *The Marginal Revolution in Economics: Interpretation and Evaluation* (Durham, NC: Duke University Press, 1973), pp. 246–66.

The best discussion of Pareto, combined with English translations of many of his articles and excerpts from his works, is in Placido Bucolo (ed.), *The Other Pareto* (London: Scolar Press, 1980). Also important is S.E. Finer's introduction, as well as the compilation in, Vilfredo Pareto, *Sociological Writings* (ed. S. Finer, London: Pall Mall Press, 1966), and S.E. Finer, 'Pareto and Pluto-Democracy: The Retreat to Galapogos', *American Political Science Review*, 62 (1968), pp. 440–50. For a current discussion see Salerno, 'Neglect'.

On Bastiat and *laissez-faire* views in Sweden, see Eli F. Heckscher, 'A Summary of Economic Thought in Sweden, 1875–1950', *The Scandinavian Economic History Review*, 1 (1953), pp. 105–25. On the libertarian, *laissez-faire* economist John Prince Smith in Germany, see the illuminating article by Ralph Raico, 'John Prince Smith and the German Free Trade Movement', in W. Block and L. Rockwell (eds.), *Man, Economy, and Liberty: Essays in Honor of Murray N. Rothbard* (Auburn University, Ala.: The Ludwig von Mises Institute, 1988), pp. 341–51. Also see W.O. Henderson, 'Prince Smith and Free Trade in Germany', *Economic History Review*, 2nd ser., 2 (1950), rprt. in Henderson, *Britain and Industrial Europe, 1750–1870* (Liverpool, 1954). On Prince Smith's associate Julius Faucher, see Andrew R. Carlson, *Anarchism in Germany, Vol. I: The Early Movement* (Metuchen, NJ: The Scarecrow Press, 1972), pp. 65–6. On Karl Heinrich Rau, see Keith Tribe, *Governing Economy: The Reformation of German Economic Discourse 1750–1840* (Cambridge: Cambridge University Press, 1988), pp. 183–201. On Rau, also see H.C. Recktenwald, 'Rau, Karl Heinrich', *The New Palgrave*, IV, p. 96.

On German liberalism generally, see Donald G. Rohr, *The Origins of Social Liberalism in Germany* (Chicago: University of Chicago Press, 1963); and James J. Sheehan, *German Liberalism in the Nineteenth Century* (Chicago: University of Chicago Press, 1978).

On British *laissez-faire* theorists heavily influenced by Bastiat, Henry Dunning Macleod's work is of interest. In particular, see his *The Elements of Political Economy* (London: Longman, Brown, 1857); *The History of Economics* (New York: Putnam, 1896); and his *Dictionary of Political Economy, Vol. I* (London: 1863). His view of *laissez-faire* and of the history of economic thought is nicely summed up in his 'On the Science of Economics and Its Relation to Free Exchange and Socialism', in Thomas Mackay (ed.), *A Policy of Free Exchange* (London: John Murray, 1894), pp. 3–46. For appreciative discussions of Macleod, see Salerno, 'Neglect', pp. 130–32; Charles Rist, *History of Monetary and Credit Theory* (1940, NY: A.M. Kelley, 1966); Israel M. Kirzner, *The Economic Point of View* (New York: Van Nostrand,

1960), pp. 73, 202–3; and Murray N. Rothbard, 'Catallactics', *The New Palgrave*, II, p. 377.

The unjustly neglected Wordsworth Donisthorpe's work in *laissez-faire* economics consists of *Individualism, A System of Politics* (London: Macmillan, 1889), and his *Law in a Free State* (London: Macmillan, 1895); his waffling chapter on 'The Limits of Liberty' in the latter work was reprinted from his article of the same name in Thomas Mackay (ed.), *A Plea for Liberty* (NY: D. Appleton & Co., 1891), pp. 63–106. For a history of Donisthorpe and the British *laissez-faire* movement, see W.H. Greenleaf, *The British Political Tradition* (London: Methuen, 1983), II, pp. 263–87. Also see Edward Bristow, 'The Liberty and Property Defence League and Individualism', *The Historical Journal*, 18 (Dec. 1975), pp. 761–89; and John W. Mason, 'Thomas Mackay: The Anti-Socialist Philosophy of the Charity Organization Society', in K.D. Brown (ed.), *Essays in Anti-Labour History* (London: Macmillan, 1974), pp. 307–9. For Donisthorpe's plutology, see his *Principles of Plutology* (London: Williams & Norgate, 1876). Also on Donisthorpe, see Peter Newman, 'Donisthorpe, Wordsworth', *New Palgrave*, I, pp. 916–7.

On William E. Hearn and economics in Australia, see Hearn, *Plutology, or the Theory of the Efforts to Satisfy Human Wants* (London: Macmillan, 1864); Salerno, 'Neglect', pp. 125–9; J.A. LaNauze, *Political Economy in Australia* (Melbourne: Melbourne University Press, 1949); and D.B. Copland, *William E. Hearn, First Australian Economist* (Melbourne: Melbourne University Press, 1935).

Joseph Dorfman's magisterial multi-volume *Economic Mind in American Civilization* is indispensable for any coverage of American economic thought; relevant to *laissez-faire* thought influenced by Bastiat are *Volume II: 1606–1865* (New York: Viking, 1946), and *Volume III: 1865–1918* (New York: Viking, 1949). Also important for the nineteenth century after the Civil War is Sidney Fine, *Laissez Faire and the General-Welfare State* (Ann Arbor, Michigan: University of Michigan Press, 1956). Also see Salerno, 'Neglect', pp. 133–8; Kirzner, *Economic Point of View*, pp. 75–77. Amasa Walker's most important work was his *The Science of Wealth* (3rd ed., Boston: Little Brown, 1867); and Arthur Latham Perry's was his *Political Economy* (21st ed., New York: Scribner, 1892). Also see the illuminating collection of essays by Perry, *Miscellanies* (Williamstown, Mass.: published by author, 1902), published for the semi-centennial celebration of the Williams College class of 1852.

Charles Holt Carroll's collected essays are published in Edward C. Simmons (ed.), *Organization of Debt into Currency, and Other Essays* (Princeton NJ: Van Nostrand, 1964). Simmons's Introduction, ibid., pp. v–xxiv, is outstanding. Also see the reprint of Carroll's essays *Congress and the Currency* (James Turk, ed., Greenwich, CT: Committee for Monetary Research and

Education, Sept. 1977), from *Hunt's Merchant's Magazine* of July 1864. For Carroll and other 100 per cent gold writers, see Skousen, *Economics of a Pure Gold Standard*. As Simmons points out, even Dorfman omits Carroll, while the standard histories of monetary thought in America: Mints, *History of Banking Theory*; and Harry E. Miller, *Banking Theories Before 1860* (Cambridge Mass.: Harvard University Press, 1932), make no reference to any of Carroll's writings after the start of the Civil War.

Index